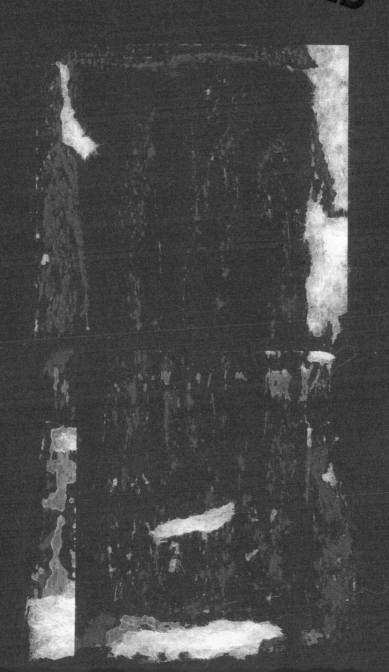

A HISTORY OF RELIGIOUS IDEAS

Translated from the French by Willard R. Trask

MIRCEA ELIADE

A HISTORY OF RELIGIOUS IDEAS

2 From Gautama Buddha to the Triumph of Christianity

The University of Chicago Press

Chicago and London

The University of Chicago Press, Chicago 60637
The University of Chicago Press, Ltd., London

Printed in the United States of America
89 88 87 86 85 84 83 82 54321

Library of Congress Cataloging in Publication Data
Eliade, Mircea, 1907–
A History of religious ideas.
Translation of Histoire des croyances et des idées religieuses.
Includes bibliographies and indexes.
CONTENTS: 1. From the stone age to the Eleusinian mysteries.—v. 2. From Gautama Buddha to the triumph of Christianity.
1. Religion—History. 2. Religions—History. I. Title.
BL48.E3813 291 77-16784
ISBN 0-226-20400-6 (v. 1) AACR1
ISBN 0-226-20402-2 (v. 2)

Originally published in French under the title *Histoire des croyances et des idées religieuses*. Vol. 2: *De Gautama Bouddha au triomphe du christianisme*. © Payot, Paris, 1978.

Mircea Eliade is the Sewell L. Avery Distinguished Service Professor in the Divinity School and professor in the Committee on Social Thought of the University of Chicago.

For Christinel

Contents

Preface

This English rendering was prepared by Willard R. Trask, an outstanding translator and close friend. Over the years, his exceptional skills have provided clear and careful versions of my works for an English readership. Unfortunately, Mr. Trask died before the manuscript could be sent to press. For corrections and improvements in this English edition I am indebted to my former student, now colleague, Professor Lawrence E. Sullivan of the University of Chicago. Throughout the entire process he labored long to take care of queries and solve problems in the text. For guiding the work to its completion, I offer him sincere thanks.

A HISTORY OF RELIGIOUS IDEAS

16 The Religions of Ancient China

126. Religious beliefs in the Neolithic period

For the historian of culture as well as for the historian of religions, China represents an unusually advantageous field of research. The earliest Chinese archeological documents, for example, go back to the sixth and fifth millenniums, and in at least some cases it is possible to follow the continuity of the different prehistoric cultures and even to define their contribution to the forming of classical Chinese civilization. For, just as the Chinese people arises from many and various ethnic combinations, its culture constitutes a complex and original synthesis in which the contributions of several sources can nevertheless be discovered.

The earliest Neolithic culture is that of Yang Shao, so termed from the name of the village in which vessels of painted clay were discovered in 1921. A second Neolithic culture, characterized by a black pottery, was discovered near Lung Shan in 1928. But it was not until after 1950 that, as a result of the numerous excavations made during the preceding thirty years, it became possible to classify all the phases and the general outlines of the Chinese Neolithic cultures. By the help of radiocarbon dating, the chronology was substantially modified. At Pan Po (in Shensi Province) the earliest site belonging to the Yang Shao culture was brought to light; radiocarbon dating indicates ca. 4115 or ca. 4365. In the fifth millennium the site was occupied for 600 years. But Pan Po does not represent the earliest stage of the Yang Shao culture.[1] According to Ping-ti Ho, the author of the latest synthetic study of Chinese prehistory, the agriculture practiced in

1. Ping-ti Ho, *The Cradle of the East*, pp. 16 ff.

the sixth millennium was a local discovery, as were the domestication of certain animals, ceramics, and the metallurgy of bronze.[2] Yet, only recently, the development of the Chinese Neolithic cultures and Bronze Age was explained by a dissemination of agriculture and metallurgy from several centers in the ancient Near East. It is not our part to take sides in this controversy. It seems indubitable that certain techniques were invented or radically modified in China. It is no less probable that protohistorical China received numerous cultural elements of Western origin, disseminated across Siberia and the Central Asian steppes.

The archeological documents can give us information about certain religious beliefs, but it would be wrong to conclude that those beliefs represent all the religious beliefs of the prehistorical populations. Their mythology and theology, the structure and morphology of their rituals, can scarcely be made out solely on the basis of the archeological finds. Thus, for example, the religious documents revealed by the discovery of the Neolithic Yang Shao culture refer almost entirely to ideas and beliefs connected with sacred space, fertility, and death. In the villages the communal building is placed at the center of the site, surrounded by small houses half underground. Not only the orientation of the village but the structure of the house, with its central mud pit and its smokehole, indicates a cosmology shared by many Neolithic and traditional societies (cf. §12). Belief in the survival of the soul is illustrated by the utensils and foodstuffs placed in the graves. Children were buried, close to the houses, in large urns having an opening at the top to permit the soul to go out and return.[3] In other words, the funerary urn was the dead person's "house," an idea that found ample expression in the cult of ancestors in the Bronze Age (the Shang period).

Certain clay vessels, painted red and decorated with the so-called death pattern, are especially interesting.[4] Three icono-

2. Ibid., pp. 43 ff., 91 ff., 121 ff., 177 ff.

3. Ibid., pp. 279 ff. Similar beliefs and practices are found in certain prehistoric cultures of the Near East and of eastern Europe.

4. See J. G. Anderson, *Children of the Yellow Earth,* p. 315; Kwang-Chih Chang, *The Archaeology of Ancient China,* p. 103; cf. Hanna Rydh, "Symbolism in Mortuary Ceramics," passim.

graphic motifs—triangle, chessboard, and cowrie—are found only on funerary vessels. But these motifs are bound up with a rather complex symbolism that associates the ideas of sexual union, birth, regeneration, and rebirth. It may be supposed that this decoration indicates the hope of survival and of a rebirth in the other world.

A design figuring two fishes and two anthropomorphic figures probably represents a supernatural being or a "specialist in the sacred," a sorcerer or priest.[5] But its interpretation is still doubtful. The fishes certainly have a symbolism that is at once sexual and connected with the calendar (the fishing season corresponds to a particular period of the yearly cycle). The distribution of the four figures may suggest a cosmological image.

According to Ping-ti Ho (pp. 275 ff.), the societies of the Yang Shao period obeyed the laws of matrilineal descent. In contrast, the following period, that of Lung Shan, indicates passage to a patrilineal society, characterized by the predominance of the ancestor cult. Following other scholars, Ho interprets certain stone objects and their reproductions on painted vases as phallic symbols. Like Karlgren, who saw the derivation of the pictogram *tsu*, designating the ancestor, from the drawing of a phallus, Ho sees in the multiplication of phallic emblems the importance attained by the ancestor cult.[6] The "death pattern," as we have seen, certainly involves a sexual symbolism. But Carl Hentze explains the various "phallic" objects and designs as representing a "house of the soul"; certain ceramics from Yang Shao represent models of little huts—which are at the same time funerary urns—comparable to the similar documents from European prehistory and to the Mongol hut. These "little houses of the soul," abundantly attested to in the prehistory of China, are the forerunners of the "ancestor tablets" of historical times.[7]

5. There is a good reproduction in Ho, *Cradle of the East,* p. 154, fig. 9.

6. Ibid., p. 282; cf. B. Karlgren, "Some Fecundity Symbols in Ancient China," pp. 18 ff.

7. See Carl Hentze, *Bronzegerät, Kultbauten, Religion im ältesten China der Shangzeit,* pp. 49 ff., 88 ff., and his *Das Haus als Weltort der Seele,* pp. 23 ff. and figs. 10–12. These two works supply a large number of parallels chosen from cultures historically or morphologically related to the archaic civilization of China.

In short, the Yang Shao and Lung Shan cultures reveal the beliefs that are typical of other Neolithic civilizations: solidarity among life, fertility, death, and the afterlife and hence the conception of the cosmic cycle, illustrated by the calendar and actualized in the rites; the importance of the ancestors, a source of magico-religious power; and the "mystery" of the conjunction of contraries (also proven by the "death pattern"), a belief that in a way anticipated the idea of the unity/totality of cosmic life, which will be the dominating idea in later periods. It is important to add that a great part of the Neolithic heritage was until recent times preserved, with the inevitable changes, in the religious traditions and practices of the Chinese villages.

127. Religion in the Bronze Age: The God of Heaven and the ancestors

We are decidedly better informed about Chinese history from the time of the Shang dynasty (ca. 1751–1028). The Shang period corresponds in general to the protohistory and the beginning of the ancient history of China. It is characterized by the metallurgy of bronze, the appearance of urban centers and capital cities, the presence of a military aristocracy, the institution of royalty, and the beginnings of writing. As for the religious life of the period, the documentation is comparatively full. First of all we have a rich iconography, best exemplified by the magnificent bronze ritual vessels. In addition, the royal tombs provide information concerning certain religious practices. But it is especially the countless oracular inscriptions, incised on animal bones or tortoise shells, that are a precious source.[8] Finally, some later works (for example, *The Book of Odes*), which Karlgren calls "free Chou texts,"[9] contain much ancient material. We should add, however, that these sources give us information concerning the

8. These exemplify a method of divination that was quite widely practiced in northern Asia: the question was asked, the bones or shells were heated, and the diviners interpreted the shapes of the resulting cracks. Then the question and answer were inscribed beside the cracks.

9. Bernhard Karlgren, "Legends and Cults in Ancient China," p. 344.

beliefs and rituals of the royal clan; as in the Neolithic period, the mythology and theology remain for the most part unknown.

The interpretation of these iconographic documents is not always certain. Scholars agree in recognizing a certain analogy with the motifs documented on the painted pottery of Yang Shao[10] and, in addition, with the religious symbolism of the following periods. Hentze (*Bronzegerät*, pp. 215 ff.) interprets the conjunction of polar symbols as illustrating religious ideas related to the renewal of Time and to spiritual regeneration. No less important is the symbolism of the cicada and of the *t'ao-t'ieh* mask, which suggests the cycle of births and rebirths, of light and life emerging from darkness and death. No less remarkable is the union of antagonistic images (feathered snake, snake and eagle, etc.), in other words the dialectic of contraries and the *coincidentia oppositorum*, a central theme for the Taoist philosophers and mystics. The bronze vessels represent urn-houses.[11] Their form is derived either from ceramics or from prototypes in wood.[12] The admirable animal art revealed by the bronze vessels probably originated in wood engravings.[13]

The oracular inscriptions inform us of a religious conception that was absent (or imperceptible?) in the Neolithic documents, namely, the preeminence of a supreme celestial god, Ti (Lord) or Shang Ti (The Lord on High). Ti commands the cosmic rhythms and natural phenomena (rain, wind, drought, etc.); he grants the king victory and insures the abundance of crops or, on the contrary, brings on disasters and sends sicknesses and death. He is offered two kinds of sacrifices: in the sanctuary of the ancestors and in the open fields. But, as is the case with other archaic celestial gods (see our *A History of Religious Ideas*, vol. 1, §§14 ff.), his cult shows a certain diminution of religious primacy. Ti is found to be distant and less active than the ancestors of the royal lineage, and he is offered fewer sacrifices. But

10. The salamander, the tiger, the dragon, etc., still in use in the iconography of Chinese popular art, are cosmological symbols that are already documented at the end of the Neolithic. See Hentze, *Bronzegerät . . . der Shangzeit*, pp. 40 ff., 55 ff., 132 ff., 165 ff.

11. Hentze, *Das Haus als Weltort der Seele*, pp. 14 ff. and passim.

12. Li Chi, *The Beginnings of Chinese Civilization*, p. 32.

13. Ibid., p. 35.

he alone is invoked in matters of fecundity (rain) and of war, the sovereign's two chief preoccupations.

In any case, Ti's position remains supreme. All the other gods, as well as the royal ancestors, are subordinate to him. Only the king's ancestors are able to intercede with Ti; on the other hand, only the king can communicate with his ancestors, for the king is the "one man."[14] The sovereign strengthens his authority with the help of his ancestors; belief in their magico-religious power legitimized the domination of the Shang dynasty. In their turn the ancestors depend on the offerings of cereals, blood, and flesh that are brought to them.[15] It is futile to suppose, as certain scholars do,[16] that, since the ancestor cult was so important for the reigning aristocracy, it was gradually adopted by the other social strata. The cult was already thoroughly implanted, and very popular, in the Neolithic period. As we have just seen (pp. 5 ff.), it formed an essential part of the religious system (structured around the anthropocosmic cycle) of the earliest cultivators. It is the preeminence of the king, whose first ancestor was supposed to descend from Ti, that gave this immemorial cult a political function.

The king offers two series of sacrifices: to the ancestors and to Ti and the other gods. Sometimes the ritual service is extended over 300 or 600 days. The word "sacrifice" designates the "year," since the annual cycle is conceived as a complete service. This confirms the importance of the calendar, which guarantees the normal return of the seasons. In the great royal tombs near Anyang, exploration has revealed, in addition to animal skeletons, numerous human victims, presumably immolated in order to accompany the sovereign into the other world. The choice of victims (companions and servants, dogs, horses) emphasizes the considerable importance of the hunt (rit-

14. The expression "I, the one man" (or perhaps, "I, the first man") is documented in the oracular inscriptions; see David N. Keightley, "Shang Theology and the Genesis of Chinese Political Culture," p. 213, n. 6.

15. As Keightley remarks (ibid., pp. 214 ff.), the cult of ancestors emphasized the royal lineage's aspect as the source of religious and political authority. The doctrine of the "Mandate of Heaven," usually considered to be an invention of the Chou dynasty, has deep roots in the theology of the Shang.

16. For example, Ho, *Cradle of the East,* p. 320.

ual hunt?) for the military aristocracy and royal clan.[17] A number of questions preserved by the oracular inscriptions are concerned with the advisability and the chances for success of the king's expeditions.

The tombs had the same cosmological symbolism and performed the same function as the urn-houses: they were the houses of the dead. A similar belief could explain human sacrifice offered at the time when buildings were newly begun, especially temples and palaces. The victims' souls insured the durability of the construction; it could be said that the building that was raised served as a "new body" for the victim's soul.[18] But human sacrifice was also practiced for other purposes, about which our information is scanty; it can be supposed that the end sought was the renewal of time or the regeneration of the dynasty.

Despite the gaps, we can make out the principal lines of religion in the Shang period. The importance of the celestial god and the ancestor cult is beyond doubt. The complexity of the sacrificial system (bound up with a religious calendar) and of techniques of divination presupposes the existence of a class of "specialists in the sacred"—diviners, priests, or shamans. Finally, the iconography shows us the articulations of a symbolism, at once cosmological and soteriological, that is still inadequately understood but that seems to anticipate the chief religious conceptions of classical China.

128. The exemplary dynasty: The Chou

In ca. 1028 the last Shang king was conquered by the duke of Chou. In a famous proclamation,[19] the latter justified his revolt against the king by the order he had received from the Celestial Lord to put an end to a corrupted and odious domination. This

17. Li Chi, *The Beginnings of Chinese Civilization,* pp. 21 ff. The author draws attention to the animal motifs (tiger, stag) in the decorations of bronze vessels (p. 33). We may add that these are emblematic animals, carrying a quite complex cosmological and initiatory symbolism.

18. See Eliade, *Zalmoxis, the Vanishing God,* pp. 182 ff.

19. The text has been preserved in the *Shu Ching;* see the translation in Bernhard Karlgren, *Shu Ching: The Book of Documents,* p. 55.

is the first statement of the famous doctrine of the "Heavenly Mandate." The victorious duke became king of the Chou; he inaugurated the longest dynasty in the history of China (ca. 1028–256). For our purpose it would be useless to summarize its moments of greatness, its crises, and its decadence.[20] We need only point to the fact that, despite wars and general insecurity, it is from the eighth to the third centuries before Christ that traditional Chinese civilization flowered and philosophic thought attained its highest point.[21]

At the beginning of the dynasty the celestial god T'ien (Heaven), or Shang Ti (The Lord on High), shows the characteristics of an anthropomorphic and personal god. He resides in the Great Bear at the center of the heavens. The texts bring out his celestial structure: he sees, observes, and hears everything; he is clairvoyant and omniscient; his decree is infallible. T'ien and Shang Ti are invoked in agreements and contracts. Later the omniscience and all-seeingness of Heaven are celebrated by Confucius and by many other philosophers, moralists, and theologians of all schools. But for these the God of Heaven increasingly loses his religious nature; he becomes the principle of cosmic order, the warrant for moral law. This process of abstraction and rationalization of a supreme god is frequent in the history of religions (cf. Brahman, Zeus, the God of the philosophers during the Hellenistic period, and the God of Judaism, Christianity, and Islam).

But Heaven (T'ien) remains the protector of the dynasty. The king is the "son of T'ien" and the "regent of Shang Ti."[22] This

20. The following are some important dates: the period of the Western Chou, which lasted until about 771, was followed by the period of the Eastern Chou (ca. 771–256). From ca. 400 to ca. 200 there were continuous wars; this is the period known as the Warring Kingdoms, which was ended by the unification of China under the Emperor Huang-ti.

21. It was during this period that the "Classic Books" were composed or edited. As Hentze observes (*Funde in Alt-China,* p. 222), under the Chou we witness a progressive desacralization of writing. The original function of writing—regulating the relations between Heaven and earth, God and mankind—is replaced by genealogical and historiographic preoccupations. In the last analysis, writing becomes a means of political propaganda.

22. See *Shu Ching,* trans. Legge, p. 426. The Chou were believed to be descended from a mythical ancestor, Hou Chi (Prince Millet) celebrated in the

is why, in principle, only the king is fit to offer him sacrifices. He is responsible for the normal progression of the cosmic rhythms; in case of disaster—drought, prodigies, calamities, floods—the king subjects himself to expiatory rites. Since every celestial god rules the seasons, T'ien also has a role in agrarian cults. Thus, the king must represent him during the essential moments of the agrarian cycle (cf. §130).

In general, the ancestor cult carries on the structures established during the Shang period (but our information extends only to the rituals practiced by the aristocracy). The urn-house is replaced by a tablet, which the son deposited in the temple of the ancestors. Ceremonies of considerable complexity took place four times a year; cooked foods, cereals, and various drinks were offered, and the ancestor's soul was invoked. The soul was personified by a member of the family, usually one of the dead man's grandsons, who shared out the offerings. Similar ceremonies are not uncommon in Asia and elsewhere; a ritual that involved a person representing the dead man was very probably practiced in the Shang period, if not as early as prehistory.[23]

The chthonic divinities and their cults have a long history, concerning which we are scantily informed. It is known that, before being represented as a mother, the earth was experienced as an asexual being or bisexual cosmic power.[24] According to Marcel Granet, the image of Mother Earth first appears "under the neutral aspect of the Sacred Place." A little later "the domestic Earth was conceived under the features of a maternal and

---

Shih Ching (poem 153) for having given them "wheat and barley at God's command." We may add that human sacrifices, documented in the royal tombs of the Shang period, disappeared completely under the Chou.

23. Portraits of men with their arms raised, depicted on clay reliefs, most probably represent ancestors or priests of an ancestral cult (see Hentze, *Funde in Alt-China,* p. 224 and pl. XL). This iconographic motif is documented in the Neolithic and in the Shang period (ibid., figs. 29, 30). An excellent example of the "folklorization" of the ancestor theme is illustrated by a bronze box from the middle of the Chou period, the cover of which bears a representation, in a naïvely naturalistic style, of a man and a woman seated face to face (see ibid., p. 228 and pl. XLIII).

24. See Eliade, "Mother Earth and the Cosmic Hierogamies," in *Myths, Dreams, and Mysteries,* p. 155.

nourishing principle."[25] In ancient times the dead were buried in the domestic enclosure, where the seed was kept. For a long time, the guardian of seeds continued to be a woman. "In Chou times, the seeds destined to sow the royal field were not kept in the Son of Heaven's room but in the apartments of the queen" (Granet, p. 200). It is only later, with the appearance of the agnate family and seigneurial power, that the sun became a god. In the Chou period there were many gods of the soil, organized hierarchically: gods of the familial soil, god of the village, gods of the royal soil and the seigneurial soil. The altar was in the open air, but it comprised a stone tablet and a tree—relics of the original cult consecrated to Earth as cosmic power. The peasant cults, structured around the seasonal crises, probably represent the earliest forms of this cosmic religion. For, as we shall see (§130), the earth was not conceived only as source of agrarian fertility. As complementary power to the sky, it revealed itself to be an integral part of the cosmic totality.

It is important to add that the religious structures that we have just sketched do not exhaust the rich documentation on the Chou period (archeological materials and, especially, a large number of texts). We shall complete our exposition by representing some cosmogonic myths and the fundamental metaphysical ideas. For the moment we will point out that scholars have recently agreed to emphasize the cultural and religious complexity of archaic China. As is the case with so many other nations, the Chinese ethnic stock was not homogeneous. In addition, in the beginning neither its language nor its culture nor its religion represented unitary systems. Wolfram Eberhard has brought out the contribution of peripheral ethnic elements—Thai, Tungus, Turco-Mongol, Tibetan, etc.—to the Chinese synthesis.[26] For the historian of religions, these contributions are precious: they help us to understand, among other things, the impact of northern

25. M. Granet, "Le dépôt de l'enfant sur le sol," in *Etudes sociologiques sur la Chine,* p. 201. "When the newborn infant or the dying man is laid on the Earth, it is for Her to say if the birth or the death is viable. . . . The rite of laying on the Earth implies the idea of an identity of substance between the Race and the Soil" (ibid., pp. 192–93, 197–98).

26. See Eberhard's *Kultur und Siedlung der Randvölker Chinas* and the two volumes of his *Lokalkulturen im alten China.*

shamanism on Chinese religiosity and the "origin" of certain Taoist practices.

The Chinese historiographers were conscious of the distance that separated their classical civilization from the beliefs and practices of the "barbarians." But among these "barbarians" we frequently find ethnic stocks that were partly or wholly assimilated and whose culture ended by becoming an integral part of Chinese civilization. We will give only one example: that of the Ch'u. Their kingdom was already established about 1100. Yet the Ch'u, who had assimilated the Chang culture, were of Mongol origin, and their religion was characterized by shamanism and techniques of ecstasy.[27] The unification of China under the Han, though it brought the destruction of Ch'u culture, facilitated the dissemination of their religious beliefs and practices throughout China. It is probable that a number of their cosmological myths and religious practices were adopted by Chinese culture; as for their ecstatic techniques, they reappear in certain Taoist circles.

129. The origin and organizing of the world

No Chinese cosmogonic myth in the strict sense has come down to us, but it is possible to discern creator gods, euhemerized and secularized, in the Chinese historiographic tradition and in a number of legends. Thus it is narrated that P'an-ku, a primordial anthropomorphic being, was born "in the time when Heaven and Earth were a chaos resembling an egg." When P'an-ku died, his head became "a sacred peak, his eyes became the sun and moon, his fat the rivers and seas, the hair of his head and his body became trees and other plants."[28] We can here see the essential features of a myth that éxplains Creation by the sacrifice of a primordial being: Tiamat (cf. § 21), Puruṣa (§ 75), Ymir (§ 173). A reference in the *Shu Ching* proves that the ancient Chinese

27. See John S. Major, "Research Priorities in the Study of Ch'u Religion," esp. pp. 231 ff.

28. Texts translated by Max Kaltenmark, "La naissance du monde en Chine," pp. 456–57. See also Norman Girardot, "The Problem of Creation Mythology," pp. 298 ff.

also knew another cosmogonic theme, documented among numerous peoples and at different levels of culture: "The August Lord (Huang-ti) ordered Tch'ong-li to break communication between Earth and Heaven, so that the descents [of the gods] should cease."[29] This particular interpretation—that the gods and spirits descended to earth to *oppress* mankind—is secondary, for the other Chinese variants of this myth (and those produced by other cultures as well) praise the paradisal nature of the primordial age, when the extreme closeness of Earth to Heaven allowed the gods to descend and mingle with men, and men to ascend to the sky by climbing a mountain, a tree, or a ladder or even by letting themselves be carried by birds. After a certain mythical event (a "ritual fault"), Heaven was violently separated from Earth, the tree or the vine was cut, or the mountain that touched Heaven was flattened. However, certain privileged beings—shamans, mystics, heroes, sovereigns—can ascend to heaven in ecstasy, thus reestablishing the communication broken off *in illo tempore*.[30] Throughout Chinese history we find what could be called the nostalgia for paradise, that is, the desire to reenact, through ecstasy, a "primordial situation": the situation represented by the original unity/totality (*hun-tun*), or the time when human beings could meet the gods directly.

Finally, a third myth tells of a brother-sister pair, Fu-hi and Nü-kua, two beings with the bodies of dragons, often represented in iconography with their tails intertwined. On the occasion of a flood, "Nü-kua repaired the blue Heaven with stones of five colors, cut off the paws of a great tortoise to raise four pillars at the four poles, killed the black dragon (Kong-kong) to save the world, piled up ashes of reeds to halt the overflowing waters."[31] Another text recounts that, after the creation of

29. Henri Maspéro, *Les religions chinoises*, pp. 186–87. This episode was later interpreted by the disorders brought on by cases of "possession" by spirits; see Derek Bodde, "Myths of Ancient China," pp. 289 ff.

30. See Eliade, *Myths, Dreams, and Mysteries*, pp. 50 ff.; *Shamanism*, pp. 275 ff.

31. Lieh Tzŭ (third century B.C.), after the translation by Kaltenmark, "La naissance du monde," p. 458.

Heaven and Earth, Nü-kua formed men from yellow earth (noblemen) and from mud (the poor and wretched).[32]

The cosmogonic theme can also be discerned in the historicized tradition of Yü the Great. Under the (mythical) Emperor Yao, "the world was not yet in order, the vast waters flowed in a disorderly way, they flooded the world." Unlike his father, who, to conquer the waters, had built dikes, Yü "dug into the ground and made [the waters] flow toward the seas; he hunted snakes and dragons and drove them into the swamps."[33] All these motifs—the earth covered with water, the multiplication of snakes and dragons—have a cosmogonic structure. Yü plays the parts of demiurge and civilizing hero. For Chinese scholars, the organizing of the world and the founding of human institutions are equivalent to the cosmogony. The world is "created" when, by banishing the forces of evil to the four quarters, the sovereign sets himself up in a Center and completes the organization of society.

But the problem of the origin and formation of the world interested Lao Tzŭ and the Taoists, which implies the antiquity of cosmogonic speculations. Indeed, Lao Tzŭ and his disciples draw on the archaic mythological traditions, and the fact that the key terms of the Taoist vocabulary are shared by the other schools proves the antiquity and pan-Chinese character of Taoism. As we shall see (p. 20), the origin of the world according to Lao Tzŭ repeats, in metaphysical language, the ancient cosmogonic theme of chaos (*hun-tun*) as a totality resembling an egg.[34]

As for the structure and rhythms of the universe, there is perfect unity and continuity among the various fundamental conceptions from the time of the Shang to the revolution of 1911. The traditional image of the universe is that of the Center traversed by a vertical axis connecting zenith and nadir and framed by the four quarters. Heaven is round (it has the shape of an egg)

32. Huai-nan Tzŭ (third century B.C.), after the translation by Kaltenmark, ibid., p. 459.

33. Mencius, after the translation by Kaltenmark, p. 461.

34. See Norman Girardot, "Myth and Meaning in the Tao Te Ching," pp. 299 ff.

and the Earth is square. The sphere of Heaven encloses the Earth. When the earth is represented as the square body of a chariot, a central pillar supports the dais, which is round like Heaven. Each of the five cosmological numbers—four quarters and one Center—has a color, a taste, a sound, and a particular symbol. China is situated at the center of the world, the capital is in the middle of the kingdom, and the royal palace is at the center of the capital.

The representation of the capital and, in general, of any city as "center of the world" is in no way different from the traditional conceptions documented in the ancient Near East, in ancient India, in Iran, etc.[35] Just as in the other urban civilizations, so too in China cities spread out from a ceremonial center.[36] In other words, the city is especially a "center of the world" because it is there that communication with both Heaven and the underground regions is possible. The perfect capital ought to be placed at the center of the universe, which is the site of a miraculous tree called "Upright Wood" (Chien-mu); it unites the lower regions with the highest heaven, and "at noon anything close to it that stands perfectly upright cannot cast a shadow."[37]

According to Chinese tradition, every capital must possess a Ming t'ang, a ritual palace that is at once *imago mundi* and calendar. The Ming t'ang is built on a square base (= the Earth) and is covered by a round thatched roof (= Heaven). During the course of a year the sovereign moves from one part of the palace to another; by placing himself at the quarter demanded by the calendar, he successively inaugurates the seasons and the months. The colors of his garments, the foods he eats, the gestures he makes, are in perfect correspondence with the various moments of the annual cycle. At the end of the third month of summer, the sovereign takes a position at the center of the Ming t'ang, as if he were the pivot of the year.[38] Like the other symbols

35. See Eliade, *The Myth of the Eternal Return,* pp. 12 ff.

36. Paul Wheatley, *The Pivot of the Four Quarters,* pp. 30 ff., 411 ff.

37. Marcel Granet, *La pensée chinoise,* p. 324.

38. Granet, ibid., pp. 102 ff.; see also Granet's *Danses et légendes de la Chine ancienne,* pp. 116 ff. It seems that this ritual taking-of-position at the center of the Ming t'ang corresponds "to a period of retreat during which the ancient chieftains were obliged to remain deep in their dwellings." The six or

of the "center of the world" (the Tree, the Sacred Mountain, the nine-story tower, etc.), the sovereign in a certain sense incarnates the *axis mundi* and forms the connection between Earth and Heaven. The spatiotemporal symbolism of the "centers of the world" is widespread; it is documented in many archaic cultures as well as in every urban civilization.[39] We should add that, just like the royal palace, the humblest primitive dwellings of China have the same cosmic symbolism: they constitute, that is, an *imago mundi*.[40]

130. Polarities, alternation, and reintegration

As stated above (p. 16), the five cosmological numbers—i.e., the four horizons and the Center—constitute the exemplary model of a classification and at the same time of a homologation that is universal. Everything that exists belongs to a well-defined class or group and hence shares in the attributes and virtues typical of the realities subsumed under that class. So we find ourselves dealing with a daring elaboration of the system of correspondences between macrocosm and microcosm, that is, of the general theory of analogies that has played a considerable part in all traditional religions. The originality of Chinese thought lies in the fact that it integrated this macrocosm-microcosm schema into a still larger system of classification, that of the cycle of antagonistic but complementary principles known by the names of Yang and Yin. Paradigmatic systems, developed on the basis of different types of bipartition and polarity, of duality and alternation, of antithetical dyads and *coincidentia oppositorum*, are found throughout the world and at every level

twelve days "were spent in rites and observations that made it possible to foretell or determine the prosperity of stock-rearing and the success of the harvest" (*La pensée chinoise*, p. 107). The twelve days represented a prefiguration of the twelve months of the coming year—an archaic conception documented in the Near East and elsewhere (see Eliade, *The Myth of the Eternal Return*, pp. 51 ff.).

39. See Eliade, "Centre du monde, temple, maison," pp. 67 ff.

40. See R. A. Stein, "Architecture et pensée religieuse en Extrême-Orient."

of culture.[41] The importance of the Yang-Yin pair of contraries is due to the fact that it not only served as the universal model of classification but, in addition, was developed into a cosmology that, on the one hand, systematized and validated numerous corporal techniques and spiritual disciplines and, on the other hand, inspired increasingly strict and systematic philosophical speculation.

As we have seen (§127), the symbolism of polarity and alternation is abundantly illustrated in the iconography of the Shang-period bronzes. The polar symbols are so placed as to bring out their conjunction; for example, the owl, or some other figure symbolizing darkness, is given "solar eyes," whereas emblems of light are marked by a "nocturnal" sign.[42] According to Carl Hentze, the Yang-Yin symbolism is documented by the earliest ritual objects, which date from long before the earliest written texts.[43] Marcel Granet calls attention to the fact that in the *Shih Ching* the word *yin* suggests the idea of cold and cloudy weather and is applied to what is within, whereas the term *yang* suggests the idea of sunny weather and heat. In other words, *yang* and *yin* indicate concrete and antithetical ideas of time.[44] A manual of divination speaks of a "time of light" and a "time of darkness," anticipating Chuang Tzŭ's expressions: "a [time of] plenitude, a [time of] decrepitude . . . a [time of] improvement, a [time of] abatement, a [time of] life, a [time of] death" (Granet, *La pensée chinoise,* p. 132). Hence the world represents "a cyclical totality [*tao pien t'ung*] constituted by the conjunction of two alternating and complementary manifestations" (ibid., p. 127). The idea of alternation appears to have won out over the idea of opposition. This is shown by the structure of the calendar. According to the philosophers, during the winter, "at the bottom of the underground springs beneath the frozen earth, the *yang,* circumvented by the *yin,* undergoes a kind of annual ordeal, from which it emerges revivified. At the beginning of spring, it emerges from its prison, striking the ground with its heel: it is

41. See our study "Prolegomenon to Religious Dualism: Dyads and Polarities" in *The Quest,* pp. 127–75.

42. See Hentze, *Bronzegerät, Kultbauten, Religion im ältesten China der Shangzeit,* pp. 192 ff.

43. See Hentze, *Das Haus als Weltort der Seele,* pp. 99 ff.

44. Granet, *La pensée chinoise,* pp. 117 ff.

then that the ice melts of itself and the streams awaken'' (ibid., p. 135). Hence the universe reveals itself to be constituted by a series of antithetical forms that alternate cyclically.

There is perfect symmetry between the cosmic rhythms, governed by the interaction of the *yang* and the *yin,* and the complementary alternation of the activities of the two sexes. And since a feminine nature has been attributed to everything that is *yin* and a masculine nature to everything that is *yang,* the theme of the hierogamy reveals a cosmic as well as a religious dimension. Indeed, the ritual opposition between the two sexes expresses both the complementary antagonism of the two life formulas and the alternation of the two cosmic principles, the *yang* and the *yin*. In the collective spring and autumn festivals, which are the keystone of the archaic peasant cults, the two antagonistic choruses, lined up face to face, challenge each other in verse. ''The *yang* calls, the *yin* replies''; ''the boys call, the girls reply.'' These two formulas are interchangeable; they indicate the rhythm that is at once cosmic and social.[45] The antagonistic choruses confront each other like darkness and light. The field in which the encounter occurs represents the whole of space, just as the participants symbolize the whole of the human group and of natural things (Granet, p. 143). And a collective hierogamy crowned the festivities, a ritual that is exemplified elsewhere in the world. Polarity, accepted as governing life during the rest of the year, is abolished, or transcended, in the union of contraries.

''A *yin* (aspect), a *yang* (aspect)—that is the Tao,'' says a brief treatise.[46] The unceasing transformation of the universe by the alternation of the *yang* and the *yin* manifests, so to speak, the exterior aspect of the Tao. But as soon as we attempt to grasp the ontological structure of the Tao, we encounter innumerable difficulties. Let us recall that the strict meaning of the word is ''road, way,'' but also ''to speak,'' whence the sense ''doctrine.'' Tao ''first of all suggests the image of a way to be followed'' and ''the idea of controlling conduct, of moral rule''; but it also means ''the art of putting Heaven and Earth, the sacred powers and men, in communication,'' the magico-religious power of the

45. See Granet, *Danses et légendes de la Chine ancienne,* p. 43; *La pensée chinoise,* p. 141.

46. The *Hsi Tz'u,* cited by Granet, *La pensée chinoise,* p. 325. This is the earliest scholarly definition of the Tao.

diviner, the sorcerer, and the king.[47] For common philosophical and religious thought, the Tao is the principle of order, immanent in all the realms of the real; there is also mention of the Heavenly Tao and the Earthly Tao (which are opposed somewhat in the manner of the *yang* and the *yin*) and of the Tao of Man (that is, of the principles of conduct that, observed by the king, make possible his function as intermediary between Heaven and Earth).[48]

Some of these meanings derive from the archaic notion of the original unity/totality, in other words, from a cosmogonic conception. Lao Tzŭ's speculations concerning the origin of the world are bound up with a cosmogonic myth that tells of Creation from a totality comparable to an egg. In chapter 42 of the *Tao Tê Ching* we read: "The Tao gave birth to One. One gave birth to Two. Two gave birth to Three. Three gave birth to the ten thousand beings. The ten thousand beings carry the Yin on their back and encircle the Yang."[49] We see in what way Lao Tzŭ made use of a traditional cosmogonic myth, at the same time giving it a new metaphysical dimension. The "One" is equivalent to the "whole"; it refers to the primordial totality, a theme familiar to many mythologies. The commentary explains that the union of Heaven and Earth (i.e., the "Two") gave birth to everything that exists, in accordance with an equally well-known mythological scenario. But for Lao Tzŭ, "One," the primitive unity/totality, already represents a stage of Creation, for it was engendered by a mysterious and incomprehensible principle, the Tao.

In another cosmogonic fragment (chap. 25), the Tao is denominated "an undifferentiated and perfect being, born before Heaven and Earth. . . . We can consider it the Mother of this

47. Max Kaltenmark, *Lao tseu et le taoïsme,* p. 30; see also Granet, *La pensée chinoise,* pp. 300 ff.

48. Kaltenmark, *Lao tseu,* p. 33: "It is this Tao which represents the ideal of Confucius, who proclaimed: 'He who in the morning has heard the Tao spoken of can die peacefully at night.' "

49. After Kaltenmark's translation in "La naissance du monde en Chine," p. 463. This scheme of serial procreations is used by almost all of the philosophical schools, from the *Yi Ching* to the Neo-Confucianists; cf. Wing-Tsit Chan, *The Way of Lao Tzu,* p. 176; Norman Girardot, "Myth and Meaning in the *Tao Te Ching,*" pp. 311 ff.

world, but I do not know its name; I will call it Tao; and, if it must be named, its name will be: the Immense (*ta*)."[50] The "undifferentiated and perfect" being is interpreted by a commentator of the second century B.C. thus: "the mysterious unity [*Hung-t'ung*] of Heaven and Earth chaotically [*hun-tun*] constitutes [the condition] of the uncarved block."[51] Hence the Tao is a primordial totality, living and creative but formless and nameless. "That which is nameless is the origin of Heaven and Earth. That which has a name is the Mother of the ten thousand beings," says another cosmogonic fragment (chap. 1, lines 3–7). However, the "Mother," which in this passage represents the beginning of the cosmogony, elsewhere designates the Tao itself. "The divinity of the Valley does not die: it is the Obscure Female. The gate of the Obscure Female—that is the origin of Heaven and Earth."[52]

The ineffableness of the Tao is also expressed by other epithets, which continue, though at the same time color, the original cosmogonic image, which is Chaos (*hun-tun*). We list the most important of them: Emptiness (*hsu*), nothingness (*wu*), the Great (*ta*), the One (*i*).[53] We shall return to some of these terms when we analyze Lao Tzŭ's doctrine, but it is important to mention at this point that the Taoist philosophers, as well as the hermits and adepts in search of long life and immortality, sought to reestablish this paradisal condition, especially the original perfection and spontaneity. It is possible to discern in this nostalgia for the primordial situation a new expression of the ancient agrarian scenario that ritually summoned up "totalization" by the collective ("chaotic") union of youths and girls, representatives of the Yang and the Yin. The essential element, common to all the Taoist schools, was exaltation of the primitive human

50. After Kaltenmark's translation, *Lao tseu,* p. 39.

51. *Huai-nan-tzŭ,* cited by Girardot, "Myth and Meaning in the *Tao Te Ching,*" p. 307. For Chuang Tzŭ, the primordial condition of perfect unity was lost when the Emperor Hun-Tun—i.e., "Emperor Chaos"—was perforated in order that, like all men, he should have a face with seven orifices; but "Chaos succumbed on the seventh day, after the seventh perforation"; see James Legge, *The Texts of Taoism,* vol. 1 (*SBE,* vol. 39, p. 267).

52. Chapter 6, trans. Kaltenmark, *Lao tseu,* p. 50.

53. Cf. Girardot, "Myth and Meaning in the *Tao Te Ching,*" p. 304.

condition that existed before the triumph of civilization. But it was precisely this "return to nature" that was objected to by all those who wanted to inaugurate a just and duly policed society, governed by the norms, and inspired by the examples, of the fabulous kings and civilizing heroes.

131. Confucius: The power of the rites

It could be said that in ancient China all the trends of religious thought shared a certain number of fundamental ideas. We will mention first of all the notion of the *tao* as principle and source of the real, the idea of alternations governed by the *yin-yang* rhythm, and the theory of the analogy between macrocosm and microcosm. This theory was applied on all the planes of human existence and organization: the anatomy, physiology, and psychology of the individual; social institutions; and the dwellings and consecrated spaces (city, palace, altar, temple, house). But while some thinkers (notably the Taoists) held that an existence conducted under the sign of the *tao* and in perfect harmony with the cosmic rhythms was possible only *in the beginning* (that is, in the stage preceding social organization and the rise of culture), others considered this type of existence especially realizable in a just and civilized society.

The most famous, and the most influential, of those who took the latter position was certainly Confucius (ca. 551–479).[54] Living in a period of anarchy and injustice, saddened by the general suffering and misery, Confucius understood that the only solution was a radical reform of the government, carried out by enlightened leaders and applied by responsible civil servants. Since he did not himself succeed in obtaining an important post in the administration, he devoted his life to teaching and was indeed the first to follow the profession of private pedagogue. Despite his success among his numerous disciples, Confucius was convinced, shortly before his death, that his mission had been a total failure. But his disciples managed, from generation to generation,

54. His family name was K'ung. "Confucius" is the Latin version of K'ung Fu-tzu, "Master Kung."

to pass on the essence of his teaching, and 250 years after his death the sovereign of the Han dynasty (ca. A.D. 206–20) decided to entrust the administration of the empire to the Confucianists. From then on the Master's doctrines guided the civil service and the making of governmental policy for more than two thousand years.

Properly speaking, Confucius is not a religious leader.[55] His ideas, and especially those of the Neo-Confucianists, are usually studied in histories of philosophy. But, directly or indirectly, Confucius profoundly influenced Chinese religion. In fact, the actual source of his moral and political reform is religious. Then, too, he rejects none of the important traditional ideas, such as the *tao,* the celestial god, the ancestor cult. Furthermore, he extols, and revalorizes, the religious function of the rites and of customary behavior.

For Confucius, *tao* was established by a decree of Heaven; "If the *tao* is practiced, that is because of the decree of Heaven" (*Lun Yü* = *Analects* 14. 38). To behave according to the *tao* is to conform to the will of Heaven. Confucius recognizes the preeminence of Heaven (T'ien). For him, this is no *deus otiosus;* T'ien is concerned for every individual separately and helps him to become better. "It is Heaven that produced virtue (*tê*) in me," he declares (5. 22). "At the age of fifty years I understood the will of Heaven" (2. 4). In fact, the Master believed that Heaven had given him a mission to perform. Like many others among his contemporaries, he held that the way of Heaven is illustrated by the example of the civilizing heroes Yao and Shun and by the kings of the Chou, Wen, and Wu dynasties (8. 20).

Confucius declared that a man must perform the sacrifices and the other traditional rituals because they form part of the life of a "superior man" (*chün tzŭ*), of a "gentleman." Heaven likes to receive sacrifices; but it also likes moral behavior and, above all, good government. Metaphysical and theological speculations concerning Heaven and life after death are useless (5. 12; 7. 20; 11. 11). The "superior man" must first of all be concerned with concrete human existence, as it is lived here and now. As for

55. But Confucius was very soon invested with the virtues and attributes typical of civilizing heroes; see some examples in Granet, *La pensée chinoise,* pp. 477 ff.

spirits, Confucius does not deny their existence, but he questions their importance. Though respecting them, he advises, "Keep them at a distance. That is wisdom" (6. 18). As for devoting oneself to their service, "If you cannot serve men, how could you serve the spirits?" (11. 11).

The moral and political reform planned by Confucius constitutes a "total education," that is, a method able to transform the ordinary individual into a "superior man" (*chün tzŭ*). Anyone at all can become a "true man" on condition that he learn ceremonial behavior in conformity with the *tao*—in other words, correct practice of the rites and customs (*li*). However, this practice is not easy to master. It is neither a matter of wholly external ritualism nor one of an emotional exaltation deliberately induced during the accomplishment of a rite. Every piece of correct ceremonial behavior releases a formidable magico-religious power.[56] Confucius calls up the image of the famous philosopher-king Shun: "He simply stood there, gravely and reverently, with his face turned toward the South [the ritual posture of sovereigns]—*and that was all*" (in other words, the affairs of the kingdom proceeded in conformity with the norm; 15. 4). For the cosmos and society are governed by the same magico-religious powers that are active in man. "With a correct behavior, it is not necessary to give orders" (13. 6). "To govern by virtue [*tê*] is as if one were the Pole Star: one remains in place while all the other stars circle around in homage" (2. 2).

A gesture made in accordance with the rule constitutes a new epiphany of the cosmic harmony. Obviously, he who is capable of such conduct is no longer the ordinary individual that he was before he was taught; his mode of existence is radically transformed; he is a "perfect man." A discipline whose object is the "transmutation" of gestures and behavior into rituals, *at the same time preserving their spontaneity,* undoubtedly has a religious intention and structure.[57] From this point of view, Confucius' method can be compared with the doctrines and techniques by which Lao Tzŭ and the Taoists held that they could recover

56. This aspect has been well brought out by Herbert Fingarette in his *Confucius: The Secular as Sacred.*

57. A similar effort is visible in Tantrism, in the Cabala, and in certain Zen practices.

the original spontaneity. Confucius' originality consists in his having pursued the "transmutation" of the gestures and conduct indispensable to a complex and highly hierarchized society into spontaneous rituals.

For Confucius, nobility and distinction are not innate; they are obtained through education. One *becomes* a gentleman through discipline and through certain natural aptitudes (4. 5; 6. 5; etc.). Goodness, wisdom, and courage are the virtues peculiar to the nobility. Supreme satisfaction lies in developing one's own virtues: "He who is really good is never unhappy" (9. 28). However, the gentleman's proper career is to govern (7. 32). For Confucius, as for Plato, the art of governing is the only means of insuring the peace and happiness of the great majority. But, as we have just seen, the art of governing, like any other skill or behavior or significant act, is the result of a teaching and learning process that is essentially religious. Confucius revered the civilizing heroes and the great kings of the Chou dynasty; they were his exemplary models. "I have transmitted what I have been taught, without adding anything of my own. I have been true to the men of old, and I have loved them!" (7. 1). Some scholars have seen in these declarations a nostalgia for a period irrevocably ended. Yet in revalorizing the ritual function of public behavior, Confucius inaugurated a new way; he showed the need to recover, and the possibility of recovering, the religious dimension of secular work and social activity.

132. Lao Tzŭ and Taoism

In his *Shih Chi* ("Historical Memoirs"), written about 100 B.C., the great historian Ssŭ-ma Ch'ien narrates that when Confucius went to consult Lao Tan (i.e., Lao Tzŭ) concerning the rites, Lao Tan replied, among other things: "Get rid of your arrogant attitude and all these desires, this self-satisfaction and this overflowing zeal: all this is of no profit for your person. That is all I can tell you." Confucius withdrew in dismay. He confessed to his disciples that he knew all animals—birds, fish, quadrupeds—and that he understood their way of behavior, "but the dragon

I cannot know; he rises into heaven on the clouds and the wind. Today I saw Lao Tzŭ, and he is like the dragon!"[58]

This meeting is certainly apocryphal, as, indeed, are all the traditions recorded by Ssŭ-ma Ch'ien. But it explains, simply and humorously, the incompatibility between these two great religious personages. For, the historian adds, "Lao Tzŭ cultivated the Tao and Tê: according to his doctrine, one must seek to live hidden and anonymously." But to live shunning public life and scorning honors was precisely the opposite of the ideal of the "superior man" advocated by Confucius. Lao Tzŭ's "hidden and anonymous" existence explains the lack of any authentic information concerning his biography. According to tradition he was for a time archivist at the Chou court, but, discouraged by the decadence of the royal house, he gave up his position and set off for the West. When he traveled through the Hsien-ku Pass, the border guard asked him to write down his doctrine. Whereupon he composed "a work in two parts, in which he set forth his ideas concerning the Tao and Tê and which contained more than 5,000 words; then he went on, and no one knows what became of him." After relating all that he had learned, Ssŭ-ma Ch'ien concludes: "No one on earth can say whether this is true or not: Lao Tzŭ was a hidden sage."

The book containing "more than 5,000 words" is the famous *Tao Tê Ching,* the most profound and most enigmatic text in all Chinese literature. As to its author and the date when it was composed, opinions are not only various but contradictory.[59] It is, however, now agreed that the text as it exists today cannot have been written by a contemporary of Confucius; it probably dates from the third century. It contains dicta that belong to various proto-Taoist schools and a certain number of aphorisms

58. After the translation by Chavannes in Kaltenmark, *Lao tseu,* p. 17.

59. At least four different positions are held: (1) Lao Tzŭ is the same person as Lao Tan of the sixth century and hence could have been visited by Confucius; (2) Lao Tzŭ lived in the so-called "Spring and Autumn" period (ca. 774–481), but he is not the author of the *Tao Tê Ching;* (3) he lived in the period of the Warring Kingdoms (ca. 404–221), but it is not certain that he wrote the *Tao Tê Ching;* (4) he is not a historical personage. See Wing-tsit Chan, *The Way of Lao Tzu,* pp. 35 ff., and Jan Yün-Hua, "Problems of Tao and *Tao Te Ching,*" p. 209 (the author summarizes the most recent views of Fung Yu-lan on Lao Tzŭ and early Taoism, pp. 211 ff.).

in verse that go back to the sixth century.[60] Yet despite its unsystematic character, the *Tao Tê Ching* expresses a thought that is consistent and original. As Kaltenmark observes, "Hence we must admit the existence of a philosopher who, if not directly its author, must at least be the master whose influence was determinative at its origin. There is no harm in continuing to call him Lao Tzŭ."[61]

Paradoxically, the *Tao Tê Ching* contains a great deal of advice directed to sovereigns and political and military leaders. Like Confucius, Lao Tzŭ affirms that the affairs of the state can be successfully managed only if the prince follows the way of the Tao, in other words, if he practices the method of *wu-wei,* "without doing" or "nonaction." For "the Tao forever remains without action, and there is nothing that it does not do" (37. 1).[62] This is why the Taoist never intervenes in the course of events. "If noblemen and kings were able, imitating the Tao, to hold to this attitude of nonintervention, the ten thousand beings would at once follow their example of themselves" (37. 2). Like the true Taoist, "the best [of princes] is the one whose existence is not known" (17. 1). Since "the heavenly Tao triumphs without striving" (73. 6), the most effective ways of obtaining power are *wu-wei* and nonviolence.[63] "The supple and the weak overcome

60. See Kaltenmark, *Lao tseu,* pp. 19 ff.

61. Ibid., p. 22. The same situation is also found in other traditional literatures: the work, attributed to a certain sage or contemplative, is usually continued and enriched by his disciples. In a certain sense the author, by becoming famous, became "anonymous."

62. Except when otherwise indicated, the translations are after those by Max Kaltenmark in his *Lao tseu.* The English version by Wing-tsit Chan, *The Way of Lao Tzu,* is valuable for its notes and commentaries; the translation by Arthur Waley, *The Way and Its Power,* is distinguished by its literary quality. [Unfortunately, Kaltenmark's version differs so often and so widely from Waley's that it has been impossible to quote the latter instead of retranslating the former.—Translator.]

63. "He who aspires to power and expects to obtain it by action—I foresee that he will fail in his attempt" (29. 1) "The good military leader is not belligerent; the good soldier is not impetuous. He who best overcomes the enemy is he who never takes the offensive. . . . This is what I call the virtue of nonviolence. This is what I call equaling Heaven. To equal Heaven was the highest idea of the ancients" (68. 1–2, 7).

the unyielding and the strong'' (36. 10; cf. 40. 2, ''weakness is the function of the Tao'').

In short, just like Confucius, who proposes his ideal of the ''perfect man'' both to sovereigns and to any man wishing to learn, Lao Tzŭ invites political and military leaders to behave in the manner of Taoists, in other words, to accept the same exemplary model: that of the Tao. But this is the only similarity between the two masters. Lao Tzŭ criticizes and rejects the Confucian system, that is, the importance of the rites, respect for social values, and rationalism. ''Let us renounce Benevolence, let us discard Justice; the people will recover the true virtues of the family'' (19. 1). For the Confucianists, benevolence and justice are the greatest virtues. Lao Tzŭ, however, regards them as attitudes that are artificial and hence useless and dangerous. ''When one abandons the Tao, one has recourse to Benevolence; when one abandons Benevolence, one has recourse to Justice; when one abandons Justice, one has recourse to the Rites. The Rites are only a thin layer of loyalty and faith and the beginning of anarchy'' (38. 9–14). Lao Tzŭ similarly condemns social values, because they are illusory and in the last analysis harmful. As for discursive knowledge, it destroys the unity of being and encourages confusion by bestowing an absolute value on relative notions.[64] ''That is why the holy man confines himself to inactivity and carries on wordless teaching'' (2. 10).

In the last analysis, the Taoist is guided by only one exemplary model: the Tao. Yet the Tao designates the ultimate, mysterious, and inapprehensible reality, *fons et origo* of all creation, foundation of all existence. When we analyzed its cosmogonic function, we pointed out the ineffable character of the Tao (see pp. 20–21). The first line of the *Tao Tê Ching* affirms: ''A tao of which it is possible to speak [*tao*] is not the permanent Tao [*ch'ang tao*]'' (1. 1). This is as much as to say that the Tao of which Lao Tzŭ is speaking, the model of the Taoist, is not the Ch'ang Tao

64. ''In this world each man affirms that what is beautiful is beautiful, thereby ugliness is instituted; and each man affirms that what is good is good, thereby the 'not good' is instituted.'' '' 'Long' and 'short' exist only comparatively; 'high' and 'low' are interconnected'' (2. 1–2, 5–6).

(permanent or supreme Tao).[65] The latter, constituted by the totality of the Real, transcends the modalities of beings and therefore is inaccessible to knowing. Neither Lao Tzŭ nor Chuang Tzŭ tries to prove its existence—an attitude well known to be shared by many mystics. In all probability, the "Obscure deeper than obscurity itself" refers to the typically Taoist experience of ecstasy, to which we shall return.

So Lao Tzŭ speaks of a "second," contingent Tao; but this cannot be apprehended either. "I gaze and I see nothing. . . . I listen and I hear nothing. . . . I find only an undifferentiated Unity. . . . Indiscernible, it cannot be named" (chap. 14).[66] But certain images and metaphors reveal some significant structures. As we have already pointed out (pp. 21–22), the "second" Tao is called the "Mother of the World" (chaps. 25 and 52). It is symbolized by the "divinity of the Valley," the "Obscure Female" that does not die.[67] The image of the valley suggests the idea of emptiness and at the same time the idea of a receptacle of waters, hence of fecundity. Emptiness, the void, is associated, on the one hand, with the notion of fertility and maternity and, on the other hand, with the absence of sensible qualities (the special modality of the Tao). The image of the thirty spokes converging toward the emptiness of the hub inspires an especially rich symbolism, evident in "the virtue of the leader who attracts to himself all beings, of the sovereign Unity that gives order to multiplicity around it," but also evident in the Taoist who, "when he is empty, that is, purified of passions and desires, is completely inhabited by the Tao" (Kaltenmark, p. 55).

By conforming to the model of the "second" Tao, the adept reanimates and strengthens his feminine potentialities, first of all

65. "Or better, the Mysterious [*Hsuang*], or still better the *Obscure deeper than obscurity itself,* for there is no end to probing deeper into the mystery" (Kaltenmark, p. 45).

66. Another passage presents the Tao as "an imperceptible, indiscernible being" that "contains in its bosom" images, beings, fecund essences, and spiritual essences (chap. 21).

67. The expression *Obscure Female* "suggests the mysterious fecundity of the Tao at the same time that it is connected with the idea of the valley or cavity in the mountain" (Kaltenmark, p. 51). On this aspect of the Tao, see the articles by Ellen Marie Chen, especially "Nothingness and the Mother Principle in Early Chinese Taoism."

"weakness," humility, nonresistance. "Know masculinity, but prefer femininity: you will be the ravine of the world. Be the ravine of the world and the Supreme Tê will not fail you, and you can return to the state of infancy" (28. 1–2). From a certain point of view, the Taoist attempts to obtain the modality of the androgyne, the archaic ideal of human perfection.[68] But the integration of the two sexes makes it easier to return to the state of infancy, that is, "to the beginning" of individual existence; such a return makes possible the periodic regeneration of life. We now better understand the Taoist's desire to recover the primordial situation, the situation that existed "in the beginning." For him, fullness of life, spontaneity, and bliss are bestowed only at the beginning of a "creation" or of a new epiphany of life.[69]

The model for the integration of contraries is always the Tao; in its unity/totality the Yang and Yin coexist. But as we have seen (p. 19), beginning in the protohistorical period the collective hierogamy of youths and girls, representing the Yang and the Yin, periodically reactualized the cosmic and social unity/totality. In this case too, Taoism is inspired by archaic religious patterns of behavior. It is important to add that the Taoists' attitude toward women contrasted sharply with the ideology that was predominant in feudal China.

The pan-Chinese idea of the cosmic circuit plays an important part in the *Tao Tê Ching*. The Tao "circulates everywhere in the universe, never being stopped" (chap. 25). The life and death of beings are also explained by the alternation of the Yang and the Yin: the former stimulates the vital energies, but the Yin brings rest. However, the holy man hopes to withdraw from the universal rhythm of life and death; by realizing emptiness in his own being, he places himself outside the circuit. As Lao Tzŭ expresses it, "there is no place in him [in the holy man] for death" (50. 13). "He who is supplied with a plenitude of Tê is comparable to a newborn infant" (55. 1). The Taoists are acquainted with several techniques for prolonging life indefinitely

68. See Eliade, *The Two and the One,* pp. 78 ff.

69. This is, of course, a common idea, shared by all traditional societies: perfection belongs to the beginning of the (cosmic or "historical") cycle, and "decadence" soon makes itself felt.

and even for obtaining a "physical immortality." The quest for long life forms part of the quest for the Tao. But Lao Tzŭ does not appear to have believed in physical immortality or in the survival of the human personality. The *Tao Tê Ching* is not explicit on this point.[70]

To put the problem in its proper context, it must be remembered that the Taoist technique of ecstasy is shamanic in origin and structure.[71] We know that during a trance the shaman's soul leaves his body and journeys in the cosmic regions. According to an anecdote narrated by Chuang Tzŭ, Confucius one day found Lao Tzŭ "completely inert and no longer having the appearance of a living being." After waiting for some time, he spoke to him: "Have my eyes deceived me, or was it real? Just now, Master, your body looked like a piece of dry wood, you seemed to have left the world and men and to have taken refuge in an inaccessible solitude." "Yes," Lao Tzŭ answered, "I went to frolic at the Origin of all things" (chap. 21). As Kaltenmark observes (p. 82), the expression "journey to the Origin of all things" sums up the essence of the Taoist mystical experience. This ecstatic journey constitutes a return "to the beginning" of all things; by freeing itself from time and space, the spirit recovers the eternal present that transcends both life and death. What we have here is a revalorization and a deepening of shamanic ecstasy. During his trance the shaman, too, frees himself from time and space: he flies away to the "center of the world"; he reconstitutes the paradisal period before the "fall," when men could ascend to heaven and converse with the gods. But Lao Tzŭ's journey to the origin of things constitutes a mystical experience of a different kind; for he transcends the limitations that characterize the human condition and hence radically alters its ontological order.

Very little is known about the life of Chuang Tzŭ, the second great master of Taoism. He probably lived in the fifth century B.C.; if this is so, some of his aphorisms are earlier than the text of the *Tao Tê Ching* as we have it. Like Lao Tzŭ, Chuang Tzŭ

70. Kaltenmark, *Lao tseu,* p. 82; cf. Ellen Marie Chen, "Is There a Doctrine of Physical Immortality in the *Tao te Ching?*"

71. See Granet, *La pensée chinoise,* pp. 501 ff.; Eliade, *Shamanism,* pp. 470 ff.

rejects both current opinions and discursive knowledge. The only perfect knowledge is ecstatic, since it does not involve the duality of the real. This is why Chuang Tzŭ identifies life and death: they are the two modalities, or the two aspects, of ultimate reality.[72] This theme of the unity life/death is constantly treated by Taoist authors.[73] A well-known anecdote illustrates Chuang Tzŭ's conception of the relativity of states of consciousness: "Long ago I, Chuang Chou, dreamed that I was a butterfly, a butterfly on the wing, and I was happy; I did not know that was Chou. Suddenly I waked, and I was myself, the real Chou. And I do not know if I was Chou dreaming that he was a butterfly, or a butterfly dreaming that it was Chou."[74] In other words, within the circling course of the Tao, states of consciousness are interchangeable.

The holy man, who has emptied his spirit of all conditionings and has emerged in the unity/totality of the Tao, lives in an unbroken ecstasy. As in the case of certain yogins, this paradoxical mode of existing in the world is sometimes expressed in extravagant terms of divine omnipotence. "The perfect man is pure spirit. He does not feel the heat of burning brush or the chill of flooding waters; the thunder that splits mountains, the storm that stirs up the ocean, cannot frighten him. For such a one, the clouds are his carriage horses, the sun and the moon are his riding horses. He wanders beyond the Four Seas; the alternations of life and death do not concern him, and still less notions of good and evil."[75] According to some Taoist authors, these ecstatic peregrinations are really inner journeys.[76] As is the case with other peoples dominated by shamanism—for example, the Turco-Mongols—the ordeals and adventures of the shaman

72. Some moving examples will be found in Chuang Tzŭ, chap. 18.

73. "I and this skull," said Lieh Tzŭ to one of his disciples, "we know that there is truly no life, that there is truly no death." "Death and life, they are a going and returning: being dead here, how do I know that it is not being alive there?" After the translation by Henri Maspéro, *Le taoïsme,* p. 240.

74. After Maspéro's translation, ibid. Chou is his personal name.

75. Chuang Tzŭ, chap. 2, after the translation by Kaltenmark, *Lao tseu,* pp. 117–18.

76. "By inner contemplation we find a way to satisfy ourselves in ourselves" (Lieh Tzŭ, after Kaltenmark's translation, p. 118).

during his ecstatic journeyings inspired poets and were glorified in epic poetry.[77]

133. Techniques of long life

Chinese terminology usually distinguishes philosophical Taoism (*Tao Chia,* literally, "Taoist school") from religious Taoism or "Taoist religion" (*Tao Chiao,* literally, "Taoist sect").[78] Some authors regard this distinction as justified and necessary; for them, the Taoism of Lao Tzŭ and Chuang Tzŭ is a "pure philosophy," in basic contrast to the search for physical immortality, the central goal of the "Taoist religion."[79] Another group of scholars maintains the fundamental unity of all the historical forms of Taoism.[80] And in fact the "metaphysicians," the "mystics," and the adepts in quest of physical immortality all shared the same paradoxical conception of the Tao and sought to reach the same result: to unite in their person the two epiphanies of ultimate reality (*yang* and *yin,* matter and spirit, life and death). But the distinction between "philosophical Taoism" and the "Taoist religion" is useful and may be preserved.

The ultimate goal of the adepts was to obtain physical immortality. The ideogram for the Immortal (*hsien*), depicting a man and a mountain, suggests a hermit; but its earliest forms represented a dancing man waving his sleeves like a bird beating its wings. The adept in the process of obtaining immortality was covered with feathers, and wings sprouted from his shoulders.[81] "To ascend to heaven in broad daylight" was the consecrated

77. See Kaltenmark, p. 120. See also Eliade, *Shamanism,* pp. 474 ff., on folklore and shamanic literature in China, and pp. 177 ff., on the shamanistic structure of Tartar epic poetry.

78. According to Sivin, this distinction is a creation of modern historiography; see his "On the Word 'Taoist,' " pp. 304 ff.

79. See, inter alia, A. C. Graham, *The Book of Lieh-tzu,* pp. 10 ff., 16 ff., and Herrlee G. Creel, *What Is Taoism?*, pp. 1–24.

80. The most important are Maspéro, Granet, Kaltenmark, and Schipper. See the discussion of these two positions in Norman Girardot, "Part of the Way," pp. 320–24.

81. On the relations among wings, down, magical flight, and Taoism, see Kaltenmark, *Le Lie-sien Tchouan,* pp. 12 ff. It is known that feathers are one

formula for the Master's final apotheosis. A second category comprised the adepts who lived for centuries in a sort of earthly paradise: the Wonderful Islands or the Sacred Mountain, K'un-lün.[82] They returned to earth from time to time to transmit the formulas for physical immortality to certain neophytes worthy to receive it. Finally, the third category included those who did not attain to the earthly paradises until after death. But this death was only apparent: in the coffin they left a staff, a sword, or a pair of sandals, to which they had given the appearance of their body. This was called the "freeing of the corpse."[83] The Immortals were sometimes represented with a disproportionately large skull, a sign that their mind had stored up a great deal of *yang* energy.

Several techniques for long life are available to the adept. Their basic principle consists in "nourishing the vital force" (*yang-hsing*). Since there is perfect correspondence between the macrocosm and the human body, the vital forces enter and leave by the nine bodily orifices; so these must be vigilantly watched. Taoists divide the body into three sections, called "Fields of Cinnabar";[84] the upper "field" is in the brain, the second is near the heart, the third is below the navel. Dietary practices have a definite goal: nourishing the organs with foods and medicinal herbs that contain the "energies" that are proper to them. It must be remembered that the inner regions of the body are inhabited not only by gods and guardian spirits but also by maleficent beings: the "Three Worms," which inhabit the three "Fields of Cinnabar," devour the adept's vitality. To get rid of them, he must give up ordinary foods (cereals, flesh, wine, etc.)

---

of the most frequent symbols of "shamanic flight"; see Eliade, *Shamanism*, s.v. "magic flight" (pp. 477 ff.).

82. We have here the exemplary image of paradisal territories that are not under the dominion of time and are accessible only to the initiated. According to the historian Ssŭ-ma Ch'ien, several kings of the fourth and third centuries B.C. had sent out expeditions in search of these supernatural islands (*Mémoires*, trans. Chavannes, vol. 3, pp. 436–37).

83. See some examples in Maspéro, *Le taoïsme*, pp. 84–85.

84. It should be borne in mind that cinnabar (mercuric sulphide) was the essential element for preparing the alchemists' "elixir of immortality."

and feed on medicinal plants and mineral substances able to kill the three demons.[85]

By freeing himself from the three inner demons, the adept begins to feed on dew or the cosmic "breaths"; he inhales not only the atmospheric air but also the solar, lunar, and stellar emanations. According to certain recipes, documented in the third century after Christ, the emanation of the sun must be absorbed at noon (when the *yang* is at its height), that of the moon (containing the *yin*) at midnight. But above all it is necessary to hold the breath; by an inner vision and by concentrating his thought, the adept is able to visualize his breath and conduct it through the three Fields of Cinnabar. If he holds his breath for the time required, for one thousand respirations, he obtains immortality.[86]

A special procedure is called "embryonic breathing" (*t'ai-si*); this is an inner, closed-circuit "breathing" similar to that of the fetus in its mother's womb.[87] "By returning to the base, going back to the origin, one drives away old age, one returns to the fetal state."[88] "Embryonic respiration" is not, like the yogic *prāṇāyāma* (see §143), a preliminary exercise for meditation. Nevertheless, the practice makes a certain experience possible. According to the *T'ai-ping ching* (third century A.D.), it is possible, by an inner vision, to discern the gods that reside in the five organs. They are, furthermore, the same as those that inhabit the macrocosm. By meditating, the adept can enter into communication with them and make them visit and strengthen his body.[89]

85. See Maspéro, *Le taoïsme,* pp. 98 ff.

86. Maspéro, "Les procédés de 'nourrir le principe vital' dans la religion taoïste ancienne," pp. 203 ff.; Maspéro, *Le taoïsme,* pp. 107 ff.

87. See Maspéro, "Les procédés," pp. 198 ff.; Eliade, *Yoga,* pp. 53 ff. We may add that the "deep and silent" breathing of ecstasy resembled the breathing of animals during hibernation, and it is known that, for the Chinese, the fullness and spontaneity of animal life constituted the supreme example of an existence in perfect harmony with the cosmos.

88. Preface to the treatise "Oral Formulas for Embryonic Respiration," trans. Maspéro, in "Les procédés," p. 198.

89. On the Taoist pantheon dwelling in the human body, see Maspéro, *Le taoïsme,* pp. 116 ff., 137 ff.; cf. M. Strickmann, "The Longest Taoist Scripture," p. 341.

Another method for obtaining longevity involves a sexual technique that is at once a ritual and a way of meditation. The practices "of the bedchamber [*fang shung*]," as they are called, go back to a very early time; their purpose is to increase vitality and to insure long life and the procreation of male offspring. But the Taoist technique, the "way of the Yin" of the Immortal Yang-cheng (first century A.D.), consists in "making the semen return to repair the brain." And in fact this is the same typically Taoist ideal of ataraxia: avoid dispersal of the vital energy. The adept must perform the sexual act without emission of semen. Retaining it makes it possible for the semen, mingled with the "breath," to circulate within the body or, more precisely, to ascend from the lower Field of Cinnabar to the one situated in the head, where it will revitalize the brain. Normally, both partners gain by the act. A text of the fifth century A.D. states that through "perfect meditation . . . men and women can practice the method of Eternal Life." Through meditation the two partners must "lose consciousness of their body and consciousness of the external world"; then, after uttering prayers, the man must concentrate on the loins and the woman on the heart. "This is the method for not dying."[90]

The Immortal Jung Ch'eng Kung's knowledge of the method of "repairing and conducting" was perfect. "He drew the essence from the mysterious Female" (see above, note 67); his principle was that the vital spirits that reside in the Valley do not die, for by them life is maintained and the breath is nourished. His hair, which was white, became black again; his teeth, which had fallen out, grew once more. His practices were exactly the same as those of Lao Tzŭ. He is also said to have been "Lao Tzŭ's master."[91] Some adepts used a method that has been termed "vampirism" (Kaltenmark) and that was condemned as not orthodox. It consisted in absorbing the vital energy of the women one approached: "this energy, coming from the very springs of life, procured a considerable degree of longevity."[92]

90. See Maspéro, "Les procédés," pp. 386–87. A fragment of this text is given by Maspéro, ibid., p. 388.

91. Kaltenmark, *Le Lie-sien Tchouan,* pp. 55–56.

92. Kaltenmark, ibid., p. 57.

One of the chief goals of the Taoist sexual technique is to mingle the semen with the breath in the lower Field of Cinnabar and there, below the navel, to form the "mysterious embryo" of the new immortal body. Nourished exclusively on the "breath," this embryo develops into a "pure body" that, upon the adept's seeming death, detaches itself from his corpse and joins the other Immortals. In order to "repair the brain," the adept had to absorb a great amount of Yin; this is why he often changed partners. This practice later gave rise to the collective "union of breaths," a ceremony that was frequently criticized, especially by the Buddhists. But this kind of "orgy" was strictly ritual; in fact, it goes back to the agrarian ceremonies of protohistory (see §130).

A certain Indian influence, especially that of "left-hand" Tantrism, which had elaborated a yogic method of obtaining the simultaneous arrest of respiration and of seminal emission,[93] is perceptible in Taoist sexual practices. Just as in Tantrism, the Taoist sexual terminology refers equally to mental operations and to mystical experiences.

134. The Taoists and alchemy

Certain rites and mythologies of metallurgists, smelters, and blacksmiths were revived and reinterpreted by the alchemists. Archaic conceptions concerning the birth of minerals in the "womb" of the earth, the natural transformation of metals into gold, the mystical value of gold, and the ritual complex "blacksmiths–initiatory brotherhoods–trade secrets" recur in the teachings of the alchemists.

The specialists are not in agreement concerning the origins of Chinese alchemy; the dates of the earliest texts mentioning alchemical operations are still in dispute. In China as elsewhere, alchemy is defined by a twofold belief: (1) in the transmutation of metals into gold and (2) in the "soteriological" value of operations performed to obtain this result. Precise references to these two beliefs are documented in China from the fourth cen-

93. See *Yoga,* pp. 254 ff., and vol. 3 of the present work (chap. 33).

tury before Christ. It is generally agreed to regard Tsu Yen, a contemporary of Mencius, as the "founder" of alchemy.[94] In the second century before Christ the relation between preparing alchemical gold and obtaining longevity-immortality is clearly recognized by Lü An and other authors.[95]

Chinese alchemy, as an autonomous discipline, is a compound of (1) the traditional cosmological beliefs; (2) the myths concerning the elixir of immortality and the Holy Immortals; and (3) the techniques whose goal was not only the prolongation of life but bliss and spiritual spontaneity. These three elements—principles, myths, and techniques—were part of the cultural inheritance from protohistory, and it would be a mistake to believe that the date of the earliest documents that attest to them also tells us their age. The solidarity between "preparing gold," obtaining the "drug of immortality," and "evoking" the Immortals is obvious: Luan Tai appears before the Emperor Wu and assures him that he can perform these three miracles, but he is able to "materialize" only the Immortals.[96] The magician Li Shao-chün instructs the Emperor Wu of the Han dynasty: "Sacrifice at the furnace (*tsao*) and you can make (supernatural) beings appear; when you have made (supernatural) beings appear, powdered cinnabar can be transformed into yellow gold; when yellow gold has been produced, you can make utensils from it for drinking and eating, and then you will have increased longevity. When your longevity is increased, you can see the blessed (*hsien*) in the island of P'ong-lai, which is in the middle of the seas. When you have seen them and have made the *feng* and *shan* sacrifices, you will not die."[97] So the quest for the elixir was connected with the quest for distant and mysterious islands in which the "Immortals" dwelt; for to encounter the Immortals is to transcend the human condition and share in a timeless and beatific existence.[98]

94. See H. Dubs, "The Beginnings of Alchemy," p. 77; cf. Joseph Needham, *Science and Civilisation in China,* vol. 5, pt. 2, p. 12.

95. Needham, p. 13.

96. Edouard Chavannes, *Les mémoires historiques de Sse-ma-Ts'ien,* vol. 3, p. 479.

97. Ibid., p. 465.

98. The search for the Immortals living in the distant islands occupied the

The search for gold also implied a spiritual quest. Gold possessed an imperial character: it was found at the "center of the earth" and was mystically related to *chüe* (realgar or sulphur), yellow mercury, and the future life (the "Yellow Springs"). It is thus presented in a text of ca. 122, *Huai-nan Tzŭ,* where we also find documentation for the belief in a hastened metamorphosis of metals.[99] So the alchemist only accelerates the growth of metals. Like his equivalent in the West, the Chinese alchemist contributes to the work of nature by accelerating the rhythm of time. Gold and jade, by the fact that they share in the Yang principle, preserve bodies from corruption. For the same reason, alchemical vessels of gold prolong life to infinity.[100] According to a tradition handed down in the *Lieh Hsien Ch'uan* (Complete Biographies of the Immortals), the alchemist We Po-yang succeeded in preparing "pills of immortality"; when, together with one of his disciples and his dog, he swallowed some of these pills, the three left earth in the flesh and went to join the other Immortals.[101]

The traditional homologation between the microcosm and the macrocosm connected the five cosmological elements (water, fire, wood, air, earth) with the organs of the human body: the heart with the essence of fire, the liver with the essence of wood, the lungs with the essence of air, the kidneys with the essence of water, the stomach with the essence of earth. The microcosm of the human body is in turn interpreted in alchemical terms: "the fire of the heart is red like cinnabar; the water of the kidneys

---

first emperors of the Ch'in dynasty (219 B.C.; see Ssŭ-ma Ch'ien, *Mémoires,* trans. Chavannes, vol. 2, pp. 141, 152; vol. 3, p. 437) and the Emperor Wu of the Han dynasty (in 110 B.C.; see ibid., vol. 3, p. 499, and Dubs, "The Beginnings of Alchemy," p. 66).

99. Fragment translated by Dubs, pp. 71–72. It is possible that this text comes from the school of Tsu Yen, if not from the Master himself, who was contemporary with Mencius, fourth century (ibid., p. 74). Belief in the natural metamorphosis of metals is of considerable antiquity in China; see, especially, Needham, *Science and Civilisation,* vol. 3, pp. 636 ff.

100. See the texts cited in Eliade, *The Forge and the Crucible,* pp. 114 ff.

101. Lionel Giles, *A Gallery of Chinese Immortals,* pp. 67 ff. "Bodily immortality" was usually obtained by absorbing elixirs prepared in a laboratory; see Needham, *Science and Civilisation,* vol. 5, pt. 2, pp. 93 ff.

is black like lead," etc.[102] Consequently, man possesses, in his own body, all the elements that make up the cosmos and all the vital forces that insure its periodic renewal. It is simply a matter of strengthening certain essences. Hence the importance of cinnabar, due less to its red color (the color of blood, the vital principle) than to the fact that, exposed to fire, cinnabar produces mercury. Hence it contains, in hidden form, the mystery of regeneration through death (for burning symbolizes death). It follows that cinnabar can insure the perpetual regeneration of the human body and, in the last analysis, can procure immortality. The great alchemist Ko Hung (283–343) writes that ten pills of a mixture of cinnabar and honey, taken in the course of a year, make white hair become black and lost teeth grow again; if one goes on for longer than a year, one obtains immortality.[103]

But cinnabar can also be created inside the human body, first of all by distillation of the sperm in the Fields of Cinnabar (see p. 37). Another name for these Fields of Cinnabar, a secret region of the brain containing the "chamber like a cave," is K'un-lün. But K'un-lün is the fabulous Mountain in the Western Sea, abode of Immortals. "To enter it through mystical meditation, one enters a 'chaotic' (*hun*) state resembling the primordial, paradisal, 'unconscious' state of the uncreated world."[104]

Let us note these two elements: (1) the homologation of the mythical mountain K'un-lün with the secret regions of the brain and the abdomen; (2) the role attributed to the "chaotic" state, which, once it is realized through meditation, permits entry into the Fields of Cinnabar and thus makes possible the alchemical preparation of the embryo of immortality. The Mountain in the Western Sea, abode of the Immortals, is a traditional and very ancient image of the "world in little"—of a miniature universe.

102. Text cited in Eliade, *The Forge and the Crucible,* p. 116.

103. James R. Ware, *The Nei P'ien of Ko Hung,* pp. 74 ff. Cinnabar as a drug of longevity is mentioned in the first century before our era in the collection of legendary biographies of the Taoist Immortals, the *Lieh-hsien chuan.* After absorbing cinnabar for several years, one master "had again become like a youth," another "was able to travel by flying," etc.; see Kaltenmark, *Le Lie-sien Tchouan,* pp. 271, 146–47, etc.

104. Rolf Stein, "Jardins en miniature d'Extrême-Orient," p. 54. See also Granet, *La pensée chinoise,* pp. 357 ff.

The K'un-lün mountain has two stories: an upright cone surmounted by an inverted cone.[105] In other words, it has the shape of a gourd, just like the alchemist's furnace and the secret region of the brain. As for the "chaotic" state realized by meditation and indispensable for the alchemical operation, it is comparable to the *materia prima,* the *massa confusa,* of Western alchemy.[106] The *materia prima* is not to be understood simply as a primordial structure of substance, for it is also an inner experience of the alchemist. The reduction of matter to its first condition of absolute undifferentiation corresponds, on the plane of inner experience, to regression to the prenatal, embryonic state. But, as we have seen, the theme of rejuvenation and longevity by a *regressus ad uterum* is one of the prime goals of Taoism. The most commonly used method is "embryonic respiration" (*t'ai-si*), but the alchemist also obtains this return to the embryonic stage by the fusion of ingredients in his furnace.[107]

After a certain period, external alchemy (*wai-tan*) is considered to be "exoteric" and is opposed to internal alchemy of the yogic type (*nei-tan*), which alone is termed "esoteric." The *nei-tan* becomes esoteric because the elixir is prepared in the alchemist's own body by methods of "subtle physiology" and without the help of mineral or vegetable substances. The "pure" metals (or their "souls") are identified with the various parts of the body, and the alchemical processes, instead of being performed in the laboratory, take place in the adept's body and consciousness. The body becomes the crucible in which the "pure" mercury and the "pure" lead circulate and fuse, together with the *semen virile* and the breath.

105. On the protohistory of this symbolism, see Carl Hentze, *Tod, Auferstehung, Weltordnung,* pp. 33 ff., 160 ff.

106. See *The Forge and the Crucible,* pp. 153 ff., and vol. 3 of the present work.

107. See *The Forge and the Crucible,* p. 119. This "return to the womb" is only the development of an earlier and more widely disseminated concept, already documented on archaic levels of culture: cure by a symbolic return to the origins of the world, that is, by reactualizing the cosmogony (see *Myth and Reality,* pp. 24 ff.). The Taoists and the Chinese alchemists took up and perfected this traditional method; that is, instead of limiting it to curing various diseases, they applied it especially to curing man from the wear and tear of time, that is, from old age and death.

By combining, the forces of Yang and Yin engender the "mysterious embryo" (the "elixir of life," the "Yellow Flower"), the immortal being that will finally escape from the body through the occiput and ascend to Heaven (cf. p. 37). The *nei-tan* can be regarded as a technique similar to "embryonic respiration," with the difference that the processes are described in the terminology of esoteric alchemy. Respiration is homologized to the sexual act and the alchemical work, and woman is assimilated to the crucible.[108]

A number of ideas and practices that we have presented in the last two sections are documented in texts from the Ch'in and Han periods (ca. 25 B.C.–220 A.D.)—which does not necessarily imply that they were unknown earlier. We have considered it useful to discuss them at this point, since the techniques for long life and, to some extent, alchemy are an integral part of ancient Taoism. But it must be added that, in the Han period, Lao Tzŭ was already deified and that Taoism, organized as an independent religious institution, had assumed a messianic mission and had inspired revolutionary movements. These more or less unexpected developments will engage our attention later (chap. 35, vol. 3). For the moment, it is enough to recall that, in a text as early as ca. 165, Lao Tzŭ was considered to be an emanation of the primordial chaos and was assimilated to P'an-ku, the cosmic anthropomorph (§129).[109]

As for the "Taoist religion" (Tao Chiao), it was founded, toward the end of the second century A.D., by Chang Tao-ling. After obtaining the elixir of immortality, Chang ascended to Heaven and received the title Heavenly Master (*t'ien shih*). In the province of Szechuan he inaugurated a "taocracy," in which the temporal and spiritual powers converged. The success of the sect owed much to its leader's talent as a healer. As we shall have occasion to see in volume 3 (chap. 35), what is involved is, rather, a psychosomatic thaumaturgy, reinforced by meals taken in common, during which those present shared in the vir-

108. See R. H. van Gulik, *Erotic Colour Prints*, pp. 115 ff.

109. "Lao Tzŭ transformed his body. His left eye became the moon; his head became Mount K'un-lün, his beard became the planets and the zodiacal houses; his flesh became the quadrupeds; his intestines became snakes; his belly became the sea, etc." (text translated in Maspéro, *Le taoïsme*, p. 108).

tues of the Tao. The monthly orgiastic ceremony, the "union of breaths," pursued the same end (see p. 37). But a similar hope of regeneration by the Tao is characteristic of another Taoist movement, the sect of "The Great Peace" (*T'ai-p'ing*). As early as the first century A.D., the founder of the movement presented a work of eschatological intent to the emperor. The book, dictated by spirits, revealed the means of regenerating the Han dynasty. This inspired reformer was put to death, but his messianism lived on in his disciples. In 184 the leader of the sect, Chang Chüeh, proclaimed the immanence of the *renovatio* and announced that the "Blue Heaven" was to be replaced by the "Yellow Heaven" (for this reason his disciples wore yellow turbans). The revolt that he precipitated very nearly overthrew the dynasty. The revolt itself was finally suppressed by the imperial troops, but the messianic fever continued throughout the Middle Ages. The last leader of the "Yellow Turbans" was executed in 1112.

17 Brahmanism and Hinduism: The First Philosophies and Techniques of Salvation

135. "All is suffering . . . "

The expansion of Brahmanism and, some centuries later, of Hinduism followed closely on the Āryanization of the subcontinent. It is probable that the Brahmans had already arrived in Ceylon by the sixth century B.C. Between the second century B.C. and the sixth century of our era, Hinduism made its way into Indochina, Sumatra, Java, and Bali. To be sure, in the course of entering Southeast Asia, Hinduism was obliged to incorporate a number of local elements.[1] But symbiosis, assimilation, and syncretism played a similar part in the conversion of central and southern India. By their pilgrimages and their journeys into distant regions the Brahmans had greatly contributed to the cultural and religious unification of the subcontinent. At the beginning of the Christian era these "missionaries" had succeeded in imposing on the local Āryan and non-Āryan populations the social structure, the cult system, and the *Weltanschauung* characteristic of the Vedas and the Brāhmaṇas, but they demonstrated both tolerance and opportunism by assimilating a large number of popular, marginal, and autochthonous elements.[2] By virtue of homologations accomplished on several levels (mythology, ritual, theology, etc.) the non-Brahmanic religious complexes were reduced, so to speak, to a common denominator and were finally absorbed by orthodoxy. Assimilation of autochthonous and

1. See Gonda, *Les religions de l'Inde,* vol. 1, pp. 268 ff. (with bibliography).
2. See ibid., p. 263.

"popular" divinities by Hinduism remains a phenomenon still active today.[3]

The transition from Brahmanism to Hinduism is imperceptible. As we have pointed out, certain specifically "Hinduistic" elements were already present within Vedic society (§ 64). But since they were not of interest to the authors of the hymns and the Brāhmaṇas, these more or less "popular" elements were not recorded in the texts. On the other hand, the process already documented in the Vedic period, especially the devaluation of certain great gods and their replacement by other figures (see § 66), continued down to the Middle Ages. Indra still retains his popularity in the Epic, but he is no longer the erstwhile champion and proud leader of the gods: *dharma* is stronger than he, and the late texts even term him a coward.[4] In contrast, Viṣṇu and Śiva obtain an exceptional position, and the female divinities begin their spectacular careers.

The Āryanization and Hinduization of the subcontinent were accomplished during the profound crises to which the ascetics and contemplatives of the Upanishads and, above all, the preaching of Gautama Buddha bear witness. In fact, for the religious elites, the horizon had changed radically after the Upanishads. "All is suffering, all is transitory," the Buddha had proclaimed. This is a leitmotiv of all post-Upanishadic religious thought. Doctrines and speculations, together with methods of meditation and soteriological techniques, have their justification in this universal suffering, for they are without value save insofar as they deliver man from "suffering." Human experience, no matter what its nature, engenders suffering. As a late writer puts it: "The body is pain, because it is the place of pain; the senses, the objects [of the senses], the perceptions are suffering, because they lead to suffering; pleasure itself is suffering, because it is followed by suffering."[5] And Īśvarakṛṣṇa, the author of the earliest Sāṃkhya treatise, affirms that the foundation of that phi-

3. Eliade, *Yoga,* pp. 431 ff.

4. See the references in Gonda, pp. 271, 275. Yama, lord of the realm of the dead, acquires a certain increase in stature; he is, moreover, assimilated to Kāla, Time (Gonda, p. 273).

5. Aniruddha (fifteenth century), commenting on *Sāmkhya Sūtra* 2. 1; cf. Eliade, *Yoga,* p. 11.

losophy is man's desire to escape from the torture of the three sufferings: from celestial misery (provoked by the gods), from terrestrial misery (caused by nature), and from inner or organic misery.[6]

However, the discovery of this universal suffering does not result in pessimism. No Indian philosophy, no Indian religious message, ends in despair. The revelation of suffering as the law of existence can, on the contrary, be considered the *sine qua non* of liberation; intrinsically, therefore, this universal suffering has a positive and stimulating value. It constantly reminds the sage and the ascetic that only one means of attaining to freedom and bliss is left to him: withdrawing from the world, detaching himself from possessions and ambitions, isolating himself completely. Besides, man is not alone in suffering; suffering is a cosmic necessity. The mere fact of existing in time, of having duration, involves suffering. Unlike the gods and animals, man is able to overcome his condition. The certainty that a way of obtaining deliverance exists—a certainty common to all Indian philosophies and mysticisms—cannot lead to either despair or pessimism. To be sure, suffering is universal; but for him who knows how to go about delivering himself from it, it is not final.

136. Methods of attaining the supreme "awakening"

Liberation from suffering is the goal of all Indian philosophies and techniques of meditation. No knowledge has any value if it does not pursue the salvation of man. "Except for that [i.e., except for the Eternal that resides in the Self], nothing is worth knowing" (*Śvetāśvatara Up*. 1. 12).[7] "Salvation" involves transcending the human condition. Indian literature employs images of binding, fettering, or captivity, of forgetting, intoxication, sleep, or unknowing to signify the human condition; to express abolition (i.e., transcendence) of the human condition—freedom, deliverance (*mokṣa, mukti, nirvāṇa,* etc.)—it employs images of deliverance from bonds and of tearing the veil (or removing a

6. *Sāṃkhya Kārikā* 1. For his part Patañjali, author of the earliest work on Yoga, writes: "All is suffering for the wise" (*Yoga Sūtra* 2. 15). Cf. *Yoga,* p. 11.

7. See other texts cited in *Yoga,* pp. 12 ff.

blindfold that covered the eyes), or of awakening, remembering, and so forth.

The *Chāndogya Upaniṣad* (6. 14. 1–2) tells of a blindfolded man taken far from his city and abandoned in a solitary place. The man begins crying out: "I have been led here blindfolded; I have been abandoned here blindfolded!" Someone then removes his blindfold and points out the direction of his city to him. Asking his way from village to village, the man succeeds in returning to his house. Even so, the text adds, he who has a competent spiritual Master is able to free himself from the blindfolds of ignorance and finally attains perfection.

Fifteen centuries later, Śaṅkara (? 788–820) commented brilliantly on this passage from the *Chāndogya*. To be sure, the famous Vedāntist metaphysician explains the fable in terms of his own system, absolute monism, but his exegesis only elaborates and clarifies the original meaning. Such is the case, Śaṅkara writes, with the man whom thieves have carried far away from Being (from *ātman-brahman*) and caught in the trap of this body. The thieves are false ideas ("merit," "demerit," etc.). His eyes are covered with the blindfold of illusion, and he is fettered by the desire that he feels for his wife, his son, his friend, his herds, etc. "I am the son of so-and-so, I am happy or unhappy, I am intelligent or stupid, I am pious, etc. How ought I to live? Or is there a way to escape? Where is my salvation?" So he reasons, caught in a monstrous net, until the moment he encounters one who is conscious of the true Being (*brahman-ātman*), who is delivered from slavery, is happy, and, in addition, is full of sympathy for others. From him he learns the way of knowledge and the vanity of the world. Thus the man, who was the prisoner of his own illusions, is freed from his dependence on worldly things. Recognizing now his true being, he understands that he is not the strayed vagabond he believed himself to be. On the contrary, he understands what Being is: it is *that* which he too is. Thus his eyes are freed from the blindfold of illusion created by ignorance (*avidyā*), and he is like the man in the fable, who returns to his house (that is, finds the *ātman*) full of joy and serenity.[8]

8. See Eliade, *Myth and Reality,* pp. 132 ff., on the analogies between these Indian symbolisms of captivity and deliverance from bonds, on the one hand, and certain aspects of Gnostic mythology on the other. See also below, § 229.

The *Maitri Upaniṣad* (4. 2) compares him who is still immersed in the human condition to one "bound by the chains produced by the fruits of good and evil," shut up in a prison or "intoxicated with alcohol" ("the alcohol of errors"), or plunged in darkness (the darkness of passion), or the victim of an illusory sleight-of-hand or of a dream that produces phantasmagorias—and it is for this reason that he no longer remembers the "highest state." Suffering, which defines the human condition, is the result of unknowing (*avidyā*). As the fable commented on by Śaṅkara shows, man suffers from the consequences of this unknowing until the day he discovers that he was only seemingly mired in the world. So, too, for Sāṃkhya and Yoga, the Self has nothing to do with the world (cf. §139).

It could be said that, after the Upanishads, Indian religious thought identifies deliverance with an "awakening" or with gaining consciousness of a situation that existed from the beginning but that one was unable to realize. Unknowing—which is, in fact, an *ignorance of oneself*—can be compared to a "forgetting" of the true Self (*ātman, puruṣa*). Gnosis (*jñāna, vidyā*), by abolishing ignorance or tearing the veil of *māyā,* makes deliverance possible; true "knowledge" is equivalent to an "awakening." The Buddha is supremely the Awakened One.

137. History of ideas and chronology of texts

Except for the early Upanishads, all the other Indian religious and philosophical texts were composed after the Buddha's preaching. At times the influence of certain characteristically Buddhist ideas is discernible. A number of works composed in the first centuries of the Christian era are concerned, among other things, with criticizing Buddhism. However, the importance of chronology must not be exaggerated. In general, every Indian philosophical treatise[9] includes concepts earlier than the

9. It should be noted that Sanskrit does not possess a word that exactly corresponds to the European term "philosophy." A particular philosophical system is called a *darśana,* "a point of view, vision, comprehension, doctrine, way of considering" (from the root *dṛś,* "to see, to contemplate, to understand").

date of its composition and often very old. When a new interpretation appears in a philosophical text, this does not mean that it was not conceived earlier. It is sometimes possible to determine, though at best only approximately, the *date of composition of certain texts* (and this only from the first centuries of our era), but it is almost impossible to establish the *chronology of philosophical ideas*.[10] In short, the fact that the religious and philosophical writings belonging to the Brahmanic tradition were composed some centuries after Gautama Buddha does not mean that they reflect conceptions articulated in the Buddhist period.

During his apprenticeship, Gautama had encountered certain representatives of the various philosophical "schools," in which it is possible to recognize the embryonic forms of Vedānta (i.e., the doctrine of the Upanishads) and of Sāṃkhya and Yoga (§148). For our purpose nothing would be gained by retracing the stages that separate these first outlines—documented in the Upanishads and the Buddhist and Jaina writings—from their systematic expressions in the classic period. It will suffice to indicate the most important transformations, to point out the modifications that radically changed the initial orientation. But it must not be forgotten that, after the period of the Upanishads, all methods and soteriologies share a common categorical framework. The sequence *avidyā-karman-saṃsāra,* the equation existence = suffering, the interpretation of ignorance as sleep, dream, intoxication, captivity—this constellation of concepts, symbols, and images was unanimously accepted. The *Śatapatha Brāhmaṇa* had proclaimed: "Man is born into a world put together by himself" (6. 2. 2. 27). It could be said that the three *darśanas* characteristic of Brahmanism—Vedānta, Sāṃkhya, and Yoga—together with Buddhism, merely endeavor to explain this axiom and elucidate its consequences.

138. Presystematic Vedānta

The term *vedānta* (literally, "end of the Veda") designated the Upanishads, which were in fact placed at the end of the Vedic

10. See *Yoga,* pp. 9 ff.

texts.[11] In the beginning the Vedānta signified the sum of the doctrines presented in the Upanishads. It was only progressively, and comparatively late (first centuries of our era), that the term became the specific appellation of a philosophical "system" opposed to the other *darśanas,* especially to the classic Sāṃkhya and Yoga. Our analysis of the Upanishadic doctrines has already set forth the governing ideas of presystematic Vedānta. As for the Vedāntist "philosophical system" properly speaking, its earliest history is unknown. The oldest work that has been preserved, the *Brahma Sūtra,* attributed to the *ṛṣi* Bādarāyaṇa, was probably composed at the beginning of our era. But it was certainly not the first, for Bādarāyaṇa cites the names and ideas of numerous authors who preceded him. For example, discussing the relations between the individual *ātmans* and *brahman,* Bādarāyaṇa refers to three different theories, and he gives the names of their most famous representatives. According to the first theory, *ātman* and *brahman* are identical; according to the second, until deliverance, *ātman* and *brahman* are completely different and separate; according to the third Vedāntist master, the *ātmans* are of divine essence but are not identical with the *brahman* (*Br. Sūtra* 1. 3. 21).

In discussing the theories previously advanced, Bādarāyaṇa very probably intended to set forth a doctrine proclaiming *brahman* as the material and efficient cause of all that exists and, at the same time, as the basis of the individual *ātmans*—a doctrine that, nevertheless, admitted that the delivered ones continue to exist externally as autonomous spiritual beings. Unfortunately, comprehending the 555 aphorisms that make up the *Brahma Sūtra* is very difficult without commentaries. Remarkably concise and enigmatic, these *sūtras* served only as a mnemonic device; their meaning had to be elucidated by a master. But the earliest commentaries were forgotten, and finally disappeared, as a result of the inspired interpretation provided by Śaṅkara, about A.D. 800. We know only the names of some authors and a few quotations from them.[12]

11. The term *vedānta* already appears in the *Muṇḍaka Up.* (3. 2. 6) and in the *Śvetāśvatara Up.* (6. 22).

12. See H. von Glasenapp, *Die philosophie der Inder,* pp. 132 ff.

However, in the *Śvetāśvatara* and *Maitri* Upanishads, in the *Bhagavad Gītā* and the *Mokṣadharma* (book 12 of the *Mahābhārata*), we find an adequate number of indications concerning the general outlines of Vedāntist thought before Śaṅkara. The doctrine of *māyā* acquires primary importance. It is above all the relations among *brahman,* the creation, and *māyā* that give rise to reflection. The old conception of the cosmic creation as a manifestation of the magical power (*māyā*) of the *brahman* yields to the role conferred on *māyā* in the experience of each individual, especially that of his blindness. In the last analysis, *māyā* is assimilated to unknowing (*avidyā*) and compared to dreaming. The multiform "realities" of the external world are as illusory as the contents of dreams. The tendency (already documented in *Ṛg Veda* 10. 129) to totalize the real in God, that is, in the One/All, leads to more and more daring formulas. If Being is the eternal unity/totality, not only the cosmos, i.e., the multiplicity of objects, is illusory (*māyā*), but the plurality of spirits is equally so. Two generations before Śaṅkara, the Vedāntist master Gauḍapāda maintains that belief in the plurality of individual *ātmans* is engendered by *māyā* (see *Māṇḍūkya Kārikā* 2. 12 and 19). In fact, only one Being—*brahman*—exists, and when the sage, by a meditation of yogic type, experientially grasps his own *ātman,* he awakens in the light and the bliss of an eternal present.

As we have seen (§ 81), the identity *brahman-ātman* constitutes the most important discovery of the Upanishads. But after the criticisms advanced by the Buddhist doctors, the Vedāntist masters were obliged to provide a systematic and rigorous foundation for their ontology, which was at once a theology, a cosmology, and, finally, a soteriology. In this effort to rethink the Upanishadic inheritance and to formulate it in accordance with the needs of his time, Śaṅkara remains unequaled. However, despite his magnificent accomplishment and the great influence of his thought in the history of Indian spirituality, Śaṅkara did not exhaust the mystical and philosophical possibilities of Vedānta. For several centuries after him, numerous masters will elaborate parallel systems. Besides, Vedānta differs from the other *darśanas* by the fact that it did not end its creativity in the period of the Sūtras and their first commentaries. Thus, while it may be said that the essential aspects of the Sāṃkhya and Yoga "philosophical systems" were set forth between the fourth and eighth centuries, Vedānta experiences its true flowering from Śaṅkara on.[13]

139. The spirit according to Sāṃkhya-Yoga

Long before the systematic articulation of the Sāṃkhya "philosophy," its characteristic terminology is documented in the *Kaṭha Upaniṣad,*[14] that is, in the fourth century B.C. The *Śvetāśvatara Upaniṣad,* which is probably later, contains numerous references to Sāṃkhya-Yoga principles and employs the technical vocabulary peculiar to those two *darśanas.* But little is known about the history of Sāṃkhya doctrines until the appearance of the first systematic treatise, whose author is Īśvarakṛṣṇa (probably of the fifth century of our era). In any case, the problem belongs, rather, to the history of Indian philosophy. For our purpose it is enough to say that presystematic Sāṃkhya—as it can be reconstructed, for example, from certain passages in the *Mokṣadharma*—is proclaimed as the saving gnosis par excellence, side by side with the eminently *practical* discipline of Yoga. In short, Sāṃkhya continues the Upanishads in insisting on the decisive role of knowledge in obtaining deliverance. The originality of the earliest Sāṃkhya masters consists in their conviction that true "science" presupposes a strict analysis of the structures and dynamisms of nature, of life, and of psychomental activity, completed by a sustained effort to grasp the unique modality of spirit (*puruṣa*).

Even in the classic period—that is, at the time when Īśvarakṛṣṇa's *Sāṃkhya Kārikā* and Patañjali's *Yoga Sūtra* were composed—the theoretical outlines of the two *darśanas* were quite similar. Two essential differences are apparent: (1) while classic Sāṃkhya is atheistic, Yoga is theistic, since it postulates the existence of a Lord (*Īśvara*); (2) whereas, according to Sāṃkhya, the only way to obtain deliverance is that of meta-

13. This is why we have deferred our presentation of the different systems of classic Vedānta until the third volume of the present work.

14. See, for example, *Kaṭha Up.* 2. 18–19, 22–23; 3. 3–4, 10–11; 7. 7–9; etc.

physical knowledge, Yoga assigns considerable importance to techniques of meditation. The other differences are negligible. Hence the Sāṃkhya doctrines that we shall briefly present can be considered equally valid for the theoretical aspects of Patañjali's *Yoga Sūtra.*[15]

For Sāṃkhya and Yoga, the world is *real* (not illusory, as it is, for example, for Vedānta). Nevertheless, if the world *exists* and *endures,* it owes its existence and endurance to the "ignorance" of the spirit (*puruṣa*). The countless forms of the cosmos, together with their process of manifestation and development, exist only insofar as the spirit, the Self, is ignorant of itself and, because of this "nescience," suffers and is enslaved. At the precise moment that the Self finds deliverance, the Creation as a whole will be reabsorbed into the primordial substance (*prakṛti*).

Just like the *ātman* of the Upanishads, the *puruṣa* is inexpressible. Its "attributes" are negative. The Self "is that which sees [*sākṣin,* literally, 'witness']; it is isolated, indifferent, a mere inactive spectator" (*Sāṃkhya Kārikā* 19). "Autonomy" and "impassibility" are traditional epithets of spirit, constantly repeated in the texts. Being irreducible, devoid of qualities, *puruṣa* has no "intelligence," for it is without desires. Desires are not eternal, hence they do not belong to spirit. Spirit is eternally free, "states of consciousness," the flux of psychomental life, being foreign to it.[16]

Now this conception of *puruṣa* at once raises difficulties. For if spirit is eternally pure, impassive, autonomous, and irreducible, how can it consent to let itself be involved in psychomental experience? And how is such a relation possible? We may profitably postpone an examination of the solution that Sāṃkhya and Yoga propose for this problem until we have become better acquainted with the possible relationships between the Self and nature. For the moment we shall state that neither the origin nor the cause of this paradoxical situation—i.e., of this strange relation that connects the *puruṣa* with *prakṛti*—has been the object of formal debate in Sāṃkhya-Yoga. The cause and the origin of

15. See Eliade, *Yoga,* pp. 7 ff.; Gerald J. Larson, *Classical Sāṃkhya,* pp. 166 ff.

16. See the texts cited in *Yoga,* pp. 15 ff.

this association between spirit and experience are the two aspects of a problem that the Sāṃkhya-Yoga masters regard as insoluble because it exceeds the present capacity of human comprehension. Man, that is, knows and understands by means of the "intellect," *buddhi*. But this intellect itself is only a product—extremely refined, to be sure—of the primordial substance (*prakṛti*). Being a product of nature, a "phenomenon," *buddhi* can enter into relations of knowledge only with other phenomena; in no case can it know the Self, for it cannot have any kind of relation with a transcendental reality. The cause, as well as the origin, of the paradoxical association between the Self and life (that is, matter) could therefore be understood only by an instrument of knowledge that did not in any way involve matter. Now such knowledge is impossible in the present human condition.

Sāṃkhya-Yoga knows that the cause of suffering is "nescience," in other words, the confusion of spirit with psychomental activity. But the precise moment when this metaphysical ignorance made its appearance cannot be established, just as it is impossible to fix the date of creation. To attempt to find a solution for this problem is vain. It is, in fact, a wrongly stated problem; and, according to an old Brahmanic custom (see Śaṅkara ad *Vedānta Sūtra* 3. 2. 17)—more than once observed by the Buddha himself—to a wrongly posed problem one replies by silence.

140. The meaning of Creation: Helping in the deliverance of spirit

Substance (*prakṛti*) is as real and as eternal as spirit (*puruṣa*); but, unlike *puruṣa*, it is dynamic and creative. Though perfectly homogeneous, this primordial substance possesses, so to speak, three "modes of being," which allow it to manifest itself in three different ways and which are called *guṇas:* (1) *sattva* (modality of luminosity and intelligence); (2) *rajas* (modality of motor energy and mental activity); (3) *tamas* (modality of static inertia and psychomental obscurity). So the *guṇas* have a twofold nature: objective on the one hand, since they constitute the phenomena of the external world, and, on the other hand, subjective, since they support, nourish, and condition psychomental life.

As soon as it departs from its original state of perfect equilibrium and assumes specific characteristics conditioned by its "teleological instinct" (to which we shall return), *prakṛti* passes from the state of *mahat* to that of *ahaṃkāra,* which means: uniform apperceptive mass, still without "personal" experience but with the obscure consciousness of being an ego (whence the term *aham* = ego). Starting from this apperceptive mass, the process of "development" bifurcates in two opposite directions, one of which leads to the world of objective phenomena, the other to that of subjective (sensible and psychomental) phenomena.

In consequence, the universe—objective or subjective—is only the transformation of an original stage of nature, *ahaṃkára,* when, for the first time, a presentiment of ego arose in the energetic mass. By a twofold process of development, the *ahaṃkāra* created a twofold universe: inner and outer, these two worlds having elective correspondences between them. Thus man's body, as well as his physiological functions, his senses, his "states of consciousness," and even his "intelligence," are all of them creations of one and the same substance: the one that produced the physical world and its structures (cf. § 75).

We should note the capital importance that Sāṃkhya-Yoga, like nearly all Indian systems, accords to the *principle of individuation through "consciousness of self."* The genesis of the world is a quasi-"psychic" act. Objective and psychophysiological phenomena have a common matrix, the only difference that separates them being the formula of the *guṇas, sattva* predominating in psychomental phenomena, *rajas* in psychophysiological phenomena (passion, activity of the senses, etc.), while the phenomena of the material world are constituted by the increasingly dense and inert products of *tamas* (atoms, vegetable and animal organisms, etc.).[17] With this physiological foundation, we understand why Sāṃkhya-Yoga regards all psychic experi-

17. Sāṃkhya-Yoga also offers a subjective interpretation of the three *guṇas* when it considers their psychic "aspects." When *sattva* predominates, the consciousness is calm, clear, comprehensible, virtuous; dominated by *rajas,* it is agitated, uncertain, unstable; overwhelmed by *tamas,* it is obscure, confused, passionate, bestial (see *Yoga Sūtra* 2. 15. 19).

ence as a simple "material" process. Morality is affected; goodness, for example, is not a quality of spirit but a "purification" of the "subtle matter" represented by consciousness. The *guṇas* impregnate the whole universe and establish an organic sympathy between man and the cosmos. In fact, *the difference between the cosmos and man is a difference only of degree, not of essence.*

By virtue of its progressive "development" (*pariṇāma*), matter has produced infinite forms, increasingly complex, increasingly varied. Sāṃkhya believes that such an immense creation, such a complicated edifice of forms and organisms, demands a justification and a meaning outside of itself. A primordial, formless, and eternally unmoving *prakṛti* can have a meaning. But the world as we see it presents, on the contrary, a considerable number of different forms and structures. The morphological complexity of the cosmos is raised by Sāṃkhya to the rank of a metaphysical argument. For common sense tells us that every compound exists in view of another. Thus, for example, a bed is a whole composed of various parts, but this provisional articulation among the parts is effected in view of man (*Sāṃkhya Kārikā* 17).

Sāṃkhya-Yoga thus brings out the *teleological* nature of Creation; for if the Creation did not have the mission of serving spirit, it would be absurd, without meaning. Everything in nature is "composite"; so everything must have a "superintendent," someone who can make use of these compounds. This superintendent cannot be either mental activity or states of consciousness (themselves extremely complex products of *prakṛti*). This is the first proof of the existence of spirit: "knowledge of the existence of spirit by combination for the profit of another."[18] Although the Self (*puruṣa*) is veiled by the illusions and confusions of cosmic Creation, *prakṛti* is dynamized by the "teleological instinct" that is wholly intent on the deliverance of *puruṣa*. For, "from *Brahman* to the last blade of grass, the Creation is for the benefit of spirit until spirit has attained supreme knowledge" (*Sāṃkhya Sutra* 3. 47).

18. *Sāṃkhya Sūtra* 1. 66; Vācaspatimiśra ad *Sāṃkhya Kārikā* 17; *Yoga Sūtra* 4. 24; cf. *Bṛhadāraṇyaka Up*. 2. 4. 5.

141. The meaning of deliverance

If the Sāṃkhya-Yoga philosophy does not explain either the cause or the origin of the strange association established between spirit and the "states of consciousness," it nevertheless attempts to explain the nature of their association. It is not a matter of *real* relations in the strict sense of the word, such as exist, for example, between external objects and perceptions. But—and for Sāṃkhya-Yoga, it is the key to this paradoxical situation—the most subtle, most transparent part of mental life, that is, intelligence (*buddhi*) in its mode of pure luminosity (*sattva*), has a specific quality: that of reflecting spirit. However, the Self is not corrupted by this reflection and does not lose its ontological modalities (eternity, impassivity, etc.). Just as a flower is reflected in a crystal, the intelligence reflects *puruṣa* (see *Yoga Sūtra* 1. 41). But only an ignorant person can attribute to the crystal the qualities of the flower (form, dimensions, color). When the object moves, its image moves in the crystal, though the latter remains motionless.

From all eternity, spirit has found itself drawn into this illusory relation with psychomental experience, that is, with life and matter. This is owing to ignorance (*Y.S.* 2. 24), and, as long as *avidyā* persists, existence is there, because of *karman,* and, with existence, suffering. Ignorance consists in confusion between the motionless and eternal *puruṣa* and the flux of psychomental life. To say: "I suffer," "I want," "I hate," "I know," and to think that this "I" refers to spirit, is to live in illusion and perpetuate it. This means that every act whose point of departure lies in illusion is either the consummation of a power created by a preceding act or the projection of another force that in its turn demands its actualization, its consummation in this present existence or in an existence to come.

This is, in fact, the law of existence. Like every law, it is transsubjective, but its validity and its universality are at the origin of the suffering by which existence is troubled. For Sāṃkhya, as for the Upanishads, there is only one way to gain salvation: adequate knowledge of spirit. And the first stage in acquiring this saving knowledge consists in one thing: *to deny that spirit has attributes*. This is equivalent to denying suffering as something that concerns us, to regarding it as an objective fact, outside of spirit, that is, *devoid of value,* of *meaning* (since all "values" and "meanings" are created by the intelligence). Pain exists only to the extent that experience is referred to the human personality regarded as identical with the Self. But since this relation is illusory, it can easily be abolished. When spirit is known and assumed, values are annulled; pain is then no longer either pain or nonpain but a mere *fact.* From the moment we understand that the Self is free, eternal, and inactive, everything that happens to us—pain, feelings, volition, thoughts, etc.—*no longer belongs to us.*

Knowledge is a simple "awakening" that unveils the essence of the Self. This knowledge is not obtained by experience but by a kind of revelation: it instantaneously reveals the ultimate reality. How, then, is it possible that deliverance is realized by the collaboration of *prakṛti?* Sāṃkhya replies with the teleological argument: matter instinctively acts in view of the enfranchisement of the *puruṣa.* The intelligence (*buddhi,*) being the most subtle manifestation of *prakṛti,* facilitates the process of deliverance by serving as the preliminary stage of revelation. As soon as this self-revelation is realized, the intelligence, as well as all the other psychomental (hence material) elements that are wrongly attributed to *puruṣa,* withdraw, detach themselves from spirit, and are reabsorbed into substance, like a "dancer who departs after satisfying her master's desire."[19] "Nothing is more sensitive than *prakṛti;* as soon as it has said to itself 'I am recognized,' it no longer shows itself before the eyes of the Spirit" (*Sām. Kār.* 61). This is the state of the man who is "liberated in this life" (*jīvan-mukta*): the sage lives on, because his karmic residue remains to be consumed (just as the potter's wheel continues to turn from the velocity it has acquired, although the pot is already finished [*Sām. Kār.* 67; *Sāṃ. Sūtra* 3. 82]). But when, at the moment of death, it abandons the body, the spirit (*puruṣa*) is completely "liberated" (*Sām. Kār.* 68).

Sāṃkhya-Yoga has, then, understood that spirit can neither be born nor be destroyed; that it is neither enslaved nor inactive

19. This comparison is very frequent, both in the *Mahābhārata* and in the Sāṃkhya treatises; see *Sāṃkhya Kārikā* 59, *Sāṃkhya Sūtra* 3. 69.

(i.e., actively seeking deliverance); that it neither thirsts for freedom nor is "liberated" (Gauḍapāda, *Māṇḍūkya Kārikā* 2. 32). "Its mode is such that these two possibilities are excluded" (*Sāṃkhya Sūtra* 1. 160). The Self is pure, eternal, and free; it cannot be enslaved because it cannot have relations with anything except itself. But man *believes* that the *puruṣa* is enslaved and *thinks* that it can be liberated. These are illusions of our psychomental life. If liberation seems to us a drama, it is because we adopt a human point of view. In reality, spirit is only a "spectator," just as "liberation" (*mukti*) is only a *becoming-conscious* of spirit's eternal freedom. Suffering simply ceases as soon as we understand that it is *outside of spirit,* that it concerns only the human "personality" (*asmitā*).

Sāṃkhya-Yoga reduces the infinite variety of phenomena to a single principle, matter (*prakṛti*), and sees the physical universe, life, and consciousness as all deriving from a single source. This doctrine, however, postulates the plurality of spirits, though by their nature these are essentially identical. Thus Sāṃkhya-Yoga unites what might appear to be so different—the physical, the vital, and the mental—and isolates what, especially in India, seems unique and universal: spirit. Each *puruṣa,* indeed, is completely isolated; for the Self can have no contact either with the world or with other spirits. The cosmos is peopled by these eternal, free, motionless *puruṣas*—monads between which no communication is possible.

In short, we are offered a tragic and paradoxical conception of spirit—and one that has been vigorously attacked both by Buddhist doctors and by Vedāntist masters.

142. Yoga: Concentration on a single object

The earliest precise references to Yoga techniques appear in the Brāhmaṇas and especially in the Upanishads. But even as early as the Vedas there is mention of certain ascetics and ecstatics who command a number of parayogic practices and enjoy "miraculous powers" (§ 78). Since the term *yoga* came quite early to designate any ascetic technique and any method of meditation, we find yogic practices widespread in India, both in Brahmanic circles and among the Buddhists and the Jains. But alongside this presystematic and pan-Indian Yoga, a *yoga-darśana,* "classic" Yoga, as it was later formulated by Patañjali in his *Yoga Sūtra,* gradually takes form. This author himself admits (*Y.S.* 1. 1) that, in general, he is only collecting and publishing the doctrinal and technical traditions of Yoga. As for Patañjali, nothing is known of him. We do not even know whether he lived in the second century B.C. or in the third, or even the fifth, century of our era. Among the technical formulas preserved by tradition, he retained those that an experience of centuries had sufficiently tested. As for the theoretical framework and the metaphysical foundation that Patañjali provides for these practices, his personal contribution is of the smallest. He simply rehandles the Sāṃkhya doctrine in its broad outlines, adapting it to a rather superficial theism.

Classic Yoga begins where Sāṃkhya ends. For Patañjali does not believe that metaphysical knowledge alone can lead man to liberation. Knowledge only prepares the ground for the conquest of freedom; freedom is obtained by means of an ascetic technique and a method of meditation. Patañjali defines Yoga as "the suppression of the states of consciousness" (*Y.S.* 1. 2). These "states of consciousness" (*cittavṛttis*) are infinite in number, but they all fall into three categories, corresponding, respectively, to three possibilities of experience: (1) errors and illusions (dreams, hallucinations, errors of perception, confusions, etc.); (2) the totality of normal psychological experiences (everything that is felt, perceived, or thought by one who does not practice Yoga); and (3) the parapsychological experiences triggered by yogic technique and, of course, accessible only to the initiated. The goal of Patañjali's Yoga is to abolish the first two categories of experience (produced, respectively, by logical error and metaphysical error) and to replace them by an enstatic, suprasensory, and extrarational "experience."

In contrast to Sāṃkhya, Yoga sets itself the task of destroying, one by one, the different groups, species, and varieties of "states of consciousness" (*cittavṛttis*). Now this destruction cannot be achieved unless one begins by knowing "experimentally," as it were, the structure, origin, and intensity of what is to be destroyed. "Experimental knowledge" here means: method, technique, practice. One can gain nothing without acting and without practicing asceticism: this is a leitmotiv of yogic literature. Books 2 and 3 of the *Yoga Sūtra* are more especially devoted to this yogic activity (purifications, bodily postures, breathing techniques, etc.). The *cittavṛttis* (literally "eddies of consciousness") cannot be controlled and, finally, abolished if they are not first known "experimentally." It is only through *experiences* that one obtains freedom.[20]

The cause of the *vṛttis* that make up the psychomental stream is, of course, ignorance (*Y.S.* 1. 8). But, for Yoga, abolition of metaphysical ignorance does not suffice to destroy the states of consciousness. For even when the present "eddies" are destroyed, others would immediately come to replace them, welling up from the immense reserves of "latencies" (*vāsanās*) buried in the subconscious. The concept of *vāsanā* is of prime importance in Yoga psychology. The obstacles that these subliminal forces raise on the road that leads to liberation are of two kinds: on the one hand, the *vāsanās* constantly feed the psychomental stream, the endless series of *cittavṛttis;* on the other hand, by virtue of their specific (subliminal) modality, the *vāsanās* are hard to control and master. Thus the yogin—even if he has the advantage of long-continued practice—is in danger of being defeated by the invasion of a powerful stream of psychomental "eddies" precipitated by the *vāsanās*. For destruction of the *cittavṛttis* to succeed, it is necessary that the subconsciousness-consciousness circuit be broken.

The point of departure of Yoga meditation is concentration (*ekāgratā*) on a single object. This object can equally well be a physical object (the point between the eyebrows, the tip of the nose, a luminous object, etc.), a thought (a metaphysical truth), or God (Iśvara). The *ekāgratā* exercise seeks to control the two generators of mental fluidity: sensory activity and the activity of the subconscious. It goes without saying that concentration on a single object cannot be accomplished except by the use of numerous exercises and techniques, in which physiology plays a capital role. *Ekāgratā* cannot be obtained, for example, if the

20. Thus the gods (*videha,* "the disincarnate")—who have no experiences because they have no body—enjoy a condition of existence inferior to the human condition and cannot attain to complete deliverance.

body is in a tiring or merely uncomfortable position or if the respiration is disorganized, that is, nonrhythmical. This is why Yoga technique includes several categories of psychophysiological practices and spiritual exercises, called *aṅgas* ("members"). These "members" of Yoga can be regarded both as forming a group of techniques and as being stages of the ascetic and spiritual itinerary whose final goal is liberation. The *Yoga Sūtra* (2. 29) presents a list that has become classic: (1) the restraints (*yamas*); (2) the disciplines (*niyamas*); (3) the bodily postures (*āsanas*); (4) control of respiration (*prāṇāyāma*); (5) emancipation from the activity of the senses, from the ascendancy of external objects (*pratyāhāra*); (6) concentration (*dhāraṇā*); (7) yogic meditation (*dhyāna*); (8) enstasis (*samādhi*).

143. Techniques of Yoga

The first two groups of practices, *yama* and *niyama,* constitute the inevitable preliminaries to any kind of asceticism. There are five "restraints" (*yamas*), namely, *ahiṃsā* ("not to kill"), *satya* ("not to lie"), *asteya* ("not to steal"), *brahmacarya* ("sexual abstinence"), and *aparigraha* ("not to be avaricious" [see *Y.S.* 2. 30]). These restraints do not bring about a yogic state but a "purified" state, superior to that of the uninitiated. In conjunction with them, the yogin must practice the *niyamas,* that is, a series of bodily and psychic disciplines. "Cleanliness, serenity, asceticism (*tapas*), study of Yoga metaphysics, and an effort to make God (Īśvara) the motive of all his actions constitute the disciplines," writes Patañjali (*Y.S.* 2. 32).[21]

It is only with the practice of *āsana* that yogic technique properly speaking begins. *Āsana* designates the well-known yogic posture that *Y.S.* 2. 46 defines as "stable and agreeable." We here have one of the characteristic practices of Indian asceticism, documented in the Upanishads and even in Vedic literature. What matters is to keep the body in the same position *without*

21. "Cleanliness" also means the inner purification of the organs (which is especially insisted upon by Haṭha Yoga). "Serenity" implies "absence of the desire to increase the necessities of existence." *Tapas* consists in tolerating contraries, such as heat and cold, etc.

effort, for only then does *āsana* facilitate concentration. "Posture becomes perfect when the effort to realize it disappears," writes Vyāsa (ad *Y.S.* 2. 47). "He who practices *āsana* must employ an effort that consists in suppressing the natural bodily efforts" (Vācaspati, ibid.).

Āsana is the first step taken toward abolition of the modalities peculiar to human existence. On the bodily plane, *āsana* is an *ekāgratā,* a concentration on a single point: the body is "concentrated" in a single position. Just as *ekāgratā* puts an end to the fluctuations and dispersion of the "states of consciousness," so *āsana* puts an end to the mobility and availability of the body by reducing the multitude of possible positions to a single motionless, hieratic posture. Furthermore, a tendency toward "unification" and "totalization" is typical of all yogic practices. Their goal is the transcendence (or the abolition) of the human condition, resulting from the *refusal* to obey one's natural inclinations.

If *āsana* illustrates refusal to move, *prāṇāyāma,* the discipline of the breath, is the refusal to breathe like the run of mankind, that is, arhythmically. The uninitiated man's respiration varies in accordance either with circumstances or with his psychomental tension. This irregularity produces a dangerous psychic fluidity and, hence, instability and dispersal of attention. One can become attentive by making an effort. But, for Yoga, effort is an "exteriorization." So, by means of *prāṇāyāma,* the attempt is made to suppress respiratory effort: achieving rhythmical respiration must become automatic, so that the yogin can forget it.

A late commentator, Bhoja, observes that "there is always a connection between respiration and the mental states" (ad *Y.S.* 1. 34). This observation is important. The relation that unites the rhythm of respiration with the states of consciousness was no doubt experienced experimentally by yogins from the very earliest times. In all probability, this relation served them as an instrument for "unifying" consciousness. By making his respiration rhythmical and progressively slower, the yogin is able to "penetrate"—that is, to experience in his own person and with complete lucidity—certain states of consciousness that in the waking state are inaccessible, and particularly the states of consciousness that are characteristic of sleep. The respiratory rhythm of a man asleep is slower than that of a man awake. In achieving, by virtue of *prāṇāyāma,* this rhythm of sleep, the yogin—though without sacrificing his lucidity—can penetrate the states of consciousness typical of sleep.

Indian psychology knows four modalities of consciousness: diurnal consciousness, the consciousness of sleep with dreams, the consciousness of dreamless sleep, and "cataleptic consciousness" (*turīya*). Each of these modalities of consciousness is related to a specific respiratory rhythm. By means of *prāṇāyāma,* that is, by increasingly prolonging exhalation and inhalation—the goal of this practice being to leave as long an interval as possible between these two moments of respiration[22]—the yogin can pass without discontinuity from the consciousness of the waking state to the three other modalities.

Āsana, prāṇāyāma, and *ekāgratā* have succeeded in suspending the human condition, if only during the time that the exercise continues. Motionless, making his respiration rhythmical, fixing his gaze and his attention on a single point, the yogin is "concentrated," "unified." He can test the quality of his concentration by *pratyāhāra,* a term usually translated by "withdrawal of the senses" or "abstraction" but which we prefer to translate by "ability to free sense activity from the domination of external objects." Instead of turning toward objects, the senses "abide within themselves" (Bhoja, ad *Y.S.* 2. 54). *Pratyāhāra* can be regarded as the ultimate stage of psychophysiological asceticism. Henceforth the yogin will no longer be "distracted" or "troubled" by the activity of the senses, by memory, etc.

Autonomy in respect to the stimuli of the external world and to the dynamism of the subconscious allows the yogin to practice

22. The rhythm of respiration is obtained by harmonizing the three "moments": inhalation, exhalation, and holding-in the air. Through practice the yogin arrives at prolonging each of these moments for a considerable time. The goal of *prāṇāyāma* being as long a suspension of respiration as possible, the yogin begins by arresting the breath for sixteen and a half seconds, then for thirty-five seconds, fifty seconds, three minutes, five minutes, and so on. Rhythmicization and retention of the breath also play an important part in Taoist practices, among the Muslim mystics, and in the methods of prayer employed by the hesychastic monks. See Eliade, *Yoga,* pp. 53–59, 431–32.

concentration and meditation. *Dhāraṇā* (from the root *dhṛ,* "to hold fast") is in fact a "fixing of the thought on a single point," having as its purpose *comprehension.* As for yogic meditation, *dhyāna,* Patañjali defines it as "a current of unified thought" (*Y.S.* 3. 2). Vyāsa adds the following gloss: "Continuum of mental effort to assimilate the object of meditation, free from any other effort to assimilate other objects."

There is no need to point out that this yogic meditation differs completely from secular meditation. *Dhyāna* makes it possible to "penetrate" objects, to "assimilate" them magically. The act of "penetration" into the essence of objects is especially difficult to explain; it is to be conceived neither as a species of poetic imagination nor as an intuition of the Bergsonian type. What distinguishes yogic meditation is its coherence, the state of lucidity that accompanies and continues to orient it. Indeed, the "mental continuum" never escapes the yogin's will.

144. The role of the God in Yoga

Unlike Sāṃkhya, Yoga affirms the existence of a God, Īśvara (literally, "Lord"). This God is, of course, not a creator. But, for certain men, Īśvara can hasten the process of deliverance. The Lord whom Patañjali mentions is rather a God of yogins. Only a man who has already chosen Yoga can be helped by him. He can, for example, bring it about that the yogin who takes him as the object of his concentration obtains *samādhi.* According to Patañjali (*Y.S.* 2. 45), this divine aid is not the result of a "desire" or a "feeling"—for the Lord can have neither desire nor emotion—but of a "metaphysical sympathy" between Īśvara and *puruṣa,* a sympathy explained by the correspondence between their structures. Īśvara is a *puruṣa* that has been free from eternity, that has never been touched by the "pains" and "impurities" of existence (*Y.S.* 1. 24). Vyāsa, commenting on this text, explains that the difference between the "enfranchised" spirit and Īśvara is as follows: the first has formerly been in some relation (if only illusory) with psychomental existence, whereas Īśvara has always been free. God cannot be attracted by rites or devotion or by faith in his "grace," but his "essence" instinctively collaborates (so to speak) with the Self that seeks to enfranchise itself by Yoga.

It would seem that this metaphysical sympathy that he shows in respect to certain yogins has exhausted Īśvara's capacity to interest himself in the fate of human beings. We get the impressions that Īśvara has entered the Yoga *darśana* from the outside, as it were. For the part that he plays in deliverance is unimportant, since *prakṛti* itself undertakes to deliver the numerous "Selves" that are caught in the illusory snares of existence. However, Patañjali felt a need to introduce God into the dialectic of deliverance because Īśvara corresponded to an experiential reality. As we have just said, some yogins obtained *samādhi* by "devotion to Īśvara" (*Y.S.* 2. 45). Undertaking to collect and classify all the yogic techniques validated by the "classic tradition," Patañjali could not neglect a whole series of experiences that only concentration on Īśvara had made possible.

In other words, side by side with the tradition of a "magical" Yoga, that is, one that called only upon the ascetic's will and forces, there was another, a "mystical" tradition, in which the final stages of Yoga practices were at least made easier by virtue of a devotion—even though extremely rarefied and intellectual—toward a god. In any case, at least as he appears in Patañjali and in the latter's earliest commentator, Vyāsa, Īśvara lacks the grandeur of the omnipotent creator god and the emotion proper to the dynamic and serious god of the various mysticisms. Īśvara, in short, is only the archetype of the yogin—a macroyogin, very probably the patron of certain yogic sects. Indeed, Patañjali states that Īśvara was the *guru* of the sages of immemorial times; for, he adds, Īśvara is not bound by time (*Y.S.* 1. 26). It is only the late commentators, Vācaspatimiśra (ca. 850) and Vijñānabhikṣu (sixteenth century) who attribute any great importance to Īśvara, and they lived at a time when the whole of India was permeated by devotional and mystical currents.[23]

23. Another late commentator, Nīlakaṇṭha, affirms that God, though inactive, helps yogins in the manner of a magnet. Nīlakaṇṭha attributes to Īśvara a "will" capable of predetermining the lives of men; for "he makes him do good deeds whom he wants to raise, and he makes him commit bad deeds whom he wants to throw down" (cited by Dasgupta, *Yoga as Philosophy and Religion,* pp. 88–89). We are far from the modest role that Patañjali assigned to Īśvara!

145. *Samādhi* and the "miraculous powers"

The passage from "concentration" to "meditation" does not require the application of any new technique. Similarly, once the yogin has succeeded in concentrating and meditating, there is no need for any supplementary yogic exercise in order to realize *samādhi*. *Samādhi,* yogic "enstasis," is the final result and the crown of all the ascetic's spiritual efforts and exercises.[24] The term is first employed in a gnoseological sense: *samādhi* is that contemplative state in which the *thought immediately grasps the form of the object,* without the help of categories and the imagination; a state in which the object reveals itself "in itself" (*svarūpa*), in its essentiality, and as if it were "empty of itself" (*Y.S.* 3. 3). There is a real coincidence between *knowledge of the object* and *the object of knowledge,* for the object, no longer presenting itself to consciousness in the relations that delimit and define it as a phenomenon, is "as if empty of itself."

However, rather than "knowledge," *samādhi* is a "state," an enstatic modality peculiar to Yoga. This "state" makes possible the self-revelation of the Self by virtue of an act that does not constitute an "experience." But it is not any *samādhi* that reveals the Self and consequently accomplishes final deliverance. When *samādhi* is obtained by fixing the thought on a point in space or on an idea, the enstasis is termed "with support" or "differentiated" (*samprajñāta-samādhi*). When, on the contrary, *samādhi* is obtained apart from any "relation," that is, when it is simply a complete comprehension of Being, there is "undifferentiated" (*asamprajñāta*) enstasis. The first state is a means of deliverance insofar as it makes comprehension of the truth possible and puts an end to suffering. But the second mode of enstasis (*asamprajñāta*) destroys the "impressions (*saṃskāra*) of all the antecedent mental functions" (*Vijñānabhikṣu*) and even succeeds in arresting the karmic forces already set in motion by the yogin's past activity. This enstasis is in fact "ravishment," since it is experienced without being provoked.

24. The meanings of the term *samādhi* are: union, totality; absorption in; complete spiritual concentration; conjunction. It is usually translated by "concentration"; but in that case there is a danger of confusion with *dhāraṇā*. That is why we have preferred to translate it by enstasis, stasis, conjunction.

Obviously, "differentiated enstasis" comprises several stages, for it is perfectible. In these phases "with support," *samādhi* proves to be a state obtained by virtue of a certain knowledge. It is necessary always to remember this passage from "knowledge" to "state," for this is the characteristic feature of all Indian meditation. In *samādhi* there is the "rupture of plane" that India seeks to realize—the paradoxical passage from knowing to Being.

It is when he has reached this stage that the yogin acquires the "miraculous powers" (*siddhis*) to which book 3 of the *Yoga Sūtra* is devoted, beginning with *sūtra* 16. By concentrating, by meditating, and by realizing *samādhi* in respect to a certain object or a whole class of objects, the yogin acquires certain occult powers concerning the objects experienced. Thus, for example, by concentrating on the subconscious residues (*saṃskāra*), he knows his former lives (*Y.S.* 3. 18). By the help of other concentrations, he obtains the extraordinary powers (flying, becoming invisible, etc.). Everything that is meditated is—by the magical virtue of meditation—assimilated, possessed. In the Indian conception, renunciation has a positive value. The force that the ascetic obtains by renouncing some pleasure by far exceeds the pleasure he has renounced. By virtue of renunciation, of asceticism (*tapas*), men, demons, or gods can grow powerful to the point of becoming a threat to the entire universe.

To avoid such an increase of sacred force, the gods "tempt" the ascetic. Patañjali himself refers to celestial temptations (*Y.S.* 3. 51), and Vyāsa gives the following explanations: when the yogin attains the final differentiated enstasis, the gods visit him and say: "Come and rejoice here, in Heaven. These pleasures are desirable, this young maiden is adorable, this elixir abolishes old age, death," and so on. They continue tempting him with celestial women, with supernatural sight and hearing, with the promise of transforming his body into a "body of diamond"—in short, they offer him a share in the divine condition (Vyāsa, ad *Y.S.* 3. 51). But the divine condition is still far from absolute freedom. The yogin owes it to himself to reject these "magical mirages," which are "desirable only for the ignorant," and to persevere in his task: obtaining final deliverance.

For as soon as the yogin succumbs to making use of the magical powers he has acquired, his possibility of acquiring new forces disappears. According to the whole tradition of classic Yoga, the yogin makes use of the countless *siddhis* in order to recover the supreme freedom, the *asamprajñāta-samādhi,* but never to obtain mastery over the elements; indeed, as Patañjali tells us (3. 37), these powers are "perfections" (this is the literal meaning of the term *siddhis*) in the waking state, but they are obstacles in the state of *samādhi.*[25]

146. Final deliverance

Vyāsa summarizes the passage from *samprajñāta* to *asamprajñāta-samādhi* as follows: by the illumination (*prajñā,* "wisdom") obtained spontaneously when the yogin arrives at the last stage of *samprajñāta-samādhi,* he realizes "absolute isolation" (*kaivalya*), that is, liberation of the *puruṣa* from the empire of *prakṛti.* It would be a mistake to consider this mode of being of the spirit as a simple trance, in which consciousness is emptied of all content. The "state" and the "knowledge" that this term simultaneously expresses refer to the total absence of objects in the consciousness and in no sense to a consciousness absolutely emptied. For, on the contrary, the consciousness is then saturated by a direct and total intuition of Being. As a late author, Mādhava, writes, "*nirodha* [final arrest of all psychomental experience] must not be imagined as a nonexistence but rather as the support of a particular condition of the spirit." It is the enstasis of total emptiness, an unconditioned state that is no longer "experience" (for in it there is no longer any relation between consciousness and the world) but "revelation." The

25. And yet the nostalgia for the "divine condition" conquered by sheer force, magically, has not ceased to obsess yogins and ascetics. And the more so since, according to Vyāsa (ad *Y.S.* 3. 26), there is a great likeness between certain gods who inhabit the celestial regions (in the *brahmaloka*) and yogins at the stage of the *siddhis*. Indeed, the four classes of gods of the *brahmaloka* have, by their very nature, a "spiritual situation" that corresponds respectively to the four classes of *samprajñāta-samādhi*. By the fact that these gods have stopped at this stage, they have not attained complete deliverance.

intellect (*buddhi*), having accomplished its mission, withdraws, detaching itself from the *puruṣa,* and reintegrates itself into *prakṛti.* The yogin attains to deliverance: he is a *jīvan-mukta,* one "delivered in life." He no longer lives under the empire of time but in an eternal present, in the *nunc stans* by which Boethius defined eternity.

Obviously, his situation is paradoxical; for he is in life, yet delivered; he has a body, yet he knows himself, and by that fact he *is* the *puruṣa;* he lives in duration and at the same time shares in immortality. *Samādhi* is, by its very nature, a paradoxical state, for it empties being and thought and at the same time fills them to repletion. Yogic enstasis takes its place on a line well known in the history of religions and mysticisms: that of the coincidence of contraries. By *samādhi,* the yogin transcends contraries and unites emptiness and fullness, life and death, being and nonbeing. Enstasis is equivalent to a reintegration of the different modalities of the real in a single modality: the primordial nonduality, the undifferentiated plenitude that existed before the bipartition of the real into object-subject.

It would be a gross error to regard this supreme reintegration as a simple regression into the primordial indistinction. Deliverance is not assimilable to the "deep sleep" of prenatal existence. The importance that all authors attribute to the yogic states of *super*consciousness shows us that the final reintegration is accomplished in that direction and not in a more or less deep "trance." In other words, the recovery through *samādhi* of the initial nonduality brings this new element into relationship with the situation that existed before the bipartition of the real into object-subject: the *knowledge* of unity and bliss. There is "return to the origin," but with the difference that he who is "delivered in life" recovers the original situation enriched by the dimensions of freedom and transconsciousness. He reintegrates the primordial plenitude after having established this new and paradoxical mode of being: *consciousness of freedom,* which exists nowhere in the cosmos, whether on the planes of life or on the planes of "mythological divinity" (the gods), for it exists only in the absolute Being (*brahman*).

It is tempting to see in this ideal—the conscious conquest of freedom—the justification proposed by Indian thought for the fact, which at first sight seems absurd and cruelly useless, that the world exists, that man exists, and that his existence in the world is an unbroken series of illusions and suffering. For, by liberating himself, man establishes the spiritual dimension of freedom and "introduces" it into the cosmos and life, that is, into modes of existence that are blind and wretchedly conditioned.

However, this absolute freedom was conquered at the price of a complete negation of life and of the human personality. So radical a negation demanded the Buddha in order to attain *nirvāṇa*. But these extreme and exclusive solutions could not exhaust the resources of the Indian religious genius. As we shall see (§§193–94), the *Bhagavad Gītā* offers another method of obtaining deliverance, one that does not require renunciation of the world as its price.

18 The Buddha and His Contemporaries

147. Prince Siddhārtha

Buddhism is the only religion whose founder declares himself to be neither the prophet of a god nor his emissary and who, in addition, rejects the idea of a God–Supreme Being. But he proclaims himself "awakened" (*buddha*) and hence guide and spiritual master. The goal of his preaching is the deliverance of mankind. It is precisely this rank of "savior" that makes his soteriological message a religion and soon transforms the historical personage, Siddhārtha, into a divine being. I say "historical," for despite the theological speculations and the fabulous inventions of the Buddhist doctors, despite certain European interpretations that have seen in Buddha a mythical figure or a solar symbol, there is no reason to deny his historicity.

The majority of scholars agree in admitting that the future Buddha was probably born in April or May, 558 B.C. (or, according to another tradition, 567), at Kapilavastu. The son of a minor king, Śuddhodana, and his first wife, Māyā, he married at the age of sixteen, left the palace at the age of twenty-nine, had the "supreme and complete Awakening" in April or May, ca. 523 (or ca. 532), and, after preaching during the rest of his life, died in November, ca. 478 (or ca. 487), at the age of eighty. But these few dates and some other events that we shall relate further on do not exhaust the Buddha's biography as it was understood by his disciples. For, once his true identity—that of the Awakened One—was publicly proclaimed and accepted by his disciples, his life was transfigured and received the mythological dimensions typical of the great saviors. This process of "mythologization" increased with time, but it was already at work during the Master's lifetime. Now it is important to keep in mind this fabulous biography, for it was what was creative, not only in Buddhist theology and mythology, but also in devotional literature and the plastic arts.

Thus, it is said that the future Buddha, the *boddhisattva* (the "Being awakening"), himself chose his parents when he was a god in the *tuṣita*-heaven. His conception was said to be immaculate, the *boddhisattva* entering his mother's right side in the form of an elephant or of an infant six months old. (The ancient versions tell only of the mother's dream: an elephant entering her body.) His gestation is likewise immaculate, for the *boddhisattva* is enclosed in a stone shrine of precious stones and not in the womb. His birth takes place in a garden; the mother clasps a tree, and the infant emerges from her right side.

As soon as he is born, the *boddhisattva* takes seven steps, facing the North, and utters the lion's "roar," exclaiming, "I am the highest in the world, I am the best in the world, I am the eldest in the world; this is my last birth; there will not be another life for me henceforth."[1] The myth of the nativity, then, proclaims that, from his birth, the future Buddha transcends the cosmos (he attains the "crest of the world") and abolishes space and time (he is, indeed, "the first" and the "oldest in the world"). Numerous miracles announce the event. When he is presented in a Brahmanic temple, the images of the gods, "having risen from their places, fall at the *boddhisattva*'s feet" and "sing a hymn [in his honor]."[2] The child receives from his father the name Siddhārtha ("Goal Attained"). Examining his body, the diviners recognize the thirty-two fundamental and the eighty secondary signs of the "great man" (*mahāpuruṣa*) and declare that he will become a universal sovereign (*cakravartin*) or a Buddha. An old *ṛṣi,* Asita, flies through the air from the Himalayas to Kapilavastu, demands to see the newborn infant, takes him in his arms, and, understanding that he will become Buddha, weeps, knowing that he, Asita, will not live to follow him.

1. *Majjhima Nikāya* 3. 123. On the symbolism of the seven steps, see Eliade, *Myths, Dreams, and Mysteries,* pp. 110 ff.

2. *Lalita Vistara,* pp. 118 ff.; A. Foucher, *La vie du Bouddha,* pp. 55 ff.

Seven days after his birth, Māyā dies, to be reborn as a god in the *tuṣita*-heaven. For seven years the child is brought up by his aunt. After that, he receives the education of every Indian prince, and he distinguishes himself both in the branches of knowledge and in physical exercises. At the age of sixteen he marries two princesses from neighboring countries, Gopā and Yaśodharā. After thirteen years the latter gives him a son, Rāhula. These details, which are embarrassing to the ascetic Buddhist tradition, are probably authentic. In any case, Siddhārtha fled from the palace soon after Rāhula's birth, in conformity with the Indian custom that does not allow renouncing the world until after the birth of a son or grandson.

A whole scenario has been elaborated around this Great Departure. According to the earliest texts, the Buddha told his disciples that it was by meditating on old age, sickness, and death that he lost the zest for life and decided to save humanity from those three evils. Legend presents the occurrence more dramatically. Warned by the diviners' predictions, Śuddhodana managed to isolate the young prince in his palace and his pleasure gardens. But the gods foiled the father's plan, for on three successive trips to the pleasure gardens, Siddhārtha encountered first a decrepit old man leaning on a stick, then, the next day, a sick man, "wasted, livid, burning with fever," and, finally, the third time, a dead man being carried to the cemetery. His coachman tells him that no one can escape from sickness, old age, and death. Finally, on his last trip, the prince sees a mendicant monk, calm and serene, and this vision consoles him, showing him that religion is able to cure the miseries of the human condition.

148. The Great Departure

In order to strengthen his decision to renounce the world, the gods wakened Siddhārtha in the middle of the night so that he could behold the naked and graceless bodies of his sleeping concubines. Then he summoned his groom, Chandaka, mounted his horse, and, the gods having put the whole city to sleep, the prince left it by the gate to the Southeast. Having ridden a dozen leagues from Kapilavastu, he stopped, cut off his hair with his sword, changed clothes with a hunter, and sent Chandaka back to the palace with his horse. When he stopped, he also dismissed the troop of gods who had escorted him until then. Henceforth the gods will play no part in the Buddha's fabulous biography. He will gain his end by his own means, without any supernatural help.

Having become a wandering ascetic under the name of Gautama (the name of his family in the Śākya clan), he traveled to Vaiśālī (Pali: Vesāli), where a Brahmanic master, Ārāḍa Kālāma, taught a kind of preclassic Sāṃkhya. He very quickly mastered this doctrine, but, considering it inadequate, he left Ārāḍa and went to Rājagṛha, the capital of Magadha. King Bimbisāra, attracted by the young ascetic, offered him half his kingdom, but Gautama rejected this temptation and became the disciple of another master, Udraka. With equal ease, he mastered the yogic techniques taught by Udraka but, dissatisfied, left him and, followed by five disciples, traveled toward Gayā. His philosophical and yogic apprenticeship had gone on for a year.

He settled down in a peaceful place near Gayā, where, for six years, he indulged in the most severe mortifications. He reached the point of subsisting on one millet seed a day but later decided on fasting completely; motionless, reduced almost to the state of a skeleton, he finally came to resemble a heap of dust. After these terrible penances he received the title of Śākyamuni ("the ascetic among the Śākyas"). When he reached the utmost limit of mortification and only the thousandth part of his vital power was left to him, he understood the uselessness of asceticism as a means of deliverance and decided to break his fast. Given the great prestige enjoyed by *tapasvins* everywhere in India, the experience was not useless. Henceforth the future Buddha could proclaim that he had mastered the ascetic practices, just as he had already mastered philosophy (Sāṃkhya) and Yoga and just as, before he forsook the world, he had experienced *all* the pleasures of princely life. Nothing of what makes up the infinite variety of human experiences was thus unknown to him—from the delights and disappointments of culture, of love, and of power to the poverty of a wandering holy man and the contemplations and trances of the yogin, by way of the solitude and mortifications of the ascetic.

When Gautama accepted a pious woman's offering of boiled rice, his five ascetic disciples, horrified, left him and set off for Benares. Miraculously restored by this food, Śākyamuni traveled to a forest, chose a pipal tree (*aśvattha; Ficus religiosa*), and sat down at the foot of it, determined not to rise until he had obtained "awakening." But before sinking into meditation, Śākyamuni underwent the assault of Māra, Death. For that great god had divined that the imminent discovery of salvation, by halting the eternal cycle of births, deaths, and rebirths, would put an end to his rule. The attack was launched by a terrifying army of demons, ghosts, and monsters, but Śākyamuni's earlier merits and his "friendly disposition" (*maitrī*) raised a zone of protection around him, and he remained steadfast.

Māra then claimed the place under the tree, by virtue of the merits he had gained, long before, as the result of a voluntary sacrifice. Śākyamuni had also accumulated merits in the course of his former lives; but, since he had no witness, he invoked "the impartial mother of all beings," and, with the gesture that has become classic in Buddhist iconography, he touched the earth with his right hand. The Earth showed herself from the waist up and vouched for Śākyamuni's statements. However, Māra, Death, is also Kāma, Eros—in the last analysis the Spirit of Life—and it is life itself that is equally threatened by the salvation that the *boddhisattva* is preparing to bestow on the world. Then countless women surrounded the ascetic, vainly seeking to tempt him by their nakedness and their many charms. Conquered, Māra withdrew before nightfall.[3]

149. The "Awakening." The preaching of the Law

This mythology of Māra's attack and temptation proclaims Śākyamuni's absolute moral purity. He can now concentrate all his spiritual forces on the central problem: deliverance from suffering. During the first watch, he passes through the four stages of meditation, which enable him to embrace, by virtue of

3. However, Māra is not irremediably damned, for, in a distant future, he too will be converted and saved.

his "divine eye" (§158), the totality of worlds and their eternal becoming, that is, the terrifying cycle of births, deaths, and reincarnations governed by *karma*. In the second watch, he recapitulates his constant former lives and in a few moments contemplates the infinite lives of others. The third watch constitutes the *boddhi,* the Awakening, for he grasps the law that makes possible this hellish cycle of births and rebirths, the law of the "twelve mutually dependent productions," as it is called (§157), and, at the same time, he discovers the conditions necessary to halt these "productions." From thenceforth he possesses the four "Noble Truths": he has become *buddha,* "the Awakened One," precisely at sunrise.

The Buddha remains for seven weeks in the "eyrie of Awakening." Among the fabulous events preserved by tradition, we mention the last temptation by Māra: let the Blessed One enter immediately into *parinirvāṇa,* without proclaiming the doctrine of salvation he had just discovered. But the Buddha replies that he will not enter until he has founded an informed and well-organized community. However, the Buddha soon afterward asks himself if it is worthwhile teaching so difficult a doctrine. The intervention of Brahmā, and especially the certainty that a certain number of human beings are capable of being saved, decide him. He goes to Benares, where, with his "divine eye," he sees the five disciples who had forsaken him. He finds them in a hermitage, on the site of the present Sarnāth, and announces to them that he has become Buddha. He expounds the four Noble Truths: on pain, the origin of pain, stopping pain, and the road that leads to the ending of pain (see §159).

This first exposition constitutes "setting in motion the wheel of the Law." The five are converted and become "saints" (*arhats*). The conversion of the son of a banker in Benares, followed by that of the other members of the family, soon occurs. Very soon the community (*saṃgha*) consists of sixty monks (*bhikkhu*), and the Buddha sends them to preach individually through the country. For his part, he goes to Uruvilvā, where, by a series of prodigies, he succeeds in converting the three Kaśyapa brothers, Brahmans who especially venerate the god Agni. The Buddha then addresses Kaśyapa's one thousand disciples; he proves to them that the whole universe is aflame with the fires of passion. They accept the doctrine, and all become *arhats*.

From then on, conversions multiply. At Rājagṛha, Bimbisāra, the young king of Magadha, gives the Buddha and the community a hermitage. Still at Rājagṛha, the Buddha converts two eminent holy monks, Śāriputra and Maudgalāyana, and an ascetic, Mahākāśyapa, all three of them destined to play a considerable part in the history of Buddhism. Some time later the Blessed One yields to his father's pleas and, with a great troop of monks, goes to Kapilavastu. The visit is the occasion for many dramatic episodes and fabulous prodigies. The Buddha succeeds in converting his father and many of his relatives. Among them are his cousins: Ānanda, thenceforth his principal lay disciple, and Devadatta, who will soon become his rival.

The Buddha does not linger at Kapilavastu. He returns to Rājagṛha, visits Śrāvastī and Vaiśālī, and more or less spectacular conversions continue. When he learns that his father is seriously ill, he again visits him and leads him to holiness. The widowed queen asks her adopted son to admit her into the community. Although he refuses, the queen, with a retinue of princesses, all wanting to become nuns, follows him on foot as far as Vaiśālī. Ānanda pleads her cause, and finally the Buddha accepts her, after giving the nuns rules more stringent than those imposed on the monks. But it is a decision made unwillingly, and he announces that, because of the admission of women, the Law, which should have lasted a thousand years, will last only five hundred.

After some of his disciples perform miracles, the Buddha objects to the display of the "marvelous powers" (see §159). However, he is himself led to perform some of the greatest miracles in the course of his combat with the "six masters," his rivals: now he causes a mango tree to grow, now he walks from the East to the West on a rainbow, or infinitely multiplies his own image in the air, or spends three months in the Heaven of Indra in order to preach to his mother. But since the accounts of these fabulous events do not go back to the primitive tradition, it is probable that the prohibition against the "miraculous powers" (*siddhis*) and the importance attributed to "wisdom" (*prajñā*) as a means of conversion form part of his original teaching.[4]

As was to be expected, the rival masters, jealous of the Blessed One's success, attempt, but vainly, to discredit him by odious calumnies. Of more consequence are the petty quarrels among the monks, like the one that, nine years after the Awakening, broke out at Kauśāmbī in regard to a detail of the monastic rule (it was a question of knowing whether the washing bowls in the latrines were to be refilled after being used). The Master tried to reconcile the opponents, but he was asked not to bother himself about such matters, and he left Kauśāmbī.[5] However, the lay disciples indignantly refused alms to the monks who had brought about the Blessed One's departure, and the recalcitrants were obliged to give in.

150. Devadatta's schism. Last conversion. The Buddha enters *parinirvāṇa*

The sources give us only very vague information concerning the middle period of the Buddha's career. During the rainy season he continued his preaching in the *vihāras* (monasteries) near to the cities. The rest of the year, accompanied by his closest disciples, he traveled about the country, preaching the Good Law. In ca. 509, his son Rāhula received final ordination. The biographies tell of certain spectacular conversions, such as that of a riddling Yakṣa, or of a famous brigand, or of a noble Bengalese merchant; these show that the Master's fame had spread far beyond the districts in which he preached.

When the Buddha was seventy-two years of age (in 486 B.C.), his jealous cousin, Devadatta, demanded that he turn over the direction of the community to him. Met with refusal, Devadatta attempted to have him killed, first by hired assassins, then by

4. However, the biographies constantly refer to the Buddha's journeys through the air.

5. The incident is significant: it may indicate that the details of monastic behavior were not necessarily decreed by the Buddha, though we have many examples of the contrary; see J. Filliozat, *L'Inde classique,* vol. 2, p. 485.

having him crushed by a falling rock or a dangerous elephant. Devadatta had instituted a schism with a group of monks by preaching a more radical asceticism; but Śāriputra and Maudgalāyana were able to call back those who had gone astray, and, according to several sources, Devadatta was precipitated alive into Hell. The Blessed One's last years were darkened by disastrous events, among them the ruin of his clan, the Śākyas, and the death of Śāriputra and Maudgalāyana.

During the rainy season of ca. 478, the Buddha, accompanied by Ánanda, settled in the "Village of Bamboos," where he fell seriously ill of dysentery. He survived the crisis, and Ānanda rejoiced because "the Blessed One would not perish before leaving his instructions concerning the community." But the Buddha replied that he had taught the Law completely, without keeping any truth secret, as certain masters did; he had become a "weak old man," life had reached its end, and henceforth the disciples must turn for help to the Law.

However, some sources[6] add a significant episode: having returned to Vaiśālī, the Buddha rested in the sacred wood of Cipala, and he thrice praised to Ānanda the charm of the place and the diversified beauty "of the continent of India," adding that, if asked to do so, the Buddha "can still subsist for a cosmic period or the rest of a cosmic period." But Ānanda thrice remained silent, and the Master asked him to go away. Then Māra approached and reminded him of his promise to enter *parinirvāṇa* when the *saṃgha* (the community) was firmly established. "Fear not, O Evil One," the Buddha replied. "You have not long to wait." Thereupon he renounced the portion of life that remained to him, and the earth shook. Ānanda asked his Master the reason for this strange phenomenon and, being told what it was, begged him to live on until the end of the cosmic period. But the Buddha could not go back on the promise he had just given to Māra. "It is your fault, Ānanda. . . . If you had asked it of the Predestined One, O Ānanda, he would have refused at the first and

6. *Divya Avadāna,* pp. 200 ff. (translated by E. Burnouf; see his *Introduction,* pp. 74 ff.) and other texts studied by Windisch, *Māra und Buddha,* pp. 33 ff. See also Foucher, *La vie du Bouddha,* pp. 303 ff.

the second asking, but the third asking he would have granted. So it is indeed your fault, O Ānanda."[7]

He then asked his disciple to gather together the monks who were at Vaiśālī, and the two of them went to Pāpā. There the blacksmith Cunda invited them to a dinner consisting of a "treat of pig"—a dish of pork or of a certain mushroom that pigs delight in. This dish brought on a bloody diarrhea, apparently a recurrence of the illness from which he had scarcely recovered. Nevertheless, he set off for Kuśinagara, capital of the Mallas. Exhausted after a difficult journey, the Buddha lay down on his right side between two trees in a wood, facing West, his head to the North, his left leg lying on his right. Ānanda burst into tears, but the dying Blessed One consoled him: "Enough, Ānanda; cease to sorrow and to moan. . . . How can you suppose that what is born does not die? It is absolutely impossible."[8] Then, in the presence of them all, he praised Ānanda's devotion and assured him that he would attain sainthood.

Warned by Ānanda, the Mallas crowded around the Blessed One. After converting a monk, Subhadra, the Buddha summoned his disciples and asked them if they still had doubts concerning the Law and the Discipline. All remained silent. Then the Buddha uttered his last words: "It is to you that I address myself, O mendicant monks: perishability is the law of things; do not slacken your efforts!" Finally, at the third and last watch of the night, he passed through the four stages of meditation and died. It was the night of the full moon of Kārtikka, November, 478 B.C. (or 487, according to another tradition).

As if to counterbalance so human a death, the Buddha's funeral gave rise to many legends. For seven days of music and dancing the Mallas honored the dead Blessed One, his body wrapped in many cloths and placed in a trough filled with oil, for he is

7. *Mahāparinibbāna Sutta* 3. 40, after the translation by Foucher, p. 303. The episode of Ānanda's fatal distraction was certainly invented in order to explain the Buddha's death. For, just as he had chosen the circumstances of his birth, the Buddha could prolong his life indefinitely. It was not his fault that he had not done so. However, since neither the legend nor the Buddhist community branded Ānanda with infamy, it is clear that the episode was interpolated for apologetic reasons.

8. *Mahāparinibbāna Sutta* 5. 14.

accorded the funeral of a king who is a *cakravartin*. Before its cremation on a pyre of scented wood, the body had been carried in procession through Kuśinagara. But the pyre was not lighted before the arrival of the disciple Mahākāśyapa, who followed the same road as his master but eight days after him. Since Mahākāśyapa became the first head of the community, he had to be present, at least at the Blessed One's cremation. Indeed, according to the legend, the Buddha's feet protruded from the coffin so that the great disciple could venerate them by touching them with his forehead. The pyre then caught fire spontaneously. Since the Blessed One had died in their country, the Mallas carried away his bones. However, the neighboring people demanded their share, in order to build *stūpas*. The Mallas refused at first, but, threatened by a coalition, they ended by allowing the bones to be divided into eight lots. Above the relics, the urn, and the dead coals from the pyre, *stūpas* were erected.

151. The religious milieu: The wandering ascetics

Toward the beginning of the sixth century, Gangetic India experienced a period of luxuriant religious and philosophical activity; it has rightly been compared with the spiritual flowering that occurred in Greece at the same period. Side by side with the monks and mystics who followed the Brahmanic tradition there were countless groups of *śramaṇas* ("those who make efforts; Pali, *samana*): wandering ascetics (*parivrājaka*), among whom there were yogins, magicians, and dialecticians ("sophists") and even materialists and nihilists, precursors of the Cārvākas and the Lokāyatas. Certain types of wandering ascetics went back to Vedic and post-Vedic times. Of most of them we know little except their names. Their doctrines are mentioned, fragmentarily, in Buddhist and Jain texts; attacked by both the Jainists and the Buddhists, they are often deliberately distorted and ridiculed.

Probably, however, all these *śramaṇas* had forsaken the world, disgusted at once by the vanity of human life and by the doctrine implied in Brahmanic ritual. It was the mechanism of transmigrations and their mysterious impelling force, the act (*karman*), that the *śramaṇas* attempted to understand and master. They made use of many and various methods, from extreme asceticism, parayogic ecstasy, and empirical analysis of matter to the most abstract metaphysics, orgiastic practices, extravagant nihilism, and vulgar materialism. The means chosen depended in part on the value attributed to the actor condemned to transmigrate by virtue of *karman*. Was this value a psychic, perishable organism or an indestructible and immortal Self? Essentially, this was the same problem raised by the earliest Upanishads (§ 80) and one that would always remain at the center of Indian thought.

The Buddhist and Jain texts sometimes speak only of the doctrines of certain religious sectarians, without mentioning their names. Thus, for example, the *Brahmajala Sutta* provides a long catalogue of doctrines: "Some speculate on the past cycles of duration, affirming the eternity of the self (*atta;* Skr. *ātman*) and the world, acquiring by a psychic discipline (which is that of *yoga* with *samādhi*) marvelous powers, such as remembering their former lives. Some affirm now an eternity, now a non-eternity, opposing, for example, eternal *brahman* to its impermanent creations. Some admit the infinity, others the finiteness, of the world. . . . Some agnostics avoid all questions. Some suppose the self and the world produced without cause. Another group speculates on the cycles to come, envisaging the becoming of the self after the dissolution of the body. This self can be conscious or even have form, or it can be without either form or absence of form, hence foreign to the realm of form, finite or infinite, suffering unhappy feelings. Or it is unconscious, or neither conscious nor unconscious, and everything is denied of it, etc." (summarized by J. Filliozat, *L'Inde classique*, vol. 2, p. 512). This catalogue is the more valuable because certain of the doctrines attacked will be taken up again and developed by various Buddhist schools.

In addition to these anonymous doctrines, the sources have preserved the names of some sects. We shall consider the most important among them further on: the Ājīvikas, whose chief master was Makkhali Gośāla, and the Nigranthas (those "Without Place"), that is, the Jains, disciples of Mahāvīra. As for Gautama's masters, Ārāḍa Kālāma and Udraka, though the Buddha exceeded them in intelligence and in power of concentration, their influence on his method of meditation was considerable.

The *Sāmaññaphala Sutta* (*Dīgha* 1. 47 ff.) also mentions the Buddha's six rival masters. Of each of them we are told that he is the "head of a community," a famous "founder of a sect, respected as a saint, venerated by a crowd of people, advanced in age." Purāṇa Kassapa seems to have preached that the act has no value; Ajita Keśakāmbala professed a materialism close to that of the Cārvākas; Pakudha Kaccāyana taught the eternity of the seven "bodies" (*kāya,* that is, the "bodies" of the earth, of water, of fire, of the wind, of pleasure, of pain, and of life); and Sañjaya probably taught skepticism, for he avoided any discussion. The two others are Makkhali Gośāla and Nigaṇṭha Nātaputta, that is, Mahāvīra; the latter is scarcely mentioned in the Buddhist sources, though he was the most important religious personality among the Buddha's contemporaries.

Several Suttas relate encounters with the *paribbājakas,* but the texts emphasize the Blessed One's answers rather than the doctrines and manners of his interlocutors. He reproaches them, for example, with being infatuated with their own asceticism, with scorning others, with believing that they have attained their goal and congratulating themselves on it, with having an exaggerated opinion of their accomplishments, etc.[9] He declares that what characterizes the true *samana* or Brahman is not his external appearance, his penitence, or his physical mortification but his inner discipline, charity, mastery of self, freedom from superstitions, and his control over his intellectual processes.[10]

152. Mahāvīra and the "Saviors of the World"

Though Mahāvīra was his contemporary, though they traveled through the same regions and frequented the same circles, the Buddha never met him. We do not know why he decided to avoid his most powerful and most original rival—the only one who

9. *Udumbarikā Sīhanāda Sutta* (*Dīgha* 3. 43 ff.; Rhys Davids, *Dialogues of the Buddha,* vol. 3, pp. 39 ff.).

10. *Kassapa Sīhanāda Sutta* (*Dīgha* 1. 169 ff.; Davids, *Dialogues,* vol. 1, pp. 234 ff.).

succeeded in organizing a religious community that still survives in our day. Certain analogies between the careers and spiritual orientations of the two masters are observable. Both belonged to the aristocratic military caste (*kṣatriya*) and exhibited the same anti-Brahmanic tendency, which was already visible in the earliest Upanishads; and both were essentially "heretics," for they denied the existence of a supreme god and the revealed character of the Vedas and denounced the uselessness and cruelty of sacrifices. On the other hand, they were of entirely different temperaments, and their doctrines are irreconcilable.

Unlike Buddhism, Jainism did not begin with Mahāvīra's preaching, for he was only the last in a fabulous series of Tīrthaṃkaras (literally, "makers of the ford," in other words, "openers of the way, announcers of salvation").[11] The first, Ṛṣabha, or Ādīśvara, "the primordial master," was said to have lived for millions of years, first as a prince, then as an ascetic, before attaining *nirvāṇa* on Mount Kailāsa. The legendary biographies of the twenty-one other Tīrthaṃkaras follow more or less the same pattern, which, in any case, is only the life of Mahāvīra transfigured into a paradigm: they are all of princely origin, renounce the world, and found a religious community. It is agreed to attribute a certain historicity to the twenty-third Tīrthaṃkara, Pārśva. Son of a king of Benares, he was said to have forsaken the world at the age of thirty, to have attained omniscience, and, after founding eight communities, to have died on a mountain at the age of one hundred, 250 years before Mahāvīra. Pārśva still enjoys an exceptional position in the cult and the mythology of the Jains in our day.

Mahāvīra was the son of Siddhārtha, the head of a noble clan, and of Tirśālā, who was related to the reigning families of Magadha. But the legend sets his birth in the traditional framework of the nativity of "saviors of the world": he who was to be the twenty-fourth and last Tīrthaṃkara decides to descend to earth to restore the doctrine and moral perfection of the communities founded by Pārśva. He became incarnate in the womb of Devānanda, wife of a Brahman, but the gods transported the embryo into a princess of Magadha. A series of prophetic dreams

11. But the Buddhists, too, soon proclaimed a long series of Buddhas.

announced to the two mothers the birth of a savior-*cakravartin*. And, just as for the Buddha and for Zarathustra, a great light illuminated the night of his birth.

The infant received the name Vardhamāna ("Prosper") and, like the Buddha, experienced the life of a prince, married a noble maiden, and had a child by her. But on the death of his parents, when he was thirty years old, and having obtained permission from his elder brother, Vardhamāna gave away all his possessions, forsook the world, and assumed the dress of a wandering ascetic. After thirteen months he renounced wearing clothes, and this is the first innovation that separates him from the tradition handed down by Pārśva. Naked, "clad in space," for thirteen years he devoted himself to the most rigorous asceticism and to meditation. Finally, after prolonged mortifications and two and a half days of recollection, on one night in summer, under a *śāla* tree on the bank of a river, he obtained "omniscience." He thus became a *jina* ("conqueror"), and his disciples would later take the name of Jains; but he is principally known as Mahāvīra, the "Great Hero." For thirty years he continued his wandering life, preaching his doctrine in the countries of Magadha, Aṅga, and Videha in the plain of the Ganges. During the monsoon, like all other holy men, Mahāvīra stopped near a city. He died at the age of seventy-two at Pāvā (near the present Patna). The date of his "entrance into *nirvāṇa*" is still disputed; it was in 468 B.C. according to some, in 477 according to Jacobi and Schubrig. In any case the event took place a few years before the Buddha's *nirvāṇa*.

153. Jain doctrines and practices

Almost nothing is known concerning Mahāvīra's personality. The mythology that celebrates his birth, like the mythology built up around the Buddha, is the traditional mythology of India. The Jain canon was edited in the fourth and third centuries B.C., but some passages are much earlier and perhaps still preserve the words used by the master. What appears to be characteristic of Mahāvīra's teaching is an interest in the structures of nature and also a passion for classification and numbers. It has been possible to say that his system is governed by number (Schubrig), and in fact it speaks of three kinds of consciousness and five kinds of right knowledge, of seven principles or categories, of five kinds of bodies, of six shades or colors (*leśya*) that mark the soul's merit and demerit, of eight kinds of "karmic matter," of fourteen stages of spiritual qualifications, etc. On the other hand, Mahāvīra differs from both Pārśva and the Buddha by his strict asceticism, which imposed permanent nudity and numerous prohibitions on his disciples.

Mahāvīra denies the existence of God but not that of the gods; the latter enjoy a certain degree of beatitude, but they are not immortal. The cosmos and life have no beginning and will have no end. The cosmic cycles repeat themselves ad infinitum. The number of souls is also infinite. Everything is governed by *karman* except the delivered soul. A characteristic feature of Jainism, and one that emphasizes its archaic structure, is panpsychism: everything that exists in the world has a soul, not only the animals but also plants, stones, drops of water, etc. And, since respect for life is the first and most important Jain commandment, this belief in panpsychism gives rise to countless difficulties. This is why the monk, as he walks, must sweep the ground before him and why he is forbidden to go out after sunset: lest he be in danger of killing some minute animal.

It seems paradoxical that a doctrine that postulates panpsychism and proclaims absolute respect for life radically disparages human life and regards suicide by starvation as the most sublime death. Respect for life—that is, for everything that exists in the three realms of the world—is not able to resanctify human life or even give it religious significance. Sharing the pessimism and the refusal of life that had become manifest in the Upanishads, Jainism conceives only a spiritual and transcosmic bliss (but see below, §190): the soul delivered from "karmic matter" flies "like an arrow" to the summit of the universe; there, in a kind of empyrean, it meets and communicates with other delivered souls, constituting a community that is purely spiritual or even divine. Such pessimism and acosmic "spiritualism" recall certain Gnostic schools (§228) and, with important differences, classic Sāṃkhya and Yoga (§§139 ff.).

Karman plays a decisive part, for it creates the karmic matter, a kind of psychocorporal organism that attaches itself to the soul and forces it to transmigrate. Deliverance (*mokṣa*) is accomplished by cessation of any contact with matter, that is, by *rejecting* the *karman* that has already been absorbed and by *halting* all new karmic influence. As was to be expected, deliverance is obtained by a series of meditations and concentrations that are yogic in type[12] and that crown a life of asceticism and recollection. Naturally, only monks and nuns can aspire to deliverance, but the monastic life is open to any child eight years of age on condition that he is in good health. After some years of study, the novice is initiated by a master and takes the five vows: to spare all life, to tell the truth, to possess nothing, to acquire nothing, and to remain chaste. He is then given a begging bowl, a short broom to clean the road ahead of him, and a small piece of muslin, with which he covers his mouth when he speaks (probably to avoid swallowing insects). The wandering life of the monks and nuns, except for the four monsoon months, exactly imitates that of Mahāvīra.

According to tradition, at the time of Mahāvīra's death there were, in addition to a huge lay community, 14,000 monks and 36,000 nuns. These figures are probably exaggerated; but what is more surprising is the great majority of women among the adepts and in the lay collectivity, especially since, according to certain Jain masters, nuns could not attain deliverance because they were forbidden to practice monastic nudity. However, the large number of women, whether nuns or lay sisters, is documented by the earliest tradition. It is believed that Mahāvīra addressed principally his social equals, members of the noble and military aristocracy. It may be presumed that women who belonged to these circles found in Mahāvīra's teaching—a teaching whose roots lay deep in the most archaic Indian spirituality—a religious way that was refused them by Brahmanic orthodoxy.

12. Certain techniques are in perfect correspondence with the tradition of classic Yoga, later fixed by Patañjali (§143). For example, concentration (*dhyāna*) consists in fixing the psychomental activity on "a single point."

154. The Ājīvikas and the omnipotence of "destiny"

The Buddha regarded Maskarin (Makkhali) Gośāla as his most dangerous rival. Disciple and companion of Mahāvīra for several years, Gośāla practiced asceticism, obtained magical powers, and became the leader of the Ājīvikas. According to the few biographical references preserved by the Buddhist and Jain scriptures, Gośāla was a powerful magician. He killed one of his disciples with his "magical fire"; however, it was after a magical tournament with Mahāvīra and as the result of the latter's curse that he died (probably between 485 and 484 B.C.).

The etymology of the word *ājīvika* remains obscure. Attacked by the Buddhists and the Jains, the doctrines and practices of the Ājīvikas are difficult to reconstruct. Except for a few quotations preserved in the books of their adversaries, nothing of their canon has survived. Yet we know that the movement is one of considerable antiquity, preceding Buddhism and Jainism by several generations.

What distinguished Gośāla from all his contemporaries was his rigorous fatalism. "Human effort is ineffective": such was the essence of his message. And the keystone of his system lay in a single word: *niyati,* "fatality," "destiny." According to a Buddhist text, Gośāla believed that "there is no cause, there is no motive, for the corruption of beings; beings are corrupted without cause or motive. There is no cause for the purity of beings; beings are purified without cause or motive. There is no act performed by oneself; there is no act performed by another. There is no human act, there is no force . . . , no energy . . . , no human vigor . . . , no human courage. All beings, all individuals, all creatures, all living things, are without will, without force, without energy; they evolve by the effort of destiny, of contingencies, by their own state" (*Sāmaññaphala Sutta* 54, after the translation by L. Renou). In other words, Gośāla rejects the pan-Indian doctrine of *karman.* According to him, every being was obliged to pass through its cycle of 8,400,000 eons (*mahākalpa*), and, at the end, deliverance was produced spontaneously, without effort. The Buddha considered this implacable determinism criminal, and that is why he attacked Makkhali Gośāla more than any other of his contemporaries; he considered his doctrine of "fatality" (*niyati*) as the most dangerous doctrine of all.

Makkhali Gośāla holds an original position in the horizon of Indian thought; his deterministic conception prompted him to study natural phenomena and the laws of life.[13] The Ājīvikas went about completely naked, following this custom earlier than the appearance of Mahāvīra and Makkhali Gośāla. Like all wandering ascetics, they begged for their food and followed very strict dietary rules; many of them put an end to their lives by letting themselves die of hunger. Initiation into the order was archaic in character: the neophyte had to burn his hands by grasping a hot object; he was buried up to the neck, and his hairs were plucked out one by one. But nothing has come down to us concerning the Ājīvikas' spiritual techniques. It must be supposed that they possessed their own ascetic traditions and methods of meditation; we deduce this from certain allusions to a kind of *nirvāṇa* comparable to the supreme heaven of the other mystical schools.[14]

13. He proposed a classification of beings according to the number of their senses; he outlined a doctrine of transformations within nature (*pariṇāmavāda*), based on precise observations of the periodicity of vegetable life.

14. Toward the tenth century A.D., the Ājīvikas, like the whole of India, became adherents of *bhakti* and ended by adopting the tenets of a Vaiṣṇava sect, the Pañcarātras; see A. L. Basham, *History and Doctrine of the Ajīvikas*, pp. 280 ff.

19 The Message of the Buddha: From the Terror of the Eternal Return to the Bliss of the Inexpressible

155. The man struck by a poisoned arrow . . .

The Buddha never consented to give his teaching the structure of a system. Not only did he refuse to discuss philosophical problems, he did not even issue pronouncements on several essential points of his doctrine—for example, on the state of the holy man in *nirvāṇa*. This silence early made possible differing opinions and finally gave rise to various schools and sects. The oral transmission of the Buddha's teaching and the composition of the canon raise numerous problems, and it would be useless to suppose that they will one day be satisfactorily solved. But if it seems impossible wholly to reconstruct the Buddha's "authentic message," it would be excessive to suppose that the earliest documents already present a radically modified version of his doctrine of salvation.

From the beginning, the Buddhist community (*saṃgha*) was organized by monastic rules (*vinaya*) that assured its unity. As for doctrine, the monks shared certain fundamental ideas concerning transmigration and the retribution for actions, the techniques of meditation that would lead to *nirvāṇa,* and the "condition of the Buddha" (what is called Buddhology). In addition to the community, there existed, even in the Blessed One's time, a mass of sympathizing laymen who, though accepting the teaching, did not renounce the world. By their faith in the Buddha, by their generosity to the community, the laymen gained "merits" that insured them a postexistence in one of the various "paradises," followed by a better reincarnation. This type of devotion is characteristic of "popular Buddhism," and it has great importance in the religious history of Asia because of the mythologies, rituals, and literary and artistic works to which it has given rise.

Essentially it may be said that the Buddha opposed both the cosmological and philosophical speculations of the Brahmans and the *śramaṇas* (magicians) and the different methods and techniques of a preclassic Sāṃkhya and Yoga. As for cosmology and anthropogony, which he refused to discuss, it is obvious that, for the Buddha, the world was created by neither a god nor a demiurge nor an evil spirit (as the Gnostics and Manicheans think; see §§ 229 ff.), but that it continues to exist, that is, it is continually created by the acts, good or evil, of men. Indeed, when ignorance and sin increase, not only is human life shortened but the universe itself wastes away. (This idea is pan-Indian, but it derives from archaic conceptions of the progressive decadence of the world, which necessitates its periodical renewal.)

As for Sāṃkhya and Yoga, the Buddha borrows and develops the analysis of the Sāṃkhya masters and the contemplative techniques of the yogins while rejecting their theoretical presuppositions, first of all the idea of the Self (*puruṣa*). His refusal to let himself be drawn into speculations of any kind is categorical. It is admirably illustrated in the famous dialogue with Māluṇkyaputta. This monk complained that the Blessed One gave no answers to such questions as: Is the universe eternal or noneternal? Finite or infinite? Is the soul the same thing as the body, or is it different? Does the Tathāgata exist after death, or does he not exist after death? And so forth. Māluṇkyaputta asks the Master to state his thought clearly and, if necessary, to admit that he does not know the answer. The Buddha then tells him the story of the man struck by a poisoned arrow. His friends and relatives fetch a surgeon, but the man exclaims: "I will not let this arrow be drawn out until I know who struck me; also, whether he is a *kṣatriya* or a Brahman . . . , to what family he belongs; whether he is tall, short, or of medium height; from what village or city he comes. I will not let this arrow be drawn out before I know what kind of bow was drawn against me, . . . what string was used on the bow, . . . what feather was used on the arrow . . . , how the point of the arrow was made." The man died without knowing these things, the Blessed One continued, just like one who would refuse to follow the way of holiness before solving one or another philosophical problem. Why did the Buddha refuse to discuss these things? "Because it is not useful, because it is not connected with the holy and spiritual life and does not contribute to disgust with the world, to detachment, to cessation of desire, to tranquillity, to profound penetration, to illumination, to Nirvāṇa!" And the Buddha reminded Māluṇkyaputta that he had taught only one thing, namely: the four Noble Truths (*Majjhima Nikāya* 1. 426).

156. The four Noble Truths and the Middle Path. Why?

These four Noble Truths contain the heart of his teaching. He preached them in his first sermon at Benares, soon after the Awakening, to his five former companions (§149). The first Noble Truth concerns suffering or pain (Pali: *dukkha*). For the Buddha, as for the majority of Indian thinkers and holy men after the period of the Upanishads, all is suffering. Indeed, "Birth is suffering, decline is suffering, sickness is suffering, death is suffering. To be joined with what one does not love means to suffer. To be separated from what one loves. . . , not to have what one desires, means to suffer. In short, any contact with [one of the] five *skandhas* implies suffering" (*Majjhima Nikāya* 1. 141). We would point out that the term *dukkha,* usually translated by "pain" or "suffering," has a much broader meaning. Various forms of happiness, even certain spiritual states obtained by meditation, are described as being *dukkha*. After praising the spiritual bliss of such yogic states, the Buddha adds that they are "impermanent, *dukkha,* and subject to change" (*Majjhima Nikāya* 1. 90). They are *dukkha* precisely because they are impermanent.[1] As we shall see, the Buddha reduces the "self" to a combination of five aggregates (*skandhas*) of the physical and psychic

1. Buddhist scholasticism distinguished *dukkha* as ordinary suffering, as suffering caused by change, and as a conditioned state (*Visuddhimagga,* p. 499; cf. Rahula, *L'Enseignement du Bouddha,* p. 40). But, since everything is "conditioned," everything is suffering.

forces. And he states that *dukkha* is, in the last analysis, the five aggregates.[2]

The second Noble Truth identifies the origin of suffering (*dukkha*) in desire, appetite, or the "thirst" (*taṇhā*) that determines reincarnations. This "thirst" continually searches for new enjoyments, of which there are three distinct kinds: desire for sensual pleasures, desire to perpetuate oneself, and desire for extinction (or self-annihilation). It is noteworthy that the desire for self-annihilation is condemned along with the other manifestations of "thirst." Being itself an "appetite," the desire for extinction, which can lead to suicide, does not constitute a solution, for it does not halt the eternal circuit of transmigrations.

The third Noble Truth proclaims that deliverance from pain (*dukkha*) consists in abolishing the appetites (*taṇhā*). It is equivalent to *nirvāṇa*. Indeed, one of the names of *nirvāṇa* is "Extinction of Thirst" (*taṇhākkaya*). Finally, the fourth Noble Truth reveals the ways that lead to the cessation of suffering.

In formulating the four truths, the Buddha applies a method of Indian medicine that first defines a disease, then discovers its cause, and finally presents the methods able to end it. The therapy elaborated by the Buddha constitutes, in fact, the fourth Truth, for it prescribes the means for curing the evils of existence. This method is known by the name of the "Middle Way." And in fact it avoids the two extremes: the pursuit of happiness by the pleasures of the senses, and the opposite way, the search for spiritual bliss by excessive asceticism. The Middle Way is also called the Eightfold Path, because it consists in: (1) right (or just) opinion, (2) right thought, (3) right speech, (4) right activity, (5) right means of existence, (6) right effort, (7) right attention, (8) right concentration.

The Buddha returns tirelessly to the eight rules of the Way, explaining them in different manners, for he addressed different audiences. These eight rules were sometimes classified according to their purposes. Thus, for example, one text of the *Majjhima Nikāya* (1. 301) defines the Buddhist teaching as: (1) ethical conduct (*śīla*), (2) mental discipline (*samādhi*), (3) wisdom (*panna;* Skr. *prajñā*). Ethical behavior, based on universal love and com-

2. See the texts cited by Rahula, p. 41.

passion for all beings, consists, in fact, in the practice of the three rules (nos. 2–4) of the Eightfold Path, namely, just or right speech and thought and right activity. Numerous texts explain what is meant by these formulas.[3] Mental discipline consists in the practice of the last three rules of the Eightfold Path (nos. 6–8): right effort, attention, and concentration. These consist in ascetic exercises of the Yoga type, on which we shall dwell later, for they are the essence of the Buddhist message. As for wisdom (*prajñā*), it is the result of the first two rules: right view or opinion, right thought.

157. The impermanence of things and the doctrine of *anattā*

By meditating on the first two Noble Truths—on pain and the origin of pain—the monk discovers the impermanence, hence the nonsubstantiality, of his own being. He finds that he is not astray among things (as is, for example, the Vedāntin, the Orphic, and the Gnostic) but shares their modalities of existence; for the cosmic totality and psychomental activity constitute one and the same universe. By employing a pitiless analysis, the Buddha showed that *all* that exists in the world can be classed in five categories—"assemblages" or "aggregates" (*skandhas*); these are (1) the sum total of "appearances," of the sensible (which includes the totality of material things, the sense organs, and their objects); (2) the sensations (provoked by contact with the five sense organs); (3) the perceptions and the notions that result from them (that is to say, cognitive phenomena); (4) psychic constructions, including both conscious and unconscious psychic activity; (5) thoughts (*vijñānas*), that is, the various kinds of knowledge produced by the sensory faculties and especially by the spirit (*manas*) that has its seat in the heart and organizes the sensory experiences. Only *nirvāṇa* is not conditioned, not "con-

3. For example, right speech means abstaining from lying, scandalmongering, and calumny, from all brutal, injurious, malevolent words, and, finally, from idle talk. The rule of right activity forbids the Buddhist to destroy life, to steal, to have illegitimate sexual relations, etc. The right way of life excludes professions that are harmful to others, etc.

structed," and, consequently, cannot be classed among the aggregates.

These aggregates or assemblages summarily describe the world of things and the human condition. Another celebrated formula even more dynamically recapitulates and illustrates the concatenation of causes and effects that govern the cycle of lives and rebirths. This formula, known as "conditioned coproduction" (*pratītya-samutpāda;* Pali, *paṭicca-samuppāda*), comprises twelve factors ("members"), the first of which is ignorance. It is ignorance that produces the volitions; these, in their turn, produce the "psychic constructions" (*saṃskāras*), which condition the psychic and mental phenomena, and so on and on—up to desire, more especially sexual desire, which engenders a new existence and finally ends in old age and death. Essentially, ignorance, desire, and existence are interdependent, and together they suffice to explain the unbroken chain of births, deaths, and transmigrations.

This method of analysis and classification was not discovered by the Buddha. The analyses of preclassic Yoga and Sāṃkhya, like the earlier speculations of the Brāhmaṇas and the Upanishads, had already dissociated and classified the cosmic totality and psychomental activity into a certain number of elements or categories. Moreover, from the post-Vedic period on, desire and ignorance were denounced as the first causes of suffering and transmigration. But the Upanishads, like Sāṃkhya and Yoga, also recognize the existence of an autonomous spiritual principle, the *ātman* or the *puruṣa*. Now the Buddha appears to have denied, or at least refrained from discussing, the existence of such a principle.

Indeed, a number of texts regarded as reflecting the Master's original teaching deny the reality of the human person (*pudgala*), of the vital principle (*jīva*), and of the *ātman*. In one of his discourses the Master brands as "completely senseless" the doctrine that affirms: "This universe is this *ātman;* after death, I shall be that, which is permanent, which remains, which endures, which does not change, and I shall exist as such for all eternity."[4] The ascetic intent and function of this negation of his are com-

4. *Majjhima Nikāya* 1. 138.

prehensible: by meditating on the unreality of the person, one destroys ignorance in its very roots.

On the other hand, the negation of a Self, subject to transmigrations but able to free itself and attain *nirvāṇa,* raised problems. This is why the Buddha on several occasions refused to answer questions concerning the existence or nonexistence of the *ātman.* Thus he remained silent when a wandering monk, Vacchagotta, questioned him concerning these problems. But he later explained to Ānanda the meaning of his silence: if he had answered that a Self exists, he would have lied; moreover, Vacchagotta would have put the Blessed One among the adherents of the "eternalist theory" (that is, he would have made him a "philosopher" like any number of others). If he had answered that there is no Self, Vacchagotta would have taken him to be a partisan of the "annihilistic theory," and, even more important, the Buddha would only have increased his confusion; "for he would have thought: formerly I did have an *ātman,* but now I no longer have one" (*Saṃyutta Nikāya* 4. 400). Commenting on this famous episode, Vasubandhu (fifth century A.D.) concluded: "To believe in the existence of the 'Self' is to fall into the heresy of permanence; to deny the 'Self' is to fall into the heresy of annihilation at death."[5]

By denying the reality of the Self (*nairātmya*), one arrives at this paradox: a doctrine that exalts the importance of the act and of its "fruit," the retribution for the act, denies the agent, the "eater of the fruit." In other words, as a late authority, Buddhaghoṣa, put it: "Only suffering exists, but no sufferer is to be found. Acts are, but there is no actor" (*Visuddhimagga,* p. 513). However, certain texts are less categorical: "He who eats the fruit of the act in a certain existence is not he who performed the act in an earlier existence; but he is not another."[6]

Such hesitations and ambiguities reflect the embarrassment occasioned by the Buddha's refusal to settle certain much-debated questions. If the Master denied the existence of an irreducible and indestructible Self, it was because he knew that the belief in *ātman* leads to interminable metaphysical controversies

5. Cited by L. de la Vallée-Poussin, *Nirvāṇa,* p. 108.
6. Cited ibid., p. 46.

and encourages intellectual pride; in the last analysis, it prevents obtaining Enlightenment. As he never ceased to repeat, he preached the cessation of suffering and the means of accomplishing it. The countless controversies concerning the Self and the nature of *nirvāṇa* found their solutions in the experience of Enlightenment: they were insoluble by thought or on the plane of verbalization.

However, the Buddha seems to have accepted a certain unity and continuity of the "person" (*pudgala*). In a sermon on the burden and the burden-bearer, he states: "The burden is the five *skandhas:* matter, sensations, ideas, volitions, knowledge; the burden-bearer is the *pudgala,* for example that venerable monk, of such and such a family, such and such name, etc." (*Saṃyutta* 3. 22). But he refused to take sides in the controversy between the "partisans of the person" (*pudgalavādin*) and the "partisans of the aggregates" (*skandhavādin*); he maintained a "middle" position.[7] However, belief in the continuity of the person continues, and not only in popular circles. The Jātakas narrate the Buddha's former existences and those of his family and his companions, and the identity of their personalities is always recognized. And how are we to understand the words uttered by Siddhārtha at the very moment he was born—"This is my last birth" (§147)—if we deny the continuity of the "true person" (even if we hesitate to call it the Self or *pudgala*)?

158. The way that leads to *nirvāṇa*

The last two Truths are to be meditated on together. First, one affirms that the halting of pain is obtained by total cessation of

7. Besides, the *pudgalavādins* approached their adversaries with a paradoxical definition of the person: "It is false that the *pudgala* is the same thing as the *skandhas;* it is false that it differs from the *skandhas.*" On the other hand, the "partisans of aggregates" ended by transforming the "personality" into a "series" (*saṃtāna*) of causes and effects, whose unity, though in motion, is not discontinuous, which makes it resemble the "soul." These two interpretations will be elaborated by later schools, but in the history of Buddhist thought the future belongs to the partisans of the soul-series. It is true, however, that the only schools whose Scriptures we possess, and which we therefore best know, profess *nairātmya* (see Vallée-Poussin, *Nirvāṇa*, pp. 66 ff.).

thirst (*taṇhā*), that is, "the act of turning away from it (from this thirst), renouncing it, rejecting it, freeing oneself from it, not attaching oneself to it" (*Majjhima N.* 1. 141). One then affirms that the ways that lead to the stopping of pain are those set forth in the Eightfold Path. The last two Truths explicitly state: (1) that *nirvāṇa* exists but (2) that it can be obtained only by special techniques of concentration and meditation. By implication, this also means that all discussion concerning the nature of *nirvāṇa* and the existential modality of the one who has achieved it has no meaning for him who has not reached even the threshold of that inexpressible state.

The Buddha does not put forth a definition of *nirvāṇa,* but he constantly returns to some of its attributes. He affirms that the *arhats* (the delivered saints) "have attained unshakable happiness" (*Udāna* 8. 10); that *nirvāṇa* "is bliss" (*Aṅguttara* 4. 414); that he, the Blessed One, has "attained the Immortal" and that the monks can attain it too: "You will make yourselves present even in this life; you will live possessing this Immortal" (*Majjhima N.* 1. 172). The *arhat,* "even in this life, cut off, nirvanaized (*nibbuta*), feeling happiness in himself, spends his time with Brahman."[8]

So the Buddha teaches that *nirvāṇa* is "visible here below," "manifest," "actual," or "of this world." But he emphasizes the fact that only he among the yogins "sees" and possesses *nirvāṇa* (by this we must understand that he means both himself and those who follow his path, his method). "Vision," called in the canon "the eye of the saints" (*ariya cakkhu*), allows "contact" with the unconditioned, the "nonconstructed"—with *nirvāṇa.*[9] Now this transcendental "vision" is obtained by certain contempla-

8. *Aṅguttara* 1. 206; *Majjhima Nikāya* 1. 341; etc. Texts cited by Vallée-Poussin, who compares *Bhagavad Gītā* 5. 24: "He who finds no happiness, joy, light, except within, the yogin identified with *brahman,* attains the *nirvāṇa* which is *brahman.*" Another Buddhist text thus describes the delivered saint: "Of this monk I say that he will go neither east nor south nor west . . . ; even in this life he is detached, nirvāṇaized, chilled, identified with Brahman (*brahma-bhūta*)" (cited by Vallée-Poussin, p. 73, n. 1).

9. A distinction must, however, be made between the "visible" *nirvāṇa,* the one that is accessible during life, and the *parinirvāṇa,* which is realized at death.

tive techniques that were practiced even from Vedic times and parallels to which are found in ancient Iran.

In short, whatever the "nature" of *nirvāṇa* may be, it is certain that no one can approach it except by following the method taught by the Buddha. The yogic structure of this method is obvious, for it comprises a series of meditations and concentrations known for many centuries. But it is a Yoga developed and reinterpreted by the religious genius of the Blessed One. The monk first practices continuous reflection on his physiological life in order to become conscious of all the acts that, until then, he has performed automatically and unconsciously. For example, "inhaling slowly, he thoroughly understands this slow inhalation; exhaling quickly, he understands, etc. And he practices being conscious of all his exhalations . . . , of all his inhalations; and he practices slowing down his exhalations . . . and his inhalations" (*Dīgha* 2. 291 ff.). Similarly, the monk seeks to "understand perfectly" what he does when he walks, raises his arm, eats, speaks, or is silent. This uninterrupted lucidity confirms to him the friability of the phenomenal world and the unreality of the "soul."[10] Above all, it contributes to "transmuting" profane experience.

The monk can now attempt with a certain confidence the techniques properly speaking. The Buddhist tradition classifies them in three categories: the "meditations" (*jhānas;* Skr. *dhyānas*), the "attainments" (*samāpattis*), and the concentrations (*samādhis*). We shall first describe them briefly and then try to interpret their results. In the first meditation (*jhāna*), the monk, detaching himself from desire, experiences "joy and felicity," accompanied by an intellectual activity (reasoning and reflection). In the second *jhāna,* he obtains the calming of this intellectual activity; in consequence, he experiences inner serenity, unification of thought, and the "joy and felicity" arising from this concentration. At the third *jhāna,* he detaches himself from joy and remains indifferent but fully conscious, and he experi-

10. Indeed, the commentary *Sumaṇgala Vilāsinī* draws the following conclusion from bodily movements: "They say that it is a living entity that walks, a living entity that rests. But is there really a living entity that walks, that rests? There is not." As for the inhalations and exhalations, the *bhikkhu* discovers that "they are founded on matter, and matter is the material body; they are the four elements, etc." (see Eliade, *Yoga,* p. 169).

ences bliss in his body. Finally, on entering the fourth stage, and renouncing both joy and pain, he obtains a state of absolute purity and indifference and awakened thought.[11]

The four *samāpattis* ("attainments" or "contemplations") pursue the process of "purifying" thought. Emptied of its various contents, the thought is concentrated successively on the infinity of space, on the infinity of consciousness, on "nothingness," and, at the fourth *samāpatti,* it attains a state that "is neither consciousness nor unconsciousness." But the *bhikkhu* must go even further in this labor of spiritual purgation by realizing the halting of all perception and of every idea (*nirodha-samāpatti*). Physiologically, the monk appears to be in a cataleptic state, and he is said "to touch *nirvāṇa* with his body." Indeed a late author declares that "the *bhikkhu* who has acquired it has nothing more to do."[12] As for the "concentrations" (*samādhis*), they are yogic exercises of lesser duration than the *jhānas* and the *samāpattis,* and they serve especially a psychomental training. The thought is fixed on certain objects or notions in order to obtain unification of consciousness and suppression of the rational activities. There are various kinds of *samādhi,* each directed toward a particular goal.

By practicing and mastering these yogic exercises, together with still others,[13] which we cannot pause to describe, the *bhikkhu* advances on the "path of deliverance." Four stages are distinguished: (1) "Having Entered the Current" is the stage attained by the monk who, freed from his errors and doubts, will be reborn on earth only seven more times; (2) the "Single Return" is the stage of him who, having reduced passion, hate, and stupidity, will have only one more rebirth; (3) the stage "Without Return" is when the monk, having definitely and completely freed himself from errors, doubts, and desires, will be reborn in a divine body and will then obtain deliverance; and (4) the final

11. *Dīgha* 1. 182 ff.; text cited in *Yoga,* pp. 170–71. Cf. also *Majjhima Nikāya* 1. 276, etc. Whatever progress the *bhikkhu* makes later, mastery of the four *jhānas* insures him rebirth among the "gods," who are perpetually plunged in these meditations.

12. Śāntideva (seventh century A.D.), cited in *Yoga,* p. 173.

13. For example, the eight "enfranchisements" (*vimokṣas*) and the "stages of mastery" (*abhibhayātanas*).

stage is that of the "Deserving One" (*arhat*), who, purged of all impurities and passions, endowed with supernatural knowledge and miraculous powers (*siddhis*), will attain *nirvāṇa* at the end of his life.

159. Techniques of meditation and their illumination by "wisdom"

It would be credulous to think that one could "understand" these yogic exercises, even by multiplying quotations from the original texts and commenting on them at length. Only practice, under the direction of a master, can reveal their structure and their function. This was true in the period of the Upanishads, and it is still true in our day.

However, we will mention some essential points. First of all, these yogic exercises are guided by "wisdom" (*prajñā*), i.e., by a perfect comprehension of the psychic and parapsychic states experienced by the *bhikkhu*. The effort to "attain consciousness" of the most familiar physiological activities (breathing, walking, moving the arms, etc.) is continued in exercises that reveal to the yogin "states" inaccessible to a profane consciousness.

Second, rendered "intelligible," the yogic experiences end by transmuting normal consciousness. On the one hand, the monk is delivered from the errors that are bound up with the very structure of an unilluminated consciousness (for example, believing in the reality of the "person" or in the unity of matter, etc.); on the other hand, by virtue of his supranormal experiences, he attains a plane of comprehension beyond any notional system, and such a comprehension cannot be verbalized.

Third, by progressing in his practice, the monk finds new confirmations of the doctrine, especially the evidence for an "Absolute," a "nonconstructed," that transcends all the modalities accessible to an unilluminated consciousness, the evident reality of an "Immortal" (or "*nirvāṇa*"), of which nothing can be said except that it exists. A late authority very aptly summarizes the experimental (i.e., yogic) origin of belief in the reality of *nirvāṇa:*

It is vain to maintain that *nirvāṇa* does not exist for the reason that it is not an object of knowledge. Obviously, *nirvāṇa* is not known directly, in the way color, sensation, etc., are known; and it is not known indirectly by its activity, in the way the sense organs are known. Yet its nature and its activity . . . are the object of knowledge. . . . The yogin, entered into contemplation, becomes conscious of *nirvāṇa,* of its nature, of its activity. When he comes out of contemplation, he exclaims: "Oh *nirvāṇa,* destruction, calm, excellent, escape!" The blind, because they do not see blue and yellow, have no right to say that the seeing do not see colors and that colors do not exist.[14]

Probably the Buddha's most inspired contribution was the articulation of a method of meditation in which he succeeded in integrating ascetic practices and yogic techniques with specific procedures for understanding. This is also confirmed by the fact that the Buddha accorded equal value to asceticism-meditation of the Yoga type and to understanding of the doctrine. But, as was to be expected, the two ways—which, furthermore, correspond to two divergent tendencies of mind—have only seldom been mastered by one and the same person. The canonical texts very early attempted to reconcile them. "The monks who devote themselves to yogic meditation (the *jains*) blame the monks who cling to the doctrine (the *dhammayogas*), and vice versa. On the contrary, they ought to think well of each other. Few indeed are they who spend their time touching with their bodies (that is, 'realizing, experiencing') the immortal element (that is, *nirvāṇa*). Few too are those who see the profound reality by penetrating it by *prajñā* (by intelligence)."[15]

All truths revealed by the Buddha were to be "realized" in the yogic way, that is, to be meditated on and "experienced." This is why Ānanda, the Master's favorite disciple, though unequaled in knowledge of the doctrine, was excluded from the council (§185): for he was not an *arhat,* that is, had not had a perfect "yogic experience." A famous text of the *Saṃyutta* (2. 115) sets Musīla and Nārada, each of them representing a certain degree of Buddhist

14. Saṃghabhadra, cited by Vallée-Poussin, *Nirvāṇa,* pp. 73–74. Cf. *Visuddhimagga:* "One cannot say that a thing does not exist because fools do not perceive it."

15. *Aṅguttara* 3. 355, cited in *Yoga,* p. 174.

perfection, face to face. Each had the same knowledge, but Nārada did not consider himself an *arhat,* since he had not experientially realized "contact with *nirvāṇa.*"[16] This dichotomy continued, only becoming more pronounced, through the whole history of Buddhism. Some authorities even affirmed that "wisdom" (*prajñā*) is able by itself to insure the acquisition of *nirvāṇa,* without any need to cultivate yogic experiences. There is perceptible in this apology for the "dry saint"—for the adept delivered by *prajñā* alone—an antimystical tendency, that is, a resistance, on the part of the "metaphysicians," to yogic excess.

We add that the road to *nirvāṇa*—just like the road to *samādhi* in classic Yoga—leads to possession of "miraculous powers" (*siddhis;* Pali, *iddhi*). This confronted the Buddha (as it later did Patañjali) with a new problem. For, on the one hand, the "powers" are inevitably acquired in the course of practice and, for that very reason, constitute precise indications of the monk's spiritual progress: they are a proof that he is in the process of "deconditioning" himself, that he has suspended the laws of nature in whose pitiless mechanism he was being crushed. But, on the other hand, the "powers" are doubly dangerous, because they tempt the *bhikkhu* with a vain "magic mastery over the world" and, in addition, they may cause dangerous confusion among the uninitiated.

The "miraculous powers" form part of the five classes of "Super Knowledges" (*abhijñās*), namely: (1) *siddhi,* (2) the divine eye, (3) divine hearing, (4) knowledge of another's thought, and (5) recollection of previous existences. None of these five *abhijñās* differs from the "powers" that can be obtained by non-Buddhist yogins. In the *Dīgha Nikāya* (1. 78 ff.) the Buddha states that the *bhikkhu* in meditation can multiply himself, become invisible, pass through solid ground, walk on water, fly through the air, or hear celestial sounds, know the thoughts of others, and remember his former lives. But he does not forget to add that possession of these powers brings with it the danger that they will deflect the monk from his true goal, which is *nirvāṇa.* In addition, the display of such powers in no way advanced the propagation of salvation;

16. See *Yoga,* p. 176. See also the texts cited in L. de la Vallée-Poussin, "Musīla et Nārada," pp. 191 ff.

other yogins and ecstatics could perform the same miracles; even worse, the uninitiated might think that no more than magic was involved. This is why the Buddha strictly forbade displaying the "miraculous powers" before lay people.

160. The paradox of the Unconditioned

If we bear in mind the transmutation of profane consciousness obtained by the *bhikkhu* and the extravagant yogic and parapsychological experiments that he performs, we understand the perplexity, the hesitations, and even the contradictions of the canonical texts in the matter of the "nature" of *nirvāṇa* and the "situation" of one who has been delivered. There has been any amount of discussion to determine whether the mode of being of the "nirvāṇaized one" is equivalent to total extinction or to an inexpressible and blissful postexistence. The Buddha compared obtaining *nirvāṇa* with the extinction of a flame. But it has been observed that, for Indian thought, the extinction of fire does not mean its annihilation but merely its regression to the mode of potentiality.[17] On the other hand, if *nirvāṇa* is supremely unconditioned, if it is the Absolute, it transcends not only the cosmic structures but also the categories of knowledge. In this case, it can be affirmed that the "nirvāṇaized" adept no longer exists (if existence is understood as being a mode of being in the world); but it can also be affirmed that he "exists" in *nirvāṇa,* in the unconditioned, hence in a mode of being that it is impossible to imagine.

The Buddha was right in leaving this problem open. For only those who have entered on the Path and have realized at least certain yogic experiences and have suitably illuminated them with *prajñā* realize that, with the transmutation of consciousness, verbal constructions and the structures of thought are abolished. One then comes out upon a paradoxical and seemingly contradictory plane on which being coincides with nonbeing; consequently, one can affirm, at one and the same time, that the "Self" exists and that it does not exist; that deliverance is ex-

17. A. B. Keith has pointed out the same image in the Upanishads, as Senart has in the Epic; see Vallée-Poussin, *Nirvāṇa,* p. 146.

tinction and is at the same time bliss. In a certain sense, and despite the differences between Sāṃkhya-Yoga and Buddhism, one can compare the "nirvāṇaized" adept to the *jīvan-mukta,* the "one delivered in life" (§146).

It is important to emphasize, however, that the equivalence between *nirvāṇa* and absolute transcendence of the cosmos, that is, its annihilation, is also illustrated by numerous images and symbols. We have already referred to the cosmological and temporal symbolism of the "Buddha's Seven Steps" (§147). The parable of the "broken egg," used by the Buddha to proclaim that he had broken the wheel of existence (*saṃsāra*)—in other words, that he had transcended both the cosmos and cyclical time—must be added. No less spectacular are the images of the "destruction of the house" by the Buddha and of the "broken roof" by the *arhats,* images that express the annihilation of any conditioned world.[18] When we remember the importance of the homology "cosmos–house–human body" for Indian thought (and, in general, for traditional, archaic thought), we can estimate the revolutionary novelty of the objective proposed by the Buddha. To the archaic ideal of "fixing one's abode in a stable dwelling place" (that is, assuming a certain existential situation in a perfect cosmos), the Buddha opposes the ideal of the spiritual elite with which he was contemporary: annihilation of the world and transcendence of every "conditioned" situation.

However, the Buddha did not claim that he preached an original doctrine. He repeated on many occasions that he was following "the ancient way," the timeless (*akālika*) doctrine shared by the "saints" and the "perfectly awakened" ones of past times.[19] It was another way of emphasizing the "eternal" truth and the universality of his message.

18. See the texts cited in Eliade, *Images and Symbols,* pp. 87 ff., and in "Briser le toit de la maison," passim.

19. "I have seen the ancient way, the old way founded by all the perfectly awakened at one time. That is the path that I claim to follow" (*Saṃyutta Nikāya* 2. 106). Indeed, "those who, in times past, were saints, perfectly awakened, all those sublime beings, guided their disciples to just such an end as, today, the disciples are guided by me; and those who, in future times, will be saints, perfectly awakened, all those sublime beings, will not fail to guide their disciples in exactly the way in which, today, the disciples are guided by myself" (*Majjhima Nikāya* 2. 3–4; cf. ibid., 2. 112; 3. 134).

20 Roman Religion: From Its Origins to the Prosecution of the Bacchanals (ca. 186)

161. Romulus and the sacrificial victim

According to the ancient historians, the founding of Rome took place about 754 B.C., and archeological discoveries confirm the validity of this tradition: the site of the *Urbs* began to be inhabited from the middle of the eighth century. The myth of the founding of Rome and the legends of the earliest kings are especially important for an understanding of Roman religion, but this mythological *summa* also reflects certain ethnographic and social realities. The fabulous events that preceded the birth of Rome emphasize (1) an assemblage of fugitives of different origins and (2) the fusion of two entirely distinct ethnic groups; for the Latin stock, from which the Roman people came, resulted from the mixture of the autochthonous Neolithic populations with the Indo-European invaders who came down from the transalpine regions. This first synthesis constitutes the exemplary model for the Roman nation and culture, for the processes of assimilation and ethnic, cultural, and religious integration continued until the end of the Empire.

According to the tradition reported by the historians, Numitor, king of Alba, was deposed by his brother Amulius. In order to consolidate his rule, Amulius slaughtered Numitor's sons and forced their sister, Rhea Sylvia, to become a Vestal. But Sylvia was pregnant by Mars and gave birth to two boys, Romulus and Remus. Exposed on the bank of the Tiber, the twins, miraculously suckled by a she-wolf, were soon rescued by a shepherd and brought up by his wife. Having grown to manhood, Romulus and Remus obtained the recognition of their grandfather and, after doing away with the usurper, reestablished Numitor on the throne. However, they left Alba and decided to found a city on the site where they had spent their childhood. To consult the gods, Romulus chose the Palatine, while Remus took his station on the Aventine hill. It was Remus who saw the first augural sign: a flight of six vultures. But Romulus saw twelve, and to him fell the honor of founding the city. With a plow, he drew a furrow around the Palatine: the turned-up earth represented the walls, the furrow symbolized the moat, and the plow was raised to indicate the future sites of the gates. To ridicule his brother's extravagant terminology, Remus jumped over the "wall" and the "moat" at one bound. Then Romulus leaped on him and killed him, crying: "So perish whoever henceforth crosses my walls!"[1]

The mythological character of this tradition is manifest. It recalls the theme of exposure of the newborn infant in the legends of Sargon, Moses, Cyrus, and other famous personages (see §§ 58, 105). The she-wolf, sent by Mars to feed the twins, foreshadows the warlike vocation of the Romans. Being exposed, then fed by the female of a wild beast, constitutes the first initiatory ordeal to be accomplished by the future hero. It is followed by the youth's apprenticeship among poor and humble people ignorant of his identity (cf. Cyrus). The theme of the "enemy (twin) brothers" and that of doing away with the uncle (or grandfather) are widespread. As for the ritual of founding a city by means of a furrow (*sulcus primigenius*), parallels to it have been found in numerous cultures. (Reciprocally, an enemy city was ritually destroyed when its walls were demolished and a furrow was drawn around their ruins.)[2] As in so many other traditions, the founding of a city in fact represents a repetition of the cosmogony. The sacrifice of Remus reflects the primordial cosmogonic sacrifice of the type exemplied by Puruṣa, Ymir, P'an-ku (see § 75). Immolated on the site of Rome, Remus insures the

1. Livy, 1. 3 ff.; Ovid, *Fasti* 2. 381 ff.; Dionysius of Halicarnassus, *Antiquit. Rom.* 1. 76 ff.; Plutarch, *Romulus* 3–11; etc.

2. Servius, ad *Aeneid* 4. 212.

fortunate future of the city, that is, the birth of the Roman people and the accession of Romulus to the kingship.[3]

It is difficult to determine the chronology and, especially, the modifications of this mythological tradition that were made *before* it was recorded by the earliest historians. Its archaism is undeniable, and certain analogies with Indo-European cosmogonies have been pointed out.[4] More instructive for our purpose are the repercussions of this legend in the consciousness of the Romans. As Grimal remarks:

> Of this blood sacrifice, the first that was offered to the divinity of Rome, the people will always preserve a terrified memory. More than seven hundred years after the Founding, Horace will still consider it a kind of original fault whose consequences would ineluctably bring about the downfall of the city by driving her sons to slaughter each other. At every critical juncture in its history, Rome will question herself in anguish, believing that she felt the burden of a curse upon her. No more than at her birth was she at peace with men, nor was she at peace with the gods. This religious anxiety will burden her destiny.[5]

162. The "historicization" of Indo-European myths

Tradition tells of the peopling of the city at first by shepherds of the region and then by outlaws and vagabonds from Latium. In order to obtain women, Romulus made use of a stratagem: during a festival that had attracted families from the neighboring cities, his companions seized the young Sabine women and dragged them into their houses. The war that then broke out between the Sabines and the Romans continued without any military decision until the women intervened between their relatives and their ravishers. The reconciliation led a number of

3. See Florus, *Rerum Romanorum epitome* 1. 1. 8; Propertius, 4. 1. 31; see also Jaan Puhvel, "Remus et frater," pp. 154 ff.

4. See Puhvel, pp. 153 ff., and Bruce Lincoln, "The Indo-European Myth of Creation," pp. 137 ff.

5. Pierre Grimal, *La civilisation romaine*, p. 27. Horace refers to the consequences of the original fratricide in *Epode* 7. 17–20.

Sabines to settle in the city. After organizing its political structure by creating the senate and the assembly of the people, Romulus disappeared during a violent thunderstorm, and the people proclaimed him a god.

Despite his crime of fratricide, the figure of Romulus became and remained exemplary in the consciousness of the Romans: he was at once founder and legislator, warrior and priest. Tradition agrees as to his successors. The first, the Sabine Numa, devoted himself to organizing the religious institutions of Rome; he especially distinguished himself by his veneration for Fides Publica, Good Faith, a goddess who governs relations among both individuals and nations. Among the kings who succeeded him, the most famous was the sixth, Servius Tullius; his name is connected with the reorganization of Roman society, with administrative reforms, and with the enlargement of the city.

There has been prolonged discussion concerning the truthfulness of this tradition, which reports so many fabulous events, from the founding of Rome to the overthrow of the last king, the Etruscan Tarquinius Superbus, and the inauguration of the Republic. In all probability, recollections of a certain number of historical personages and events, already modified by the working of the collective memory, were interpreted and organized in conformity with a particular historiographic conception. Georges Dumézil has shown that the Romans "historicized" the great themes of Indo-European mythology (see § 63) to such an extent that it is possible to say that the earliest Roman mythology—the mythology that existed before Etruscan and Greek influences—is to be found, disguised, in the first two books of Livy.

Thus, in regard to the war between the Romans and the Sabines, Dumézil notes the astonishing symmetry between it and a central episode of Scandinavian mythology, that is, the conflict between two groups of gods, the Aesir and the Vanir. The former are grouped around Óðinn and Thór. Óðinn, their chief, is the god-king-magician; Thór, the god with the hammer, is the great celestial champion. In contrast, the Vanir are the gods of fecundity and wealth. Attacked by the Aesir, the Vanir resist; but, as Snorri Sturluson puts it, "now one side, now the other, gained the victory." Wearied by this costly alternation of semisuccesses, the Aesir and the Vanir make peace; the chief Vanir divinities settle among the Aesir, thus completing, by the fecundity and wealth that they represent, the class of gods grouped around Óðinn. In this way the fusion of the two divine peoples is accomplished, and there will never be another conflict between the Aesir and the Vanir (see §174, below).

Georges Dumézil emphasizes the analogies with the war between the Romans and the Sabines: on the one side, Romulus, son of Mars and protégé of Jupiter, and his companions, redoubtable warriors but poor and without women; on the other side, Tatius and the Sabines, characterized by wealth and fecundity (for they possess the women). In fact, the two groups are complementary. The war ends, not as the result of a victory, but through the initiative of the wives. Reconciled, the Sabines decide to fuse with Romulus' companions, thus bringing them wealth. The two kings, having become colleagues, found cults: Romulus to Jupiter alone, Tatius to the gods connected with fertility and the soil, among whom is Quirinus. "Never again, either under this double reign or later, will we hear talk of dissension between the Sabine element and the Latin, Alban, Romulean element of Rome. The society is complete."[6]

To be sure, it is possible, as a number of scholars think, that this war, followed by a reconciliation, reflects a certain historical reality—the fusion between the "autochthons" and the Indo-European conquerors.[7] But it is significant that the "historical events" were rethought and organized in accordance with a mythological schema proper to the Indo-European societies. The surprising symmetry between a Scandinavian mythological episode and a Roman historical legend reveals its deep meaning when we examine the whole of the Indo-European heritage at Rome. First of all, it must be remembered that the earliest Roman triad—Jupiter, Mars, Quirinus—expresses the tripartite ideology documented among other Indo-European peoples, that is, the function of magical and juridical sovereignty (Jupiter; Varuṇa

6. Georges Dumézil, *L'héritage indo-européen à Rome,* pp. 127–42; *La religion romaine archaïque,* pp. 82–88 (the quotation is from the English translation of this work, p. 70).

7. But it would be risky to identify the ethnic components in accordance with funeral rites, assigning burial to the Sabines and cremation to the Latins; see H. Müller-Karpe, cited by Dumézil, *La rel. rom. arch.,* p. 10.

and Mitra; Óðinn), the function of the gods of warlike force (Mars; Indra; Thór), and, finally, that of the divinities of fecundity and economic prosperity (Quirinus; the twin Nāsatyas; Freyr). This functional triad constitutes the ideal model for the tripartite division of the Indo-European societies into three classes: priests, warriors, and stock-breeders/agriculturalists (*brāhmanas, kṣatriyas,* and *vaiśyas,* to mention only the Indian example; see § 63). At Rome the social tripartition was disrupted quite early, but it is possible to make out the memory of it in the legendary tradition of the three tribes.

However, the essence of the Indo-European heritage was preserved in a strongly historicized form. The two complementary tendencies of the first function—magical sovereignty and juridical sovereignty, illustrated by the pair Varuṇa-Mitra—recur in the two founders of Rome, Romulus and Tatius. The former, a violent demigod, is the protégé of Jupiter Feretrius; the latter, level-headed and wise, establisher of the *sacra* and the *leges,* is the devotee of Fides Publica. They are followed by the exclusively warmongering King Tullus Hostilius and by Ancus Marcius, under whose reign the city becomes open to wealth and long-distance commerce.[8] In short, the divine representatives of the three functions have been metamorphosed into "historical personages" and, precisely, into the series of the earliest Roman kings. The original hierarchic formula—divine tripartition—was expressed in temporal terms, as a chronological succession.

Georges Dumézil has brought to light other examples of the historicization of Indo-European myths at Rome. We mention the victory of the third Horatius over the three Curiatii, which transposes Indra's and Trita's victory over the Three-Headed One. Or the legend of the two maimed figures, Cocles and Scaevola ("Cyclops" and "Lefty") and its parallel in the pair of the one-eyed god and the one-armed god of the Scandinavians, that is, Óðinn and Thór.[9]

The results of these comparative researches are of great consequence. They show first of all that the origins of Roman religion

8. See, most recently, G. Dumézil, *Mythe et épopée,* vol. 1, pp. 271 ff.; vol. 3, pp. 211 ff.

9. Dumézil, *La rel. rom. arch.,* p. 90, with references to his earlier works.

must not be sought in "primitive" beliefs,[10] for the Indo-European religious ideology was still active at the time the Roman people was formed. To recognize that this heritage comprised not only a specific mythology and ritual technique but also a consistent and clearly formulated theology, we need only read Dumézil's analyses of the terms *maiestas, gravitas, mos, augur, augustus,* etc.[11]

The historicization of Indo-European mythological themes and mythico-ritual scenarios is also important for another reason. This process reveals one of the characteristic features of the Roman religious genius: its ametaphysical tendency and its "realistic" vocation. Indeed, we are struck by the passionate *religious* interest of the Romans in the immediate realities of cosmic life and of history, by the considerable importance they attributed to unusual phenomena (regarded as so many portents), and, above all, by their solemn confidence in the power of rites.

In short, the survival of the Indo-European mythological heritage, camouflaged in the earliest history of the city, in itself constitutes a religious creation able to reveal to us the specific structure of Roman religiosity.

163. Specific characteristics of Roman religiosity

Their ametaphysical disposition and extremely keen interest (religious in nature!) in *immediate realities,* cosmic as well as historical, are early revealed in the Romans' attitude toward anomalies, accidents, and innovations. For the Romans, as for rural societies in general, the ideal norm was manifested in the regularity of the annual cycle, in the orderly succession of the

10. An approach illustrated especially by H. J. Rose, who identified *numen* with *mana,* overlooking the fact that "for centuries *numen* was only *numen dei,* the expressed will of such and such a god" (Dumézil, *La rel. rom. arch.,* p. 47).

11. See Dumézil, *Idées romaines,* pp. 31–152. To be sure, alongside this general system of theoretical explanation and, at the same time, of empirical mastery of the world there existed a number of beliefs and divine figures of foreign origin; but at the period of the ethnogenesis of the Roman people this allogeneous religious heritage affected, above all, the rural stocks.

seasons. Every radical innovation constituted an attack on the norm; in the last analysis, it involved the danger of a return to chaos (cf. a similar conception in ancient Egypt, § 25). In the same way, every anomaly—prodigies, unusual phenomena (birth of monsters, rains of stones, etc.)—denoted a crisis in the relations between gods and men. Prodigies proclaimed the gods' discontent or even anger. Aberrant phenomena were equivalent to enigmatic manifestations of the gods; from a certain point of view, they constituted "negative theophanies."

Yahweh, too, announced his plans by means of cosmic phenomena and historical events: the prophets continually commented on them, emphasizing the terrible threats that they proclaimed (see §§116 ff.). For the Romans, the precise meaning of a prodigy was not obvious; it had to be deciphered by professionals of the cult. This explains the considerable importance of divinatory techniques and the respect, mingled with fear, enjoyed by the Etruscan haruspices and, later, by the Sibylline Books and other oracular collections. Divination consisted in interpretation of presages either seen (*auspicia*) or heard (*omina*). Only the magistrates and military leaders were authorized to explain them. But the Romans reserved the right to refuse presages (see, inter alia, Cicero, *De divinatione* 1. 29), and a certain consul, who was also an augur, had himself carried about in a closed litter so that he could ignore any signs that might thwart his plans (*De div.* 2. 77). Once the meaning of the prodigy was deciphered, lustrations and other rites of purification were performed, for these "negative theophanies" proclaimed the presence of a defilement, which must be sedulously removed.

At first sight this exaggerated fear of prodigies and defilement might be interpreted as terror fathered by superstition. It is, however, a special type of religious experience. For it is through such unusual manifestations that the dialogue between gods and men is carried on. This attitude toward the sacred is the direct consequence of the religious valorization of natural realities, human activities, and historical events—in short, of the *concrete*, the *particular*, the *immediate*. The proliferation of rites is another aspect of this behavior. Since the divine will manifests itself *hic et nunc,* in an endless series of unusual signs and incidents, it is important to know which ritual will be the most efficacious.

The need to recognize, even in their details, the specific manifestations of all the divine entities fostered a rather complex process of personification. The many epiphanies of a deity, as well as its different functions, tended to be distinguished as autonomous "persons."

In certain cases these personifications do not reach the point of shaping a true divine figure. They are invoked one after the other, but always as a group. Thus, for example, agricultural activity is carried on under the sign of a number of entities, each of whom governs a particular moment—from turning over fallow land and plowing to harvesting, carting, and storing. Similarly, as Saint Augustine humorously notes (*Civ. dei* 7. 3), Vaticanus and Fabulinus were invoked to help the newborn infant cry and speak, Educa and Polina to make it eat and drink, Abeona to teach it to walk, and so on and so on. But these supernatural entities are invoked only in connection with agricultural tasks and in the private cult. They have no real personality, and their "power" does not extend beyond the limited area in which they act.[12] Morphologically, such entities do not share in the condition of the gods.

The rather impoverished mythological imagination of the Romans and their indifference to metaphysics are made up for, as we have just seen, by their passionate interest in the concrete, the particular, the immediate. The Roman religious genius is distinguished by pragmatism, the search for effectiveness, and, above all, by the "sacralization" of organic collectivities: family, *gens*, fatherland. The famous Roman discipline, their honoring of obligations (*fides*),[13] their devotion to the state, and the religious prestige they attributed to law are expressed by depreciation of the human person: the individual mattered only insofar as he belonged to his group. It was not until later, under the influence of Greek philosophy and the Oriental cults of salvation, that the Romans discovered the religious importance of the person; but this discovery, which will have marked consequences (see § 206), more especially affected the urban populations.

12. What is more, even in these limited areas these entities are not important; see Dumézil, *La rel. rom. arch.*, pp. 52 ff.

13. On *fides*, see ibid., p. 156, n. 3 (recent bibliography).

The social character of Roman religiosity,[14] and first of all the importance attributed to relations with others, are clearly expressed by the term *pietas*. Despite its relations with the verb *piare* ("to pacify, to do away with a defilement, an evil omen," etc.), *pietas* means not only scrupulous observance of the rites but also respect for the natural relationships (i.e., relationships *in conformity with the norm*) among human beings. For a son, *pietas* consists in obeying his father; disobedience is equivalent to a monstrous act, contrary to natural order, and the guilty son must expiate the defilement by his own death. Together with *pietas* toward the gods, there is *pietas* toward the members of the groups to which one belongs, toward the city, and, finally, toward all human beings. The "law of peoples" (*jus gentium*) prescribed duties even toward foreigners. This conception reached its full development when, "under the influence of Hellenic philosophy, the concept of *humanitas* became clear—the idea that the mere fact of belonging to the human race constituted a true kinship, similar to that which linked the members of one *gens* or one city, and created duties of solidarity, of friendship, or at least of respect."[15] The "humanitarian" ideologies of the eighteenth and nineteenth centuries only return to and elaborate, though at the same time they desacralize, the old conception of Roman *pietas*.

164. The private cult: Penates, Lares, Manes

Until the end of paganism the private cult—under the direction of the *pater familias*—maintained its autonomy and importance side by side with the public cult carried on by professionals, who were dependents of the state. Unlike the public cult, which was continually modified, the domestic cult, performed around the

14. A similar tendency will be found in the effort of certain Christian churches to become "current" in the desacralized society of the twentieth century (see vol. 3).

15. Grimal, *La civilisation romaine,* p. 89. Against Latte's "political" hypothesis concerning *pietas* (*Römische Religionsgeschichte,* pp. 236–39), see P. Boyancé, *La religion de Virgile* (1963), p. 58, and Dumézil, *La rel. rom. arch.,* p. 400.

hearth, seems not to have changed perceptibly during the twelve centuries of Roman history. It is without any doubt an archaic cult system, for it is documented among other Indo-European peoples. Just as was the case in Āryan India, the domestic fire constituted the center of the cult; it was offered daily sacrifices of food, flowers three times a month, etc. The cult was addressed to the Penates and the Lares, mythico-ritual personifications of the ancestors, and to the *genius,* a kind of "double" that protected the individual. The crises brought on by birth, marriage, and death called for specific rites of passage, governed by certain spirits and minor divinities. We mentioned above (p. 115) the entities invoked in the case of the newborn infant. The religious ceremony of marriage was performed under the auspices of the chthonic and domestic divinities (Tellus, later Ceres, etc.) and of Juno as protectress of the conjugal oath, and it included sacrifices and circumambulations of the hearth.

Funeral rites, performed on the ninth day after entombment or burial, were continued in the regular cult of deceased relatives (*divi parentes*) or Manes. Two festivals were consecrated to them: the Parentalia, in February, and the Lemuria, in May. During the first, the magistrates no longer wore their emblems, the temples were closed, the fires on the altars were extinguished, and no marriages were contracted (Ovid, *Fasti* 2. 533, 557–67). The dead returned to earth and ate the food on their tombs (ibid., 2. 565–76). But it was, above all, *pietas* that pacified the ancestors (*animas placare paternas:* ibid., 2. 533). Since in the ancient Roman calendar February was the last month of the year, it shared in the fluid, "chaotic" condition that characterizes the intervals between two temporal cycles. The norms being in abeyance, the dead could return to earth. It was also February that saw the performance of the ritual of Lupercalia (§165), the collective purifications that prepared the universal renewal symbolized by the "New Year" (= ritual re-creation of the world).[16]

During the three days of Lemuria (May 9, 11, and 13) the dead (*lemures;* etymology unknown) returned again and visited their descendants' houses. In order to pacify them and keep them

16. See Eliade, *The Myth of the Eternal Return,* chap. 2, "The Regeneration of Time."

from taking some of the living away with them, the head of the family filled his mouth with black beans and, spitting them out, uttered the following formula nine times: "By these beans I redeem myself—myself and those who are mine." Finally, making a noise with some bronze object to frighten the shades, he repeated nine times: "Manes of my fathers, leave this place!" (ibid., 5. 429–44). Ritually seeing off the dead after their periodical visits to earth is a ceremony widely spread through the world (cf. the Anthesteria, §123).

Another rite connected with the Manes deserves mention: the *devotio*. Livy (8. 9–10) describes it in detail in his account of a battle against the Samnites. Seeing his legions on the verge of yielding, the consul Decius "devotes" his life for victory. Guided by a pontiff, he recites a ritual formula, invoking a great number of gods, beginning with Janus, Jupiter, Mars, and Quirinus and ending with the Manes and the goddess Tellus. Together with his own life, Decius offers to the Manes and to Earth the enemy armies. The ritual of *devotio* illustrates an archaic conception of human sacrifice as "creative murder." In short, there is a ritual transfer of the sacrificed life for the benefit of the operation that has just been undertaken—in Decius' case, military victory. Almost the entire pantheon is invoked, but it is the *offering to the Manes*—that is, Decius' self-sacrifice and the mass immolation of the Samnites—that saves the Roman army.

We do not know how the ancient inhabitants of Latium pictured the realm of the dead; the representations that have come down to us reflect the influence of Greek and Etruscan ideas. In all probability the archaic funerary mythology of the Latins continued the traditions of the Neolithic cultures of Europe. In any case, the conceptions of the other world held by the rural, Italic stocks were only superficially modified by later Greek, Etruscan, and Hellenistic influences. On the other hand, the Hades evoked by Vergil in book 6 of the *Aeneid*, the funerary symbolism of the sarcophaguses of the imperial period, and Oriental and Neo-Pythagorean conceptions of celestial immortality will become extremely popular, from the first century B.C. on, in Rome and the other cities of the Empire.

165. Priesthoods, augurs, and religious brotherhoods

The public cult, controlled by the state, was performed by a certain number of officiants and religious brotherhoods. In the period of the monarchy the king held the highest rank in the priestly hierarchy: he was *rex sacrorum* ("king of the sacred"). Unfortunately, we know little of the services as they were celebrated. We do know, however, that in the Regia, the "king's house," three categories of rites were performed, dedicated respectively to Jupiter (or to Juno and Janus), to Mars, and to a goddess of agricultural abundance, Ops Consina. Thus, as Dumézil[17] rightly points out, the king's house was the meeting place, and the king the synthesizing agent, of the three fundamental functions that, as we shall see in a moment, the *flamines maiores* administered separately. It is legitimate to suppose that, even in the pre-Roman period, the *rex* was surrounded by a body of priests, just as the Vedic *rājan* had his chaplain (*purohita*) and the Irish *ri* his Druids. But Roman religion is characterized by a tendency to division and specialization. Unlike Vedic India and the Celts, where the priesthoods were interchangeable and consequently able to celebrate any ceremony, in Rome every priest, every college or sodality, had a specific competence.[18]

After the *rex* there followed, in the priestly hierarchy, the fifteen *flamines,* first of all the major flamens, those of Jupiter, (*flamines Dialis*), of Mars, and of Quirinus. Their name is connected with Sanskrit *brahman,* but the flamens did not form a caste. They did not even make up a college, for each flamen was autonomous and attached to the divinity from whom he took his name. The institution is certainly archaic; the flamens were distinguished by their ritual costume and by a large number of prohibitions. Because of the antiquarian passion of Aulus Gellius, we are best informed concerning the status of the *flamen Dialis:* he could not leave Rome and could not wear anything knotted (if a chained man managed to enter his house, he had to be set free); he must not appear under the sky naked or see

17. *La rel. rom. arch.,* p. 576; see also ibid., pp. 184–85.
18. Ibid., p. 571.

the army or ride horseback; he had to shun contact with defilements and with the dead or anything that suggested death, etc. (*Noctes Atticae* 10. 15; cf. Plutarch, *Quaest. Rom.* 111).

For the flamens of Mars and Quirinus, the obligations and the prohibitions were less severe. We have no direct information concerning the cult services rendered by the *flamen Martialis,* but he probably took part in the horse sacrifice offered to Mars on October 15. As for the *flamen Quirinalis,* he officiated in three ceremonies: the first two (the summer Consualia, on August 21, and the Robigalia, on April 25) were certainly connected with grain.[19]

We know little of the origin of the pontifical college. From a statement of Cicero's (*De domo* 135 and *Har. resp.* 12), it can safely be deduced that the college contained, in addition to the *pontifices,* the *rex sacrorum* and the major flamens. Contrary to the opinion of Kurt Latte,[20] Dumézil has shown the antiquity of this institution. Beside the *flamen Dialis,* the *pontifex* represented a complementary function in the sacred entourage of the *rex.* The flamens did their duties "outside of history" in a way; they regularly performed the prescribed ceremonies but had no power to interpret or resolve new situations. Despite his intimacy with the celestial gods, the *flamen Dialis* did not express the will of heaven; this was the responsibility of the augurs. On the other hand, the pontifical college—more precisely, the *pontifex maximus,* of whom the others were only the extension—enjoyed both freedom and initiative. He was present at the meetings at which religious acts were decided upon, and he saw to the performance of cults that had no titular officials; he was also in control of the festivals. Under the Republic, it is the *pontifex maximus* who "creates the major flamens and the Vestals, over whom he has disciplinary powers; and, in respect to the Vestals, he is their

19. Dumézil, ibid., pp. 166 ff., 277–80. The twelve *flamines minores* were attached to divinities who had fallen into desuetude in the classic period: Volcanus, Volturnus, Palatua, Carmenta, Flora, Pomona, etc.

20. This author presupposes a revolution "that brought the great pontiff and the college that was subordinated to him to the head of the religious organization of Rome" (*Römische Religionsgeschichte,* p. 195). See Dumézil's critique, *La rel. rom. arch.,* pp. 116 ff.

counselor, sometimes their representative."[21] Hence it is very probable that the institutions of the major flamens and of the *pontifex* are not the creation of royal Rome; as Dumézil remarks, "the strict status of the former and the freedom of the latter are not to be explained by successive creations, by evolutions, but correspond to different, pre-Roman functions that can still be read in their names; . . . in short, it was natural that the greater part of the religious heritage of the royal function should pass to the pontifex."[22]

The six Vestals were attached to the pontifical college. Chosen by the *pontifex maximus* from among virgins between the ages of six and ten years, the Vestals were consecrated for a period of thirty years. They safeguarded the Roman people by keeping alight the fire of the city, which they must never allow to go out. Their religious power depended on their virginity; if a Vestal failed in chastity, she was shut up alive in an underground tomb, and her sexual partner was executed. As Dumézil observes, this is a decidedly original type of priesthood, one "for which ethnography has not discovered many parallels" (p. 576).

The augural college was as ancient and as independent as the pontifical college. But the secret of its discipline has been well kept. We know only that the augur was *not* expected to decipher the future. His role was limited to discovering if one or another project (the choice of a cult site, of a religious functionary, etc.) was *fas* (proper). He asked the gods: "*Si fas est . . . ,* send me such and such a sign!" However, as early as the end of the royal period the Romans began to consult other specialists, both native and foreign (§167). With the passing of time, certain divinatory techniques of Greek or Etruscan origin were introduced into Rome. The method of haruspices (which consisted in examining the entrails of victims) was entirely borrowed from the Etruscans.[23]

21. Dumézil, *La rel. rom. arch.,* p. 574.

22. Ibid., p. 576.

23. As for oracular activity, which implied the direct inspiration of a god, it was suspect by the mere fact that it escaped state control. The collection known as the Sibylline Books must have been accepted because it was supposed to contain the secrets of Rome's future. But it was carefully guarded by priests and was consulted only in cases of extreme danger.

Side by side with these colleges, the public cult comprised a number of closed groups, or "sodalities" (from *sodalis*, "companion"), each specializing in a particular religious technique. The twenty Fetiales sacralized declarations of war and peace treaties. The Salii, "dancers" of Mars and Quirinus, each group having twelve members, performed in March and October, when there was passage from peace to war and from war to peace. The Fratres Arvales protected cultivated fields. The brotherhood of the Luperci celebrated the Lupercalia on February 15, a rite that had its place among the ceremonies belonging to the period of crisis brought on by the end of the year (cf. §§12, 22).[24] After the sacrifice of a he-goat at the cave of the Lupanar, the Luperci, naked except for a goatskin apron, began their purifying run around the Palatine. As they ran, they struck passers-by with thongs cut from the skin of a he-goat. The women bore the strokes to obtain fertility (Plutarch, *Romulus* 21. 11–12, etc.). The rites were at once purifying and fertilizing, like many ceremonies celebrated in connection with the New Year. We certainly have here an archaic ritual complex, which also includes vestiges of an initiation of the *Männerbund* type; but the meaning of the scenario appears to have been forgotten before the Republic.

In the public as well as the private cult, sacrifice consisted in the offering of some foodstuff: firstfruits of cereal, grapes, sweet wine, and especially animal victims—bovines, ovines, porcines, and, at the Ides of October, the horse. Except for the October horse, the sacrifices of animal victims followed the same scenario: preliminary libations were performed on the portable hearth (*foculus*), representing the sacrificer's own *foculus* and placed in front of the temple, beside the altar. The sacrificer then symbolically immolated the victim by passing the sacrificial knife over its body from head to tail. Originally he himself slaughtered the animal, but in the classic ritual certain priests (*victimarii*) took over the task. The portion reserved for the gods—liver, lungs, heart, and some other pieces—was burned on the altar. The flesh was eaten by the sacrificer and his companions in the

24. *Februum*, which gave its name to the month of Februarius, is translated by Varro (*De lingua latina* 6. 13) as "purgamentum," and the verb *februare* means "to purify."

private cult, by the priests in the sacrifices celebrated for the state.

166. Jupiter, Mars, Quirinus, and the Capitoline triad

Unlike the Greeks, who had early organized a well-defined pantheon, the Romans at the beginning of the historical period had only a single hierarchic group of divinities, namely, the archaic triad Jupiter, Mars, Quirinus, completed by Janus and Vesta. As patron god of "beginnings," Janus headed the list, and Vesta, protectress of the city, closed it. However, the literary sources mention a large number of divinities, either aboriginal or borrowed from the Greeks or the Etruscans. But neither the classification nor the hierarchy of these gods and goddesses was settled.[25] Certain ancient authors distinguished the *di indigetes* and the *divi novensiles,* the former national (*patrii*), the latter divinities who were accepted later (Varro, *De lingua latina* 5. 74; Vergil, *Georg*. 1. 498). Of greater value is the sequence displayed in the formula of *devotio* handed down by Livy: the four great gods (Janus, Jupiter, Mars, Quirinus) were followed by Bellona and the Lares (patrons of war and of the soil), then by the *divi novensiles* and *di indigetes,* and finally by the Manes and Tellus (§164).

In any case there can be no doubt concerning the archaic character of the triad Jupiter, Mars, Quirinus. The statutes and functions of the three major flamens sufficiently indicate the structure of the gods for whose cults they were responsible. Jupiter[26] is above all the sovereign god, the celestial thunderer, source of the sacred and regent of Justice, guarantor of universal fecundity and cosmocrat, though he does not govern war. That is the domain of Mars (Mavors, Mamers), who, for all the Italics, represents the war god. Sometimes Mars is also associated with peaceful rites, but this represents a phenomenon that is well known in the history of religions: the totalitarian, "imperialistic"

25. Varro divided them into *certi* ("determined) and *incerti,* among which he distinguished twenty as principal (*selecti*) gods; see Augustine, *Civ. dei* 7. 2.

26. The name is found in Oscian, in Umbrian, and in the Latin dialects.

tendency of certain gods to go beyond the proper sphere of their activity. This appears especially in the case of Quirinus.[27] However, as we have seen (§165), the *flamen Quirinalis* takes part only in three ceremonies connected with cereals. Moreover, etymologically Quirinus is closely related to the assembly (*co-virites*) of the Roman people; in short, he represents the "third function" in the Indo-European tripartite division. But at Rome, as elsewhere, the third function underwent a decided fragmentation, explicable by its plurivalence and its dynamism.

As for Janus and Vesta, their being added to the archaic triad probably continues an Indo-European tradition. According to Varro, the *prima* belong to Janus, the *summa* to Jupiter. Jupiter, then, is the *rex,* for the *prima* are outclassed by the *summa,* the former having their advantage only in the order of time, the latter in the order of *dignitas*.[28] Spatially, Janus is on thresholds of houses and at gates. In the temporal cycle, it is he who governs the "beginnings of the year." Similarly, in historical times Janus is placed at the beginning: he was the first king of Latium and the sovereign of a golden age when men and gods lived together (Ovid, *Fasti* 1. 247–48).[29] He is imagined as *bifrons* (two-faced) because "every passage supposes two places, two states, the one that is left and the one that is entered" (Dumézil, p. 337). His archaism is beyond doubt, for the Indo-Iranians and the Scandinavians also know "first gods."

The name of Vesta derives from an Indo-European root meaning "to burn"; the perpetual fire of the *ignis Vestae* constitutes the hearth of Rome. The fact that only the sanctuary of the Vesta is round (all other temples being quadrangular) is explained, as Dumézil has shown, by the Indian doctrine of the symbolism of Earth and Heaven. Temples must be inaugurated and oriented

27. This god is sometimes found grouped with Mars Gradivus; they both possess sacred shields (*ancilia,* Livy, 5. 52); and Romulus, son of Mars, representative of magical and martial royalty, is assimilated to Quirinus after his death.

28. Varro, cited by Saint Augustine, *Civ. dei* 7. 9. 1; see Dumézil's commentary, *La rel. rom. arch.,* p. 333.

29. Similarly, Janus presides over certain natural "beginnings": he insured the conception of the embryo, he is held to have founded religion, to have built the first temples, to have instituted the Saturnalia, etc.; see the sources cited by Dumézil, *La rel. rom. arch.,* p. 337.

in accordance with the four celestial directions; but the house of Vesta must not be inaugurated, since all the power of the goddess is from the earth; her sanctuary is an *aedes sacra,* not a *templum.*[30] Vesta was not represented by images; fire was enough to represent her (Ovid, *Fasti* 6. 299). This is yet another proof of archaism and conservatism, for the absence of images was originally characteristic of all the Roman divinities.

Under the Etruscan domination, the old triad of Jupiter, Mars, and Quirinus loses its actuality; it is replaced by the triad Jupiter, Juno, Minerva, instituted in the days of the Tarquins. The Etrusco-Latin influence, also bringing with it some Greek elements, is evident. The divinities now have statues. Jupiter Optimus Maximus, as he will henceforth be called, is presented to the Romans under the Etruscanized image of the Greek Zeus. His cult undergoes changes. Moreover, the triumph granted by the Senate to a victorious general takes place under the sign of Jupiter. During the ceremony, the triumphing general becomes Jupiter's double: he makes his way in a chariot and is crowned with laurel, wearing the trappings of the god.[31] Despite the presence of Juno and Minerva in his temple, the one master is Jupiter; it is to him that the vow and the dedication are addressed.

"Juno," Dumézil observes, "is the most important of the Roman goddesses but also the most disconcerting" (p. 299). Her name, *Jūnō,* derives from a root that expresses "the vital force." Her functions are many; she rules over various festivals connected with the fertility of women (as Lucina, she is invoked during childbearing) but also with the beginnings of the months, the "rebirth" of the moon, etc. However, on the Capitoline she was Regina, a title that reflected a tradition strong enough to be accepted under the Republic. In short, Juno was associated with the three functions of the Indo-European ideology: sacred royalty, military force, and fertility. Dumézil compares this multivalence with a conception common to Vedic India and Iran,

30. See Dumézil, p. 323; similarly, in Iran, Atar, Fire, was put at the end of the list of the Amesha Spentas (Dumézil, p. 329).

31. Servius, ad Vergil, *Eclogue* 4. 27. Plutarch, *Aemilius Paulus* 32–34, gives a detailed description of Aemelius Paulus' famous triumph after the victory of Pydna (ca. 168); see Dumézil's commentary, pp. 296–98.

namely, the goddess who assumes all three functions and reconciles them, thus constituting the model of woman in society.[32]

As for Minerva, she was the patroness of arts and artisans. The name is probably Italic (derived from the Indo-European root **men-*, meaning any mental activity); however, the Romans received it through the Etruscans. But in Etruria Menrva (Minerva) already represented an adaptation of Pallas Athena.

In the last analysis, the Capitoline triad does not continue any Roman tradition. Only Jupiter represented the Indo-European heritage. The association of Juno and Minerva was the work of the Etruscans. For them, too, the divine triad played a part in the hierarchy of the pantheon. We know, for example, that it presided over the foundation of temples (see Servius ad *Aeneid* 1. 422). But that is almost all that we know.

167. The Etruscans: Enigmas and hypotheses

Rome was early confronted by the Etruscan world. Yet it is hard to define the reciprocal influences of their cultures. The archeological documentation (tombs, frescoes, statues, various objects) testifies to a highly developed civilization, but we do not know the Etruscan language. Then, too, no historian of antiquity presented the religion, culture, and history of the Etruscans as had been done for the Thracians, the Celts, or the Germans. Furthermore, the essential data concerning certain aspects of Etruscan religion are not supplied by Latin authors before the first century B.C., when the original heritage had undergone Hellenistic influences. Finally, even the origin of the Etruscan people is disputed, which lessens the value of comparative deductions.

According to the tradition transmitted by Herodotus (1. 94), the Etruscans descended from the Lydians. And in fact their Asian origin appears to be confirmed by some inscriptions discovered at Lemnos. But the cultural forms developed in Etruria do not reflect Asian realities. What is certain is the symbiosis early realized between the conquerors from overseas and the

32. See Dumézil, pp. 307 ff., where he analyzes the function of Sarasvatī and Anāhitā.

original populations settled between the Po and the Tiber, that is, in the region that, in the sixth century, constituted Etruria. The civilization of the Etruscans was certainly superior: they possessed a considerable fleet, practiced commerce, used iron, and built fortified cities. Their principal political organization was the federation of cities; the metropolis had twelve of these. But the population of these cities was Etruscan only in part; the remainder was made up of Umbrians, Veneti, Ligurians, and other Italic peoples.

Greek influences were soon felt, in both art and religion. The Etruscan god Fufluns was represented as Dionysus, beside Semla (Semele) and Areatha (Ariadne). We find Artumes (Artemis) and Aplu (Apollo). On the other hand, a number of authentic Etruscan divinities bear Latin or Faliscan names: Uni (Juno), Nethuns (Neptune), Maris (Mars), Satres (Saturn). The name of the mythological hero Mastarna (Etruscan: *maestrna*) derives from the Latin *magister.* The assimilation of Roman to Greek divinities had the Etruscan precedent as its model: Juno, Minerva, and Neptune became Hera, Athena, and Poseidon, in imitation of the Etruscan Uni, Menrva, and Nethuns. In short, Etruscan culture, and especially Etruscan religion, are characterized by an early assimilation of Italic and Greek elements.[33] To be sure, the synthesis is an original one, for the Etruscan people developed borrowed ideas in accordance with its own genius. But we do not know Etruscan mythology and theology. We do not dare consider even Hercle (Heracles) to be an exception; for, despite Jean Bayet's efforts, we know only that he was extremely popular in Etruria and that he had an original mythology, different from the Greek tradition and even including some elements of Oriental origin (Melkart).[34] As for Etruscan theology, it would be vain to believe that it could be reconstructed on the basis of some late statements concerning the

33. F. Altheim observes that the Asian and Mediterranean heritage is more perceptible at the end, not at the beginning, of Etruscan history; see his *A History of Roman Religion,* p. 50.

34. J. Bayet, "Heraclès-Herclé dans le domaine étrusque," in his *Les origines de l'Hercule romain* (1926), pp. 70–120; see also Bayet's *Herclé, étude critique des principaux monuments relatifs à l'Hercule étrusque* (1926).

Etruscan "books." As we shall see, these statements deal almost exclusively with various divinatory techniques.

In default of texts, scholars have concentrated on detailed study of the archeological material. The archaic structure of the cult of the dead and of the chthonic goddesses is reminiscent of the tombs and statues of Malta, Sicily, and the Aegean (see §34). The necropolises—veritable cities of the dead—rose beside the cities of the living. The tombs were richly furnished, especially with weapons for men and jewels for women. Human sacrifice was practiced; the custom later gave rise to the gladiatorial combats. The funerary inscriptions give only the dead person's maternal ancestry. Whereas men's tombs were decorated with a phallus, women's tombs displayed cippi in the shape of houses. Woman incarnated the house itself, hence the family.[35] Bachofen spoke of "matriarchy"; what appears to be certain is the eminent position of women in Etruscan society. Women took part in banquets side by side with men. Greek writers had observed with surprise that Etruscan wives enjoyed a freedom granted in Greece only to *hetairai.* In fact they showed themselves before men without veils, and funerary frescoes represent them in their transparent dresses, encouraging combats between naked athletes by their cries and gestures.[36]

At the end of the Republic the Romans knew that the Etruscan religion possessed "books" that had been communicated by supernatural personages—by Tages or the nymph Vegoie. According to the legend, the former one day emerged from a furrow; he had the appearance of a child but the wisdom of an old man. The crowd that quickly gathered around Tages carefully wrote down his teaching, and this was the origin of the *haruspicinae disciplina.*[37] The mythical motif of the revelation of a "sacred book" (or a book containing a secret doctrine) by a supernatural

35. Funerary phalli make their appearance beginning with the fourth century, whereas cippi in the shape of houses are documented much earlier. The Etruscan funerary inscription mentioned the father's first name and the family name of the mother: "the mother was regarded less as a personality than as a member of her lineage" (Altheim, *A History of Roman Religion,* pp. 51 ff.

36. Altheim, ibid., pp. 61 ff.

37. Cicero, *De Div.* 2. 51. Lydus states that Greeks assimilate the child Tages to the chthonian Hermes.

being is documented from Egypt and Mesopotamia down to medieval India and Tibet. This scenario became especially popular during the Hellenistic period. The epiphany of Tages as *puer aeternus* suggests Hermeticism (see §209), which does not necessarily imply an alchemical (hence late) "reading" of the Etruscan tradition. For our purpose what is important is the fact that, at the beginning of the first century B.C., the Etruscans were believed to have preserved certain supernatural revelations in their *libri*. Essentially these texts can be classified as *libri fulgurales* (the theory of thunderbolts), *libri rituales* (to which the *acherontici* are joined), and *libri haruspicini* (completed by the *libri fatales*).

The doctrine of thunderbolts, as we know it by the explanations of Seneca and Pliny,[38] comprised a repertory that gave the meaning of thunder for each day of the year. In other words, the sky, divided into sixteen sections, constituted a virtual language, actualized by meteorological phenomena. The meaning of a thunderbolt was revealed by the portion of the sky from which it came and the portion in which it ended. The eleven different types of thunderbolt were manipulated by different gods. Hence the message was of divine origin and was transmitted in a "secret language," accessible only to specialized priests, the haruspices. The analogies with Chaldean doctrine have been aptly brought out.[39] But in the form in which it has been transmitted to us, the theory of thunderbolts shows certain influences exercised by Hellenistic science, from the *Meteorologica* of the pseudo-Aristotle to the conceptions of the "Chaldean magi."[40] However, in the last analysis these influences modified principally the language, by adapting it to the style of the contemporary *Zeitgeist*. The fundamental idea, and especially the homology macrocosm/microcosm, is archaic.

So, too, haruspicy—that is, the interpretation of signs inscribed on the entrails of victims—presupposed correspondence among the three planes of reference: divine, cosmic, human. The peculiarities of different areas of the organ indicated the gods'

38. *Naturales quaestiones* 2. 31–41 and 47–57; *Naturalis historia* 2. 137–46.

39. Most recently by A. Piganiol, "Les Etrusques, peuple d'Orient," pp. 340–42.

40. See, especially, S. Weinstock, "Libri Fulgurales," pp. 126 ff.

decision and, in consequence, predicted the imminent unfolding of historical events. The bronze model of a sheep's liver, discovered at Piacenza in 1877, contains a certain number of lines drawn by a graver and the names of some forty divinities.[41] The model represents both the structure of the world and the distribution of the pantheon.

The doctrine of the homology macrocosm/microcosm also informs what we may call the Etruscan conception of history. According to the *libri fatales,* a human life extends over twelve hebdomads; after the twelfth, men "go out of their minds" and the gods no longer send them any sign.[42] Similarly, peoples and states, Etruria as well as Rome, have a term fixed by the same norms that govern the cosmos. Some scholars have referred to the pessimism of the Etruscans, especially in connection with their belief in strong cosmic and existential determinism. But what we have here is an archaic conception, held by many traditional societies: man is in solidarity with the major rhythms of the Creation, because all the modes of existence—cosmic, historical, human—iterate, on their specific plane of reference, the exemplary model revealed by the cyclical trajectory of life.

It is difficult to reconstruct the Etruscan beliefs concerning death and existence beyond the grave. From the fourth century the tomb paintings depict underworlds that are "different from the Greek ones but inspired by them: the dead man travels on horseback or in a chariot; he is received into the other world by a group of men who are perhaps his ancestors; a feast awaits him, presided over by Hades and Persephone, who here are called Eita and Phersipnai."[43] On the other hand, the paintings represent a whole demonology that is not Greek in origin. The protagonist, Charun, despite his Greek name, is an original creation of Etruscan mythology. "His hooked nose suggests a bird of prey and his ears a horse; his grinding teeth, on the monuments

41. The age of the model is still in dispute; it probably dates from the third or second century B.C. The analogies with Mesopotamian hepatoscopy are obvious; they were presumably strengthened by later influences.

42. Varro, text cited and commented on by Bouché-Leclerq, *Histoire de la divination,* vol. 4, pp. 87 ff.; cf. C. O. Thulin, *Die Ritualbücher,* pp. 68 ff.; Dumézil, *La rel. rom. arch.,* pp. 653 ff.

43. Dumézil, *La rel. rom. arch.,* pp. 676–77.

where the cruel grin on his lips reveals them, suggest the image of a carnivore ready to devour its victims."[44] After killing him, Charun accompanies his victim on his journey to Hades. But his part ends at the entrance to the other world, where, to judge from the scenes painted on tomb walls, the dead man enjoys a postexistence that is rich in pleasures.

The fragments of the *libri acherontici* are too few to permit any comparison with the Egyptian *Book of the Dead.* According to the Christian writer Arnobius (fourth century): "In its *libri acherontici,* Etruria promises that by offering the blood of certain animals to certain divinities, souls may become divine and will escape the condition of mortality" (*Adversus nationes* 2. 62). Servius adds an important detail: after certain sacrifices, souls are transformed into gods who are termed *animales* to recall their origin (ad *Aeneid* 3. 168). We should then have here a deification obtained as the result of blood rituals, which may be interpreted either as an indication of archaism or as a sacrifice-sacrament comparable to initiation into the Mysteries of Mithra (see § 217). In any case, the "deification of souls" adds a new dimension to Etruscan eschatology.

In the last analysis, the essence of Etruscan religious thought escapes us. The prestige that the Etruscans' methods of divination, of *orientatio,* and of the building of cities and sacred edifices enjoyed from the beginnings of Rome indicates the cosmological structure of their theology and seems to explain their efforts to solve the enigma of historical time. In all probability these conceptions contributed to the maturing of Roman religion.

168. Crises and catastrophes: From the Gallic suzerainty to the Second Punic War

In ca. 496, soon after the expulsion of the last Etruscan king and the inauguration of the Republic, a temple was erected at the foot of the Aventine to a new triad: Ceres, Liber, and Libera. Probably politics played a part in the founding of this new cult, devoted to three divinities who were patrons of fertility. The

44. F. de Ruyt, *Charun, démon étrusque de la mort,* pp. 146–47.

sanctuary, a place long consecrated to agrarian cults, belonged to representatives of the plebs.[45] Etymologically, Ceres means "Growth" personified. The existence of a *flamen Cerealis* and the special character of the rituals celebrated on the occasion of the Cerealia (April 19) confirm the goddess's archaism. As for Liber, his name appears to be derived from the Indo-European root **leudh*, whose meaning is "he of germination, he who assures birth and the harvest."[46] According to Saint Augustine (*Civ. dei* 7. 3), the pair Liber-Libera were favorable to procreation and to universal fecundity by "liberating" the semen in the course of sexual union (*Civ. dei* 7. 9). In some parts of Italy their festival, the Liberalia (March 17), included licentious elements: procession of a phallus, which the chastest matrons had to crown publicly, obscene words, etc. (*Civ. dei* 7. 21). But the triad Ceres, Liber, Libera was very soon assimilated (the *interpretatio graeca!*) to the trio Demeter, Dionysus (Bacchus), Persephone (Proserpine).[47] Become famous under the name Bacchus, Liber will have exceptional good fortune as the result of the spread of the Dionysiac cult (see below, pp. 135–36).

Rome was already familiar with the Greek gods in the sixth century, during the rule of the Etruscan kings. But from the beginnings of the Republic we witness the rapid assimilation of Greek divinities: the Dioscuri in 499, Mercury in 495, Apollo in 431 (on the occasion of pestilences; so it was the "healer god" who was first introduced). Venus, originally a common noun meaning a magical charm, was identified with the Greek Aphrodite; but the goddess's structure changed later, under the influence of the Trojan legend. A similar process characterizes the assimilation of Latin and Italiot divinities. Diana was received from the Albans and was finally homologized to Artemis. In ca. 396 Juno Regina, the patron goddess of Veii, was ceremonially invited to establish herself in Rome. Livy, in a famous passage (5. 21. 3–22), describes the rite of the *evocatio:* the dictator Camillus addressed the goddess of the beseiged: "I beseech thee,

45. According to tradition, the temple was the result of the first consultation of the Sibylline Books, but there is anachronism here.

46. E. Benveniste, "Liber et liberi"; Dumézil, *La rel. rom. arch.*, p. 383.

47. See J. Bayet, "Les 'Cerealia,' altération d'un culte latin par le mythe grec," in *Croyances et rites dans la Rome antique;* see esp. pp. 109 ff.

Queen Juno, that dwellest now in Veii, to come with us, when we have gotten the victory, to our city—soon to be thine, too—that a temple meet for thy majesty may there receive thee.'' The people of Veii did not know ''that they were already given up by their own soothsayers and by foreign oracles; that some of the gods had already been invited to share in their despoiling, while others, having been entreated to quit their city, were beginning to look to new homes in the temples of their enemies; or that this was the last day they were themselves to live.''[48]

The invasion by the Celts during the first quarter of the fourth century had interrupted contacts with Hellenism. The devastation of Rome (ca. 390) was so thorough that some Romans had thought of abandoning the ruins forever and establishing themselves at Veii. Like Egypt after the Hyksos incursion (see § 30), the burning of the city shook the Romans' confidence in their historical destiny. It was not until after the victory of Sentinum (ca. 295) that Rome and Italy freed themselves from Gallic suzerainty. Communications with the Greek world were reestablished, and the Romans resumed their policy of conquest. Toward the end of the third century Rome was the greatest power in Italy. Thenceforth, political vicissitudes will have repercussions, sometimes serious, on the traditional religious institutions. For a people who were inclined to read in historical events so many divine epiphanies, their military victories or disasters were charged with religious meanings.

When, soon afterward, the Second Punic War threatened the very existence of the Roman state, religion underwent a transformation in depth. Rome appealed to all the gods, whatever their origin. The haruspices and the Sibylline Books revealed that the causes of military disasters lay in ritual faults of various kinds. Obeying the indications of the Sibylline Books, the Senate promulgated saving measures: sacrifices, lustrations, ceremonies, and unusual processions, even human sacrifices. The disaster at Cannae (ca. 216), made all the more threatening by many prodigies and by incest committed by two Vestals, decided the Senate to send Fabius Pictor to consult the oracle at Delphi. At Rome the Sibylline Books prescribed human sacrifices: two

48. [After the translation by B. O. Foster.—Trans.]

Greeks and two Gauls were buried alive (Livy, 21. 57. 6).[49] We probably have here a rite that is archaic in structure: "creative murder."[50]

Finally, in ca. 205–204, on the eve of the victories over Hannibal and following a suggestion in the Sibylline Books, Rome introduced the first Asiatic divinity, Cybele, the Great Mother of Pessinonte (Livy, 29. 10 ff.). The famous black stone symbolizing the goddess was brought to Pergamum by a Roman fleet. Solemnly received at Ostia, Cybele was installed in her temple on the Palatine.[51] However, the orgiastic nature of the cult and, above all, the presence of eunuch priests were too strongly in contrast with Roman austerity. The Senate lost no time before carefully regulating the manifestations of the cult. Sacrifices were strictly confined to the interior of the temple, except for an annual procession that conducted the sacred stone to its bath. Roman citizens were forbidden to sacrifice to Cybele according to the Anatolian rite. The personnel was limited to a priest, a priestess, and their assistants, but neither Romans nor their slaves had the right to perform these functions. As for the official Roman cult, it was controlled by an urban praetor.

However, in ca. 204 the Senate permitted the organization of sodalities, consisting exclusively of members of the aristocracy, whose principal function was limited to banquets in honor of Cybele. In short, the introduction of the first Asiatic divinity was the work of the aristocracy. The patricians considered that Rome was called to play an important part in the Orient. But Cybele's presence had no consequences. The invasion by Oriental cults will take place more than a century later. Certainly, after the

49. In ca. 226, likewise after a consultation of the Sibylline Books, two Greeks and two Gauls were buried alive to ward off the threat of a Gallic invasion (Plutarch, *Marcellus* 3. 4). Similar immolations took place at the end of the second century (Plutarch, *Quaest. Rom.* 83). Human sacrifices were forbidden by the Senate, ca. 97.

50. In order to make sure of victory, Xerxes had nine youths and nine girls buried alive when he set sail for Greece. We know, too, that on the eve of the Battle of Salamis Themistocles, in obedience to an oracle, had three young prisoners sacrificed (Plutarch, *Vita Them.* 13). On this mythical theme, see Eliade, *Zalmoxis, the Vanishing God,* pp. 183 ff.

51. It should be pointed out that, because of the legend of Aeneas, Cybele was no longer a foreign goddess.

dreadful sufferings and the terror of the Second Punic War, Rome was doubly attracted by the Asiatic divinities. But here, once again, we find the characteristically Roman ambiguity: at once the need to control foreign cults and fear of losing their benefits.[52] However, the consequences of these two wars, and of the overwhelming final victory, could not be avoided. On the one hand, a considerable number both of refugees from all the regions of Italy and of foreign slaves gathered in Rome. On the other hand, certain sections of the population increasingly broke away from the traditional religion. In Rome, as throughout the Mediterranean world from the fourth century on, the need for a personal religious experience became more and more intense. Such a religious experience was accessible especially in the conventicles and closed societies of the Mystery-religion type—in other words, in the secret associations that escaped state control. This is why the Senate had forbidden Roman citizens, and even their slaves, to take part in the Anatolian cult of Cybele.

In ca. 186 the authorities discovered, with surprise and indignation, the existence in Rome itself of bacchanalia, that is, of nocturnal "orgiastic mysteries." The cult of Dionysus had become widely disseminated in the Mediterranean world, especially in the Hellenistic period (see § 206). Following the Roman conquest of Magna Graecia, esoteric associations of mystai spread through the peninsula, especially in Campania. Indeed, it was a Campanian priestess-seeress who had introduced into Rome a secret cult, modified according to her own directions and including certain rites comparable to those of the Mysteries. In consequence of a denunciation that was immediately made public by the consul, an investigation revealed the size of the cult and its orgiastic character. Its adherents, who numbered more than 7,000, were accused of many abominations: not only did they swear to reveal nothing, but they practiced pederasty and organized murders in order to obtain fortunes. The rites were performed in the greatest secrecy. According to Livy (39. 13. 12), men, their bodies tossing as if they were demented, uttered prophecies; women "in the dress of bacchantes, with disheveled hair," ran to the Tiber, "carrying blazing torches,"

52. See Jean Bayet, *Histoire . . . de la religion romaine*, p. 154.

which they thrust into the water and withdrew still on fire, for "they contained live sulphur mixed with calcium."[53]

Some of the accusations resemble the clichés used later in all trials for heresy and witchcraft. The promptness and intensity of the investigation and the severity of the suppression (several thousands of executions) show the political nature of the prosecution. The authorities denounced the danger of secret associations, hence the danger of a plot able to attempt a *coup d'état*. No doubt the Bacchic cult was not entirely abolished, but Roman citizens were forbidden to practice it. In addition, all Bacchic ceremonies, which were strictly limited to five participants, had to be authorized by a decision of the Senate. The cult buildings and objects were destroyed, except for those that had "something sacred."

All these panicky measures show how greatly the Senate suspected religious associations that were not under its control. The *senatus consultum* against the bacchanals was never to lose its validity; three centuries later, it served as a model for the persecutions of Christians.

53. They were further accused of causing those who refused to join in their crimes and debauches to disappear in some horrible manner (Livy, 39. 13. 13). For a detailed analysis of Livy's text and of the *senatus consultum* of 186 concerning the bacchanals, see Adrien Bruhl, *Liber Pater*, pp. 82–116.

21 Celts, Germans, Thracians, and Getae

169. Persistence of prehistoric elements

The impact of the Celts on the ancient history of Europe was felt for less than two centuries: from the conquest of northern Italy in the fifth century (Rome was attacked ca. 390) to the pillage of the sanctuary of Apollo at Delphi, ca. 279. Soon afterward, the doom of the historical destiny of the Celts was sealed: caught between the expansion of the Germanic tribes and the pressure from Rome, their power steadily declined. But the Celts were inheritors of a protohistory that was remarkably rich and creative. As we shall very soon see, information contributed by archeology is of great importance for an understanding of Celtic religion.

The proto-Celts were, in all probability, the authors of the so-called Urnfield[1] culture, which was developed in central Europe between ca. 1300 and ca. 700. They lived in villages, practiced agriculture, used bronze, and burned their dead. Their first migrations (tenth and ninth centuries) took them to France, Spain, and Great Britain. Between ca. 700 and ca. 600 the use of iron spread in central Europe; this was the so-called Hallstatt culture, characterized by a marked social stratification and by different funerary rites. Probably these innovations were the result of Iranian cultural influences carried by the Cimmerians (of Black Sea origin). It was then that the Celtic military aristocracy originated. Corpses (at least those of chiefs) were no longer burned but, accompanied by their weapons and other precious objects,

1. So termed because the dead were cremated and their ashes put in urns that were later buried in a cemetery.

were laid in a four-wheeled chariot, which was then buried in a funerary chamber covered by a mound. About 500, during the second Iron Age, known by the name of La Tenel, the artistic creativity of the Celtic genius reached its height. The jewelry and countless metal objects brought to light by excavations have been termed a "glory of barbarian art, a great, if limited, contribution by the Celts to European culture."[2]

In view of the scarcity of written sources for Celtic religion, the archeological documents are of inestimable value. As the result of excavations, we know that the Celts attributed great importance to sacred space, that is, to places that had been consecrated, in accordance with definite rules, around an altar on which sacrifices were performed. (As we shall see, the ritual delimitation of the sacred space and the symbolism of the "center of the world" are reported by ancient authors and are found in Irish mythology.) Again as the result of excavations, we know that different kinds of offerings were placed in ritual pits from two to three meters deep. Just like the Greek *bothros* or the Roman *mundus,* these ritual pits insured communication with the divinities of the world underground. Such pits are documented from the second millennium; they were sometimes filled with objects of gold and silver, heaped up in richly decorated ceremonial caldrons.[3] (Recollections of these pits communicating with the other world, and of underground treasures, are found in medieval legends and Celtic folklore.)

No less important is the confirmation furnished by archeology concerning the dissemination and continuity of the cult of skulls. From the limestone cylinders decorated with stylized heads found in Yorkshire, dating back to the eighteenth century B.C. and continuing on into the Middle Ages, skulls and representations of "severed heads" are documented in all the areas inhabited by the Celtic tribes. Excavations have brought to light skulls placed in niches or inserted into the walls of sanctuaries, heads sculptured in stone, and countless wooden images immersed in springs. Indeed, the religious importance of skulls was noted by the classic authors, and, despite ecclesiastical inter-

2. Anne Ross, *Pagan Celtic Britain,* p. 35. See a selection of reproductions in the book by J. J. Hatt, *Les Celtes et les Gallo-Romains,* pp. 101 ff.

3. Stuart Piggott, *Ancient Europe,* pp. 215 ff.; Piggott, *The Druids,* pp. 62 ff.

dicts, the glorification of the severed head plays an important part in medieval legends and in British and Irish folklore.[4] It is indubitably a cult whose roots go deep into prehistory and that still survived down to the nineteenth century in several Asiatic cultures.[5] The original magico-religious value of the severed head was later reinforced by beliefs that localized in the skull the original source of *semen virile* and the seat of the "mind." Among the Celts the skull was outstandingly the receptacle of a sacred force, of divine origin, which protected its owner from all kinds of dangers and at the same time insured him health, wealth, and victory.

In short, the archeological discoveries bring out, on the one hand, the archaism of Celtic culture and, on the other hand, the continuity, from protohistory to the Middle Ages, of certain central religious ideas. A number of these ideas and customs belonged to the old religious stock of the Neolithic, but they were early assimilated by the Celts and partially integrated into the theological system they had inherited from their Indo-European ancestors. The astonishing cultural continuity demonstrated by archeology allows the historian of Celtic religion to make use of late sources, first of all the Irish texts composed between the sixth and eighth centuries, but also the epic legends and the folklore that still survived in Ireland down to the end of the nineteenth century.

170. The Indo-European heritage

The archaism of Celtic culture is corroborated by other sources. We find in Ireland a number of ideas and customs that are documented in ancient India, and Irish prosody is similar to that of Sanskrit and Hittite; as Stuart Piggott expresses it, this represents "fragments of a common heritage from the second millennium."[6] Just like the Brahmans, the Druids attributed great importance to memory (see §172). The ancient Irish laws were

4. See Ross, *Pagan Celtic Britain,* pp. 97–164 and figs. 25–86 and pls. 1–23.

5. See Eliade, *Yoga,* pp. 301, 419–20; *Shamanism,* pp. 421 ff.

6. Piggott, *The Druids,* p. 88. According to Myles Dillon, the Druids and the Brahmans preserved Indo-European practices and beliefs that survived in the

composed in verse in order to facilitate memorizing them. The parallelism between the Irish and the Hindu judicial treatises is shown not only in their form and technique but also, at times, in their diction.[7] Other examples of Indo-Celtic parallelism are: fasting as a means of strengthening a judicial petition; the magico-religious value of truth;[8] insertion of passages in verse into epic narrative prose, especially in dialogues; the importance of bards, and their relations with sovereigns.[9]

Because writing was ritually prohibited by the continental Celts we have not even one text on their religion composed by a native. Our only sources are the few descriptions by Greco-Latin authors and a large number of figured monuments, most of them from the Gallo-Roman period. In contrast, the insular Celts, concentrated in Scotland, Wales, and especially Ireland, produced an abundant epic literature. Despite the fact that it was composed after the conversion to Christianity, this literature in large part continues the pre-Christian mythological tradition, and this is also true of the rich Irish folklore.

The information given by the classic authors is frequently confirmed by Irish documents. In his *De Bello Gallico* (6. 13), Caesar states that the Gauls have two privileged classes—the Druids and the knights—and a third, oppressed, class, the "people." This is the same social tripartition, reflecting the well-known Indo-European ideology (§ 63), that is found in Ireland soon after

---

Gaelic world until the eighteenth century and in India down to our day; see his "The Archaism of Irish Tradition," p. 246. See also, by the same author, *Celts and Aryans,* pp. 52 ff. Studying Irish and Indian funerary rites, Hans Hartmann concludes (*Der Totenkult in Irland,* p. 207) that the structure of the Irish mentality is closer to that of ancient India than to the mentality of England or Germany.

7. D. A. Binchy, "The Linguistic and Historical Value of the Irish Law Tracts," cited by Dillon, "The Archaism," pp. 247.

8. See the references in Dillon, "The Archaism," pp. 247, 253 ff. See also his *Celts and Aryans*.

9. G. Dumézil, *Servius et la Fortune,* pp. 221 ff. and passim; J. E. Caerwyn Williams, "The Court Poet in Medieval Ireland," pp. 99 ff. We add that analogies are also found with the Sumero-Akkadian world. These can be explained by contacts of the Indo-Europeans with the peoples of the ancient Near East (see H. Wagner, "Studies in the Origins of Early Celtic Tradition," pp. 6 ff. and passim).

its conversion to Christianity: under the authority of the **rig* (the phonetic equivalent of Sanskrit *rāj-*, Latin *rēg-*), society is divided into the class of Druids, the military aristocracy (the *flaith,* properly "power," the exact phonetic equivalent of Sanskrit *kṣatra*), and the stock-breeders "the *bó airig,* the free (*airig*) men, who are defined as owners of cows (*bó*)."[10]

We shall have occasion further on to point out other survivals of the Indo-European religious system among the Celts. But at this point it is important to state that "the survivals common to the Indo-Iranian and Italo-Celtic societies" are explained by "the existence of powerful colleges of priests, who were the repositories of sacred traditions that they maintained with formalistic strictness."[11] As for the tripartite Indo-European theology, it can still be recognized in the list of their gods handed down to us by Caesar, and, radically historicized, it survives in Irish tradition. Georges Dumézil and Jan de Vries have shown that the chiefs of the legendary people the Tuatha Dé Danann actually represent the gods of the first two functions, while the third is embodied in the people of the Fomorṡ, considered to be the previous inhabitants of the island.[12]

Caesar presents the Celtic pantheon in an *interpretatio romana*. "Among the gods," the consul wrote, "they most worship Mercury. There are numerous images of him; they declare him the inventor of all arts, the guide for every road and journey, and they deem him to have the greatest influence for all money-making and traffic. After him they set Apollo, Mars, Jupiter, and Minerva. Of these deities they have almost the same idea as all other nations: Apollo drives away diseases, Minerva supplies the first principles of arts and crafts, Jupiter holds the empire of heaven, Mars controls the wars" (*B.G.* 6. 17; trans. H. J. Edwards).

The authenticity, and hence the value, of this *interpretatio romana* of the Gallic pantheon have been much discussed. Caesar had considerable knowledge of the customs and beliefs of

10. G. Dumézil, *L'idéologie tripartite des Indo-Européens,* p. 11.

11. E. Benveniste, *Le vocabulaire des institutions indo-européennes,* vol. 1, p. 10. Cf. Vendryès's observations in n. 38, below.

12. See Dumézil, *Mythe et épopée,* vol. 1, p. 289; Jan de Vries, *La religion des Celtes,* pp. 157 ff. (originally published in German; see the Critical Bibliographies, §169).

the Celts. He had already been proconsul of Cisalpine Gaul before he began his campaign in Transalpine Gaul. But since we know nothing of continental Celtic mythology, we know very little about the gods mentioned by Caesar. It is surprising that he does not put "Jupiter" at the head of the list. Presumably the great celestial god had lost his primacy among the inhabitants of cities that, for at least four centuries, had been exposed to Mediterranean influences. The phenomenon is common in the history of religions, as well in the ancient Near East (see §§ 48 ff.) and among the Vedic Indians (§ 62) as among the ancient Germans (§ 176). But the "gigantic Jupiter" type of column, found in great numbers especially between the Rhine, the Moselle, and the Saône and also erected by certain Germanic tribes, carries on an archaic symbolism, namely, that of the celestial supreme being. The first point to be noted is that these columns did not celebrate military triumphs, like those of Trajan and Marcus Aurelius. They were not set up in forums or streets but far from cities. What is more, this Celtic Jupiter was often represented with a wheel,[13] and the wheel plays an important part among the Celts. The wheel with four spokes represents the year, that is, the cycle of the four seasons. Indeed, the terms designating the "wheel" and the "year" are identical in the Celtic languages.[14] As Werner Müller well saw, this Celtic Jupiter is consequently the celestial cosmocrator god, lord of the year, and the column symbolizes the *axis mundi*. On the other hand, the Irish texts mention Dagda, "the good god," and there is agreement in identifying him with the Gallic god whom Caesar designated by the divine name "Jupiter."[15]

Archeology has confirmed Caesar's statement concerning the popularity of "Mercury": witness more than two hundred statues and bas-reliefs and nearly five hundred inscriptions. We do not know his Gallic name, but presumably it was the same as that of the god Lug, who plays an important part among the

13. See the information given by Werner Müller, *Die Jupitergigantensäulen und ihre Verwandten*, pp. 46 ff.

14. See the examples cited by Müller, ibid., pp. 52 ff. Figurations of the *annus* by a being carrying a wheel with four or twelve spokes are documented in the Middle Ages; see the drawings reproduced by Müller, p. 51.

15. Jan de Vries, *La religion des Celtes*, pp. 45 ff.

insular Celts. Several cities bear the name Lug (e.g., Lugdunum, modern Lyons), and his festival was celebrated in Ireland, a proof that the god was known in all the Celtic countries. The Irish texts present Lug as the leader of an army, using magic on the battlefield, but also as a master poet and the mythical ancestor of an important tribe. These characteristics make him comparable to Wodan-Óðinn, whom Tacitus also assimilated to Mercury. We may conclude from this that Lug represented sovereignty in its magical and military aspect: he is violent and to be feared, but he protects warriors as well as bards and magicians. Just like Óðinn-Wodan (§175), he is characterized by his magico-spiritual capacities, which explains why he was homologized with Mercury-Hermes.[16]

"To Mars," writes Caesar (*B.G.* 6. 17), "when they have determined on a decisive battle," the Gauls "dedicate whatever spoils they may take. After a victory they sacrifice such living things as they have taken, and all the other effects they gather into one place." We do not know the Celtic name of the Gallic war god. The numerous votive inscriptions to Mars often include surnames: Albioriz, "King of the World," Rigisamos, "Most Royal," Caturix, "King of Combat," Camulus, "Powerful," Segomo, "Victorious," etc. Certain surnames are incomprehensible, but even when they can be translated they do not increase our knowledge. The same may be said of more than a hundred inscriptions dedicated to Hercules; like those dedicated to Mars, they indicate no more than the existence of a war god.

If we take into account other pieces of information, the structure of this god appears to be comparatively complex. According to the Greek historian Lucian of Samosata (second century A.D.), the Celtic name of Hercules was Ogmios. Lucian had seen an image of the god: it represented a bald old man with wrinkled skin, dragging along a great number of men and women fastened to his tongue by small gold and amber chains. Though the fastening was weak, they did not want to escape but followed him "gay and joyous, praising him." A native of the country explained the image to him: they, the Celts, do not represent the

16. Jan de Vries, ibid., p. 62, who adds: "But it must not be forgotten that this assimilation accounts for only one detail of an extremely complex personality."

art of words by Hermes, like the Greeks, but by Hercules, "because Hercules is much stronger" (Lucian, *Heracles* 1–7). This text has inspired contradictory interpretations.[17] The chained men have been compared to the Maruts who accompany Indra and to the troop of Einherjar who escort Óðinn-Wodan (J. de Vries). On the other hand, Ogmios has been compared to Varuṇa, the "master binder" (F. Le Roux). Probably the Celtic "Mars" had assimilated certain attributes proper to the sovereign god-magician, at the same time strengthening his function as psychopomp. (As we shall see in §175, among the Germans Óðinn had, on the contrary, partly supplanted the war god.) To Ogmios there corresponds, in Irish epic literature, the god Ogma, the exemplary champion. But he is also credited with having invented "Oghamic" writing—which is as much as to say that he combines martial force with "science" of the Óðinnic type.

Caesar presents "Apollo" as a physician-god. We do not know his Gallic name, but his epithets, found in inscriptions, generally confirm his healing character. Now the Irish texts mention Diancecht, who cures and resuscitates the Tuatha Dé Danann; he is also invoked in an ancient formula of exorcism. His name is cited side by side with Grobniu, the blacksmith-god. So he may be regarded as representing the gods whom Dumézil considers to be characteristic of the "third function." As for "Minerva," whose Gallic name is also unknown but whom Caesar defines as the goddess of artisans and the trades (hence also belonging to the third function), she has been compared with the goddess Brigantia, daughter of Dagda and patroness of poets, blacksmiths, and physicians.

171. Is it possible to reconstruct the Celtic pantheon?

The pantheon disguised by Caesar's *interpretatio romana* camouflages a religious reality that comparison with the traditions of the insular Celts makes accessible to us only in part. As for the divine names supplied by the monuments and inscriptions

17. Some of them are discussed by Francoise Le Roux, "Le Dieu celtique aux liens: de l'Ogmios de Lucien à l'Ogmios de Dürer," pp. 216 ff.; J. de Vries, *La religion des Celtes*, pp. 73 ff.

of the Gallo-Roman period, they are, for the most part, merely descriptive or topographical epithets of the member gods of the pantheon; some scholars have wrongly regarded them as designating autonomous divinities.

The only information that we have concerning the Gallic names of the gods has been handed down to us by the poet Lucan (first century A.D.). He mentions "those who propitiate with horrid victims ruthless Teutates and Esus, whose savage shrine makes men shudder, and Taranis, whose altar is no more benign than that of Scythian Diana" (*Civil War* [Pharsalic] 1. 444–46). The authenticity of these names is confirmed by the Gallo-Roman inscriptions that mention Esus, Taranucus (or Jupiter Taranucus), and Mars Toutatis. The author of a medieval commentary[18] tried to explain them, but his glosses are contradictory. However, his commentary furnishes precise information about the kind of sacrifice offered to each of these gods: for Teutates, a man is suffocated by being plunged into a vat; for Esus, the victim is hung on a tree and bled to death; for Taranis—"the lord of combats and the greatest of the gods of heaven"—men are burned in a wooden manikin.

One of the images on the Gundestrup caldron represents a clothed personage throwing the human victim, head first, into a receptacle. Several warriors on foot are approaching the receptacle; above them, horsemen are moving away from it. Jan de Vries (*La religion des Celtes,* p. 55) thinks that an initiatory rite may be represented here but that there is no connection with Teutates. (Irish epic poetry returns more than once to the theme of the king who, in a house heated white-hot, drowns in the vat into which he had thrown himself to escape the fire. There is certainly a reference here to a ritual involving human sacrifice.)[19] Since the eighteenth century, the name Teutates has been translated as "Father of the Tribe." The god certainly played an

18. *Commenta Bernensia,* reproduced by J. Zwicker, *Fontes historiae religionis Celtica,* vol. 1, pp. 51 ff.

19. M. L. Sjoestedt cites some continental parallels in her *Dieux et héros des Celtes* (p. 75). For C. Ramnoux, these sacrifices, performed at the end of a reign or of a cycle of reigns, sought the regeneration of a time become decrepit (they were, in fact, celebrated at certain dates of the calendar); see his "La mort sacrificielle du Roi," p. 217.

important part in the tribe's life: he was the patron of war, but his function was more complex.[20]

As for Taranis, the meaning of his name is clear: its root is **taran,* "thunder.' In his secondary form, Taranos, he is close to the god of the Germans, Donar.[21] Like Donar, he was assimilated to Jupiter. So it is likely that the "giant Jupiter" columns were consecrated to Taranis, the "Thunderer," the ancient Celtic sky god. The divine name Esus is found in proper names, but its etymology has not been determined.[22] On the bas-reliefs of two altars, Esus is depicted striking a tree: are we to think of a sacrifice by hanging? Jan de Vries holds that Esus was a Gallic god comparable to the Scandinavian Óðinn.[23] The fact is that we know nothing definite.

Sculpture, iconography, and inscriptions have revealed the names and images of other Gallo-Roman divinities. In certain cases we are able to make out their structure and define their religious function with the help of the mythology camouflaged in the traditions of the insular Celts. But precisely because of the conservative tendency that is characteristic of the Celtic religious genius, the results of the analysis are often indecisive. We cite as a well-known example the bas-relief bearing the name Cernunnos and representing an old man, perhaps bald-headed, with a stag's ears and antlers. It has been natural to compare a scene from the Gundestrup caldron: a person wearing stag's antlers on his head and seated in what has been mistakenly described as the "position of the Buddha" holds a necklace in one hand and in the other a ram-headed snake; he is surrounded by wild animals, among them a very fine stag. Similar images

20. See Duval, "Teutates, Esus, Taranis," p. 50, and Duval, *Les dieux de la Gaule,* pp. 29 ff. (war god); for J. de Vries, he "could as well have been a Mercury as a Mars" (p. 53); J. J. Hatt credits him with "a twofold countenance, now warlike, now peaceful" ("Essai sur l'évolution de la religion gauloise," p. 90).

21. See, most recently, H. Birkhan, *Germanen und Kelten,* vol. 1, pp. 310 ff., 313 ff.

22. J. de Vries connects it with the root **eis,* which means approximately "energy, passion" (*Rel. des Celtes,* p. 106).

23. Ibid., p. 108; to the same effect, Duval, "Teutates, etc.," pp. 51 ff.; *Les dieux de la Gaule,* pp. 34–35. See also Hatt, "Essai," pp. 97 ff. (unconvincing).

have been found in Great Britain.[24] We know that the iconography and religious symbolism of the stag are archaic. An engraved scene from Val Cammonica that goes back to the fourth century B.C. represents a god with stag's antlers and a horned snake. But, as we saw (§ 5), the "Great Magician" or "Lord of Wild Beasts" of the Trois Frères cave also wore a stag's head with many-branched antlers. So Cernunnos could be interpreted as a god of the type of the "Master of Wild Beasts."[25]

However, the religious symbolism of the stag is extremely complex. On the one hand, in an area that, in the protohistorical period, extended from China to western Europe, the stag, because of the periodical renewal of its antlers,[26] is one of the symbols of continual creation and of *renovatio*. On the other hand, the stag was held to be a mythical ancestor of the Celts and the Germans;[27] in addition, it was one of the best-known symbols of fecundity, but it was also a funerary animal and guide of the dead; finally, it was the game animal preferred above all others by kings and heroes, and its death at the end of the hunt was symbolically one with the tragic death of heroes.[28] Hence it is probable that Cernunnos combined other functions with those of Master of Wild Beasts. We need think only of the long, hard struggle waged by the Church against ritual dressing-up as a stag (*cervulo facere*) to understand the religious importance of the stag (the preferred game of the military aristocracy!) among the popular strata.

The example of Cernunnos illustrates the difficulty of correctly interpreting a multivalent religious complex in the absence of its particular mythico-ritual context. The attempt to analyze the archeological documents concerning female divinities encounters a like difficulty; all that we can say is that the considerable number of statues and ex-votos confirms their importance. The

24. Ross, *Pagan Celtic Britain*, pp. 104 ff.

25. See the legends cited ibid., p. 183.

26. See Eliade, *Images and Symbols*, p. 164. On the religious role of the stag, see Eliade, *Zalmoxis, the Vanishing God*, pp. 147 ff.

27. See Otto Höfler, *Siegfried, Arminius und die Symbolik*, pp. 32 ff. and notes 66–94.

28. See *Zalmoxis, the Vanishing God*, pp. 147 ff.; H. Birkhan, *Germanen und Kelten*, pp. 454 ff.

plastic representations of *Matres* and *matronae* emphasize their being in part goddesses of fertility and maternity (baskets of fruits, horns of plenty; children at the breast or held on the lap, etc.). As Camille Jullian writes, they "were perhaps at once anonymous and myrionymous divinities, who were not named and who had a hundred epithets."[29] But the texts of the insular Celts supply significant details. The mother of the gods was a goddess: Danu in Ireland, Dôn in Wales. What is more: he who would become king of Ireland (Eriu) could do so only by marrying the tutelary goddess who bore the same name; in other words, he attained to sovereignty by a *hieros gamos* with the Earth Goddess. This mythico-ritual scenario is one of the commonest and most persistent themes in Irish vernacular literature.[30]

In all probability we have here a variant of the ancient Near Eastern mythico-ritual scenario involving the sacred marriage between the God of Heaven (or of the storm or the sun) and the Earth Mother, the two being personified by the reigning sovereign and a hierodule. This *hieros gamos* insured the fertility of the country and the good fortune of the reign for a certain period. The survival of the archaic heritage in Ireland is illustrated by the rite of royal consecration, documented in the twelfth century: before the eyes of his subjects, the king copulates with a white mare, which is then killed and cooked; the meat is shared between the king and his men.[31] In other words, sovereignty is attained by the *hieros gamos* between the king and a hippomorphic Earth Mother. Now a Gallic goddess, Epona (Regina), is represented on the monuments as sitting on a horse or standing in front of a horse or between two or more horses. Epona has been interpreted as a Mother Goddess and psychopomp;[32] her

29. *Histoire de la Gaule,* vol. 6, p. 42, n. 2, cited by Duval, *Les dieux,* p. 57.

30. See Proinsias Mac Cana, "Aspects of the Theme of King and Goddess in Irish Literature"; Rachel Bromwich, "Celtic Dynastic Themes and the Breton Lays."

31. Geraldus Cambrensis, *Topographia Hibernica*. F. R. Schröder was the first to compare this to the Vedic ritual episode of the *aśvamedha;* see his "Ein altirischer Krönungsritus und das indogermanische Rossopfer."

32. See H. Hubert, "Le mythe d'Epona."

Irish counterpart, Rhiannun (< *Rīgantona, "Queen") was also hippomorphic.[33]

Like the iconography of Great Britain during the Roman period, the vernacular literature preferred to present the mother goddesses grouped in triads. The most famous are the three Machas, personifying the tutelary goddess of the capital of Ulster.[34] Accession to the throne is possible only by sleeping with one of the Machas. Sometimes the goddess appears as a hideous old woman and demands to share a young hero's bed, but, as soon as he lies down beside her, the old woman turns out to be a singularly beautiful girl; by marrying her, the hero obtains the sovereignty.[35] The mythico-ritual theme of the old woman transformed by a kiss, which is found in the Breton Grail romances, was already known in India during the period of the Brāhmaṇas.[36]

In the epic, Queen Medb has many lovers—which is as much as to say that she had belonged to all the kings of Ireland. But it must be added that in the Celtic societies woman enjoyed considerable religious and social prestige. The ritual of the couvade, documented in Europe only among the Celts and the Basques (a pre-Indo-European people), emphasizes the magico-religious importance of woman. Together with other archaic customs (e.g., certain funerary rituals, the mythology of death, etc.), the couvade indicates the survival of pre-Indo-European elements that presumably belonged to the autochthonous Neolithic populations.

As for the goddesses, their multiple functions as divinities governing fecundity, war, destiny, and fortune are also documented among the goddesses of the Germans, which indicates, at least in part, an Indo-European heritage.[37] To this religious complex, which goes back to European prehistory and to the protohistory of the Celts, there were progressively added Med-

33. J. Gricourt, "Epona-Rhiannon-Macha," pp. 25 ff.

34. Gricourt (ibid., pp. 26 ff.) points out the relations between Macha and the horse.

35. The sources are analyzed by A. C. L. Brown, *The Origin of the Grail Legend,* chap. 7, "The Hateful *Fée* Who Represents Sovereignty."

36. See A. K. Coomaraswamy, "On the Loathly Bride," pp. 393 ff.

37. See Birkhan, *Germanen und Kelten,* p. 542.

iterranean, Roman (more precisely, Hellenistic-syncretistic), and Christian influences. To estimate the Celtic religious genius, it is necessary to take into account both the persistence with which certain archaic elements—most importantly, the customs and beliefs connected with the "mysteries" of femininity, destiny, death, and the otherworld—were preserved and their continual revalorization from antiquity down to the premodern period.

172. The Druids and their esoteric teaching

The pages that Julius Caesar devoted to the Druids (*De Bello Gallico* 6. 13) represent one of the most important sources for Celtic religion. Though he does not cite him, the consul uses the information supplied by Posidonius (second century B.C.), but he also had other sources. The Druids, Caesar writes, "are concerned with divine worship, the due performance of sacrifices, public and private, and the interpretation of ritual questions: a great number of young men gather about them for the sake of instruction and hold them in great honor." It is the Druids who "decide in almost all disputes, public and private"; those who do not accept their decision are forbidden to attend the sacrifices, which is equivalent to a kind of civil death. A single chief exercises supreme authority. "At his death, either any other that is preeminent in position succeeds, or, if there be several of equal standing, they strive for the primacy by the vote of the Druids, or sometimes even with armed force. These Druids, at a certain time of the year, meet within the borders of the Carnutes, whose territory is reckoned as the center of all Gaul."

The Druids are dispensed from military service and from the obligation to pay taxes. Attracted by such great advantages, many come to study under them. "Report says that in the schools of the Druids they learn by heart a great number of verses, and therefore some persons remain twenty years under training. And they do not think it proper to commit these utterances to writing, although in almost all other matters, and in their public and private accounts, they make use of Greek letters." Caesar states that the Druids established this usage "because they do not wish the rule to become common property" and also because, by relying on writing, the apprentice Druids would be in danger of neglecting memory. Their conviction is "that souls do not die but, after death, pass from one body to another; and this belief, as the fear of death is thereby cast aside, they hold to be the greatest incentive to valor. Besides this, they have many discussions about the stars and their movement, the size of the universe and that of the earth, the order of nature, the strength and the powers of the immortal gods; and they hand down their lore to the young men."

Like the Brahmans, the Druids are priests (it is they who perform the sacrifices); but they are also teachers, men of learning, and philosophers.[38] Their annual reunion in a "consecrated spot . . . reckoned as the center of all Gaul" is extremely significant. We certainly have here a ceremonial center regarded as "center of the world."[39] This symbolism, documented more or less throughout the world (see §12), is bound up with the religious concept of sacred space and the techniques for consecrating places; as we have seen (p. 138), the construction of a sacred space was practiced by the Celts from protohistory. It is obvious that the annual gatherings of the Druids presuppose the unity of their religious ideas, despite the inevitable variety in the names of gods and in the beliefs peculiar to various tribes. In all probability the public sacrifices performed by the Druids in the territory of Gaul had as their model the liturgy of the great sacrifice celebrated at the *locus consecratus,* at the "center" of the country of the Carnutes.[40]

The Celts also practiced human sacrifice and, according to the information from Posidonius used by Diodorus Siculus (5. 31) and by Strabo (4. 4), they practiced it in different ways: the victim was struck with a sword (and the future was predicted in

38. Vendryès has shown the unity of religious vocabulary (especially terms designating abstract notions) among the Vedic Indians, the Latins, and the Celts ("L'écriture ogamique et ses origines"). This fact demonstrates the speculative possibility that there were "specialists in the sacred" among these three Aryan-speaking groups even in the protohistorical period; see above, page 141 and note 11.

39. See the examples cited by Françoise Le Roux, *Les druides,* pp. 109 ff.

40. See J. de Vries, *Rel. des Celtes,* p. 218. Caesar's statement concerning the "single chief" who exercises "supreme authority" among the Druids is not confirmed by other classical authors.

accordance with his convulsions and his fall), or pierced by arrows, or impaled. Caesar (*B.G.* 6. 16) reports that "those who are smitten with the more grievous maladies and who are engaged in the perils of battle either sacrifice human victims or vow so to do, employing the Druids as ministers for such sacrifices." Certain scholars have interpreted these facts as proof of the "barbarity" of the Celts or of the "primitive" nature, at once savage and childish, of Druidic theology. But in all traditional societies human sacrifice was fraught with a cosmological and eschatological symbolism that was singularly powerful and complex, which explains its persistence among the ancient Germans, the Geto-Dacians, the Celts, and the Romans (who, incidentally, did not forbid it until ca. 97 A.D.). This bloodstained ritual in no way indicates an intellectual inferiority or a spiritual poverty in the peoples who practice it. To give only one example: the Ngadju Dayaks of Borneo, who have elaborated one of the most consistent and elevated theologies known to the history of religions, were headhunters (like the Celts) and practiced human sacrifice.[41]

All the sources emphasize the great importance of the Druids in the education of the youth. In all probability only the disciples who were preparing to join the Druidic order, and so had to study theology and the sciences thoroughly, were taught by their masters for the twenty years Caesar mentions. The rejection of writing (which explains our ignorance of the Druidic doctrine) and the importance attributed to memory and the oral transmission of lore continue the Indo-European tradition (see vol. 1, p. 432). What was taught was secret because it was esoteric, that is, inaccessible to the uninitiated—a conception that recalls the esotericism of the Upanishads (§§ 80 ff.) and the Tantras.

As for the belief in metempsychosis, the explanation advanced by Caesar—that it was a doctrine that, "as the fear of death is thereby cast aside," is especially "calculated to stimulate courage"—is simply the rationalistic interpretation of a belief in the survival of the soul. According to the Celts, Lucan writes (*Civil War* 1. 450 ff.), "the same breath still governs the limbs in a

41. See Eliade, *The Quest*, pp. 77 ff., commenting on Hans Schärer's work, *Die Gottesidee der Ngadju Dajak in Süd-Borneo* (Leiden, 1946).

different scene.'' Pomponius Mela (3. 3) and Timagenes (cited by Ammianus Marcellinus, 15. 9. 2) add that, in the teaching of the Druids, ''souls are immortal, and after a prescribed number of years they commence upon a new life, the soul entering into another body.'' The belief in metempsychosis is also documented in Irish literature.[42] In the absence of any direct testimony it is difficult to determine whether the postexistence of the soul implied for the Druids ''immortality'' and at the same time psychosomatosis (as in the Upanishads) or whether it consisted merely in an indeterminate ''survival'' of the soul.

Since some ancient authors brought up the Orphico-Pythagorean doctrine of metempsychosis in connection with the Celts, a number of modern scholars have concluded that the Greco-Latin writers interpreted the Celtic beliefs in the language of Pythagoras—in other words, that they ''invented'' a belief unknown to the Celts themselves. But in the fifth century B.C. Herodotus explained in the same way—i.e., by the influence of Pythagoras—the belief of the Getae in the ''immortality'' of the soul, a belief that, furthermore, the Greek historian did not deny (§179). In fact, the ancient authors brought up Pythagoras precisely because the conceptions of the Getae and the Celts were reminiscent of the Orphico-Pythagorean doctrine.

Doubt has also been cast on Caesar's statements concerning the scientific interests of the Druids: ''they have many discussions [concerning] the stars and their movement, the size of the universe and of the earth,'' etc. However, the fragment of a calendar found at Coligny shows a considerably advanced astronomical knowledge. Indeed, it was possible to construct a cycle of 19 solar years, equivalent to 235 lunar months, which enabled the two calendrical systems (solar and lunar) to be reconciled. Numerous authors have looked with the same suspicion on Strabo's information concerning the astronomical knowledge of the Geto-Dacians, but, as we shall see further on (§179), excavations have brought to light the remains of two ''calendaristic temples'' at Sarmizegetuza and at Costesti, which were the ceremonial centers of the Geto-Dacians.

42. See some examples in Le Roux, *Les druides*, pp. 128–29. This author observes, however, that in Ireland metempsychosis is limited to certain mythical or divine beings (p. 130).

The suppression of the Druids under the emperors Augustus, Tiberius, and Claudius aimed at annihilating Gallic nationalism. Yet in the third century, when Roman pressure lessened considerably, there was a surprising renaissance of Celtic religion, and the Druids regained their authority. But it was in Ireland that the Druids, as well as the principal religious structures, survived until the Middle Ages. What is more, the creativity of the Celtic religious genius will experience a new apogee in the literature created, beginning in the twelfth century, around the heroes engaged in the quest for the Grail (see vol. 3).

173. Yggdrasill and the cosmogony of the ancient Germans

Though having at their disposition far fuller information than the Celticists command, the historians of Germanic religion emphasize the difficulties of their undertaking. Their sources are of different kinds and of unequal value: archeological finds, writings from the Roman period (most importantly, the *Germania* of Tacitus), descriptions by Christian missionaries, and, above all, the poems composed by the Icelandic skalds, supplemented by a valuable manual compiled by Snorri Sturluson in the thirteenth century. Add to this that it is only in Iceland, converted to Christianity comparatively late (in the year 1000), that a sufficiently consistent oral tradition was preserved to enable us to reconstruct, at least in their chief outlines, both mythology and cult. This is as much as to say that, without supplementary proofs, our information about the beliefs of the Norwegian immigrants into Iceland cannot be regarded as valid for the generality of the German tribes.

However, despite serious gaps (our lack of information concerning the Goths and the Burgundians) and despite the heterogeneousness of beliefs, resulting from the various influences (Celtic, Roman, Oriental, North Asian, and Christian) undergone by the various tribes during their dispersal through half of Europe, we cannot doubt a certain fundamental unity of the religion of the Germans. To begin with, a number of elements characteristic of the Indo-European heritage are still recognizable in the traditions of several tribes (first of all, the divine tripartition, the antagonistic and complementary pair of sovereign gods, the eschatology). In addition, the names of the days indicate that all the Germanic peoples venerated the same great gods. When, in the fourth century, the Germans adopted the seven-day week, they replaced the names of the Roman divinities by those of their own gods. Thus, for example, *dies Mercuri* was replaced by "day of Óðinn-Wodan": Old High German *Wuotanestac,* English *Wednesday,* Dutch *Woensdag,* Old Norse *Óðinnsdagr.* This proves that Mercury was identified with a god known, throughout the Germanic world, by one and the same name: Óðinn-Wodan.

It has been observed that the last phase of Germanic religion was dominated by intense interest in the myth of the end of the world. This interest is, in any case, a general phenomenon, documented from the second century B.C. in the Near East, Iran, Palestine, and the Mediterranean and, a century later, in the Roman Empire. But what characterizes Germanic religion is the fact that *the end of the world is already announced in the cosmogony.*

The fullest account of the Creation is handed down by Snorri (*Gylfaginning* 4–9); his chief source is an admirable poem, *Völuspá* ("Prophecy of the *Völva,*" i.e., "of the Seeress"), composed toward the end of the pagan period. According to these "Prophecies" (strophe 3), in the beginning there was "neither earth nor the vault of heaven" but a "giant abyss," Ginnungagap.[43] The image, familiar to Oriental cosmogonies, is also found in other texts.[44] Snorri adds that in the North lay a cold and foggy region, Niflheimr, identified with the world of the dead and from which flowed a spring that gave birth to eleven rivers; in the South there was a burning country, Múspell, guarded by the giant Surtr (the "Black"). As the result of the meeting of ice and fire, an anthropomorphic being, Ymir, was born in the intermediate region. While he slept, there were born of the sweat under his arms a man and a woman, and one of his feet engendered, with the other, a son. From the melting ice there came

43. Jan de Vries interprets the word *ginnunga* as expressing the idea of deceit by magic, hence "spell, magic" ("*Ginnungagap,*" pp. 41 ff.).

44. According to the "Wessobrun Prayer," a poem of Christian origin written in southern Germany in the ninth century, "there was neither earth nor high

into being a cow, Auðmbla: it was she who fed Ymir on her milk. By licking the salted ice, Auðmbla gave it the form of a man, Búri. Búri married the daughter of a giant and had three children by her: Óðinn, Vili, and Vé. These three brothers decided to kill Ymir; his outpouring blood swallowed all the giants except one, who mysteriously saved himself with his wife. Then the brothers took Ymir to the middle of the great abyss and, dismembering him, produced the world from his body: from his flesh they formed the earth, from his bones the rocks, from his blood the sea, from his hair the clouds, from his skull the sky.

The cosmogony based on killing and dismembering an anthropomorphic Being is reminiscent of the myths of Tiamat (§ 21), Puruṣa (§73), and P'an-ku (§129). The creation of the world is, then, the result of a blood sacrifice, and this archaic and widely disseminated religious idea justifies human sacrifice for the Germans just as it does for other peoples. In short, such a sacrifice—a repetition of the primordial divine act—insures the renewal of the world, the regeneration of life, the cohesion of society. Ymir was bisexual:[45] he engendered a human couple by himself. Bisexuality is, of course, the most effective expression of totality. Among the ancient Germans the idea of the primordial totality is strengthened by other mythological traditions, according to which Ymir, ancestor of the gods, also engendered the demonic giants (who will threaten the cosmos until the final catastrophe).

Pursuing their cosmogonic labor, the three brothers created the stars and the heavenly bodies from sparks thrown out by Múspell, and they also regulated their motions, thus fixing the quotidian cycle (night and day) and the succession of the seasons. The earth, circular in shape, was surrounded on the outside by the great Ocean; on its shores the gods established the dwelling place of the giants. Within, they built Miðgarð (literally, "middle dwelling"), the world of men, defended by a fence made from

---

heaven, neither tree nor mountain. . . . No sun shone, no moon gave light. There was no glorious sea" (trans. A. R. Ellis Davidson, *Gods and Myths of Northern Europe*, p. 197).

45. The name Ymir has been compared to Sanskrit Yima, "of two sexes." According to Tacitus (*Germania* 2), the mythical ancestor of the Germans was Tuisto. Now this name is associated with Old Swedish *tvistra*, "separated," and, like Ymir, it designates an androgynous being.

Ymir's eyelashes. With the help of Hoenir, the taciturn god, and of Lóður, a figure of which we know almost nothing, Óðinn created the first human pair from two trees, Askr and Embla,[46] found on the beach. He animated them; then Hoenir gave them intelligence, and Lóður gave them the senses and shape of men. Another myth tells of two human beings emerging from the cosmic tree, Yggdrasill, and peopling the world. During the great winter of the Ragnarök (see §177), they will find refuge in Yggdrasill's trunk and will be fed by the dew from its branches. According to Snorri, this couple, sheltered in the cosmic tree, will survive the destruction of the world and will set out to repeople the new world that will emerge afterwards.

The tree Yggdrasill, situated at the Center, symbolizes, and at the same time constitutes, the universe. Its top touches the sky and its branches spread over the world. Of its three roots, one plunges into the land of the dead (Hel), the second into the realm of the giants, and the third into the world of men.[47] From the time of its emergence (that is, from the time that the world was organized by the gods), Yggdrasill was threatened with ruin: an eagle set out to eat its foliage, its trunk began to rot, and the snake Níðhögg began gnawing at its roots. On some not distant day, Yggdrasill will fall, and that will be the end of the world (Ragnarök).

Obviously, we have here the well-known image of the Universal Tree, situated at the "center of the world" and connecting the three planes: Heaven, Earth, and Hades.[48] We have more than once pointed out the archaism and the considerable dissemination of this cosmological symbol. Certain Oriental and North Asian concepts have probably influenced the image and myth of Yggdrasill. But it is important to emphasize the specif-

46. Askr suggests the cosmic ash tree; Embla is perhaps the same word as *elmla*, "elm." Anthropogony from trees is a rather widely disseminated theme in archaic mythologies; it is also documented among the Indo-Europeans. See Bonfante, "Microcosmo e macrocosmo nel mito indoeuropeo," pp. 1 ff.

47. According to Snorri, each of the three roots descends into a well, the most famous of them being the well of the wisest of the gods, Mímir, in which Óðinn will put his eye in pledge (§174), and that of destiny (Urðarbrunnr). But probably the original tradition knew of only one well.

48. The same symbolism appears in the column Irminsul, which, the Saxons believed, held up the sky.

ically Germanic features: the Tree—that is, the cosmos—announces by its very appearance the coming decadence and the final ruin, for destiny, Urðar, is hidden in the subterranean well into which Yggdrasill's roots plunge; in other words, it is hidden at the very center of the universe. According to the *Völuspá* (strophe 20), the goddess of destiny determines the fate of every living creature, not only men but also giants and gods. It could be said that Yggdrasill incarnates the exemplary and universal destiny of existence itself: every mode of existence—the world, the gods, life, men—is perishable and yet capable of rising again at the beginning of a new cosmic cycle.

174. The Aesir and the Vanir. Óðinn and his "shamanic" powers

After establishing the ancestral pair in Miðgarð, the gods built their own dwelling place, Asgarð, still at the center of the world, but elevated.[49] The pantheon is divided into two divine groups: the Aesir and the Vanir. The most remarkable among the Aesir are Týr, Óðinn, and Thór; the first two correspond to the binomial of the sovereign gods (in Vedic India, Mitra and Varuṇa), while Thór, the god with the hammer, the most inveterate enemy of the giants, is reminiscent of Indra's martial character. On the other side, the most important among the Vanir—Njörð, Freyr, and Freyja—are characterized by their wealth and by their relations with fecundity, pleasure, and peace. When we analyzed the mythical structure of the war between the Romans and the Sabines (§162), we alluded to the conflict that opposed the Aesir to the Vanir. This long, hard-fought, and indecisive war ends in a definitive reconciliation. The principal Vanir divinities settle down among the Aesir and, by the fecundity and wealth that they represent, complement the Aesirs' powers of juridical sovereignty, magic, and martial force.

A number of authors have made every effort to interpret this fabulous episode as the memory of a historical conflict between

49. As is well known, the topographical indications of the "center of the world" reflect a mythical geography, constructed in accordance with an imaginary geometry.

different religious beliefs: the autochthonous agriculturalists (for some, the "Megalithenvölker") and their conquerors (the "Streitaxtvölker," that is, the Āryan-speaking invaders). But Georges Dumézil has shown that what we have here is an Indo-European mythological theme, greatly historicized in Snorri's narrative.[50] To be sure, the invasions of the territories inhabited by the Neolithic agricultural populations, the conquest of the autochthons by militarily superior invaders, followed by a symbiosis between these two different types of societies, or even two different ethnic groups, are facts documented by archeology; indeed, they constitute a characteristic phenomenon of European protohistory, continued, in certain regions, down to the Middle Ages. But the mythological theme of the war between the Aesir and the Vanir precedes the process of Germanization, for it is an integral part of the Indo-European tradition. In all probability, the myth served as the model and the justification for a number of local wars, ended by reconciliation of the adversaries and their integration into a common society.

We will add, however, that if the principal Aesir—Týr, Óðinn, and Thór—preserve certain features characteristic of the gods of the first two functions, sovereignty and war, their figures underwent decided modifications; for they were shaped, on the one hand, in conformity with the Germanic religious genius and, on the other hand, under the impact of Mediterranean and North Asian influences. Óðinn-Wodan is the most important of the gods, their father and sovereign. His analogies with Varuṇa have been emphasized: both are the model of the sovereign and are masters of magic; they "bind" and paralyze their adversaries; they delight in human sacrifices.[51] But, as we shall soon see, the differences between them are no less noteworthy.

In a passage of the poem *Hávamál* ("Words of the High One," strophes 139–42) Óðinn tells how he obtained the runes, symbol of wisdom and magical power. Hanging for nine nights from the tree Yggdrasill, "wounded by the spear and sacrificed to Óðinn, myself to myself, without food or drink, lo! the runes revealed

50. See, most recently, Dumézil's *Les dieux des Germains*, pp. 17 ff. and p. 39 (bibliography), and his *Du mythe au roman*, pp. 22 ff. (English trans., *From Myth to Fiction*, pp. 98 ff.).

51. See Dumézil, *Les dieux des Germains*, pp. 62 ff.

themselves at my call." He thus obtained occult knowledge and the art of poetry. We certainly have here an initiatory rite that is parashamanic in structure. Óðinn remains hanging from the cosmic tree;[52] Yggdrasill means "the horse (*drasil*) of Ygg," one of Óðinn's names. The gallows is called the hanged man's "horse," and we know that victims sacrificed to Óðinn were hung on trees. By wounding himself with his spear, by abstaining from water and food, the god undergoes ritual death and acquires secret wisdom of the initiatory type. Óðinn's shamanic aspect is confirmed by his horse with eight legs, Sleipnir, and by the two ravens that tell him everything that goes on in the world. Like the shamans, Óðinn can change his shape and send out his spirit in the form of an animal; he searches among the dead for secret knowledge and obtains it; he declares in *Hávamál* (strophe 158) that he knows a charm that can make a hanged man come down from the gallows and talk with him; he is skilled in the art of *sieðr,* an occult technique of shamanistic type.[53]

Other myths show the stratagems to which Óðinn has recourse, and the price he is willing to pay, in order to obtain wisdom, omniscience, and poetic inspiration. A giant, Mímir, was famous for his occult knowledge. The gods cut his head off and sent it to Óðinn. Óðinn preserved it by means of plants, and from then on he consulted the giant's head whenever he wanted to learn certain secrets.[54] According to Snorri (*Gylfaginning* 8), Mímir was the guardian of the spring of wisdom, situated at the foot of Yggdrasill. Óðinn did not obtain the right to drink from it until he had sacrificed an eye by hiding it in the spring (*Völuspá,* strophe 25).

An important myth relates the origin of the "drink of poetry and wisdom": when peace was concluded between the Vanir

52. On the role of the cosmic tree in the initiations of North Asian shamans, see our *Shamanism,* pp. 38 ff., 157 ff., 171 ff.

53. It is difficult to determine the "origin" of the shamanic elements in ancient German religion, especially in the mythology and cult of Óðinn-Wodan. Some of them go back to the Indo-European heritage, but we must not exclude North Asian influences. In any case, the importance attributed to ecstatic techniques and to beliefs that are shamanic in structure bring Germanic religion close to Asiatic shamanism.

54. The Yukagir shamans consult the skulls of their shaman ancestors; see *Shamanism,* p. 245. Cf. also the head of Orpheus (§180).

and the Aesir, all the gods spat into a caldron; from this ceremonial spitting there emerged a being of extraordinary wisdom, named Kvasir.[55] Two dwarfs killed him, mixed his blood with honey, and thus made mead. He who drinks it becomes a poet or a sage. The drink is hidden in the other world, in a place difficult to get to, but Óðinn manages to obtain it, and from then on it is accessible to all the gods. The skalds call poetic inspiration "Ygg's cup," "Ygg's mead," but also "mead of the dwarfs," "Kvasir's blood," etc.[56] To conclude: after his initiation (which allowed him to obtain the runes), the sacrifice of his eye (which gave him the right to drink from the well of Mímir), and the theft of mead, Óðinn became the undisputed master of wisdom and of all the occult sciences. He is at once the god of poets and sages, of ecstatics and warriors.

175. War, ecstasy, and death

Unlike Varuṇa, Óðinn-Wodan is a god of war; for, as Dumézil writes, "in the ideology and practice of the Germans, war invaded everything, colored everything" (*Les dieux des Germains,* p. 65). But in the traditional societies, and especially among the ancient Germans, war constitutes a ritual that is justified by a theology. First of all there is the assimilation of military combat to sacrifice: both the victor and the victim bring the god a blood offering. In consequence, heroic death becomes a preferred religious experience. In addition, the ecstatic nature of the warrior's death brings him close to the inspired poet as well as to the shaman, the prophet, and the seer. It is by virtue of this glorification of war and ecstasy and death that Óðinn-Wodan acquires his particular character.

The name Wodan derives from the term *wut,* literally, "fury." The reference is to an experience typical of young warriors: by an excess of aggressive and terrifying fury, their humanity was transmuted—they became like raging carnivores. According to

55. This is the personification of an intoxicating drink, sealing an agreement between two social groups. Dumézil has illuminated an Indian parallel in his *Loki,* pp. 102 ff.; cf. his *Les dieux des Germains,* pp. 31 ff.

56. The sources are listed by Turville-Petre, *Myth and Religion of the North,* p. 38. [Turville-Petre's spellings of the Germanic names have been used throughout.—Trans.]

the *Ynglinga Saga* (chap. 6), Óðinn's companions "went without body armor, savage as dogs or wolves, chewed their shields, and were as strong as bears and bulls. They slaughtered men, and neither fire nor steel could do anything against them. This was called the fury of the *berserkir*" (literally, "warriors with the covering, *serkr,* of a bear"). They were also known as *úlfhéðnar,* "man with the skin of a wolf."

One became *berserkr* as the result of an initiatory combat. Thus among the Chatti, Tacitus writes (*Germania* 31), the postulant cut neither his hair nor his beard before he had killed an enemy. Among the Taifali the young man had to kill a boar or a bear, and among the Heruli he had to fight without weapons.[57] Through these ordeals the postulant acquired the mode of being of a wild beast; he became a redoubtable warrior to the extent that he behaved like a carnivore. Beliefs in lycanthropy, obtained by dressing ritually in a wolfskin, become extremely popular in the Middles Ages, and in the North they persist down to the nineteenth century.

God of war, Óðinn-Wodan is also god of the dead. By magical means he protects the great heroes, but he ends by betraying and killing his protégés. The explanation for this strange and contradictory behavior seems to be the need to gather around him the most redoubtable fighters in view of the eschatological battle of the Ragnarök. And in fact notable warriors, fallen in battle, were led by the Valkyries to the heavenly palace, Valhalla.[58] Welcomed by Óðinn, they spend their days fighting, preparing themselves for the final battle.

Protector of the *Männerbunde,* which, like all societies of ecstatic and martial structure, terrorized the villages, Óðinn-Wodan could not be the favorite god of the rural population. His

57. See Eliade, *Rites and Symbols of Initiation,* p. 81 and note 4, and "Dacians and Wolves," in *Zalmoxis, the Vanishing God,* esp. pp. 17 ff. Tacitus describes the Harii (who lived along the upper Oder and the upper Vistula) with their black shields and their bodies painted black, like an "army of phantoms" (*exercitus feralis*), the sight of which no enemy could bear (*Germania* 43).

58. Valhöll, "the hall of the fallen." The Valkyries (whose name means "they who choose the dead on the battlefield") were, primitively, spirits who looked after the needs of the dead (they provided food, shelter, etc.).

cult, which involved human sacrifices by hanging, was chiefly celebrated by the families of kings and military leaders and among their immediate followers. Yet a number of toponyms containing the word Óðinn have been found, and in some of these his name is combined with the vocables for "field" and "meadow." This does not prove the "agrarian" structure of Óðinn but rather his "imperialistic" character, his tendency to take over the functions and attributes of other divinities.

The leading part played by Óðinn-Wodan in the religious life of the Germans is explained by his many and various powers of magical sovereignty. Óðinn is the chief author of the creation of the world, of gods, and of men. (Of the other divine personages active in the mythical time of the beginnings, the collective memory has retained only the names.) Similarly, he is called upon to play the chief part in the final battle of the Ragnarök. His quality of sovereign god and, at the same time, of god of war and death makes comprehensible both the sacred character of royalty and the religious valorization of death on the battlefield—conceptions characteristic of the culture of the Germanic High Middle Ages (see vol. 3).

176. The Aesir: Týr, Thór, Baldr

The first of the Aesir, Týr (*Tiwaz, Ziu), is far paler. Originally he was a supreme god,[59] for one of the names of the gods, *tîwar,* is the plural of Týr. Since the *interpretatio romana* identified him with Mars, he is usually classed among the war gods, and in fact he presents a well-developed military aspect. But his original vocation of "jurist god" (homologue of Mitra) is still visible. He has organic relations with the *thing*—the assembly of the people before which legal cases were tried. It is true that the assemblies in peacetime resembled those in time of war, since the people gathered together in arms and approved decisions by brandishing

59. His name, *Tiwaz, is related to the other Indo-European names of the (god of the) sky: Dyaus, Zeus, Jupiter. Probably, at least among some Germanic tribes, the celestial god continued to be venerated under the name Irmin-Hermin; see below, §178.

sword or axe in the air or by striking their shields with their swords.[60]

The most important mythical episode, which characterizes Týr's vocation, took place at the beginning of time. The gods knew that the wolf Fenrir, which a giantess had conceived by Loki, was to devour them. By convincing it that they were only playing a game, they managed to tie it to a magical thong, so fine that it was invisible. Suspicious, the young wolf had consented to play the game on condition that one of the gods would put a hand down its throat, as a pledge that no harm would be done it. Only Týr dared to make the gesture, and, as soon as the wolf felt that it could not get loose, it bit off his hand (*Gylfaginning* 13. 21). Georges Dumézil rightly observes that such a gesture, necessary as it was to save the pantheon, constitutes a violation of an oath and hence indicates the degradation of the god who is at once sovereign and jurist.[61]

Thór (Donar) was one of the most popular gods. His name means "thunder," his weapon is the hammer Mjöllnir ("the crusher"), mythical image of the thunderbolt, analogous to Indra's *vajra* (see § 68). His red beard and his fabulous appetite make him resemble the Vedic champion. Thór is the defender of the Aesir and of their divine dwelling place. Numerous stories show him confronting the giants and annihilating them with his hammer.[62] His chief adversary is the cosmic snake, Jörnungan, who encircles the world and who will threaten the gods at the Ragnarök; several texts and some drawings show him pulling this dragon out of the sea.

60. As Jan de Vries observes, "from the Germanic point of view, there is no contradiction between the concepts of the 'god of battles' and the 'god of law' " (*Altgermanische Religionsgeschichte,* vol. 2, p. 13).

61. Dumézil, *Les dieux des Germains,* p. 75: "What the divine society thus gained in effectiveness it lost in moral and mystical power; it is no longer anything but the exact projection of the earthly bands or states, whose only concern was gain and conquest. To be sure, the life of all human groups is made up of violence and ruse; at least theology describes divine Order, in which everything is not perfect either, but in which Mitra, or Fides, keeping watch and ward, shines as a divine model."

62. The relations between Thór and the personage brandishing an axe in the rock drawings of the Scandinavian Bronze Age are difficult to determine.

Images of Thór, always with his hammer, were found in many temples. The witnesses mention these images more than they do those of the other gods. As master of storms, Thór was popular among farmers, though he was not an agrarian god. But he insured harvests and protected villages from demons. In his function of war god he was supplanted by Óðinn. The erotic tendency that is characteristic of Indra can perhaps be detected in the ritual role of the hammer on the occasion of marriages. The "folklorization" of certain mythological tales featuring Thór, Mjöllnir, and the giants has been observed; for example, Thór disguises himself as a bride in order to deceive the giant who had stolen his hammer. The meaning of the underlying rituals having been forgotten, these mythological tales survived by virtue of their narrative qualities. Similar processes explain the "origin" of numerous literary themes.

By his purity and nobility, by his tragic fate, Baldr is the most interesting of the gods. Son of Óðinn and the goddess Frigg, he is, Snorri writes, "the best of them, and everyone sings his praises. He is so fair of face and bright that a splendour radiates from him. . . . He is the wisest of the gods, and the sweetest-spoken, and the most merciful" (*Gylfaginning*, chap. 22; trans. Jean I. Young). Little is known about his cult, but he is known to have been universally loved. Yet it is by his death that Baldr revealed his importance in the drama of the world. His myth is, in any case, the most touching in all Germanic mythology.

According to Snorri's version, Baldr had ominous dreams, and the gods decided to make him invulnerable. His mother gathered the oaths of all the things in the world that they would not harm him. Then the Aesir assembled at the place of the *thing,* around Baldr, and amused themselves by striking him with swords and throwing all sorts of things at him. "When Loki saw that, it displeased him." Disguised as a woman, he went to see Frigg and asked her if *all* beings had sworn to spare Baldr. Frigg replied: "There is a young shoot of wood that is called *Mistilteinn,* 'shoot of mistletoe'; it seemed to me too young for me to ask for an oath from it." Loki pulled it up and went to the *thing.* Höð (Hödhr), Baldr's brother, being blind, had remained at the rear, but Loki gave him the branch and said: "Do like the others, attack him, I will show you the direction where he is." Guided by Loki, Höð threw the shoot of mistletoe at his brother. "The stroke pierced Baldr, who fell dead to the ground. It was the greatest misfortune that has ever been among gods and among men." Nevertheless, because they were in a sacred place, no one could punish Loki (*Gylfaginning,* chaps. 33–35).

"This drama, as is apparent from the structure of the *Völuspá,* is the keystone of the history of the world. Through it, the mediocrity of the present age became irremediable. To be sure, Baldr's goodness and clemency had been ineffectual until then, since, by a kind of evil fate, 'none of his judgments held, became a reality'; at least he existed, and that existence was protest and consolation."[63]

Because he had not fallen on a battlefield, Baldr did not go to Valhalla but to the domain of Hel. To the messenger sent by Óðinn, demanding Baldr's release, Hel replied that she would release him on condition that "all things in the world" bewailed him. Informed by the gods, men and animals, stones and trees, all did so. Only one witch refused to weep for Baldr, and "it is suppposed that it was Loki." Finally Thór catches Loki, and the gods chain him to a stone. Above him they hang a venomous snake, which lets poison fall on his face. His wife, Snorri writes, is with him and holds a basin under the poisoned liquid. When the basin is full, she goes to empty it, but in the meanwhile he receives the venom on his face; he writhes, and then the earth trembles. However, Loki will succeed in freeing himself at the time of the Ragnarök, on the eve of the end of the world.

177. The Vanir gods. Loki. The end of the world

The Vanir are all more or less directly connected with fertility, peace, and wealth. Njörðr, the eldest of them, married his sister and had by her the twins Freyr and Freyja. Since the ancient Germans abhorred incest, this mythological tradition can be interpreted either as reflecting the customs of the aboriginal, pre-Indo-European populations[64] or as emphasizing the orgiastic na-

63. Dumézil, *Les dieux des Germains,* pp. 95–96.

64. Snorri states that marriage between brother and sister was customary among the Vanir.

ture characteristic of divinities of fecundity, especially agrarian fecundity. Tacitus (*Germania* 40) speaks of the goddess Nerthus, "that is, the Earth Mother"; this is the same name as Njörðr. The goddess traveled about among the tribes in a chariot drawn by a cow; her cult was celebrated in a sacred wood on an island in the "Ocean"—and, the Roman historian adds, "it is the only time when peace and tranquillity are known and enjoyed." The goddess's chariot and statue were then bathed, and the slaves who performed the rite were drowned in the same lake. Tacitus' account was probably influenced by what he knew about the ritual of Cybele at Rome; however, a study preserved in the saga of King Olaf confirms the existence of this type of cult.[65]

In the last phase of Scandinavian paganism Njörðr was supplanted by Freyr. The latter's image in the temple at Uppsala was phallic; his cult involved many orgiastic acts and human sacrifice. But his mythology is not interesting. As for Freyja, like Frigg (*Frija)[66]—which may be no more than a surname—she was above all the goddess of love and procreation. According to Snorri, she was the only divinity whom the people still venerated when he composed his work, and the great number of toponyms containing the name of Freyja confirms this opinion. Snorri adds that Freyja was originally a priestess of the Vanir who first taught the Aesir the divinitory technique of the *seiðr*. She had the power to communicate with the other world, and she could assume the form of a bird.

Loki is an enigmatic and ambiguous god. The etymology of his name is uncertain; he had no cult, and no temples were consecrated to him. Although himself one of the Aesir, he tries to harm the gods, and at the end of the world he will fight against them; it is he who will kill Heimdallr. His behavior is disconcerting: on the one hand he is a companion of the gods,[67] and he likes to fight their enemies, the giants; he makes the dwarfs forge certain magical objects that are true attributes of the gods (the ring Draupnir for Óðinn, the hammer for Thór, etc.). On the

65. Summarized by Davidson, *Gods and Myths of Northern Europe*, pp. 93 ff.

66. She was assimilated to Venus: *dies Veneris, Freitag*, Friday.

67. He undertakes a journey to the land of the demons and giants with Thór; he accompanies Óðinn and Hoenir and helps them rob the dwarf Andvari, etc.

other hand, he is malicious, amoral, criminal: he is the author of Baldr's murder and boasts of it. His demonic nature is confirmed by his offspring: the wolf Fenrir and the Great Snake are his sons; Hel is his daughter—she to whose gloomy land the dead go who have not earned the right to reside in Valhalla.

There is a multitude of myths about Loki, but they often resemble popular and farcical tales. He boasts of his conquests: he has given Týr's wife a son, he has taken Thór's place beside his wife, etc. He plays a role in almost all the farcical episodes and tales that bring the gods and giants on the stage. A famous and terrible poem, *Lokasenna,* tells how Loki, entering the chamber in which the gods were feasting, insulted them in the most insolent way. It is only Thór's appearing that silences his vituperations.

For more than a century scholars have successively explained Loki as a god of fire, as a god of thunder or of death, as a reflection of the Christian devil, or as a civilizing hero comparable to Prometheus.[68] In 1933, Jan de Vries compared him to the "trickster," an ambivalent personage who occurs only in North American mythologies. Georges Dumézil proposed a more plausible interpretation, because it accounts at the same time for Loki, Höð, Baldr, and the end of the world. Loki's role as an impostor, his malevolence, and his presence among the enemies of the gods during the eschatological battle make him homologous with the sinister personage in the *Mahābhārata,* Duryodhana, the supreme incarnation of the demon of our age (see §191). According to Dumézil, the extent and regularity of the harmony between the *Mahābhārata* and the *Edda* show the existence of a vast eschatological myth recounting the relations between Good and Evil and the destruction of the world, a myth already in existence before the dispersal of the Indo-European peoples.[69]

As we observed (§173), in the last period of paganism the Germans were extremely concerned with eschatology. The end of the world was made an integral part of their cosmogony, and,

68. See the account of the chief theories proposed down to 1932 in Jan de Vries, *The Problem of Loki,* pp. 10–22, and Dumézil, *Loki,* pp. 109 ff.

69. See Dumézil, *Les dieux des Germains,* pp. 97 ff., and his *Mythe et épopée,* vol. 1, pp. 238 ff.

as in India, Iran, and Israel, the scenario and the principal actors in the apocalypse were known. The most complete and dramatic description is supplied by the poem *Völuspá* and by Snorri's paraphrase. The well-known clichés of all apocalyptic literature make their appearance: morality declines and disappears, men kill one another, the earth trembles, the sun grows dark, the stars fall; freed from their chains, the monsters descend on the earth; the Great Snake emerges from the Ocean, bringing on catastrophic inundations. But more specific details are also found: a winter three years long (*fimbulvetr*) will occur; a horde of giants will arrive in a boat built from the fingernails of the dead; other giants, commanded by Surtr, will advance by land and climb up the rainbow to attack and destroy Asgarð, the home of the gods. Finally, the army of the gods and heroes meets the army of the monsters and giants on a vast plain for the decisive battle. Each of the gods assails an adversary. Thór confronts the Cosmic Snake and kills him but immediately falls, poisoned by its venom. Óðinn is devoured by Fenrir; his young son Vidar kills the Wolf but dies soon afterward. Heimdallr attacks Loki, and they destroy each other. In fact, all the gods and all their opponents fall in this eschatological battle, with the exception of Surtr; surviving, he lights the cosmic conflagration—and all trace of life disappears; finally, the whole earth is swallowed by the Ocean, and the sky crumbles.

Yet it is not the end. A new earth emerges, green, beautiful, fertile as never before, purified of all suffering. The sons of the dead gods will return to Asgarð; Baldr and Höð will emerge from Hel, reconciled. A new sun, more brilliant than the former one, will take its course through the sky. And the human pair sheltered by Yggdrasill will become the founders of a new humanity.[70] Some authors have believed that they could identify various Oriental influences (Iranian, Christian, Manichaean, etc.) in the myth of the Ragnarök. But, as Dumézil has shown, what we have here is the Scandinavian version of the Indo-European eschatological myth; the possible later influences have only added a more highly colored imagery and touching details.

70. This last detail contradicts the eschatological scenario that we have just summarized, in which the collapse of Yggdrasill completes the end of the world.

Judged by the fragments of it that have been preserved, the religion of the Germans was one of the most complex and original in Europe. What first strikes us is its ability to enrich and renew the Indo-European heritage by assimilating a number of allogeneous religious techniques, of Mediterranean, Oriental, or North Asian origin. A similar process has been observed in the Hindu synthesis (§135) and in the formation of Roman religion (§161). But among the Germans religious creativity was not paralyzed by the conversion to Christianity. One of the most beautiful epic poems, *Beowulf,* composed in England in the eighth century, presents the heroic mythology more completely and more profoundly than similar continental compositions, thanks precisely to the influence of Christian ideas.[71] One of the most impressive descriptions of the Ragnarök is carved on a stone cross at Gosforth (Cumberland); the other side of the monument represents the Crucifixion.[72] In fact, certain Germanic religious creations flowered during the High Middle Ages as the result of symbiosis with, or opposition to, Christianity. The religious prestige of medieval royalty derives in the last analysis from the old Germanic conception that the king is the representative of the divine Ancestor: the sovereign's "power" depends on a supraterrestrial sacred force that is at once the foundation and the warrant for universal order.[73] As for the heroic mythology, it is continued, in enriched and revalorized form, in the institution of chivalry and in the legends of Saint George, Sir Galahad, and Parsifal (see vol. 3).

178. The Thracians, "great anonyms" of history

The earliest Thracian culture appears as a synthesis between an important substratum of the Bronze Age and the contribution of

71. See A. Margaret Arendt, "The Heroic Pattern," pp. 149, 164 ff. For its part, the hagiographic literature imitates the model of heroic life proclaimed in the *Heldensagen* (ibid., p. 165).

72. K. Berg, "The Gosforth Cross," pp. 27 ff.; Davidson, *Gods and Myths,* pp. 207 ff. A stone (probably a fragment of a cross) showing Thór fishing up the Great Snake has been found in the same church.

73. See Otto Höfler, *Germanische Sakralkönigtum,* vol. 1, pp. xii ff., 350 ff.

seminomadic peoples arriving from the Ukraine. The ethnogenesis of the Thracians took place in a region of considerable extent, between the Dniester, the Northern Carpathians, and the Balkans. Toward the end of the eighth century B.C. the incursions of the Cimmerians introduced certain Caucasian elements into art and armament. Writing in the fifth century, Herodotus stated that the Thracians were the most numerous people after the Indians. But their role in political history was slight. The kingdom of the Odryses (in the valley of the Maritsa), strong enough to attack Macedonia in ca. 429, lost its autonomy less than a century later to Philip II. Alexander the Great continued his father's expansionist policy: about 335 he crossed the Danube to conquer and subdue the Geto-Dacians. The failure of his campaign allowed these Thracian tribes to remain independent and to improve their national organization. While the southern Thracians were definitively integrated into the orbit of Hellenism, Dacia did not become a Roman province until the year 107 of our era.

An equally unfortunate destiny seems to have pursued the religious creations of the Thracians and the Geto-Dacians. The Greeks had early recognized the originality and force of Thracian religiosity. Various traditions localized in Thrace (or in Phrygia) the origin of the Dionysiac movement (§122) and a large part of the mythology of Orpheus (§180). And in the *Charmides* (156e), Socrates speaks admiringly of the physicians of the "Thracian king Zalmoxis," whose doctrine and practice were superior to those of the Greek physicians. But except for some valuable details communicated by Herodotus in connection with the mythico-ritual scenario of Zalmoxis, sources for information concerning Thracian and Thraco-Getan religion are few and vague. It is true that, especially in the period of the Roman Empire, religious monuments abound; however, in the absence of written testimony their interpretation is uncertain and provisional. Just as among the Celts, the Thracian and Geto-Dacian priests and monks were suspicious of writing. The little that we know about their mythology, theology, and rites has been transmitted to us by Greek and Latin authors, through their *interpretatio graeca* and *latina*. If Herodotus had not recorded certain conversations with Hellespontine Greeks, we should have known nothing of the mythico-ritual scenario of Zalmoxis or even the name of

Gebeleïzis. To be sure, as among the Slavs and the Balts, to say nothing of the ancient Germans and the descendants of the Celts, the religious heritage of the Thracians was preserved, with inevitable changes, in the popular customs and folklore of the Balkan peoples and the Romanians. But analysis of European folklore traditions from the point of view of the general history of religions is still in its beginnings.

According to Herodotus (5. 7), the Thracians worshipped "Ares, Dionysus, and Artemis"; however, their kings venerated "Hermes," from whom they believed themselves descended. On the basis of this brief account, made still more enigmatic by the *interpretatio graeca,* the attempt has been made to reconstruct the original pantheon of the Thracians. From Homer (*Iliad* 13. 301, etc.) to Vergil (*Aen.* 3. 357), tradition put the native country of Ares, the god of war, in Thrace. Then, too, the Thracians were renowned for their military virtues and their indifference in the face of death; hence it could be accepted that a god of the "Ares" type was the head of their pantheon. However, as we saw (§176), the ancient celestial god of the Germans, Tiwaz, was assimilated by the Romans to Mars. So it is possible that the Thracian "Ares" was originally a celestial god who had become a god of storms and of war.[74] In this case, "Artemis" was a chthonian divinity, analogous to the Thracian goddesses Bendis and Cotyto (Cotys); Herodotus had chosen to call her "Artemis" (instead of, for example, "Demeter") because of the wildness of the Thracian forests and mountains.

If this "reading" is accepted, we may also suppose the existence, among the earliest Thracians, of the exemplary myth of the hierogamy between the storm god and the Earth Mother; "Dionysus" would be the fruit of that union. The Greeks knew the Thracian names of Dionysus; those most commonly used were Sabos and Sabazius.[75] The cult of the Thracian "Dionysus"

74. Moreover, we know of the god Zbelsurdos, the second part of whose name, *-surdos,* appears to derive from the root **suer,* "to low, to hum"; hence he was a storm god, whom the Greeks incorrectly named Zeus Keraunos. See Eliade, *Zalmoxis, the Vanishing God,* p. 51 and n. 87.

75. See the sources cited by E. Rohde, *Psyche,* p. 304, n. 1. Another divine name was Bassareus, meaning "clad in a long foxskin." On the rites of Sabazius at Athens, see volume 1 of the present work, pp. 367–68.

is reminiscent of the rites presented by Euripides in the *Bacchae* (see §124). The ceremonies took place at night, in the mountains, by torchlight; a wild music (the sounds of bronze caldrons, cymbals, and flutes) inspired believers to joyous outcries and to dances in furious circles. "It was especially women who indulged in these disorderly and exhausting dances; their costume was strange; they wore '*bessares,*' long, floating garments made, it seems, from foxskins; above those, deerskins, and probably horns on their heads."[76] In their hands they held snakes consecrated to Sabazius, daggers, or thyrsi. Attaining paroxysm, "sacred madness," they seized animals chosen to be sacrificed and tore them to pieces, eating the raw flesh. This ritual omophagy produced identification with the god; the participants now called themselves Sabos or Sabazius.[77]

Undoubtedly there is here, as among Greek bacchantes, a temporary "divinization." But the ecstatic experience could inspire specific religious vocations, first of all oracular gifts. Unlike Greek Dionysianism, prophecy in Thrace was connected with the cult of "Dionysus." A certain tribe, that of the Bessi, managed the oracle of "Dionysus"; the temple was on a high mountain,[78] and the prophetess predicted the future in "ecstasy," like the Pythia at Delphi.

Ecstatic experiences strengthened the conviction that the soul is not only autonomous but that it is capable of an *unio mystica* with the divinity. The separation of soul from body, determined by ecstasy, revealed on the one hand the fundamental duality of man and, on the other, the possibility of a purely spiritual postexistence, the consequence of "divinization." The vague and uncertain archaic beliefs in some form of survival of the soul were progressively modified, ending, in the last analysis, in the idea of metempsychosis or in various conceptions of spiritual immortality. It is probable that the ecstatic experiences that

76. Rohde, *Psyche,* p. 257.

77. See the sources cited by Rohde, *Psyche,* p. 272, n. 32. On the "enthusiasm" that brings about ecstatic union with the god, see the references ibid., pp. 272–73, nn. 32–36.

78. Herodotus (7. 111) regards the Bessi as a family of the Satrae tribe, but other authors (Polybius, Strabo, Pliny, etc.) describe them, more correctly, as an autonomous people. On Thracian prophecy, see Rohde, *Psyche,* pp. 260 ff.

opened the way for such conceptions were not always of the "Dionysiac" (i.e., orgiastic) type. Ecstasy could also be brought on by certain herbs or by asceticism (solitude, vegetarian diet, fasting, etc.) and by prayer.[79]

It is in such circles that the religious practices and concepts known by the name of Orphism (see §§180 ff.) developed in Greece. Among certain Thracian tribes, the belief in immortality and the certainty of bliss for the disincarnate soul end in an almost morbid exaltation of death and a depreciation of existence. The Trausi wailed at the birth of a child, but they buried their dead joyfully (Herodotus, 5. 4). A number of ancient authors explained the exceptional courage of the Thracians in battle by their eschatological convictions. Martianus Capella (6. 656) even credited them with an actual "appetite for death" (*appetitus maximus mortis*), for "they thought it beautiful to die." This religious valorization of death is recognizable in certain creations of the folklore of Romania and of other peoples of southeastern Europe.[80]

As for the "Hermes" who, according to Herodotus, was worshiped exclusively by the "kings," that is, by the military aristocracy, it is hard to identify him. Herodotus makes no reference to the solar god, though such a god is well documented in other sources.[81] So we could see a solar divinity in the Thracian "Hermes." Some centuries later the so-called "Hero on Horseback" monuments become frequent in the Balkans; now the

79. Hemp seeds among the Thracians (Pomponius Mela, 2. 21) and among the Scythians (Herodotus, 4. 73); the smoke of certain "fruits" among the Massagetae (Herodotus, 1. 202). Strabo (7. 3. 3), following Posidonius, reports that the Mysians abstain from all flesh food, contenting themselves with honey, milk, and cheese, and that for this reason they are called both "those who fear God" (*theosebeis*) and "those who walk in smoke" (*kapnobatai*). These terms probably designate certain religious personages, not the whole people. The *kapnobatai* would be dancers and "shamans" who used the smoke of hemp to bring on ecstatic trances (see *Zalmoxis*, pp. 42, 61). Strabo adds that, among the Thracians, there are pious solitaries, known by the name of *ktistai*, who live apart from women, consecrate themselves to the gods, and live "freed from all fear" (8. 3. 3).

80. See *Zalmoxis*, chaps. 5 and 8.

81. See Pettazzoni, "The Religion of Ancient Thrace," pp. 84 ff.

Hero on Horseback is identified with Apollo.[82] However, this is a late conception, which throws no light on the "royal" theology mentioned by Herodotus.

179. Zalmoxis and "immortalization"

The same historian declares that the Getae are "the bravest and most law-abiding of the Thracians" (4. 93). They "claim to be immortal," Herodotus goes on, and in this sense: "They believe that they do not die but that he who perishes goes to the god [*daimon*] Zalmoxis or Gebeleïzis, as some of them call him" (4. 94). This is the first—and the last—time that the name Gebeleïzis appears in the literature. Tomaschek had already recognized in this divine name a parallel to the Thracian god Zbelsurdos, Zbeltiurdos.[83] Like Zbelsurdos, Gebeleïzis would be a storm god or, rather, an ancient celestial god, if we follow Walde-Pokorny and Dečev, who derive his name from the Indo-European root **guer*, "to shine."[84] After narrating the sacrifice of a messenger to Zalmoxis, a ritual that we shall consider further on, Herodotus adds: "When there is thunder and lightning, these same Thracians shoot arrows skyward as a threat to the god, believing in no other god but their own" (4. 94).

Despite Herodotus' testimony (expressed, it is true, with astonishing carelessness, both grammatically and stylistically), it is difficult to regard Zalmoxis and Gebeleïzis as one and the same god. Their structures are different, their cults are not at all alike. As we shall see further on, Zalmoxis has none of the characteristics of a storm god. As for the shooting of arrows, we may wonder if Herodotus had rightly grasped the meaning of the ritual. In all probability, it was not the god (Gebeleïzis) who was

82. See Gavril Kazarow, *Die Denkmäler des thrakischen Reitergottes in Bulgarien,* vol. 1, figs. 528, 835, etc.; Pettazzoni, "Religion of Ancient Thrace," pp. 87 ff.

83. "Die alten Thraker," p. 62.

84. A. Walde and J. Pokorny, *Vergleichendes Wörterbuch der indogermanischen Sprachen,* vol. 1, p. 643; D. Dečev, *Charakteristik der thrakischen Sprache,* pp. 73, 81. But see also C. Poghirc, "Considérations philologiques et linguistiques sur Gebeleïzis," p. 359.

threatened but the demonic powers manifested in the clouds. In other words, it was a positive cult act: it imitated, and indirectly helped, the god of lightning by shooting arrows at the demons of darkness.[85] However this may be, we must resign ourselves: we cannot reconstruct the function and "history" of Gebeleïzis on the basis of a single document. The fact that Gebeleïzis is not mentioned again after Herodotus does not necessarily imply his disappearance from the cult. We can imagine either his coalescence with another divinity or his survival under a different name.[86]

The most valuable information furnished by Herodotus has to do with the myth and the cult of Zalmoxis. According to what he had learned from the Greeks of the Hellespont and the Black Sea region, Zalmoxis was a former slave of Pythagoras: "freed and gaining great wealth, he returned to his own country. Now the Thracians were a meanly-living and simple-witted folk"; so Zalmoxis undertook to civilize them. He "made himself a hall, where he entertained and feasted the chief among his countrymen and taught them that neither he nor his guests nor any of their descendants should ever die, but that they should go to a place where they would live forever and have all good things." Meanwhile, "he was making himself an underground chamber," into which he "descended [and] lived for three years, the Thracians wishing him back and mourning him for dead; then in the fourth year he appeared to the Thracians, and thus they came to believe what Zalmoxis had told them. . . . For myself," Herodotus adds, "I neither disbelieve nor fully believe the tale about Zalmoxis and his chamber; but I think that he lived many years before Pythagoras; and whether there was a man called Zalmoxis, or this be a name among the Getae for a god of their country, I have done with him" (4. 95–96).

85. See *Zalmoxis*, pp. 51 ff.

86. The fact that the Romanian folk mythology of the Prophet Elijah contains a number of elements belonging to a storm god proves at least that Gebeleïzis was still active at the time of the Christianization of Dacia, whatever his name at that period may have been. We may also admit that a religious syncretism encouraged by the high priest and the priestly class finally ended by confusing Gebeleïzis with Zalmoxis (see below, p. 179).

As was natural, this text made a great impression in the ancient world, from Herodotus' contemporaries to the Neo-Pythagoreans and Neo-Platonists. The story he tells is consistent: the Hellespontine Greeks, or Herodotus himself, had integrated what they had learned about Zalmoxis, his doctrine, and his cult into a spiritual horizon that is Pythagorean in structure. Now this is as much as to say that the cult of the Geto-Dacian god comprised belief in the immortality of the soul and certain rites that were initiatory in type. Through the rationalism and euhemerism of Herodotus, or of his informants, we divine that the cult had the character of a "mystery."[87] The Getae, Herodotus writes, "pretend to be immortal" (4. 93), for "they believe that they do not die, but that he who perishes goes to . . . Zalmoxis" (4. 94). However, the verb *athanatizein* (5. 4) does not mean "pretend to be immortal" but "make oneself immortal."[88] This "immortalization" was obtained by means of an initiation, which brings the cult inaugurated by Zalmoxis close to the Greek and Hellenistic Mysteries (see § 205). We know nothing of the ceremonies properly speaking, but the information transmitted by Herodotus indicates a mythico-ritual scenario of "death" (occultation) and "return to earth" (epiphany).

The Greek historian also tells (4. 94) of the ritual peculiar to Zalmoxis: the sending, every four years, of a messenger "charged to tell [the god] of their needs." A number of men held three javelins, and the man chosen by lot was tossed into the air; when he fell, he was run through by the javelin points. The sacrifice made possible the communication of a message, in other words, *reactualized the direct relations between the Getae and their god as they existed in the beginning,* when Zalmoxis was among them. The sacrifice and sending of the messenger were in some sense a symbolic (since ritual) repetition of the founding of the

87. This may be the reason why Herodotus hesitates to give details (if—which is not certain—his informants had supplied him with them), for his discretion in regard to the Mysteries is well known. But Herodotus admits that he does not believe in the story that Zalmoxis was a slave of Pythagoras; on the contrary, he is convinced that the Getan *daimon* is far earlier—and this detail is important.

88. See I. M. Linforth, "*Hoi athanatizontes,* Herodotus, IV. 93–94," *Classical Philology* 93 (1918): 23–33.

cult; there was a reactualization of Zalmoxis' epiphany after his three years of occultation, with all that his epiphany implied, especially an assurance of the immortality and bliss of the soul.

Certain ancient authors, as well as a number of modern scholars, have connected Zalmoxis with Dionysus and Orpheus, on the one hand, and, on the other, with mythical or strongly mythologized personages[89] whose characteristic feature was either a shamanic technique or the gift of prophecy or descents to Hell (*katabaseis*). But what Herodotus tells us about Zalmoxis does not fit into the system of shamanic or shamanizing mythologies, beliefs, and techniques. On the contrary, as we have just seen, the most characteristic elements of his cult—*andreia* (ceremonial banquets), occultation in the "underground chamber" followed by epiphany after four years, "immortalization" of the soul, and teachings concerning a happy existence in another world—make it comparable to the Mysteries.[90]

At the beginning of the Christian era Strabo (*Geography* 7. 3. 5) provides a new version of the myth of Zalmoxis, chiefly drawing on the documentation collected by Posidonius (ca. 135–ca. 50 B.C.). According to this, Zalmoxis was Pythagoras' slave; however, it was not the doctrine of immortality that he learned from his master but "certain things about the heavenly bodies," that is, the art of predicting future events in accordance with celestial signs. To this Strabo adds a journey to Egypt, supremely the land of magic. It is by virtue of his astronomical knowledge and his magical and prophetic powers that Zalmoxis persuaded the king to associate him with the government. High priest and prophet of "the most honored god in their country," Zalmoxis retired to a cave at the summit of the sacred mountain Kogaionon, where he received no one but the king and his own servants, and later he "was called a god." Strabo adds that "when Boerebista ruled over the Getae, this office was held by Decaeneus," and that "in one way or another the Pythagorean

89. Abaris, Aristeas of Proconnesus, Hermotimus of Clazomenae, Epimenides of Crete, Pythagoras, etc.; see p. 194, below.

90. It is also in this sense that Zalmoxis can be compared to the Dionysus of the Dionysiac Mysteries; see § 206.

command to abstain from eating living beings still existed as it had been taught by Zalmoxis."[91]

In the new stage of Geto-Dacian religion concerning which we are informed by Posidonius and Strabo, the character of Zalmoxis proves to be decidedly modified. First of all, there is the identification of the *god* Zalmoxis with *his high priest,* who ends by being deified under the same name. What is more, there is no reference to a cult with a structure resembling that of the Mysteries, such as Herodotus presented. In short, the cult of Zalmoxis is dominated by a high priest who lives alone at the top of a mountain, though being at the same time the king's associate and chief councilor; and this cult is "Pythagorean" because it excludes flesh food. We do not know to what extent the initiatory and eschatological structure of the "Mystery" of Zalmoxis survived in Strabo's time. But the ancient authors speak of certain hermits and holy men, and it is possible that these "specialists in the sacred" carried on the "Mystery" tradition of the cult of Zalmoxis.[92]

91. In another passage (7. 3. 11), in which he gives an account of the career of Boerebista (70–44), Strabo describes Decaeneus as "a magician (*goēs*), a man who not only had traveled in Egypt but also had thoroughly learned certain signs through which he claimed to know the divine will; and in a short time he had come to be considered a god."

92. See *Zalmoxis,* pp. 61 ff. Another detail seems equally important for Strabo: that Zalmoxis—like Decaeneus more recently—had managed to have so prodigious a career above all because of his astronomical and mantic knowledge. In the sixth century of our era, but relying on earlier sources, Jordanes described in extravagant terms the Dacian priests' interest in astronomy and the natural sciences (*Getica* 11. 69–71). The insistence on knowledge of the heavenly bodies may reflect correct information. Indeed, the temples of Sarmizegetuza and Costeşti, whose urano-solar symbolism is obvious, seem to have a calendrical function. See Hadrian Daicoviciu, "Il Tempio-Calendario dacico di Sarmizegetuza" and also his *Dacii,* pp. 194 ff., 210 ff.

22 Orpheus, Pythagoras, and the New Eschatology

180. Myths of Orpheus, lyre-player and "founder of initiations"

It seems impossible to write about Orpheus and Orphism without irritating one or the other of two groups of scholars: on the one hand, the skeptics and "rationalists," who minimize the importance of Orphism in the history of Greek spirituality; on the other, the admirers and "enthusiasts," who regard it as a movement of considerable significance.[1]

Analysis of the sources enables us to distinguish two groups of religious realities: (1) the myths and fabulous traditions concerning Orpheus and (2) the ideas, beliefs, and customs regarded as "Orphic." The lyre-player is first mentioned in the sixth century by the poet Ibycus of Rhegium, who speaks of "Orpheus of famous name." For Pindar, he is "the player on the phorminx, father of melodious songs" (*Pyth*. 4. 177). Aeschylus describes him as he who "haled all things by the rapture of his voice" (*Agamemnon* 1630). In a vase painting he is depicted on board a boat, lyre in hand, and he is expressly named on a sixth-century metope of the Treasury of the Sicyonians at Delphi. Beginning

1. Even the evaluation of the sources differs radically from one group to the other. The skeptics emphasize the fewness of the documents and their late date. The others hold that the date of composition of a document must not be confused with the age of its contents and that, in consequence, by using all the valid testimonies in the proper critical spirit, we can grasp the essential message of Orphism. The tension between these two methodologies corresponds to a deeper philosophical opposition, documented in Greece from the sixth century and still perceptible in our day. "Orpheus" and "Orphism" are prime examples of subjects that trigger polemical passions almost automatically.

in the fifth century the iconography of Orpheus becomes continually richer: vase paintings show him playing the lyre and surrounded by birds or wild animals or else by Thracian disciples. He is torn to pieces by maenads, or he is in Hades with other divinities. From the the fifth century, too, are the first references to his descent to the underworld to bring back his wife, Eurydice (Euripides, *Alcestis* 357 ff.). He fails in this because he looks back too soon[2] or because the infernal powers oppose his undertaking.[3] Legend makes him live in Thrace "a generation before Homer," but on fifth-century ceramics he is always represented in Greek costume, charming wild beasts or barbarians by his music.[4] It is in Thrace that he dies. According to Aeschylus' lost play the *Bassarides,* Orpheus every morning ascended Mount Pangaeus to worship the sun, identified with Apollo; angered, Dionysus sent the maenads against him; the lyre-player was torn to pieces, and the parts of his body were scattered.[5] His head, thrown into the Hebron, floated to Lesbos, singing. Piously recovered, it served as an oracle.

We shall have occasion to mention other references to Orpheus in the literature of the sixth and fifth centuries. For the moment we will observe that Orpheus' powers and the most important episodes in his biography are strangely reminiscent of shamanic practices. Like the shamans, he is both healer and musician; he charms and masters wild animals; he goes down to the underworld to bring back the dead; his head is preserved and serves as an oracle, just as the skulls of Yukagir shamans did even as late as the nineteenth century.[6] All these elements are archaic and contrast with the Greek spirituality of the sixth and fifth centuries; but we know nothing of their protohistory in ancient Greece, that is, their possible mythico-religious function before

2. The sources are analyzed by W. K. C. Guthrie, *Orpheus and Greek Religion,* pp. 29 ff., and by Ivan M. Linforth, *The Arts of Orpheus.*

3. He lacked "the courage to die as Alcestis did for love, choosing rather to scheme his way, living, into Hades. And it was for this that the gods doomed him, and doomed him justly, to meet his death at the hands of women" (Plato, *Sympos.* 179d).

4. See Guthrie, *Orpheus,* pp. 40 ff., 66, and fig. 9; cf. plate 6.

5. O. Kern, *Orphicorum Fragmenta,* no. 113, p. 33. The Muses gathered the scattered parts together and buried them at Leibethria, on Mount Olympus.

6. Eliade, *Shamanism,* pp. 391–92.

they were incorporated into the Orphic legend. In addition, Orpheus had connections with a series of fabulous personages—such as Abaris, Aristeas, etc.—who were also characterized by shamanic or parashamanic ecstatic experiences.

All this would be enough to put the legendary singer "before Homer," as was reported by tradition and repeated by Orphic propaganda. It does not matter much if this archaizing mythology was perhaps the product of a claim inspired by certain deeply felt experiences. (It is possible to discern, behind the mythology, the desire to put Orpheus back into the prestigious time of "origins" and therefore to proclaim him "Homer's ancestor"—older, that is, and more venerable than the representative, the very symbol, of the official religion.) What is important is the fact that there was a deliberate choice of the most archaic elements accessible to the Greeks of the sixth century.[7] Thus the emphasis placed on his living in Thrace, on his preaching and his tragic death there,[8] corroborated the "primordial" structure of his personage. It is equally significant that, among the few descents to the underworld that are documented in Greek tradition, the one accomplished by Orpheus became the most popular.[9] *Katabasis* is bound up with initiation rites. Now our singer was famous as "founder of initiations" and Mysteries. According to Euripides, he showed "the torch-march of those veiled mysteries" (*Rhesus* 943). The author of *Against Aristogeiton* (25. 11 = Kern. *Orph. Frag.*, no. 23) stated that Orpheus "has shown us the most sacred initiations," referring, in all probability, to the Eleusinian Mysteries.

Finally, his relations with Dionysus and Apollo confirm his fame as "founder of Mysteries," for these are the only Greek gods whose cult involved initiations and "ecstasy" (ecstasy, of course, of different and even irreconcilable types). From antiq-

7. This was the time when the "barbarian" peoples of Thrace, and even the Scythians who led a nomadic life north of the Black Sea, were becoming better known.

8. For a list of the sites of the Orpheus cult in Thrace, see R. Pettazzoni, *La religion dans la Grèce antique*, p. 114, n. 16

9. The *Katabasis eis Hadou* (Kern, *Orph. Frag.*, nos. 293 ff., pp. 304 ff.). The *katabasis* in the *Odyssey* (book 11, especially lines 566–631) probably represents an "Orphic" interpolation.

uity on, these relations have inspired controversy. When Dionysus brings his mother Semele up from Hades, Diodorus (4. 25. 4) observes the analogy with Orpheus' descent in quest of Eurydice. Orpheus' being torn to pieces by the maenads can also be interpreted as a Dionysiac ritual, the *sparagmos* of the god in the form of an animal (see §124). But Orpheus was known primarily as the disciple of Apollo. According to one legend, he was even the son of the god and the nymph Calliope. He owes his violent death to his devotion to Apollo. Orpheus' musical instrument was the Apollonian lyre.[10] Finally, as "founder of initiations," Orpheus attributed great importance to purifications, and *katharsis* was a specifically Apollonian technique.[11]

A number of characteristic features must be borne in mind. (1) Although his name and certain references to his myth are documented only from the sixth century on, Orpheus *is* a religious personage of the archaic type. It is easy to imagine him as having lived "before Homer," whether this expression is understood chronologically or geographically (that is, in a "barbarous" region not yet touched by the spiritual values distinctive of Homeric civilization). (2) His "origin" and prehistory escape us, but Orpheus certainly belongs neither to the Homeric tradition nor to the Mediterranean heritage. His relations with the Thracians are enigmatic, for, on the one hand, among the barbarians he behaves like a Greek, and, on the other hand, he enjoys pre-Hellenic magico-religious powers (mastery over animals, shamanic *katabasis*). Morphologically, he is close to Zalmoxis (§179), who was also a founder of Mysteries (by means of *katabasis*) and a civilizing hero of the Getae, those Thracians who "claimed to be immortal." (3) Orpheus is presented as the outstanding founder of initiations. If he is proclaimed "ancestor of Homer," it is the better to emphasize the importance of his religious message, which is in radical contrast to the Olympian

10. Guthrie cites line 578 of Euripides' *Alcestis*, where Apollo is surrounded by lynxes and lions and a doe, "dancing to the sound of the lyre" (*The Greeks and Their Gods*, p. 315).

11. Apollo silences the oracles produced by Orpheus at Lesbos (Philostratus, *Vita Apoll.* 4. 14). Is this a jealous gesture on the god's part, or does it signify incompatibility between two oracular techniques, the shamanic and the Pythian?

religion. We do not know the fundamentals of the initiation that was supposed to have been "founded" by Orpheus. We know only its preliminaries: vegetarianism, asceticism, purification, religious instruction (*hieroi logoi,* sacred books). We also know its theological presuppositions: the transmigration, and therefore the immortality, of the soul.

As we have seen (§ 97), the postmortem destiny of the soul constituted the goal of the Eleusinian initiations, but the cults of Dionysus and Apollo also involved the destiny of the soul. So it seems plausible that the sixth and fifth centuries saw in the mythical figure of Orpheus a founder of Mysteries who, though inspired by traditional initiations, proposed a more appropriate initiatory discipline, since it took into account the transmigration and immortality of the soul.

From the beginning, the figure of Orpheus arises under the joint signs of Apollo and Dionysus. "Orphism" will develop in the same direction. This is not the only example. Melampus, the seer of Pylos, though the "favorite of Apollo," was at the same time he "who introduced the name of Dionysus into Greece, together with the sacrifice in his honor and the *phallic* procession" (Herodotus, 2. 49). Furthermore, as we have seen (§ 90), Apollo had a certain relation with Hades. On the other hand, he had ended by making peace with Dionysus, who had finally been admitted among the Olympians. This coming-together of the two antagonistic gods is not without significance. Is it possible that the Greek spirit thereby attempted to express its hope of finding, by the expedient of this coexistence of the two gods, a solution to the religious crisis brought on by the ruin of the Homeric religious values?

181. Orphic theogony and anthropogony: Transmigration and immortality of the soul

In the sixth century B.C. religious and philosophical thought was dominated by the problem of the One and the Many. The religious minds of the age asked: "What is the relation of each individual man to the divine, to which we feel we are akin, and how can we best realize . . . the potential unity which underlies the two?"[12] A certain union of the divine and the human took place during the Dionysiac *orgia,* but it was temporary and was obtained by a lowering of consciousness. The "Orphics," while accepting the Bacchic lesson—that is, man's participation in the divine—drew the logical conclusion from it: the *immortality,* and therefore the *divinity,* of the soul. So doing, they replaced *orgia* by *katharsis,* the technique of purification taught by Apollo.

The lyre-player became the symbol and the patron of a whole movement, at once "initiatory" and "popular," known by the name of Orphism. What suffices to distinguish this religious movement is, first of all, the importance given to written texts, to "books." Plato refers to many books attributed to Orpheus and Musaeus (who was supposed to be his son or his disciple) and dealing with purifications and life after death. He also cites some hexameters of theogonic content as being "by Orpheus." Euripides likewise speaks of Orphic "writings," and Aristotle, who did not believe in the historicity of Orpheus, was familiar with the theories of the soul contained in "the so-called Orphic verses."[13] It seems plausible that Plato knew some of these texts (they could be bought at the booksellers').

A second characteristic is the considerable variety of so-called "Orphics." Side by side with authors of theogonies and with ascetics and visionaries there were what later on, in the classic period, Theophrastus called "Orpheotelestes" ("Orphic initiators"), not to mention the vulgar purifying thaumaturges and diviners whom Plato describes in a famous passage.[14] The phe-

12. Guthrie, *The Greeks and Their Gods,* p. 316. The Ionians, who were little attracted to religion, asked the philosophical question: "What is the relation between the multiple variety of the world in which we live and the one and original substance from which everything came to birth?" See also, by the same author, *A History of Greek Philosophy,* vol. 1, p. 132.

13. Plato, *Rep.* 364e, *Crat.* 402b, *Phileb.* 66c; Euripides, *Hipp.* 954; Aristotle, *De an.* 410b28. Suidas gives a long list of works attributed to Orpheus (Kern, *Orph. Frag.,* no. 223). See the critical analysis in L. Moulinier, *Orphée et l'Orphisme à l'époque classique,* pp. 74 ff.

14. "Begging priests and soothsayers go to rich men's doors and make them believe that they by means of sacrifices and incantations have accumulated a treasure of power from the gods that can expiate and cure with pleasurable festivals any misdeed of a man or his ancestors. . . . And they produce a bushel

nomenon is common enough in the history of religions: every ascetic, gnostic, and soteriological movement gives rise to countless pseudo-morphoses and initiations that are sometimes puerile. We need only remember the false ascetics who have swarmed in India from the time of the Upanishads and the grotesque imitators of the yogins and Tantrics. Parodies abound, especially when there is emphasis on the revealed and initiatory character of a soteriological gnosis. Let us think, for example, of the countless "initiations" and "secret societies" that sprang up in western Europe after the appearance of Freemasonry or in connection with the Rosicrucian "mystery." So it would be simpleminded to be so impressed by the Orpheotelestes and the thaumaturges that we are led to doubt the reality of the Orphic ideas and rituals. On the one hand, similar ecstatics, diviners, and healers are documented from the most ancient times; they are one of the characteristic features of "popular religions." On the other hand, the fact that, from the sixth century on, a number of these thaumaturges, diviners, and purifiers invoked the name of Orpheus proves that there were in existence certain soteriological techniques and gnoses that appeared to be superior, more effective, and more highly reputed and that attempts were made to imitate them or at least to benefit by the prestige connected with the fabulous personage's name.

Some references in Plato enable us to glimpse the context of the Orphic conception of immortality. As punishment for a primordial crime, the soul is shut up in the body (*sōma*) as in a tomb (*sēma*).[15] Hence, incarnate existence is more like a death, and the death of the body is therefore the beginning of true life. However, this "true life" is not obtained automatically; the soul is judged according to its faults or its merits, and after a certain time it is incarnated again. As in India after the Upanishads, there is here a belief in the indestructibility of the soul, con-

---

of books of Musaeus and Orpheus, the offspring of the Moon and the Muses, as they affirm, and these books they use in their ritual, and make not only ordinary men but states believe that there really are remissions of sins and purifications . . . and that there are also special rites for the defunct . . . that deliver us from evil in the other world" (*Rep.* 364b–365a).

15. *Cratylus* 400c; cf. *Phaedo* 62b, on the "jail" or "prison" of the soul. These passages have given rise to endless controversies.

demned to transmigrate until its final deliverance. Even in his day, for Empedocles, who lived the "Orphic life," the soul was a prisoner in the body, exiled far from the Blessed, clothed in "a fresh garment of flesh" (frags. 115 and 126). For Empedocles, too, immortality implied metempsychosis; it was, moreover, the justification for his vegetarianism (the butchered animal may have in it the soul of one of our close relatives).

But vegetarian practices had a more complex and deeper religious justification. By refusing flesh food, the Orphics (and the Pythagoreans) abstained from blood sacrifices, which were obligatory in the official cult. Such a refusal, to be sure, expressed the decision to detach oneself from the city and, in the last analysis, to "renounce the world"; but above all it proclaimed rejection, *in toto,* of the Greek religious system, a system established by the first sacrifice, originated by Prometheus (§ 86). By reserving the eating of the flesh for human beings, and intending the offering of bones for the gods, Prometheus aroused the anger of Zeus; he also set in motion the process that put an end to the "paradisal" period, when men lived in communion with the gods.[16] The return to vegetarian practices indicated at one and the same time the decision to expiate the ancestral fault and the hope of recovering, at least in part, the original state of bliss.

What was called the "Orphic life" (Plato, *Laws,* bk. VI, 782c) involved purification, asceticism, and a number of particular rules; but salvation was obtained primarily by an "initiation," that is, by cosmological and theosophical revelations. By collating the few testimonies and references of the ancient authors (Aeschylus, Empedocles, Pindar, Plato, Aristophanes, etc.), as well as those furnished by documents, we are able to reconstruct at least the outlines of what, for want of a better term, may be called the "Orphic doctrine." We discern a theogony carried on in a cosmogony, and we find also a rather strange anthropology. It is essentially the anthropogonic myth that is the foundation

16. Hesiod, *Works and Days* 90 ff., 110 ff. On the mystical and eschatological values of vegetarianism, see the texts cited and commented on by Guthrie, *Orpheus,* pp. 197 ff., and, especially, Sabbatucci's interpretation, *Saggio sul misticismo greco,* pp. 69 ff. See also Detienne, "La cuisine de Pythagore," pp. 148 ff.

of the Orphic eschatology, which contrasts with both that of Homer and that of Eleusis.

The theogony of the so-called "Rhapsodies"[17] retains only a few details of the genealogy transmitted by Hesiod. Time (Kronos) produces in the Aither the primordial egg, from which emerges the first of the gods, Eros, also called Phanes. It is Eros, the principle of generation, who creates the other gods and the world. But Zeus swallows Phanes and the whole creation and produces a new world. The mythical theme of the absorption of a divinity by Zeus was well known. Hesiod relates that the Olympian had swallowed his wife Metis before the miraculous birth of Athena (§ 84). But in the Orphic theogony the meaning is more subtle; we see in it the effort to make a cosmocrator god into the *creator* of the world that he rules. In addition, the episode reflects philosophical speculation concerning the production of a multiple universe from an original unity.[18] Despite rehandlings, the myth still has an archaic structure. Its analogies with the Egyptian and Phoenician cosmogonies have been rightly emphasized.

Other traditions postulate as first principle Nyx (Night), who engendered Uranus and Gaea; or Oceanus, from whom emerged Time (Kronos), who then produced Aither and Chaos; or the One, who gave birth to Conflict, by whose efforts the Earth was separated from the Waters and the Sky. Recently, the Derveni Papyrus[19] has revealed a new Orphic theogony, centered around Zeus. A verse attributed to Orpheus proclaims that "Zeus is the beginning, he is the middle, and he brings all things to fulfillment" (col. 13, line 12). Orpheus called Moira (destiny) the "thought" of Zeus. "When men say, . . . 'Moira has spun,' they mean to say that the thought of Zeus has determined what is and what is yet to be and also what is yet to come" (col. 15, lines 5–7). Oceanus is only a hypostasis of Zeus, just as Ge (Demeter),

17. In the fifth century A.D. Damascius was still reading a work entitled *Rhapsodies of Orpheus*. Some fragments of it are certainly old (sixth century B.C.); see Guthrie, *Orpheus*, pp. 77 ff., 137–42.

18. Guthrie, *The Greeks and Their Gods*, p. 319.

19. Discovered in 1962 near the city of Derveni in Thessalonica, and dated to the fourth century B.C. It is a commentary on an Orphic text, which confirms both the antiquity of such writings and their richly speculative nature.

the Mother, Rhea, and Hera are only different names of the same goddess (col. 18, lines 7–11). The cosmogony has a structure that is at once sexual and monistic: Zeus made love "in the air" (or: "from above") and so created the world. But the text does not mention his partner.[20] The author proclaims the unity of existence by affirming that the *logos* of the world is similar to the *logos* of Zeus (col. 15, lines 1–3). It follows that the name designating the "world" is "Zeus" (cf. Heraclitus, frags. 1, 32). The text preserved in the Derveni Papyrus is important in several respects; on the one hand, it confirms the existence, at an early period, of actual Orphic conventicles; on the other hand, it illustrates the monistic, or even "monotheistic," tendency of at least this Orphic theogony.

As for the myth of the origin of man from the ashes of the Titans, it is clearly documented only in some late authors (first–second centuries A.D.).[21] But as we attempted to show in connection with the mythico-ritual theme of Dionysus-Zagreus (§125), references are found in earlier sources. Despite the skepticism of certain scholars, it is permissible to see references to man's Titanic nature in Pindar's expression "the penalty of their pristine woe" (frag. 133 Schr.) and in a passage in Plato's *Laws* (701c) concerning those who show "the 'Titanic nature' of which old legends speak." According to information supplied by Olympiodorus, we may suppose that Xenocrates, Plato's disciple, associated the idea of body as "prison" with Dionysus and the Titans.[22]

Whatever interpretation is put on these few obscure references, it is certain that, in antiquity, the myth of the Titans was regarded as "Orphic." According to this myth, man shared both in the Titanic nature and in divinity, since the ashes of the Titans also contained the body of the infant Dionysus. However, by purifications (*katharmoi*) and initiation rites (*teletai*) and by lead-

20. This type of cosmogony is reminiscent of the Memphite theology (§26), Pherecydes' system, and the autogenous creation of Prajāpati (§76).

21. Plutarch, *De esu carn.* 1. 7 (Kern, *Orph. Frag.*, no. 210); Dio Chrysostom, 30. 55. The most complete version occurs in Clement of Alexandria, *Protrept*. 2. 17. 2 and 2. 18. 2.

22. Olympiodorus, p. 84 Norvin (= Xenocrates, frag. 20 Heinze), commenting on *Phaedo* 62b.

ing the "Orphic life," one was able to eliminate the Titanic element and so become a *bakkhos;* in other words, one separated out and assumed the divine, Dionysiac, condition.

There is no need to emphasize the novelty and originality of this conception. Let us remember the Mesopotamian precedent: man's creation by Marduk from earth (that is, from the body of the primordial monster Tiamat) and from the blood of the archdemon Kingu (see § 21). But the Orphic anthropogony, somber and tragic as it seems to be, paradoxically contains an element of hope that is absent not only from the Mesopotamian *Weltanschauung* but also from the Homeric conception. For, despite his Titanic origin, man shares, through the mode of being that is his, in divinity. He is even able to free himself from the "demonic" element manifest in all profane existence (ignorance, flesh diet, etc.). We can make out, on the one hand, a dualism (spirit/body) very close to the Platonic dualism and, on the other hand, a series of myths, beliefs, behaviors, and initiations that insure the separation of the "Orphic" from his fellow men and, in the last analysis, the separation of the soul from the cosmos. All this is reminiscent of a number of Indian soteriologies and techniques (§195), and it anticipates various Gnostic systems (§§ 229 ff.).

182. The new eschatology

As for the "Orphic" eschatology, its general outline can be reconstructed on the basis of certain references made by Plato, Empedocles, and Pindar. According to the *Phaedo* (108a) and the *Gorgias* (524a), the road "is neither straightforward nor single . . . ; there are many forkings and crossroads." The *Republic* (614c–d) adds that the just are allowed to take the right-hand road, while the wicked are sent to the left. Similar indications are found in the verses inscribed on gold plates found in both southern Italian and Cretan tombs and going back at least to the fifth century: "Hail to thee who dost travel by the right-hand road toward the sacred fields and grove of Persephone." The text contains precise indications: "To the left of the abode of

Hades, thou wilt find a spring beside which rises a white cypress; do not go too near to this spring. But thou wilt find another: from the lake of Memory (Mnemosyne) cool waters spring and guardians are on duty there. Say to them: 'I am the child of Earth and starry Heaven; that you know; but I am parched with thirst, and I am dying. Give me quickly of the cool water that flows from the lake of Memory.' And the guardians will of themselves give you to drink from the sacred spring, and after that you will reign with the other heroes."[23]

In the myth of Er, Plato tells that all souls destined for reincarnation must drink of the spring of Lethe in order to forget their experiences in the other world. But the souls of "Orphics" were believed not to be reincarnated; this is why they were to avoid the water of Lethe. "I have leaped up from the cycle of heavy punishments and sufferings, and I have sped with prompt feet to the desired crown. I have taken refuge under the breast of the Lady, queen of Hell." And the goddess replies: "O fortunate, O happy one! Thou hast become a god, having been a man" (after the translation by A. Boulanger).[24]

The "cycle of heavy punishments" involves a certain number of reincarnations. After death the soul is judged, is then sent temporarily to a place of punishment or of bliss, and returns to earth after a thousand years. An ordinary mortal has to go through the cycle ten times before he escapes. The "Orphics" described at length the torments of the guilty, "the infinite ills

23. Plates from Petelia and Eleuthernae. See Guthrie, *Orpheus,* pp. 171 ff., and Zuntz's new interpretation, *Persephone,* pp. 364 ff.

24. The beginning is very significant. The initiate addresses the infernal gods: "I come from a community of the pure, O pure sovereign of Hades, Eucles, Eubouleus, and you other immortal gods. For I also flatter myself that I belong to your blessed race. But fate laid me low and the other immortal gods" (but see Zuntz's reading, *Persephone,* p. 318). Another tablet reveals important details: "I have undergone the punishment that my unjust acts deserved. . . . Now I come praying before the shining Persephone so that, in her beneficence, she will send me to the dwelling of the blessed." The goddess receives him mercifully: "Hail to thee, who hast undergone the suffering thou hadst never suffered before. . . . Hail, hail, hail to thee, take the right-hand road toward the sacred fields and the grove of Persephone" (after the translation by Boulanger, "Le salut selon l'Orphisme," p. 40).

in store for the damned."[25] Kern even goes so far as to say that Orphism was the first creator of Hell.[26] In fact, Orpheus' *katabasis* in search of Eurydice justified all kinds of descriptions of the infernal world. Again we come upon the shamanic element, a dominating feature of the myth of Orpheus; it is well known that, throughout central and northern Asia, it is the shamans who, telling in infinite detail of their ecstatic descents to the underworld, have elaborated and popularized a vast and spectacular infernal geography.[27]

The landscape and the itinerary sketched in the gold plates—the spring and the cypress, the right-hand road—as well as the "thirst of the deceased" have parallels in many funerary mythologies and geographies. Certain Oriental influences must not be excluded. But more probably the entire complex represents an immemorial common heritage, the result of millennial speculations on ecstasies, visions, and raptures, oneiric adventures and imaginary journeys—a heritage, to be sure, that was differently valorized by various traditions. The tree beside a spring or a fountain is an exemplary image of "Paradise"; in Mesopotamia what corresponds to it is the garden with a sacred tree and a spring, guarded by the Gardener King, representative of the god (§22). The religious importance of the plates, then, consists in the fact that they present a different conception of the soul's postexistence from the one documented in the Homeric tradition. It is possible that what we have here are archaic Mediterranean and Oriental beliefs and mythologies that, long pre-

25. "Sunk in mud, they will see themselves punished in a manner befitting their moral pollution (*Republic* 363d; *Phaedo* 69c), like pigs, loving to wallow in filth (see Plotinus, 1. 6. 6), or they will exhaust themselves in vain efforts to fill a pierced cask or to carry water in a sieve (*Gorgias* 493b; *Rep*. 363e), an image, according to Plato, of the madmen who insatiably surrender themselves to ever unsatisfied passions, perhaps actually the punishment of those who, not having submitted to cathartic ablutions, must, in Hades, constantly but vainly carry the water of the purifying bath" (F. Cumont, *Lux perpetua*, p. 245).

26. Pauly-Wissowa, *Realencyklopädie*, s.v. "Mysterien," col. 1287. Cumont (*Lux perpetua*, p. 46) tends to identify in Orphism the origin of all "that hallucinating literature" that, by way of Plutarch's myths and the Apocalypse of Peter, leads to Dante.

27. See Eliade, *Shamanism*, pp. 487 ff.

served in "popular" or marginal milieux, had for some time enjoyed a certain repute among the "Orphics," the Pythagoreans, and all those who were haunted by the eschatological enigma.

More significant, however, is the new interpretation of the "thirst of the soul." Funerary libations to slake the thirst of the dead are documented in numerous cultures.[28] The belief that the "Water of Life" insured the hero's resurrection is also widespread in myths and folklore. For the Greeks, death is assimilated to forgetting; the dead are those who have lost the memory of the past. Only a few privileged persons, such as Tiresias or Amphiaraus, keep their memories after death. In order to make his son Aethalides immortal, Hermes gives him "an unfailing memory."[29] But the mythology of memory and forgetting changes when a doctrine of transmigration is introduced. Lethe's function is reversed: its waters no longer welcome the newly departed soul in order to make it forget earthly existence; on the contrary, Lethe blots out memory of the celestial world in the soul that returns to earth to be reincarnated. Thus "forgetting" no longer symbolizes death but returning to life. The soul that has been so rash as to drink at the fountain of Lethe ("burdened with a load of forgetfulness and wrongdoing," as Plato describes it in *Phaedrus* 248c) becomes reincarnated and is again hurled into the cycle of becoming. Pythagoras, Empedocles, and still others who believed in the doctrine of metempsychosis claimed to remember their former lives; in other words, they had succeeded in preserving memory in the beyond.[30]

The fragments inscribed on the gold plates seem to form part of a canonical text, a sort of guide to the beyond, comparable to the Egyptian or Tibetan "books of the dead." Some scholars

28. See Eliade, "Locum refrigerii."

29. "Not even now, though he has entered the unspeakable whirlpools of Acheron, has forgetfulness swept over his soul" (Apollonius Rhodius, *Argonautica* 1. 642 ff.).

30. See Eliade, *Myth and Reality,* pp. 114 ff. The exercise and cultivation of memory played an important part in the Pythagorean brotherhoods (Diodorus, 10. 5; Iamblichus, *Vita Pyth.* 78 ff.). The theme of forgetting and remembering, the earliest testimonies to which refer to certain fabulous Greek personages of the sixth century, has played a considerable part in Indian contemplative techniques and speculations; it will be revived by Gnosticism (§130).

have denied their "Orphic" character, holding that they are Pythagorean in origin. It has even been maintained that the majority of the supposedly "Orphic" ideas and rituals really represent Pythagorean creations or rehandlings. The problem is too complex to be settled in a few pages. Yet we will say that the possible contribution of Pythagoras and the Pythagoreans, even if of considerable magnitude, does not change our understanding of the "Orphic" phenomenon. To be sure, analogies between the legends of Orpheus and Pythagoras are obvious, just as the parallel between their respective reputations is undeniable. Just like the fabulous "founder of initiations," Pythagoras, a historical personage and yet an outstanding example of the "divine man," is characterized by a grandiose synthesis of archaic elements (some of them shamanic) and daring revalorizations of ascetic and contemplative techniques. Indeed, the legends of Pythagoras refer to his relations with gods and spirits, to his mastery over animals, to his presence in several places at the same time. Burkert explains Pythagoras' famous "golden thigh" by comparing it to a shamanic initiation. (We know that during their initiation Siberian shamans are believed to have their organs renewed and their bones sometimes fastened together with iron.) Finally, Pythagoras' *katabasis* is another shamanic element. Hieronymus of Rhodes relates that Pythagoras descended into Hades and there saw the souls of Homer and Hesiod atoning for all the evil they had spoken of the gods.[31] Such shamanic characteristics, moreover, are not found solely in the legends of Orpheus and Pythagoras, for the Hyperborean Abaris, priest of Apollo, flew on an arrow (§ 91); Aristeas of Proconnesus was famous for his ecstasy that could be confused with death, for his bilocation, and for his metamorphosis into a crow; and Hermotimus of Clazomenae, whom some ancient authors held to be a former incarnation of Pythagoras, was able to leave his body for long periods.[32]

31. Eliade, *Zalmoxis, the Vanishing God,* pp. 39 ff. For a list of miraculous legends having to do with Pythagoras, with their sources and the recent bibliography, see Walter Burkert, *Weisheit und Wissenschaft,* pp. 118 ff., 133 ff., 163 ff. (Eng. trans., *Lore and Science in Ancient Pythagoreanism,* pp. 120 ff., 141 ff., 166 ff.). Among these legends, however, there are none referring to ecstatic journeys of the shamanic type.

32. See Eliade, *Zalmoxis,* p. 37, notes 44–45, and, for similar examples, ibid., pp. 37–39.

In addition to the similarities in the legendary biographies of their "founders," there are these analogies between the doctrines and practices of the "Orphics" and the Pythagoreans: a belief in immortality and metempsychosis and in the soul's punishment in Hades and final return to heaven; vegetarianism; the importance attributed to purifications; and asceticism. But these similarities and analogies do not prove the nonexistence of "Orphism" as an autonomous movement. It is possible that a certain number of "Orphic" writings are the work of Pythagoreans, but it would be simpleminded to imagine that the "Orphic" eschatological myths, beliefs, and rituals were invented by Pythagoras or his disciples. The two religious movements developed in parallel, as expressions of the same *Zeitgeist.* Yet there is a marked difference between them: under the direction of its founder, the Pythagorean "sect" not only became organized as a closed society, esoteric in type, but the Pythagoreans cultivated a system of "complete education."[33] What is more, they did not disdain active politics; during a certain period Pythagoreans even held power in several cities in southern Italy.

Pythagoras' great merit is to have laid the foundations for a "total science," holistic in structure, in which scientific knowledge was integrated into a complex of ethical, metaphysical, and religious principles accompanied by various "corporal techniques." In short, knowledge had a function that was at once gnoseological, existential, and soteriological. It is the "total science" of the traditional type,[34] which can be recognized in Plato's thought as well as in the humanists of the Italian Renaissance, in Paracelsus, and in the alchemists of the sixteenth century—

33. By completing their ascetic and moral rules by the study of music, mathematics, and astronomy. But, as is well known, the real goal of these disciplines was mystical in nature. In fact, if "All is number" and "All is a harmony of contraries," everything that lives (the cosmos included, for it, too, "breathes") is akin.

34. The fact that, after Aristotle, this type of "total science" loses its prestige and that scientific research orients itself toward a methodology that, in Europe, will produce its first brilliant results in the sixteenth and seventeenth centuries in no way implies the inadequacy of the holistic approach. It is simply a matter of a new point of view and a different *telos.* Alchemy was not an embryonic chemistry; it was a discipline bound up with a different system of significances and pursuing a different end.

a "total science" such as was realized, above all, by Indian and Chinese medicine and alchemy.

Some authors tend to consider the Orphic movement a sort of "church," or a sect comparable to that of the Pythagoreans. Yet it is not at all probable that Orphism set itself up as a "church" or as a secret organization, similar to the Mystery religions. What characterizes it—a movement at once "popular" and attractive to elites, involving "initiations" and possessing "books"—brings it closer to Indian Tantrism and to Neo-Taoism. These religious movements do not constitute "churches" either, but they include "schools," representing parallel traditions, made illustrious by a series of sometimes legendary masters, and possessing a very large literature.[35]

On the other hand, we may recognize in the "Orphics" the successors to the initiatory groups that in the archaic period performed various functions under the names of Cabiri, Telchines, Curetes, and Dactyls—groups whose members jealously guarded certain "trade secrets" (they were metallurgists and smiths, but also healers, diviners, masters of initiation, etc.). It was simply that, with the "Orphics," these trade secrets connected with various techniques for obtaining mastery over matter had given place to secrets connected with the soul's destiny after death.

Although the prestige of Orphism declined after the Persian Wars, its central ideas (the dualism, the immortality, and therefore the divinity of man, the eschatology), especially through Plato's interpretation, continued to influence Greek thought. The trend also survived on the "popular" level (the "Orpheotelestes"). Later on, in the Hellenistic period, we can identify the influence of certain Orphic conceptions in the Mystery religions; still later, in the first centuries of the Christian era, Orphism will arouse a new interest, due especially to the Neo-Platonists and Neo-Pythagoreans. It is precisely this ability to develop and renew itself, to take part creatively in a number of religious syncretisms, that reveals the scope of the "Orphic" experience.

35. And, just as in the case of Tantrism, certain Orphic texts of more recent date are presented as revelations of an ancient doctrine—which, at least in certain cases, may well be true.

As for the figure of Orpheus, it continued to be reinterpreted, independently from "Orphism," by Jewish and Christian theologians, by the Hermeticists and philosophers of the Renaissance, by poets from Poliziano to Pope and from Novalis to Rilke and Pierre Emmanuel. Orpheus is one of the very few Greek mythical figures that Europe, whether Christian, rationalistic, romantic, or modern, has not been willing to forget (see volume 3).

183. Plato, Pythagoras, and Orphism

According to A. N. Whitehead's celebrated formulation, the history of Western philosophy is only a series of glosses on the philosophy of Plato. Plato's importance in the history of religious ideas is also considerable: late antiquity, Christian theology, especially from the fourth century on, Ismaelitic gnosis, the Italian Renaissance, all were profoundly, if differently, marked by the Platonic religious vision. The fact is all the more significant because Plato's first and most tenacious vocation was not religious but political. In fact, Plato aspired to build the ideal city, organized in accordance with the laws of justice and harmony, a city in which each inhabitant was to perform a definite and specific function. For some time Athens and the other Greek cities had been undermined by a series of political, religious, and moral crises that threatened the very foundations of the social edifice. Socrates had identified the prime source of the disintegration in the relativism of the Sophists and the spread of skepticism. By denying the existence of an absolute and immutable principle, the Sophists implicitly denied the possibility of objective knowledge. In order to show the faultiness of their reasoning, Socrates had concentrated on maieutics, a method of arriving at self-knowledge and the discipline of the soul's faculties. Investigation of the natural world did not interest him. But Plato attempted to complete his master's teaching; and, to provide a scientific basis for the validity of knowledge, he studied mathematics. He was fascinated by the Pythagorean conception of universal unity, of the immutable order of the cosmos, and of the harmony that governs both the course of the planets and the musical scale.[36] In elaborating the theory of Ideas—extraterrestrial and immutable archetypes of terrestrial realities—Plato replied to the Sophists and the skeptics: objective knowledge is, then, possible, since it is based on preexisting and eternal models.

For our purpose it does not matter that Plato sometimes speaks of the world of Ideas as the model of our world—in which material objects "imitate" the Ideas to the extent of their ability—and sometimes affirms that the world of sensible realities "participates" in the world of the Ideas.[37] Still, once this universe of eternal models was duly postulated, it was necessary to explain when, and how, men are able to know the Ideas. It is to solve this problem that Plato took over certain "Orphic" and Pythagorean doctrines concerning the soul's destiny. To be sure, Socrates had already insisted on the inestimable value of the soul, for it *alone* was the source of knowledge. Taking his stand against the traditional opinion, sanctioned by Homer, that the soul was "like smoke," Socrates had emphasized the need to "take care of one's soul." Plato went much further: for him, the soul—*and not life!*—was the most precious thing, for it belonged to the ideal and eternal world. So he borrowed from the "Orphico"–Pythagorean tradition, at the same time adapting it to his own system, the doctrine of the transmigration of the soul and of "recollecting" (*anamnēsis*).

For Plato, in the last analysis, knowing amounts to recollecting (see esp. *Meno* 81 c–d). Between two terrestrial existences the soul contemplates the Ideas: it enjoys pure and perfect knowledge. But in the course of being reincarnated, the soul drinks from the spring of Lethe and forgets the knowledge it had acquired by direct contemplation of the Ideas. However, this knowledge is latent in incarnate man, and, by virtue of the work of philosophy, it can be recalled. Physical objects help the soul to withdraw into itself, and, by a kind of "backward return," to

36. Aristotle writes, not without malice, that the only difference between Plato and Pythagoras is terminological (*Metaphysics* 987b10 ff.). But, as Burkert rightly observes (*Lore and Science*, p. 44), for Pythagoras things *are* numbers.

37. See Guthrie, *The Greeks and Their Gods*, p. 345, and his *A History of Greek Philosophy*, vol. 4, pp. 329 ff.

find again and recover the original knowledge that it possessed in its extraterrestrial condition. Death is therefore the return to a primordial and perfect state, periodically lost during the soul's reincarnation.[38]

Philosophy is a "preparation for death" in the sense that it teaches the soul, once delivered from the body, how to maintain itself in the world of the Ideas continually and therefore to avoid a new reincarnation. In short, not only valid knowledge but the only policy that could save the Greek cities from impending ruin was based on a philosophy that postulated an ideal and eternal universe and the transmigration of the soul.[39]

Eschatological speculations were highly fashionable. To be sure, the doctrines of the soul's immortality and of transmigration and metempsychosis were not novelties. In the sixth century Pherecydes of Syros had been the first the maintain that the soul is immortal and that it returns to earth in successive reincarnations.[40] It is difficult to identify the possible source of this belief. In Pherecydes' day it was clearly formulated only in India. The Egyptians considered the soul to be immortal and capable of assuming different animal forms, but we find no trace of a general theory of transmigration. The Getae also believed in the possibility of "making oneself immortal," but they knew nothing of metempsychosis and transmigration.[41]

In any case, Pherecydes' eschatology had no echo in the Greek world. It is "Orphism," and especially Pythagoras, his disciples, and his contemporary, Empedocles, who popularized, and at the same time systematized, the doctrine of transmigration and

38. Eliade, *Myth and Reality,* pp. 121–22. See ibid., pp. 122 ff., for some observations on the analogies between the theory of Ideas and Platonic *anamnēsis* and the behavior of man in archaic societies; see also *The Myth of the Eternal Return,* pp. 34 ff.

39. It may be recalled that Indian metaphysics laboriously developed the doctrine of transmigration (*saṃsāra*) but did not relate it to the theory of knowledge, to say nothing of politics (§ 80).

40. Cicero, *Tuscul.* 1. 38 (= Diels A 5). See other references in M. L. West, *Early Greek Philosophy and the Orient,* p. 25, nn. 1–2. According to another tradition, Pherecydes had used "the secret books of the Phoenicians"; but this is a cliché without documentary value (West, p. 3), though Oriental influences on Pherecydes' thought appear to be considerable (West, pp. 34 ff.).

41. Herodotus, 4. 93 ff. (cf. §179, above).

metempsychosis. But the cosmological speculations of Leucippus and Democritus, recent astronomical discoveries, and, above all, Pythagoras' teaching had radically changed the conception of the survival of the soul and hence of the structures of the beyond. Since it was now known that the Earth was a sphere, neither Homer's underground Hades nor the Isles of the Blessed, supposed to lie in the farthest West, could any longer be localized in a terrestrial mythogeography. A Pythagorean maxim proclaimed that the Isles of the Blessed were "the Sun and the Moon."[42] Gradually a new eschatology and a different funerary geography became dominant: the beyond is now localized in the region of the stars; the soul is declared to be of celestial origin (according to Leucippus and Democritus, it is "of fire," like the sun and the moon), and it will end by returning to the heavens.

To this eschatology Plato brought a decisive contribution. He elaborated a new and more consistent "mythology of the soul," drawing from the "Orphico"–Pythagorean tradition and using certain Oriental sources but integrating all these elements into a personal vision. He does not draw at all on the "classical" mythology, based on Homer and Hesiod. A long process of erosion had ended by emptying the Homeric myths and gods of their original meaning.[43] In any case, the "mythology of the soul" could have found no support in the Homeric tradition. On the other hand, in his youthful dialogues Plato himself had opposed *mythos* to *logos;* at best, myth is a mixture of fiction and truth. However, in his early masterpiece, the *Symposium,* Plato does not hesitate to discourse at length on two mythological motifs, the cosmogonic Eros and, above all, the primitive man, imagined as a bisexual being, spherical in form (*Symp.* 189e and 193d). But these are myths that are archaic in structure. The androgyny of the First Man is documented in several ancient traditions (for

42. But another tradition, describing Pythagoras' *katabasis,* implied belief in an underground Hades.

43. Xenophanes (born ca. 565) already did not hesitate openly to attack the Homeric pantheon, especially the anthropomorphism of the gods. He maintained the existence of "a god above all the gods and all men; neither his form nor his thought has anything in common with that of mortals" (frag. 23). Even so profoundly religious an author as Pindar objects to "unbelievable" myths (*Olymp.* 1. 28 ff.).

example, among the Indo-Europeans).[44] The message of the myth of the androgyne is obvious: human perfection is conceived of as an unbroken unity. However, Plato adds new meaning to it: the spherical form and the movements of the anthromorph resemble the heavenly bodies, from which this primordial being was descended.

What most needed to be explained was man's celestial origin, since it was the basis for Plato's "mythology of the soul." In the *Gorgias* (493) we come for the first time upon an eschatological myth: the body is the tomb of the soul. Socrates defends this eschatology, citing Euripides and the "Orphico"–Pythagorean tradition. Transmigration is here only implied, but this theme, which is of capital importance for the Platonic eschatology, is, as we have just seen, analyzed in the *Meno* (81a–e). In the *Phaedo* (107e) it is further stated that the soul returns to earth after a long time. The *Republic* uses the old symbolism of macrocosm/microcosm but develops it in a specifically Platonic way by showing the homology among the soul, the state, and the cosmos. But it is above all the myth of the Cave (*Rep.*, bk. 7) that bears witness to Plato's powerful mythological creativity.

The eschatological vision attains its high point in the *Phaedrus;* there, for the first time, the soul's destiny is declared to be bound up with the motions of the heavens (246b ff.). The first principle of the cosmos is found to be identical with the first principle of the soul. It is significant that the same dialogue employs two exotic symbolisms: that of the soul as a charioteer driving his chariot, and that of the "wings of the soul." The first is found in the *Katha Upaniṣad* (1. 3. 3–6), but with the difference that, in Plato, the soul's difficulty in controlling the two horses is due to the antagonism between them. As for the "wings of the soul," they "begin to grow" when man "beholds the beauty of this world [and] is reminded of true Beauty" (249e). The growth of wings as the result of an initiation is documented in China, among the Taoists, and in the secret traditions of the Australian medicine

44. This conception will be persistently revived, from Neo-Platonism and Christian Gnosticism to German romanticism. See Eliade, *The Two and the One*, pp. 101 ff.

men.[45] The image is bound up with the conception of the soul as a volatile spiritual substance, comparable to the bird or the butterfly. "Flight" symbolizes intelligence, comprehension of secret things or metaphysical truths.[46] There is nothing surprising in the use of this immemorial symbolism. Plato "rediscovers" and develops what may be called the archaic ontology: *the theory of Ideas carries on the doctrine of exemplary models that is characteristic of traditional spirituality.*

The cosmogonic myth of the *Timaeus* elaborates certain suggestions contained in the *Protagoras* and the *Symposium,* but it is a new creation. And it is significant that it is a Pythagorean, Timaeus, who, in this supreme cosmogonic vision of Plato's, affirms that the Demiurge created just as many souls as there are stars (*Tim.* 41d ff.). Plato's disciples later arrive at the doctrine of "astral immortality." Now it is by virtue of this grandiose Platonic synthesis that the "Orphic" and Pythagorean elements it had incorporated will achieve their widest dissemination. This doctrine, in which a Babylonian contribution is also discernible (the divinity of the stars), will become dominant from the Hellenistic period on.[47]

The political reform of which Plato dreamed never became more than a project. A generation after his death the Greek city-states were collapsing before Philip of Macedon's dizzying advance. It is one of the rare moments in universal history when the end of a world is almost indistinguishable from the beginning of a new type of civilization: the civilization that is to flower in the Hellenistic period. It is significant that Orpheus, Pythagoras, and Plato are among the sources of inspiration for the new religiosity.

45. The Taoists believe that, when a seeker obtains the *tao,* feathers begin to sprout from his body. On Australian medicine men, see Eliade, *Australian Religions,* pp. 134 ff. These images will be revived and developed by the Neo-Platonists, the Church Fathers, and the Gnostics.

46. "Intelligence (*manas*) is the swiftest of birds" says the *Ṛg Veda* (6. 9. 5). "He who comprehends has wings" (*Pancavimca Brāhmaṇa* 4. 1. 13).

47. See Burkert, *Lore and Science,* p. 360. The belief that the soul is related to the heavens and the stars—and even that it comes from the heavens and returns there—is held by the Ionian philosophers, beginning at least with Heraclitus and Anaxagoras (Burkert, p. 362).

184. Alexander the Great and Hellenistic culture

When, on June 13th of a year that was probably 323, Philip's son, Alexander, died at Babylon at less than thirty-three years of age, his kingdom extended from Egypt to the Punjab. In the course of the twelve years and eight months of his reign he had put down rebellions in Greece, had subdued Asia Minor and Phoenicia, had conquered the empire of the Achaemenides, and had defeated Porus. And yet, despite his genius and his half-divine aura—for he was held to be the son of Zeus-Ammon—Alexander learned at the Beas the limits of his power. His army had mutinied, refusing to cross the river and continue the advance into India, and the "master of the world" was forced to yield. It was his greatest defeat and the ruin of his fabulous project: the conquest of Asia even as far as the "outer Ocean." However, when Alexander gave the order to retreat, the immediate future of India, as well as the future of the historical world in general, was already outlined: Asia was now open to Mediterranean influences; from then on, communications between East and West would never be completely severed.

Since the biography by J. G. Droysen (1833), and especially since the book by W. W. Tarn (1926), a number of historians have applied different, not to say contradictory, points of view to interpreting the goal that Alexander pursued in his conquest of Asia.[48] It would be foolish to attempt, in a few pages, an analysis of a controversy that has gone on for a century and a half. But from whatever point of view Alexander's campaigns are judged, there is agreement that their consequences were profound and irrevocable. After Alexander the historical profile of the world was radically changed. The earlier political and religious structures—the city-states and their cult institutions, the *polis* as "center of the world" and reservoir of exemplary models, the anthropology elaborated on the basis of a certainty that there was an irreducible difference between Greeks and "barbarians"—all these structures collapse. In their place the notion of the *oikoumenē* and "cosmopolitan" and "universalistic" trends

48. It is enough, for example, to compare the monographs by A. R. Burn, R. D. Milns, F. Schachermeyr, F. Altheim, Peter Green, and R. L. Fox.

become increasingly dominant. Despite resistances, the discovery of the fundamental unity of the human race was inevitable.

Aristotle, Alexander's tutor, maintained that slaves are slaves simply by their nature and that the "barbarians" are slaves *naturaliter.*[49] But at Susa Alexander married two Achaemenid princesses and, using the Persian rite, united ninety of his close companions to the daughters of noble Iranian families. At the same time, the marriages of ten thousand Macedonian soldiers were performed, again according to the Persian rite. Afterwards Persians were given leading positions in the army and were even integrated into the phalanx. The Macedonians were far from sharing in their sovereign's political concept. Since they were victorious and conquerors, they saw in the "barbarians" only subjected peoples. When the Macedonians mutinied at Opis—because, as one of them put it, "You have made Persians your relatives"—Alexander exclaimed: "But I have made you *all* my relatives!" The sedition ended in a banquet of reconciliation to which, according to tradition, 3,000 persons were invited. At the end of it Alexander uttered a prayer for peace and wished that all the peoples on earth could live together in harmony and in unity of heart and mind (*homonoia*). "He had previously said that all men were sons of one Father, and that his prayer was the expression of his recorded belief that he had a mission from God to be the Reconciler of the World."[50]

Alexander never proclaimed himself the son of Zeus; however, he accepted the title from others. To insure fusion between the Greeks and the Persians, he introduced the Iranian ceremonial of "obeisance" (*proskynēsis*) to the king. (He had already adopted the dress and etiquette of the Achaemenid sovereigns.) For the Iranians, *proskynēsis* varied in accordance with the social rank of the person performing it. A bas-relief from Persepolis represents Darius I seated on his throne and a noble Persian kissing his hand to him. But Herodotus states that subjects of lower rank prostrated themselves before the sovereign. However, sur-

49. Aristotle, frag. 658 Rose. Cf. Plato, *Rep.* 470c–471a. But Isocrates, Aristotle's rival, maintained on the contrary that the term "Hellene" denotes, not the descendant of a particular ethnic stock, but one who has a certain education (*Panegyric.* 50).

50. Tarn, *Alexander the Great,* p. 117.

prised by his companions' resistance, Alexander renounced *proskynēsis* at the same time that he renounced the idea of becoming the god of his empire.[51] Probably this latter idea had been inspired in him by the example of the pharaohs, but account must also be taken of certain tendencies that were beginning to develop in Greece. To give only one example: Aristotle wrote—certainly with Alexander in mind—that, when the supreme sovereign would come, he would be a god among men (*Politics* 3. 13; 1284a). In any case, Alexander's successors in Asia and Egypt will not hesitate to accept deification.

After twenty years of wars among the Diadochi, what was left of the empire was divided among the three Macedonian dynasties: Asia fell to the Seleucids, Egypt to the Lagids (Ptolemies), and Macedonia to the Antigonids. But from ca. 212 on, Rome began to interfere in the affairs of the Hellenistic kingdoms and ended by absorbing the entire Mediterranean world. When Octavius conquered Egypt (ca. 30), the new *oikoumenē* extended from Egypt and Macedonia to Anatolia and Mesopotamia. But the establishment of the Imperium Romanum also marked the end of Hellenistic civilization.

The unification of the historical world begun by Alexander was accomplished initially by the massive emigration of Hellenes into the eastern regions and by the spread of the Greek language and of Hellenistic culture. Common Greek (*koinē*) was spoken and written from India and Iran to Syria, Palestine, Italy, and Egypt. In the cities, whether ancient or recently founded, the Greeks built temples and theaters and established their *gymnasia*. Schooling of the Greek type was increasingly adopted by the rich and privileged of all the Asiatic countries. From one end to the other of the Hellenistic world, the value and importance of education and "wisdom" were glorified. Education—almost always based on a philosophy—enjoyed an almost religious prestige. Never before in history had education been so sought after,

51. Tarn, ibid., p. 80. The philosopher Callisthenes, who had advised Alexander to restrict this custom to Asiatics, was later involved in a plot and executed. On the "*proskynēsis* project," see, most recently, Peter Green, *Alexander of Macedon*, pp. 372 ff.

both as a means of social advancement and as an instrument of spiritual perfection.[52]

The fashionable philosophies—first of all Stoicism, founded by a Cyprian Semite, Zeno of Citium,[53] but also the doctrines of Epicurus and the Cynics—became dominant in all the cities of the *oikoumenē*. What has been called the "Hellenistic Enlightenment" encouraged individualism and at the same time cosmopolitanism. The decadence of the *polis* had freed the individual from his immemorial civic and religious ties; on the other hand, this freedom showed him his solitude and alienation in a cosmos that was terrifying by its mystery and vastness. The Stoics did their utmost to support the individual by showing him the homology between the city and the universe. Diogenes, Alexander's contemporary, had already proclaimed that he was a *cosmopolitēs,* a "citizen of the world"[54] (in other words, Diogenes refused to accept citizenship in any city, any country). But it was the Stoics who popularized the idea that all men are *cosmopolitai*—citizens of the same city, i.e., the cosmos—whatever their social origin or geographical situation.[55] "Zeno's earliest work, his *Republic,* exhibited a resplendent hope which has never quite left man since; he dreamt of a world which should no longer be separate states, but one great City under one divine law, where all were citizens and members of one another, bound together, not by human laws, but by their own willing consent or (as he phrased it) by Love."[56]

Epicurus, too, fostered "cosmopolitanism," but his principle object was the well-being of the individual. He admitted the

52. In western and central Europe we must wait until the seventeenth century before we find a similar glorification—that of the "new science," that is, of a new method of education and scientific research, by virtue of which it was hoped to purify and reform the Christian world. See vol. 3.

53. Arriving in Athens ca. 315, Zeno opened his school in the Portico of the Painters (Stoa Poikile) in ca. 300. Epicurus, born at Samos of an Athenian father, taught at Athens beginning in ca. 306.

54. Diogenes Laertius, *Lives of the Philosophers* 6. 22. But, concerned exclusively with the well-being of the individual, the Cynics took no interest in the community.

55. M. Hadas, "From Nationalism to Cosmopolitanism," pp. 107 ff.; see also, by the same author, *Hellenistic Culture,* pp. 16 ff.

56. W. W. Tarn, *Hellenistic Civilization,* p. 79.

existence of the gods. However, the gods had nothing to do with either the cosmos or with mankind. The world was a machine, which had come into being in a purely mechanical way, without author or purpose. It followed that man was free to choose the mode of existence that best suited him. Epicurus' philosophy undertook to show that the serenity and happiness obtained by *ataraxia* were the characteristics of the best possible existence.

The founder of Stoicism articulated his system in opposition to the doctrine of Epicurus. According to Zeno and his disciples, the world developed from the primordial epiphany of God, the fiery seed that gave birth to "seminal reason" (*logos spermatikos*), that is, to universal law. Similarly, the human intelligence emerges from a divine spark. In this monistic pantheism, which postulates a single *logos* (reason), the cosmos is "a living being full of wisdom" (*Stoicorum veterum fragmenta,* vol. 1, nos. 171 ff.; vol. 2, nos. 441–44). Now the wise man discovers in the utmost depths of his soul that he possesses the same *logos* as that which animates and governs the cosmos (a conception reminiscent of the oldest Upanishads; see §81). So the cosmos is intelligible and welcoming, since it is suffused by reason. By practicing wisdom, man realizes identity with the divine and freely assumes the destiny that is proper to him.

It is true that the world and human existence unfold in accordance with a strictly predetermined plan; but, by the mere fact that he cultivates virtue and does his duty—that, in short, he accomplishes the divine will—the wise man proves that he is free and transcends determinism. Freedom is equivalent to discovering the soul's self-sufficiency (*autarkeia*). In relation to the world and to other men, the soul is invulnerable; one can harm only oneself. This glorification of the soul at the same time proclaims the fundamental equality of men. But, to obtain freedom, one must free oneself of the emotions and renounce everything—"body, property, reputation, books, office"; for otherwise man is "a slave to each thing he desires," he is "under the control of others" (Epictetus, 4. 4. 33). The equation possessions and desires = slavery is reminiscent of Indian doctrines, especially Yoga and Buddhism (§§143 ff., 156 ff.). Similarly, Epictetus' exclamation addressed to God, "I am of one mind with Thee; I am Thine" (2. 16. 42), suggests countless Indian parallels.

The analogies between the Indian metaphysical systems and soteriologies and those of the Mediterranean world will multiply during the first centuries before and after Christ. We shall return to the significance of this spiritual phenomenon.

Like the new philosophies, the innovations typical of the Hellenistic religions were directed to the individual's salvation. The closed organizations, involving eschatological initiation and revelation, multiply. The initiatory tradition of the Eleusinian Mysteries (see chap. 12) will be taken over and amplified by the various mysteriosophic religions centered around divinities held to have experienced and conquered death (§ 205). Such divinities were closer to man; they took an interest in his spiritual progress and insured his salvation. Side by side with the gods and goddesses of the Hellenistic Mysteries—Dionysus, Isis, Osiris, Cybele, Attis, Mithra—other divinities became popular, and for the same reason: Helios, Heracles, Asclepius protect and help the *individual*.[57] Even deified kings seem to be more efficacious than the traditional gods: the king receives the title "savior" (*sōtēr*); he incarnates the "living law" (*nomos empsychos*).

The Greco-Oriental syncretism that characterizes the new Mystery religions at the same time illustrates the powerful spiritual reaction to the Orient that Alexander had conquered. The Orient is glorified as the fatherland of the earliest and most respected "sages," the land where the masters of wisdom have best preserved and guarded esoteric doctrines and methods of salvation. The legend of Alexander's discussion with the Indian Brahmans and ascetics, a legend that will become strangely popular in the Christian period, reflects the prevailing, almost religious, admiration for Indian "wisdom." It is from the Orient that certain apocalypses (bound up with particular conceptions of history) will be disseminated, together with new magical and angelological formulas and a number of "revelations" obtained as the result of ecstatic journeys to heaven and the other world (see § 202).

Further on we shall analyze the importance of the religious creations of the Hellenistic period (§ 205). For the moment we

57. See Carl Schneider, *Kulturgeschichte des Hellenismus,* vol. 2, pp. 800 ff., 838 ff., 869 ff.

will add that, from the point of view of the history of religions, the unification of the historical world begun by Alexander and completed by the Roman Empire is comparable to the unity of the Neolithic world brought about by the dissemination of agriculture. On the level of rural societies, the tradition inherited from the Neolithic constituted a unity that was maintained for millennia, despite influences from urban centers. Compared to this fundamental unity, clearly visible among the agricultural populations of Europe and Asia, the urban societies of the first millennium B.C. presented a considerable religious diversity. (We need only contrast the religious structures of some Oriental, Greek, and Roman cities.) But during the Hellenistic period the religiosity of the *oikoumenē* will end by adopting a common language.

23 The History of Buddhism from Mahākāśyapa to Nāgārjuna. Jainism after Mahāvīra

185. Buddhism until the first schism

The Buddha could have no successor. He had revealed the Law (*dharma*) and established the community (*saṃgha*); it now became necessary to codify the Law, that is, to collect the Blessed One's sermons and settle the canon. The great disciples, Śāriputra and Maudgalāyana, had died.[1] As for Ānanda, who was the Master's faithful servant for twenty-five years, he was not an *arhat:* he had not had time to learn the techniques of meditation. The first steps toward holding a council of 500 *arhats* were taken by Mahākāśyapa; he too had been highly esteemed by the Buddha, but he was rigid and intolerant in character, unlike the amiable Ānanda.

According to unanimous tradition, the council took place in a huge cave near Rājagṛha, during the rainy season that followed the Master's death, and it went on for seven months. Most of the sources report a serious tension between Mahākāśyapa and Ānanda. Not being an *arhat,* the latter found that he was refused the right to take part in the council. Ānanda retired into solitude and very soon achieved sanctity. He was then admitted or, according to other versions, miraculously made his way into the cave, thus displaying his yogic powers. In any case, his presence was indispensable, for Ānanda alone had heard and memorized all the Master's discourses. In answer to Mahākāśyapa's questions, Ānanda recited them. His answers made up the body of

1. Śāriputra, who had died only six months after the Blessed One, had had a great influence on the *bhikkhus:* he excelled them all in "wisdom" and learning. Some schools held him to be the greatest saint after the Buddha.

the Sūtras. The texts that composed the "basket" (*piṭaka*) of the Discipline, *vinaya,* were communicated by another disciple, Upāli.

Soon afterward Mahākāśyapa was said to have accused Ānanda of having been guilty of a number of faults (five or ten) while he served the Blessed One. The most serious ones were having supported the admission of nuns and having failed to ask the Blessed One to prolong his life until the end of the present cosmic cycle (see §150). Ānanda had to confess his faults in public, but he finally triumphed and became the leading figure in the *saṃgha*. He was said to have lived the rest of his life (for forty, or at least twenty-four, years after the *parinirvāṇa*) following his Master's example, that is, traveling and preaching the Way.

Little is known of the history of Buddhism after the council at Rājagṛha. The various lists of patriarchs who were supposed to have guided the *saṃgha* during the following century provide no valid information. What appears to be certain is the expansion of Buddhism westward and its entrance into the Deccan. It is also probable that doctrinal differences and divergent interpretations of the Discipline increased. A hundred or a hundred and ten years after the *parinirvāṇa,* a comparatively serious crisis made a new council necessary. Yaśas, a disciple of Ānanda's, was indignant at the behavior of the monks of Vaiśālī, especially at their accepting gold and silver. He managed to bring about a meeting of 700 *arhats* at Vaiśālī itself. The council condemned the questionable practices, and the guilty were constrained to accept the decision.[2]

The disagreements, however, not only continued but grew worse, and it seems certain that different sects already existed toward the middle of the fourth century B.C. A few years after the council at Vaiśālī a monk named Mahādeva proclaimed at Pāṭaliputra five unorthodox theses concerning the condition of being of an *arhat*. He maintained that an *arhat* (1) can be seduced in a dream (that is, the daughters of Māra can make him have a seminal emission); (2) can still be in some degree ignorant;

2. This second council is the last historical event reported in the various books of discipline (*Vinaya Piṭaka*). Thereafter the history of Buddhism will be related, always fragmentarily and inconsistently, in works of later date.

(3) can have doubts; (4) can progress in the Way by the help of another; and (5) can achieve concentration by uttering certain words. Such a diminishing of the *arhat* expressed a reaction against the exaggerated self-esteem of those who considered themselves to be "delivered in life." The communities very quickly divided into partisans and adversaries of Mahādeva. The council, meeting at Pāṭaliputra, could not prevent the *saṃgha*'s dividing between the partisans of the "five points"—who, claiming to be the more numerous, took the name of Mahāsāṃghika—and their opponents, who, maintaining that they represented the opinion of the elders (*sthavira*), called themselves Sthaviras.

186. The time between Alexander the Great and Aśoka

The first schism was decisive and exemplary, for other differences followed it. The unity of the *saṃgha* was irremediably broken, though without halting the spread of Buddhism. During the quarter of a century after the schism, two events of unparalleled importance for the future of India took place. The first was the invasion by Alexander the Great, which had decisive consequences for India, which was thenceforth open to Hellenistic influences. However, indifferent as it was to history and completely without historiographic consciousness, India preserved no memory of Alexander or of his prodigious enterprise. It is only by way of the fabulous legends that circulated later (the so-called "Alexander Romance") that Indian *folklore* became conscious of the most extraordinary adventure in the ancient history. But the results of this first real encounter with the West were very soon felt in Indian culture and policy. The Greco-Buddhist sculptures of Gandhāra are only one example, but an important one, for they initiated the anthropomorphic representation of the Buddha.

The second notable event was the founding of the Maurya dynasty by Chandragupta (? 320–296), a prince who, in his youth, had known Alexander. After reconquering several regions in the Northwest, he overcame the Nandas and became king of Magadha. Chandragupta laid the foundations for the first Indian "empire," which his grandson, Aśoka, was destined to enlarge and consolidate.

At the beginning of the third century, Vātsīputra, a Brahman converted by the Sthaviras, defended the doctrine of the continuity of the person (*pudgala*) through its transmigrations (see §157). He was able to found a sect, and it became powerful. Soon afterward, during the reign of Aśoka, the Sthaviras underwent a new division because of the theory supported by some that "everything exists" (*sarvam asti*)—things past, present, and future. Aśoka summoned a council, but without result. The innovators were given the name Sarvāstivādins. Since the sovereign was opposed to them, they took refuge in Kashmir, thus introducing Buddhism into that Himalayan region.

The great event in the history of Buddhism was the conversion of Aśoka (who reigned from 274 to 236 or, according to another computation, from 268 to 234). According to his own confession (published in the Thirteenth Edict), Aśoka was deeply troubled after his victory over the Kaliṅgas, which cost the enemy 100,000 dead and 150,000 prisoners. But thirteen years earlier Aśoka had been guilty of an even more odious crime. When the death of his father, King Bindusāra, appeared imminent, Aśoka had his brother murdered and seized power. However, this pitiless conqueror and fratricide was to become "the most virtuous of Indian sovereigns and one of the greatest figures in history" (Filliozat). Three years after his victory over the Kaliṅgas he was converted to Buddhism. He publicly announced his conversion and for years went on pilgrimages to the holy places. But despite his deep devotion to the Buddha, Aśoka exhibited great tolerance; he was generous toward the other religions of the empire, and the *dharma* that he professed is at once Buddhist and Brahmanic. The Twelfth Edict, chiseled in stone, states: "King Priyadarśī honors men of all faiths, members of religious orders and laymen alike, with gifts and various marks of esteem. Yet he does not value either gifts or honors as much as growth in the qualities essential to religion in men of all faiths" (trans. N. A. Nikam and Richard McKeon, *The Edicts of Aśoka,* University of Chicago Press, 1959). In the last analysis, we here have the old idea of a cosmic order whose exemplary representative is the cosmocratic sovereign.[3]

Nevertheless, this last of the great Mauryas, who reigned over almost all of India, was also an ardent propagator of the Law, for he considered it the most suited to human nature. He propagated Buddhism everywhere, sending missionaries as far as Bactria, Sogdiana, and Ceylon. According to tradition, Ceylon was converted by his son or by his younger brother. This event had marked consequences, for that island has remained Buddhist down to our day. The impetus that Aśoka gave to missionary work continued during the following centuries, despite persecution by the Mauryas' successors and invasions by Scythian peoples. From Kashmir, Buddhism spread into eastern Iran and, by way of Central Asia, reached even China (first century A.D.) and Japan (sixth century). From Bengal and Ceylon it made its way, in the first centuries of our era, into Indochina and the Indian Archipelago.

Aśoka proclaimed: "All men are my children. Just as I seek the welfare and happiness of my own children in this world and the next, I seek the same things for all men" (trans. N. A. Nikam and Richard McKeon). His dream of an empire—that is, of the *world*—unified by religion perished with him. After his death the Maurya empire rapidly declined. But Aśoka's messianic faith and his energy in propagating the Law made it possible for Buddhism to be transformed into a universal religion, the only universal religion of salvation that Asia has accepted.

187. Doctrinal tensions and new syntheses

By his messianic policy Aśoka had insured the universal triumph of Buddhism. But the swift flowering and the creativity of Buddhist thought have their sources elsewhere. To begin with, the tension between the "speculatives" and the "yogins," encouraged, in both alike, a notable effort of exegesis and doctrinal investigation. Next, the theoretical discrepancies, not to say con-

3. Indirectly, this is another proof that Buddhism accepted a number of the fundamental ideas of traditional Indian thought.

tradictions, present in the canonical texts, obliged the disciples constantly to go back to the source, that is, to the fundamental principles of the Master's teaching. This hermeneutic effort resulted in a marked enrichment of thought. The schisms and the sects in fact provide proof that the Master's teaching could neither be exhausted by an orthodoxy nor be rigidly straitjacketed into scholasticism.[4]

Finally it must be remembered that, like every other Indian religious movement, Buddhism was syncretistic in the sense that it continually assimilated and integrated non-Buddhist values. The example had been set by the Buddha himself, who had accepted a large part of the Indian heritage—not only the doctrine of *karman* and *saṃsāra,* yogic techniques and analyses of the Brāhmaṇa and Sāṃkhya type, but also the pan-Indian mythological images, symbols, and themes—on condition that he might reinterpret it from his own point of view. Thus it is probable that the traditional cosmology, with its innumerable heavens and hells and their inhabitants, was already accepted in the Buddha's day. The cult of relics became obligatory immediately after the *parinirvāṇa;* it certainly had antecedents in the veneration paid to certain famous yogins. The *stūpas* are the center for a cosmological symbolism that is not lacking in originality but that, in its chief outlines, existed before Buddhism. That so many architectural and artistic monuments have disappeared, added to the fact that a great part of the early Buddhist literature has been lost, makes chronologies only approximate, but it is beyond doubt that a number of symbolisms, ideas, and rituals precede, sometimes by several centuries, the earliest documents that testify to them.

Thus to the philosophical creativity illustrated by the new "schools" there corresponds a slower, but equally creative, process of syncretism and integration, which is realized especially among the mass of laymen.[5] The *stūpa,* which was presumed to contain relics of the Buddha or of the saints, or sacred objects,

4. It is true that each school and each sect felt obliged to elaborate its own scholasticism, but this process of systematization was set in motion and fed by genuine philosophical creativity.

5. It must not be regarded as a "popular" phenomenon, for it is chiefly inspired by representatives of traditional Indian culture.

probably derives from the tumulus in which the ashes were buried after cremation. The dome, surrounded by a circular corridor that served for circumambulation, rose from the center of a terrace. The *caitya* was a pillared sanctuary, comprising a vestibule, a deambulatory, and a small walled-up chamber containing texts written on various materials. With time, the *caitya* comes to resemble the temple and finally disappears as a separate unit. The cult consisted in prostrations and ritual greetings, circumambulation and offerings of flowers, perfumes, parasols, etc. The paradox—worshiping a Being that no longer had any relation with this world—is only a seeming one. For approaching the traces of the Buddha's "physical body," reactualized in the *stūpa*, or his "architectonic body," symbolized in the structure of the temple, is equivalent to assimilating the doctrine, that is, to absorbing his "theoretical body," the *dharma*. The cult later rendered to the Buddha's statues and the pilgrimages to various places sanctified by his presence (Bodh-Gayā, Sārnāth, etc.) are justified by the same dialectic; that is, the various objects or activities belonging to *saṃsāra* are able to facilitate the disciple's salvation by virtue of the grand and irreversible soteriological action of the Awakened One.[6]

For centuries, and probably immediately after his death, the Blessed One was represented—and venerated—in aniconic form: his footprint, the Tree, the Wheel. These symbols made the Law present by suggesting, respectively, the Buddha's missionary activity, the Tree of his Awakening, and "setting the wheel of the Law in motion." When, at the beginning of the Christian era, the first statues of the Buddha were made (the Greco-Indian sculptures of Gandhāra), the human figure did not hide the fundamental symbolism. As Paul Mus has shown, the image of the Buddha inherits the religious values of the Vedic altar. On the other hand, the nimbus that shines around the heads of the Buddhas (and around Christ in the Christian art of the same period, first–fifth centuries) derives from a prototype of the Achaemenid period, especially the shining halo of Ahura Mazdā. (Besides,

6. The earliest tradition holds that, before the *parinirvāṇa*, the Buddha accepted all the gifts and all the homage that were to be rendered to him by his disciples through the ages; see Vasubandhu, *Abhidharmakośa*, vol. 4, pp. 236–46.

this prototype carries on the old Mesopotamian conceptions; see § 20). In the Buddhist iconography the symbolism preponderantly emphasizes the identity of the Buddha's nature with light, and, as we have seen (§ 81), from the *Ṛg Veda* on, light was regarded as the most adequate image and expression for "spirit."

The life of the monks underwent some changes with the building of monasteries (*vihāras*). The only change that concerns us is the multiplication of doctrinal writings and works of erudition. Despite the immense number of lost books (as the result of which we know almost nothing of many schools and sects), Buddhist literature in Pali and Sanskrit[7] is impressive by its bulk. The texts that make up the "Supreme Doctrine"—the third "basket," the *Abhidharma Piṭaka*—were produced between 300 B.C. and A.D. 100. It is a literature that contrasts in style with the Sūtras, consisting, as it does, of works that are rationalistic, didactic, dry, impersonal. The Buddha's message is reinterpreted and presented in the form of a philosophical system, and the authors make every effort to explain the abundant contradictions in the Sūtras.

Obviously, each sect has an *abhidharmakośa* of its own, and the differences between these versions of the Supreme Doctrine gave rise to fresh controversies. The innovations are sometimes important. We will give but one example: originally, *nirvāṇa* was the only thing "uncompounded" (*asaṃskṛta*), but now, with few exceptions, the schools confer the rank of "Uncompounded" on space, the Four Truths, the Way (*mārga*), *pratītya samutpāda* (conditioned coproduction), or even certain yogic "contemplations." As for the *arhat:* according to certain schools he can fall, whereas for others even his body is supremely pure; some state that it is possible to become an *arhat* even in the embryonic state or in dream, but such doctrines are severely criticized by other masters.

Still more important by its consequences was the reinterpretation of Buddhology. For the Sthaviravādins, Śākyamuni was a man who *made himself the Buddha* and therefore became "god." But for other doctors the historicity of Buddha-Śākyamuni was humiliating. On the one hand, how can a great god *become*

7. A part of it has been preserved only in Tibetan and Chinese translations.

god? On the other hand, it was necessary to accept a savior who was held to be lost in his *nirvāṇa*. One school, the Lokottara, proclaimed that Śākyamuni, having become a Buddha several cosmic periods earlier, had not left the heaven that he inhabited; he whom men saw born at Kapilavastu, preach, and die was only a phantom (*nirmita*) created by the real Śākyamuni. This docetistic Buddhology will be taken up again and enlarged by the Mahāyāna.

The Ceylonese Theravādins were not free from schismatic dissidences. But it was especially on the continent that the fragmentation and multiplication of schools continued with ever increasing intensity. Like their opponents, the Sthaviras, the Mahāsāṃghikas also underwent divisions, first into three groups, then into a number of sects whose names it would serve no purpose to record. But what is important is the fact that the Mahāsāṃghikas inspired, or made possible, a radical renewal of Buddhism, known by the name of the Mahāyāna, literally the "Great Vehicle."

188. The "Way of the *boddhisattvas*"

The earliest manifestations of the Mahāyāna are documented toward the end of the first century B.C.; they are the *Prajñāpāramitā Sūtras* ("Sermons on the Perfection of Wisdom"), works of various lengths, rather hard to understand, and introducing a new style into Buddhist thought and literature. The terms Mahāyāna and Hinayāna (literally, "Little Vehicle," applied to the old Buddhism, Theravāda) are apparently late. The disciples of the new way called it the "Way of the *boddhisattvas*." They are distinguished by their greater tolerance in respect to discipline and by their Buddhology, which is more mystical in structure. Scholars agree in recognizing the influence of lay devotion. The ideal is no longer the solitary *arhat* in quest of his *nirvāṇa* but the *boddhisattva*, a lay personage, model of benevolence and compassion, who indefinitely defers his own deliverance in order to help in the salvation of others. This religious hero, who resembles Rāma and Kṛṣṇa, does not demand of his disciples the austere way of the monk but personal devotion of the *bhakti* type. It must be added, however, that the old Buddhism was not without this type of devotion. According to the *Majjhima Nikāya* (1. 142), the Buddha himself had declared that whoever expressed "a simple feeling of faith or affection [in regard to him] will go to paradise."[8] But now it is enough *to make the resolve to become a Buddha "for the good of others,"* for the Mahāyāna radically changed the conception of the adept: he no longer aspires to *nirvāṇa* but to the condition of a Buddha.

All the Buddhist schools recognized the importance of the *boddhisattvas*. But the Mahāyānists proclaimed the *boddhisattvas'* superiority to the *arhat;* for the latter is not wholly delivered from the "self"; that is why he seeks *nirvāṇa* for himself alone. According to those who criticize them, the *arhats* developed wisdom but not enough compassion. In contrast, as the texts of the *Prajñā-pāramitā* repeat, the *boddhisattvas* "do not wish to attain their own private *nirvāṇa*. On the contrary, they have surveyed the highly painful world of being, and yet, desirous of winning supreme enlightenment, they do not tremble at birth-and-death. They have set out for the benefit of the world, for the ease of the world, out of pity for the world. They have resolved: "We will become a shelter for the world, a refuge for the world, the world's place of rest, the final relief of the world, islands of the world, lights of the world, the guides of the world's means of salvation."[9]

This doctrine of salvation is all the more courageous because the Mahāyāna elaborated a new and even more radical philosophy, that of "universal emptiness" (*śūnyatā*). Indeed, it is said that two things are necessary for the *boddhisattva* and his practice of wisdom: "Never to abandon all beings, and to see into the truth that all things are empty."[10] It seems paradoxical that at the very moment of triumph of compassion for all beings—not only human beings but phantoms, animals, plants—the entire world is "emptied" of reality. The old Buddhism had insisted

8. There are many more such texts; see *Dīgha Nikāya* 2. 40; *Dhammapada* 288 ("He who takes refuge in the Buddha . . . will enter the assembly of the gods").

9. *Aṣṭasāhasrikā* 15. 293, trans. E. Conze, *Buddhism: Its Essence and Development* (New York: Harper & Bros., 1954), p. 125.

10. *Vajracchedikā* 3, quoted by Conze, ibid., p. 130.

on the unreality even of the soul (*nairātmya*). The Mahāyāna, while glorifying the *boddhisattva's* career, proclaims the unreality, the nonexistence in itself, of "things," of the *dharmas* (*dharma śūnyatā*). Yet this paradox is really not one. The doctrine of universal emptiness, by emptying the universe of reality, makes detachment from the world easier and leads to doing away with the self—the primary goal of the Buddha Śākyamuni and of the old Buddhism.

We shall come upon this problem again when we present the *śūnyatā* philosophy. For the moment let us examine the specifically Mahāyānic religious creations. For what is characteristic of the Great Vehicle is, on the one hand, the limitless increase of lay devotion and of the soteriological mythologies that it implies and, on the other hand, the prodigious metaphysics, at once visionary and extremely strict, of its masters. These two tendencies are by no means in conflict;[11] on the contrary, they complete and influence each other.

There are many *boddhisattvas*, for there have always been saviors who, becoming a Buddha, have taken the vow to put off Awakening for the salvation of all beings. The most important among them are Maitreya, Avalokiteśvara, and Mañjuśrī. The *boddhisattva* Maitreya (from *maitrī*, "goodness") is the next Buddha, the successor to Śākyamuni. Avalokiteśvara[12] is the most famous. He is certainly a more recent creation, typical of the devotion (not only Buddhistic) that begins to be felt in the first centuries of our era. Avalokiteśvara appears as a synthesis of the three great gods of Hinduism. He is Lord of the Universe; the sun and moon come from his eyes, the earth comes from his feet, the wind comes from his mouth; he "holds the world in his hand," and "each pore of his skin contains a system of the world"—formulas that are found again in references to Viṣṇu and Śiva. Avalokiteśvara protects against all kinds of danger and denies no requests, not even the prayer to grant sterile women children. Mañjuśrī ("Smooth Fortune"), closely connected with

11. As is sometimes the case in the Hinayāna, when the *bhikkhus* seem to be embarrassed by certain extravagant manifestations of popular devotion.

12. Scholars are in disagreement concerning the meaning of his name: "Lord (*īśvara*) who looks from on high" (Burnouf) or "who looks down with compassion" (Conze) seems the most convincing.

the Buddha Akṣobhya, personifies wisdom and protects learning. He will enjoy an exalted position in Chinese Buddhism.

The *boddhisattva* Avalokiteśvara is mystically connected with the Buddha Amitābha, but the latter did not become popular in India until very late—in the seventh century; before that, his reputation depended on his relations with Avalokiteśvara. In contrast, after the eighth century Amitābha will enjoy an extraordinary reputation in Tibet, China, and Japan. It is fitting to present him at this point in the context of Mahāyānist devotion, since his mythology and cult represent a surprising innovation. When he was a simple monk, Amitābha vowed to become a Buddha and to acquire a "miraculous land," whose inhabitants, by virtue of his merits, would enjoy unequaled happiness until they entered *nirvāṇa.* This land, Sukhāvatī ("the Happy"), is situated at an incomprehensible distance in the West; it is bathed in light and resembles a paradise in its jewels and flowers and birds. Its inhabitants are, in fact, immortal; they also feast on Amitābha's word-of-mouth teaching.

Such paradises were already known in India. The distinctive feature of Sukhāvatī consists in the *extreme ease with which believers enter it.* In fact, it is enough to have heard the name of Amitābha and to have thought of him; at the moment of death the god will descend and will himself lead his disciple into the paradise of Sukhāvatī. It is the absolute triumph of devotion. However, its doctrinal justification can be found in the earliest Buddhism. In the Chinese version of the *Milinda-pañha,* it is said that "men who in one existence have done evil for up to a hundred years, if they think of the Buddha at the moment of death, will all, after their death, obtain being born in the height of heaven."[13] To be sure, the paradise of Sukhāvatī is not *nirvāṇa;* but those who reach it by virtue of *a single thought* or *a single word* are destined to obtain final deliverance in the future without any effort. If we remember the extreme strictness of the Way as preached by the Buddha and the old Buddhism, we can gauge the boldness of this new theology. But obviously it is a mystical and devotional theology, which does not hesitate to apply, in

13. After the translation by Paul Demiéville, *Version chinoise du Milinda-pañha,* p. 166. The Pali version is a rehandling, under the influence of Sinhalese monasticism, and shows interpolations.

everyday practice, the metaphysical discoveries of the great masters of Mahāyāna.

Since there is an infinite number of Buddhas, there is an infinite number of "Buddha lands" or "Buddha fields" (*buddha-kṣetras*). Sukhāvatī is only one among these countless Buddha lands. They are transcendent universes, created by the merits or the thoughts of the saviors. The *Avataṃsaka* declares that they are "as innumerable as particles of dust," coming out of a "thought cherished in the mind of the *boddhisattva* of mercy." All these Buddha lands "rise from one's own mind and have infinite form."[14] The imaginary nature of these universes is constantly emphasized by the texts. The "Buddha fields" are mental constructions, raised in the thoughts of men in order to achieve their conversion. This time, too, the Indian genius has not hesitated to valorize the creative imagination by using it as a means to salvation.

189. Nāgārjuna and the doctrine of universal emptiness

These mythological theologies are accompanied by certain new theories, which also arose from the same preoccupation with the need to annihilate egocentric impulses. The first is the doctrine of the *transfer of merit* (*pariṇāma*). It seems to contradict the law of *karman*, yet it continues the old Buddhism's conviction that the example of a *bhikkhu* striving to become an *arhat* helps and inspires lay people. But as it is interpreted by the Mahāyāna, the doctrine of the transfer of merit is a creation typical of the time. Adepts are invited to transfer or dedicate their merits to the illumination of all beings. As Śāntideva (seventh century) writes in a work that became famous, *Bodhicaryāvatāra:*

> By the merit emanating from all my good deeds, I wish to soothe the suffering of all creatures, to be the physician, the healer, the nurse of the sick as long as there is sickness. . . . My life with all my rebirths, all my possessions, all the merit that I have acquired or will acquire—all of that I abandon

14. *Avataṃsaka Sūtra,* quoted by Conze, *Buddhism: Its Essence and Development,* p. 154.

without hope of gain for myself, so that the salvation of all beings shall be forwarded.[15]

Another new idea reveals that the "Buddha nature" is present in every human being and even in each grain of sand. This is as much as to say that it is our own "Buddha-ness" that forces us to become Buddha. It is an idea bound up with the Upanishadic discovery (the identity *ātman-brahman*) and the Hindu axiom that a man cannot worship divinity except by himself becoming a divinity. The theory will have important developments in the Mahāyāna, especially in the famous doctrine of the "embryo of Tathāgata" (*tathāgata-garbha*). It is also bound up with another original interpretation of the nature of Buddhas: the doctrine of the Buddha's three bodies (*trikāya*). The first body, that of the Law (*dharmakāya*), is transcendent, absolute, infinite, eternal; indeed, it is the spiritual body of the *dharma;* that is, it is at once the *Law preached by Buddha* and *absolute reality, pure being*. (We may think of the body of Prajāpati, constructed—in certain cases—from sacred syllables and magical formulas; see § 77.) The second body, the *saṃbhogakāya,* or "body of enjoyment," is the glorious epiphany of the Buddha, accessible only to *bodhisattvas*. Finally, the "body of magical creation" (*nirmāṇakāya*) is the phantom that men confront on earth and that resembles them, for it is material and ephemeral; but it plays a decisive part, for it is only through this phantom body that human beings are capable of receiving the Law and attaining salvation.

As we have observed, the goal of these doctrinal elaborations and mythological constructions that are characteristic of the Mahāyāna is to make salvation easier for laymen. By accepting and integrating a certain number of Hindu elements, whether "popular" (cults, *bhakti,* etc.) or learned, the Mahāyāna renewed and enriched the Buddhist heritage, though without thereby betraying it. Indeed, the doctrine of universal emptiness (*śūnyatāvāda*), elaborated by the genius of Nāgārjuna (second century A.D.), was also known by the name "[the doctrine] of the middle," corresponding to the "middle way" preached by Śākyamuni. Certainly, as if to balance the tendency toward "easiness," evident in Mahāyānist devotion, the doctrine of

15. *Bodhicaryāvatāra* 3. 6 ff., after the translation by Finot.

emptiness (*śūnyatāvāda*) stands out by its philosophical depth and difficulty.

Nāgārjuna's Indian adversaries, and some Western scholars, have declared that the *śūnyatāvāda* is a nihilistic philosophy, since it appears to deny the fundamental doctrines of Buddhism. In reality, it is an ontology, paralleled by a soteriology, that seeks to free itself from the illusory structures that are dependent on language; so the *śūnyatāvāda* employs a paradoxical dialectic that ends in the *coincidentia oppositorum*, which in a way suggests Nicholas of Cusa, an aspect of Hegel, and Wittgenstein. Nāgārjuna criticizes and rejects any philosophical system by demonstrating the impossibility of expressing ultimate truth (*paramārthatā*) by language. First of all, he points out that there are two kinds of "truths": truths that are conventional or "hidden in the world" (*lokasaṃvṛti-satya*), which have their practical use, and ultimate truth, which alone can lead to deliverance. The *Abhidharma*, which claims to convey "high learning," really works with conventional knowledge. What is worse, the *Abhidharma* obscures the way to deliverance with its countless definitions and categories of existences (as, for example, *skandhas, dhātus*, etc.), which are basically only products of the imagination. Nāgārjuna sets out to liberate, and rightly direct, the mental energies trapped in the net of discourse.

From a demonstration of the emptiness, that is, the nonreality, of everything that seems to exist or can be felt, thought, or imagined, several consequences follow. The first is that all the famous formulas of the old Buddhism, as well as their systematic redefinitions by *Abhidharma* authors, prove to be false. Thus, for example, the three stages of the production of things—"origin," "duration," "cessation"—do not exist; and equally nonexistent are the *skandhas*, the irreducible elements (*dhātus*), and desire, the subject of desire, and the situation of the person who desires. They do not exist because they possess no nature of their own. *Karman* itself is a mental construction, for there is neither "act" nor "actor," properly speaking. Nāgārjuna likewise denies the difference between the "world of composites" (*saṃskṛta*) and the "unconditioned" (*asaṃskṛta*). "From the point of view of ultimate truth, the notion of impermanence (*anitya*) cannot be considered more true than the notion of permanence'' (*Mūlamadhyamaka Kārikā* 23. 13, 14). As for the famous law of ''conditioned coproduction'' (*pratītya-samutpāda*), it is useful only from the practical point of view. In reality, ''conditioned coproduction—we call it *śūnya*, 'empty' '' (ibid., 24. 18). So too, the Four Holy Truths proclaimed by the Buddha have no nature of their own: they are merely conventional truths, which can serve only on the plane of language.

The second consequence is even more radical: Nāgārjuna denies the distinction between ''him who is bound'' and ''the delivered one'' and, consequently, the distinction between *saṃsāra* and *nirvāṇa*. ''There is nothing that differentiates *saṃsāra* from *nirvāṇa*'' (ibid., 25. 19).[16] This does not mean that the world (*saṃsāra*) and deliverance (*nirvāṇa*) are ''the same thing''; it means only that they are undifferentiated. *Nirvāṇa* is a ''fabrication of the mind.'' In other words, from the point of view of ultimate truth, the Tathāgata himself does not enjoy an autonomous and valid ontological condition.

Finally, the third consequence of universal emptiness is the basis for one of the most original ontological creations known to the history of thought. Everything is ''empty,'' without any ''nature of its own''; yet it must not be inferred from this that there is an ''absolute essence'' to which *śūnyatā* (or *nirvāṇa*) refers. When it is said that ''emptiness,'' *śūnyatā*, is inexpressible, inconceivable, and indescribable, there is no implication that there is in existence a ''transcendent reality'' characterized by these attributes. Ultimate truth does not unveil an ''absolute'' of the Vedānta type; it is the mode of existence discovered by the adept when he obtains complete indifference toward ''things'' *and their cessation*. The ''realization,'' by thought, of universal emptiness is, in fact, equivalent to deliverance. But he who attains *nirvāṇa* cannot ''know'' it, for emptiness transcends both being and nonbeing. Wisdom (*prajñā*) reveals ultimate truth by making use of the ''truth hidden in the world'': the latter is not rejected but is transformed into ''truth that does not itself exist.''[17]

16. Chapter 25 of the *Mūlamadhyamaka Kārikā* is entirely devoted to analysis of *nirvāṇa*. See Frederick J. Streng, *Emptiness*, pp. 74 ff.

17. See Streng, p. 96.

Nāgārjuna refuses to consider the *śūnyatāvāda* a "philosophy"; it is a practice, at once dialectical and contemplative, which, by ridding the adept of every theoretical construction not only of the world but *of salvation,* enables him to obtain imperturbable serenity and freedom. Nāgārjuna utterly rejects the idea that his arguments, or any other philosophical affirmation, are valid because of a foundation that exists outside of or beyond language. One cannot say of *śūnyatā* that it exists or that it does not exist or that it exists and at the same time does not exist, etc. To the critics who observe, "If all is empty, then Nāgārjuna's negation is likewise an empty proposition," he replies that his adversaries' affirmations as well as his negations have no autonomous existence: they exist only on the plane of conventional truth (*Mūlamadh.* 24. 29).

Buddhism, as well as Indian philosophical thought in general, was changed profoundly after Nāgārjuna, though the change was not immediately evident. Nāgārjuna carried to the extreme limit the innate tendency of the Indian spirit toward the *coincidentia oppositorum.* Nevertheless, he succeeded in showing that the career of the *boddhisattva* retains all its greatness despite the fact that "all is empty." And the ideal of the *boddhisattva* continued to inspire charity and altruism, although, as the *Avataṃsaka* expresses it, "though dwelling in *nirvāṇa,* he manifests the *saṃsāra.* He knows that there are no beings, but he tries to convert them. He is definitively pacified (*śānta*), but he appears to experience passions (*kleśas*). He inhabits the Body of the Law (*dharmakāya*), but he manifests himself everywhere, in countless bodies of living beings. He is always deep in profound ecstasies (*dhyānas*), but he enjoys the objects of desire."[18]

190. Jainism after Mahāvīra: Erudition, cosmology, soteriology

Mahāvīra's immediate successor was the *sthavira* (the "Ancient") Sudharman, who is held to have transmitted his master's

18. After the French version of the Chinese translation by Siksānanda, cited by E. Lamotte, *L'Enseignement de Vimalakīrti,* p. 36.

sayings to his disciple Jambū. So they are the last of the "omniscient ones" (*kevalins*), for only they knew the whole of the sacred texts. We know the names of the *sthaviras* who succeeded Jambū. The most important of them is a third-century figure, Bhadrabāhu, a contemporary of King Chandragupta (Bhadrabāhu died in 270 or 262 B.C). It was he who established the Jaina canon and even composed several works himself. But he also witnessed, and was probably one of the causes for, the crisis that led to the division of the Jaina church.

According to tradition, Bhadrabāhu, foreseeing a twelve-year-famine, emigrated into the Deccan with part of the community. He charged his disciple Sthūlabhadra to look after those who did not emigrate. Some years later a council was summoned at Pāṭaliputra for the purpose of collecting all the sacred texts, which until then had been transmitted by word of mouth. Bhadrabāhu was on his way to Nepal. Emissaries were sent to him so that he could recite to them certain old texts that he alone knew. But the emissaries listened carelessly and managed to remember only fragments of these treatises that preserved the original doctrine. Only Sthūlabhadra memorized ten works out of a total of fourteen. This episode, which is probably legendary, will later justify the differences between the two canons.

When the emigrants, maintaining their practice of nudity, returned to Magadha, they were shocked by the laxity of the monks who had remained there. The tension continued for several generations, aggravated by controversies over certain details of ritual and by doctrinal differences. Finally, in 77 B.C., a split became inevitable, and the community divided into Śvetāmbaras, the "white-clad," and Digambaras, those "clad in space." The latter denied deliverance to those who did not observe total nakedness (hence they also denied it to women). In addition, they rejected certain elements in Mahāvīra's biography (for example, that he was married), and, because they held that the ancient texts were lost, the "space-clad" monks questioned the authenticity of the canon established by the Śvetāmbaras. A second council was held at Valabhī, in the second half of the fifth century; it was organized by the Śvetāmbaras to establish the definitive version of the sacred texts.

We will not discuss the different categories of works that make up the immense body of Jaina canonical literature. As for the postcanonical texts, they are many.[19] Unlike Buddhism, Jainism preserved its original structures. In its extensive philosophical and ritual literature we find few new and creative ideas. The most famous treatises, such as the *Pravacanasāra* by Kuṇḍakunda (first century A.D.) and *Tattvārtha* by Umāsvāti (undated, but later than Kuṇḍakunda's work), are essentially nothing but scholastic systematizations of the conceptions that Mahāvīra or his immediate successors had already formulated.[20]

The doctrine is also a soteriology. It is concentrated in the "Three Jewels" of Jainism: Right Seeing, Right Knowledge, Right Conduct. This last is realized only by monastic discipline. Four kinds of "Right Seeing" are distinguished, the first of which is merely visual, whereas the last constitutes an unlimited transcendental perception. We shall not analyze the five kinds of "Right Knowledge." We will merely mention two theses that are typical of Jaina logic: the "doctrine of points of view" (*naya-vāda*) and the "doctrine of can be" (*syād-vāda*). The first maintains that, in regard to anything at all, various complementary affirmations may be made. True from a certain point of view, an assertion is no longer true if it is looked at from a different viewpoint, but it remains compatible with the total tenor of the statements. The doctrine of "can be" (*syād*) implies the relativity or the ambiguity of the real. It is also called the "rule with seven divisions," because it comprises seven forms of affirmations: (1) something can be such; (2) something can be not such; (3) something can be such or can be not such; etc. The doctrine was

19. Side by side with philosophical treatises, we find epics (adapted from the Hindu epics and the Purāṇas), legendary biographies of the Tīrthaṃkaras, and even tales, romances, and dramas, to say nothing of didactic and scientific literature. Except for the narrative literature (which itself is not without a tiresome didacticism), the immense Jaina production is characterized by monotony and aridity.

20. This type of conservatism is typical of traditional India and, in itself, does not constitute a negative characteristic. But the Jaina writings are unusual in their heavy, arid texture.

condemned by the other Indian philosophical schools.[21] Nevertheless, these two logical methods constitute one of the most original creations of Jaina thought.

Analyses of matter, of the soul, of time and space (these last two categories were regarded as "substances"), of "karmic matter," etc., were elaborated and systematized, with a multiplication of classifications and enumerations. A characteristic feature, perhaps borrowed by Mahāvīra from Makkhali Gośāla, is the belief that acts mark the soul like a dye (*leśya*) and that these colors also impregnate bodies. Thus the soul's merit or demerit is expressed by the six colors of bodies; black, blue-black, and gray are characteristic of the inhabitants of the infernal regions, while yellow, pink, and white designate beings who live on earth—pure and intense white belonging only to those who rise toward the summit of the universe. This is certainly an archaic conception, bound up with certain yogic practices. In fact, in the classification of beings in accordance with their spiritual qualifications, the eighth stage, when the "first contemplative withdrawal of the soul into its pure essence" is accomplished, is also called the "first white contemplation." The equivalence color/spiritual stage is also found in other Indian traditions and elsewhere as well.

Like nature (*prakṛti*) in the Sāṃkhya-Yoga conception, matter is spontaneously and unconsciously organized in order to serve the soul. Although eternal and without beginning, the universe exists in order that souls may deliver themselves from its structures. But, as we shall see in a moment, deliverance does not imply total and definitive escape from the cosmos. The originality of the Jaina cosmology lies precisely in its archaism. It has preserved and revalorized traditional Indian conceptions overlooked by Hindu and Buddhist cosmologies. The cosmos (*loka*) is represented in the form of a man standing with his arms bent and his fists on his hips. This macranthrope is made up of a lower world (the lower members), a median world (the region of the waist), and an upper world (the chest and head). A vertical tube

21. The Buddha was probably referring to the *syād-vāda* when he attacked certain monks who dodged every question that was put to them (*Dīgha* 1. 39–42).

traverses the three cosmic regions after the fashion of the *axis mundi*. The lower world comprises seven superimposed "earths" (*bhūmis*), each having a different color, from the most opaque black to the light produced by the brightness of sixteen kinds of precious stones. The upper zones of the first "earth" are inhabited by eighteen categories of divinities. The six other "earths" constitute true hells, of which there are 8,400,000, peopled by different classes of the damned, who are colored gray, blue-black, and black. Their deformed bodies, the torments inflicted on them in fiery or icy hells, are reminiscent of the traditional clichés. Those guilty of unforgivable crimes are shut up for all eternity in the most terrifying infernal abyss, *nigroda*, which lies at the feet of the macranthrope.

This image of an anthropomorphic universe, whose various zones—identified with the organs of the cosmic man—are inhabited by beings of different colors, is archaic. Nowhere else in India has it been better preserved and more aptly harmonized with the experiences of "mystical light" than in Jainism. The middle world corresponds in general to the world described by the Hindu and Buddhist cosmologies.[22] The upper world, situated above Mount Meru, is divided into five superimposed zones, corresponding to the macranthrope's ribs, neck, chin, five facial openings, and topknot. Each zone in turn comprises several "paradises" inhabited by various types of divinities. As for the fifth zone, the summit of the universe and topknot of the macranthrope, it is reserved for liberated souls. This is as much as to say that *he who is delivered does not transcend the cosmos* (as is the case with the Buddhist *nirvāṇa*) but only its many ascending levels. The liberated soul enjoys inexpressible and eternal bliss in the *siddha-kṣetra*, the "field of the perfect," in company with his peers but within the macranthropic universe.

22. It has the shape of a disk, with, at its center, Mount Meru, whose base reaches down into the infernal regions. Around this cosmic mountain there are fifteen concentric continents (called "islands," *dvīpas*), separated by circular oceans. The central continent, Jambudvīpa, is divided into seven transverse zones by Bhāratavarṣa (India). The other island-continents are "lands of enjoyments" (*bhoga-bhūmis*), for their inhabitants need not work in order to live. They are also the home of the stellar divinities.

As early as in Bhadrabāhu's time Jainism made its way into Bengal and Orissa. Later the Digambaras established themselves in the Deccan, and the Śvetāmbaras moved westward, settling especially in the Gujarat. The traditions of the two churches delighted in counting among their converts or sympathizers a large number of kings and princes. Like all the other Indian religions, Jainism underwent persecution by the Muslims (pillage, destruction of temples, prohibition of nudity). It also became the target of the Hindu counteroffensive, and, from the twelfth century on, its decline was irreversible. Unlike Buddhism, Jainism never became a popular and dominant religion in India, and it did not spread beyond the frontiers of the subcontinent. But whereas Buddhism has completely disappeared from its country of origin, the Jaina community still has 1,500,000 members today, and, because of their social position and cultural distinction, its influence is considerable.

24 The Hindu Synthesis: The *Mahābhārata* and the *Bhagavad Gītā*

191. The eighteen-day battle

With its 90,000 verses, the *Mahābhārata* is the longest epic in world literature. As it has come down to us, the text includes visions and numerous interpolations, the latter chiefly in the "encyclopedic" sections (books 12 and 13). However, it would be illusory to believe that we could reconstruct the "original form" of the poem. As to its date, "the idea makes no sense for the epic" (L. Renoü). It is assumed that the epic poem was already finished between the seventh and sixth centuries before our era and acquired its present form between the fourth century B.C. and the fourth century A.D. (Winternitz).

Its principal theme is the conflict between the two lines of Bhāratas: the descendants of the Kurus (the one hundred Kauravas) and the descendants of the Pāṇḍus (the five Pāṇḍavas). Duryodhana, the eldest of the Kauravas, son of the blind king Dhṛtarāṣṭra, is devoured by a demonic hate for his cousins; as a matter of fact, he is the incarnation of the demon Kali, that is, the demon of the most evil age of the world. The five Pāṇḍavas—Yudhiṣṭira, Arjuna, Bhīma, Nakula, and Sahadeva—are the sons of Pāṇḍu, younger brother of Dhṛtarāṣṭra. Actually, they are the sons of the gods Dharma, Vāyu, Indra, and the two Aśvins, and we shall later perceive the meaning of this divine parentage. On Pāṇḍu's death, Dhṛtarāṣṭra becomes king for the period before Yudhiṣṭhira grows old enough to take power. But Duryodhana does not resign himself. Among the traps that he set for his cousins, the most dangerous was the burning of a lacquer house in which he had persuaded them to live. The Pāṇḍavas escape by an underground passage and, with their mother, take refuge in the forest, incognito. A number of adventures follow. Disguised as a Brahman, Arjuna succeeds in obtaining the hand of Princess Draupadī, incarnation of the goddess Śrī, and takes her to the Pāṇḍavas' hermitage in the forest. Not seeing Draupadī, and believing that Arjuna is bringing only the food he had obtained as alms, his mother exclaims: "Enjoy this together." Thus the young woman becomes the common wife of the five brothers.

Learning that the Pāṇḍavas did not die in the fire, the blind king Dhṛtarāṣṭra decides to let them have half of the kingdom. They build a capital, Indraprastha, where their cousin Kṛṣṇa, head of the Yādava clan, joins them. Duryodhana challenges Yudhiṣṭhira to a game of dice. One of the dice being false, Yudhiṣṭhira successively loses his possessions, his kingdom, his brothers, and their wife. The king annuls the game and restores their possessions to the Pāṇḍavas. But soon afterward he permits a second game of dice; it is agreed that the losers shall live for twelve years in the forest and a thirteenth year incognito. Yudhiṣṭhira plays, loses again, and goes into exile with his brothers and Draupadī. The third book, *Vana-parvan* ("Book of the Forest"), which, with its 17,500 couplets, is the longest, is also the richest in literary episodes: the hermits tell the Pāṇḍavas the dramatic stories of Nala and Damayantī, Sāvitrī, Rāma, and Sītā. The following book describes the adventures of the thirteenth year, which the exiles succeed in spending without being recognized. In the fifth book ("Book of Preparations"), war seems inevitable. The Pāṇḍavas send Kṛṣṇa as ambassador; they demand the restoration of their kingdom, or at least of five villages, but Duryodhana refuses. Immense armies gather on either side, and war breaks out.

The sixth book contains the most famous episode in the epic—the *Bhagavad Gītā,* which we shall discuss further on. In the following books the various moments of the battle, which rages for eighteen days, are laboriously narrated. The ground is covered with the dead and wounded. The leaders of the Kurus fall one after the other, Duryodhana the last. Only three Kauravas escape, among them Aśvatthāman, into whom the god Śiva had just entered. With a horde of demons produced by Śiva, Aśvatthāman makes his way into the sleeping Pāṇḍavas' camp by night and butchers them, except the five brothers, who were away. Saddened by so much killing, Yudhiṣṭhira wants to renounce the throne and live as a hermit; but his brothers, helped by Kṛṣṇa and several sages, are able to make him abandon his decision, and he regally performs the horse sacrifice (the *aśvamedha;* see § 73). After collaborating with his nephew for fifteen years, Dhṛtarāṣṭa retires to the forest with a few companions. Not long afterward, they are killed in a conflagration started by their own sacred fires. Thirty-six years after the great battle, Kṛṣṇa and his people perish in a strange way: they kill one another with reeds magically transformed into maces. The capital crumbles and disappears into the ocean. Feeling that he is growing old, Yudhiṣṭhira leaves power to his grandnephew Parikṣit (who, stillborn, was resuscitated by Kṛṣṇa), and, with his brothers, Draupadā, and a dog, sets out for the Himalayas. One after the other, his companions fall on the journey. Only Yudhiṣṭhira and the dog (which is really his own father, Dharma) hold out to the end. The epic concludes with a short description of Yudhiṣṭhira descending to the underworld and then ascending to heaven.

192. Eschatological war and the end of the world

This monstrous war was decided on by Brahmā, in order to relieve the earth of a population that did not cease to multiply. Brahmā asked a certain number of gods and demons to become incarnate in order to provoke a terrifying war of extermination. The *Mahābhārata* describes the end of a world (*pralaya*), followed by the emergence of a new world under the reign of Yudhiṣṭhira or Parikṣit.[1] The poem shows an eschatological structure: a gigantic battle between the forces of "good" and "evil" (analogous to the combats between *devas* and *asuras*); destruction on a cosmic scale by fire and water; resurgence of a new and pure world, symbolized by the miraculous resurrection of Pa-

1. Georges Dumézil sees in Yudhiṣṭhira's reign the restoration of the world; see his *Mythe et épopée,* vol. 1, pp. 152 ff. Alf Hiltebeitel, following the traditional Indian interpretation, holds that the "new age" begins with the reign of Parikṣit ("The *Mahābhārata* and Hindu Eschatology," p. 102).

rikṣit. In a certain sense we may speak of a grandiose revalorization of the old mythico-ritual scenario of the New Year. However, this time it is not a matter of the end of a year but of the conclusion of a cosmic age.

The cyclical theory becomes popular from the time of the Purāṇas. This does not mean that the eschatological myth is necessarily a creation of Hinduism. The conception of it is archaic and enjoys a considerable dissemination. What is more, similar myths are documented in Iran and Scandanavia. According to Zoroastrian tradition, at the end of history Ohrmazd will seize Ahriman, the six Ameśa Spentas will each lay hold of an archdemon, and these incarnations of evil will be definitively cast into darkness (see §216). As we have seen (§177), a similar eschatology is found among the ancient Germans: in the course of the final battle (the Ragnarök), each god will take on a demonic being or a monster, with the difference that the gods and their adversaries will kill one another down to the last of them and the earth will burn and finally be plunged into the sea; however, the earth will rise again from the aquatic mass, and a new humanity will enjoy a happy existence under the reign of the young god Baldr.

Stig Wikander and Georges Dumézil have brilliantly analyzed the structural analogies among these three eschatological wars. It may thus be concluded that the myth of the end of the world was known by the Indo-Europeans. The divergences are certainly marked, but they can be explained by the different orientations characteristic of the three Indo-European religions. It is true that the eschatological myth is not documented in the Vedic period, but this does not prove that it did not exist.[2] As Dumézil expresses it (*Mythe et épopée,* vol. 1, pp. 218 ff.), the *Mahābhārata* is the "epic transposition of an eschatological crisis," of what Hindu mythology calls the end of a *yuga*. Now the *Mahābhārata* contains certain Vedic, or even pre-Vedic, ele-

2. "The thought of the Vedic singers is concentrated on the present, on present services of the gods, which their past mythical exploits guarantee; the distant future does not interest them" (Dumézil, *Mythe et épopée,* vol. 1, p. 221).

ments.[3] So it is permissible to put the myth of the end of an age among these archaic Āryan traditions, and the more so because it was known by the Iranians.

But we must immediately add that the poem represents a grandiose synthesis, decidedly richer than the Indo-European eschatological tradition that it continues. In describing the annihilation of the limitless human masses and the telluric catastrophes that follow, the *Mahābhārata* borrows the flamboyant language of the Purāṇas. More important are the theological developments and innovations. The "messianic" idea of the *avatāra* is set forth forcefully and rigorously. In the famous theophany of the *Bhagavad Gītā* (11. 12 ff.) Kṛṣṇa reveals himself to Arjuna as an incarnation of Viṣṇu. As has been observed,[4] this theophany also constitutes a *pralaya,* which in some way anticipates the "end of the world" described in the last books of the epic. Now the revelation of (Kṛṣṇa-)Viṣṇu as lord of the *pralaya* is pregnant with theological and metaphysical consequences. Indeed, behind the dramatic events that make up the plot of the *Mahābhārata,* it is possible to decipher the opposition and complementarity of Viṣṇu(-Kṛṣṇa) and Śiva. The latter's "destructive" function is counterbalanced by the "creative" role of Viṣṇu(-Kṛṣṇa). When one of these gods—or one of their representatives—is present in an action, the other is absent. But Viṣṇu(-Kṛṣṇa) is also the author of "destructions" and "resurrections." In addition, the epic and the Purāṇas emphasize this god's negative aspect.[5]

3. Stig Wikander has observed that the fathers of the five Pāṇḍavas—Dharma, Vāyu, Indra, and the Twins—correspond to the trifunctional list of the Vedic gods: Mitra-Varuṇa (= Dharma), Indra (= Vāyu and Indra), and the Aśvins. This list does not reflect the religious situation at the time when the poem was finished (a period dominated by Viṣṇu and Śiva), nor that of Vedic days, when Soma and Agni played important parts. It follows that the *Mahābhārata* presents a para-Vedic and pre-Vedic state of things (see Dumézil, *Mythe et épopée,* vol. 1, pp. 42 ff.).

4. See M. Biardeau, "Etudes de mythologie hindoue" (1971), p. 54.

5. In the Purāṇas, Viṣṇu is often described as savage, dangerous, irresponsible, "mad"; in contrast, Śiva is more than once presented as he who is able to pacify him. See the texts cited by David Kinsley, "Through the Looking Glass," pp. 276 ff.

This is as much as to say that Viṣṇu, as supreme being, is the ultimate reality; hence he governs both the creation and the destruction of worlds. He is beyond good and evil, like all the gods. For "virtue and sin exist, O King, only among men" (12. 238. 28). Among yogins and contemplatives the idea had been familiar from the time of the Upanishads, but the *Mahābhārata*—particularly, the *Bhagavad Gītā*—makes it accessible, and therefore popular, on all levels of Indian society. While glorifying Viṣṇu as the Supreme Being, the poem emphasizes the complementarity of Śiva and Viṣṇu.[6] From this point of view, the *Mahābhārata* can be considered the cornerstone of Hinduism. Indeed, these two gods, together with the Great Goddess (Śakti, Kālī, Durgā), have dominated Hinduism from the first centuries of our era to the present.

The complementarity Śiva-Viṣṇu in a way corresponds to the complementarity of antagonistic functions that is characteristic of the great gods (creativity/destruction, etc.). Understanding this structure of divinity is equivalent to a revelation and also constitutes the model to follow in obtaining deliverance. Indeed, the *Mahābhārata* describes and glorifies, on the one hand, the struggle between good and evil, *dharma* and *adharma,* a struggle that acquires the weight of a universal norm, for it governs cosmic life, society, and personal existence; on the other hand, however, the poem is a reminder that the ultimate reality—the *brahman-ātman* of the Upanishads—is beyond the pair *dharma/adharma* and every other pair of contraries. In other words, deliverance involves comprehension of the relations between the two "modes" of the real: *immediate*—that is, historically conditioned—reality and *ultimate* reality. Upanishadic monism had denied the validity of immediate reality. The *Mahābhārata,* especially in its didactic sections, proposes a broader doctrine: on the one hand, Upanishadic monism, colored by theistic (Vaiṣṇava) experiences, is reaffirmed; on the other hand, there is acceptance of any soteriological solution that is not explicitly contrary to the scriptural tradition.

6. For the different aspects of this complementarity, see J. Gonda, *Viṣṇuism and Śivaism,* pp. 87 ff.

193. Kṛṣṇa's revelation

At first sight it may appear paradoxical that the literary work that depicts a frightful war of extermination and the end of a *yuga* is at the same time the exemplary model for every spiritual synthesis accomplished by Hinduism. The tendency to reconcile contraries is characteristic of Indian thought from the period of the Brāhmaṇas, but it is in the *Mahābhārata* that we see the importance of its results. Essentially, we can say that the poem[7] (1) teaches the equivalence of Vedānta (i.e., the doctrine of the Upanishads), Sāṃkhya, and Yoga; (2) establishes the equality of the three "ways" (*mārgas*), represented by ritual activity, metaphysical knowledge, and Yoga practice; (3) makes every effort to justify a certain mode of existing in time, in other words, assumes and valorizes the historicity of the human condition; and (4) proclaims the superiority of a fourth soteriological "way": devotion to Viṣṇu(-Kṛṣṇa).

The poem presents Sāṃkhya and Yoga in their presystematic stages. The former means "true knowledge" (*tattva-jñāna*) or "knowledge of the Self" (*ātman-bodha*); in this respect, Sāṃkhya carries on Upanishadic speculation. Yoga designates any activity that leads the Self to *brahman* at the same time that it confers countless "powers." Most often, this activity is equivalent to asceticism. The term *yoga* sometimes means "method," sometimes "force" or "meditation."[8] The two *darśanas* are regarded as equivalent. According to the *Bhagavad Gītā*, "only narrow minds oppose Sāṃkhya and Yoga, but not the wise (*paṇḍitas*). He who is truly master of the one is assured of the fruit of both. . . . Sāṃkhya and Yoga are but one" (5. 4–5).

It is also in the *Bhagavad Gītā* that the homology of the three soteriological "ways" is strictly demonstrated. This celebrated episode begins with Arjuna's "existential crisis" and ends with an exemplary revelation concerning the human condition and the "ways" of deliverance. Seeing him depressed by the war, in which he will have to kill friends and his own cousins, Kṛṣṇa reveals to Arjuna the means of doing his duty as a *kṣatriya*

7. Especially in the "pseudo-epic" and didactic sections (books 12, 13, etc.).

8. This variety of meanings corresponds to a real morphological diversity; see Eliade, *Yoga: Immortality and Freedom*, pp. 143 ff.

without letting himself be bound by *karma*. Generally speaking, Kṛṣṇa's revelations concern (1) the structure of the universe, (2) the modalities of Being, and (3) the ways to obtain final deliverance. But Kṛṣṇa takes care to add that the "ancient Yoga" (4. 3), which is the "supreme secret," is not an innovation; he had already taught it to Vivasvant, who revealed it to Manu, and Manu transmitted it to Ikṣvāku (4. 1). "It is by this tradition that the *ṛṣi*-kings knew it; but, with time, this Yoga disappeared here below" (4. 2). Every time that order (*dharma*) is shaken, Kṛṣṇa manifests himself (4. 7), that is, he reveals, in a manner suited to the given "historical moment," this timeless wisdom. (This is the doctrine of the *avatāra*.) In other words, if the *Bhagavad Gītā* appears historically as a new spiritual synthesis, it seems "new" only to the eyes of beings who, like ourselves, are conditioned by time and history.[9]

It could be said that the essence of the doctrine revealed by Kṛṣṇa lies in this brief admonition: Believe me and imitate me! For all that he reveals concerning his own being and concerning his "behavior" in the cosmos and in history is to serve as exemplary model for Arjuna: Arjuna finds the meaning of his historical life and, in conjunction with it, obtains deliverance by understanding what Kṛṣṇa *is* and what he *does*. Moreover, Kṛṣṇa himself insists on the exemplary and soteriological value of the divine model: "whatever the Chief does, other men imitate: the rule he follows, the world obeys" (3. 21). And he adds, referring to himself: "In the three worlds, there is nothing that I am obliged to do . . . yet I remain in action" (3. 23). Kṛṣṇa hastens to reveal the deep meaning of this activity: "If I were not always tirelessly in action, everywhere, men would follow my example. The

9. This is not without its bearing on all Western interpretations of Indian spirituality; for, if we have the right to reconstruct the history of Indian doctrines and techniques and to attempt to define their innovations, their developments, and their successive modifications, we must not forget that, from the Indian point of view, the historical context of a "revelation" has only a limited bearing: the "appearance" or "disappearance" of a soteriological formula on the plane of history can teach us nothing concerning its "origin." According to Indian tradition, so strongly reaffirmed by Kṛṣṇa, the various "historical moments"—which are at the same time moments of cosmic becoming—do not *create* doctrine but merely bring to birth *appropriate formulas* for the timeless message. See Eliade, *Yoga*, pp. 155 ff.

worlds would cease to exist if I did not perform my work; I should be the cause of universal confusion and the end of creatures'' (3. 23–24 [after the translation by E. Sénart]).

Consequently, Arjuna must imitate Kṛṣṇa's behavior: that is, in the first place, to continue acting, so that his passivity shall not contribute to ''universal confusion.'' But in order for him to act ''as Kṛṣṇa does,'' he must understand both the essence of divinity and its modes of manifestation. This is why Kṛṣṇa *reveals himself:* by knowing God, man at the same time knows the model to imitate. Now Kṛṣṇa begins by revealing that Being and nonbeing reside in him and that the whole of creation—from the gods to minerals—descends from him (7. 4–6; 9. 4–5; etc.). He continually creates the world by means of his *prakṛti,* but this ceaseless activity does not bind him: *he is only the spectator of his own creation* (9. 8–10). Now it is precisely this (seemingly paradoxical) valorization of activity (of *karman*) that is the chief lesson revealed by Kṛṣṇa: in imitation of God, who creates and sustains the world *without participating in it,* man will learn to do likewise. ''It is not enough to abstain from action in order to free oneself from the act; inaction alone does not lead to perfection,'' for ''everyone is condemned to action'' (3. 4–5). Even if he abstains from acting in the strict sense of the word, a whole unconscious activity, caused by the *guṇas* (3. 5), continues to chain him and integrate him into the karmic circuit. (The *guṇas* are the three modes of being which impregnate the whole universe and establish an organic sympathy between man and the cosmos.)

Condemned to action—for ''action is superior to inaction'' (3. 8)—man must perform the prescribed acts—in other words, the ''duties,'' the acts that fall to him because of his particular situation. ''It is better to perform, even if imperfectly, one's own duty (*svadharma*) than to perform, even perfectly, the duty of a different condition (*paradharma*)'' (3. 35). These specific activities are conditioned by the *guṇas* (17. 8 ff.; 18. 23 ff.). Kṛṣṇa repeats on several occasions that the *guṇas* proceed from him but do not bind him: ''not that I am in them; it is they that are in me'' (7. 12). The lesson to be drawn from this is the following: while accepting the ''historical situation'' created by the *guṇas* (and one must accept it, for the *guṇas,* too, derive from Kṛṣṇa) and acting in accordance with the necessities of that "situation," man must refuse to *valorize* his acts and, in consequence, to attribute an *absolute value* to his own condition.

194. "Renouncing the fruits of one's acts"

In this sense it can be said that the *Bhagavad Gītā* attempts to "save" all human acts, to "justify" every profane action; for, by the mere fact that he no longer enjoys their "fruits," *man transforms his acts into sacrifices,* that is, into transpersonal dynamisms that contribute to the maintenance of the cosmic order. Now, as Kṛṣṇa declares, only acts whose object is sacrifice do not bind (3. 9). Prajāpati created sacrifice so that the cosmos could manifest itself and human beings could live and propagate (3. 10 ff.). But Kṛṣṇa reveals that man, too, can collaborate in the perfection of the divine work, not only by sacrifices properly speaking (those that make up the Vedic cult) but by *all his acts,* whatever their nature. When the various ascetics and yogins "sacrifice" their psychophysiological activities, they detach themselves from these activities, they give them a transpersonal value (4. 25 ff.), and, in so doing, they "all have the true idea of sacrifice and, by sacrifice, wipe out their impurities" (4. 30).

This transmutation of profane activities into rituals is made possible by Yoga. Kṛṣṇa reveals to Arjuna that the "man of action"[10] can save himself (in other words, escape the consequences of his taking part in the life of the world) *and yet continue to act*. The only thing that he must do is this: *he must detach himself from his acts and from their results,* in other words, "renounce the fruits of his acts" (*phalatṛṣṇavairāgya*); he must *act impersonally,* without passion, without desire, as if he were acting by proxy, in another's stead. If he strictly obeys this rule, his actions will not sow the seeds of new karmic potentialities or any longer enslave him to the karmic circuit. "Indifferent to the fruit of action, always satisfied, free from all ties, no matter how active he may be, in reality he does not act" (4. 20).

10. The "man of action" is he who cannot retire from civil life in order to gain his salvation through knowledge, asceticism, or mystical devotion.

The great originality of the *Bhagavad Gītā* is its having insisted on this "Yoga of action," which one realizes by "renouncing the fruits of one's acts." This is also the principal reason for its unprecedented success in India. For henceforth every man is allowed to hope for deliverance, by virtue of *phalatṛṣṇavairāgya,* even when, for reasons of very different kinds, he is obliged to continue to take part in social life, to have a family, to be concerned, to hold a position, even to do "immoral" things (like Arjuna, who must kill his enemies in war). To act placidly, without being moved by "desire for the fruit," is to obtain a self-mastery and a serenity that, undoubtedly, Yoga alone is able to confer. As Kṛṣṇa teaches: "While acting without restriction, one remains faithful to Yoga." This interpretation of the Yoga technique is characteristic of the grandiose synthetic effort of the *Bhagavad Gītā,* which sought to reconcile all vocations: whether ascetic, mystic, or devoted to activity in the world.

In addition to the Yoga that is accessible to everyone and consists in renouncing the "fruits of one's acts," the *Bhagavad Gītā* briefly expounds a yogic technique properly speaking, which is restricted to contemplatives (6. 11 ff.). Kṛṣṇa decrees that "Yoga is superior to asceticism (*tapas*), even superior to knowledge (*jñāna*), superior to sacrifice" (6. 46). But yogic meditation does not attain its ultimate end unless the disciple concentrates on God: "With soul serene and fearless . . . , mind firm and ceaselessly thinking of Me, he must practice Yoga taking Me as his supreme end" (6. 14). "He who sees Me everywhere and sees all things in Me, him I never abandon, and he never abandons Me. He who, having established himself in unity, worships Me, who dwell in all beings, that yogin dwells in Me, *whatever be his way of life*" (6. 30–31; our italics).

This is at once the triumph of Yoga practices and the raising of mystical devotion (*bhakti*) to the rank of supreme "way." In addition, the *Bhagavad Gītā* marks the appearance of the concept of grace, foretelling the luxuriant development that it will attain in medieval Vaiṣṇava literature. But the decisive part that the *Bhagavad Gītā* played in the expansion of theism does not exhaust its importance. That incomparable work, keystone of Indian spirituality, can be valorized in many and various contexts. By the fact that it puts the emphasis on the historicity of man, the solution that the *Gītā* offers is certainly the most comprehensive one and, it is important to add, the one best suited to modern India, already integrated into the "circuit of history." For, translated into terms familiar to Westerners, the problem faced in the *Gītā* is as follows: how is it possible to resolve the paradoxical situation created by the twofold fact that man, on the one hand, finds himself existing in time, *condemned to history,* and, on the other hand, knows that he will be "damned" if he allows himself to be exhausted by temporality and by his own historicity and that, consequently, he must at all costs find *in the world* a way that leads into a transhistorical and atemporal plane?

We have seen the solution offered by Kṛṣṇa: doing one's duty (*svadharma*) in the world but doing so without letting oneself be prompted by desire for the fruits of one's actions (*phalatṛṣṇavairāgya*). Since the whole universe is the creation, or even the epiphany, of Kṛṣṇa(-Viṣṇu), to live in the world, to participate in its structures, does not constitute an "evil act." The "evil act" is to believe that the world and time and history possess an independent reality of their own, that is, to believe that *nothing else exists* outside of the world and temporality. The idea is certainly pan-Indian, but it is in the *Bhagavad Gītā* that it received its most consistent expression.

195. "Separation" and "totalization"

To realize the importance of the part played by the *Bhagavad Gītā* in the religious history of India, we must remember the solutions offered by Sāṃkhya, by Yoga, and by Buddhism. According to these schools, deliverance demanded, as a *sine qua non,* detachment from the world or even the negation of human life as a mode of existing in history.[11] The discovery of "universal

11. To be sure, the "classical" stage of the Sāṃkhya and Yoga *darśanas* is several centuries later than the composition of the *Bhagavad Gītā*. But their characteristic tendencies—especially the methods they elaborated for separating the spirit from psychomental experience—are already documented in the period of the Upanishads.

suffering'' and the infinite cycle of reincarnations[12] had oriented the search for salvation in a particular direction: deliverance *must* involve *refusal* to yield to the impulses of life and to the social norms. Withdrawal into solitude and ascetic practices constituted the indispensable preliminaries. On the other hand, salvation by gnosis was compared to an ''awakening,'' a ''freeing from bonds,'' the ''removal of a blindfold that covered the eyes,'' etc. (see §136). In short, salvation presupposed a break, a dislocation from the world, which was a place of suffering, a prison crowded with slaves.

The religious devalorization of the world was made easier by the disappearance of the creator god. For Sāṃkhya-Yoga, the universe came into being by virtue of the ''teleological instinct'' of the primordial substance (*prakṛti*). For the Buddha, the problem does not even arise; in any case, Buddha denies the existence of God. The religious devalorization of the world is accompanied by a glorification of the spirit or the Self (*ātman, puruṣa*). For Buddha himself, though he rejects the *ātman* as autonomous and irreducible monad, deliverance is obtained by virtue of an effort that is ''spiritual'' in nature.

The progressive hardening of the dualism spirit/matter is reminiscent of the development of religious dualism, ending in the Iranian formula of two contrary principles, representing good and evil. As we have observed more than once, for a long time the opposition good/evil was but one of many examples of dyads and polarities—cosmic, social, and religious—that insured the rhythmical alternation of life and the world. In short, what was isolated in the two antagonistic principles, good and evil, was in the beginning only *one* among the many formulas by means of which the antithetical but complementary aspects of reality were expressed: day/night, male/female, life/death, fecundity/sterility, health/sickness, etc.[13] In other words, good and evil formed part of the same cosmic (and therefore human) rhythm that Chinese thought formulated in the alternation of the two principles *yang* and *yin* (§130).

12. It must be borne in mind that the fatality of transmigration made suicide unavailing.

13. See Eliade, *The Quest: History and Meaning in Religion,* pp. 232 ff.

The devalorization of the cosmos and life, adumbrated in the Upanishads, finds its most rigorous expressions in the "dualistic" ontologies and the methods of separation elaborated by Sāṃkhya-Yoga and Buddhism. The hardening process characteristic of these stages of Indian religious thought can be compared with the hardening of Iranian dualism from Zarathustra to Manichaeanism. Zarathustra likewise considered the world a mixture of the spiritual and material. The believer, by correctly performing the sacrifice, separated his celestial essence (*mēnōk*) from its material manifestation (*gētik*).[14] For Zarathustra and for Mazdaism, however, the universe was the work of Ahura Mazdā; the world was corrupted only later, by Ahriman. But Manichaeanism and a number of Gnostic sects on the contrary attributed the Creation to the demonic powers. The world, life, and man himself are the product of a series of sinister or criminal dramatic activities. In the last analysis, this vain and monstrous creation is doomed to annihilation. Deliverance is the result of a long and difficult effort to separate spirit from matter, light from the darkening that holds it captive.

To be sure, the various Indian methods and techniques of seeking deliverance of the spirit by a series of more and more radical "separations" continued to have proselytes long after the appearance of the *Bhagavad Gītā*. For refusal of life—and especially of existence conditioned by sociopolitical structures and by history—had, after the Upanishads, become a highly regarded soteriological solution. Nevertheless, the *Gītā* had succeeded in integrating into a daring synthesis all the Indian religious orientations, hence also the ascetic practices involving abandoning the community and social obligations. But above all the *Gītā* had effected the resacralization of the cosmos, of universal life, and even of man's *historical existence*. As we have just seen, Viṣṇu-Kṛṣṇa is not only the creator and lord of the world, he resanctifies the whole of nature by his presence.

On the other hand, it is still Viṣṇu who periodically destroys the universe at the end of each cosmic cycle. In other words, *all* is created and governed by God. In consequence, the "neg-

14. See §104. We follow G. Gnoli's interpretations; see Eliade, "Spirit, Light, and Seed," pp. 18 ff.

ative aspects'' of cosmic life, of individual existence, and of history receive a religious meaning. Man is no longer the hostage of a cosmos-prison that created itself, since the world is the work of a personal and omnipotent God. What is more: he is a God who did not abandon the world after its creation but continues to be present in it and active on all planes, from the material structures of the cosmos to the consciousness of man. Cosmic calamities and historical catastrophes, even the periodical destruction of the universe, are governed by Viṣṇu-Kṛṣṇa; *hence they are theophanies*. This brings the God of the *Bhagavad Gītā* close to Yahweh, creator of the world and lord of history, as the prophets understood him (see §121). In any case, it is not without interest to point out that, just as the revelation advocated by the *Gītā* took place during a horrible war of extermination, the prophets preached under the ''terror of history,'' under the threat of the imminent disappearance of the Jewish people.

The tendency to totalization of the real that is characteristic of Indian thought finds in the *Bhagavad Gītā* one of its most convincing expressions. Accomplished under the sign of a personal God, this totalization confers a religious value even on undeniable manifestations of ''evil'' and ''misfortune,'' such as war, treachery, and murder.[15] But it is above all the resacralization of life and of human existence that had important consequences in the religious history of India. In the first centuries of our era, Tantrism will similarly attempt to transmute the organic functions (alimentation, sexuality, etc.) into sacraments. However, this type of sacralization of the body and life will be obtained by an extremely complex and difficult yogic technique; in fact, Tantric initiation will be restricted to an elite. But the message of the *Bhagavad Gītā* was addressed to all categories of men and encouraged all religious vocations. This was the privilege of devotion paid to a God who was at once personal and impersonal, creative and destructive, incarnate and transcendent.

15. From a certain point of view, it could be said that the *Bhagavad Gītā* recovers the archaic conception of total reality imagined as the alternation of opposing but complementary principles.

25 The Ordeals of Judaism: From Apocalypse to Exaltation of the Torah

196. The beginnings of eschatology

Chapters 40 to 55 of the Book of Isaiah make up a separate work, known as Deutero-Isaiah ("Second Isaiah"). The text was composed during the last years of the Babylonian Exile by an unknown author, who was probably executed after a trial (see Is. 52:13–53:12). Its message is in strong contrast to the other prophecies, first of all by its optimism but also by a daring interpretation of contemporary history: the Great King, Cyrus, Yahweh's instrument (41:42), is preparing the destruction of Babylon; those who believe in the superiority of the Babylonian gods will be quickly confounded, for those gods are idols, inert and powerless (40:19 ff.; 44:12–20; etc.); Yahweh alone is God: "I am the first and the last; there is no other God besides me" (44:6; see also 45:18–21); "I am God unrivaled / God who has no like" (46:9).

We have here the most radical affirmation of a systematic monotheism, since even the existence of other gods is denied. "Did you not split Rahab in two, and pierce the Dragon through? Did you not dry up the sea, the waters of the great Abyss, to make the seabed a road for the redeemed to cross?" (59:9–10). The creation as well as history, and consequently both the Exile and the Liberation, are Yahweh's work. The liberation of the deportees is interpreted as a new Exodus. But this time it is a triumphant return: "I am making a road in the wilderness, paths in the wild" (43:19). "Mountains and hills will break into joyful cries before you. . . . Cypress will grow instead of thorns, myrtle instead of briars" (55:12–13; cf. 40:9–11; 54:11–14). The new Exodus will not be made in haste: "You are not to hurry away, you are not to leave like fugitives. No, Yahweh will go in front of you, and the God of Israel will be your rearguard'' (52:12). Other nations will be included in the redemption that is to come. ''Turn to me and be saved, all the ends of the earth, for I am God unrivaled'' (45:22; see 56:1–7 on the converts to Yahweh). However, Israel will always enjoy its privileged situation, that of dominant nation.

The fall of Jerusalem, the disappearance of the kingdom of Judah, and the Exile were in fact the divine judgments announced by the great prophets. Now that the punishment was completed, Yahweh would renew the Covenant, which this time would be eternal (55:3) and the redemption irrevocable (45:17; 51:6, 8). For ''with everlasting love I have taken pity on you, says Yahweh, your redeemer'' (54:8). Liberated by Yahweh, the deportees will return to Zion ''shouting for joy, everlasting joy in their faces; joy and gladness go with them, sorrow and lament are ended'' (51:11).

The enthusiasm, the exaltation, the beatific visions inspired by the certainty of imminent salvation are unparalleled in the earlier literature. Hosea, Jeremiah, and Ezekiel proclaimed their faith in the redemption of Israel. But the author of Deutero-Isaiah is the first prophet who works out an eschatology. In fact, he announces the dawn of a new age. Between the two periods—the one that had just ended and the new one that was to begin at any moment—there is a fundamental difference. The other prophets did not preach the end of a tragic era and the coming of another that would be perfect and happy; they preached the end of Israel's immoral behavior, its regeneration by a sincere return to God. In contrast, Second Isaiah presents the inauguration of the new age as a dramatic history comprising a series of prodigious acts determined by God: (1) the ruin of Babylon by Yahweh (43:14–15; etc.), by his instrument Cyrus (41:24; etc.) or by Israel (41:14–16); (2) the redemption of Israel, that is, the liberation of the exiles (49:25–26), the crossing of the wilderness (55:12–13), the arrival in Jerusalem (40:9–11), and the gathering-together of all who were scattered through the world (41:8–9); (3) Yahweh's return to Zion (40:9–11); (4) the transformation of the land by rebuilding (44:26), by the increase of the community

(44:1–5), and even by changes little short of reconstituting an Eden (51:3); (5) the conversion of the nations to Yahweh and the repudiation of their gods (51:4–5).[1] This eschatological scenario will be returned to and developed by the later prophets (§197). But none of them will be able to equal the visionary power and spiritual depth of Second Isaiah.

Four poems, called "Songs of the Servant" (42:1–4; 49:1–6; 50:40; 52:13; 53:12), are an original and dramatic expression of the sufferings of the Jewish people. Their interpretation has given rise to countless controversies. Very probably the "Servant of Yahweh" (*ebhed yahveh*) personifies the elite of the Jewish exiles. His torments are regarded as an expiation for the sins of the whole people. The Servant of Yahweh had accepted every tribulation: "I offered my back to those who struck me. . . . I did not cover my face against insults and spittle" (50:6). The ordeal of the deportation is a sacrifice by virtue of which Israel's sins were wiped out. "Ours were the sufferings he bore, ours the sorrows he carried. . . . He was pierced through for our faults, crushed for our sins. On him lies a punishment that brings us peace, and through his wounds we are healed" (53:5).

Christian exegesis saw in the Servant of Yahweh an anticipation of the Messiah. A number of passages encouraged this interpretation. For "Yahweh burdened him with the sins of all of us. . . . Like a lamb that is led to the slaughterhouse . . . for our faults [he was] struck down in death" (53:6–8). Voluntary victim, the Servant was "taken for a sinner, while he was bearing the faults of many and praying all the time for sinners" (53:12). But "his soul's anguish over, he shall see the light and be content . . . , [and] he shall divide the spoil with the mighty" (53:11–12). Even more: Yahweh will make his Servant "the light of the nations so that my salvation may reach to the ends of the earth" (49:6).

These texts take their place among the high points of Hebrew religious thought. The proclamation of universal salvation through the ordeals of the Servant of Yahweh announces Christianity.

1. See Fohrer, *History of Israelite Religion*, pp. 328 ff.

197. Haggai and Zechariah, eschatological prophets

As soon as they returned (ca. 538), the deportees were faced, among other urgent problems, with rebuilding the Temple. The new sanctuary no longer belonged to the dynasty but to the people, who had undertaken to defray the expenses. The cornerstone was laid in ca. 537; however, work was stopped soon afterward. It was not until ca. 520, following a political change, that construction was resumed. The crisis that was shaking the Persian Empire brought a new wave of eschatological exaltation. Zerubbabel, who had just been appointed high commissioner, and the High Priest Joshua, supported by the prophets Haggai and Zechariah, concentrated their efforts on rebuilding the sanctuary. In ca. 515 the Temple was consecrated, but Zerubbabel, considered untrustworthy by the Persian regime, had already left.

For the enthusiasts, intoxicated by the recent prophecies, this was the beginning of a new series of disappointments. Since the divine judgment was now accomplished, when, they asked, would the eschatological age announced by Second Isaiah appear? For Haggai, the new age had begun at the moment when Zerubbabel laid the cornerstone (2:15–19). And he announced that the day that the work was ended would see an earthquake, the fall of the "kings of the nations," the annihilation of their armies, and the installation of Zerubbabel as messianic king (2:20–23).[2] However, when the Temple was finally consecrated, why, it was asked, did the *eschaton* still not arrive? One of the most plausible answers explained the delay by the corruption of the community. But, as happened many times in history, the postponement of the universal transfiguration predicted by Second Isaiah altered the concept of salvation, and the eschatological hope was gradually extinguished.

We shall evaluate, further on, the consequences of this state of confusion for the later history of Israel. However, the importance of eschatological prophecy must not be underestimated. Haggai and Zechariah insist on the radical difference between the two ages, the old and the new. For Zechariah, the former

2. Similar ideas occur in Zechariah (8:9–13; etc.).

was characterized by Yahweh's will to destroy, the latter by his desire to save (1:1–6; 8:14–15). First there will be the destruction of the peoples responsible for Israel's tragedy (1:15), followed by a very great "prosperity" dispensed by Yahweh (1:17; 2:5–9; etc.). God will banish the sinners from Judah (5:1–4), drive iniquities from the land (5:5–11), and gather the exiles together. Finally the reign of the Messiah will be inaugurated in Jerusalem, and the nations will come "to seek Yahweh Sabaoth in Jerusalem and to entreat the favor of Yahweh" (8:20–22; cf. 2:15).

Similar prophecies occur in the text known as the "Apocalypse of Israel" (Isaiah, chap. 24–27).[3] The same themes will be treated again in the fourth century by Deutero-Zechariah (9:11–17; 10:3–12) and by the prophet Joel.[4] The eschatological scenario contains all or some of the following motifs: annihilation of the nations, deliverance of Israel, gathering of the exiles in Jerusalem, paradisal transfiguration of the country, establishing divine sovereignty or a messianic reign, final conversion of the nations. In these images of an Eden we can see the eschatological modification of the pre-Exilic "optimistic prophets."[5]

From Deutero-Isaiah onward, the dawn of the *eschaton* was held to be imminent (see Is. 56:1–2; 61:2). Sometimes the prophet makes bold to remind Yahweh that he is late in restoring Jerusalem (Is. 62:7). However, he knows that the fault lies with the sinners, for "your iniquities have made a gulf between you and your God" (59:2).[6] For Second Isaiah, as for the post-Exilic prophets, the inauguration of the new age will be preceded by great historical upheavals (the fall of Babylon, the nations' attack on Jerusalem, followed by their destruction).

3. God will judge all of Israel's enemies, their capitals will be ruined, yet the survivors will share in the messianic festival in Yahweh's presence on Mount Zion (24:21–25:12).

4. After the eschatological battle against the nations that have been guilty toward Yahweh and Israel, a paradisal period of wealth and peace will begin (Joel 4:2–3, 12; 4:18–21). ("Deutero-Zechariah" is composed of chapters 9–14 of the Book of Zechariah.)

5. Fohrer, *History of Israelite Religion*, p. 340.

6. The prophet Malachai (fifth century) refuses to specify the date of the "day of Yahweh." The essential thing is to prepare oneself inwardly, for "the day of his coming" may arrive at any time (3:2).

The extension of the eschatological redemption to other peoples is fraught with consequences for the later development of the religion of Israel. In Deutero-Isaiah (Is. 51:4–6), Yahweh, addressing all the nations, speaks of his "salvation," which will "come like the light." "That day, man will look to his creator and his eyes will turn to the Holy One of Israel" (17:7). Universal redemption is still more clearly proclaimed by Zephaniah (3:9): "Yes, I will then give the peoples lips that are clean, so that they may invoke the name of Yahweh and serve him under the same yoke." However, salvation is most often promised to all, but it will be accessible only at Jerusalem, the religious and national center of Israel (Is. 2:2–4; 25:6 ff.; 56:7; Jer. 3:17; Zech. 8:20 ff.).

Side by side with such prophecies, which concern only the historical world, there are other predictions more archaic in type (cf. §12) that concern the cosmos in its totality. Haggai (2:6) announces that Yahweh will "shake the heavens and the earth, the sea and the dry land." The Last Judgment will be accompanied by cosmic catastrophes that will destroy the world (Is. 34:4; 51:6). But Yahweh will create "new heavens and a new earth, and the past will not be remembered" (Is. 65:17). The new creation will be indestructible (66:22), and Yahweh will be an "everlasting light" (60:20). Even Jerusalem will be renewed (Zech. 2:5–9) and will be called "by a new name, one which the mouth of Yahweh will confer" (Is. 62:2). As in so many other eschatological scenarios, the renewal of Creation will include certain "paradisal" elements: countless riches, unequaled fertility, disappearance of sicknesses, long life, eternal peace between men and animals, elimination of impurities, etc. But the pivot of the universe, restored to its first perfection, will be Jerusalem, true "center of the world."

198. Expectation of the messianic king

According to the eschatological prophecies, the renewed world will be ruled over by Yahweh[7] or by a king whom God will

7. Is. 24:23; 33:22; 43:15; 44:6; "Then will Yahweh reign over them on the mountain of Zion" (Micah 4:7; cf. 2:13); Zechariah 9:1–8; etc.

designate and who will govern in his name. This king, usually called the "Anointed" (*masiah*), was supposed to descend from David. Isaiah speaks of a "child," a "son . . . for the throne of David" (9:1–6), of a "shoot . . . from the stock of Jesse" (11:1), who will reign with justice in a paradisal world in which "the wolf lives with the lamb, the panther lies down with the kid, calf and lion cub feed together with a little boy to lead them" (11:6). Zechariah divides the messianic dignity between the temporal authority and the spiritual power, Zerubbabel and the High Priest Joshua (4:1–6; 10:6–14). In another prediction he describes the messianic king entering Jerusalem, "victorious, . . . triumphant, humble and riding on a donkey" (9:9–10).

It is important to make it clear that the formula the "Anointed of Yahweh" was originally applied to the reigning king. Hence the eschatological personage was compared to a king. Later the term "anointed" was applied to priests, prophets, and patriarchs.[8] To be "anointed" by Yahweh indicated a more intimate relation with God. But in the Old Testament the eschatological Messiah is not a supernatural being, descended from heaven to save the world. The *redemption* is *exclusively the work of Yahweh*. The Messiah is a mortal, an offspring of the line of David, who will sit on the throne of David and reign with justice. Some historians have concluded that the messianic expectation arose in circles animated by eschatological enthusiasm yet at the same time faithful to the Davidic monarchy. But these groups represented no more than a minority, and that is why the messianic expectation had no significant influence.[9] Yet the problem is more complex. The originality of Hebrew religious thought is beyond doubt, but the royal ideology that it had elaborated included analogies with the "redeeming" role of the king in the great Oriental monarchies.[10]

The eschatological prophecies have been contrasted with the message of the great pre-Exilic prophets. For these later prophets did not hope for a radical transformation of man and a new quality of existence but rather for a new age and therefore the

8. See S. Mowinckel, *He That Cometh*, pp. 56 ff.

9. See Fohrer, *History of Israelite Religion*, p. 350.

10. See, inter alia, G. Widengren, *Sakrales Königtum*, pp. 30 ff.; Mowinckel, *He That Cometh*, 280 ff. and passim; and Ringgren, "König und Messias."

creation of a new world; man would be transformed indirectly, and in a way automatically, by this miracle, performed by Yahweh. As a result, the eschatological prophecies contained a misunderstanding of the message of the great prophets and an optimistic illusion concerning God's will to save Israel.[11] Yet it must be observed that the hope of a cosmic renovation, involving man's restoration to his original integrity, is a central conception of archaic religiosity, especially that of the paleo-cultivators (see §§12 ff.). Every eschatology returns to, continues, and revalorizes the idea that the Creation, supremely the divine work, is alone capable of renewing and sanctifying human existence. To be sure, the eschatological expectation after the Exile came out of a different religious experience from that of the great prophets, but it was not less significant. In the last analysis, it was a matter of renouncing any hope of a spiritual perfection that could be realized by personal efforts, and of strengthening faith in the omnipotence of God and in his promises of salvation.

It is true that the delay in the arrival of the *eschaton* ended by reinforcing the authority of the opposing legalistic and ritualistic orientations. But the eschatological hopes never finally disappeared (see § 203).

199. The progress of legalism

During the two centuries of peace under Persian suzerainty, the legalistic reform, begun before the Exile and continued during the Captivity, was definitively consolidated. At Babylon, circumcision was revalorized as the supreme symbol of membership in the people of Yahweh. Respect for the Sabbath became proof of fidelity to the Covenant (Is. 56:1–8; 58:13–14). The code of ritual prescriptions contained in Leviticus (chaps. 17–26) was given its definitive form during the Exile. Called the "Law of Holiness" and attributed to Moses, it regulated sacrifices of animals, sexual relations and prohibitions, the calendar of festivals, and the details of the cult, with insistence on ritual purity and impurity. Like the Brāhmaṇas (see § 76), the "Law of Holiness"

11. See Fohrer, p. 352.

ritualizes the functions of life and social behavior. Its purpose is to preserve the purity of Israel in order to prepare it for a new conquest of the land promised by Yahweh. The survival of the people will be possible only if its ethnic and spiritual identity is safeguarded in the midst of a foreign and impure world.

The reconstruction of the national life is no longer expected, as it was by the great prophets, to result from an inner conversion, brought about by the spirit, but from the effective organization of the community under the absolute authority of the Law (*torah*). In the cult, the glorification of God is subordinated to the "holiness" of Israel, that is, to its ritual purity, which is constantly threatened by sins. The public expiation of sins acquires a considerable importance, confirmed by the institution of the Great Pardon (*yom kippurim*). "The expiatory apparatus is so well set up that it scarcely leaves room to hope for a new and better order. There is not a trace of eschatology or of messianism in the sacerdotal narratives. For them, Israel possesses all the institutions necessary for its salvation, for its perpetuation through the centuries."[12] The priesthood was the only authority able to supervise the application of the Law. The hierocracy, which dominated religious life during the Persian period, had already built up its structures during the Exile.

About 430, Nehemiah, a Jew living at the court of Artaxerxes I, became governor of Judaea and obtained authorization to rebuild the walls of Jerusalem. He also undertook religious reforms (among other things, he insisted on the elimination of priests married to non-Israelitish women). Not much is known of the history of another religious leader, Esdras, who (probably during the latter years of the fifth century) continued Nehemiah's mission.[13] He too attributed prime importance to the ritual purity of Israel and prescribed the dissolution of mixed marriages. This was certainly no racial measure. The danger was religious, for intermarriages threatened the integrity of Yahwism. Nevertheless, Esdras' reform led to an ethnic segregation, and he con-

12. A. Caquot, "Le judaïsme depuis la captivité de Babylone," p. 143.

13. But according to Morton Smith (who accepts Kellermann's conclusions), it was Nehemiah who continued the reform begun by Esdras; see his *Palestinian Parties and Politics That Shaped the Old Testament*, pp. 120 ff. See also ibid., pp. 126 ff., his analysis of the work undertaken by Nehemiah.

solidated the legalism that thenceforth dominated the religion of Israel. According to tradition (Nehemiah, chap. 8), Esdras summoned an assembly "of men, women, and all who had reached the age of reason," to which he read "the book of the Law of Moses." It is impossible to determine if the Pentateuch is meant or only a portion of that work. But, from the time of this solemn reading, the religion of Israel "officially" possesses sacred scriptures.

The Law (*torah*) was very soon confused with the books of the Pentateuch. Oral transmission is replaced by the study and explication of written texts. Esdras was considered to be the first "scribe" or "doctor of the Law." The scribe became a veritable model of religious behavior. (See, further on, p. 261, the eulogy of the scribe by Ben Sirach.) But little by little a new idea develops—that of the oral Torah. It was held that, in addition to the written Law, Moses received supplementary instructions from God, which were transmitted orally from then on. This corpus of exegesis made up the Mishnah ("repetition"). Fundamentally, it was a way of legitimating what can already be called "esotericism," that is, an initiatory transmission of secret doctrines.[14] With time, the work of the "doctors" was invested with an authority approaching that of the Torah (see § 201).

For our purpose, it would be useless to refer to all the works that were elaborated, rehandled, or edited during the centuries that followed Esdras' reform. It was this period that saw the composition of the Book of Chronicles, a certain number of the Psalms and the prophetic writings,[15] and the rehandling of many earlier texts. It was also this period that saw an increase in the tension between two opposed religious tendencies, to which we may give the approximate designations "universalist" and "nationalist." The universalists continued the eschatological prophets' hope of some day seeing the "nations" worship Yahweh, recognized as the one God. The nationalists, on the other hand, proclaimed the exclusive character of the Revelation and con-

14. A similar exegesis justified the validity of the Mahāyāna doctrines and the Tantric techniques, as well as the Hermetic, apocalyptic, and Gnostic "revelations."

15. It should be noted that several historians date the Book of Job from the post-Exilic period.

centrated their efforts on the defense of Israel's ethnic integrity. In fact the conflict was more complex and more subtle.

200. The personification of divine Wisdom

The most important event, and one that will have considerable consequences for the history of Judaism, was its confrontation with Hellenism. As early as the Late Bronze Age the Greeks had continuing relations with Palestine. During the first millennium their influx steadily increased, and it continued even under the Persian domination.[16] But it was especially after Alexander's victories that the influence of Hellenistic culture attained formidable proportions. The Greek language, culture, and institutions (schools, gymnasia, etc.), spread everywhere, not only in the Diaspora but also in Palestine, which after Alexander's death (ca. 323) was governed by the Ptolemies, the sovereigns of Egypt.[17]

Just as for the Romans, history, especially after the prophets, was fraught with religious meanings. In other words, historical events, by transforming and modeling Israel's political destiny, were equally able to represent important moments in the history of salvation. For the Hebrews, national policy was not separate from religious activity, for ritual purity—and hence the preservation of Israel—was bound up with political autonomy. The growing influence of Hellenism made itself felt in Palestine in various political, religious, and cultural orientations. The aristocracy and certain sections of the bourgeoisie strove to introduce the ideas and institutions promoted by the Hellenistic *Aufklärung*. This "liberal" and cosmopolitan policy, which threatened the national identity itself, was rejected by other social categories, first of all by the conservative religious circles and by the rural population. The tension between these two

16. See Smith, *Palestinian Parties and Politics That Shaped the Old Testament*, pp. 58 ff., 228 ff.

17. E. Bickerman, *Der Gott der Makkabäer*, pp. 59 ff.; V. Tcherikover, *Hellenistic Civilization and the Jews*, pp. 90 ff.; Martin Hengel, *Judaism and Hellenism*, vol. 1, pp. 65 ff.

opposing tendencies will lead to the revolt of the Maccabees (§ 202).

The differing ideological and religious orientations that split the Jewish people, from the time of Alexander's conquest (ca. 332) until the transformation of Palestine into a Roman province (ca. 69), left their mark on a number of works composed in Jerusalem or in the Diaspora. But it is important to point out that the force of the *Zeitgeist* was such that traces of Hellenistic conceptions are found even in texts composed to criticize and reject them.

The personification of Wisdom (*hokmā*) belongs among the most original religious creations of this period. The first nine chapters of Proverbs (a book probably written in the middle of the third century B.C.) glorify the divine origin of Wisdom and enumerate her qualities. "Yahweh created me when his purpose first unfolded, before the oldest of his works. From everlasting I was firmly set, from the beginning, before earth came into being. The deep was not, when I was born" (8:22–24). Wisdom is "the inventor of lucidity of thought"; by her, "monarchs rule . . . , rulers govern, and the great impose justice on the world" (8:12 ff.). Certain authors have seen the influence of Greek philosophy in this conception, but Sophia (Gk. *sophia* = wisdom) as a divine and personified entity appears comparatively late; she is found especially in the Hermetic writings, in Plutarch, and among the Neo-Platonists.[18] Other scholars have adduced Semitic parallels earlier than Greek influences, especially the Elephantine "Wisdom of Ahikar."[19] The antecedents of *hokmā* have even been sought in the cult of the Mother Goddesses (Isis or Ashtarte); but Wisdom is not God's companion; engendered by the Lord, she emerged from his mouth.

Bousset and Gressmann have rightly emphasized the importance in Jewish religious thought of "intermediate beings" be-

18. Hengel, *Judaism and Hellenism*, vol. 1, p. 154, and vol. 2, p. 98, n. 298 (ancient sources and bibliography).

19. See the studies by W. A. Albright, C. I. K. Story, and H. Donner, analyzed by Hengel, ibid., vol. 1, pp. 154 ff.; vol. 2, p. 99.

tween man and God, especially in the Hellenistic period.[20] Certain schools of wisdom promoted *hokmā* to the rank of supreme authority, as mediatrix of the Revelation. But as we shall see in a moment, the various and contradictory interpretations and revalorizations of Wisdom reflect a crisis in depth that could radically have changed the profile of Judaism.

201. From despair to a new theodicy: The Qoheleth and Ecclesiasticus

Ecclesiastes (or the Qoheleth)[21] is generally regarded, with the Book of Job, as a moving testimony to the shock brought on by the collapse of the doctrine of retribution. Against the theology of the Wisdom literature, the author of the Qoheleth dwells on the inexplicability of God's acts. Not only does the same destiny await the fool and the wise man (2:15 ff.), man and beast ("one dies, the other too," 3:19), but "crime is where the law should be, the criminal where the good should be" (3:16). The author judges from his own experience: he has seen "the virtuous man perishing for all his virtue, for all his godlessness the godless living on" (7:15). Calm, almost detached, like a philosopher, he keeps returning to this theme: "the good, I mean, receive the treatment the wicked deserve" (8:14; cf. 9:2). In the last analysis, it is no longer possible to speak of God's "justice" (5:7; etc.). What is more, it is no longer possible to understand the significance of the Creation or the meaning of life: "no one can discover what the work is that goes on under the sun or explain why man should toil to seek yet never discover" (8:17). For no one can "comprehend the work of God from beginning to end" (3:11). God no longer lavishes either his anger or his mercy.

20. W. Bousset and H. Gressmann, *Die Religion des Judentums im späthellenistischen Zeitalter,* 3d ed., pp. 319, 342 ff.; cf. Hengel, *Judaism and Hellenism,* vol. 1, p. 155.

21. The meaning of the term Qoheleth is uncertain; it probably means "master of the assembly" or "the orator"; see Hengel, *Judaism and Hellenism,* vol. 1, p. 129.

Feelings of guilt and hopes of forgiveness are equally vain. God has withdrawn from men; he no longer cares what befalls them.

The celebrated refrain "Vanity and chasing of the wind" has its justification in the discovery of the precariousness and iniquity of human existence. The author congratulates "rather than the living . . . the dead" and especially him "who is yet unborn" (4:2–3). Even wisdom is vanity (1:16–17; 2:15; 9:11). However, Ecclesiastes does not revolt against God. On the contrary, since men's fate is "in the hands of God" (9:11), a man must take advantage of "the few days God has given him to live, since this is the lot assigned to him" (5:17). The only "right happiness" for man is hedonistic. "Go, eat your bread with joy and drink your wine with a glad heart . . . . Spend your life with the woman you love . . . , for this is the lot assigned to you . . . . Whatever work you propose to do, do it while you can, for there is neither achievement, nor planning, nor knowledge, nor wisdom in Sheol, where you are going"(9:7–10).

This pessimistic rationalism has been compared with certain Greek philosophical schools. From the time of Voltaire a number of historians and interpreters have suggested the influence of Stoicism, of Epicurus, or of the Cyrenaic hedonists.[22] Influences from Hellenistic culture on post-Exilic Judaism were powerful and long-lasting (see § 202). Nevertheless, they are not found in the Qoheleth. The Greek philosophers and writers had drastically criticized the traditional mythologies and theologies, but the author of the Qoheleth, far from denying the existence of God, proclaims his reality and omnipotence[23] and never ceases to repeat that we must profit by his gifts. What is more, the Qoheleth rejects neither the cult practices nor piety. So there is no question of atheism; what is being expressed is, rather, a tension between despair and resignation, brought on by the discovery of God's indifference. This invitation to enjoy life has been rightly compared with the Egyptian *Song of the Harper* (§ 30) and with Siduri's advice to Gilgamesh (§ 23).

Less moving than the Qoheleth, the work by Ben Sirach, known as Ecclesiasticus, nevertheless better reveals the crisis under

22. See the bibliographical references in Hengel, vol. 2, p. 77, n. 52.
23. See Hengel, vol. 1, p. 124.

which Israel is laboring. Probably composed between ca. 190 and ca. 185 by a scribe (*sōpēr*), teacher of a school of wisdom, the book is addressed to the young Hebrews who were fascinated by the Hellenistic *Aufklärung*. Ben Sirach is a patriot who is convinced of the decisive importance (both religious and political) of the purity of the Law. He attacks the rich (13:3, 18–23), since they are the most active supporters of cosmopolitanism and universalism. From the beginning of his book Ben Sirach protests against the secular ideology of Hellenism: "All wisdom is from the Lord," he exclaims (1:1). This allows him to identify Wisdom (preexisting in God) with the Torah. The eulogy of Wisdom, the great hymn of chapter 24, is the high point of his book. Wisdom proclaims both her exalted position ("I came forth from the mouth of the Most High") and her descent to Jerusalem ("Thus was I established on Zion . . . , and in Jerusalem I wield my authority" (24:11).

Against the opinion defended by the "cosmopolites," representatives of the "Enlightenment," Sirach describes the teacher of wisdom, the ideal scribe, as a scholar wrapped up in study of the Scriptures: he "devotes his soul to reflecting on the Law of the Most High. He researches into the wisdom of all the Ancients, he occupies his time with the prophecies. He researches into the hidden sense of proverbs, he ponders the obscurities of parables," etc. (39:1 ff.). For "wisdom consists entirely in fearing the Lord, and wisdom is entirely constituted by the fulfilling of the Law" (19:20). In the Wisdom literature, especially in the Proverbs and in certain Psalms, the true "just man" was the sage who recognized the divine origin of the cosmic order and moral life. *Hence wisdom was accessible to men independently of their religion*. But Sirach rejects this "universalist" interpretation; he identifies wisdom with piety and the cult. The Torah is "no other than . . . the Law that Moses enjoined on us" (24:23).[24] In other words, wisdom is the exclusive

24. In the "Eulogy of the Ancestors" (44:1–49:16), Ben Sirach praises the great figures of biblical history: Enoch, Noah, Abraham, Isaac and Jacob, Moses, etc. It is a peculiar text, unparalleled in the Wisdom literature. (Hengel compares it to the glorification of heroes in Hellenistic literature, *de viris illustribus* [*Judaism and Hellenism*, vol. 1, p. 136].) But the author loses his inspiration, and the "eulogy" becomes didactic and finally monotonous.

gift made by God to Israel. For God set a governor over each nation, "but Israel is the Lord's own portion" (17:17).

In theology Ben Sirach returns to the traditional positions. He criticizes the opinion that God is indifferent to the lot of human beings; in other words, he repudiates both the Qoheleth and the Greek philosophy that was fashionable in the cosmopolitan circles of Jerusalem. Above all, he attempts to justify the doctrine of retribution: he glorifies the perfection of the divine work (39:16, 42:15, 22:25); he repeats that the pious have a different fate from the wicked, for "good things were created from the beginning for good men, as evils were for sinners" (39:25). After long "pondering," he concludes: "the Lord alone will be found righteous" (18:2).

This bold restoration of the traditional theodicy is accompanied by a bitter critique of the "enemies of Wisdom," identified with the Hellenophile apostates and "libertines." Sirach prays for Israel's deliverance from "foreign nations": "Rouse your fury, pour out your rage, destroy the opponent, annihilate the enemy . . . . Let . . . destruction overtake those who use your people badly"(36:6, 8).

Yet, in the famous chapter 24, Wisdom declares: "Alone I encircled the vault of the sky, and I walked on the bottom of the deeps. Over the waves of the sea and over the whole earth, and over every people and nation I have held sway" (24:5). In other words, Wisdom is presented as a "power that fills the whole world, nature and humanity (and not only the Jews)."[25] But Ben Sirach was obliged to limit and, in the last analysis, to forget the universalistic dimension of Wisdom. At grips with Hellenism and its Sophia, "a Wisdom could impose itself in Judaism only by allying itself with the factor that played the decisive part in the struggle: the Law. . . . The importance of *hokmā* for the formation of the Jewish religion in this struggle against Hellenism and its *Sophia* must not be underestimated."[26]

25. W. Schencke, *Die Chokma (Sophia) in der jüdischen Hypostasenspekulation*, p. 29. Hengel (vol. 1, p. 160) compares the Logos of the Stoic philosophers, which penetrates and gives form to the Cosmos: "The universal Law [*logos*], which is the true wisdom penetrating everywhere, is identical with Zeus" (Zeno, cited by Diogenes Laertius, 7. 88).

26. J. Fichtner, *Die altorientalische Weisheit in ihrer israelitisch-jüdischen Ausprägung*, p. 127; cf. Hengel, vol. 1, p. 162.

202. The first apocalyses: Daniel and 1 Enoch

The confrontation with Hellenism reached its highest point under the reign of Antiochus IV Epiphanes (ca. 175–164). The opposition between the two parties—the Tobiads (the universalists) and the Oniads (the nationalists)—had for some time been threatening to degenerate into violence. The philhellenes demanded a radical reform, designed to transform biblical Judaism into a "modern" religion, comparable to the other contemporary syncretistic creations. In ca. 167, taking advantage of a failed attempt at a revolt by the Oniads, their adversaries advised Antiochus to abrogate the Torah by a royal decree.[27] The Temple was transformed into a syncretistic sanctuary of Olympian Zeus, identified with the Phoenician Baal. On pain of death, the decree forbade observance of the Sabbath and feast days, the practice of circumcision, and the possession of biblical books. Everywhere in Palestine altars were raised to the gods of the Gentiles, and the populace was obliged to bring sacrifices to be offered to them.

Ever since the conquest of Canaan, and especially under the monarchy, the Israelites had experienced the temptation and the danger of religious syncretism (§§113 ff.). But Antiochus Epiphanes' aggression was far more serious. It is true that he did not intend to substitute Olympian Zeus for Yahweh; his intention was to give a name to a god who, for the pagans, was essentially nameless.[28] Besides, a number of Greek and Roman authors had compared Yahweh with Zeus.[29] Such a comparison, sacrilegious for the traditionalists, could be accepted by a great many of the philhellenic intelligentsia, fascinated by the grandiose religious and philosophical vision of Stoicism. But a philosophical interpretation of this kind was beyond the ken of the majority of Israelites; they saw in Zeus only one of the many gods honored by the Gentiles. In addition, as the historian Flavius Josephus later recognized (*Antiq. Jud.* 12. 220, 253), Antiochus was guilty of numerous instances of sacrilege (first of all, in the polytheistic

27. According to Bickerman, it was the extreme hellenophiles of Jerusalem who drove Antiochus to the exacerbated violence of the repression: see his *Der Gott der Makkabäer,* pp. 120 ff. and passim. The authors of the edict of persecution were the Tobiads themselves (Hengel, vol. 1, p. 289).

28. Bickerman, pp. 92 ff.

29. See Hengel, vol. 1, pp. 261 ff.; M. Simon, "Jupiter-Yahvé," pp. 49 ff.

nature of the cult established in Jerusalem) and of brigandage, intolerance, and, above all, persecution of the Jews.[30]

A priest named Mattathias, of the family of the Hasmoneans, gave the signal for armed revolt. From the outset he was supported by a group of zealots, the "pious" (*hassidim*). After Mattathias' death, one of his sons, Judas Maccabaeus, took over the direction of the war. In ca. 164 he occupied the Temple and restored the cult. This religious victory was regarded as sufficient by the *hassidim*. But the Maccabees continued the struggle for political freedom as well, which they succeeded in obtaining in ca. 128. After a lapse of several centuries, there were, once again, Jewish kings, now elected from the family of the Hasmoneans.[31] Their reign was disastrous, and in ca. 63 the people accepted Roman suzerainty with relief.

The century that elapsed between Antiochus Epiphanes' aggression and Pompey's reduction of Palestine to a Roman province was decisive for both the history and the religion of the Jewish people. On the one hand, the attempt at enforced paganization produced a trauma that the Jews of Palestine would never be able to forget: they could no longer believe in the innocence of the pagans, and thenceforth an abyss separated them from Hellenistic culture.[32] On the other hand, the military victory of the Maccabees had as its consequence a surprising increase in the political influence of the Jewish kingdom. What is more, the charismatic figure of Judas Maccabaeus later encouraged other armed insurrections, this time against the Romans. But the revolt in 66–70 ended in the destruction of the second Temple and of Jerusalem itself by Titus's legions. And the insurrection led by Bar Cochba in 132–35 was savagely put down by Hadrian.

For the purpose of the present work, it is especially the religious creations of this period that will engage our attention. As

30. See Simon, "Jupiter-Yahvé," p. 51.

31. For analysis of the persecution and the war of the Maccabees see Bickerman, *Der Gott der Makkabäer;* Tcherikover, *Hellenistic Civilization and the Jews*, pp. 176–234; S. K. Eddy, *The King Is Dead*, pp. 213–56; and Hengel, *Judaism and Hellenism*, vol. 1, pp. 277 ff.

32. But syncretistic tendencies continued to develop in Samaria and Transjordania and, above all, in the Greek-speaking Diaspora; see Hengel, vol. 1, p. 308.

was to be expected, contemporary historical events are transfigured, freighted with messages in cipher, integrated into a particular vision of universal history. It is in the circles of the "pious" (the *hassidim*) that the earliest apocalyptic writings appear—the Book of Daniel and the oldest section of the Book of Enoch. The "pious" made up a strictly closed community; they insisted on absolute respect for the Law and the need for repentance. The considerable importance accorded to repentance was the immediate consequence of an apocalyptic conception of history. And in fact the terror of history had attained proportions previously unknown. Therefore, Daniel and 1 Enoch predicted, the world is nearing its end; the pious must prepare themselves for God's imminent judgment.

In its present form the Book of Daniel was completed about 164. The author describes recent or contemporary events in the form of prophecies uttered several centuries earlier. This procedure (*vaticinia ex eventu*) is characteristic of apocalyptic literature:[33] it strengthens faith in the prophecies and hence helps believers to bear the ordeals of the present. Thus the Book of Daniel recounts a dream of Nebuchadnezzer (ca. 605–562). The king had seen a statue: its head was of gold, its chest and arms were of silver, its belly and thighs of bronze, its legs of iron and earthenware. Suddenly a stone broke away and struck the statue: "and then iron and earthenware, bronze, silver, gold, all broke into small pieces as fine as chaff on the threshing floor in summer. The wind blew them away, leaving not a trace behind" (2:32–36). Daniel interprets the dream: the golden head is Nebuchadnezzer; after him another, lesser kingdom will arise, and then a third kingdom, this one of bronze, will rule the whole world. The fourth kingdom, "hard as iron," will crush the others, but will end by being destroyed. Then "the God of heaven will set up a kingdom which will never be destroyed, and this kingdom will not pass into the hands of another race" (2:44). The successive kingdoms of the Assyrians (i.e., the neo-Babylonian kingdom), of the Medes and the Persians, and finally that of Alexander indicate an accelerating process of decadence. But it is especially

33. Cf. the Egyptian "Oracle of the Potter," the Oracles of Hystaspes and the Sibyl, etc.

during the fourth kingdom (that is, the kingdom of Antiochus Epiphanes) that the existence of the people of Israel is seriously threatened. However, Daniel gives his assurance, the end of this decayed world is drawing near, and after it God will build the eternal kingdom. Daniel further relates one of his own dreams, in which he saw four huge beasts coming out of the sea. The beasts represent the four kingdoms that are destined to perish; after that, rule over all the empires will be given "to the people of the saints of the Most High" (7:27).

In short, by reminding them of the grandiose events of the past, especially the sequence of catastrophes that had destroyed the military empires, the author of Daniel had a definite end in view: to encourage and strengthen his coreligionists. But at the same time, the dramatic succession of the four kingdoms expresses *a unitary conception of universal history.* It is true that the mythological imagery shows an Oriental origin. The theme of the four successive kingdoms, symbolized by the four metals, is found in Hesiod and in Iran. As for the four beasts, they have numerous precedents: Babylonian, Iranian, Phoenician.[34] Similarly, the "great eon" of 1 Enoch (16:1) is comparable to the doctrine of the "Great Year."[35] However, Daniel and the Jewish apocalypses present an element that is unknown in the other traditions: the events that make up universal history no longer reflect the eternal rhythm of the cosmic cycle and no longer depend on the stars; *they develop in accordance with God's plan.*[36] In this preestablished plan, Israel plays the central part. History is hastening to its end; in other words, Israel's definitive triumph is imminent. This triumph will not be simply political; in fact, the accomplishment of history is equivalent to the salvation of Israel, a salvation determined by God from all eternity and inscribed in the plan of History, despite the sins of his people.

34. See W. Baumgartner, "Danielforschung," pp. 214–22; A. Bentzen, *Daniel*, pp. 57–67; A. Lacoque, *Le Livre de Daniel*, pp. 49 ff.

35. See Eliade, *The Myth of the Eternal Return*, pp. 134 ff.; Hengel, *Judaism and Hellenism*, vol. 1, pp. 191 ff.

36. In his ecstatic journey to heaven, Enoch sees the tablets on which the whole of history is inscribed (1 Enoch 81:1 ff.). On this motif see Widengren, *The Ascension of the Apostle*, esp. pp. 27 ff.

203. The only hope: The end of the world

As in the other traditions, in the Jewish apocalypse the end of the world is announced by a number of cataclysms and strange cosmic phenomena: the sun will shine by night and the moon by day, blood will flow in the fountains, the stars will leave their orbits, the trees will drip blood, fire will spring from the bowels of the earth, stones will cry out, etc. (4 Esdras 5:4–12). The year will be shortened, men will kill one another, there will be drought and famine, etc.[37] And, just as in the Iranian tradition, the end of the world will see the universal judgment and hence also the resurrection of the dead.

The Book of Isaiah (26:19) had already referred to the resurrection ("Your dead will come to life, their corpses will rise"), but it is difficult to date this passage. The earliest incontrovertible reference occurs in Daniel 12:13: "you will rise for your share at the end of time."[38] There is here very probably an Iranian influence; but we must also bear in mind the paleo-Oriental conceptions of the vegetation gods (see §117). The doctrine of resurrection will be assiduously proclaimed in the apocalyptic literature (4 Esdras; 1 Enoch 51:1–3, 61:5, 62:14 ff.; the Syriac Apocalypse of Baruch) and by the Pharisees. At the time of Jesus' preaching, it was universally accepted, except by the Sadducees.

As for the Last Judgment, Daniel (7:9–14) describes it as taking place before "one of great age," his "robe white as snow," seated on a throne of flames: "a court was held and the books were opened." In his ecstatic dream Enoch had also seen the Lord seated on his throne and the "sealed books," and he witnessed the judgment of the fallen angels and of the apostates, condemned to be cast into a burning gulf (90:20 ff.; see Charles, *Apocrypha*, vol. 1, pp. 259–60). The image of the "Most High" seated on "the throne of judgment" reappears in 4 Esdras, where sinners are destined to the "furnace of Gehenna" and the virtuous are rewarded in the "Paradise of delight" (7:33–37; Charles, vol. 2,

37. See Eliade, *The Myth of the Eternal Return*, pp. 147 ff.; P. Volz, *Die Eschatologie*, pp. 150 ff. These clichés, which are typical of apocalyptic literature, derive from an archaic mythico-ritual scenario: the end of the world, followed by a new creation (§12; see also Eliade, *Myth and Reality*, chaps. 4–5).

38. From the same period is 1 Enoch 90:33 and the work by Jason of Cyrene, composed soon after the death of Judas Maccabaeus; see Hengel, vol. 1, p. 196.

p. 583). After the Judgment, evil will be abolished forever, corruption will be vanquished, and truth will reign everywhere (4 Esdras 6:26–28; Charles, vol. 2, pp. 576–77). The conception of the eschatological judgment by fire is very probably of Iranian origin (see §104).

In the same vision of the "one of great age" and the Judgment, Daniel witnesses the descent from heaven of "one like a son of man," who was led into the presence of the "one of great age" and "on him was conferred sovereignty, glory, and kingship" (7:13–14). In the "Son of Man" (i.e., "Man") Daniel symbolizes the people of Israel at the supreme moment of eschatological triumph. The expression will enjoy a great success during the first century before our era; in addition, it is the title that Jesus will bestow on himself. What we have here is a comparatively familiar figure in the Hellenistic world, that of the Anthropos or Primordial Man. The myth is Indo-Iranian in origin (cf. Puruṣa, Gayōmart), but the immediate precedents for the "Son of Man" (= "Man") are to be sought in Irano-"Chaldean" religious syncretism (see § 216). The idea of the First Man invested with an eschatological mission is not biblical. It is only in late Judaism that the notion appears of an Adam who existed before the Creation.[39]

Thus the unitarian concept of universal history allowed the eschatological meaning of the contemporary period to be deciphered. Contrary to the old cosmologies, which explained the progressive and ineluctable decline of the world by a cyclical theory (whose strictest expression was the Indian doctrine of the four *yugas*), the *hassidim* proclaimed Yahweh sole Lord of History. In the Book of Daniel and 1 Enoch, God remains the central figure: Evil is not clearly personified in an Adversary of Yahweh. Evil is engendered by man's disobedience (1 Enoch 98:4 ff.) and by the revolt of the fallen angels.

39. In fact Judaism did not know that the Son of Man was a variant of the myth of the Primordial Man. The Jewish apocalyptical writings glorify the eschatological role of the Son of Man but make no reference to his preexistence (see Mowinckel, *He That Cometh*, pp. 420 ff.). F. A. Borsch has well brought out the Oriental mythologem of the king as primordial Son of Man: see his *The Son of Man in Myth and History*, pp. 89 ff.

But the background changes markedly in the apocalyptic literature. The world and history are now regarded as dominated by the forces of evil, that is, by the demonic powers commanded by Satan. The first mentions of Satan (Job 1:6 ff.; Zechariah 3:1 ff.) present him as belonging to Yahweh's celestial court. He was the "Enemy" because he was the celestial personage hostile to man (see §115). Now, however, *Satan incarnates the principle of Evil: he becomes the Adversary of God.* In addition, a new idea takes form: that of the two ages (or two kingdoms): "this reign" and "the other reign." In fact it is written: "the Most High has made not one Age but two" (4 Esdras 7:50).[40] In this age the "kingdom of Satan" is destined to triumph. Saint Paul calls Satan "the god of this world" (2 Corinthians 4:4). His power will attain its culminating point at the approach of the messianic era, when there will be a multiplication of the catastrophes and aberrant phenomena briefly mentioned above (p. 267). But in the eschatological battle, Yahweh will conquer Satan, annihilate or overcome all the demons, extirpate evil, and then build his Kingdom, dispensing eternal life, joy, and peace.[41] Certain texts speak of a return to Paradise and hence of the abolition of death (4 Esdras 8:52–54). Yet, despite its perfection and perenniality, this newly created world *remains a physical one.*

The figure of Satan probably developed under the influence of Iranian dualism.[42] In any case, it presents a mitigated dualism, for Satan does not coexist from the beginning with God, and he is not eternal. On the other hand, account must be taken of an earlier tradition, which conceived Yahweh as absolute totality of the real, that is, as a *coincidentia oppositorum* in which all contraries coexisted—including "evil" (see § 59). We must remember the celebrated example of Samuel: "Now the spirit of

40. The same work contains the archaic idea of the inevitable degeneration of the world: "Creation is already old; it has already passed the strength of youth" (4 Esdras 14:10).

41. The date of the *eschaton* can be calculated by the "wise"; see, inter alia, Daniel 9:22 ff.; 1 Enoch 10:12, 89, 90, 97; 2 Esdras 4:5, 14:11; etc. See also W. Bousset, *Religion des Judentums,* 2d ed., pp. 283 ff.; P. Volz, *Eschatologie,* 2d ed., pp. 141 ff.

42. The Qumran texts refer to two spirits created by God, one good and one evil (see § 233), a doctrine that is reminiscent of Zurvanism (§ 213).

Yahweh had left Saul and *an evil spirit from Yahweh* filled him with terror'' (1 Sam. 16:14). As in other religions, dualism assumes clear form after a spiritual crisis that raises doubts concerning both the language and the postulates of the traditional theology and that ends, among other things, in a personification of the negative aspects of life, reality, and divinity. What until then was conceived as *a moment in the universal process* (based on the alternation of contraries: day/night; life/death; good/evil; etc.) is thenceforth isolated, personified, and invested with a specific and exclusive function, especially that of Evil (cf. §195). Probably Satan is at once the result of a ''splitting'' of the archaic image of Yahweh (a consequence of reflecting on the mystery of divinity) and of the influence of Iranian dualistic doctrines. In any case, the figure of Satan, as incarnation of Evil, will play a considerable part in the formation and history of Christianity before becoming the famous personage, with his countless metamorphoses, of eighteenth- and nineteenth-century European literature.

In regard to the *eschaton* and the new Creation, the apocalyptic literature does not present a unified conception. Its authors agree in terming the calamities and torments of the present time ''childbirth'' or ''messianic'' pains, for they precede and announce the coming of the Messiah. Just as in Isaiah and the post-Exilic prophets, the Messiah is always regarded as a human being: he is the King of God's people.[43] To mention only one example, the Psalms of Solomon (a work composed in the first century B.C.) contain a prayer to hasten the coming of the Messiah, son of David, in order that he may crush ''unrighteous rulers and purge Jerusalem'' of the presence of the pagans (17:22–24). He is a ''righteous king . . . and there shall be no unrighteousness in his days; for all shall be holy and their king [will be] the anointed of the Lord'' (17:26 ff., 29, 30).

For some, the Messiah's Kingdom still belongs to the present eon; in a sense it constitutes an intermediate reign, the *millennium*.[44] This messianic kingdom is destined to endure for 400,

43. See Mowinckel, *He That Cometh*, pp. 280 ff. (with a valuable bibliography).

44. The idea will be elaborated by rabbinic speculation: see G. F. Moore, *Judaism in the First Centuries of the Christian Era*, vol. 2, pp. 375 ff.

500, or 1,000 years. It will be followed by the universal judgment and the destruction of the world. The Messiah himself will die, and all will return to the primordial "silence," that is, to Chaos. "After seven days the age which is not yet awake shall be roused" (4 Esdras 7:28 ff.; Charles, vol. 2, p. 582); in other words, there will be the new Creation, resurrection, and eternal bliss.[45]

Several texts rank the Messiah among eternal beings, together with Enoch, Elijah, and other personages who were taken up to Heaven by God. According to certain rabbinic sources, immediately after his birth the Messiah was hidden in Paradise or, with Elijah, in Heaven.[46] The *Testament of the XII Patriarchs* and the texts from Qumran mention two messiahs, a priest and a king, the priestly Messiah having the primacy. The Testament of Levi states that under his priesthood "all sin will disappear . . . and he himself will open the gates of Paradise . . . and to the Saints he will give to eat of the Tree of Life" (18:9–12). In short, the priestly Messiah will annul the consequences of original sin.[47]

We may add that the preaching of Jesus and the swift rise of Christianity are bound up with the same spiritual ferment that is characteristic of Jewish messianic hopes and eschatological speculations between the revolt of the Maccabees and the destruction of the second Temple (see § 224).

45. *Sanhedrin* 99a, where various rabbinic opinions are cited; see also Moore, *Judaism,* vol. 2, pp. 375 ff.

46. Strack and Billerbeck, *Kommentar zum Neuen Testament aus Talmud und Midrasch,* vol. 2, p. 340.

47. Ringgren, *La religion d'Israël,* p. 350; Mowinckel, *He That Cometh,* p. 382. Speculations concerning the messianic age continued in rabbinic circles in the first centuries after Christ. The same motifs constantly recur: destruction of the pagans, triumph of the Jews, the blessings God bestows on the faithful, etc. (see the sources cited by Moore, *Judaism,* vol. 2, pp. 345 ff.). Certain texts add that on the day that the Messiah comes all peoples will be converted to the worship of the one God, Yahweh (Moore, ibid., p. 371). But the conviction cherished by the authors of the apocalypses that the date of the *eschaton* can be calculated is abandoned. The Messiah will arrive at the moment chosen by God. Until then the faithful must practice penitence, repent, and obey the Law (Moore, ibid., pp. 350 ff.).

204. Reaction of the Pharisees: Glorification of the Torah

In Judaism, as in other traditions, apocalyptic visions strengthened defenses against the terror of history. The instructed could decipher a comforting presage in contemporary catastrophes. The worse the situation of the Jewish people became, the more the certainty increased that the present eon was nearing its end. In short, the worsening of the terror announced the imminence of salvation. In future, the religious valorization of the sufferings brought on by historical events will be reiterated time and again, and not only by the Jews and the Christians.

There is here neither a running-away from the pressure of history nor an optimism fed on fantasies. Apocalyptic literature constituted a sacred science, divine in origin and essence. As the author of Daniel writes (2:20–22), it is God who confers "wisdom on the wise," it is "his to uncover depths and mysteries, to know what lies in darkness." Enoch, that fabulous personage, exemplary image of the sage and prophet of the primordial period,[48] now becomes highly popular: he had predicted the imminent Judgment of the prediluvian generation and the fallen angels. Now he proclaims a new revelation and demands repentance, for the second Judgment is coming. Like Daniel, Enoch receives sacred knowledge in his dreams and visions (1 Enoch 13:8, 14:1, 83:1 ff., 93:1 ff.). Angels introduce him to celestial mysteries, and he undertakes ecstatic journeys to Heaven (chaps. 12–36), where God allows him to see the tablets on which universal history is written from beginning to end.

At the dawn of time, God had revealed secret knowledge to certain personages famed for their piety and their visionary powers. This teaching was esoteric, "sealed"—in other words, inaccessible to the profane. It was then transmitted to a few exceptional beings. But since the primordial period corresponds to the end of time (*eschaton*), sacred knowledge is now revealed again, and always to a small group of initiates. In 1 Enoch 1:6

48. According to tradition, Enoch was one of the prediluvian patriarchs: he "walked with God. Then he vanished, for God took him" (Genesis 5:24). What follows is much indebted to Hengel's analyses in *Judaism and Hellenism*, vol. 1, pp. 204 ff.

the Son of Man is described as the initiate par excellence, "master of all secrets." When he is seated on his throne "his mouth shall pour forth all the secrets of wisdom" (ibid., 51:3). His most characteristic qualities are wisdom and intelligence.[49] We will add that the theme of a saving "hidden knowledge" is very popular during the Hellenistic period (§ 209), and it constitutes the justification for all the Gnostic schools (§ 229).[50]

The authors of the Apocalypse fully developed this conception of a wisdom hidden in Heaven and inaccessible to human beings,[51] and ecstatic visions and experiences also played a leading role in the apocalyptic literature (as everywhere else in the Hellenistic world); for visions and ecstasies confirmed the authenticity of the true "prophet and sage," and, what is more, ecstatic experiences progressively enriched the sum of revealed knowledge. The Book of Daniel disclosed only universal history, whereas the texts that claimed to belong to the "tradition of Enoch" embraced the whole world, visible and invisible: terrestrial and celestial geography, astronomy and astrology, meteorology and medicine. For the "tradition of Enoch," the cosmological mysteries at once revealed and glorified the work of God. As Hengel observes (vol. 1, p. 208), the masters of wisdom (*hassidim*) were engaged even more vigorously than Ben Sirach in the controversy with Hellenism. For basically, by virtue of "apocalyptic revelations," they possessed a knowledge superior to that of the Greeks. Indeed, their knowledge embraced the cosmos, history, and the celestial world and, in addition, the destiny of man at the moment of the *eschaton*—a knowledge inaccessible to reason. This conception of a total, esoteric, and saving knowledge, which could be apprehended in ecstatic visions or transmitted by an initiation, is also documented in other religious traditions and will be shared by ancient Christianity.

No other current of Jewish thought borrowed Hellenistic-Oriental ideas as freely as did the apocalyptic. Nevertheless, its

49. See other examples in Mowinckel, *He That Cometh*, pp. 375 ff., 385 ff.

50. In India the doctrine of a secret gnosis, communicated by initiation, is documented from the time of the Upanishads, but it will be principally elaborated in Tantric literature (see vol. 3).

51. See Hengel, *Judaism and Hellenism*, vol. 1, pp. 206 ff.; vol. 2, p. 137, n. 630.

foundation still rests on the Old Testament conception of the history of salvation.[52] We have to do with an extremely important spiritual phenomenon: the *religious creativity inspired by syncretism*. Indeed, the *hassidim*, authors of the earliest apocalyptic literature, received and assimilated ideas derived from several syncretistic systems; but these ideas enriched Judaism and sustained the hope of the Jewish people during an extremely difficult period. A similar process can be seen in other religious currents. Under the leadership of the "Teacher of Righteousness," the Hassidic group known as the Essenes separated from the rest of the community and resolved to live a monastic life in the desert (§ 223); now the closest analogy to the cenobitic organization of the Essenes is the closed conventicle of the Greek type. Even the Pharisees, the second group derived from the *hassidim*, incorporated a number of Hellenistic ideas into their doctrine of the Law.[53]

In the last analysis, Antiochus Epiphanes' sacrilegious aggression and the victorious revolt of the Maccabees determined the orientation and future structures of Judaism. The "zeal against the Torah" that animated Antiochus' partisans encouraged "zeal *for* the Torah" and ended by consolidating the ontology of the Law.[54] The Torah was raised to the rank of an absolute and eternal reality, exemplary model of the Creation. According to Rabbi Simon ben Laqisch (third century A.D.), the existence of the world depends on the fact that Israel accepts the Torah; without that, the world will return to Chaos.[55] Each of the 248 commandments and 365 prohibitions that make up the Torah receives a cosmic meaning. Man, created with 248 members and 365 veins, reflects in his very structure at once the work of God

52. Hengel, vol. 1, p. 251.

53. See Hengel, vol. 1, p. 312, which contains also a summary of the beliefs and ideas borrowed by the Jews from the Oriental-Hellenistic cultural milieu.

54. Hengel, vol. 1, pp. 292 ff. Eschatology—that is, the "second fruit in the confrontation with Hellenism"—represented the only force able to limit the omnipresence of the Torah; in fact, the Torah will end by dominating both the historical present and the cosmic rhythms (ibid., p. 312).

55. Rabbi Eliezer ben Hyrcanus (ca. 100 A.D.) is reported to have said: "If the Torah were not there, Heaven and Earth would not have existed" (text cited by Hengel, vol. 1, p. 172). See other sources in Moore, *Judaism*, vol. 1, pp. 266 ff., 450 ff.

(the Cosmos) and his revelation (the Law).[56] As absolute reality, the Torah is the source of life. As Hillel writes, "Where there is much Torah, there is much life" (*Pirkê Abhot* 3. 7).

But the glorification of the Torah radically altered the destiny of Judaism. From the time of the prophets, Hebraic religiosity was stimulated by the tension between universalist and particularist tendencies. The cause of this vigorous and creative opposition was essentially the paradoxical character of Revelation. In fact, a revelation from God *in history,* that is, *limited to the Jewish people,* was proclaimed *universally valid* while at the same time being considered as *exclusively* for the Israelites. In the second half of the second century B.C., by virtue of the surprising development of the Diaspora and also, in part, because of missionary propaganda, Judaism was becoming a *universal religion*. But the reaction against Antiochus' sacrilege ended in what has been called "fixation on the Torah."[57] Now, such a "fixation" hampered the rise of a universal religion. To be sure, the Law played the decisive role in the defense of the national identity, but the consciousness of a universal mission could not develop freely beside a powerful and nationalistic current. This, by the way, explains the decision of the primitive Christian church, animated by the Jewish prophetic spirit, to send missionaries to the Samaritans, who were so greatly detested by the Israelites (Acts 8:4 ff.), and, a little later, to the non-Jews of Antioch (Acts, chaps. 11–19, etc.). "Christology took the place of Torah ontology as an expression of the free and sovereign revelation of God in history, which no longer recognized national or historically conditioned limitations."[58] The immutability of the Torah and the triumph of legalism together put an end to eschatological hopes. "Even apocalyptic literature gradually died out and was replaced by Jewish mysticism."[59]

56. Two centuries later, Tantrism will present a similar anthropocosmic system and a similar ritual; see vol. 3.

57. See Hengel, vol. 1, p. 312. Even in the Diaspora the primacy of the Torah was not denied. Allegorical interpretation did not annul the literal meaning of the Scriptures, and Philo accepted the prescribed laws and prohibitions.

58. Hengel, vol. 1, p. 314.

59. Ibid., p. 175.

It must be added, however, that, from the point of view of Judaism, abandonment of the universal mission was the price that had to be paid for safeguarding the Israelitish community. In the last analysis, what was essential was the historical continuity of the Jewish people. It was not a matter solely of "nationalism" but, above all, of a theology built up around the idea of the "chosen people." Israel was chosen by Yahweh; it was *his* people. Hence the Jewish people constituted a historical reality sanctified by the will of God. National alienation was equivalent to an apostasy, that is, to *profanation of an ethnic structure consecrated by its very origin*. Hence the first duty of the Jewish people was to maintain its identity intact, even to the end of history: in other words, always to remain at the disposal of God.

26 Syncretism and Creativity in the Hellenistic Period: The Promise of Salvation

205. The Mystery religions

As we observed earlier (§184), the *promise of salvation* constitutes the novelty and principal characteristic of the Hellenistic religions. Uppermost, of course, was individual salvation (although the dynastic cults had a similar purpose—salvation of the dynasty).[1] The divinities who were believed to have undergone death and resurrection were closer to individual men than were the tutelary gods of the *polis*. Their cult included a more or less elaborate initiation (catechesis, rites, esoteric teaching), after which the neophyte was granted admission to the conventicle. Membership in a Mystery society did not preclude initiation into other secret brotherhoods. Like all of the spiritual currents of the time, the hope of salvation developed under the sign of syncretism.

Indeed, syncretism is the dominant characteristic of the period. An immemorial and abundantly documented phenomenon, syncretism had played an important part in the formation of the Hittite, Greek, and Roman religions, in the religion of Israel, in Mahāyāna Buddhism, and in Taoism, but what marks the syncretism of the Hellenistic and Roman period is its scale and its surprising creativity. Far from manifesting attrition and sterility, syncretism seems to be the condition for every religious creation. We have seen its importance in post-Exilic Judaism (§ 202). We

1. For example, the elevation of a traditional god to the rank of protective divinity of the dynasty: Apollo for the Seleucids, Zeus for the Lagids, Athena for the Attalids. The deification of sovereigns and the syncretistic state cults—for example, that of Serapis in Ptolemaic Egypt—sought the same end.

shall later discover a similar process in certain creations of Iranian religiosity (§ 212). Primitive Christianity also develops in a syncretistic environment. It is true that, in the period we are considering, only one god, Serapis, is the result of a deliberate fusion of two divine figures. But the Greco-Oriental Mysteries, the eschatological and apocalyptic speculations, and the cult of sovereigns—to cite only a few examples—illustrate the importance and strength of syncretistic thought.

It could be said that the promise of salvation attempts to exorcise the redoubtable power of the goddess Tyche (Chance; Latin, Fortuna). Capricious and unpredictable, Tyche indifferently brings good or evil; she manifests herself as *anangkē* ("necessity") or *heimarmenē* ("destiny") and shows her power especially in the lives of the greatest, such as Alexander.[2] Destiny ends by being associated with astral fatalism. The existence of individuals as well as the duration of cities and states is determined by the stars. This doctrine and, with it, astrology—the technique that applies its principles—develop under the impulse given by the Babylonians' observations of the revolutions of the heavenly bodies. To be sure, the theory of micro-macrocosmic correspondences had long been known in Mesopotamia (§ 24) and elsewhere in the Asian world. However, this time man not only feels that he shares in the cosmic rhythms but discovers that his life is *determined by* the motions of the stars.[3]

This pessimistic conception is not discredited until the conviction arises that certain divine beings are independent of Destiny, that they are even superior to it. Bel is proclaimed Master of Chance, *Fortunae rector.* In the Mysteries of Isis, the goddess assures the initiate that she can prolong life beyond the term fixed by fate. In the *Praises of Isis and Osiris* the goddess pro-

2. See Tarn, *Hellenistic Civilisation*, p. 340.

3. The Stoics set themselves to correct this astrological amoralism: they interpreted Destiny as a Providence that takes morality into account; indeed, it was Providence that had created the planets. On the other hand, it must be pointed out that, as the result of the astronomical calculations made by the Babylonians, the history of the world was thereafter divided into periods and crises dominated by the planets. This new cosmo-historical vision inspires certain eschatological speculations (e.g., the Jewish apocalyptic visions [see § 202], the Golden Age inaugurated by Augustus at the end of the Civil Wars, etc.).

claims: "I have conquered Destiny, and Destiny obeys me." What is more, Tyche (or Fortuna) becomes an attribute of Isis.[4] A number of mysteriosophic and Hermetic texts state that initiates are no longer determined by fate.[5]

Unlike initiation into the Eleusinian Mysteries, which took place only in the *telestērion* and only at a particular date (see § 97), initiations into the other religions of salvation could take place anywhere and at any time. All these initiatory cults boasted of an immemorial antiquity even if their establishment, in certain cases, did not date back even a century. This is certainly a cliché of the *Zeitgeist* of the Hellenistic and Roman periods; but, as we shall see, the religions of salvation reactualize certain archaic religious elements. With the exception of Dionysianism, all of the Mysteries are of Oriental origin: Phrygian (Cybele and Attis), Egyptian (Isis and Osiris), Phoenician (Adonis), Iranian (Mithra). But in the Hellenistic period, and especially under the Empire, these Oriental cults no longer had an ethnic character; their structures and soteriologies proclaimed a universalist aim. We know the principal features of their public cults; as for their secret rituals—that is, initiation properly speaking—we are reduced to a few brief and enigmatic indications.

We know that the postulant took an oath of secrecy concerning all that he would see and hear in the course of the ceremonies. He then learned the sacred history (the *hieros logos*), which related the myth of the cult's origin. Probably the myth was already known to the neophyte, but he was now given a new, esoteric, interpretation of it—which was equivalent to revealing the true meaning of the divine drama. The initiation was preceded by a period of fasting and mortification, at the end of which the novice was purified by lustrations. In the Mysteries of Mithra and Attis, bulls and rams were sacrificed over a pit covered by a grill; the blood dripped onto the mystes, who was placed un-

4. See A. D. Nock, *Conversion*, pp. 101, 288–89; J. Bergman, "I Overcame Fate, Fate Harkens to Me," pp. 39 ff.

5. See Nock, *Conversion*, p. 102. Chance (*casus infestus*) no longer has power over those who serve and honor Isis (Apuleius, *Met*. 11. 15). The Gnostics are no longer prisoners of *fatum* (Lactantius, *Institutiones* 2. 16); for spirit (*nous*) is master of Destiny (*heimarmenē*) as well as of Law (*Corp. Herm*. 12. 9).

derneath. In some way that has not been elucidated, the neophyte took part ritually in a scenario centered around the death and resurrection (or rebirth) of the divinity. In short, the initiation realized a kind of *imitatio dei*. Most of the fragmentary indications at our disposal refer to the symbolic death and resurrection of the mystes. During his initiation into the Mysteries of Isis, Lucius, the hero of Apuleius' romance, the *Metamorphoses*, undergoes a "voluntary death" and "approaches the kingdom of death" in order to obtain his "spiritual birthday" (11. 21, 24). In the Mysteries of Cybele, the neophyte is regarded as *moriturus*, "in the process of dying."[6] This mystical death was followed by a new, spiritual, birth. In the Phrygian rite, Sallust writes, the new initiates "were fed on milk as if they were reborn" (*De diis et mundo* 4). And in the text known as the *Liturgy of Mithra*, but which is filled with Hermetic gnosis, we read: "Today, having been born again by Thee out of so many myriads . . . " or "Born again for rebirth of that life-giving birth . . . ."[7]

In the course of the ceremonies the neophyte contemplated or handled certain sacred objects. At the same time, he was told the interpretation of their symbolism; this probably amounted to an esoteric exegesis that defined and justified their value as means of salvation. At a certain time in his initiation the mystes partook of a ritual banquet. At the period with which we are concerned, this immemorial practice had chiefly an eschatological meaning.[8] In the Mysteries of Mithra the bread and wine gave the initiates strength and wisdom in this life and a glorious immortality in the afterlife.[9] By virtue of his initiation, the neophyte became the equal of the gods. Apotheosis, deification,

6. Firmicus Maternus, *De errore profanorum religionum* 18. See other examples in Eliade, *Rites and Symbols of Initiation: The Mysteries of Birth and Rebirth*, pp. 103 ff.

7. A. Dieterich, *Eine Mithrasliturgie*, p. 10, cited in *Rites and Symbols of Initiation*, p. 103.

8. See the documents cited by F. Cumont, *Les religions orientales*, p. 219, n. 43; p. 256, n. 52.

9. F. Cumont, *Textes et monuments figurés relatifs aux Mysteres de Mithra*, vol. 1 (Brussels, 1896), pp. 320 ff.

"de-mortalization" (*apathanatismos*) are conceptions that are familiar to all of the Mysteries.[10]

206. The mystical Dionysus

In the Hellenistic and Roman period the most popular Greek god was Dionysus. His public cult was "purified" and spiritualized by the elimination of ecstasy (which, however, continued to play a part in the Dionysiac Mysteries).[11] What is more, the mythology of Dionysus was the most lively, vivid, mythology. The plastic arts, especially the decoration of sarcophaguses, were freely inspired by the famous mythological episodes of the god's career, first of all his childhood (his miraculous birth, the winnowing basket), then his rescue of Ariadne, followed by the *hieros gamos*. The mythology, the sites of the cult, the monuments, all pointed to Dionysus' twofold nature, born of divine Zeus and a mortal woman, persecuted yet victorious, murdered yet resuscitated. At Delphi his tomb was shown, but his resurrection was depicted on many monuments elsewhere. He had succeeded in raising his mother to the rank of an Olympian; above all, he had brought Ariadne back from Hades and married her. In the Hellenistic period the figure of Ariadne symbolized the human soul. In other words, Dionysus not only delivered the soul from death; he also united himself with it in a mystical marriage (Schneider, *Kulturgeschichte des Hellenismus,* vol. 2, p. 802).

Dionysus' popularity was also spread by the societies of *technitai,* or Dionysiac artists, associations documented in Athens as early as ca. 300. These are parareligious brotherhoods,[12] but without any Mystery characteristics. As for the Dionysiac Mysteries *stricto sensu,* we have already presented their essential character (§125). We repeat that in the *Bacchae* Dionysus proclaims the Mystery structure of his cult and explains the necessity for initiatory secrecy: "Their secrecy forbids communicating

10. See R. Reitzenstein, *Die hellenistischen Mysterienreligionen*, pp. 29 ff.; S. Angus, *The Mystery Religions and Christianity*, pp. 106 ff.

11. See Carl Schneider, *Kulturgeschichte des Hellenismus*, vol. 2, p. 801.

12. See H. Jeanmaire, *Dionysos*, pp. 425 ff.

them to those who are not bacchants." "What use are they to those who celebrate them?" Pentheus asks. "It is not permitted thee to learn that, but they are things worthy to be known" (lines 470–74). In the last analysis, initiatory secrecy was well maintained. The texts referring to the liturgical service have almost all disappeared, except for some late Orphic hymns. The archeological documents from the Hellenistic and Roman periods are numerous enough, but the interpretation of their symbolism, even when it is accepted by the majority of scholars, is not enough to elucidate the initiation.

There can be no doubt of the closed, hence ritual (that is, initiatory), structure of the Dionysiac *thiasoi*. An inscription from Cumae (beginning of the fifth century) proves that the brotherhoods had their own cemeteries, to which only initiates into the Mysteries of Bacchus were admitted.[13] It has been possible to show (contrary to the opinion of some scholars, who saw in them only a favorable setting for profane banquets and jollifications) that the Dionysiac caverns were cult sites. The earliest iconographic testimonies, going back to the sixth century, show Dionysus lying in a cave or a maenad dancing before a huge mask of the god set inside a cavern. Now the texts refer to sacred dances and ritual banquets in front of Dionysiac caves; on the other hand, they also state that the ceremonies take place at night to insure their secrecy. As for the initiatory rituals, we are reduced to hypotheses. In his essay on the figured scenes, Friedrich Matz (though following the example of other scholars) concludes that the central act of the initiation consisted in the unveiling of a phallus hidden in a winnowing fan (*liknon*).[14] It is probable that this scene, which is abundantly illustrated, had a ritual importance, but Boyancé has cogently shown that the texts mention the *liknon* in connection with all kinds of initiations, not only with that of Dionysus.

On the other hand, in a stucco relief preserved at the Museum of Ostia (Matz's plate XXV), in which Dionysus and three other personages are designated by name, the cist bears the word

13. See Cumont, *Religions orientales*, p. 197, fig. 12; *Lux perpetua*, p. 252, fig. 6; see also ibid., pp. 405–6.

14. F. Matz, *Dionysiakē teletē*, p. 16. Cf. Boyancé, "Dionysiaca," p. 35, n. 2; Eliade, *A History of Religious Ideas*, vol. 1, pp. 357 ff.

Mysteria. Now the cist contained the *crepundia* or *signa*, that is, the "mystical playthings" (top, bull-roarer, knucklebones, mirror) that are already documented in the third century B.C. in the Gorub papyrus. It is with these playthings that the Titans succeeded in attracting the infant Dionysus-Zagreus, whom they later slaughtered and cut to pieces (§125). This myth has been transmitted to us primarily by a few Christian authors, but it was also known to two who had been initiated into the Mysteries—Plutarch and Apuleius—and also to the Orphic brotherhood of Hellenistic Egypt.[15] To judge from the monuments, the showing of the phallus seems to have formed part "of the somewhat terrifying rites that precede access to the god's presence."[16] Boyancé holds that "what could engender faith in the mystes—certainty of a divine support able to insure him a privileged lot in the beyond—cannot have been the sight of such an object" (p. 45). The central act of the initiation was the divine presence made perceptible by music and dance, an experience that engendered "belief in an intimate bond established with the god."[17]

These observations are indubitably well justified, but they do not advance our knowledge of the initiatory ritual. In any case, it is necessary to state that the showing of the phallus constituted a religious act, for the generative organ was that of Dionysus himself, at once *god and mortal who had conquered death*. We need only remember the sacrality of Śiva's *liṅgam* to understand that, in certain cultural and religious contexts, the generative organ of a god not only symbolizes the mystery of his creativity but also conveys his *presence*. In the modern Western world such a religious experience is, of course, inaccessible. For, unlike the Mysteries, Christianity ignored the sacramental value of sex-

15. Boyancé, "Dionysiaca," p. 55. On the *crepundia*, see also R. Turcan, *Les sarcophages romains à représentation dionysiaque*, pp. 407 ff.

16. Boyancé, p. 45. Cf. Turcan, "Du nouveau sur l'initiation dionysiaque," p. 108.

17. Boyancé, p. 44. Other initiatory scenes are analyzed by Turcan, *Les sarcophages*, pp. 402 ff. The celebrated frescoes of the Villa Item (the "Villa dei Misteri") at Pompeii presumably refer to the Dionysiac cult. But contrary to the opinion of those who see initiatory episodes in the frescoes, other authors consider that they do not reveal Mysteries and do not illustrate either the god's myth or the stages of an initiation; see G. Zuntz, "On the Dionysiac Fresco in the Villa dei Misteri," pp. 180–81.

uality. The same could be said of the Dionysiac ritual meals, when the initiates, crowned with flowers, surrendered to a joyous intoxication, regarded as a divine possession. It is difficult for us to grasp the sacrality of such rejoicings. Yet they anticipated the otherworld bliss promised to initiates into the Mystery of Dionysus.[18]

Late texts reflecting the Orphic eschatology emphasize the role of Dionysus as king of the new age. Though a child, he was made by Zeus to reign over all the gods in the universe (Kern, *Orphicorum Fragmenta*, no. 207). The epiphany of the divine infant announces the new youth of the universe, the cosmic palingenesis.[19] (The infant, as sign of rebirth and renewal, continues the religious symbolism of the phallus.) The hopes attached to the triumph of Dionysus, hence to a periodical regeneration of the world, imply belief in an imminent return of the Golden Age. This explains the popularity of the title "New Dionysus," which was bestowed on several personages (or which they bestowed on themselves) around the beginning of our era.[20]

207. Attis and Cybele

Even better than other contemporary religious forms, the cult of Cybele and the Mysteries of Attis illustrate the structural diversity that characterizes the syncretistic creations of the period. The Phrygian goddess, who was introduced into Rome in ca. 205–204 to save the Republic when it was being seriously threatened by the Carthaginian armies (§168), had a multimil-

18. See F. Cumont, *Religions orientales*, p. 203, *Etudes sur le symbolisme funéraire*, p. 372, and *Lux Perpetua*, pp. 255 ff.

19. "The concept of palingenesis and the idea that a new god is a god who reappears periodically not only have obvious affinities with the concept implying the alternation of the epiphanies and disappearances (*aphanismoi*) of a god who manifested himself in his *parousiai*, whether annual or biennial (*trietērides*). On the plane of cosmic duration, this concept can easily be transposed in the form of a cycle of return on an equally cosmic scale" (Jeanmaire, *Dionysos*, pp. 413–14). On the Dionysiac symbolism of the infant, see also Turcan, *Les sarcophages*, pp. 394 ff., 405 ff., 433 ff.

20. Jeanmaire (p. 416) cites Ptolemy XI, the triumvir Antony, and, later, Trajan, Hadrian, and Antoninus Pius.

lennial history. The black stone in which Cybele was ritually present testifies to the archaism of her cult: rock is one of the oldest symbols of the Earth Mother. And it is again a rock—in other words, the Great Mother Cybele—that is at the origin of Attis and his cult. According to the myth reported by Pausanias (7. 17. 10–12), a hermaphroditic monster, Agdistis, was born of a stone fecundated by Zeus.[21] The gods decided to castrate it and turn it into the goddess Cybele. According to another variant, the hermaphrodite's blood engendered an almond tree. Eating an almond, Nana,[22] daughter of the River Sangarius, becomes pregnant and gives birth to a child, Attis. Grown up, Attis is celebrating his marriage to the king's daughter when Agdistis, who loves him, enters the hall in which the festivities are taking place. All those present are stricken with madness, the king cuts off his genital organs, and Attis flees, mutilates himself under a pine tree, and dies. In despair, Agdistis tries to resuscitate him, but Zeus forbids it; all that he will grant is for Attis' body to remain incorruptible, his only sign of life being the growth of his hair and the motion of his little finger.[23] Since Agdistis is only an epiphany of the androgynous Great Mother, Attis is at once the son, the lover, and the victim of Cybele. The goddess regrets her jealousy, repents, and bewails her sweetheart.

This archaic mythology and the bloodstained rites that we shall describe in a moment constitute the source of a religion of salvation that became extremely popular throughout the Roman Empire during the first centuries of the Christian era. It is certain that its mythico-ritual scenario illustrated the "mystery" of vegetation (see §12): the blood and the sexual organs offered to Cybele insured the Earth Mother's fertility. With the passing of time, however, this immemorial cult became invested with new religious meanings; its bloodstained rites became so many means of redemption. Probably the soteriological function of the cult had been known for some time. At Pessinus there was a closed

21. This episode is reminiscent of a Hurrito-Hittite myth: Kumarbi, "the Father of the Gods," impregnated a rock with his semen (see § 46).

22. Nana is another epiphany of the Mother (hence of Agdistis).

23. According to another variant, Attis is killed by a boar—an ancient tradition, for Herodotus (1. 34 ff.) relates it in euhemerized form.

brotherhood of the Mystery-religion type.[24] Long before it was introduced into Rome, the cult of Attis and Cybele had spread into Greece, where it probably underwent some changes. In Greece as at Rome, the repulsion aroused by the bloodstained rites of castration and by the eunuch priests had kept Attis in a subordinate position. For a long time the god enjoyed no public cult in Rome, though a number of terra-cotta statuettes that go back to the second century B.C. testify to his presence. It was only under Claudius and his successors that Attis and the rites he had established were raised to the first rank—an event whose importance we must point out.

The festivals were celebrated at the spring equinox,[25] from March 15 to March 28. On the first day (*canna intrat*, "the entrance of the reed") the brotherhood of reed-bearers brought cut reeds to the temple (according to the legend, Cybele had found the infant Attis exposed on the bank of the river Sangarius). After seven days the brotherhood of tree-bearers brought a cut pine tree from the forest (*arbor intrat*). Its trunk was wrapped in narrow bands, like a corpse, and an image of Attis was fastened to the middle of it. The tree represented the dead god. On March 24, "the day of blood" (*dies sanguinis*), the priests (the Galloi) and the neophytes indulged in a savage dance to the sound of flutes, cymbals, and tambourines, whipped themselves until the blood flowed, and gashed their arms with knives; at the height of their frenzy some neophytes cut off their virile organs and offered them to the goddess in oblation.

The funereal lamentations of the night of March 24–25 were suddenly succeeded by an explosion of joy when, in the morning, the god's resurrection was announced.[26] It was the day of "joy,"

24. See Hepding, *Attis*, pp. 202 ff.; H. Graillot, *Le culte de Cybèle*, pp. 396 ff.

25. Our information concerning the calendar of festivals is late (third and fourth centuries A.D.): see the Present Position of Studies, § 207. But it is important to present the structure of the cult at its apogee.

26. Several authors have connected with this scene a passage in the Christian writer Firmicus Maternus (fourth century) describing the nocturnal lamentations around a divine statue on a bier. Suddenly a light is brought, and the priest consoles the congregation: "Be of good heart, you novices, because the god is saved; deliverance from distress will come for us as well" (*De errore profanarum religionum* 22; trans. Vermaseren). Firmicus Maternus does not

the Hilaria. After a day of "rest" (*requietio*), March 27 saw the great procession to the river, where the statue of Cybele was bathed (the *lavatio*). According to some authors, individual initiations were performed on March 28; the neophyte was sanctified by the blood of a sacrificed bull or ram (*taurobolium* or *criobolium*). Presumably this sacrifice took the place of the mystes' self-mutilation, for he offered the victim's genital organs to the goddess. He was admitted to the "nuptial chamber" (*pastos, cubiculum*) as mystical husband of Cybele, just like the Gallos, who entered this sacrosanct place to offer the Mother the fruits of his mutilation.[27]

As for the initiation proper, the only document we have is the formula quoted by Clement of Alexandria, which served initiates as a password: "From the tambourine I have eaten; from the cymbal I have drunk; I have become the *kernos;* the room I have entered" (*Protrept*. 2. 15; trans. Vermaseren). The analogy with the Eleusinian *synthēma* is obvious (see § 98); it can be explained either by a borrowing from one side or the other or by derivation from a common formula used in several Mysteries during the Hellenistic period. The formula refers to certain initiation rites. The tambourine and cymbal are Cybele's favorite instruments. Since Attis was called "the ear harvested green" (*Philosophoumena* 5. 8), it is likely that the ritual meal consisted essentially of bread and wine; indeed, Firmicus Maternus (*De errore* 18) interprets it as the demonic and baneful equivalent of the Christian communion. As for the *kernos,* it is probable that in the initiatory cult of Attis this terra-cotta vessel was not used to hold

state which cult is referred to, but his description seems most appropriate to Osiris; see Hepding, *Attis,* p. 106; Loisy, *Les mystères païens et le mystère chrétien,* p. 102. However, we must not forget that there is a structural analogy between the two religions; see M. J. Vermaseren, *Cybele and Attis,* p. 116.

27. The Gallos was one of the priests of Cybele, usually a eunuch. (The name comes from the Phrygian river Gallos.) See Hepding, *Attis,* pp. 190 ff. According to another interpretation, the *pastos* (literally, "bridal chamber") was a cave or a subterranean place in the temple itself or in the vicinity; by entering it, the mystes effected a *descensus ad inferos;* see Vermaseren, *Cybele and Attis,* pp. 117–18. It should be added that, in the Imperial period, the *taurobolium* and the *criobolium* could be performed at any season. They were also celebrated for the health of the emperor.

an oblation of food but to carry the sexual organs of the bull or the ram to the Mother "under the canopy."[28]

As we shall see, the Mysteries of Attis and Cybele, at least after a certain date, promised the "immortalization" of initiates. For the moment, we must look more closely into the meaning of the principal rites—that is, the alimentary prohibitions and the self-castration of the Galloi. Despite their "spiritualization," the Hellenistic Mystery religions had preserved a number of archaic elements. This, of course, is characteristic of religious movements that require individual initiation. Omophagia, supremely the Dionysiac rite, was able to reactualize a religious experience typical of primitive hunters (§124). As for the initiation into the Eleusinian Mysteries, it made possible an anamnesia, a remembrance, of archaic sacraments, first of all, the sacramental value of wheat and bread (§ 99). In general it may be said that ceremonies that are initiatory in structure rediscover certain archaic modes of behavior and revalorize a number of ritual objects that have fallen into disuse. Examples are the flint knives employed for initiatory circumcisions, the role of the bullroarer in Orphic mythology and initiation, and the religious function of secrecy (§ 99).

The Hellenistic Mysteries drew on archaic ritual modes of behavior—savage music, frenetic dances, tattooing, the use of hallucinogenic plants—in order to force the divinity to approach or even to obtain an *unio mystica*. In the Mysteries of Attis the fast imposed on the neophytes consisted chiefly in abstaining from bread,[29] for the god was "the ear harvested green." The first initiatory meal amounted to no more than the experience of the sacramental value of bread and wine, an experience seldom accessible to urban populations. As for the self-mutilation of the Galloi and of certain disciples during their ecstatic trances, it insured their absolute chastity, in other words, their total gift of

28. We follow the interpretation in Hepding, *Attis*, pp. 190 ff., and in Loisy, *Les mystères*, pp. 109 ff. See also Vermaseren, *Cybele and Attis*, p. 118.

29. Which did not entail abstaining from pheasant! Saint Jerome (*Ep.* 107 *ad Lactam*) called it "gluttonous abstinence," *gulosa abstinentia* (cited by Loisy, *Les mystères*, p. 89, n. 4).

themselves to the divinity.[30] It is difficult to analyze such an experience; in addition to the more or less unconscious impulses that governed the neophyte, we must take into account the nostalgia for a ritual androgyny, or the desire to increase one's reserve of "sacred powers" by a unique or spectacular infirmity, or even the will to feel expelled from the traditional structures of society by a total *imitatio dei*. In the last analysis, the cult of Attis and Cybele made it possible to rediscover the religious values of sexuality, of physical suffering, and of blood. The disciples' trances freed them from the authority of norms and conventions; in a certain sense, it was the discovery of freedom.

The tendency to recover immemorial experiences was counterbalanced by the effort to "sublimate" the divine pair Attis-Cybele and to reinterpret their cults. This time, too, we are dealing with a phenomenon typical of the religious syncretisms of the time: the will to restore the virtues of the most distant past and, at the same time, to glorify the most recent creations. Allegorical interpretation, laboriously practiced by the theologians and philosophers of the first centuries A.D., identified Attis with the very principles of both creation and the dialectical process life-death-rebirth. Paradoxically, Attis ended by being assimilated to the sun and became the center of the solar theology that was so popular toward the end of paganism. The original meaning of the initiation—mystical assimilation to the god—was enriched with new values. A Roman inscription of 376 proclaims that he who accomplishes the *taurobolium* and the *criobolium* is "reborn for eternity."[31] There is probably Christian influence here. But the promise of "resurrection" or "rebirth" was implicit in the mythico-ritual scenario of the Hilaria. It is likely that, faced by

30. See Michel Meslin's pertinent observations, "Réalités psychiques et valeurs religieuses dans les cultes orientaux," p. 297. It must be made clear that absolute devotion to the divinity does not necessarily imply sexual self-mutilation. Ceremonial chastity could be insured by a symbolic marriage. In the second grade of the Mithraic initiation, called Nymphus, the mystes became the bride of the god, but the rite was wholly spiritual; see Meslin, pp. 302–3.

31. *Taurobolio criobolioque in aeternum renatus;* inscription cited by Hepding, *Attis*, p. 89. But sometimes the *taurobolia* were repeated after twenty years; see Loisy, *Les mystères*, pp. 119 ff.; Vermaseren, *Cybele and Attis*, p. 106.

the success of the Christian mission, the theologians of the Mysteries strongly emphasized the idea of immortality as a consequence of the redemption accomplished by Attis. However this may be, it is certain that the Roman emperors, especially the last Antonines, vigorously fostered the Phrygian cult in the hope of halting the rise of Christianity.

208. Isis and the Egyptian Mysteries

The Egyptian Mysteries differ from similar religious associations by the fact that we know their "origin" and the stages of their spread through Asia and Europe. At the beginning of the third century B.C. Ptolemy Soter decided to strengthen his rule by the help of a divinity accepted as supreme by both Egyptians and Greeks. So he raised Serapis (Sarapis) to the rank of a great national god. According to the tradition transmitted by Plutarch (*De Iside* 28), Ptolemy had seen the god's statue in a dream. In ca. 286 (or ca. 278) the statue was brought from Sinope and set up in the temple that had been newly built in Alexandria. The etymology of Serapis and his country of origin are still in dispute. His name is usually derived from Oserapis, that is, "Osiris-Apis."[32] As for his cult, Ptolemy Soter ordered two learned theologians to establish its structure: the Egyptian priest Manetho and the Greek Timotheus. The former, author of several works, among them a history of Egypt, was well versed in Greek culture; the latter, a member of the famous family of the Eumolpids of Eleusis, had been initiated into several Mysteries.

The success of the new cult was insured by the great prestige enjoyed by Isis and Osiris. As we saw (§ 33), the theologians of the New Empire had elaborated a grandiose religious synthesis by associating Osiris and Re; regarded as complementary, these two great gods ended by being identified. Osiris' popularity did not cease to grow, for he was the only Egyptian god who, murdered, triumphed over death and was "reanimated" by the efforts of Isis and Horus. At Abydos and elsewhere, ritual scenarios representing various episodes of his legend were per-

32. But see Ruth Stiehl, "The Origin of the Cult of Sarapis."

formed before the temples. Herodotus had been present at similar ceremonies at Saïs; he assimilated them to the Greek Mysteries, and that is why he abstained from describing them (2. 61).[33] It is beyond doubt that certain secret Osirian rituals, performed inside the temples, had reference to the future life.[34] But it would be risky to interpret these secret rites as actual initiation ceremonies performed for the benefit of a living individual to obtain his "salvation." On the other hand, it is difficult to imagine that such a knowing theologian as Manetho did not incorporate earlier religious traditions into the Mysteries of Isis. It has been possible to show, for example, that the aretalogies of Isis do not represent a recent innovation; on the contrary, they repeat archaic ritual formulas associated with the royal ideology.[35] In addition, as we shall soon see, the Mysteries of Isis continue certain ceremonies practiced in ancient Egypt.

For our purpose it would be otiose to summarize the chronology and the incidents of the cult's dissemination beyond the frontiers of Egypt. Spreading first into Asia Minor and Greece, it entered Italy in the second century B.C. and Rome at the beginning of the first century. The Egyptian cult became so popular that the Romans more than once fiercely opposed the Senate's decision to demolish its temples. Like the other Mysteries of the Hellenistic and Imperial periods, the Mysteries of Isis and of Serapis comprised public festivals, a daily cult, and secret rites that constituted the initiation proper. We know the principal features of the first two ceremonial systems. As for the initiation, Apuleius' testimony in book 11 of his *Metamorphoses* is regarded—and rightly—as the most valuable document of all ancient writings on the Mysteries.

The two great public festivals reactualized certain episodes of the myth of Osiris and Isis. The first, the Navigium, or "Vessel of Isis," opened the spring navigation season. The second, the

33. He had shown the same scrupulousness in regard both to the Mysteries of Samothrace (2. 51) and Eleusis (2. 171) and to Orphism (2. 123).

34. See some bibliographical indications in Cumont, *Religions orientales*, pp. 243–44, notes 96–101; see also Loisy, *Les Mystères*, pp. 136 ff.; G. Nagel, "The 'Mysteries' of Osiris in Ancient Egypt," pp. 124 ff. (texts from the temple at Abydos).

35. Jan Bergman, *Ich bin Isis*, pp. 121–240.

Inventio of Osiris, took place from October 29 to November 1. The three days of fasting, lamentation, and pantomimes depicting the search for the murdered and dismembered Osiris and the funeral rites performed by Isis (see § 29) were followed by the joy and jubilation of the disciples when it was announced to them that the god's body had been found, reconstructed, and reanimated.[36] The daily services were celebrated at dawn and in the afternoon. The gates of the sanctuary were opened very early in the morning, and the spectators could contemplate the statues of the divinities and be present at the cult performed by the priests. According to Apuleius, on the day set in advance by the goddess the pontiff sprinkles the neophyte with water and imparts to him "certain secret things unlawful to be uttered." Then, before all those present, he urges him to abstain for ten days from flesh food and from wine. On the evening of the initiation the company of disciples offers the initiate various presents; after this, wearing a linen tunic, he is led by the priest into the inmost chapel of the sanctuary.

> Thou wouldst peradventure demand, thou studious reader, what was said and done there: verily I would tell thee if it were lawful for me to tell; thou wouldst know if it were convenient for thee to hear . . . . Howbeit I will not long torment thy mind, which peradventure is somewhat religious and given to some devotion; listen therefore and believe it to be true. Thou shalt understand that I approached near unto hell, even to the gates of Proserpine, and after that I was ravished throughout all the elements, I returned to my proper place: about midnight I saw the sun brightly shine, I saw likewise the gods celestial and the gods infernal, before whom I presented myself and worshipped them. [*Met.* 11. 23; trans. Aldington, rev. Gaselee]

We undoubtedly have here an experience of death and resurrection, but its specific content is not known. The neophyte descends to Hades and returns by way of the four cosmic elements: he sees the sun shining in the darkness of night, an image that could refer to Osiris-Re's nightly journey through the un-

36. The antecedents of these festivals go back to sacred representations performed at Abydos as early as the Twelfth Dynasty.

derground world; he then approaches other gods, contemplates them, and worships them close by. Attempts have been made to discover in this enigmatic account references to the neophyte's passing through various halls ornamented with statues of the gods and representing the underworld, then suddenly coming out into a brightly lit chamber. Other scholars have referred to parapsychological experiences or hypnotism. As a matter of fact, all that can safely be said is that the mystes ends by feeling that he is identified with Osiris-Re or with Horus. For in the morning, clad in twelve ritual garments symbolizing the twelve signs of the zodiac, the mystes mounts a platform in the very center of the temple, with a crown of palm leaves on his head. Thus, "adorned like unto the sun, and made in fashion of an image," he appeared before the eyes of the disciples in front of the statue of Isis. For the hero of the *Metamorphoses*, this day was the anniversary of his rebirth in the bosom of the Mysteries. On the third day, the initiation was completed by a ritual banquet. However, after a year, and still at the goddess's command, the neophyte is introduced to the "ceremonies of the great god: which were done in the night" (11. 28), a rite presumably connected with the Inventio of Osiris. Finally, another vision of the goddess advises a third initiation; but Apuleius reveals nothing concerning these final initiatory ordeals.

As we saw (§ 33), in ancient Egypt the individual hoped for a posthumous identification with Osiris. But by virtue of his initiation the neophyte obtained, here and now on earth, this mystical identification with the god; in other words, it was the *living* individual who was "divinized," not the soul in its postmortem condition. Just as Osiris was "reanimated" by Isis, the neophyte's "divinization" was essentially the work of the goddess. We do not know the "existential situation" of the mystes; it is certain, however, that no initiate doubted his privileged lot, in the presence of the gods, after death. If, so far as the initiation proper is concerned, we are reduced to conjectures, what Apuleius tells us allows us to perceive the syncretistic structures of the new cult. The Egyptian elements play an important part: the mythico-ritual scenario of Isis and Osiris inspires the two public festivals and probably, at least in part, the initiation rites; the elevation of Isis to the rank of universal (or, indeed, of sole) goddess and of Osiris to the rank of supreme god continues the tendency, already documented in the archaic period (see § 33), to raise various divinities to the highest plane. On the other hand, the mystes' descent to the underworld and his ascent through the cosmic elements bear witness to a specifically Hellenistic conception.

The great popularity of the Egyptian Mysteries during the first centuries of the Christian era, together with the fact that certain features of the iconography and mythology of the Virgin Mary were borrowed from Isis, shows that we have here a genuine religious creation and not an artificial or obsolescent revival. The gods of the Mysteries must be regarded as new epiphanies of Isis and Osiris. What is more, it is these Hellenistic interpretations that will be developed by the neo-Orphic and neo-Platonist theologians. Assimilated to Dionysus (who was also killed, dismembered, and resuscitated), Osiris admirably illustrated the neo-Orphic theology: the cosmology conceived as a self-sacrifice of the divinity, as the dispersal of the One in the Many, followed by "resurrection," that is, by the gathering of Multiplicity into the primordial Unity.[37]

The mutual identification of all the gods ends in a "monotheism" of the syncretistic type dear to the theosophers of late antiquity. It is significant that such a "monotheistic" universalism glorifies especially the typically suffering gods, such as Dionysus and Orpheus. As for Isis and Osiris, it is the last interpretations and revalorizations of them by the theologians of the Mysteries and the neo-Platonist philosophers that, for centuries, will be regarded as illustrating the true, and the deepest, Egyptian religious genius.[38]

209. The revelation of Hermes Trismegistus

The name of Hermetism is applied to the whole body of beliefs, ideas, and practices transmitted in the Hermetic literature. This

37. See Macrobius, *In Somnium Scipionis* 1. 12.
38. See vol. 3.

is a collection of texts of unequal value, composed between the third century B.C. and the third century A.D. Two categories are distinguished: writings pertaining to popular Hermetism (astrology, magic, occult sciences, alchemy) and learned Hermetic literature, first of all the seventeen treatises, in Greek, of the *Corpus Hermeticum*.[39] Despite their differences in structure, content, and style, the two groups of texts have a certain unity of intention, reminiscent of the relations between philosophical and popular Taoism (§133) and of the continuity between the "classic" and "baroque" expressions of Yoga. Chronologically, the texts of popular Hermetism are the earlier, some of them going back to the third century B.C.; the philosophical Hermetism developed especially in the second century of the Christian era.

As might be expected, this literature more or less reflects Judeo-Egyptian syncretism (hence certain Iranian elements as well), and the influence of Platonism is also apparent; but, from the second century A.D., Gnostic dualism becomes predominant. "By its actors, its setting, its myths, Hermetic literature seeks to be Egyptian. This claim, at least for some early texts, is based on a certain knowledge of Ptolemaic or Roman Egypt, a knowledge whose reality must not be underestimated."[40] The personages (Thoth, Agathodaimon, Ammon, etc.), the settings (Memphis, Hermopolis, Saïs, Aswan, etc.), certain motifs of pharaonic theology (for example, the emergence of the primordial mound at Thebes or Hermopolis), familiarity with ancient Egyptian traditions,[41] are all indications that must be taken into account. The identification of Thoth with Hermes was already known to Herodotus (2. 152). For the writers of the Hellenistic period, Thoth was the patron of all the sciences, the inventor of hieroglyphs, and a redoubtable magician. He was held to have created the

39. We also have the Latin translation, known as the *Asclepius*, of a "Perfect Discourse" (*Logos teleios*), the original of which has been lost, and some thirty extracts preserved, also in translation, in Stobaeus' *Anthologium* (ca. 500 A.D.).

40. Jean Doresse, "L'Hermétisme égyptianisant," p. 442.

41. In fact the papyri have restored the true Hellenic versions of certain myths, for example that of the goddess Tefnut, in which Thoth-Hermes plays a part; see Doresse, p. 449.

world by his word; now, as we know, the Stoics had identified Hermes with the *logos*.[42]

The writings of popular Hermetism played an important part during the Roman Imperial period. This was first of all because of their "operative" character: in an age terrorized by the omnipotence of Destiny, these texts revealed the "secrets of nature" (the doctrine of analogy, the "sympathetic" relations among the different planes of the cosmos), by virtue of which the *magus* became possessed of their secret forces. Even astral fatalism could be turned to advantage. In one of the astrological writings, the *Liber Hermeticus*,[43] there was not a single reference to the problem of death and the future life; what mattered was how to live happily on earth. Yet knowledge of nature, and hence mastery over it, was made possible by the divinity. "Since it is a matter of discovering a whole network of sympathies and antipathies that nature maintains secretly, how can this secret be penetrated unless a god reveals it?"[44] In consequence, Hermetic science is at once a mystery and the initiatory transmission of that mystery; knowledge of nature is obtained by prayer and the cult or, on a lower plane, by magical control.[45]

In the amorphous corpus of magical recipes and treatises on natural magic and the occult sciences, we sometimes find conceptions characteristic of the learned literature. In the *Korē Kosmou* (14–18) the creation of souls is described as an alchemical operation. The prayer with which the *Asclepius* ends is found, in Greek, in a magical recipe. The importance of this "popular" Hermetic literature must not be underestimated. It inspired and provided material for Pliny's *Natural History* and a famous medieval work, the *Physiologus;* its cosmology and its governing ideas (the doctrine of sympathies and correspondences, espe-

42. A. J. Festugière, *La Révélation d'Hermès Trismégiste*, vol. 1, pp. 71 ff. A tradition going back to the reigns of the Ptolemies related that Thoth, the first Hermes, lived "before the flood"; the second Hermes, Trismegistus, succeeded him, and then his son Agathodaimon and his grandson Tat. These personages are all cited in the treatise *Korē Kosmou*. The genealogy is genuinely Egyptian.

43. The Greek original goes back to the third century B.C.: see Festugière, *La Révélation*, vol. 1, pp. 122 ff.

44. Festugière, *Hermétisme et mystique païenne*, p. 43.

45. Ibid., p. 44.

cially the correspondences between macrocosm and microcosm) were markedly successful from the late Middle Ages until about the end of the eighteenth century; they are to be found not only among the Italian Platonists and Paracelsus but also among scholars as different as John Dee, Ashmole, Fludd, and Newton.[46]

Like the category of popular texts, the writings that make up the learned Hermetic literature are held to have been revealed by Hermes Trismegistus. These treatises differ in their literary forms and especially in their doctrine. As early as 1914 Bousset had observed that the *Corpus Hermeticum* presents two irreconcilable theologies: one optimistic (monistic-pantheistic in type), the other pessimistic, characterized by a strong dualism. For the first, the cosmos is beautiful and good, since it is imbued with God.[47] By contemplating the beauty of the cosmos, one arrives at the divinity. God, who is at once One (*C.H.* 11. 11; etc.) and All (12. 22), is the creator and is called "Father." Man occupies the third place in the triad, after God and the cosmos. His mission is "to admire and worship celestial things, to take care of and govern terrestrial things" (*Asclepius* 8). In the last analysis, man is the necessary complement of the Creation; he is "the mortal living being, ornament of the immortal living Being" (*C.H.* 4. 2).

In the pessimistic doctrine, the world is, on the contrary, fundamentally bad: "It is not the work of God, in any case of the First God, for this First God resides infinitely above all matter, he is hidden in the mystery of his being; hence one cannot attain to God except by fleeing the world, one must behave here below like a stranger."[48] Let us consider, for example, the genesis of the world and the pathetic drama of man according to the first treatise in the *Corpus*, the *Poimandres:* the androgynous superior Intellect (Nous) first produces a demiurge, who forms the world, then the Anthropos, the celestial man; the latter descends to the lower sphere, where, "deceived by love," he unites with

46. See vol. 3; in the meantime, consult Eliade, *The Forge and the Crucible: The Origins and Structures of Alchemy*, pp. 153 ff., 185 ff.

47. The world is an "immortal living being" (*Corpus Hermeticum* 8. 1); it is called "god" or "great god"; it is through the world that "the invisible god" manifests himself (ibid. 5. 2).

48. Festugière, *Hermétisme*, p. 37; cf. his *Révélation*, vol. 1, pp. 84 ff.

Nature (Physis) and engenders terrestrial man. Thenceforth the divine Anthropos ceases to exist as a separate person, for he animates man: his life is transformed into the human soul, and his light into *nous*. This is why, alone among terrestrial beings, man is at once mortal and immortal. However, by the help of knowledge, man can "become god." This dualism, which devalorizes the world and the body, emphasizes the identity between the divine and the spiritual element in man; just like the divinity, the human spirit (*nous*) is characterized by *life* and *light*. Since the world is "the totality of Evil" (*C.H.* 6. 4), it is necessary to become a "stranger" to the world (13. 1) in order to accomplish the "birth of the divinity" (13. 7); indeed, the regenerated man has an immortal body, he is "son of God, All in All" (13. 2).

This theology, which is bound up with a particular cosmology and soteriology, has an essentially "Gnostic" structure (see § 229). But it would be risky to attribute to Gnosticism properly speaking the Hermetic treatises that express dualism and pessimism. Certain mythological and philosophical elements of the "gnostic" type are part of the *Zeitgeist* of the period—for example, contempt for the world, the saving value of a primordial science revealed by a God or a superhuman Being and communicated under the sign of secrecy. We add that the decisive importance attributed to knowledge, transmitted in an initiatory manner to a few disciples, is reminiscent of the Indian tradition (the Upanishads, Sāṃkhya, and Vedānta), just as the "immortal body" of regenerated man shows analogies with Hatha Yoga, Taoism, and Indian and Chinese alchemy.

210. Initiatory aspects of Hermetism

Some scholars (Reitzenstein and Geffcken) have regarded Hermetism as a religious brotherhood in the strict sense, with its dogmas, rites, and liturgy, of which the *Corpus Hermeticum* would have been the Sacred Book. Following Bousset, E. Kroll, and Cumont, Father Festugière rejects this hypothesis. First of all, the presence of two opposed and irreconcilable doctrines is incompatible with the idea of a brotherhood made up of "a group of men who have deliberately chosen a system of thought and life''; second, the Hermetic literature shows no trace of ''ceremonies peculiar to the disciples of Hermes. There is nothing that resembles the sacraments of the Gnostic sects, neither baptism nor communion nor confession of sins nor laying-on of hands to consecrate ministers of the cult. There is no clergy, no appearance of a hierarchic organization or degrees of initiation. Only two classes of individuals are distinguished: those who hear the word and those who refuse it. Now this distinction had become banal; it had entered the literature at least as early as Parmenides.''[49]

Nevertheless, if the hypothesis of a secret, hierarchically organized brotherhood is not persuasive, the great treatises of learned Hermetism presuppose the existence of closed groups practicing an initiation comparable to that of the alchemists and the Tantrics. To use an expression in the *Asclepius* (sec. 25), what is involved is a *religio mentis:* God ''receives pure spiritual sacrifices'' (*C.H.* 1. 3). Nevertheless, we detect a specific religious atmosphere and certain ritual patterns of behavior: the disciples gather together in a sanctuary; they obey the rule of silence and keep the revelations secret; the catechesis takes place with ceremonial seriousness; the relations between the teacher and his disciples have religious overtones. The myth of baptism in a *kratēr* indicates familiarity with the rituals of the Mysteries.[50] We may also assume knowledge of certain practices leading to ecstasy; Hermes tells his disciple Tat of an ecstatic experience after which he entered an ''immortal body,'' and Tat was able to imitate him (*C.H.* 13. 3, 13).

It could be said that what we have here is a new model for communicating esoteric wisdom. Unlike the closed associations involving a hierarchical organization, initiation rites, and progressive revelation of a secret doctrine, Hermetism, like al-

49. Festugière, *Hermétisme*, p. 38; cf. *Révélation*, vol. 1, pp. 81 ff.

50. According to the fourth treatise of the *Corpus Hermeticum*, at the beginning of time God had filled a *kratēr* with *nous;* those who submerge themselves in it become ''perfect men.'' Festugière has shown that this represents a mixture of two rites practiced in the Mysteries: (1) ingestion of a sacred drink drawn from a *kratēr* (mixing bowl) and (2) a purifying and initiatory bath; see his ''Le baptême dans le cratère,'' p. 108 (reprinted in *Hermétisme*, pp. 100–112).

chemy, implies only a certain number of revealed texts, transmitted and interpreted by a "master" to a few carefully prepared disciples (that is, made "pure" by asceticism, meditation, and certain cult practices). We must not lose sight of the fact that the revelation contained in the great treatises of the *Corpus Hermeticum* constitutes a supreme Gnosis, that is, the esoteric knowledge that insures salvation; the mere fact of having understood and assimilated it is equivalent to an "initiation."[51] This new type of individual and wholly spiritual "initiation," made possible by attentively reading and meditating on an esoteric text, developed during the Imperial period and especially after the triumph of Christianity. It follows, on the one hand, from the considerable prestige enjoyed by "Sacred Books," reputedly of divine origin, and, on the other hand, after the fifth century of our era, from the disappearance of the Mysteries and the eclipse of other secret organizations. From the point of view of this new model of initiation, transmission of esoteric doctrines does not imply an "initiatory chain"; for the sacred text can be forgotten for centuries, but if it is rediscovered by a competent reader its message becomes intelligible and contemporary.

The transmission of Hermetism constitutes a fascinating chapter in the history of esotericism. It took place through the Syriac and Arabic literatures and especially through the efforts of the Sabaeans of Harran, in Mesopotamia, who survived in Islam until the eleventh century.[52] Recent research has revealed certain Hermetic elements in Wolfram von Eschenbach's *Parzival* and in several thirteenth-century Spanish texts.[53] However, the real renaissance of Hermetism in Western Europe began with the

51. Festugière has aptly analyzed a characteristic cliché of the Hellenistic period: the transposition of a rite of the cult Mysteries into a metaphor in what the author calls "literary Mystery." But such a transposition still retains a religious value: it stimulates the reader's imagination and reveals to him the deep meaning of the Mysteries.

52. The Sabaeans had, as "prophets," Hermes and Agathodaimon and were acquainted with the fourth treatise of the *Corpus Hermeticum*, the title of which is "*Kratēr.*" According to Henry and Renée Kahane, *kratēr* is the same word as "grail."

53. See R. and H. Kahane, *The Krater and the Grail: Hermetic Sources of the Parzival*, and, by the same authors, "Hermetism in the Alfonsine Tradition."

Latin translation of the *Corpus Hermeticum* undertaken by Marsilius Ficinus at the request of Cosmo de' Medici and finished in 1463. But, as we shall see (vol. 3), the rediscovery of the *Corpus Hermeticum* in fact constitutes a new, creative, and daring interpretation of Hermetism.

211. Hellenistic alchemy

Historians of the sciences distinguish three periods in the formation of Greco-Egyptian alchemy:[54] (1) the period of technical recipes for the operations of alloying, coloring, and imitating gold (for example, the Leiden and Stockholm papyri, which date from the third century B.C.); (2) the philosophical period, probably inaugurated by Bolos of Mendes (second century B.C.), which is manifested in the *Physika kai Mystika,* an apocryphal treatise attributed to Democritus; (3) finally, the period of alchemical literature properly speaking, that of Zosimus (third–fourth centuries) and his commentators (fourth–fifth centuries). Although the problem of the historical origin of Alexandrian alchemy has not yet been solved, the sudden appearance of alchemical *texts* around the Christian era could be explained as the result of a meeting between the esoteric current represented by the Mysteries, neo-Pythagoreanism and neo-Orphism, astrology, the "wisdom of the East" in its various revelations, Gnosticism, etc. (this current was especially the concern of cultivated people, of the intelligentsia), and the "popular" traditions, which were the guardians of trade secrets and magical and technical systems of great antiquity. A similar phenomenon is found in China with Taoism and neo-Taoism and in India with Tantrism and Hatha Yoga. In the Mediterranean world these "popular" traditions had continued into the Hellenistic period a spiritual behavior that is archaic in structure. As we saw (§ 209), the growing interest in the traditional techniques and sciences having to do with substances, precious stones, and plants is characteristic of this whole period of antiquity.

54. See Eliade, *The Forge and the Crucible,* pp. 127 ff.

To what historical causes are we to attribute the birth of alchemical practices? Doubtless we shall never know. But it is not likely that alchemy became an autonomous discipline on the basis of recipes for counterfeiting or imitating gold. The Hellenistic East had inherited all of its metallurgical techniques from Mesopotamia and Egypt, and we know that from the fourteenth century before our era the Mesopotamians had perfected the assaying of gold. Attempting to connect a discipline that has haunted the Western world for two thousand years with efforts to counterfeit gold is to forget the extraordinary knowledge of metals and alloying that the ancients possessed; it is also to underestimate their intellectual and spiritual capabilities. Transmutation, the chief end of Hellenistic alchemy, was not an absurdity in the contemporary condition of science, for the unity of matter had been a dogma of Greek philosophy for some time. But it is hard to believe that alchemy came out of experiments undertaken to validate that dogma and provide experimental proof of the unity of matter. It does not look as if a spiritual technique and a soteriology could have had their source in a philosophical theory.

On the other hand, when the Greek intelligence applied itself to science, it demonstrated an extraordinary sense of observation and reasoning. Now what strikes us in reading the texts of the Greek alchemists is precisely their lack of the scientific spirit. As Sherwood Taylor observes:

> No one who had used sulphur, for example, could fail to remark the curious phenomena which attend its fusion and the subsequent heating of the liquid. Now while sulphur is mentioned hundreds of times, there is no allusion to any of its characteristic properties except its action on metals. This is in such strong contrast to the spirit of the Greek science of classical times that we must conclude that the alchemists were not interested in natural phenomena other than those which might help them to attain their object. Nevertheless, we should err were we to regard them as mere gold-seekers, for the semi-religious and mystical tone, especially of the later works, consorts ill with the spirit of the seeker of riches . . . . At no time does the alchemist employ a scientific procedure.[55]

55. F. Sherwood Taylor, *A Survey of Greek Alchemy,* p. 110. See also, by the same author, "Origins of Greek Alchemy," pp. 42 ff.

The texts of the ancient alchemists show "that these men were not really interested in making gold and were not in fact talking about gold at all. The practical chemist examining these works feels like a builder who should try to get practical information from a work on Freemasonry" (Taylor, *A Survey,* p. 138).

So if alchemy could arise neither from the wish to counterfeit gold (assaying gold had been known for at least twelve centuries) nor from a Greek technique (we have just seen the alchemists' lack of interest in physico-chemical phenomena as such), we are forced to look elsewhere for the "origins" of this unique discipline. Far rather than the philosophical theory of the unity of matter, it is probably the old conception of the Earth Mother bearing minerals as embryos in her womb (see §15) that crystallized belief in an artificial transmutation, that is, a transmutation performed in a laboratory. It is contact with the symbolisms, mythologies, and techniques of miners, smelters, and smiths that in all probability gave rise to the earliest alchemical operations. But it is above all the experimental discovery of *living* substance, as it was felt to be by artisans, that must have played the decisive part. Indeed, it is the conception of a complex and dramatic *life of matter* that constitutes the originality of alchemy in contrast to classical Greek science. We have good reason to suppose that the experience of the dramatic life of matter was made possible by knowledge of the Greco-Oriental Mysteries.

The scenario of the "sufferings," "death," and "resurrection" of matter is documented in Greco-Egyptian alchemical literature from its beginning. Transmutation, the *opus magnum* whose result is the Philosopher's Stone, is obtained by making matter pass through four phases, denominated, in accordance with the colors the ingredients assume, *melansis* (becoming black), *leukansis* (white), *xanthosis* (yellow), and *iosis* (red). "Black" (the *nigredo* of medieval authors) symbolizes "death." But it must be emphasized that the four phases of the *opus* are already documented in the *Physika kai Mystika* of the pseudo-Democritus, hence in the earliest properly alchemical text (second–first centuries B.C.). With countless variants, the four (or five) phases of the work (*nigredo, albedo, citrinitas, rubedo,* sometimes *viriditas,* sometimes *cauda pavonis*) are maintained through the entire history of Arabic and Western alchemy.

Even more to the point: it is the mystical drama of the god—his passion, his death, his resurrection—that is projected on matter in order to transmute it. In short, the alchemist treats matter as the divinity was treated in the Mysteries: the mineral substances "suffer," "die," and "are reborn" to another mode of being, that is, are transmuted. In his *Treatise on the Art* (3. 1. 2–3) Zosimus reports a vision that he had in a dream: a personage named Ion reveals to him that he was wounded by a sword, cut to pieces, beheaded, flayed, and burned by fire, and that he suffered all this "in order to be able to change his body into spirit." When he woke, Zosimus asked himself if all that he had seen in his dream did not refer to the alchemical process of the combination of water, if Ion was not the figure, the exemplary image, of Water. As Jung has shown, the Water is the *aqua permanens* of the alchemists, and its "tortures" by fire correspond to the operation of *separatio*.[56]

It should be noted not only that Zosimus' description is reminiscent of the dismemberment of Dionysus and the other "dying gods" of the Mysteries (whose "passion" can, on a certain plane, be homologized with various moments of the vegetable cycle, especially the torture, death, and resurrection of the "Corn Spirit") but that it exhibits striking analogies with the initiatory visions of shamans and, in general, with the fundamental schema of all archaic initiations. In shamanic initiations the ordeals, though undergone "at a remove," are sometimes extremely cruel: the future shaman is present in dream at his own dismemberment, beheading, and death.[57] If we bear in mind the universality of this initiatory schema and, on the other hand, the solidarity among metalworkers, smiths, and shamans, and if we consider that the ancient Mediterranean brotherhoods of metallurgists and smiths very probably had their own Mysteries, we are led to place Zosimus' vision in a spiritual universe typical of the traditional societies. With this, we become aware of the great innovation of the alchemists: *they projected on matter the initiatory function of suffering*. By virtue of alchemical operations, homologized with the "tortures," "death," and "resur-

56. C. G. Jung, "The Visions of Zosimus," pp. 38 ff.
57. See Eliade, *Shamanism*, pp. 33 ff. and passim.

rection'' of the mystes, substance is transmuted, that is, obtains a transcendental mode of being: it becomes ''Gold.'' Gold, we know, is the symbol of immortality. So alchemical transmutation is equivalent to perfecting matter[58] and, for the alchemist, to the accomplishment of his ''initiation.''

In the traditional cultures, minerals and metals were regarded as living organisms, having their gestation, growth, and birth, even their marriages (§115). The Greco-Oriental alchemists took over and revalorized all of these archaic beliefs. The alchemical combination of sulphur and mercury is almost always expressed in terms of ''marriage.'' But this marriage is also a mystical union between two cosmological principles. Therein lies the novelty of the alchemical point of view: the life of matter is no longer expressed in terms of ''vital'' hierophanies, as it was from the point of view of archaic man; instead it acquires a ''spiritual'' dimension. In other words, by assuming the initiatory meaning of the spirit's drama and suffering, matter also assumes the destiny of spirit. The ''initiatory ordeals'' that, on the plane of spirit, result in freedom, illumination, and immortality, lead, on the plane of matter, to transmutation, to the Philosopher's Stone. This daring revalorization of an immemorial mythico-ritual scenario (the gestation and growth of minerals in the womb of the Earth Mother; the furnace assimilated to a new telluric womb, where the mineral completes its gestation; the miner and the metallurgist taking the place of the Earth Mother in hastening and perfecting the ''growth'' of minerals) could be compared to the ''transmutation'' of the old agrarian cults into Mystery religions. We shall later evaluate the consequences of this effort to ''spiritualize'' matter, to ''transmute'' it.[59]

58. C. G. Jung, *Psychology and Alchemy*, pp. 222 ff., speaks of the redemption, by the alchemical work, of the *anima mundi*, captive in matter. This conception, which is Gnostic in origin and structure, was certainly held by certain alchemists; in any case, it is consonant with this whole current of eschatological thought, which was to end in the conception of the apocatastasis of the cosmos. But, at least in its beginnings, alchemy did not postulate the captivity of the *anima mundi* in matter, though the latter was still obscurely felt as being the Terra Mater—the Earth Mother.

59. See vol. 3 of the present work.

27 New Iranian Syntheses

212. Religious orientations under the Arsacids (ca. 247 B.C. to 226 A.D.)

After the fall of the Achaemenid Empire (ca. 330 B.C.) Iranian religion was drawn into the vast and complex syncretistic movement that is characteristic of the Hellenistic period (see § 205). The reconquest of the independence of a part of Iran by the Parthian chief Arsaces, who, by proclaiming himself king (ca. 247), founded the new national dynasty of the Arsacids, did not halt this process. To be sure, the Parthians brought with them a whole religious and cultural tradition originated by the horsemen of the steppes, and it is very probable that certain elements of the royal ideology that began to define themselves after the Arsacids took power represent the heritage of these unconquerable tribes, who for centuries had led a nomadic life on the margin of the great empires. But the attraction of Hellenism proved irresistible, and, at least until the first century A.D., the Arsacids encouraged Hellenization (likenesses of the Greek gods are engraved on their coins). We must, however, remember that the model they sought to imitate, Alexandrian Hellenism, had itself absorbed a number of Semitic and Asian elements.

The contemporary documents are numerous and of many kinds: writings by Greek and Latin authors, monuments, inscriptions, coins. But the information they supply concerning Iranian religious beliefs and ideas is rather disappointing. The religious creativity under the Arsacids can be better perceived by the help of later documents. Recent researchers have shown that late texts express beliefs and ideas articulated or valorized during the Parthian period. Moreover, this was the way of the age: after numberless cultural confrontations and exchanges, new religious forms arose out of earlier conceptions.

Essentially, the sources show us (1) that Mithra was worshiped throughout the Empire and that he had a special relation to the kings;[1] (2) that the Magi made up the caste of sacrificing priests, especially performing the sacrifices involving the shedding of blood (cows and horses); Strabo writes that the Magi worshiped Anāhitā, but there are indications that they also took part in the cult of Mithra (they had a role in his Mysteries); (3) that the cult of fire was extremely popular; and (4) that in the second and first centuries B.C. an apocalypse written in Greek was in circulation under the title *Oracles of Hystaspes* (Hystaspes is the Greek form of Vishtaspa); it was directed against Rome (whose fall was announced) but formed part of the Iranian eschatological literature.[2]

However, the great religious creations of the Parthian period are of a different order. It was in the first century B.C. that the Mysteries of Mithra began to spread through the Mediterranean world (the earliest document dates from 67 B.C.); it is legitimate to conjecture that the same period (more or less) begins to define the idea of the messianic king, still in connection with a mythico-ritual scenario elaborated around Mithra; despite controversies, it seems probable, as Widengren has shown, that the myth of the savior, as it is presented in the Gnostic "Hymn of the Pearl," took shape in the period of the Arsacids. Finally, it was also this period that saw the development of the Zurvanite theology, with its elaboration of ideas concerning time, eternity, the precedence of the "spiritual" over the physical creation, and absolute dualism—conceptions that were to be systematized and sometimes laboriously organized some centuries later, under the Sassanids.

1. The deification of living sovereigns, a phenomenon characteristic of the Hellenistic period, is also documented among the Arsacids; at least three examples are known. See J. Duchesne-Guillemin, *La religion de l'Iran ancien,* pp. 225, with bibliography (English trans., by K. M. JamaspAsa, *Religion of Ancient Iran* [Bombay, 1973]).

2. J. Bidez and F. Cumont, *Les Mages hellénisés,* vol. 1, p. 217; G. Widengren, *Les religions de l'Iran,* pp. 228 ff.; J. R. Hinnells, "The Zoroastrian Doctrine of Salvation," pp. 147 ff.

It is important not to lose sight of the fundamental solidarity among all these religious forms. The variety of their expressions is explained by the differences in the ends sought. It would be useless, for example, to look for elements of the royal ideology in the concurrent manifestations of the popular religion or in theological speculations. A characteristic common to all these creations is the fact that, while they continue conceptions that are earlier, sometimes even archaic, they remain "open" in the sense that they go on developing during the following centuries. The *Oracles of Hystaspes* take up classical eschatological motifs, probably of Indo-Iranian origin (the shortening of the year, universal decadence, the final battle, etc.), that will be elaborated in the Pahlavi apocalypse of the Sassanid period, first of all in the *Bahman Yašt*. On the other hand, the *Oracles* justify their prophecies on the basis of an eschatological chronology of 7,000 years, each millennium being dominated by a planet, which shows Babylonian influence (cf. the well-known series: seven planets, seven metals, seven colors, etc.). But the interpretation of this chronological schema is Iranian: during the first six millennia, God and the Spirit of Evil fight for supremacy; Evil appears to be victorious; God sends the solar god Mithra (= Apollo, Helios), who dominates the seventh millennium; at the end of this last period, the power of the planets ends and a universal conflagration renews the world.[3] Now these mytho-chronologies with eschatological aims will have a great popularity in the Western world at the beginning of the Christian era.

The eschatological hope can also be deciphered in the traditions regarding the birth of a king-savior, assimilated to Mithra. The traditional conception of the divine king and cosmocrator, mediator between men and gods, is enriched by new soteriological meanings—a process easy to understand in a period dominated by expectation of the savior. The fabulous biography of Mithradates Eupator admirably illustrates this eschatological hope: his birth is announced by a comet; lightning strikes the newborn infant but leaves only a scar; the future king's education amounts to a long series of initiatory ordeals; when he is

3. F. Cumont, "La fin du monde selon les Mages occidentaux," pp. 93 ff.; Bidez and Cumont, *Les Mages hellénisés,* vol. 1, pp. 218 ff.

crowned, Mithradates (like so many other kings) is held to be an incarnation of Mithra.[4] A similar messianic scenario animates the Christian legend of the Nativity.

213. Zurvan and the origin of evil

The problems raised by Zurvan and Zurvanism are still far from being solved. The god is certainly archaic.[5] Ghirshman claims to have identified Zurvan in a bronze from Luristan representing the winged and androgynous god giving birth to twins (who emerge from his shoulders); three processions, symbolizing the three ages of man, bring him the *barsom* (bundle of twigs) in homage.[6] If this interpretation is correct, it follows that the myth of Zurvan as father of Ohrmazd and Ahriman was already known at a time long before that of the earliest written testimonies. According to the information supplied by Eudemus of Rhodes (second half of the fourth century B.C.), "the Magi . . . call the one and intelligible All sometimes 'Space,' sometimes 'Time'; therefrom are said to be born Ohrmazd and Ahriman, that is, Light and Darkness."[7] This information is important: it assures us that, toward the end of the Achaemenid period, speculations on time-space as the common source of the two principles, Good and Evil, incarnated in Ohrmazd and Ahriman, were familiar to the Iranians.

The Avestan term for "time" is *thwâša,* literally "the in-haste one" or "he who hurries," and Widengren thinks that from the beginning it designated the celestial vault, an epithet proper to

4. Justin, 37. 2; Plutarch, *Quaest. Conviv.* 1. 6. 2; Widengren, *Les religions de l'Iran,* pp. 266 ff.; Widengren, "La légende royale de l'Iran antique," passim.

5. Widengren (*Hochgottglaube im alten Iran,* p. 310) believed that he recognized his name in the Nuzi tablets (thirteenth–twelfth centuries). But E. A. Speiser has shown that the name ought to read *Zarwa(n),* the name of a Hurrian goddess; see *Annual of the American Schools of Oriental Research* 16 (1936): 99, nn. 47–48.

6. Ghirshman, "Notes iraniennes XV: Deux bronzes des rois d'Urartu," *Artibus Asiae* 28 (1958): 37 ff.; Duchesne-Guillemin, *La religion de l'Iran,* p. 146.

7. Eudemus' text has been published by Bidez and Cumont in *Les Mages hellénisés,* vol. 2, pp. 69–70; cf. ibid., vol. 1, pp. 62 ff.

a celestial god who determines destinies.[8] So it is probable that Zurvan was originally a celestial god, source of time and distributor of good and evil fortune—in the last analysis, master of destiny.[9] In any case, Zurvan's structure is archaic: he is reminiscent of certain primitive divinities in whom cosmic polarities and all kinds of antagonisms coexist.

In the late Avesta (texts probably redacted in the fourth century B.C.) Zurvan is seldom mentioned, but he is always related to time or destiny. One text (*Vidēvdāt* 19. 29) states that before reaching the Činvat Bridge (see §103), "created by Mazdā," the souls of the just and the impious advance along "the road created by Zurvan." The eschatological function of time/destiny—in other words, of the temporal duration granted to each individual—is clearly emphasized. In another passage Zurvan is presented as infinite time (*Vidēvdāt* 19. 13 and 16); elsewhere a distinction is made between *Zurvan akarana,* "infinite time," and *Zurvan darego xvadhāta,* "long autonomous time" (*Yašt* 72. 10).

All this presupposes a theory of temporal duration pouring from the breast of eternity. In the Pahlavi works, "long autonomous time" emerges from "infinite time" and, after lasting 12,000 years, returns to it (*Bundahišn* 1. 20; *Dēnkart* 282). The theory of cycles made up of a certain number of millennia is ancient, but it was differently expressed in India, Iran, and Mesopotamia. Although it became popular toward the end of antiquity and was used in countless apocalypses and prophecies, the theory of millennia was particularly developed in Iran, especially in Zurvanite circles. In fact, speculations on time and destiny are frequent in Zurvanite writings: they are used to explain both the origin of evil and its present predominance in the world and to propose a stricter solution to the problem of dualism.

8. Widengren, *Hochgottglaube,* pp. 232 ff.; Zaehner, *Zurvan, a Zoroastrian Dilemma,* pp. 89 ff.

9. Since, according to Eudemus, Zurvan was worshiped by the Magi—that is, originally in the land of the Medes—it is difficult to decide whether Zarathustra's silence is explained by polemical reasons or simply denotes the small importance, perhaps even the absence, of this god of time and destiny in the prophet's circles.

In his treatise on Isis and Osiris (secs. 46–47), Plutarch, using fourth-century B.C. sources, reports the doctrine of the "Magus Zoroaster": "Oromazdes, born of the purest light," and "Aremanos, born of darkness"; each wields power for 3,000 years, then they fight each other for another 3,000 years. The belief that the world will last for 9,000 years, divided into three equal periods (Ohrmazd's domination gives place to Ahriman's, which is followed by 3,000 years of warfare), occurs in a late treatise that is full of Zurvanite elements, the *Menōk i Khrat* (7. 11). Since Zoroastrianism excludes the idea of a period ruled by Ahriman, it is probable that the sources used by Plutarch refer to Zurvanistic conceptions. In addition, Plutarch writes that Mithra, who is placed between Ohrmazd and Ahriman (this is why he is called "mediator"), had taught the Persians to offer these gods characteristic sacrifices, an offering of the chthonic-infernal type being intended for the "Evil Demon"—which is not a Zoroastrian conception either.[10]

Plutarch does not mention Zurvan, but the myth of the Twins and the explanation of their alternating sovereignty are presented in several late sources as being specifically Zurvanistic. According to an Armenian Church Father, Eznik of Kolb, when nothing existed, Zurvan ("Zrwan, which means 'Destiny' or 'Glory' ") had for a thousand years offered a sacrifice in order to have a son.[11] And because he had doubted the efficacy of his sacrifice ("What use can the sacrifice that I offer be?"), he conceived two sons: Ohrmazd "by virtue of the offered sacrifice" and Ahriman "by virtue of the above-mentioned doubt." Zurvan decided that the first to be born should be king. Ohrmazd knew his father's thought and revealed it to Ahriman. The latter tore open the womb[12] and emerged. But when he told Zurvan that he

10. Plutarch's text is discussed by Widengren, *Rel. de l'Iran,* pp. 244 ff., which also gives the recent bibliography.

11. Eznik, *De Deo,* after the translation by L. Mariès, cited by Zaehner, *Zurvan,* pp. 420–28. See also Eznik, *Against the Sects,* trans. Zaehner, pp. 438–39.

12. Eznik clearly understood that Zurvan was a hermaphrodite. But other late authors speak of Zurvan's "mother" or "wife"; see Zaehner, *Zurvan,* pp. 63 ff., 423, 428. See other texts of Eznik and of Theodore bar Konai, reproduced in Bidez and Cumont, *Les Mages,* vol. 2, pp. 89–92, and in Zaehner, *Zurvan,* pp. 421 ff.; for discussion of them, see Zaehner, pp. 54 ff.

was his son, Zurvan replied: "My son is perfumed and luminous, and thou, thou art dark and stinking." Then Ohrmazd was born, "luminous and sweet-smelling," and Zurvan wanted to consecrate him king. But Ahriman reminded him of his vow to make his firstborn son king. In order not to break his oath, Zurvan granted him the kingship for 9,000 years, after which Ohrmazd should reign. Then, Eznik goes on, Ohrmazd and Ahriman "fell to making creatures. And all that Ohrmazd created was good and straight, and what Ahriman made was evil and crooked." It should be noted that both gods are creators, although Ahriman's creation is entirely evil. Now this negative contribution to the cosmogonic work (mountains, snakes, noxious animals, etc.) is an essential element in many popular cosmogonic myths and legends, disseminated from eastern Europe to Siberia,[13] in which God's Adversary plays a part.

As the important Pahlavi treatise the *Greater Bundahišn* (3. 20) expresses it, "By the performance of sacrifice, all creation was created." Both this conception and the myth of Zurvan are certainly Indo-Iranian, for they are also found in India. To obtain a son, Prajāpati offered the *dākṣāyaṇa* sacrifice,[14] and he, too, as he sacrificed, felt a doubt ("Ought I to offer? Ought I not to offer?"). Now Prajāpati is the Great God who produces the universe from his own body, and he also represents the year, the temporal cycle (§ 76). Doubt, with its disastrous consequences, constitutes a ritual error. Hence, *evil is the result of a technical accident, of an inadvertence on the part of the divine sacrificer.* The Evil One does not possess an ontological condition of his own: he is dependent on his involuntary author, who, furthermore, hastens to limit, in advance, the terms of his existence.

The mythological theme of the fateful consequences of doubt has numerous parallels in the myths—documented more or less all over the world—that explain the origin of death or of evil by lack of vigilance or foresight on the part of the Creator. The difference from the earlier conception, also held by Zarathustra, is plain: Ahura Mazdā engenders the two spirits, but the Evil Spirit *freely chooses his mode of being* (see § 103). Thus the Wise

13. See our study "The Devil and God," in *Zalmoxis, the Vanishing God,* pp. 76–130.

14. See S. Lévi, *La doctrine du sacrifice dans les Brāhmanas* (1898), p. 138.

Lord is not directly responsible for the appearance of evil. Similarly, in many archaic religions the supreme being comprises a *coincidentia oppositorum,* since he constitutes the totality of the real. But in the Zurvanite myth, as in other myths of the same tenor, evil is produced, although involuntarily, by the Great God himself. In any case, at least in the tradition transmitted by Eznik, Zurvan plays no part in the cosmic creation; he himself recognizes that he is a *deus otiosus,* since he offers his twin sons the symbols of sovereignty (the *barsom* to Ohrmazd and, to Ahriman, according to the Pahlavi book *Zâtspram,* "a tool made of the proper substance of shadow").

214. The eschatological function of time

Insofar as it is possible for us to orient ourselves among the successive strata of the Pahlavi texts and their rehandlings (made when Mazdaism became the official church of the Sassanian Empire [226–635] and even after the Moslem conquest), Zurvanism appears to be a syncretistic theology, elaborated by the Median Magi,[15] rather than an independent religion. In fact, no sacrifices are offered to Zurvan. What is more, this primordial god is always mentioned in association with Ohrmazd and Ahriman. But it must also be made clear that the doctrine of millennia always, in one way or another, involved Zurvan—whether as cosmic god of time or simply as symbol or personification of time. The 9,000 or 12,000 years that make up the history of the world are interpreted in relation to the actual person of Zurvan. According to certain Syriac sources,[16] Zurvan is surrounded by three gods—in reality, his hypostases, Ašōqar, Frašōqar, Zārōqar. These names are explained by the Avestan epithets *aršōkara* ("the one who makes virile"), *frašokara* ("the one who makes

15. Widengren has brought out the relations between Zurvanism and the Median Magi; see his *Rel. de l'Iran,* pp. 320 ff.

16. The texts are translated by Zaehner, *Zurvan,* pp. 435, 439, 440 ff. For commentary on them, see Duchesne-Guillemin, pp. 186 ff., and Widengren, *Rel. de l'Iran,* pp. 317 ff.

splendid''), and maršokara (''the one who makes old'').[17] Obviously, the reference is to time as lived, as it can be perceived in the three stages of human existence: youth, maturity, and old age. On the cosmic plane, each of these three temporal moments can be connected with a period of 3,000 years. This ''formula of the three times'' can be found in the Upanishads and in Homer.[18] On the other hand, a similar formula is used in the Pahlavi texts; for example, Ohrmazd ''is, was, and will be,'' and it is said that the ''time of Ohrmazd,'' *zamân i Ohrmazd,* ''was, is, and will always be.''[19] But Zurvan (= Zaman) is also he ''who was and will be all things.''[20]

In short, temporal images and symbolisms are documented in both Zorastrian and Zurvanite contexts. The same situation obtains in regard to the 12,000-year cycle. It plays a part in Zurvanite speculations. Zurvan is presented as a god with four faces, and different cosmological tetrads serve to circumscribe him, as befits an ancient celestial god of time and destiny.[21] If we recognize Zurvan in ''unlimited time,'' *zaman i akanārak,* it appears that he transcends Ohrmazd and Ahriman, since it is proclaimed that ''Time is stronger than the two creations.''[22]

We can follow the polemics between Mazdean orthodoxy, which had progressively hardened its dualism, and the Zurvanite theology. The idea that Ohrmazd and Ahriman are brothers engendered by Zurvan is naturally condemned in a passage in the *Dēnkart.*[23] This is why the problem of the origin of the two adversaries is not raised in the orthodox Pahlavi books. Ohrmazd and Ahriman exist from eternity, but the Adversary will cease to be at a certain moment in the future. We understand, then,

17. Nyberg, ''Questions de cosmogonie et de cosmologie mazdéennes,'' pp. 89 ff.; Zaehner, *Zurvan,* pp. 221 ff.; Widengren, *Rel. de l'Iran,* pp. 317 ff.

18. See Widengren, p. 319, n. 4; Homer, *Iliad* 1. 70.

19. See the text translated by Zaehner, *Zurvan,* p. 278.

20. Texts in Zaehner, pp. 232 and 283; cf. Widengren, pp. 318 ff.

21. Nyberg, ''Questions de cosmogonie,'' p. 57; Zaehner, *Zurvan,* pp. 54, 97 ff.

22. Fragment of the first chapter of the *Bundahišn,* after the translation by Widengren, p. 325.

23. *Dēnkart* (M 829. 1–5), in reference to exegesis of the Gathic text on the two Spirits (*Yasna* 30. 3); cf. Duchesne-Guillemin, pp. 185 ff.

why time and the doctrine of millennia are of prime importance for the Mazdeans too.

According to Mazdean theology, time is not only indispensable for the Creation; it also makes possible the destruction of Ahriman and the banishing of evil.[24] In fact, Ohrmazd created the world in order to conquer and annihilate evil. The cosmology already presupposes an eschatology and a soteriology. This is why cosmic time is no longer circular but linear: it has a beginning and will have an end. Temporal duration is the indirect consequence of Ahriman's attack. By creating linear and limited time as the interval in which the battle against evil will take place, Ohrmazd gave it both a meaning (an eschatology) and a dramatic structure (a war continued without interruption until the final victory). This is as much as to say that he created limited time as *sacred history.* It is, in fact, the great originality of Mazdean thought that it interpreted the cosmogony, the anthropogony, and Zarathustra's preaching as moments constituting one and the same sacred history.

215. The two Creations: *mēnōk* and *gētik*

According to the first chapter of the *Bundahišn,* Ohrmazd and Ahriman exist from eternity; but whereas Ohrmazd, infinite in time, is delimited by Ahriman in space, Ahriman is limited in both space and time, for at a certain moment he will cease to exist. In other words, in Mazdaism God is originally finite, since he is circumscribed by his opposite, Ahriman.[25] This situation would have continued for eternity if Ahriman had not attacked. Ohrmazd counterattacks by creating the world, which enables him also to become infinite in space. Thus Ahriman contributes to the perfection of Ohrmazd. In other words, unconsciously and involuntarily, Evil advances the triumph of Good—a con-

24. In the *Bundahišn* 1. 1 (see Zaehner, *The Teachings of the Magi,* p. 35), Ohrmazd has three more names: Time, Space, and Religion. The quaternity is adapted from Zurvanism, but it is necessary to explain the Creation; see Duchesne-Guillemin, pp. 309–10.

25. Zaehner, *Teachings of the Magi,* p. 30.

ception that is rather often encountered in history and that aroused Goethe's impassioned interest.

In his omniscience, Ohrmazd foresees the attack and produces an "ideal" or "spiritual" Creation. The term employed, *mēnōk,* is hard to translate, for it refers both to a perfect and to an embryonic world. According to the *Dātastān i Dēnīk* (37. 3 ff.), what is *mēnōk* is perfect, and the *Dēnkart* (9. 37. 5) states that the world was immortal in the beginning. On the other hand, the *Bundahišn* (1. 6) describes the Creation in the *mēnōk* state, during the 3,000 years that it lasted, as being "without thought, without motion, impalpable."[26] But it is, above all, the celestial and spiritual character of the *mēnōk* state that is emphasized. "I have come from the celestial world (*mēnōk*)," says a fourth-century text; "it is not in the terrestrial world (*gētik*) that I began to be. I was originally manifested in the spiritual state; my original state is not the terrestrial state."[27] It must be made clear, however, that there is no question here of an abstract existence, of a world of Platonic Ideas: the *mēnōk* state can be defined as a mode of being that is at once spiritual and concrete.

Four stages are distinguished in the cosmic drama and the history of the world. During the earliest period, the attack by Ahriman and darkness against Ohrmazd's world of light takes place. (We here have a dualism that is acosmic, for in Zarathustra's doctrine Ahura Mazdā is the creator of both light and darkness; see *Yasna* 44. 5.) Before transposing the Creation from the spiritual state (*mēnōk*) to the material state (*gētik*), Ohrmazd asks the Fravashis (preexisting spirits dwelling in Heaven) if they will accept a corporeal existence, on earth, in order to combat the forces of evil,[28] and the Fravashis consent. This testifies to the attachment for incarnate life, for work, and, in the last analysis, for matter—an attachment that is a specific characteristic of Zarathustra's message. The difference between this and Gnostic and Manichaean pessimism is manifest.[29] Indeed, before Ah-

26. See other texts cited and commented on by Duchesne-Guillemin, pp. 310–11; see also Mary Boyce, *A History of Zoroastrianism,* vol. 1, pp. 229 ff.

27. *Pand Nāmak i Zartušt* (= *The Book of the Counsels of Zartušt*), strophe 2, after the translation by H. Corbin, "Le temps cyclique dans le mazdéisme," p. 151.

28. *Bundahišn,* chap. 1, trans. Zaehner, *Zurvan,* p. 336.

29. For Mazdaism, Mani's radical dualism represented the extreme of heresy.

riman's aggression, the material Creation (*gētik*) was in itself good and perfect. It is only Ahriman's attack that corrupts it, by introducing evil. The result is the state of "mixture" (*gumēcišn*), which is thereafter that of the entire Creation, a state that will not disappear until after the final purification. Ahriman and his demonic troops spoil the material world by entering it and soiling it with their harmful creations, and especially by taking up residence in the bodies of men. Indeed, certain texts suggest that Ahriman does not reply to Ohrmazd's material Creation with a negative *gētik* Creation: to ruin the world, he has only to enter it and dwell in it. "Consequently, when he shall no longer have his dwelling in the bodies of men, Ahriman will be eliminated from the entire world."[30]

Ahriman's aggression is described in moving terms: he tears the periphery of Heaven, enters the material world (*gētik*), pollutes the waters, poisons vegetation, and thus causes the death of the primordial Bull.[31] He attacks Gayōmart, the First Man, and the Prostitute befouls him and, through him, all men. (However, Gayōmart was predestined to live for thirty more years after the aggression.) After that, Ahriman throws himself on the sacred fire and soils it, making it smoke. But at the height of his power Ahriman is still captive in the material world, for, by closing itself, Heaven shuts him up in the material Creation, as in a trap.[32]

216. From Gayōmart to Saoshyant

Gayōmart is the son of Ohrmazd and Spandarmat, the Earth; like other mythical macranthropoi, he is round in shape and "shines like the sun" (cf. Plato, *Symp.* 189d ff.). When he dies,

30. *Dēnkart,* bk. 6, sec. 264, translated by S. Shaked, "Some Notes on Ahriman," p. 230.

31. Edible and medicinal plants spring from his marrow, and his sperm produces useful animals. The memory of a myth of the Hainuwele type is recognizable (see §113). On the murder of the Bull, see Duchesne-Guillemin, pp. 323–24; Mary Boyce, *History of Zoroastrianism,* pp. 138 ff., 231.

32. Ahriman can no longer attack Heaven, for the Fravashis, armed with lances, now defend the "fortresses of the Sky" (Zaehner, *Dawn and Twilight of Zoroastrianism,* p. 270.

the metals proceed from his body; his semen is purified by the light of the sun, and a third of it falls to the ground and produces the rhubarb, from which the first human pair, Mašye and Mašyāne, will be born. In other words, the primordial couple is born from the mythical Ancestor (Gayōmart) and the Earth Mother, and their first form is vegetable—a mythologem rather widely disseminated in the world. Ohrmazd orders them to do good, not to worship the demons, and to abstain from food. Though Mašye and Mašyāne proclaim Ohrmazd the Creator, they yield to Ahriman's temptations and exclaim that he is the author of the earth, water, and plants. Because of this "lie," the pair is damned, and their souls will remain in Hell until the resurrection.

For thirty days they live without food, but then they suck the milk of a she-goat and pretend to dislike it; this was a second lie, which strengthened the demons. This mythical episode can be interpreted in two ways: as illustrating (1) the sin of lying or (2) the sin of having eaten, that is, of establishing the human condition (in a number of archaic myths the primordial pair has no need of food, and, what is more, according to Iranian belief, at the end of time men will forgo the practice of eating and drinking).[33] After thirty more days Mašye and Mašyāne slaughter a head of cattle and roast it. They offer part of it to the fire and another part to the gods, throwing it into the air; but a vulture carries off this part. (Soon afterward a dog is the first to eat flesh.) This may mean that God has not accepted the offering, but it may also mean that man is not meant to be carnivorous. For fifty years Mašye and Mašyāne feel no sexual desire. But they copulate, and a pair of twins is born, "so delicious" that the mother eats one of them, and the father eats the other. Then Ohrmazd takes away the flavor of children so that their parents will thenceforth let them live.[34] After that, Mašye and Mašyāne have other pairs of twins, who become the ancestors of all the human races.

33. *Bundahišn,* trans. by Zaehner, *Teachings of the Magi,* p. 145; see also Zaehner, *Zurvan,* p. 352.

34. *Greater Bundahišn,* 14. 14, trans. by Zaehner, *Teachings of the Magi,* p. 73; for another translation, see A. Christensen, *Les types du premier homme et du premier roi,* vol. 1, pp. 19–20.

The myth of Gayōmart (Avestan *gaya maretan,* "mortal life") is highly significant for an understanding of the Zoroastrian theologians' reinterpretation of the traditional mythology. Like Ymir or Puruṣa, Gayōmart is a primordial and androgynous macranthropos, but his slaying is differently valorized. It is no longer the whole of the world that is created from his body but only the metals—in other words, the planets—and, from his semen, the rhubarb that engenders the first human pair. Just as, in late Jewish speculation, Adam is endowed both with cosmological attributes and with eminent spiritual virtues, Gayōmart is raised to an exceptional position. In Mazdean sacred history he ranks close to Zarathustra and Saoshyant. In fact, in the material Creation (*gētē*), Gayōmart is the first to receive the revelation of the Good Religion.[35] And, since he survived Ahriman's aggression by thirty years, he was able to transmit the revelations to Mašye and Mašyāne, who then communicated it to their descendants. Mazdean theology proclaims Gayōmart to be the Just and Perfect Man, equal to Zarathustra and Saoshyant.[36]

The work of late theologians, the glorification of Gayōmart ends by redeeming the human condition. Man, in fact, was created good and endowed with a soul and an immortal body, just like Gayōmart. Death was introduced into the material world by Ahriman, in consequence of the Ancestor's sin. But, as Zaehner observes,[37] for Zoroastrianism the original sin is less an act of disobedience than an error of judgment: the Ancestors were mistaken in considering Ahriman the Creator. Nevertheless, Ahriman did not succeed in killing Gayōmart's soul or, in consequence, the souls of men. Now man's soul is Ohrmazd's most powerful ally; for in the material world only man possesses free will. But the soul can act only through the body that it inhabits; the body is the instrument or "garment" of the soul. What is more, the body is not made of darkness (as the Gnostics affirm) but of the same substance as the soul; in the beginning the body was shining and sweet-smelling, but concupiscence made it stink-

35. *Dēnkart* 7. 1, 4, translated by Molé, *Culte, mythe et cosmologie dans l'Iran ancien,* p. 504.

36. See the texts cited by Molé and his commentary on them, ibid., pp. 485 ff., 521.

37. *The Dawn and Twilight of Zoroastrianism,* p. 267.

ing. However, after the eschatological Judgment, the soul will recover a resuscitated and glorious body.[38]

In short, by virtue of his freedom to choose between good and evil, man not only insures his salvation, but he can collaborate in Ohrmazd's work of redemption. As we saw (§104), every sacrificer contributes to the "transfiguration" of the world by reestablishing in his own person the condition of purity that preceded the "mixture" (*gūmecišn*) produced by Ahriman's attack. For, in the eyes of Mazdaism, the material Creation—that is, matter and life—*is good in itself* and worthy to be purified and restored. Indeed, the doctrine of the resurrection of bodies proclaims the inestimable value of the Creation. This is the most rigorous and the most daring religious valorization of matter that we know of before the Western chemist-philosophers of the seventeenth century (see vol. 3).

During the 3,000 years that separate the murder of Gayōmart and the emergence of the primordial couple from the coming of Zarathustra, there was a series of legendary reigns, the most famous of which are those of Yim (Yima), Aždahāk, and Frēton. Zarathustra *appears at the center of history,* at an equal distance from Gayōmart and from the future savior, Saoshyant. (According to a tradition of the fourth century A.D., Saoshyant will be born of a virgin who will bathe in Lake Kasaoya, in whose waters Zarathustra's semen is miraculously preserved.) As we saw (§§104, 112) the final Renovation (*frašō-kereti*) will take place after a sacrifice performed by Saoshyant. The Pahlavi books give more detailed descriptions of the episodes of this eschatological scenario. First, during the final three millennia, men will gradually abstain from meat, milk, and plants, until their only food is water. According to the *Bundahišn,* this is precisely what happens in the case of the aged, who are nearing their end.

The eschatology, in fact, repeats, in order to annul them, the deeds and gestures of the Ancestors. That is why the demoness Āz (Covetousness), having no more power over men, will be forced to devour demons. Ahriman's murder of the primordial Bull will have its counterpart in the eschatological sacrifice of

38. See the passages from the *Dēnkart* translated and commented on by Zaehner, ibid., pp. 273 ff.

the ox Hathayōs, performed by Saoshyant and Ohrmazd. The drink prepared from its fat or its marrow, mixed with white *haoma,* will make resuscitated men immortal. As First Man, Gayōmart will be the first to be resuscitated. The battles that took place in the beginning will be repeated: the dragon Aždahāk will reappear, and it is required that Frēton, who had conquered it *in illo tempore,* will be resuscitated. In the final battle the two armies will face each other, each combatant having his precisely determined adversary. Ahriman and Āz will be the last to fall, under the blows of Ohrmazd and Srōz.[39]

According to some sources, Ahriman is reduced to impotence forever; according to others, he is thrust back into the hole through which he had entered the world, and there he is annihilated.[40] A gigantic conflagration makes the metals of the mountains flow, and in this stream of fire—burning for the wicked, like warm milk for the just—the resuscitated bodies are purified for three days. The heat finally makes the mountains vanish, the valleys are filled, and the openings that communicate with Hell are blocked. (A flattened earth is, as we know, the image of the paradisal world, primordial as well as eschatological.) After the Renovation, men, freed from the danger of sinning, will live eternally, enjoying bliss that is at once carnal (e.g., families will be reunited) and spiritual.

217. The Mysteries of Mithra

According to Plutarch (*Pompey* 24. 5), the Cilician pirates "secretly celebrated the Mysteries" of Mithra; conquered and captured by Pompey, they disseminated this cult in the West. This

39. See *Bundahišn* 34. 23; Duchesne-Guillemin, pp. 350 ff.; Zaehner, *Dawn and Twilight,* pp. 309 ff. There is certainly here an Indo-European eschatological myth, still preserved in Brāhmanic India and among the Germans; see §§177, 192.

40. *Mēnōk ī Krat* 8. 11–15; *Dēnkart,* bk. 12, sec. 291; see the other sources cited by Duchesne-Guillemin, p. 351, Zaehner, pp. 314 ff., 351, and Widengren, *Rel. de l'Iran,* pp. 230 ff.

is the first explicit reference to the Mysteries of Mithra.[41] We do not know by what process the Iranian god glorified by the *Mihr-yašt* (see § 109) was transformed into the Mithra of the Mysteries. Probably his cult developed in the circle of the Magi established in Mesopotamia and Asia Minor. Supremely a tutelary or champion god, Mithra had become the protector of the Parthian sovereigns. The funerary monument of Antiochus I of Commagene (69–34 B.C.) shows the god clasping the king's hand. But it seems that the royal cult of Mithra did not include any secret ritual; from the end of the Achaemenid period the great ceremonies known as the Mithrakana were celebrated publicly.

The mythology and theology of the Mithraic Mysteries are accessible to us chiefly through figured monuments. Literary documents are few and for the most part refer to the cult and the hierarchy of the initiatory grades. One myth told of the birth of Mithra from a rock (*de petra natus*), just like the anthropomorphic being Ullikummi (§ 46), the Phrygian Agdistis (§ 207), and a celebrated hero of Ossetic mythology.[42] This is why the cave played a primary part in the Mysteries of Mithra. On the other hand, according to a tradition transmitted by al-Bîrûni, on the eve of his enthronement the Parthian king retired to a cave, where his subjects approached and venerated him like a newborn infant—more precisely, like an infant of supernatural origin.[43] Armenian traditions tell of a cave in which Meher (i.e., Mihr, Mithra) shut himself up and from which he emerged once a year. In fact the new king *was* Mithra, reincarnated, born again.[44] This Iranian theme is found again in the Christian legends of the Nativity in the light-filled cave at Bethlehem.[45] In short, Mithra's miraculous birth was an integral part of a great Irano-syncretistic myth of the cosmocrator-redeemer.

41. All the other sources—literary, epigraphic, and archeological—on the cult and its spread into the West go back no further than the first century of the Christian era.

42. See G. Dumézil, *Légendes sur les Nartes*, pp. 192 ff.

43. al-Bîrûni, *India* (trans. by Sachau), vol. 2, p. 10.

44. G. Widengren, *Iranisch-semitische Kulturbegegnung*, p. 65; see also his *Les religions de l'Iran*, p. 269, and other examples in S. Hartmann, *Gayōmart*, p. 60, n. 2, p. 180, n. 6; also I. Gershevitch, in J. R. Hinnells, ed., *Mithraic Studies*, pp. 85 ff., 356.

45. See Eliade, *The Two and the One*, pp. 50 ff., and *Zalmoxis*, pp. 27 ff.

The essential mythological episode involves the theft of the bull by Mithra and its sacrifice, undertaken (to judge from certain monuments) by order of the Sun (Sol). The immolation of the bull is depicted on almost all the Mithraic bas-reliefs and paintings. Mithra performs his mission unwillingly; turning his head away, he grasps the bull's nostrils with one hand and plunges the knife into its side with the other. "From the body of the dying victim were born all herbs and health-giving plants . . . . From its spinal marrow sprouted bread-bestowing wheat, from its blood the vine, which produces the sacred drink of the mysteries."[46] In the Zoroastrian context, Mithra's sacrifice of the bull appears enigmatic. As we saw (§ 215), the murder of the primordial Bull is the work of Ahriman. A late text (*Bundahišn* 6. E. 1–4), however, reports beneficent effects from this immolation: from the primordial Bull's semen, purified by the light of the moon, the animal species are born and the plants grow from its body. From the morphological point of view, this "creative murder" is explained better as part of an agrarian religion than of an initiatory cult.[47] On the other hand, as we have just seen (§ 216), at the end of time the ox Hathayōs will be sacrificed by Saoshyant and Ohrmazd, and the drink produced from its fat or its marrow will make men immortal. So Mithra's exploit could be compared with this eschatological sacrifice; in that case, it could be said that initiation into the Mysteries anticipated the final Renovation, in other words, the salvation of the mystes.[48]

The immolation of the bull takes place in the cave in the presence of the Sun and the Moon. The cosmic structure of the sacrifice is indicated by the twelve signs of the zodiac, or the seven planets, and the symbols of the winds and the four seasons. Two personages, Cautes and Cautopates, dressed as Mithra and

46. After the translation by F. Cumont, *Les Mystères de Mithra*, 2d ed., p. 13. See also Cumont, *Textes et monuments figurés relatifs aux Mystères de Mithra*, vol. 1, pp. 179 ff., 186 ff.

47. G. Widengren compares a late Babylonian ritual, Kalu, involving the sacrifice of a bull for the purpose of insuring cosmic fecundity (*Iranisch-semitische Kulturbegegnung*, pp. 51 ff.).

48. For a similar interpretation of the bull-slaying, see J. R. Hinnells in *Mithraic Studies*, pp. 305 ff. In addition, since H. Windischmann (1859), several Iranologists have noted the striking similarities between Mithra and Saoshyant. See, most recently, Hinnells, ibid., p. 311 (bibliography in n. 132).

each holding a lighted torch, watch the god's exploit attentively; they represent two other epiphanies of Mithra as solar god (indeed, Pseudo-Dionysius speaks of the "triple Mithra," *Epist.* 7).

The relations between Sol and Mithra raise a problem that has not yet been solved; on the one hand, though he is inferior to Mithra, Sol orders him to sacrifice the bull; on the other hand, the inscriptions term Mithra "Sol invictus." Certain scenes present Sol kneeling before Mithra; others show the gods clasping hands. However this may be, Mithra and Sol seal their friendship by a banquet in which they share the flesh of the bull. The feast takes place in the cosmic cave. The two gods are served by persons wearing animal masks. This banquet constitutes the model for ritual meals, at which the mystai, wearing masks that indicate their initiatory grades, serve the chief (*pater*) of the conventicle. It is assumed that Sol's ascension to Heaven, a scene depicted in several bas-reliefs, takes place soon afterward. In his turn, Mithra mounts to the sky; some images show him running behind the Sun's chariot.

Mithra is the only god who does not suffer the same tragic destiny as the gods of the other Mysteries, so we may conclude that the scenario of Mithraic initiation did not include ordeals suggesting death and resurrection. Before their initiation the postulants undertook on oath (*sacramentum*) to keep the secret of the Mysteries. A passage in Saint Jerome (*Ep.* 107, *ad Laetam*) and a number of inscriptions have supplied us with the nomenclature of the seven grades of initiation: Crow (*corax*), Bride (*nymphus*), Soldier (*miles*), Lion (*leo*), Persian (*Perses*), Courier of the Sun (*heliodromus*), and Father (*pater*). Admission to the first grades was granted even to children from the age of seven; presumably they received a certain religious education and learned chants and hymns. The community of the mystai was divided into two groups: the "servitors" and the "participants," the latter group being made up of initiates of the grade of *leo* or higher.[49]

We know nothing of the initiations into the different grades. In their polemic against the Mithraic "sacraments" (inspired by

49. See Cumont, *Textes et monuments figurés,* vol. 1, p. 317, and vol. 2, p. 42, where a fragment of Porphyry, *De abstinentia* 4. 16, is quoted.

Satan!), the Christian apologists refer to a "baptism," which presumably introduced the neophyte into his new life.[50] Probably this rite was reserved for a neophyte preparing for the grade *miles*.[51] We know that he was offered a crown, but the mystes had to refuse it, saying that Mithra "was his only crown."[52] He was then marked on the forehead with a redhot iron (Tertullian, *De praescr. haeret.* 40) or purified with a burning torch (Lucian, *Menippus* 7). In the initiation into the grade of *leo,* honey was poured on the candidate's hands and his tongue was smeared with it. Now honey was the food of the blessed and of newborn infants.[53]

According to a Christian author of the fourth century, the candidates' eyes were blindfolded, and a frantic troop then surrounded them, some imitating the cawing of crows and the beating of their wings, others roaring like lions. Some candidates, their hands tied with the intestines of chickens, had to jump over a ditch filled with water. Then someone appeared with a sword, cut the intestines, and announced himself as the liberator.[54] Initiation scenes depicted in paintings in the mithraeum at Capua probably represent some of these initiatory ordeals. Cumont describes one of the best-preserved of these scenes as follows: "The naked mystes is seated, with his eyes blindfolded and his

50. Tertullian, *De praescr. haeret.* 40 (cf. Cumont, *Textes et monuments,* vol. 2, p. 51).

51. Loisy, *Mystères païens et mystère chrétien,* p. 173. We do not know the initiatory ordeal for the *corax;* according to Porphyry (*De abst.* 4. 16), the "Crows" are auxiliaries. (The crow, be it said, is the messenger who brings Mithra the Sun's order to immolate the bull.) The emblems belonging to the grade of *nymphus* were a torch (the marriage torch), a diadem (allusion to Venus), and a lamp, symbol of the "new light" thenceforth accessible to the mystes.

52. Tertullian, *De corona* 15 (= Cumont, *Textes et monuments,* vol. 2, p. 50).

53. Porphyry, *De antro nymph.* 15 (Cumont, *Textes et monuments,* vol. 2, p. 40). Honey was put on the tongues of newborn infants. In the Iranian tradition, honey had come from the moon. See Cumont, vol. 1, p. 320.

54. Pseudo-Augustine, *Quaest. vet. et novi Test.* 114. 12 (Cumont, *Textes et monuments,* vol. 2, p. 8). Some authors doubt the genuineness of this information, but, as Loisy puts it, "its coarseness testifies to its authenticity; what our author says of it would lead to the supposition that it was given a symbolic interpretation whose meaning he did not understand or which he did not want to repeat" (*Mystères païens,* p. 183).

hands perhaps bound behind his back. The mystagogue approaches him from behind, as if to push him forward. Facing him, a priest in Oriental dress, with a high Phrygian cap on his head, comes forward, holding out a sword. In other scenes the naked mystes kneels or even lies on the floor.''[55] We also know that the mystes had to be present at a simulated murder, and he was shown a sword stained with the victim's blood.[56] Very probably, certain initiatory rituals involved fighting a bugbear. Indeed, the historian Lampridius writes that the Emperor Commodus desecrated the Mysteries of Mithra by an actual homicide (*Commodus* 9; Cumont, *Textes et monuments*, vol. 2, p. 21). Presumably in acting as ''Father'' in initiating a postulant into the grade of *miles*, Commodus in fact killed him when he was supposed only to simulate killing him.

Each of the seven grades was protected by a planet: *corax* by Mercury, *nymphus* by Venus, *miles* by Mars, *leo* by Jupiter, *Perses* by the Moon, *heliodromus* by the Sun, and *pater* by Saturn. These astral relations are clearly illustrated in the mithraea at Santa Prisca and Ostia.[57] On the other hand, Origen (*Contra Celsum* 6. 22) speaks of a ladder with seven rungs made of different metals (lead, tin, bronze, iron, alloy, silver, and gold) and associated with different divinities (lead with Kronos, tin with Aphrodite, etc.). Very probably such a ladder played a ritual part—a part of which we know nothing—while at the same time serving as a symbol for the Mithraic conventicle.

218. "If Christianity had been halted . . . "

When the Mysteries of Mithra are discussed, it appears inevitable to quote Ernest Renan's famous sentence: ''If Christianity had been halted in its growth by some mortal illness, the world would have been Mithraist'' (*Marc Aurèle*, p. 579). Presumably Renan

55. F. Cumont, *Les religions orientales*, p. 142, plate XIII. Other scenes from the mithraeum at Capua have been reproduced by Vermaseren, *Mithras, the Secret God*, figs. 51–53, pp. 132–33.

56. Cumont, *Les Mystères de Mithra*, p. 135.

57. Ferrua, *Il mitreo sotto la chiesa di Santa Prisca*, pp. 72 ff.; G. Becatti, *Scavi di Ostia*, vol. 2: *I Mitrei* (Rome, 1954), pp. 108 ff.

was impressed by the prestige and popularity that the Mysteries of Mithra enjoyed in the third and fourth centuries; he was certainly struck by their dissemination through all the provinces of the Roman Empire. In fact this new Mystery religion inspired respect by its power and originality. The secret cult of Mithra had succeeded in combining the Iranian heritage with Greco-Roman syncretism. In its pantheon the principal gods of the classical world rubbed shoulders with Zurvan and other Oriental divinities. In addition, the Mysteries of Mithra had assimilated and integrated the spiritual currents characteristic of the Imperial period: astrology, eschatological speculations, solar religion (interpreted, by the philosophers, as solar monotheism). Despite its Iranian heritage, its liturgical language was Latin. Unlike other Oriental religions of salvation, which were governed by an exotic body of priests (Egyptians, Syrians, Phoenicians), the chiefs of the Mysteries, the *patres,* were recruited among the Italic populations and those of the Roman provinces. In addition, Mithraism differed from the other Mysteries by the absence of orgiastic or monstrous rites. A religion especially of soldiers, the cult impressed the profane by the discipline, temperance, and morality of its members—virtues that were reminiscent of the old Roman tradition.

As for the dissemination of Mithraism, it was immense: from Scotland to Mesopotamia, from North Africa and Spain to Central Europe and the Balkans. Most of its sanctuaries have been discovered in the old Roman provinces of Dacia, Pannonia, and Germania. (The cult appears not to have made its way into Greece or Asia Minor.) However, it must be taken into account that a conventicle accepted, at most, one hundred members. Consequently, even in Rome, where at a certain moment there were a hundred sanctuaries, the number of adepts did not number above 10,000.[58] Mithraism was almost exclusively a secret cult reserved for soldiers; its dissemination followed the movements of the legions. The little that we do know of its initiatory rituals resembles the initiations into the Indo-European "men's societies" (see §175) more than the initiations into the Egyptian or Phrygian Mysteries. For, as we have observed, Mithra was

58. See Widengren, "The Mithraic Mysteries," p. 453.

the only god of Mysteries who had not suffered death. And, alone among the other secret cults, Mithraism did not admit women. Now at a time when the participation of women in cults of salvation had reached a degree never before known, such a prohibition made the conversion of the world to Mithraism difficult if not decidedly unlikely.

Yet the Christian apologists feared the possible "competition" of Mithraism, for they saw in the Mysteries a diabolical imitation of the Eucharist. Justin (*Apol.* 66) accused the "evil demons" of having prescribed the sacramental use of bread and water; Tertullian (*De praescr.* 40) spoke of the "oblation of bread." In fact, the ritual meal of initiates commemorated the banquet of Mithra and Sol after the sacrifice of the bull. It is difficult to determine if, for Mithraic initiates, such feasts constituted a sacramental meal or if they were more like other ritual banquets that were common during the Imperial period.[59] However this may be, there can be no denying the religious significance of the Mithraic banquets (or, for that matter, that of the other Mystery cults), since they followed a divine model. The mere fact that the Christian apologists vigorously denounced them as diabolical imitations of the Eucharist testifies to their sacred character. As for initiatory baptism, it was also practiced by other cults. But for the Christian theologians of the second and third centuries, the similarity with Mithraism here is even more disquieting, for the sign marked on the forehead with a hot iron reminded them of the *signatio*, the rite that completed the sacrament of baptism; in addition, from the second century on, the two religions celebrated the nativity of their God on the same day (December 25) and shared similar beliefs concerning the end of the world, the Last Judgment, and the resurrection of bodies.

But these beliefs and mythico-ritual scenarios belonged to the *Zeitgeist* of the Hellenistic and Roman period. In all probability the theologians of the various syncretistic religions of salvation did not hesitate to borrow certain ideas and formulas whose value and success they had recognized (we have already mentioned this in connection with the Phrygian Mysteries, § 207).

59. See I. P. Kane, "The Mithraic Cult Meal in Its Greek and Roman Environment," pp. 343 ff.

In the last analysis, what was important was the personal experience and theological interpretation of the mythico-ritual scenario revealed by conversion and the initiatory ordeals (it is enough to remember the numerous valorizations of sacraments both among non-Christians and in the history of Christianity).[60]

Several emperors supported Mithraism, especially for political reasons. At Carnutum in 307 or 308 Diocletian and other Augusti consecrated an altar to Mithra, "the benefactor of the Empire." But Constantine's victory at the Milvian Bridge in 312 sealed the fate of Mithraism. The cult would recover its prestige under the very short reign of Julian; that philosopher-emperor declared himself a Mithraist. His death in 363 was followed by a period of tolerance, but Gratian's edict in 382 ended official support of Mithraism. Like all the religions of salvation and all the esoteric conventicles, the secret cult of Mithra, forbidden and persecuted, disappears as a historical reality. But other creations of the Iranian religious genius continue to make their way into a world that is in the process of being Christianized. Beginning in the third century, the success of Manichaeanism shakes the foundations of the Church, and the influence of Manichaean dualism continues all through the Middle Ages. On the other hand, a number of Iranian religious ideas—notably, some motifs of the Nativity, angelology, the theme of the magus, the theology of Light, and certain elements of Gnostic mythology—will end by being assimilated by Christianity and Islam; in some instances their traces can still be recognized in the period extending from the High Middle Ages to the Renaissance and the Age of Enlightenment.[61]

60. See John R. Hinnells, "Christianity and the Mystery Cults," p. 20.
61. See volume 3 of the present work.

28 The Birth of Christianity

219. An "obscure Jew": Jesus of Nazareth

In the year 32 or 33 of our era a young Pharisee named Saul, who had distinguished himself by the zeal with which he persecuted Christians, was traveling from Jerusalem to Damascus. "Suddenly, . . . there came a light from heaven all around him. He fell to the ground, and then he heard a voice saying 'Saul, Saul, why are you persecuting me?' 'Who are you, Lord?' he asked, and the voice answered, 'I am Jesus, and you are persecuting me. Get up now and go into the city, and you will be told what you have to do.' The men traveling with Saul stood there speechless, for though they heard the voice they could see no one. Saul got up from the ground, but even with his eyes wide open he could see nothing at all, and they had to lead him into Damascus by the hand. For three days he was without his sight, and took neither food nor drink." Finally a disciple, Ananias, taught by Jesus in a vision, laid his hands on Saul, and Saul recovered his sight. "So he was baptized there and then, and after taking some food he regained his strength."[1]

This happened two or three years after the Crucifixion. (The exact date of Jesus' execution is unknown; it could have taken place in 30 or in 33. Hence Paul's conversion can be put at the earliest in 32 and at the latest in 36.) As we shall see, faith in the resurrected Christ constitutes the fundamental element of Chris-

1. Acts of the Apostles 9:3–5, 18–19. The author of Acts gives two more accounts of his encounter with the resurrected Christ on the road to Damascus: 2:4–21; 26:12–20.

tianity, especially of the Christianity of Saint Paul.[2] This fact is of great importance, for his Epistles constitute the earliest documents that narrate the history of the Christian community. Now all the Epistles are infused with an unequaled fervor: certainty of the Resurrection, hence of salvation through Christ. "At last," wrote the great Hellenist Wilamowitz-Moellendorff, "at last the Greek language expresses an intense and burning spiritual experience."[3]

It is important to emphasize another fact: the short time—a few years—that separates Paul's ecstatic experience from the event that revealed the vocation of Jesus. In the fifteenth year of the principate of Tiberius (hence in 28–29 A.D.), an ascetic, John the Baptist, began traveling about the Jordan district "proclaiming a baptism of repentance for the forgiveness of sins" (Luke 3:1 ff.). The historian Flavius Josephus describes him as an "honest man" who exhorted the Jews to practice virtue, justice, and piety (*Ant. Jud.* 18. 5. 2. 116–19). In fact, he was a true prophet, illuminated, irascible, and vehement, in open rebellion against the Jewish political and religious hierarchies. Leader of a millenarianistic sect, John the Baptist announced the imminence of the Kingdom, but without claiming the title of its Messiah. His summons had considerable success. Among the thousands of persons who flocked from all over Palestine to receive baptism was Jesus, a native of Nazareth in Galilee. According to Christian tradition, John the Baptist recognized the Messiah in him.

It is not known why Jesus chose to be baptized. But it is certain that his baptism revealed the messianic dignity to him. In the Gospels the mystery of the revelation is translated by the image of the Spirit of God descending in the form of a dove and a voice coming from heaven and saying: "This is my Son, the Beloved" (Matthew 3:16; cf. Mark 1:11, Luke 3:22). Immediately after his baptism Jesus withdrew into the wilderness. The Gospels state that "the Spirit drove him out into the wilderness" in order for him to be tempted there by Satan (Mark 1:12, Matt. 4:1–10, Luke 4:1–13). The mythological character of these temp-

2. In the First Epistle to the Corinthians (15:1–2) he is careful to draw up a list of all those to whom the resurrected Christ appeared.

3. Wilamowitz-Moellendorff, cited by G. Bornkamm, *Paul,* pp. 9–10.

tations is obvious, but their symbolism reveals the specific structure of the Christian eschatology. Morphologically, they are a series of initiatory ordeals, similar to those of Gautama Buddha (see §148). Jesus fasts for forty days and forty nights, and Satan "tempts" him: he first orders him to perform miracles ("tell these stones to turn into loaves"; he takes him to the parapet of the Temple in Jerusalem and says, "If you are the Son of God, throw yourself down"), and he then offers him absolute power: "all the kingdoms of the world and their splendor." In other words, Satan offers him power to destroy the Roman Empire (and so effect the military triumph of the Jews announced by the apocalypses) on condition that Jesus will fall at his feet.[4]

For some time, Jesus practiced baptism, like John the Baptist and probably more successfully (see John 3:22–24; 4:1–2). But learning that the prophet had been arrested by Herod, Jesus left Judaea for his native land. Flavius Josephus explains Herod's act as due to fear: Herod was afraid of the Baptist's influence over the masses and dreaded a rebellion. However this may have been, John's imprisonment triggered Jesus' preaching. As soon as he arrived in Galilee, Jesus proclaimed the Good News, that is, the Gospel. "The time has come, . . . and the Kingdom of God is close at hand. Repent, and believe the Good News."[5] The message expresses the eschatological hope that with few exceptions had dominated Jewish religiosity for more than a century. Following the prophets, following John the Baptist, Jesus predicted the imminent transfiguration of the world: this is the essence of his preaching (see § 220).

Surrounded by his first disciples, Jesus preached and taught in the synagogues and in the open air, especially addressing the humble and the disinherited. He used the traditional didactic

4. To be sure, the scenario of the "temptations" was later integrated into the fabulous traditions collected in the Gospels, after the defeat of the insurrection of 66–70, that is, after the Romans had destroyed the Temple. But in the symbolic horizon in which the Church was developing, the "temptations" prefigured the miracles of Jesus (for soon afterward he will change water to wine and multiply the loaves and fishes) and the triumph of Christianity (for, though the Roman Empire was not destroyed by an armed insurrection, it would end by being conquered, that is, by becoming Christian).

5. Mark 1:15. Matthew 4:17 refers to the "Kingdom of Heaven," but the two formulas are synonymous.

means, referring to sacred history and the most popular biblical personages, drawing from the immemorial reservoir of images and symbols, making use especially of the figurative language of parables. Like so many other "divine men" of the Hellenistic world, Jesus was a physician and thaumaturge, curing all kinds of sicknesses and relieving the possessed. It was after certain prodigies that he became suspected of sorcery, a crime punishable by death. "It is through Beelzebub, the Prince of devils, that he casts out devils," said some. "Others asked him, as a test, for a sign from heaven."[6] His reputation as an exorcist and thaumaturge was not forgotten by the Jews: a tradition of the first or second century mentions Yeshu, who "practiced sorcery and led Israel astray."[7]

Jesus' preaching soon began to disquiet the two politically and religiously influential groups, the Pharisees and Sadducees. The former were irritated by the liberties the Nazarene took in regard to the Torah. As for the Sadducees, they sought to avoid the disturbances that were likely to break out after any messianic propaganda. In fact, the Kingdom of God that Jesus preached suggested to some the religious fanaticism and political intransigence of the Zealots. The latter refused to recognize the authority of the Romans because, for them, "God is the only ruler and lord" (Josephus, *Ant. Jud.* 18. 1. 6. 23). At least one of the twelve Apostles, Simon, called the Zealot,[8] was a former adherent of that sect (Mark 3:18). And Luke reports that, after the Crucifixion, a disciple said: "Our own hope had been that he would be the one to set Israel free" (24:21).

In addition, one of the most spectacular and mysterious episodes recounted by the Gospels brings out the misunderstanding

6. Luke 11:15–16. Luke well saw that the demand for a "sign" and the accusation of sorcery constitute a narrative unity; the other Gospels report them separately: Mark 3:22, 8:11; Math. 12:24, 38; 16:1. See C. H. Dodd, *The Founder of Christianity*, p. 179, n. 11.

7. See B. *Sanhedrin* 43. 2. The same text gives other details, whose importance will appear further on, for they are independent of the Christian sources (see n. 12, below). The rabbinic sources are cited and discussed by J. Klausner, *Jesus of Nazareth*, pp. 17–47.

8. See S. C. F. Brandon, *Jesus and the Zealots*, pp. 44–47, 243–45.

concerning the Kingdom proclaimed by Jesus.[9] After preaching for part of a day, Jesus learned that the five thousand people who had followed him to the shores of the Sea of Galilee were without food. He made them sit down and miraculously multiplied a few loaves and fishes, whereupon they all ate together. We here have an archaic ritual act by means of which the mystical solidarity of a group is affirmed or restored. In this case, the common meal might signify a symbolic anticipation of the *eschaton,* for Luke (9:11) states that Jesus had just been speaking to them of the Kingdom of God. But, excited by this new wonder, the crowd did not understand its deep meaning and saw in Jesus the feverishly awaited "prophet-king," him who was to deliver Israel. "Jesus . . . could see that they were about to come and take him by force and make him king" (John 6:15). At that, he sent away the crowd, took refuge in a boat with the disciples, and crossed the Sea of Galilee.

The misunderstanding could be interpreted as an abortive revolt. In any case, Jesus was abandoned by the crowd. According to John (6:66–67), only the Twelve remained faithful to him. It was with them that, in the spring of 30 (or 33), Jesus decided to celebrate the Feast of Passover at Jerusalem. The purpose of this expedition has long been—and still is—discussed. In all likelihood, Jesus wanted to proclaim his message in the religious center of Israel in order to force a definite answer one way or the other.[10] When he came near Jerusalem, people "imagined that the kingdom of God was going to show itself then and there" (Luke 19:11). Jesus entered the city like a messianic king (Mark 11:9–10), drove the buyers and sellers from the Temple, and preached to the people (11:15 ff.). The next day he entered the Temple again and told the parable of the murderous vine-dressers who, after killing the servants sent by their master, seized and killed his son. "What will the owner of the vineyard do?" Jesus concluded. "He will come and make an end of the tenants and give the vineyard to others" (12:19).

9. The episode is narrated by the four Evangelists (Mark and Matthew tell it twice): Mark 6:30–44, 8:1–110; Matt. 14:13–21, 15:32–39; Luke 9:10–17; John 6:1–15.

10. Dodd, *The Founder of Christianity,* pp. 139 ff.; R. M. Grant, *Augustus to Constantine,* p. 43.

For the priests and the scribes the meaning of the parable was transparent: the prophets had been persecuted, and the last emissary, John the Baptist, had just been killed. According to Jesus, Israel still represented God's vineyard, but its religious hierarchy was condemned; the new Israel would have other leaders.[11] What is more, Jesus gave his hearers to understand that he himself was the heir to the vineyard, the "beloved son" of the master—a messianic proclamation that could provoke bloody reprisals on the part of the incumbent. Now as the High Priest Caiaphas will say, "it is better for one man to die for the people, than for the whole nation to be destroyed" (John 11:50). It was necessary to intervene quickly, yet without alerting Jesus' partisans. The arrest must be made secretly, by night. On the eve of Passover Jesus celebrated his last meal with his disciples. This final agape will become the central rite of Christianity: the Eucharist, whose meaning will engage our attention further on (§ 220).

"After psalms had been sung, they left for the Mount of Olives" (Matt. 26:30). Of this touching night, tradition has preserved the memory of two incidents that still haunt Christian consciences. Jesus announces to Peter that "before the cock crows" he will deny him three times (Matt. 26:34; cf. Mark 14:26–31). Now, Jesus saw in Peter his most constant disciple, him who was to sustain the community of the faithful. To be sure, the denial was only a confirmation of human weakness. However, such an act does not annul Peter's dignity and charismatic virtues. The meaning of this painful incident is obvious: in the economy of salvation, human virtues matter no more than human sins; what counts is to repent and not to lose hope. A great part of the history of Christianity would be hard to justify without the precedent of Peter; his denial and his repentance (Matt. 26:74) have become in a way the exemplary model for every Christian life.

No less exemplary is the next scene, which occurs in a place "called Gethsemane." Jesus took Peter and two other disciples with him and said: "My soul is sorrowful to the point of death. Wait here and keep awake with me" (Matt. 26:38). And going a little distance away, "he fell on his face and prayed. 'My

11. See Dodd, p. 150.

Father,' he said, 'if it is possible, let this cup pass me by. Nevertheless, let it be as you, not I, would have it' " (26:39). But when he came back, he found his disciples sleeping. He said to Peter: "So you had not the strength to keep awake with me one hour" (26:40). "You should be awake and praying," he urged them again. It was in vain: when he returned, he "found them sleeping, their eyes were so heavy" (26:41; cf. Mark 14:32–42, Luke 22:40–46). Now, since Gilgamesh's adventure (§ 23) it has been well known that conquering sleep, remaining "awake," constitutes the most difficult initiatory ordeal, for it seeks a transformation of the profane condition, a conquest of "immortality." At Gethsemane the "initiatory vigil"—though limited to a few hours—proved to be beyond human strength. This defeat, too, will become an exemplary model for the majority of Christians.

Soon afterward, Jesus was arrested by the High Priest's guards, probably reinforced by Roman soldiers. It is hard to determine the succession of events. The Gospels report two separate judgments. The Sanhedrin found Jesus guilty of blasphemy. For, asked by the High Priest, "Are you the Christ (that is, the Messiah), . . . the Son of the Blessed One?" he answered, "I am" (Mark 14:61–62; cf. Matt. 26:57–68, Luke 22:54, 66–71). Blasphemy was punishable by stoning, but it is not certain that at this period the Sanhedrin had the right to inflict capital punishment. In any case, Jesus was next judged by Pontius Pilate, the prefect of Judaea. Accused of sedition ("Are you the king of the Jews?"), he was condemned to death by crucifixion, a typically Roman torture. Subjected to derision (clad in a purple cloak and a crown of thorns, he was saluted by the soldiers with "Hail, king of the Jews!"), Jesus was crucified between two "thieves." Josephus often used this term—*lēistai*—to signify revolutionists. "The context of Jesus' execution was thus clearly the suppression of Jewish revolt against the rule of Romans and their collaborators in Judaea. Any proclamation of the coming reign of God immediately suggested to the Jerusalem authorities that the restoration of a Jewish kingdom was involved."[12]

12. Grant, *Augustus to Constantine*, p. 43. The rabbinic tradition reports that Jesus was judged by the Jewish authorities and sentenced to be hanged on the eve of Passover; see Klausner, *Jesus of Nazareth*, pp. 18 ff.

The arrest, trial, and sacrifice of Jesus scattered the faithful. Soon after the arrest, Peter, Jesus' favorite disciple, denied him three times. It is certain that Jesus' preaching, and perhaps even his name, would have sunk into oblivion but for a strange episode that is incomprehensible except to believers: the resurrection of the victim. The tradition transmitted by Paul and the Gospels attributes decisive importance to the empty tomb and the numerous appearances of the resurrected Jesus. Whatever the nature of these experiences may be, they constitute the source and foundation of Christianity. Faith in the resurrected Jesus Christ transformed the handful of demoralized fugitives into a group of resolute men, certain that they were invincible. It could almost be said that the Apostles themselves also experienced the initiatory ordeal of despair and spiritual death before they were reborn to a new life and became the first missionaries of the Gospel.

220. The Good News: The Kingdom of God is at hand

Rudolf Bultmann spoke of the "intolerable platitudinousness" of the biographies of Jesus. And in fact the testimonies are few and uncertain. The earliest—Paul's Epistles—almost entirely neglect the historical life of Jesus. The Synoptic Gospels, composed between 70 and 90, collect the traditions transmitted orally by the earliest Christian communities. But these traditions concern Jesus as well as the resurrected Christ. This does not necessarily lessen their documentary value, for the essential element of Christianity—as is also the case with any religion laying claim to a founder—is precisely *memory.* It is the *memory of Jesus* that constitutes the model for every Christian. But the tradition handed down by the earliest witnesses was "exemplary," not simply "historical"; it preserved the significant structures of events and the preaching, not any precise recollection of Jesus' activity. The phenomenon is well known, and not only in the history of religions.

On the other hand, it must be borne in mind that the earliest Christians, Jews of Jerusalem, constituted an apocalyptic sect within Palestinian Judaism. They were in daily expectation of the Second Coming of Christ, the parousia; it was the *end of history* that preoccupied them, not the historiography of the eschatological expectation. In addition, as was to be expected, around the figure of the resurrected Master there had early crystallized a whole mythology reminiscent of that of the savior gods and the divinely inspired man (*theios anthropos*). This mythology, which we shall outline further on (§ 222), is especially important: it helps us to understand not only the specifically religious dimension of Christianity but its later history as well. The myths that projected Jesus of Nazareth into a universe of archetypes and transcendent figures are as "true" as his acts and words; indeed, these myths confirm the strength and creativity of his original message. Besides, it is due to this universal mythology and symbolism that the religious language of Christianity became ecumenical and accessible beyond its original homeland.

It is generally agreed that the Synoptic Gospels have brought us the essence of the message, first of all the proclamation of the Kingdom of God. As we mentioned (p. 332), Jesus began his ministry in Galilee by preaching the "Good News from God: 'The time has come, . . . and the Kingdom of God is close at hand' " (Mark 1:15).[13] The *eschaton* is imminent: "There are some standing here who will not taste death before they see the Kingdom of God come with power" (Mark 9:1; cf. 13:30). "But as for that day or hour, nobody knows it, neither the angels of heaven, nor the Son; no one but the Father" (Mark 13:32).

However, other expressions used by Jesus imply that the Kingdom is already present. After an exorcism he said: "But if it is through the finger of God that I cast out devils, then know that the Kingdom of God has overtaken you" (Luke 11:20). On another occasion Jesus affirmed that since the time of John the Baptist "the Kingdom of Heaven has been subjected to violence, and the violent are taking it by storm" (Matt. 11:12). The meaning seems to be: the Kingdom is impeded by the violent, but it

13. Contemporary exegesis accepts as authentic four declarations concerning the Kingdom of God: Mark 1:15a; Luke 11:20 and 17:20–21; and Matt. 11:12. See Perrin, *Rediscovering the Teachings of Jesus*, pp. 63 ff., and Perrin, *The New Testament: An Introduction*, pp. 288 ff.

is already present.[14] Unlike the apocalyptic syndrome abundantly set forth in the literature of the period, the Kingdom arrives without cataclysms, even without external signs. "The coming of the Kingdom of God does not admit of observation and there will be no one to say 'Look here! Look there!' For you must know, the Kingdom of God is among you" (Luke 17:20–21). In the parables, the Kingdom is compared to the gradual maturing of the seed that is sprouting and growing (Mark 4:26–29), to the mustard seed (30–32), to the yeast that makes the dough rise (Matt. 13:33).

It is possible that these two differing proclamations of the Kingdom—in a very near *future,* in the *present*—correspond to successive phases of Jesus' ministry.[15] It is also conceivable that they express two translations of the same message: (1) the imminence of the Kingdom, announced by the prophets and the apocalypses—in other words, "the end of the historical world"—and (2) anticipation of the Kingdom, accomplished by those who, by virtue of the mediation of Jesus, already live in the atemporal present of faith.[16]

It is especially this second possible translation of the message that emphasizes the messianic dignity of Jesus. It is beyond doubt that his disciples had recognized him as the Messiah, as is proved by the appellation "Christ" (the Greek equivalent of the "Anointed," that is, the "Messiah"). Jesus never used this term in regard to himself; however, he accepted it when it was spoken by others (Mark 8:29, 14:61). Probably Jesus avoided the appellation Messiah in order to emphasize the difference between the Good News that he preached and the nationalistic forms of Jewish messianism. The Kingdom of God was not the theocracy that the Zealots wanted to establish by force of arms. Jesus principally defined himself by the expression "Son of Man." This term, which in the beginning was only a synonym

14. See Ernst Käsemann, "The Problem of the Historical Jesus," pp. 42 ff.; Perrin, *Rediscovering,* pp. 76 ff.

15. See M. Simon and A. Benoit, *Le Judaïsme et le Christianisme antique,* p. 86.

16. Following Bultmann, Perrin speaks of an "experience of existential reality"; see his *The New Testament,* p. 290.

for "man" (see § 203), ended by designating—implicitly in Jesus' preaching and explicitly in Christian theology—Son of God.

But insofar as it is possible to reconstruct the "personage" of Jesus, at least in its general outlines, it is to the figure of the Suffering Servant (Isaiah 40–55; see §196) that he can be compared.

> Nothing warrants our rejecting, as not authentic, the verses in which he speaks of the ordeals that await him. It is his entire ministry that becomes inexplicable if we refuse to admit that he faced and accepted the possibility of sufferings, of humiliations, and doubtless of death itself. By going up to Jerusalem, he certainly—though perhaps without entirely dismissing the possibility of a victorious intervention on the part of God—assumed the risks of his course of conduct.[17]

"Do not imagine," Jesus declares, "that I have come to abolish the Law of the Prophets. I have come not to abolish but to complete them" (Matt. 5:17). Just like the prophets, he glorifies purity of heart at the expense of ritual formalism; he returns tirelessly to the love of God and one's neighbor. In the Sermon on the Mount (Matt. 5:3–12, Luke 6:20–23) Jesus describes the blessings that await the merciful and the pure in heart, the gentle and the peacemakers, the afflicted and those who are persecuted in the cause of right. It is the most popular Gospel text beyond the Christian world. Yet for Jesus Israel always remains the people chosen by God. It was to the lost sheep of the House of Israel that he was sent (Matt. 15:24), and only exceptionally does he turn to the pagans: he teaches his disciples to shun them (Matt. 10:6). But he seems to have accepted "all the nations" at the establishment of the Kingdom (Mark 13:10, Matt. 8:11). Like the prophets and John the Baptist, Jesus sought the radical transformation of the Jewish people, in other words, the emergence of a New Israel, a new people of God. The Lord's Prayer (Luke 11:2–4, Matt. 6:9–13) admirably summarizes the "method" for achieving this end. An expression of Hebrew

17. Simon and Benoit, *Le Judaïsme*, p. 87. On the fusion of the two ideal figures of the Messiah and the Suffering Servant in the person of Jesus, see Dodd, *The Founder*, pp. 103 ff.

piety, the prayer does not use the first person in the singular but only in the plural: *our* Father, give *us* this day *our* daily bread, forgive us *our* trespasses, deliver *us* from evil. The content derives from the *kaddish* prayer of the ancient synagogue; it reflects the nostalgia to recover a primitive religious experience: the epiphany of Yahweh as *Father*. But the text put forth by Jesus is more concise and more moving.[18] However, every prayer must be imbued with *true faith,* that is, the faith shown by Abraham (§ 57). "Because everything is possible for God" (Mark 10:27). Similarly, "everything is possible for anyone who has faith" (Mark 9:23). Due to the mysterious virtue of Abrahamic faith, the mode of being of fallen man is radically changed. "Everything that you ask and pray for, *believe* that you have it already, and *it will be yours*" (Mark 11:24; cf. Matt. 21:22). In other words, the New Israel emerges mysteriously by the power of Abrahamic faith. This, furthermore, explains the success of the Christian mission of preaching faith in the resurrected Jesus Christ.

When he celebrated the Last Supper with his disciples, Jesus "took some bread, and when he had said the blessing he broke it and gave it to them. 'Take it,' he said, 'this is my body.' Then he took a cup, and when he had returned thanks he gave it to them, and all drank from it, and he said to them, 'This is my blood, the blood of the covenant, which is to be poured out for many.' "[19] A modern exegete does not hesitate to write: "No other words of his are more firmly attested."[20] Only Luke reports Jesus' command: "Take this and share it among you" (22:18). Though Paul confirms the authenticity of this tradition (1 Cor. 11:24), there is no way of proving that these words were uttered by Jesus. The rite continues the Jewish domestic liturgy, especially the blessing of the bread and wine. Jesus often practiced

18. The exegetes also emphasize the difference between the formula of the earliest *kaddish* text ("May God establish his Kingdom during thy life and thy days") and the one used by Jesus: "Thy Kingdom come." See Perrin, *Rediscovering the Teachings,* pp. 57 ff., and the literature cited there.

19. Mark 14:22–24; cf. Matt. 26:26, Luke 22:19, 1 Cor. 11:24. John (6:51) transmits a parallel version, presumably based on a different translation of the original Aramaic of the statement.

20. Dodd, *The Founder,* p. 10.

it; when publicans and sinners were present, the meal presumably proclaimed the Kingdom.[21]

For the earliest Christians, the "breaking of bread" (Acts 2:24) constituted the most important cult act. On the one hand, it was the reactualization of the presence of Christ and hence of the Kingdom that he had established; on the other hand, the rite anticipated the messianic banquet at the end of time. But Jesus' words contain a deeper meaning: the need for his voluntary sacrifice in order to insure the "new covenant,"[22] foundation of the New Israel. This implies the conviction that a new religious life arises only through a sacrificial death; the conception is well known to be archaic and universally disseminated. It is difficult to determine if this ritual communion with his body and his blood was regarded by Jesus as a mystical identification with his person. This is what Paul states (1 Cor. 1:16; cf. 12:27; Rom. 12:5; Eph. 4:12), and, despite the originality of his thought and his theological language, it is possible that he is continuing a genuine Jerusalemite tradition.[23] In any case, the meal taken in common by the first Christians imitated Jesus' last act; it was at once a memorial of the Last Supper and the ritual repetition of the voluntary sacrifice of the Redeemer.

Morphologically, the Eucharist is reminiscent of the cult agapes practiced in Mediterranean antiquity, especially in the Mystery religions.[24] Their goal was the consecration, and hence the salvation, of the participants through communion with a divinity who was mysteriosophic in structure. The convergence with the Christian rite is significant: it illustrates the hope—common enough in that period—of a mystical identification with the divinity. Some authors have tried to explain the Eucharist by influences from the Oriental religions of salvation, but the hy-

21. Certainly, the presence of "untouchables" offended and angered the Jewish rigorists.

22. The Qumran community also regarded itself as having been granted the benefit of a New Covenant; see § 223.

23. Paul elaborates this idea and at the same time gives it a deeper meaning; he identifies the Christian community, the New Israel, with the "body of Christ," each Christian being "in Christ," just as Christ is "in him"; see p. 348, below.

24. See, inter alia, A. D. Nock, *Early Gentile Christianity and Its Hellenistic Background,* pp. 73 ff., 138 ff.

pothesis is groundless (see p. 348). Insofar as it sought an *imitatio Christi,* the primitive agape virtually constituted a sacrament. It must be said even now that in the course of the centuries this central rite—together with baptism, the most important in the Christian cult—inspired many and various theologies; in our own day, the interpretation of the Eucharist still separates Roman Catholicism from the reformed churches (see vol. 3).

221. The birth of the Church

On the day of Pentecost in the year 30, Jesus' disciples were all together "when suddenly they all heard what sounded like a powerful wind from heaven, the noise of which filled the entire house in which they were sitting; and something appeared to them which seemed like tongues of fire; these separated and came to rest on the head of each of them. They were all filled with the Holy Spirit, and began to speak foreign languages" (Acts 2:1–4). Fiery epiphanies of the Holy Spirit are a rather well-known theme in the history of religions: they are found in Mesopotamia (§ 20), in Iran (§ 104), in India (Buddha, Mahāvīra, etc.; § 152). But the context of the Pentecost has a more definite aim: the violent wind, the tongues of fire, and the glossolalia are reminiscent of certain traditions concerning the theophany on Sinai[25] (see § 59). In other words, the descent of the Holy Spirit is interpreted as a new revelation from God, similar to the revelation on Sinai. The day of Pentecost sees the birth of the Christian Church. It was not until after they had received the Holy Spirit that the Apostles began preaching the Gospel and producing many "miracles and signs" (Acts 2:43).

On that day Peter addressed to the crowd the first summons to conversion. He and his companions bore witness to the Resurrection of Jesus Christ; it was God who resurrected him (2:24, 32, etc.). The miracle had already been predicted by David (2:31); hence the Resurrection is the eschatological event foretold by the prophets (2:17–21). Peter adjured the Jews to repent,

25. The sources are cited by E. Trocmé, *Le livre des Actes et l'histoire,* pp. 202 ff.

adding that "every one of you must be baptized in the name of Jesus Christ for the forgiveness of your sins, and you will receive the gift of the Holy Spirit" (2:38). This first harangue, which became the exemplary model for the *kerygma* (the Christian "proclamation"), was followed by numerous conversions (three thousand according to Acts 2:41). On another occasion (he had just cured a man crippled from birth; Acts 3:1–9), Peter exhorted the Jews to recognize that they had been wrong, though out of ignorance, when they condemned Jesus, and to repent and accept baptism (Acts 3:13–19).

The Acts of the Apostles afford us a glimpse of the life of the first Christian community in Jerusalem (to which the author gives the Greek name *ecclēsia*). Apparently its members still followed the traditional religious discipline (circumcision of male infants, ritual purifications, rest on the Sabbath, prayers in the Temple). But they often met for instruction, breaking bread, the agapes, and to pray and praise God (2:42, 46). However, the Book of Acts (which cites many examples of preaching to unbelievers) tells us nothing of the instruction given to members of the community. As for economic organization, it states that "the faithful all . . . owned everything in common; they sold their goods and possessions and shared out the proceeds among themselves according to what each one needed" (2:44–45). They awaited the Second Coming of Christ.

Despite their strict obedience to the Mosaic usages, the Christians of Jerusalem aroused the hostility of the High Priests and the Sadducees (4:1–3). Peter and John were arrested when they preached in the Temple, were summoned before the Sanhedrin, but were later released (4:1–3). On another occasion all the Apostles were arrested, then released by the Sanhedrin (5:17–41). Later, presumably in the year 43, one of the Apostles was beheaded at the order of Herod Agrippa I (12:1 ff.), who wanted to obtain the support of the family of Annas. The attitude of the Pharisees was less decided. Gamaliel—Saul's teacher—defended the Apostles before the Sanhedrin. But the Pharisees, favorable to the converts of Jerusalemite stock (the "Hebrews") were hostile to the proselytes recruited among the Jews of the Diaspora (the "Hellenists"); they reproached them for their detachment from the Temple and the Law (6:13–14). This was the reason for the stoning, in 36–37, of Stephen, the first martyr to the Christian faith (7:58–60). "Saul entirely approved of the killing" (8:1). On that same day the "Hellenists" were expelled from Jerusalem into the country district of Judaea and Samaria (8:1). Thenceforth the Hebrews and their leader James, "brother of the Lord," will hold sway over the Church of Jerusalem.

It is possible already to detect a certain tension between the "Hebrews" and the "Hellenists." The former are more conservative and legalistic, despite their expectation of the parousia. They faithfully follow the Jewish code of ritual prescriptions and are the typical representatives of the movement designated by the term "Judaeo-Christianity."[26] It was their strict obedience to the Law that Paul refused to accept (see p. 348). And in fact it is difficult to understand a rabbinical legalism practiced precisely by those who proclaimed the Resurrection of Christ and bore witness to it. The "Hellenists" were a small group of Jews established in Jerusalem and converted to Christianity. They had no great esteem for the cult celebrated in the Temple. In his speech Stephen exclaimed: "The Most High does not live in a house that human hands have built" (Acts 7:48). The dispersal of the "Hellenists" hastened missionary work among the Jews of the Diaspora and, exceptionally, at Antioch, among the pagans (11:19). It was in the Diaspora that Christology developed. The title "Son of Man"—which, in Greek, has no further meaning—is replaced by "Son of God" or "Lord" (Kyrios); the term Messiah is translated into Greek, Christos, and ends by becoming a proper name: Jesus Christ.

Very soon the mission was directed to the pagans. At Antioch, in Syria, the first important community of converts of pagan stock was organized; it is there that the term "Christians" was

26. Norman Perrin makes them the source of the narratives and sayings of Jesus that are preserved in the Gospels; the Judaeo-Christians were also characterized by their interest in prophecy; see Perrin, *The New Testament*, pp. 45 ff. But the problem is more complex; see Jean Daniélou, *Théologie du Judéo-Christianisme*, pp. 17 ff.; M. Simon and A. Benoit, *Le Judaïsme et le Christianisme antique*, pp. 258 ff.

first used (Acts 11:26).[27] It was from Antioch that the Christian mission spread out into the Hellenistic world. The confrontation of a Jewish messianic movement with Greek thought and religiosity will have decisive consequences for the development of Christianity. It is Saint Paul's inestimable contribution that he rightly grasped the elements of the problem and had the courage to fight untiringly for the only solution that he considered just and consistent.

Born probably at the beginning of the first century at Tarsus in Cilicia,[28] he came to study in Jerusalem with Gamaliel, "a doctor of the law and respected by the whole people" (Acts 5:34). He describes himself as a "Hebrew born of Hebrew parents. As for the Law, I was a Pharisee; as for working for religion, I was a persecutor of the Church" (Phil. 3:5; cf. Gal. 1:13–14). When on his anti-Christian mission, he saw Christ appear to him on the road to Damascus. He is the only one of those who did not know Jesus to have been given the title of Apostle. In fact, he was converted by the resurrected Christ: he had received or learned the Gospel that he preached not from a human being but "only through a revelation of Jesus Christ" (Gal. 1:11–12; 1 Cor. 2:16). Become the "Apostle to the Gentiles," Paul undertook long missionary journeys through Asia Minor, Cyprus, Greece, and Macedonia. He preached in many cities, founded churches, spent a long time in Corinth and in Rome. Denounced by the Jews and arrested in Jerusalem, after two years in prison he was referred to the emperor's tribunal. At Rome he lived for two years in freedom but watched by guards. Acts breaks off at this point, and we do not know the full story of the Apostle's end. He died a martyr in Rome, between 62 and 64.

Despite the fifteen chapters (out of twenty-eight) that Acts devotes to him, despite the fourteen Epistles that are attributed

27. E. Peterson has shown the political resonance of the name: "partisans of Christ"; see his *Frühkirche, Judentum und Gnosis*, pp. 64 ff. Suetonius, the first Latin author to mention the new sect, reports that the Emperor Claudius expelled the Jews from Rome in 49 because they were in tumult "at the instigation of Christ" (*Judaei impulsore Christi tumultuantes*).

28. He added to his biblical name Saul the Roman cognomen Paul, his father being a Roman citizen.

to him,[29] our knowledge of the life, apostolate, and thought of Saint Paul remains fragmentary. His profound and personal interpretation of the Gospel was expounded orally—and probably differently to believers and unbelievers. The Epistles do not constitute consecutive chapters of a systematic treatise. They continue, clarify, and define certain questions of doctrine or practice—questions that are carefully discussed in his teachings but that were not correctly understood by the community or questions whose typically Pauline solutions were criticized or sometimes even rejected by other missionaries. Despite this, it must immediately be added that the Epistles represent the earliest and most important document of the primitive Church, for they reflect not only the most serious crises of nascent Christianity but also the creative daring of the first Christian theologian.

222. The Apostle to the Gentiles

Saint Paul's theology and *kerygma* derive from his ecstatic experience on the road to Damascus. On the one hand, he recognized in the resurrected Christ[30] the Messiah, the Son sent by God to deliver men from sin and death. On the other hand, his conversion established a relationship of mystical participation with Christ. Paul interprets his experience as analogous to the Crucifixion (Gal. 2:19): he now possesses "the mind of Christ" (1 Cor. 2:16) or "the Spirit of God" (7:40). He does not hesitate to proclaim: "It is Christ speaking in me" (2 Cor. 13:3; Rom. 15:18). He refers to being mystically caught up "into the third heaven" and to "revelations" that he had received from the Lord (2 Cor. 12:1–4, 7). These "signs and wonders" were granted him by the Spirit of God "to win the allegiance of the pagans" (Rom. 15:18). Despite this privileged experience, Paul does not demand an exceptional status, different from that of others. Every believer accomplishes mystical union with Christ through the sacrament of baptism. For "when we were baptized in Christ

29. There is now agreement as to the authenticity of five or six, among them the most important ones: the Epistle to the Romans, 1 and 2 Corinthians, and Galatians. But the other Epistles express or continue the same Pauline thought.

30. Paul was the last to whom the resurrected Christ appeared (1 Cor. 15:8).

Jesus we were baptized in his death . . . we went into the tomb with him and indeed joined him in death, so that as Christ was raised from the dead by the Father's glory, we too might live a new life'' (Rom. 6:3–4). Through baptism, the Christian ''is in Christ'' (2 Cor. 5:17); he has become a member of a mystical body. Baptized in one Spirit, to ''make one body,'' ''Jews as well as Greeks, slaves as well as citizens, . . . one Spirit was given us all to drink'' (1 Cor. 12:13).

Death and resurrection by immersion in water constitute a well-known mythico-ritual scenario that is bound up with a universally documented aquatic symbolism.[31] But Saint Paul connects the sacrament of baptism *with a recent historical event: the death and resurrection of Jesus Christ.* In addition, baptism not only insures the new life of the believer but accomplishes his transformation into a member of the mystical body of Christ. Such a conception was unthinkable for traditional Judaism. On the other hand, it differs from the other contemporary baptismal practices, for example that of the Essenes, in which the numerous lustrations had an essentially purifying value (see p. 355). The sacrament of the Eucharist is equally foreign to Judaism. Just like baptism, the Eucharist integrates the believer into the mystical body of Christ, the Church. By communicating with the consecrated bread and wine, he assimilates the body and blood of the Lord (1 Cor. 10:16–17; cf. 11:27–29). For Saint Paul, salvation is equivalent to mystical identification with Christ. Those who have faith have Jesus Christ within them (2 Cor. 13:5). Redemption is brought about by a gratuitous gift of God, namely, the death and resurrection of Jesus Christ.

The prime importance that Saint Paul attributes to grace (Rom. 3:24; 6:14, 23; etc.) presumably derives from his own experience: despite all that he had thought and done—even to approving the stoning of Stephen—God granted him salvation. Hence it is useless, for a Jew, to obey the ritual and moral prescriptions of the Torah: by himself, man cannot obtain salvation. Properly speaking, it is in consequence of the establishment of the Law that man became conscious of sin; before knowing the Law, he was

31. See Eliade, *Patterns of Comparative Religion,* §§ 64 ff., and *Images and Symbols,* chap. 5.

not aware if he was or was not a sinner (Rom. 7:7 ff.). To be under the Law is equivalent to being "slaves to the elemental principles of this world" (Gal. 4:3). This is as much as to say that "those who rely on the keeping of the Law are under a curse" (Gal. 3:10). As for the pagans, though they can know God through the works of his creation, "the more they called themselves philosophers, the more stupid they grew"; they sank into idolatry, the source of degrading passions and perversion (Rom. 1:20–32). In short, for the Jews as for the pagans, redemption is accomplished only by faith and the sacraments. Salvation is "the free gift given of God, eternal life in Christ Jesus our Lord" (Rom. 6:23).[32]

Such a theology inevitably opposed Saint Paul to the Judaeo-Christians of Jerusalem. The latter demanded the preliminary circumcision of converted pagans and forbade their presence at meals taken in common and at the celebration of the Eucharist. After a conflict, of which Paul (Gal. 2:7–10) and Acts (15) give contradictory accounts, the two parties, meeting in Jerusalem, reached a compromise solution. The converted pagans were bound to abstain only "from food sacrificed to idols, from blood, from the meat of strangled animals, and from fornication" (Acts 15:29). This decision was probably arrived at in Paul's absence. The Apostle to the Gentiles would certainly not have accepted it, for it preserved a part of Jewish observance. In any case, the meeting in Jerusalem confirmed the unexpected success of the Christian mission among pagans—a success that contrasted with the partial failure experienced in Palestine.

But Saint Paul was also called on to face certain crises that threatened his own churches, the communities that he had founded. At Corinth the faithful coveted the spiritual gifts or

32. It should be pointed out that the Epistle to the Romans—in which the theology of grace and the soteriology of the Cross are developed—is the most important of Saint Paul's writings. Many theologians consider the Epistle to the Romans the most important book of the New Testament. Exegesis of this profound, daring, and enigmatic text has given rise to numerous speculations and has brought on crises that have divided and at the same time renewed Christianity for fifteen centuries. One of the most significant contemporary theologies was inaugurated by Karl Barth's famous commentary on it (see vol. 3).

"charisma" received from the Holy Spirit. As a matter of fact, we have here a religious practice of considerable popularity in the Hellenistic world: the quest for *enthousiasmos*. "Charisma" included the gift of healing, the ability to perform miracles, prophecy, glossolalia, the gift of interpreting languages, etc. (1 Cor. 12:4 ff.). Intoxicated by their ecstasies and their powers, some of the faithful believed they had obtained possession of the Spirit and hence of freedom; they held that henceforth everything was allowable to them (6:12), even prostitution (6:15–16).[33] Paul reminds them that their bodies are "members making up the body of Christ" (6:15). He further elaborates the hierarchy of charismata: the most important is that of the Apostle, next that of the prophet, followed, in the third place, by the spiritual gift of the *didaskalos* or teacher (12:28; cf. 14:1–5). In short, Saint Paul does not reject aspiration to the higher gifts, but he adds: "I am going to show you a way that is better than any of them." Then follows the hymn to charity, one of the summits of Pauline thought: "If I have all the eloquence of men or of angels, but speak without love, I am simply a gong booming or a cymbal clashing. If I have the gift of prophecy, understanding all the mysteries that are, and knowing everything, and if I have faith in all its fullness, to move mountains, but without love, then I am nothing at all," and so forth (13:1–13).

In all probability, Saint Paul accepted the quest for charisma, for he had understood the need to translate the message of the Gospel into a religious language familiar to Hellenistic circles. Better than anyone else, he knew the difficulty of preaching "a crucified Christ; to the Jews an obstacle that they cannot get over, to the pagans madness" (1 Cor. 1:23). The resurrection of bodies, a belief held by the majority of Jews, seemed senseless to the Greeks, who were exclusively interested in the immortality of the soul.[34] No less difficult to understand was the hope of an

33. The phenomenon is abundantly documented in the history of Indian religions (see §146) and of Gnosticism (§ 230); it will also be found in certain mystical currents of Christianity and Islam (see vol. 3).

34. The Resurrection of the Redeemer insures the resurrection of Christians (1 Cor. 15:12 ff.). Paul also accepts the (originally Greek) conception of an immortality obtained immediately after death (Phil. 1:23; cf. 2 Cor. 5:8). However, postexistence is not purely disincarnate; it is the "spiritual [*pneumatikos*]

eschatological renewal of the world; the Greeks, on the contrary, sought more certain means of freeing themselves from matter. The Apostle tried to adapt himself; the more deeply he penetrated into Hellenistic circles, the less he spoke of the eschatological expectation. We also note innovations of considerable significance. Not only did he often use the Hellenistic religious vocabulary (*gnōsis, mystērion, sophia, kyrios, sōtēr*), but he adopted certain conceptions that were foreign to Judaism and to primitive Christianity. Thus, for example, Saint Paul took over the dualistic idea, fundamental to Gnosticism, of a "psychic man" inferior and opposed to the "spiritual man."[35] The Christian seeks to cast off the carnal man in order to become purely spiritual (*pneumatikos*). Another dualistic characteristic opposes God to the world, dominated by its "masters" (1 Cor. 2:8), in other words, by the "elemental principles" (Gal. 4:3, 9). However, Paul's theology remains fundamentally biblical. He rejects the distinction, insisted on by the Gnostics, between the supreme God and redeemer and the evil Demiurge, responsible for the Creation. The cosmos is dominated by evil after the fall of man; but redemption is equivalent to a second creation, and the world will recover its original perfection.

Paul's Christology develops around the Resurrection; that event reveals the nature of Christ: he is the Son of God, the Redeemer. The christological drama is reminiscent of a soteriological scenario well known at the time but whose earliest expressions are far older:[36] the savior comes down from heaven to earth for the good of men and then returns to heaven after accomplishing his mission.

---

body" that survives death (or, to use his expression, that is "raised": 1 Cor. 15:44 ff.). The doctrine of the "spiritual body" is documented in other traditions (India, Tibet, etc.). Saint Paul's originality is in having associated immortality with resurrection; but this solution raised other problems.

35. 1 Cor. 2:14–15. "The first man, being from the earth, is earthly by nature; the second man is from heaven" (15:47).

36. Archaic mythologies are aware of several types of supernatural beings (sons of God, demiurges, civilizing heroes, messianic and millenaristic figures, etc.) who descend to teach or to save men and then return to heaven. Similar conceptions occur in the theologies of Hinduism (*avatar*) and Buddhism (the *boddhisattvas*).

In his earliest letter, the First Epistle of Paul to the church in Thessalonia, written in 51 from Corinth, Paul makes known a "word of the Lord"[37] concerning the parousia: "At the trumpet of God, the voice of the archangel will call out the command and the Lord himself will come down from heaven; those who have died in Christ will be the first to rise, and then those of us who are still alive will be taken up in the clouds, together with them, to meet the Lord in the air. So we shall stay with the Lord for ever" (4:16–17). Six years later, in 57, he reminds the Romans that "our salvation is even nearer than it was when we were converted. The night is almost over, it will be daylight soon" (Rom. 13:11–12). However, expectation of the parousia must not trouble the life of the Christian communities. He insists on the need to work in order to deserve the food that one eats (2 Thess. 3:8–10), and he demands respect for the laws in force, submission to the authorities, and payment of taxes, direct or indirect (Rom. 13:1–7). The consequences of this ambivalent valorization of the *present* (while awaiting the parousia, history continues and must be respected) were soon to make themselves felt. Despite the countless solutions proposed from the end of the first century, the problem of the *historical present* still haunts contemporary Christian thought.

Saint Paul's considerable authority in the ancient Church is largely the result of a catastrophe that shook Judaism and paralyzed the development of the Judaeo-Christian tendency. During his lifetime the Apostle's importance was not very great. But soon after his death the war of the Jews against Rome broke out, in 66; it ended, in 70, with the ruin of Jerusalem and the destruction of the Temple.

223. The Essenes at Qumran

During the war, at the beginning of the summer of 68, a contingent of Vespasian's army attacked and destroyed the "monastery" of Qumran, situated in the open desert on the shore of the Dead Sea. In all likelihood the defenders were massacred; but on the eve of the disaster they had had time to hide a considerable

37. Cf. 1 Cor. 15:51: "I will tell you something that has been secret."

number of manuscripts in large clay vessels. Their discovery, between 1947 and 1952, renewed our knowledge of the Jewish apocalyptic movements and the origins of Christianity. In fact, scholars have seen in the Dead Sea monastic community the mysterious sect of the Essenes, known until then only through the scanty information supplied by Josephus, Philo, and Pliny the Younger.[38] Among the manuscripts so far deciphered and published, there are, in addition to commentaries on certain books of the Old Testament, some original treatises. We mention the most important among them: the "Scroll of the War of the Sons of Light against the Sons of Darkness," the "Treatise of Discipline," the "Thanksgiving Psalms," and the "Commentary on Habakkuk."

With the help of these new documents it is possible to reconstruct the general outline of the sect's history. Its ancestors were the *hassidim,* whose religious fervor and whose role in the War of the Maccabees will be remembered (see § 202). The founder of the Qumran community, known to his disciples as the "Teacher of Righteousness," was a Zadokite priest, hence a member of the legitimate and ultraorthodox priestly class. When Simon (142–134) was proclaimed "prince and high priest for ever," and the office of high priest was irrevocably transferred from the Zadokites to the Hasmoneans, the Teacher of Righteousness left Jerusalem with a group of disciples and took refuge in the desert of Judah. In all probability the "Evil Priest" execrated in the Qumran texts was Simon; he had persecuted the Teacher of Righteousness in his exile and was even contemplating attacking Qumran when he was assassinated by the governor of Jericho (1 Mac. 16:11 ff.). It is not known under what circumstances the Teacher of Righteousness died.[39] His disciples and followers venerated him as God's messenger. Just as Moses

38. The contradictions between the two classes of documents—the Qumran manuscripts and the reports of the classical authors—are explained, in part, by the latter's inadequate information and, in part, by the complexity of this apocalyptic sect. The Qumran community does not represent Essenism as a whole; it seems certain that Essene groups existed in other regions of Palestine.

39. A. Dupont-Sommer, followed by other scholars, accuses the "impious priest" of having inspired his assassination; see *Les écrits esséniens*, pp. 375 ff. (Eng. trans., *The Essene Writings from Qumran*, pp. 349 ff.). However, this crime is not explicitly attested in the documents; see the analysis of the texts in F. M. Cross, *The Ancient Library of Qumran*, pp. 157–60.

had made the old Covenant possible, the Teacher of Righteousness had renewed it; by founding the eschatological community at Qumran, he had anticipated the messianic era.

From the publication of the first texts, the specialists observed significant similarities between the Essenian religious practices and those of Christianity. Through these new documents we are now better informed concerning the historical and spiritual milieu (the *Sitz im Leben*) of a Jewish apocalyptic sect. The Essenian parallels illuminate certain aspects of Jesus' preaching and numerous expressions often used by the authors of the New Testament. But there are also differences, and they are not less important. The Qumran community was strictly monastic; the earliest Christians lived in the world, they made up a missionary community. Both sects were apocalyptic and messianic: like the Christians, the Essenes regarded themselves as the people of the New Covenant. But they awaited an eschatological prophet (who, in the New Testament, had already come in the person of John the Baptist) and two messiahs: the Priest Messiah, who would sanctify them, and the Royal Messiah, who would lead Israel in the war against the Gentiles, a war that God himself would bring to a triumphant end. Indeed, the "Scroll of the War of the Sons of Light against the Sons of Darkness" constitutes the plan of battle for this eschatological conflagration. A mobilization lasting six years would be followed by twenty-nine years of war. The army of the Sons of Light would be made up of 28,000 infantry and 6,000 cavalry, reinforced by a large number of angels.[40] The Christians, too, hoped for the Second Coming of Christ in glory, as judge and Redeemer of the world; but, following Jesus' teaching, they did not accept the ideology of the holy war.

For the Essenes as for the Christians, the Messiah would appear at the end of time and would receive an eternal kingdom; in both messianic doctrines the priestly, royal, and prophetic elements coexisted. However, in the Qumran literature the idea of a preexistent Messiah (the Second Adam, the Son of Man) is not documented; what is more, the Messiah has not yet become

40. See Y. Yadin, *The Scroll of the War of the Sons of Light against the Sons of Darkness;* Dupont-Sommer, *Les écrits esséniens*, pp. 369 ff. (Eng. trans., pp. 343 ff.).

the celestial Redeemer, and the two messianic figures are not unified, as in the Christology of the primitive Church.[41] As eschatological personage, the Teacher of Righteousness would inaugurate the new age. His disciples accorded him the rank of Messiah: that of the Master who reveals the real, esoteric meaning of the Scriptures and who also possesses prophetic powers. Some texts imply that the Master will be resurrected at the end of time.[42] But as one expert, Father Cross, concludes, "if the Essenes expected the return of their Master as a Priestly Messiah, they expressed their hope in an extremely indirect manner" (p. 299); this is in contrast to the insistence with which the New Testament develops this idea.

The organization and the ritual systems of the two apocalyptic sects present astonishing similarities, but certain differences are observable, and they are not less important. The Essenes made up a community that was at once priestly and lay. Its religious activity (teaching, cult, exegesis) was directed by hereditary priests; the laymen were responsible for the community's material resources. The directing group was termed the *rabbîm* (literally, the "numerous"), a term found also in the New Testament (where it designates the "assembly" that chooses its representatives; Acts 15:12). Twelve laymen and three priests formed the inner circle. The highest office was that of "inspector" (*mbaqqên*); this supreme leader was bound to behave as a "shepherd" (the "Damascus Document," 13:7–9). His function is reminiscent of that of the "shepherd" or *episkopos* among the Christians.

At Qumran, initiatory baptism, which integrated the neophyte into the community, was followed by annual ritual lustrations. And, like the "breaking of bread" for the Christians, their com-

41. See Cross, *The Ancient Library of Qumran,* pp. 221 ff. The Epistle to the Hebrews presents Jesus as a Messiah who is at once priestly and royal, "of the order of Melchizedek" (6:20; 7:1–25; etc.). Cross sees in this interpretation the effort of the primitive Church to adapt Christology to the messianic expectation of the Essenes or, more precisely, to present in a single figure the fulfillment of all the messianic nostalgias of the past (p. 221).

42. The most important text, and the one most discussed, is a passage in the "Damascus Document" commenting on Numbers 21:18; see the translations and analyses in Dupont-Sommer, *Les écrits,* pp. 145 ff. (Eng. trans., pp. 124 ff.), and Cross, *The Ancient Library,* pp. 226 ff.

mon meal was understood by the Essenes as an anticipation of the messianic banquet.[43] The members of the community abstained from marriage, for they considered themselves all to be soldiers in the holy war. This was not a true, disciplinary, asceticism but a provisional one, imposed by the imminence of the *eschaton*.[44] Another point of resemblance must be emphasized: the similar hermeneutic method employed by the Essenian exegetes and the authors of the New Testament—a method without analogies either in rabbinic Judaism or in Philo. By applying a special procedure (*pesher*), the Essenes read in the prophecies of the Old Testament precise references to contemporary history and hence predictions concerning certain imminent events. Those who had access to "knowledge"—that is, those initiated into the apocalyptic gnosis revealed by the Teacher of Righteousness—knew that the supreme war was on the point of breaking out. Moreover, as we have seen (§ 202), the whole of Jewish apocalyptic literature glorified esoteric knowledge. Similarly, especially from the second generation, the Christians accorded a special value to gnosis: they were impatient to decipher the precursory signs of the parousia. For the Essenes, religious knowledge was essentially a revealed knowledge, eschatological in nature. A parallel conception has been shown to exist in Paul's Epistles and in the Gospels of Matthew and John. Higher teaching, and even the community sacraments, were regarded as esoteric. For the Kingdom of God is not accessible to the "flesh" but only to the "spirit."[45] In short, among the Jews as among the Christians, secret gnosis and esotericism form part of the apocalyptic "method." After the destruction of Qumran and the dispersal of the Essenes, some of those who escaped probably

43. See the texts cited and commented on by Cross, pp. 85–91, 235–36.

44. The texts are analyzed by Cross, pp. 96–99, 237–38. Cf. 1 Cor. 7:29–31: "Our time is growing short. Those who have wives should live as though they had none."

45. See John 3:5: "unless a man is born through water and the Spirit, he cannot enter the Kingdom of God." For the esoteric character of "knowledge" (= gnosis) in the literature of Qumran and in the New Testament, see F. Nötcher, *Zur theologischen Terminologie der Qumranischen Texte,* pp. 15 ff.; W. D. Davies, " 'Knowledge' in the Dead Sea Scrolls and Matthew 11:25–30"; J. Jeremias, *Die Abendmahlsworte Jesu,* pp. 58 ff.; K. G. Kuhn, "Die Sektenschrift und die iranische Religion," esp. pp. 299 ff.

joined the Christian communities of Palestine. In any case, the apocalyptic and esoteric traditions were maintained in the Christianity of the first two centuries, and they encouraged certain Gnostic tendencies (see § 228).

The analogies between the Essenian theological language and that of the Gospel of John are equally remarkable. The Qumran texts contain a number of specifically Johannine expressions, for example "light of the world" (8:12), "sons of light" (12:36), "the man who lives by the truth comes out into the light" (3:21), "the spirit of truth from the spirit of falsehood" (1 John 4:6).[46] According to the doctrine of the Essenes, the world is the field of battle between two spirits whom God created from the beginning: the Spirit of Truth (called also the Prince of Light and the Angel of Truth) and the Spirit of Wickedness or Perversity; the latter is none other than Belial, the Prince of Darkness, Satan. The war between these two spirits and their spiritual armies also takes place between men and in the heart of each "Son of Light" ("Treatise of Discipline," 4:23–26). The Essenian eschatological scenario has been compared to certain Johannine texts. The "Treatise of Discipline" (3:17–23) states that, though they are guided by the Prince of Light, the Children of Justice sometimes fall into error, driven by the Angel of Darkness. Similarly, the First Epistle of John speaks of "children of God" and "children of the devil"[47] and exhorts believers not to let the devil lead them astray (3:7–10, 4:1–6). But while the Essenes await the eschatological war, in the Johannine literature, despite the fact that the combat still continues, the crisis has passed, for Jesus Christ has already triumphed over evil.

Another difference must be pointed out: in the Johannine literature, the Spirit is usually understood as the Spirit of God or

46. The equivalents in the Qumran texts are cited by Cross, p. 207, nn. 13–17. The dualism light/darkness and especially the glorification of light as the supreme epiphany of the Spirit show the influence of Iranian ideas. But it must not be forgotten that a similar imagery is found in the Old Testament and in other Semitic religions; see Eliade, *The Two and the One*, pp. 55 ff.

47. [The English version of the Jerusalem Bible (whose texts I have for the most part reproduced) does not use the expression "children of the devil." However, it is used in both the Authorized Version and the New English Bible.—Translator.]

of Christ (1 John 4:13); in the "Treatise of Discipline," the Prince of Light or the Spirit of Truth proves to be the helper of the Son of Light. However, the figure of the Paraclete, described by John (14:17; 15:26; 16:13, etc.), seems to derive from a theology similar to that of Qumran. Christ promised to send him to bear witness and to intercede for the faithful, but the Paraclete will not speak in his own name. Such a function, which was not expected of the Holy Spirit, has always aroused the curiosity of exegetes. The Qumran texts allow us to understand the origin of the Paraclete; morphologically, he is one with a personage of Yahweh's celestial court, especially the divine angel or messenger.[48] But Iranian influences, first of all religious dualism and angelology, have transformed the two angels of Yahweh's court (see § 203) into the incarnation of two opposed principles: good/evil, truth/falsehood, light/darkness. The Essenes, as well as the author of the Johannine corpus, shared in this Palestinian syncretistic theology and eschatology, which were strongly influenced by Iranian dualism.

Despite the numerous resemblances that we have just mentioned, Essenism and primitive Christianity present different structures and pursue different ends. The Essenian eschatology derives from the priestly tradition; the Christian eschatology has its deep roots in the prophetic tradition of the Old Testament. The Essenes maintained and strengthened priestly separatism; the Christians, on the contrary, sought to reach all social strata. The Essenes excluded from the messianic banquet those who were physically or spiritually impure or deformed; for the Christians, one of the signs of the Kingdom was precisely the curing of the infirm (the blind who see, the dumb who speak, etc.) and the resurrection of the dead. Finally, the Resurrection of Jesus and the gift of the Holy Spirit, the spiritual freedom that succeeded to the discipline of the Law, constitute the central "event" that discriminates between these two messianic communities.[49]

48. Cross, p. 214, n. 82, mentions the Canaanite prototype of the angel messenger.

49. Cross, pp. 241 ff.

224. Destruction of the Temple. Delay in the occurrence of the parousia

Refusing to take part in the messianic war against the Romans, a group of Judaeo-Christians was evacuated, in 66, to Pella, in Transjordania; others sought refuge in the cities of Syria and Asia Minor and in Alexandria. The significance of the refusal did not escape the insurgents: the Christians[50] were separating themselves from the national destiny of Israel (Eusebius, *Ecclesiastical History* 3. 5. 3). The event marks the breaking-away of the Church from Judaism. However, Judaism will survive, by virtue of a similar action. The most important religious leader of the century, Rabbi Johanan ben Zakkai, who had strongly opposed the armed insurrection, was evacuated in a coffin during the siege of the city. Soon afterward he obtained leave from Titus to establish an elementary school at Jabneh, a village not far from Jaffa. It would be the founding of this school by Rabbi Johanan that would save the spiritual values of the Jewish people, conquered on the national plane and threatened with disappearance.

The ruin of the holy city and the destruction of the Temple brutally changed the religious orientation of the Jews as well as that of the Christians. For the former, the destruction of the Temple raised a problem still more serious than the one their ancestors had faced six centuries earlier. For then the prophets, in predicting the catastrophe, had at the same time revealed the reason for it: Yahweh was preparing to punish his people for their countless infidelities. This time, on the contrary, the apocalypses had proclaimed as certain the final victory of God in the eschatological battle against the forces of evil. The answer to this unexpected and incomprehensible catastrophe was given at Jabneh: Judaism will continue, but "reformed," that is, rid of vain apocalyptic hopes and messianisms and exclusively following the teaching of the Pharisees (see § 204). The consequences of this decision were, first, the strengthening of the Law and the synagogue and then the valorization of the Mishnayoth and,

50. Four years earlier, in 62, James, leader of the Judaeo-Christian community of Jerusalem, had died a martyr.

finally, of the Talmud. But the second destruction of the Temple profoundly marked the development of Judaism: deprived of the sanctuary—the only sacred space where the *cult* could be performed—the faithful were reduced to *prayers* and *religious instruction*.[51]

During the war, the Christians, too, experienced a resurgence of apocalyptic enthusiasm: the hope that God would soon intervene, and precisely by hastening the Second Coming of Christ. The Gospel of Mark reflects and continues this apocalyptic hope.[52] But the delay in the parousia prompted embarrassing questions. Essentially, the answers given may be classified in three categories: (1) the imminence of the parousia is reaffirmed even more strongly (e.g., in the Second Epistle of Peter); (2) the parousia is deferred to a more distant future, and a theological justification is offered for this long interval: it is the period set aside for the missionary activity of the Church (see, e.g., the Gospels of Matthew and Luke); (3) the parousia has already taken place, for the Crucifixion and Resurrection of Jesus are in fact the true "final event" (*eschaton*), and the "new life" is already accessible to Christians (see, e.g., the Gospel of John).[53]

It was this third explanation that ended by being accepted. In point of fact, it continued the paradoxes faced by the earliest believers: for Jesus the Messiah was not different from other human beings; though the Son of God, he was humiliated and died on the Cross. But the Resurrection confirmed his divinity. Yet this irrefragable proof was not generally accepted. (For the majority of Jews, the coming of the Messiah necessarily implied national deliverance and the *obvious* transfiguration of the world.) Henceforth, the parousia was awaited in order to force the conversion of unbelievers. The author of the Gospel of John and his circle of followers give a daring reply to the delay in the parousia. The Kingdom of God has already been inaugurated; it is not automatically universally *obvious*, just as the Messiah, incarnated in the historic personage of Jesus, was not obvious

51. See Judah Goldin, "On Change and Adaptation in Judaism," pp. 290 ff.

52. After the catastrophe of 70, the Christians began to collect and write down the Jerusalemite traditions concerning the life, ministry, death, and resurrection of Jesus; thus the first Gospels came into existence.

53. See Perrin, *The New Testament: An Introduction*, p. 41.

to the majority of Jews—and the divinity of Christ still is not so for unbelievers. In short, there is here the same dialectical process that is well known in the whole history of religions: the epiphany of the sacred in a profane object is at the same time a camouflage; for the sacred is not *obvious* to all those who approach the object in which it has manifested itself. This time the sacred—the Kingdom of God—manifested itself in a human community that was historically circumscribed: the Church.

This revalorization of the parousia opens numerous possibilities for religious experience and theological speculation. Instead of the familiar scenario—the parousia as concrete and unmistakable manifestation of the triumph of God, confirmed by the annihilation of evil and the end of history—there emerges the conviction that the spiritual life can progress and be perfected *in this world* and that history can be transfigured; in other words, that historical existence is capable of reaching the perfection and bliss of the Kingdom of God. To be sure, the Kingdom will be "obvious" first of all to believers, but every Christian community can become the exemplary model of a sanctified life and hence an incitement to conversion. This new interpretation of the dialectic of the sacred, inaugurated by the identification of the Kingdom with the Church, continues in our day; paradoxically, it is manifested especially in the multitude of "desacralizations" (demythicizations of the Gospels and of tradition, banalization of the liturgy, simplification of sacramental life, antimystical tendencies and depreciation of religious symbolism, exclusive interest in the ethical values and social function of churches, etc.)—"desacralizations" that are in the course of being brought about in the contemporary Christian world (see vol. 3).

29 Paganism, Christianity, and Gnosis in the Imperial Period

225. *Jam redit et Virgo . . .*

If the cult of the Great Mother Cybele was patronized by the Roman aristocracy (see p. 134), the success of other Oriental religions, introduced later, was insured by the urban proletariat and by the large number of foreigners settled in Rome. During the last two centuries of the Republic the traditional religion—that is, the public cults—had gradually lost its prestige. Certain priestly functions (e.g., those of the *flamen Dialis*) and a number of sodalities had fallen into desuetude. As everywhere else in the Hellenistic period, religiosity displayed itself under the sign of the goddess Fortuna (Tyche) and in astral fatalism (§ 205). Magic and astrology attracted not only the masses but also certain philosophers (the Stoics recognized the validity of astrology). During the civil wars a large number of apocalypses of Oriental origin were in circulation; those known by the name of the *Sibylline Oracles* announced the imminent collapse of Roman power. What is more, the old obsession with the end of Rome[1] seemed, this time, to be confirmed by the bloodstained events

1. "At every historical crisis two crepuscular myths obsessed the Roman people: (1) the life of the city is ended, its duration being limited to a certain number of years (the 'mystic number' revealed by the twelve eagles seen by Romulus); and (2) the Great Year will put an end to all history, hence to that of Rome, by a universal *ekpyrōsis* [conflagration]. Roman history itself undertook to show the baselessness of these fears, down to a very late period. For at the end of 120 years after the foundation of Rome, it was realized that the twelve eagles seen by Romulus did not signify 120 years of historical life for the city, as many had feared. At the end of 365 years, it became apparent that there was no question of a Great Year, in which each year of the city

of contemporary history. Horace did not hide his fear of the approaching fate of the city (see his *Sixteenth Epode*).

When Caesar crossed the Rubicon, the Neo-Pythagorean Nigidius Figulus announced the beginning of a cosmico-historical drama that would put an end to Rome and even to the human race (Lucan, *Pharsalia* 639, 642–45). But the reign of Augustus, coming after the long and disastrous civil wars, seemed to inaugurate a *pax aeterna*. The fears inspired by the two myths—the "age" of Rome and the Great Year—now proved to be groundless. For, on the one hand, Augustus had just founded Rome anew, hence there was nothing to fear as to its duration; on the other hand, the passage from the Iron Age to the Age of Gold had taken place without a cosmic catastrophe. Indeed, Vergil replaced the last *saeculum,* that of the Sun—which was to bring on the universal combustion—by the century of Apollo; he thus avoided the *ekpyrōsis* and considered that the civil wars themselves actually indicated the passage from the Iron Age to the Age of Gold. Later, when Augustus' reign seemed really to have inaugurated the Golden Age, Vergil tried to reassure the Romans as to the duration of the city. In the *Aeneid* (1. 255 ff.) Jupiter, speaking to Venus, assures her that he will impose no kind of spatial or temporal limitation on the Romans: "I have given them endless rule" (*imperium sine fine dedi*). After the publication of the *Aeneid,* Rome was named *urbs aeterna,* Augustus being proclaimed the city's second founder. His birthday, September 23, was regarded "as the point of departure of the Universe, whose existence Augustus had saved as he had changed its face."[2] Then the hope spread that Rome could be periodically regenerated ad infinitum. It was thus that, freed from the myths of the twelve eagles and the *ekpyrōsis,* Rome could spread, as Vergil announced (*Aeneid* 6. 798), even to the regions "that lie beyond the roads of the Sun and the year" (*extra anni solisque vias*).

We have to do with a supreme effort to free history from astral destiny and from the law of cosmic cycles and, by the myth of

---

would be equivalent to a day, and it was supposed that destiny had granted Rome another kind of Great Year, composed of twelve months of 100 years" (Eliade, *The Myth of the Eternal Return,* p. 134; trans. by Willard R. Trask).

2. J. Carcopino, *Virgile et le mystère de la IVe églogue,* p. 200.

the eternal renewal of Rome, to recover the archaic myth of the annual regeneration of the cosmos by means of its periodic re-creation (by sacrificers or by the sovereign). It is likewise an attempt to valorize history on the cosmic plane, that is, to regard historical events and catastrophes as true cosmic combustions or dissolutions, which must periodically put an end to the universe to allow its regeneration. The wars, the destructions, the sufferings brought on by history are no longer the precursory signs of the passage from one cosmic age to another: *they are themselves that passage*. Thus, at each period of peace, history is renewed, and, in consequence, a new world begins; in the last analysis (as is shown by the myth that arose around Augustus), the sovereign repeats the creation of the cosmos.[3]

In his *Fourth Eclogue* Vergil announces that the Age of Gold is about to begin again under the consulate of Asinius Pollio (ca. 40 B.C., that is, before Octavius' final victory). "It is the birth of a new cycle of ages [*magnus ab integro saeclorum nascitur ordo*]. Now the Virgin returns [*jam redit et Virgo*], returns now the reign of Saturn." A "golden race" springs up throughout the world, and Apollo is its sovereign (5–10). Now Vergil associates all these signs pointing to the return of the Age of Gold with the birth of a child whose identity is unknown but whom numerous scholars suppose to be the son of Pollio. The meaning of this inspired and enigmatic poem has long been discussed and is still under discussion. For our purpose, it is enough to emphasize Vergil's visionary power: like a true *vates,* he grasped the simultaneously cosmic and religious context of the end of the civil wars, and he divined the eschatological function of the peace inaugurated by the victory of Octavius Augustus.

And in fact the reign of Augustus marks a creative rebirth of the traditional Roman religion.[4] According to Suetonius (*Aug.* 90–92), Augustus behaved like a true Roman of the olden times, taking into account dreams and other warnings, observing the manifestations of the gods, practicing *pietas* in regard to divinities and men. "It is this *religio,* and not the Stoic theology, that

3. *The Myth of the Eternal Return,* pp. 119–20.

4. It is to Franz Altheim's credit that he has insisted on the authenticity of Augustus' religious reforms; see his *A History of Roman Religion,* pp. 350 ff. The following pages owe much to his analyses.

always dictated the emperor's decisive acts. . . . Through *pietas* and *religio,* the religious attitude and the ideals of the Roman past were consciously recovered and renewed."[5] Augustus decreed the restoration of ruined sanctuaries and built many new temples. He reestablished sacerdotal positions that had long been vacant (e.g., the position of *flamen Dialis*), and he revived sodalities as venerable as that of the Titii, the Luperci, and the Arval Brothers. His contemporaries did not doubt the authenticity of the change. "The advent of the new age was celebrated in the songs of poets as well as in public manifestations" (Altheim, *History of Roman Religion,* p. 372). And works of art of Augustus' century brilliantly show the renewal of religious experience and thought.

History set itself to give the lie to the Age of Gold as soon as Augustus died, and the Romans returned to living in expectation of imminent disaster. But the century of Augustus remained the exemplary model for the civilization of the Christian West. What is more, Vergil, and Cicero in part, inspired the theology of literature and, in general, the theology of culture that was typical of the Middle Ages and that continued into the Renaissance.

226. The tribulations of a *religio illicita*

After his death Julius Caesar was proclaimed a god among the gods, and in ca. 29 a temple was consecrated to him in the Forum. The Romans consented to the postmortem apotheosis of their great leaders but refused them deification in their lifetimes.[6] Augustus accepted divine honors nowhere but in the provinces; at Rome he was only "son of god," *Divi filius*. However, the imperial genius (attendant spirit) was venerated at official and private banquets.

The deification of the "good" emperors and, in consequence, the organization of the imperial cult became general after

5. Altheim, *History of Roman Religion,* p. 375.

6. Nevertheless, Caesar had his statue at the Capitol and another at the Temple of Quirinus, bearing the inscription "Deo invicto." In ca. 44 he had officially received the title "divine Julius."

Augustus.[7] But Tiberius was not deified, because Caligula failed to present the request for it to the Senate. As for Caligula, he had seen to it that he was deified before his death; however, his memory was officially condemned by the senators. Claudius, Vespasian, and Titus were apotheosized, but not Galba, Otho, and Vitellius, who did not deserve it; nor was Domitian, enemy of the Senate. Once the apparatus of succession was firmly established, all the great emperors of the second century were deified; this did not happen in the third century, when the emperors succeeded one another too rapidly.[8]

From the second century on, refusal to celebrate the imperial cult was the chief basis for the persecutions of Christians. At first, except for the slaughter ordered by Nero, anti-Christian measures were chiefly encouraged by the hostility of Roman public opinion. During the first two centuries, Christianity was considered a *religio illicita,* and Christians were persecuted because they practiced a clandestine religion, one that had no official authorization. In 202 Septimus Severus published the first anti-Christian decree, forbidding proselytizing. Soon afterward, Maximus attacked the ecclesiastical hierarchy, but unsuccessfully. Until the reign of Decius, the Church developed in peace. But in 250 Decius published an edict requiring all citizens to offer sacrifices to the gods of the Empire. The persecution, though short, was extremely severe, which explains the large number of abjurations. However, chiefly by virtue of its confessors and martyrs, the Church emerged from the ordeal victorious. The repression decided on by Valerian in 257–58 was followed by a long period of peace (260–303). Christianity was able to infiltrate everywhere in the Empire and on every social level (even into the emperor's family).

The last persecution—Diocletian's (303–5)—was the longest and the most sanguinary. Despite the dramatic situation of the Empire, public opinion this time showed itself less hostile to the Christians. Now Diocletian had made up his mind to destroy this exotic and antinational religion precisely in order to strengthen

7. This is not due to an influence from the Hellenistic East. Cicero had already written that "the spirits of good and brave men are intrinsically divine" (*De Leg*. 2. 11. 27).

8. The sources are given in Robert Grant, *Augustus to Constantine*, p. 17.

the idea of Empire; he wanted to reanimate the old Roman religious traditions and, above all, to glorify the quasi-divine image of the emperor. But the heritage of Augustus' reform had been gradually eroded. Cults native to Egypt and Asia Minor enjoyed an astonishing popularity; they also benefited from imperial protection. Commodus (185–92) had been initiated into the Mysteries of Isis and those of Mithra, and Caracalla (211–17) had encouraged the cult of the Syrian solar god, Sol Invictus. Some years later, the Emperor Heliogabalus, himself a Syrian and a priest of the god of Emesa, introduced this cult into Rome. Heliogabalus was assassinated in 222, and the Syrian god was then banished from the city. However, as we shall see (p. 411), Aurelian (270–75) successfully reintroduced the cult of Sol Invictus. Aurelian understood that it was useless simply to glorify the great religious past of Rome; it was necessary also to integrate into the venerable Roman tradition a monotheistic solar theology, the only religion that was in the process of becoming universal.

Even before the great persecutions, toward the end of the second century, several Christian theologians and controversialists tried to justify and defend their religion before the authorities and the pagan intelligentsia. But their attempt was doomed to fail. Naïve or unskillful, certain apologists (Tatian, Tertullian) virulently attacked paganism and Hellenistic culture. The most important of them, Justin (martyred ca. 165), attempted to show that Christianity did not scorn pagan culture; he praised Greek philosophy but pointed out that it was inspired by the biblical revelation. Repeating the arguments of Alexandrian Judaism, Justin affirmed that Plato and the other Greek philosophers knew the doctrine that had been professed, long before their time, by the "prophet" Moses. In any case, the failure of the apologists was foreseeable. For the authorities, Christianity was not only clearly guilty of atheism and *lèse-majesté*, it was suspected of all kinds of crimes, from orgies and incest to infanticide and cannibalism. For the pagan elite, the essence of Christian theology—the incarnation of the Savior, his sufferings and resurrection—was simply unintelligible. In any case, the fanatical intransigence of this new religion of salvation made any hope of peaceful coexistence with the polytheistic religions illusory.

For the Christian mission, the persecutions constituted the greatest peril; but they were not the only danger threatening the Church. The Mysteries of Isis and of Mithra and the cult of Sol Invictus and solar monotheism represented a competition greatly to be feared, and the more so since they had the benefit of official protection. In addition, a far more subtle danger threatened the Church from within: the various heresies, and first of all Gnosticism. The heresies and gnoses make their appearance from the very beginning of Christianity. In the absence of a canon, the only way to verify the authenticity of beliefs and ritual practices was the apostolic tradition. By about the year 150 all the Apostles and those who had known them personally had died, but transmission of their testimony was insured by a number of texts they had composed or inspired and by oral tradition.

However, the two currents of apostolic tradition—written and oral—were both subject to more or less dubious innovations. Besides the four Gospels and the Acts of the Apostles, which were accepted by all of the Christian communities,[9] other texts were in circulation under the names of Apostles: the Gospel of Thomas, the Gospel of Truth, the Gospel of the Pseudo-Matthew, the Acts of Peter, of John, etc. The majority of these works, termed "apocrypha" (since they contained revelations previously "hidden"), involved the revelation of an esoteric doctrine, communicated to the Apostles by the resurrected Christ and concerning the secret meaning of the events of his life. It was to this secret teaching, preserved and transmitted by oral tradition, that the Gnostics appealed as their authority.

227. Christian gnosis

The problem of esotericism, and consequently of initiation, was to inspire countless controversies, especially and first of all during the crisis brought on by Gnosticism. In the face of the extravagant pretensions of certain Gnostic authors, the Fathers of

9. It is significant that in the second half of the second century these texts were adopted by all the great churches of the period as the only writings representing the apostolic tradition. Thenceforth Christianity possesses its canon—the New Testament—and becomes a "religion of the Book."

the Church, later followed by the majority of ancient and modern historians, denied the existence of an esoteric teaching practiced by Jesus and continued by his disciples. But this opinion is contradicted by the facts. Esotericism—in other words, the initiatory transmission of doctrines and practices restricted to a limited number of adepts—is documented in all the great religions in both the Hellenistic period and near the beginning of the Christian era. In varying degrees we find the initiatory scenario (secret teaching and rites, segregation of believers, oath of silence, etc.) in normative Judaism and in the Judaic sects, among the Essenes (for example, in the "Treatise of Discipline" 9. 16 ff.; 6. 13–23), and among the Samaritans and the Pharisees.[10]

The practice of a certain esoteric teaching is likewise mentioned in the Gospel of Mark (4:10 ff., 7:17 ff., 10:10 ff.). From the beginnings of the Church, three degrees—which presuppose initiatory apprenticeship—are distinguished within the community. They are: the "Beginners," the "Progressing," and the "Perfect." According to Origen, "Jesus explained all things to his own disciples privately, and for this reason the writers of the Gospels concealed the clear exposition of the parables" (*Commentary on Matthew* 14. 12). Clement of Alexandria is still more explicit. He mentions his teachers, who preserved "the true tradition of the blessed teachings, come directly from the holy Apostles Peter, James, John, and Paul, transmitted from father to son [and which] came down to us, thanks be to God" (*Stromateis* 1. 11; 2. 3). This refers to teachings restricted to a certain number of believers and which, transmitted orally (13. 2), must remain secret; these teachings constitute the gnostic tradition. In another work Clement states: "James the Righteous, John, and Peter were entrusted by the Lord, after his resurrection, with the higher knowledge. They imparted it to the other apostles, the other apostles to the seventy, one of whom was Barnabas."[11]

10. See the sources cited and commented on by Morton Smith, *Clement of Alexandria and a Secret Gospel of Mark*, pp. 197–99. It is from this tradition of secret doctrines and practices of Judaism that the literature of the *Merkabah* will be elaborated, first of all the *Hekalat* texts (see Smith, p. 198).

11. Fragment of the *Hypotuposeis*, transmitted by Eusebius, *Hist. Eccl.* 2. 1. 3–4; see Jean Daniélou, "Les traditions secrètes des Apôtres," p. 200.

It is impossible to determine the criteria that guided the selection of disciples worthy of being initiated into the gnosis, and especially the circumstances and the stages of their initiation. A certain instruction, "esoteric" in type, was gradually given to all believers; it dealt with the symbolism of baptism, the Eucharist, and the Cross, with the archangels, and with the interpretation of the apocalypse. As for the secrets revealed to the "perfect" and those in the course of becoming such, they probably referred to the mysteries of the descent and ascension of Christ through the seven heavens inhabited by the angels (see Ephesians 4:9) and to individual eschatology, that is, to the mystical itinerary of the soul after death. Now this mystical itinerary is connected by Pseudo-Dionysius to the oral tradition of the Apostles. "Thus we are brought to see the existence of a succession of gnostic masters or spiritual masters, separate from the succession of bishops, who transmit the faith of the Apostles . . . but who continue the charismatic tradition of apostolic times and of the Apostles."[12]

However, the esoteric traditions of the Apostles carry on a Jewish esotericism concerning the mysteries of the ascent of the soul and the secrets of the celestial world. But these doctrines are also found among the Mandaeans. What is more, they are similar to certain Egyptian (see § 53) and Iranian eschatological conceptions. Side by side with other ideas and beliefs that differ from those held in common by Judaism and Christianity, they are found in a number of Gnostic, pagan, and heterodox Christian authors. We understand why, from a certain moment, gnosis and esotericism became suspect in the eyes of the ecclesiastical hierarchy. By citing the authority of an oral and secret apostolic tradition, certain Gnostics could introduce into Christianity doctrines and practices radically opposed to the ethos of the Gospel. It was not esotericism and gnosis as such that were found to be dangerous but the heresies that infiltrated themselves under the cloak of initiatory secrecy.

To be sure, as long as the "Book" and the dogmas were not fixed, it could seem an abuse to apply the term "heretical" to certain daring interpretations of Christ's teaching. But in a num-

12. Daniélou, "Les traditions secrètes," pp. 208 ff.

ber of cases the heresy—that is, the false interpretation of the Gospel message—was obvious: for example, when the validity of the Old Testament was rejected and God the Father was regarded as a malevolent and stupid demiurge; similarly, when the world was condemned and life was denigrated as accidental or demonic creations, or when the incarnation, death, and resurrection of the Son were denied. It is true that Saint Paul himself regarded this world as dominated by Satan, and the Jewish and Christian apocalypses predicted the imminent destruction of the earth. But neither Saint Paul nor the authors of the apocalypses denied the divine origin of the Creation.

228. Approaches of Gnosticism

It is difficult to determine the origin of the spiritual current known by the name of "Gnosticism," but it must be distinguished from the numerous earlier or contemporary gnoses that formed an integral part of various religions of the time (Zoroastrianism, the Mysteries, Judaism, Christianity)—gnoses that, as we have just seen, included an esoteric teaching. It must be added that almost all the mythological and eschatological themes employed by the Gnostic authors are earlier than Gnosticism *stricto sensu*. Some of them are documented in ancient Iran and in India of the Upanishadic period, in Orphism and Platonism; others are characteristic of Hellenistic syncretism, biblical and intertestamentary Judaism, or the earliest expressions of Christianity. However, what defines Gnosticism *stricto sensu* is not the more or less organic integration of a certain number of disparate elements but the daring, and strangely pessimistic, reinterpretation of certain myths, ideas, and theologoumena that were in wide circulation at the time.[13]

A formula of Valentinian gnosis, transmitted by Clement of Alexandria, declares that one obtains deliverance by learning

13. Thus, for example, the Gnostic doctors reinterpreted the myth of Christ's descent into the world by detaching it from its biblical context—the Messiah sent by the creator God—and connecting it with an entirely different "secret history" (the Creation is a sinister tragedy and must therefore be attributed to a demiurge or a demonic being, a true incarnation of evil).

"what we were and what we have become; where we were and where we have been cast; toward what end we hasten and whence we are redeemed; what is birth and what is regeneration" (*Extracts from Theodotus* 78. 2). Unlike the Upaṇishads, Sāṃkhya-Yoga, and Buddhism—which deliberately avoid discussing the original cause of the fall of humanity—the redeeming knowledge taught by the Gnostics consists above all in the revelation of a "secret history" (more precisely, a history kept secret from the uninitiated) of the origin and creation of the world, the origin of evil, the drama of the divine redeemer come down to earth to save men, and the final victory of the transcendent God—a victory that will find expression in the conclusion of history and the annihilation of the cosmos. This is a *total* myth: it reports all the decisive elements, from the origin of the world to the present and, by demonstrating their interdependence, insures the credibility of the *eschaton*. This total myth is known to us in numerous versions. We shall mention some of them further on, especially emphasizing the most grandiose among them, the version elaborated by Mani (§ 233).

To return to the Valentinian formula, the Gnostic learns that his true being (i.e., his spiritual being) is divine by origin and by nature, though at present it is captive in a body; he also learns that he lived in a transcendent region but that he was later cast into this world below, that he is rapidly advancing toward salvation, and that he will end by being freed from his fleshly prison; in short, he discovers that, whereas his birth was equivalent to a fall into matter, his rebirth will be purely spiritual. The following fundamental ideas are to be noted: the dualism of spirit/matter, divine (transcendent)/antidivine; the myth of the fall of the soul (= spirit, divine particle), that is, incarnation in a body (assimilated to a prison); and the certainty of deliverance (salvation) obtained by virtue of gnosis.

At first sight, we would seem to be dealing with an exaggerated, anticosmic, and pessimistic development of Orphico-Platonic dualism.[14] In reality the phenomenon is more complex. The

14. Cf. §§181 ff. For Plato, of course, the demiurge is not the incarnation of evil. The world is a "cosmos," hence perfect and harmonious. For Plotinus, as for the Stoics, the stars are gods, and contemplating them facilitates the coming-together of intelligible beings; see *Enneads* 2. 9; 4. 8; etc. As for the

drama of humanity—in particular, its fall and redemption—reflects the divine drama. God sends a primordial being, or his own son, into the world in order to save men. This transcendent being undergoes all the humiliating consequences of incarnation but is able to reveal the true, redeeming gnosis to a few chosen spirits before finally returning to heaven. Some variants give a more dramatic amplification to the descent of the son or the transcendent being: he is captured by demonic powers and, brutalized by immersion in matter, forgets his own identity; God then sends a messenger who, by "awakening" him, helps him recover consciousness of himself. (This is the myth of the "saved Savior," admirably narrated in the "Hymn of the Pearl"; see § 230.)

Despite certain Iranian parallels, the *immediate* model of the savior-messenger sent by God is obviously Jesus Christ. The texts discovered in 1945 at Nag Hammadi in Upper Egypt demonstrate the Judaeo-Christian origin of some important Gnostic schools.[15] Yet their theologies and ethics are radically different from those professed by Judaism and Christianity. First of all, for the Gnostics, the true God is not the creator God, that is, Yahweh. The Creation is the work of lower or even diabolical powers, or, alternatively, the cosmos is the more or less demonic counterfeit of a superior world—conceptions inconceivable both for the Jews and the Christians. To be sure, in late paganism the cosmogony had lost all positive religious meaning. But the Gnostics go still further. Not only is the creation of the world no longer a proof of God's omnipotence; it is explained by an accident that occurred in the higher regions or as the result of the primordial aggression of Darkness against Light (see the Manichaean myth, § 233). As for incarnate existence, far from being a part of a "sacred history," as the Jews and the Christians thought, it confirms and illustrates the fall of the soul. For the

---

incarnation of the soul, for Plotinus it is a "fall," since the soul loses its spiritual plenitude and its autonomy (4. 8; 5. 16); but it is also a descent freely accepted in order to help existences placed in the lower world (4. 8; 7. 1).

15. Thus, for example, the Gospel according to Thomas, found at Nag Hammadi, constitutes the complete version of the logia attributed to Jesus in the Oxyrynchus papyri and known since 1897; see H.-C. Puech, *En quête de la Gnose*, vol. 2, pp. 33 ff., 65 ff., and passim.

Gnostic, the only object worth pursuing was the deliverance of that divine particle and its reascent to the celestial spheres.

As we saw (§§181 ff.), the "fall" of man, that is, the incarnation of the soul, was already a prime object of speculation for the Orphic and Pythagorean theologians; it was explained either as the punishment for a sin committed in heaven or as the result of a disastrous choice made by the soul itself. During the earliest centuries of the Christian era, these two myths were amplified and modified by numerous Gnostic and other authors.[16]

Since the world is the result of an accident or a catastrophe, since it is dominated by ignorance and ruled by the powers of evil, the Gnostic finds himself completely alienated from his own culture and rejects all of its norms and institutions. The inner freedom obtained by gnosis enables him to comport himself freely and to act as he pleases. The Gnostic forms part of an elite, the result of a selection decided by the Spirit. He belongs to the class of Pneumatics or "Spirituals"—the "Perfect," the "Sons of the King"—who alone will be saved.[17] Just like the *ṛṣis,* the *sannyasis,* and the yogins, the Gnostic feels that he is freed from the laws that govern society: he is beyond good and evil. And, to pursue the comparison with Indian phenomena: to the sexual techniques and orgiastic rituals of the Tantric schools of "the left hand" (see vol. 3, chap. 38) there correspond the orgies of the libertine Gnostic sects (first of all, the Phibionists).[18]

16. The Orphico-Pythagorean idea of incarnation as punishment, combined with the biblical myth of the fall of the angels, was borrowed by certain Christian or semi-Christian Gnostics (Valentinus, Marcion, Bardesanes), by Mani, by the author of the *Korē Kosmou,* and, probably, by Origen. As for the soul's voluntary descent, it resulted from narcissism (the soul fell in love with its own image reflected in the material world) or from ambition. This conception is documented in Numenius of Apamaea, in the author of the *Poimandres,* and in Plotinus; see the references brought together by E. R. Dodds, *Pagan and Christian in an Age of Anxiety,* pp. 23–24.

17. A second class, the Psychics, includes those who have a soul (*psychē*) and, as such, can be drawn upward, but who lack spirit (*pneuma*). Finally, the third class, the "carnal" (the Somatics or Hylics), are totally immersed in matter and condemned to disappear. The vain agitation of these two categories of individuals necessitates the secret, esoteric, transmission of the teaching.

18. "More than a critique or a refutation, we have here a revolt . . . obstinate, violent, of vast scope and grave consequences: against the human condition,

229. From Simon Magus to Valentinus

The Christian apologists denounce in Simon Magus the first heretic and the ancestor of all heresies. According to some historians, Simon is not a Gnostic *stricto sensu,* but his disciples became such after the catastrophe of the year 70.[19] The Apostle Peter ran afoul of the Simonian movement in Samaria, where Simon proclaimed himself "the divine Power that is called great."[20] And in fact he was worshiped as the "first God," and his companion, Helen, discovered by Simon in a brothel at Tyre, was regarded as the last and most fallen incarnation of the Thought (Ennoia) of God; redeemed by Simon, Helen-Ennoia became the means of universal redemption. Simon Magus is of interest to the historian of religions especially for the glorification of Helen and the mythology that she inspired. The union of the "magician" with the prostitute insured universal salvation because their union is, in reality, the reunion of God and divine Wisdom.

The memory of this eccentric couple in all probability gave rise to the legend of Faust, the archetype of the magician. In fact, Simon was known in Rome as Faustus ("Favored"), and his companion had, in a previous existence, been Helen of Troy. But in the first centuries of the Christian era, emphasis was laid on the supreme confrontation between the Apostle Peter and the magician. According to the legend, Simon, in the presence of a large number of spectators in Rome, announced his ascent to

---

existence, the world, God himself. It can lead equally well to imagining a final event that will be an *eversio, revolutio*—an overturning and reversal of the present situation, reciprocal substitution of left and right, outer and inner, higher and lower—or to nihilism: a nihilism of the 'libertine Gnostics' who, freed from all natural or moral law, use and abuse their body and the world in order to profane them, to 'exhaust,' deny, and annihilate them; the nihilism of a Basilides, for whom every being, every thing, the universe in the totality of its becoming, is destined to find its definitive fulfillment in the darkness of the 'Great Ignorance,' in the peace of 'nonbeing' " (H.-C. Puech, *En quête de la Gnose,* vol. 1, p. xxii).

19. See R. M. Grant, *Gnosticism and Early Christianity,* pp. 70 ff.; J. Daniélou and H. Marrou, *Nouvelle histoire de l'Eglise,* vol. 1, p. 87.

20. Acts 8:10. However, it is not certain that Simon Magus and the Simon of Acts are the same person; see Jonas, *The Gnostic Religion,* p. 103.

heaven, but a prayer uttered by the Apostle made him fall lamentably.

The example of Marcion is instructive for several reasons. He was born ca. 85 in Pontus; son of the bishop of Sinope, he largely adhered to orthodox practices. But he developed the Pauline anti-Judaism to excess. Marcion rejected the Old Testament and established his own canon, which was reduced to Luke's Gospel and Paul's ten Epistles. He added a manual, the *Antitheses*, in which he set forth the principles of his theology. At Rome about 144 Marcion tried in vain to obtain the support of the presbyters. Excommunicated, he elaborated his doctrine more and more radically and actually founded a church. An excellent organizer, he succeeded in converting a large number of Christian communities in the Mediterranean Basin. This new theology had considerable success and hence was tirelessly attacked by orthodox writers. But from the beginning of the third century Marcionism was in decline, and it disappeared in the West in less than a century.

Marcion accepted the essentials of Gnostic dualism, but without embracing its apocalyptic implications. His dualistic system opposes the Law and justice, instituted by the creator god of the Old Testament, to the love and the Gospel revealed by the good God. The latter sends his son, Jesus Christ, to deliver men from slavery to the Law. Jesus assumes a body capable of feeling and suffering, though it is not material. In his preaching, Jesus glorifies the good God but is careful to state that he does *not* mean the god of the Old Testament. Indeed, it is from Jesus' preaching that Yahweh learns of the existence of a transcendent God. He avenges himself by delivering Jesus to his persecutors. But the death on the Cross brings salvation, for by his sacrifice Jesus redeems humanity from the creator god. However, the world continues to be under the domination of Yahweh, and believers will be persecuted until the end of time. It is only then that the good God will make himself known: he will receive the faithful into his Kingdom, while the rest of mankind, together with matter and the creator, will be definitively annihilated.

Another Samaritan, Menander, introduced Gnosticism into Antioch. He presented himself as the redeemer come down from heaven to save men (Irenaeus, *Adversus haereses* 1. 23. 8), and claimed that those whom he baptized would become superior to the angels. His heir, Satornil (active at Antioch between ca. 100 and 130), opposed the hidden God to the God of the Jews, mere leader of the creator angels. He condemned marriage, which he declared to be the work of Satan (Irenaeus, 1. 24. 2). His theology was dominated by dualism. According to Irenaeus, Satornil was the first to speak of the two categories of men, those who have and those who do not have the celestial light.

Cerinthus, a Judaeo-Christian contemporary of John (Irenaeus, 3. 3. 4), teaches that the world was created by a demiurge who did not know the true God; this is the first expression of Gnosticism *stricto sensu*. According to Cerinthus, Jesus is the son of Joseph and Mary; at his baptism Christ descended upon him in the form of a dove and revealed the Unknown Father to him and then, before the Passion, reascended to God the Father (Irenaeus, 1. 28).

Judaeo-Christian Gnosticism, disseminated in Asia and Syria, also made its way into Egypt. Cerinthus settled in Alexandria, where, about 120, Carpocrates proclaimed a similar doctrine: Jesus is the son of Joseph, but a "power" sanctified him (Irenaeus, 1. 23. 1). He who receives this power becomes the equal of Jesus and is able to perform the same miracles. A characteristic feature of Carpocrates' gnosis is his radical amoralism, "which seems to arise from the Gnostic revolt not only against the Jewish God but against the Law."[21] Basilides, another Alexandrian, contemporary with Carpocrates, gave the first synthesis of the doctrines taught by the disciples of Simon Magus. He elaborated a vast and complex cosmogony of the Gnostic type, spectacularly multiplying the heavens and the angels that rule them: he reckoned their number at 365![22] Basilides entirely rejected the Jewish Law and regarded Yahweh as only one of the angels who created the world, though he attempts to dominate and subject them all (Irenaeus, 1. 24. 4).

The most important Gnostic teacher is indubitably Valentinus, who ranks among the greatest theologians and mystics of his

21. Daniélou and Marrou, *Nouvelle histoire de l'Eglise*, vol. 1, p. 96.

22. See the texts reproduced and commented on by H. Leisegang, *La Gnose*, pp. 143 ff. See also Grant's pertinent remarks, *Gnosticism and Early Christianity*, pp. 142 ff.

time. Born in Egypt and educated in Alexandria, he taught at Rome between 135 and 160. But since he did not succeed in obtaining the position of bishop, he broke with the Church and left the city.[23] In elaborating his grandiose system, Valentinus set out to explain the existence of evil and the fall of the soul not from a dualistic point of view—i.e., by the intervention of an anti-God—but by a drama that took place *within* the divinity. No summary does justice to the magnificence and boldness of the Valentinian synthesis, yet a summary has the advantage of omitting the countless genealogies, "emanations," and "projections" summoned up with touching monotony to explain the origin and relate the drama of all cosmic, vital, psychic, and spiritual realities.[24]

According to Valentinus, the Father, absolute and transcendent First Principle, is invisible and incomprehensible. He unites with his companion, Thought (Ennoia), and engenders the fifteen pairs of eons that, together, constitute the Pleroma.[25] The last of the eons, Sophia, blinded by desire to know the Father, brings on a crisis, as the result of which evil and the passions make their appearance. Precipitated from the Pleroma, Sophia and the aberrant creations that she had occasioned produce an inferior wisdom. Above, a new couple is created, Christ and his feminine partner, the Holy Spirit. Finally, restored to its original perfection, the Pleroma engenders the Savior, also named Jesus. Descending to the lower regions, the Savior forms "invisible

23. Until about 1950 our only sources for Valentinus' theology were the extracts and summaries preserved by Irenaeus, Clement of Alexandria, and Hippolytus, who in any case had chiefly used the works of his disciples. But the Gospel of Truth, discovered at Nag Hammadi, though it is not the work of Valentinus, certainly represents his thought. Other texts from Nag Hammadi (for example, the "Treatise of the Three Natures" and the "Letter to Rhegius on the Resurrection") are connected with the Valentinian school.

24. The fascination exercised by such cascading genealogies and series of manifestations is one of the specific characteristics of the period. The tendency to multiply the intermediate stages and the mediating agents between the Absolute and the various classes of realities is also present in the philosophers (for example, Plotinus); but among the Gnostic authors—especially Basilides, Valentinus, and Mani—it became at once an obsession and a stereotype.

25. The term Pleroma (Gk. *plērōma*, "plenitude") designates the spiritual world around the primordial divinity; it is constituted by the totality of the eons.

matter'' with the hylic (material) elements proceeding from the lower Wisdom, and with the psychic elements he makes the Demiurge, i.e., the God of Genesis. The latter knows nothing of the existence of a higher world and considers himself the only God. He creates the material world and, animating them with his breath, forms two categories of men, the Hylics and the Psychics. But the spiritual elements, proceeding from the higher Sophia, introduce themselves into the Demiurge's breath, unknown to him, and give birth to the class of Pneumatics.[26] In order to save these spiritual particles, captive in matter, Christ descends to earth and, without incarnating himself in the strict sense of the word, reveals the liberating knowledge. Thus, awakened by gnosis, the Pneumatics, and *they alone,* ascend to the Father.

As Hans Jonas observes, in Valentinus' system matter has a spiritual origin and is explained by divine history. Indeed matter is a state or an ''affection'' of the absolute Being—more precisely, the ''solidified external expression'' of that state. Ignorance (the ''blindness'' of Sophia) is the first cause of the existence of the world[27]—an idea that is reminiscent of Indian conceptions (held by certain Vedāntic and Sāṃkhya-Yoga schools). And, just as in India, ignorance and knowledge characterize two types of ontologies. Knowledge constitutes the original condition of the Absolute; ignorance is the consequence of some disorder produced within this same Absolute. But the salvation procured by knowledge is equivalent to a cosmic event (see Jonas, p. 175). The redemption of the last Pneumatic will be accompanied by the annihilation of the world.

230. Gnostic myths, images, and metaphors

Amnesia (in other words, forgetting one's own identity), sleep, drunkenness, torpor, captivity, fall, and homesickness are among the specifically Gnostic images and symbols, though they are not the creation of the teachers of Gnosis. In turning toward matter

26. This is the explanation for the existence of the three classes of men, a belief held in common by all the Gnostics; see p. 374 and n. 17, above.

27. Hans Jonas, *The Gnostic Religion,* p. 174.

and wanting to know the pleasures of the body, the soul forgets its own identity. "It forgets its original dwelling place, its true center, its eternal being."[28] The most dramatic and moving presentation of the Gnostic myth of amnesia and anamnesia is found in the "Hymn of the Pearl,"[29] preserved in the apocryphal Acts of Thomas. A prince arrives in Egypt from the East to seek

> the one pearl
> Which is in the midst of the sea
> Hard by the loud-breathing serpent.

In Egypt he is captured by men of the country. They give him some of their food to eat, and the prince forgets his identity:

> I forgot that I was a son of kings,
> And I served their king;
> And I forgot the pearl for which my parents had sent me.
> And by reason of the burden of their foods
> I lay in a deep sleep.

But the prince's parents learned what had happened to him, and they wrote him a letter:

> "Up and arise from thy sleep
> And listen to the words of our letter!
> Call to mind that thou art a son of kings!
> See the slavery—whom thou servest.
> Remember the pearl for which thou
> Didst speed to Egypt!"

The letter flew in the likeness of an eagle, alighted beside him, and became speech.

> At its voice and the sound of its rustling
> I started and arose from my sleep,
> I took it up and kissed it,
> I loosed its seal [?], [and] read. . . .
> I remembered that I was a son of kings. . . .
> I remembered the pearl for which I had been sent to Egypt,
> And I began to charm . . .

28. Doctrine of a late Gnostic sect, the Harranites; see Jonas, p. 63.

29. The text has been translated and commented on by H. Leisegang, *La Gnose*, pp. 247–48; Jonas, *The Gnostic Religion*, pp. 112–24; R. M. Grant, *Gnosticism: A Source Book*, pp. 116 ff.; and by others. The translation used here is Grant's.

> The . . . loud-breathing serpent.
> I hushed him to sleep . . . ,
> For my Father's name I named over him . . . ;
> And I snatched away the pearl,
> And turned to go back to my Father's house.

This is the myth of the "saved Savior," *Salvator salvatus,* in its best version. It must be added that parallels for each mythical motif are found in the various Gnostic texts.[30] The meaning of the images is easy to apprehend. The sea and Egypt are common symbols for the material world, in which man's soul and the savior sent to deliver it are both taken captive. Descending from the celestial regions, the hero lays off his "bright robe" and puts on the "filthy garb" in order not to differ from the inhabitants of the country; it is the "fleshly envelope," the body in which he is incarnated. At a certain moment during his ascension he is met by his glorious garment of light, "like unto himself," and he understands that this "double" is his true Self. His meeting with his transcendent "double" is reminiscent of the Iranian conception of the celestial image of the soul, the *dāenā,* which meets the deceased on the third day after his death (see vol. 1, pp. 329 ff., 472). As Jonas observed, the discovery of this transcendent principle within one's Self constitutes the central element of the Gnostic religion.[31]

The theme of the amnesia brought on by immersion in "life" (= matter) and of the anamnesia obtained by the gestures, songs, or words of a messenger is also found in the religious folklore of medieval India. One of the most popular legends tells of the anamnesia of Matsyendranāth. This master yogin fell in love with a queen and went to live in her palace, completely forgetting his identity, or, according to another version, he became a pris-

30. Jonas cites a certain number of parallels for the "filthy garb" and the "bright robe," for the snake, the letter, and the ascension; see his *Gnostic Religion,* pp. 116 ff. See also Puech, *En quête de la Gnose,* vol. 2, pp. 118 ff.

31. Jonas, *Gnostic Religion,* p. 124. In the apocryphal Gospel according to Thomas (logion 84), Jesus says to his disciples, "When you see your images, which came into existence before you, [which] neither die nor are manifested, how much will you bear!" The "image" (*eikōn*), that is, the transcendent Self, is also described as an "angel"; see Puech, *En quête,* vol. 2, pp. 130 ff., 142 ff.

The meeting of the transcendent Self with the "angel" can be compared to the ineffable experience of the unity *ātman-brahman.*

oner of the women "in the land of Kadalī." Learning of Matsyendranāth's captivity, his disciple Goraknāth comes before him in the form of a dancing girl and falls to dancing, at the same time singing enigmatic songs. Little by little Matsyendranāth remembers his true identity: he understands that the "fleshly way" leads to death, that his "forgetting" was, fundamentally, a forgetting of his true and immortal nature, and that the "charms of Kadalī" represent the mirages of profane life. Goraknāth explains to him that it was the goddess Durgā who had brought on the "forgetting" that had almost cost him immortality. This spell, Goraknāth adds, symbolizes the eternal curse of ignorance laid by nature (i.e., Durgā) on the human being.[32]

The "origins" of this folklore theme go back to the period of the Upanishads. We earlier summarized the fable in the *Chāndogya Upaniṣad* about the man captured by robbers and carried far from his village with his eyes blindfolded, and Śankara's commentary on it: the robbers and the blindfold are the teacher who reveals true knowledge; the house to which the man succeeds in returning symbolizes his *ātman*, his Self, identical with the absolute being, *brahman* (see above, §136). Sāṃkhya-Yoga presents a similar position: the Self (*puruṣa*) is, above all, a "stranger"; it has nothing to do with the world (*prakṛti*). Just as for the Gnostics, the Self (the spirit, the *pneuma*) "is isolated, indifferent, inactive, a mere spectator" in the drama of life and history (see §§136 ff.).

Influences, in one direction or the other, are not excluded, but it is more probable that this is a case of parallel spiritual currents, developing out of crises brought on several centuries earlier in India (the Upanishads), in Greece and the eastern Mediterranean (Orphism and Pythagoreanism), in Iran, and in the Hellenistic world. A number of images and metaphors used by the Gnostic authors have a venerable history—even a prehistory—and an immense dissemination. One of the favorite images is that of sleep assimilated to ignorance and death. The Gnostics maintain that men not only sleep but love to sleep. "Why will you always love sleep and stumble with those that stumble?" asks the

32. See Eliade, *Yoga*, pp. 294 ff.

Ginzā.[33] "Let him who hears wake from heavy sleep," it is written in the Apocalypse of John.[34] As we shall see, the same motif is found in Manichaeanism. But such formulas are no monopoly of the Gnostic authors. Paul's Epistle to the Ephesians (5:14) contains this anonymous quotation: "Wake up from your sleep, rise from the dead, and Christ will shine on you." Sleep (Hypnos) being the twin brother of Thanatos (Death), in Greece as in India and in Gnosticism, the act of "awakening" had a soteriological meaning (in the broad sense of the term: Socrates "awakens" his interlocutors, sometimes against their will).

This is an archaic and universally disseminated symbolism. Victory over sleep and prolonged wakefulness are a rather typical initiatory ordeal. Among certain Australian tribes the novices who are being initiated must not sleep for three days; alternatively, they are forbidden to go to bed before dawn.[35] We have seen the initiatory ordeal in which the famous hero Gilgamesh fails miserably: he cannot stay awake, and he loses his chance to obtain immortality (see § 23). In a North American myth of the Orpheus-and-Eurydice type, a man succeeds in descending to the underworld, where he finds his wife, who had just died. The lord of the underworld promises him that he can take his wife back to earth if he can stay awake all night. But twice, and even after sleeping during the day in order not to be tired, the man fails to stay awake until dawn.[36] It is clear, then, that "not to sleep" is not only to overcome physical fatigue; it is, above all, to demonstrate the possession of spiritual strength. To remain "awake," to be fully conscious, means: *to be present to the world of the spirit*. Jesus constantly told his disciples to "stay awake" (see, for example, Matt. 24:42). And the night of Gethsemane is made especially tragic by the disciples' inability to "keep awake" with Jesus (see above, p. 336).

33. Cited by Jonas, *Gnostic Religion*, p. 70. In another context the *Ginzā* tells how Adam "awoke from his slumber and lifted his eyes to the place of the light" (Jonas, p. 74).

34. See J. Doresse, *Les livres secrets des gnostiques d'Egypte*, vol. 1, p. 227. "I am the voice that wakens from sleep in the Eon of night": so begins a Gnostic fragment preserved by Hippolytus (*Refut*. 5. 14. 1).

35. Eliade, *Rites and Symbols of Initiation*, pp. 14–15.

36. Eliade, *Shamanism*, pp. 311–12.

In Gnostic literature, ignorance and sleep are also expressed in terms of "intoxication." The apocryphal Gospel of Truth compares him "who is to have knowledge" with "one who, having become drunk, has turned away from his drunkenness, [and] having returned to himself, has set right what are [*sic*] his own."[37] "Awakening" implies anamnesia, the rediscovery of the soul's true identity, that is to say, re-cognition of its celestial origin. "Awake, soul of splendor, from the slumber of drunkenness into which thou hast fallen," says a Manichaean text. "Follow me to the place of the exalted earth where thou didst dwell at the beginning." In the Mandaean tradition the celestial messenger addresses Adam, after waking him from his deep sleep: "Slumber not nor sleep, and forget not that with which the Lord hath charged thee."[38]

In the last analysis, the majority of these images—ignorance, amnesia, captivity, sleep, intoxication—become, in Gnostic preaching, metaphors to indicate spiritual death. Gnosis bestows *true* life, that is, redemption and immortality.

231. The martyred Paraclete

Mani was born on April 14 of the year 216, at Seleucia-Ctesiphon in Babylonia. According to tradition, for three days his father, Patek, heard a voice bidding him not to eat flesh, not to drink wine, and to remain apart from women. Troubled, Patek joined a Gnostic baptismal sect, the Elchasaites.[39] The child came into the world sickly (he was probably lame). When he reached the age of four, his father took him to live with him in order that he should be brought up in the Elchasaite community. For more than twenty years (from 219/220 to 240) Mani grew up and was educated in a milieu of great Judaeo-Christian fervor. Hence the importance of the Christian elements in the Manichaean synthesis must not be underestimated. Yet Mani's religious vocation

37. The "Gospel of Truth" 22:18–20, from James M. Robinson, *The Nag Hammadi Library,* p. 40 (the text is translated by George W. MacRae).

38. See Jonas, *Gnostic Religion,* pp. 83–84; Puech, *En quête,* vol. 2, pp. 210–11; see also Eliade, *Myth and Reality,* pp. 127 ff.

39. A heterodox Judaeo-Christian sect, founded in 100 in Parthia by Elchai.

manifested itself in opposition to the theology, the eschatology, and the rituals of Christianity. Two revelations, received, respectively, at the ages of twelve and twenty-four years, by disclosing his own mission to him obliged him to break with the Elchasaite sect. Mani himself has informed us of the content of these revelations. An angel brought him messages from the "King of the Paradise of Lights" (the supreme and good God of Manichaeanism). In the first message he was ordered to abandon his father's community. Twelve years later, in 240, the second message urged him to act: "The time is now come for thee to manifest thyself publicly and to proclaim thy doctrine aloud."[40]

We know almost nothing of the spiritual travail that transformed the young weakling into the tireless apostle of a new religion of salvation. Nor do we know the reasons that decided him to undertake his first apostolic journey to India, which lasted from 240/41 to the beginning of 242 or 243.[41] In any case, contact with certain representatives of Indian spirituality had consequences both for Mani and for India. Summoned back to Persia by the new king, Shapur I, Mani journeyed to Balapat (Gundev Shapur), the capital of the Sassanids. Shapur was deeply impressed by the prophet and gave him, as well as his missionaries, permission to preach throughout the empire. This amounted to official recognition of the new religion, and the date has been piously preserved: March 21, 242 (or, according to a different calculation, April 9, 243).

We are poorly informed concerning Mani's biography during the reign of Shapur I (from 242 to 273). This is as much as to say that we know almost nothing of the prophet's life except its beginning (the two revelations, the "conversion" of Shapur) and

40. *Fihrist,* p. 50, after the translation by H.-C. Puech, *Le Manichéisme,* p. 43. According to Manichaean tradition, the prophet left the baptismal sect of his own free will. However, it seems more likely that he was expelled by the hierarchy.

41. "Was it to avoid some measure of the government, alarmed by the beginnings of Manichaean propaganda? Was it to learn from Buddhist beliefs, or, on the contrary, to follow in the footsteps of the Apostle Thomas and gain by his preaching the Christian communities already established in the country?" (Puech, p. 44).

its end (disgrace, death). What seems certain is that he remained on good terms with the king and that he undertook long journeys as a preacher through the whole Iranian empire, as far as its eastern boundary. He also sent numerous missions to the interior of the empire and abroad (to Egypt, Bactriana, etc.).

In April, 272, Shapur died, and his son Hormizd succeeded him. Mani hastened to meet him. From the new sovereign he obtained the renewal of the letters of protection, together with permission to go to Babylonia. But scarcely a year later Hormizd died and the throne passed to his brother, Bahram I. Summoned to appear before the king, Mani arrived at Gundev Shapur after a journey that can be considered his "supreme pastoral tour," the "apostle's farewell visit to the scenes of his youth and the churches that he had founded."[42]

And in fact, as soon as he arrived, he was accused by the leader of the Magians, the inflexible *mobēd,* Kartēr: Mani's preaching, this prime mover in Mazdaean intolerance maintained, led the king's subjects away from the official religion. Mani's interview with the king was stormy. When Mani proclaimed the divine character of his mission, Bahram burst out: "Why was this revelation made to thee, and not to Us, who are the masters of the land?" Mani could answer only "Such is the will of God."[43] Condemned, he was chained and put in prison. The chains (three on his hands, three on his feet, and one on his neck) made it impossible for him to move, and their weight (about twenty kilos) caused atrocious suffering. This passion—which the Manichaeans have designated by the Christian term "crucifixion"—continued for twenty-six days.[44] Nevertheless, the prophet was able to receive visits from his coreligionists, and

42. Puech, *Le Manichéisme*, p. 50. According to tradition, Mani addressed his companions: "Look at me and feast your fill on me, my Children, for as for my body I shall depart from you"(cf. François Decret, *Mani et la tradition manichéenne*, p. 67).

43. Puech, p. 51; cf. Decret, p. 68.

44. In a moving prayer, Mani implores his god: "I have shown the way to the sons of height. I have executed your order, for which I was sent into this world. Now let me be united again with the peace of deliverance so that I shall no longer see the face of enemies and no longer hear their powerful voice. This time, give me the great crown of victory" (F. C. Andreas, *Mitteliranische Manichaica aus Chinesisch-Turkestan*, vol. 3, p. 863).

tradition, though embroidering on them, has preserved several edifying episodes. Mani died on February 26, 277, aged sixty years. His body was cut to pieces. The head was exposed at the gate of the city; the rest was thrown to the dogs.

Immediately after the prophet's death, Bahram ordered a merciless repression of the movement. The Manichaean church seemed on the point of disappearing forever. Yet it continued to progress for centuries, propagating itself in the West as far as the Iberian Peninsula and in the East as far as China.

232. The Manichaean gnosis

Manichaeanism is above all a gnosis and, as such, forms part of the great Gnostic current that we have just presented. But unlike the other founders of sects, Mani sought to create a universal religion, accessible to all and not limited to an esoteric teaching restricted to initiates. He recognized the value of certain earlier religions but considered them incomplete. On the other hand, he proclaimed that he had integrated into his church the essentials of all scriptures and all wisdoms: "As a river joins another river to form a strong current, so the old books are added together in my Scriptures; and they have formed a great Wisdom, such as has not existed in previous generations" (*Kephalia* 154, after the translation by Puech, *Le Manichéisme*, p. 69). And in fact Mani attributes an eminent role to Jesus and makes his own the idea of the Paraclete; he borrows from India the theory of transmigration; above all, he goes back to the central Iranian ideas, first and foremost the dualism Light/Darkness and the eschatological myth. Syncretism was a syndrome characteristic of the period. In Mani's case, it was also a tactical necessity. He wanted to extend his church to the two ends of the Persian Empire, so he was obliged to use the religious languages that were familiar to both the eastern and the western regions. Nevertheless, despite seemingly heterogeneous elements, Manichaeanism possesses the inner unity of a powerful and original creation.

A universal religion, like Buddhism and Christianity, Manichaeanism was obliged, like them, to be a missionary religion. According to Mani, the preacher must "wander perpetually through the world, preaching the doctrine and guiding men in the truth."[45] Finally, and here, too, in harmony with the *Zeitgeist,* Manichaeanism is a "religion of the book." In order to avoid the controversies and heresies that had shaken Zoroastrianism, Buddhism, and Christianity, Mani himself composed the seven treatises that make up the canon. Except for the first, the *Shābuhragān,* which he composed in Middle Persian, the others are written in Syriac and or in Eastern Aramaic. Of this large production, very little has been preserved, and that only in translations; but the number and variety of the languages in which these fragments have come down to us (Sogdian, Coptic, Turkish, Chinese, etc.) proclaim the unprecedented success of Manichaean preaching.

As in all gnoses, and as is also the case for Sāṃkhya-Yoga and Buddhism, the journey to deliverance begins with a rigorous analysis of the human condition. By the mere fact that he lives on this earth, that is, that he is endowed with an incarnate existence, man suffers, which is as much as to say that he is the prey of evil. Deliverance cannot be obtained except through gnosis, the only true science, *the knowledge that saves.* In conformity with the Gnostic doctrine, a cosmos dominated by evil cannot be the work of God, the good and transcendent, but of his adversary. So the existence of the world presupposes an earlier, precosmic, state, just as the miserable, fallen condition of man supposes a blissful primordial situation. The essence of the Manichaean doctrine can be summarized in two formulas: the *two principles* and the *three moments.*[46] Now these two formulas also constitute the foundation of post-Gathic Iranian religiosity. So it could be said that Manichaeanism is the Iranian expression, during the syncretistic period, of Gnosticism. On the one hand, Mani reinterpreted certain traditional Iranian concep-

45. al-Bîrûni, *Chronology,* p. 190; Puech, p. 64.

46. According to a text from Turfan, translated by Pelliot (*JA* 1913, pp. 110 ff.), he who wished to "enter religion" had to know that there are two principles, absolutely different in nature, light and obscurity, and three moments: the anterior moment, when the world had not yet come into being and when light was separated from darkness; the median, intermediate moment, after darkness had attacked the region of light; and, finally, the moment beyond, when the two principles will be separated again.

tions; on the other hand, he integrated into his system a number of elements of diverse origin (Indian, Judaeo-Christian, and Gnostic).

For believers, Manichaeanism furnished not only a soteriological ethics and method but also, and above all, a total, absolute science. Salvation is the inevitable effect of gnosis. "Knowing" is equivalent to an anamnesia: the adept recognizes that he is a particle of light, hence of divine nature, for there is consubstantiality between God and souls. Ignorance is the result of the mingling of spirit and body, of spirit and matter (a conception that was dominant in India and elsewhere from the fifth century B.C.). But for Mani, as for all Gnostic teachers, the redeeming gnosis also included knowledge of the secret (or forgotten) history of the cosmos. The adept obtained salvation because he *knew* the origin of the universe, the cause of the creation of man, the methods employed by the Prince of Darkness and the countermethods elaborated by the Father of Light. The "scientific explanation" of certain cosmic phenomena, first of all the phases of the moon, impressed contemporaries. And in fact, in the great cosmogonic and eschatological myth elaborated by Mani, nature and life play an important part: the drama of the soul is reflected in the morphology and the destiny of universal life.

233. The great myth: The fall and redemption of the divine soul

In the beginning, in the "anterior time," the two "natures" or "substances," light and obscurity, good and evil, God and matter, coexisted, separated by a frontier. In the North reigned the Father of Greatness (assimilated to God the Father of the Christians and, in Iran, to Zurvan); in the South, the Prince of Darkness (Ahriman or, for Christians, the Devil). But the "disorderly motion" of matter drove the Prince of Darkness toward the upper frontier of his kingdom. Seeing the splendor of light, he is fired by the desire to conquer it. It is then that the Father decides that he will himself repulse the adversary. He "evokes," i.e., projects from himself, the Mother of Life, who, in her turn, projects a new hypostasis, the Primordial Man (Ohrmizd in the Iranian transpositions). With his five sons, who are, in fact, his "soul," and "armor" made from five lights, the Primordial Man descends to the frontier. He challenges the darkness, but he is conquered, and his sons are devoured by the demons (the Archontes). This defeat marks the beginning of the cosmic "mixture," but at the same time it insures the final triumph of God. For obscurity (matter) now possesses a portion of light—that is, part of the divine soul—and the Father, preparing its deliverance, at the same time arranges for his definitive victory against darkness.

In a second Creation, the Father "evokes" the Living Spirit, which, descending toward obscurity, grasps the hand of the Primordial Man[47] and raises him to his celestial homeland, the Paradise of Lights. Overwhelming the demonic Archontes, the Living Spirit fashions the heavens from their skins, the mountains from their bones, the earth from their flesh and their excrements. (We here recognize the old myth of creation through the sacrifice of a primordial giant or monster, of the type of Tiamat, Ymir, Puruṣa.) In addition, he achieves a first deliverance of light by creating the sun, the moon, and the stars from portions of it that had not suffered too much from contact with obscurity.

Finally, the Father proceeds to a last evocation and projects by emanation the Third Messenger. The latter organizes the cosmos into a kind of machine to collect—and, in the last analysis, to deliver—the still-captive particles of light. During the first two weeks of the month, the particles rise to the moon, which becomes a full moon; during the second two weeks, light is transferred from the moon to the sun and, finally, to its celestial homeland. But there were still the particles that had been swallowed by the demons. Then the messenger displays himself to the male demons in the form of a dazzling naked virgin, while the female demons see him as a handsome naked young man (sordid, "demonic" interpretation of the androgynous nature of the celestial messenger). Fired by desire, the male demons, or Archontes, give forth their semen and, with it, the light that they

47. The handclasp will become the Manichaean ritual par excellence.

had swallowed. Fallen to the ground, their semen gives birth to all the vegetable species. As for the female devils who were already pregnant, at the sight of the handsome young man they give birth to abortions, which, cast onto the ground, eat the buds of trees, thus assimilating the light that they contained.

Alarmed by the Third Messenger's tactics, matter, personified in Concupiscence, decides to create a stronger prison around the still-captive particles of light. Two demons, one male, the other female, devour all the abortions in order to absorb the totality of light, and they then couple. Thus Adam and Eve were engendered. As Henri-Charles Puech writes,

> so our species is born of a succession of repulsive acts of cannibalism and sexuality. It keeps the stigmata of this diabolic origin: the body, which is the animal form of the Archontes; *libido*, desire, which drives man to couple and reproduce himself in his turn, that is, in accordance with the plan of Matter, indefinitely to maintain in its captivity the luminous soul that generation transmits, "transvasates," from body to body. [*Le Manichéisme*, p. 81]

But since the greatest quantity of light is now collected in Adam, it is he, with his progeny, that becomes the principal object of redemption. The eschatological scenario is repeated: just as the Primordial Man was saved by the Living Spirit, Adam, degraded, unknowing, is awakened by the savior, the "Son of God," identified with Ohrmizd or with "Jesus, the Light." It is the incarnation of the saving intelligence ("the god of Nous," the "Nous") that comes to save in Adam its own soul, astray and chained in Darkness (Puech, p. 82). As in the other Gnostic systems, deliverance involves three stages: awakening, revelation of the saving knowledge, and *anamnēsis*. "Adam examined himself and knew who he was"; "The soul of the blessed one, become intelligent again, revived."[48]

This soteriological scenario became the model for all redemption through gnosis, present and future. Until the end of the

48. Theodore bar Konai, in F. Cumont, *Recherches sur le Manichéisme*, vol. 1, p. 47; Turfan fragment S 9, published by Henning and translated by Puech, p. 82.

world, a portion of the light, that is, of the divine soul, will attempt to "awaken" and, in the last analysis, to deliver the other part of it that is still immured in the world, in the bodies of men and animals and in all the vegetable species. It is especially the trees, which contain a large quantity of the divine soul, that serve as gallows for the suffering Christ, Jesus Patibilis. As the Manichaean Faustus expressed it, "Jesus, who, as hanging from every tree, is the life and salvation of men."[49] The continuation of the world carries on the crucifixion and agony of the historical Jesus. It is true that the particles of light, that is to say, the souls of the blessed dead, are continually conveyed to the heavenly paradise by the "vessels" of the moon and the sun. On the other hand, however, the final redemption is delayed by all those who do not follow the road pointed out by Mani, that is, who do not avoid procreation. For, since light is concentrated in the sperm, each infant that comes into the world only prolongs the captivity of a divine particle.

In describing the Third Time, the eschatological finale, Mani sometimes borrows from the apocalyptic imagery familiar throughout western Asia and in the Hellenistic world. The drama opens with a series of terrible ordeals (called by the Manichaeans the "Great War"), which precede the triumph of the Church of Justice and the Last Judgment, when souls will be judged before the tribunal (*bēma*) of Christ. After a short reign, Christ, the Elect, and all the personifications of Good will ascend to heaven. The world, enveloped and purified in a conflagration that will continue for 1,468 years, will be annihilated. The last particles of light will be brought together in a "statue," which will ascend to heaven.[50] Matter, with all its personifications, its demons, and its victims, the damned, will be imprisoned in a kind of "globe" (the *bōlos*) and cast into the bottom of a huge pit, sealed by a rock. This time, the separation of the two substances will be definitive, for Obscurity can never again invade the kingdom of Light.

49. Expression reported by Saint Augustine, *Contra Faustum* 20. 2 (trans. Richard Stothert in *The Works of Aurelius Augustinus* [Edinburgh, 1872]).

50. However, according to certain Manichaean schools, not all the particles of light will be saved; in other words, a certain number of souls will remain prisoners of matter for all eternity.

234. Absolute dualism as *mysterium tremendum*

This grandiose mythology clearly contains the essential themes of Iranian spirituality and Hellenistic gnosis. Laboriously, with a plethora of details, Mani "explains" the causes of humanity's decline, retracing the various episodes of the fall and captivity of the divine soul in matter. Compared, for example, to the succinctness or even the silence of the Indian gnoses (Sāmkhya-Yoga and Buddhism), the Manichaean theology, cosmogony, and anthropogony seem to answer any and every question concerning "origins." It is understandable why the Manichaeans regarded their doctrine as more true, that is, more "scientific," than the other religions: it is because it explained the totality of the real by a chain of causes and their effects. In truth, there is a certain likeness between Manichaeanism and scientific materialism, both ancient and modern: for the one as for the other, the world, life, and man are the result of a chance happening. Even the conflict between the two Principles had broken out because of an accident: the Prince of Darkness happened to be close to the Light because of what Alexander of Lycopolis called the "disorderly motion" of Matter. And, as we have just seen, all the "creations," from the forming of the world to the appearance of man, are only defensive acts on the part of one or the other of the protagonists.

Seldom does an acosmic philosophy or gnosis attain the tragic pessimism that informs the Mani system. The world was created from a demonic substance, the bodies of the Archontes (although the cosmogonic *act* was performed by a divine being). And man is the work of the demonic powers in their most repulsive incarnation. It is improbable that a more tragic and more humiliating anthropogonic myth exists. (Here too we may observe an analogy with contemporary science; for Freud, for example, saw cannibalism and incest as contributing in no small measure to making man such as he is.)

Human existence, like universal life, is only the stigma of a divine defeat. Indeed, if the Primordial Man had conquered from the beginning, neither the cosmos nor life nor man would have existed. The cosmogony is a despairing gesture on the part of God to save something of himself, just as the creation of man is a despairing gesture on the part of Matter to keep the particles of light captive. Despite his ignoble origin, man becomes the center of the drama and its stake, for he bears within him a particle of the divine soul.[51] However, a misunderstanding is involved, for God is not interested in *man* as such but in the *soul,* which is of divine origin and precedes the appearance of the human species. In short, what is involved is always the effort of God to save himself; in this case, too, we may speak of a "saved Savior." It is, furthermore, the only moment in which the divinity is active, for in general the initiative and the action fall to the Prince of Darkness. This is what makes Manichaean literature so moving, especially the hymns that describe the fall and tribulations of the soul. Certain Manichaean psalms are of great beauty, and the image of Jesus Patibilis ranks among the most touching creations of human piety.

Since the body is demonic by nature, Mani prescribes, at least for the "Elect,"[52] the strictest asceticism, at the same time forbidding suicide. Once its premises—the two Principles and the primordial aggression of Evil—are accepted, the whole system seems to be solidly constructed. One cannot, one *must* not, religiously valorize what belongs to the adversary of God: nature, life, human existence. The "true religion" consists in escaping from the prison built by the demonic forces and in contributing to the definitive annihilation of the world, of life, and of man. The "illumination" obtained through gnosis suffices for salvation because it inspires a particular behavior that separates the believer from the world. Rites are useless, except for a few symbolic gestures (the kiss of peace, the fraternal greeting, the handclasps), together with prayers and songs. The principal festival, the Bema, though it commemorates Mani's passion, glorifies the apostle's "chair" (*bēma*), that is, the teaching of the redeeming gnosis.

Indeed, preaching, "teaching," constitutes the true religious activity of the Manichaeans. In the third, but especially in the fourth, century, missions multiply all through Europe and in

51. Paradoxically, this divine spark is located in the sperm. Mani takes over the archaic Indo-Iranian idea of the identity spirit, light, and *semen virile*.

52. Like the other Gnostic sects, Manichaeanism divides believers into a lower class, the Auditors or catechumens, and an elite, the Elect.

North Africa and Asia Minor. The fifth century marks a certain retrogression, and in the sixth century Manichaeanism seems on the point of disappearing in Europe, though it survives in certain centers (for example, in Africa in the eighth century). In addition, in the Sassanid Empire it inspires the movement of Mazdak in the fifth century, and it is probable that the Paulicians in Armenia in the seventh century and Bogomilism in Bulgaria in the tenth century revived certain Manichaean themes (see vol. 3). On the other hand, beginning with the end of the seventh century a new and powerful thrust carries the preaching into Central Asia and China, where Manichaeanism survives into the fourteenth century.[53] It must be added that, directly or indirectly, Manichaean cosmological ideas had a certain influence in India and Tibet (see vol. 3, chap. 36). What is more, a certain "Manichaean tendency" is still an integral part of European spirituality.

All these successes with its preaching must not make us lose sight of the fact that Manichaeanism was regarded by the Christians as the heresy par excellence and that it was also violently criticized, not only by the Magi, the Jews, and the Muslims, but also by such Gnostics as the Mandaeans and by the philosophers—for example, Plotinus.

53. In 763 the *qaghan* of the Ugrians was converted, and Manichaeanism became the state religion in all the Ugrian Empire, until its destruction by the Kirghiz in 840. In China, Manichaean "temples" were built in the seventh century, and the "Religion of Light" was still active, on the margins of Taoism and Buddhism, until the fourteenth century (Puech, *Le Manichéisme,* pp. 64–67 and n. 257).

30 The Twilight of the Gods

235. Heresies and orthodoxy

The first systematic theology is the consequence of the dangerous crises that shook the Church during the second century. It was in the course of criticizing the "heresies" of the Gnostic sects—first of all, anticosmic dualism and rejection of the incarnation, death, and resurrection of Jesus Christ—that the Fathers gradually elaborated orthodox doctrine. Essentially, orthodoxy consisted in fidelity to the theology of the Old Testament. The Gnostics were regarded as the worst of heretics precisely because they repudiated, either wholly or in part, the principles of Hebrew thought. And in fact there was complete incompatibility between the ideas of Gnosticism—preexistence of the soul in the bosom of the original One, the accidental nature of the Creation, the soul's fall into matter, etc.—and the theology, cosmogony, and anthropology of the Bible. It was impossible to call oneself a Christian and not accept the doctrines of the Old Testament concerning the origin of the world and the nature of man: God had begun his cosmogonic work by creating matter, and he completed it by creating man, corporeal, sexual, and free, in the image and likeness of his Creator. In other words, man was created with the powerful potencies of a god. "History" is the temporal span during which man learns to practice his freedom and to sanctify himself—in short, to serve the apprenticeship of his calling as god.[1] For the end of Creation is a sanctified hu-

1. We follow the interpretation of that admirable expounder of Hebrew thought, Claude Tresmontant; see his *La métaphysique du christianisme*, pp. 53 ff., and his *Essai sur la pensée hébraïque*, chaps. 1 and 2.

manity. This explains the importance of temporality and history and the decisive role of human freedom; for a man cannot be made a god despite himself.

These conceptions were taken over by Christianity. Saint Paul glorifies the new birth assured by Christ: "For anyone who is in Christ there is a new creation" (2 Cor. 5:17). Neither circumcision nor uncircumcision matters; "what matters is . . . to become an altogether new creature" (Gal. 6:15), "one single new man in himself" (Eph. 2:15). As Claude Tresmontant writes,

> from this point of view, it is not a matter of *returning* to our previous, primitive condition, as in the Gnostic myth, but, on the contrary, of aiming, without a backward glance, at that which is ahead, at the creation that is coming and becoming. Christianity is not a doctrine of *return,* like Gnosticism or Neo-Platonism, but a doctrine of creation.[2]

Paradoxically, despite the delay of the parousia and the increase in persecutions, Christianity appears as an optimistic religion. The theology elaborated against the Gnostics glorifies the Creation, blesses life, accepts history—even when history becomes nothing but terror. Just like Rabbi Johanan ben Zakkai, who, in his school at Jabneh, insured the continuity of Judaism, the Church looked at the future with hope and confidence. To be sure, as we shall soon see, certain attitudes expressive of a refusal of life (asceticism, monasticism, praise of virginity, etc.) are accepted, and sometimes glorified, in the various churches. However, in a period dominated by despair and characterized by philosophies almost as anticosmic and pessimistic[3] as those of the Gnostics, the theology and practice of the Church are distinguished by their balance.

For the Fathers, orthodoxy was bound up with the apostolic succession: the Apostles had received the teaching directly from

2. *La métaphysique du christianisme,* p. 71. It is significant that, in general, the Fathers followed the principles of normative Judaism and ignored Jewish speculations of the Gnostic type.

3. It is important to bear in mind a paradox that is often ignored by historians: the most important Gnostic teachers, as well as Marcion and certain classic authors (Epictetus, Plutarch), elaborated their tragic and extremely pessimistic philosophies in a period of peace and prosperity, the "Golden Age" of the Antonines; see E. R. Dodds, *Pagan and Christian in an Age of Anxiety,* p. 4.

Christ and had transmitted it to the bishops and their successors.[4] As for the cause of heresies, Irenaeus and Hippolytus found it in the corruption of the Scriptures by Greek philosophy.

This thesis was criticized by Walter Bauer[5] in 1934. This German scholar observes first of all that the opposition orthodoxy/heresy became explicit rather late, at the beginning of the second century. Primitive Christianity was comparatively complex, taking many and various expressions into account. In fact, the earliest Christian forms were closer to those that were later considered heretical. Bauer comes to the conclusion that three great Christian centers—Edessa, Alexandria, and Asia Minor—were heretical during the first two centuries; orthodoxy was not introduced until later. From the beginning, the only orthodox center was Rome. Hence the victory of orthodoxy in antiquity is equivalent to the victory of Roman Christianity. "Thus, in a primitive Christianity, with many and shifting forms, with many and often opposing currents, Rome succeeded in fixing a particular form that takes the name of orthodoxy because it succeeded in imposing itself and over against which the other tendencies were then termed heretical."[6]

However, as André Benoit observes, Bauer's explanation remains purely historical; it does not take into consideration the doctrinal content belonging to orthodoxy and to heresy. We are indebted to H. E. Turner for having undertaken a theological analysis of these two opposing positions.[7] According to Turner, as Benoit remarks, heresy

4. The heretics also claimed descent from one or another of the Apostles (e.g., Basilides claimed to be descended from the interpreter of Peter and hence from Peter himself), but the Fathers rejected these would-be successions on the ground that they were secret and unverifiable. As Irenaeus wrote (*Adv. haer.* 3. 4. 3), "prior to Valentinus, those who follow Valentinus had no existence; nor did those from Marcion exist before Marcion" (trans. from *The Ante-Nicene Fathers*).

5. *Rechtglaubigkeit und Ketzerei im ältesten Christentum.* The second edition (1964) has been translated into English under the title *Orthodoxy and Heresy in Earliest Christianity* (1971). See also the short but clear presentation by André Benoit, *Le Judaïsme et le Christianisme antique*, pp. 297 ff.

6. Benoit, ibid., p. 300.

7. E. H. W. Turner, *The Pattern of the Christian;* this book is discussed by Benoit, pp. 302 ff.

> is distinguished from orthodoxy, on the one hand, by rejecting doctrines explicitly defined by the Church and, on the other hand, by corrupting the specific content of the Christian faith; in short, it represents a deviation from the traditional faith. [Benoit, p. 303]

> Orthodoxy appears as a consistent and well-coordinated system of thought, whereas heresy, by increasingly departing from the primitive doctrinal bases and introducing factors of dilution, mutilation, distortion, and archaism, appears as a congeries of fragmentary and incomplete systems that are finally inconsistent. [Ibid., p. 306]

From the point of view of the history of Christian thought,

> the victory of orthodoxy is the victory of consistency over inconsistency, of a certain logic over fantasizing elucubrations, of a theology scientifically elaborated as opposed to unorganized doctrines. . . . Orthodoxy appears as bound up with a juridical institution, with a society that has its history and its policy. But it also appears as bound up with a system of thought, a doctrine. It is at once a juridical institution and a theology. [Ibid., p. 307]

In short, orthodoxy is defined by (1) fidelity to the Old Testament and to an apostolic tradition attested by documents; (2) resistance to the excesses of the mythologizing imagination; (3) a high regard for systematic thought (hence for Greek philosophy); (4) importance accorded to social and political institutions—in short, to juridical thought, a category specifically characteristic of the Roman genius. Each of these elements gave rise to significant theological creations and contributed, to a greater or lesser extent, to the triumph of the Church. Yet, at a certain moment in the history of Christianity, each of these elements precipitated crises, often extremely serious, and contributed to the improvement of the primitive tradition.

236. The Cross and the Tree of Life

Because of the anti-Gnostic polemic, the esoteric teaching and the tradition of Christian gnosis were almost stifled in the Church.

(Later, the ecclesiastical hierarchy will show a similar suspicion in regard to mystical experiences; see vol. 3.) This is perhaps the highest price that Christianity had to pay to safeguard the unity of the Church. Henceforth Christian gnosis and esoteric teaching will survive, in diminished and camouflaged form, on the margin of the official institutions. Certain esoteric traditions (predominantly those preserved in apocalypses and apocryphas) will enjoy great currency in popular circles, but in connection with myths and legends derived from heretical Gnostic systems, especially Manichaeanism (see pp. 405–6).

For the purpose of this chapter, it would be useless to dwell on certain difficulties of the primitive Church, for example, the controversies concerning the paschal question (toward the end of the second century) or questions of discipline (e.g., forgiveness of believers guilty of mortal sins after their baptism, etc.).

More serious and of greater significance for the general history of religions are the controversies and crises brought on by dogmatic formulations of Christology, a problem that will engage our attention further on. For the moment, it may be said that it is possible to distinguish two parallel and complementary tendencies at work in the process of integrating the pre-Christian religious heritage, in the repeated and varied efforts to give a universal dimension to the message of Christ. The first (and earlier) tendency appears in the assimilation and revalorization of symbolisms and mythological scenarios of biblical origin, whether Oriental or pagan. The second tendency, chiefly illustrated by theological speculations from the third century on, attempts to universalize Christianity by the help of Greek philosophy, especially Neo-Platonic metaphysics.

Saint Paul had already invested the sacrament of baptism with a symbolism that is archaic in structure: ritual death and resurrection, new birth in Christ. The earliest theologians elaborated the scenario: baptism is a descent into the abyss of the Waters for a duel with the marine monster; the model is Christ's going down into the Jordan. According to Justin, Christ, the new Noah, risen victorious from the Waters, has become the head of a new race. Baptismal nudity, too, has a meaning that is at once ritual and metaphysical: it is abandoning the old garment of corruption and sin with which Adam was clothed after the Fall. Now all these themes are found elsewhere: the "Waters of Death" are a leitmotiv of paleo-Oriental, Asiatic, and Oceanic mythologies. Ritual nudity is equivalent to integrity and plenitude: "Paradise" implies the absence of "clothing," that is, the absence of "wear and tear" (archetypal image of Time). Encountering the monsters of the abyss is an initiatory ordeal of heroes. To be sure, for the Christian, baptism is a sacrament because it was instituted by Christ. But, despite that, it repeats the initiatory ritual of the ordeal (= battle with the monster), of symbolic death and resurrection (= birth of the new man).[8]

Still according to Saint Paul, by baptism one obtains the reconciliation of contraries: "there are no more distinctions between . . . slave and freeman, male and female" (Gal. 3:28). In other words, the baptized person recovers the primordial condition of the androgyne. The idea is clearly expressed in the Gospel of Thomas: "And when you shall make one thing of male and female, so that the male is not male and woman is not woman . . . then you shall enter the Kingdom."[9] There is no need to insist on the archaism and the universal dissemination of the symbol of the androgyne as the exemplary expression of human perfection. It is probably because of the marked importance accorded to androgyny by the Gnostics that this symbolism was less and less used after Saint Paul. But it never entirely disappeared from the history of Christianity.[10]

Even more daring is the assimilation, by Christian imagery, liturgy, and theology, of the symbolism of the World Tree. In this case too we have to do with an archaic and universally disseminated symbol. The Cross, made from the wood of the Tree of

8. See Eliade, *Patterns in Comparative Religion,* §§ 64, 65; *Images and Symbols,* pp. 151–60.

9. Logion 22, after Puech's translation; cf. logion 106: "When you shall make one of two, you will become sons of man."

10. See Eliade, *The Two and the One,* pp. 78 ff., and Wayne A. Meeks, "The Image of the Androgyne: Some Uses of a Symbol in Earliest Christianity," esp. pp. 180 ff. The mythology of the androgyne reappears with Scotus Erigena, continues with Jacob Boehme, Baader, and German Romanticism, and is revived in certain contemporary theologies.

Good and Evil, is identified with, or replaces, the Cosmic Tree; it is described as a tree that "rises from earth to heaven," an immortal plant "that stands at the center of heaven and earth, firm support of the universe," "the Tree of Life planted on Calvary." Numerous patristic and liturgical texts compare the Cross to a ladder, a pillar, or a mountain, characteristic expressions for the "center of the world." This shows *that the image of the Center imposed itself naturally* on the Christian imagination. To be sure, the image of the Cross as Tree of Good and Evil and Cosmic Tree has its origin in biblical traditions. But it is by the Cross (= the Center) that communication with heaven is conducted and that, at the same time, the entire universe is "saved." Now the notion of *salvation* merely takes up and completes the notions of *perpetual renewal* and *cosmic regeneration*, of universal *fecundity* and *sacrality*, of *absolute reality*, and, in the last analysis, of *immortality*—all notions that coexist in the symbolism of the World Tree.[11]

More and more archaic themes became integrated into the scenario of the Crucifixion. Since Jesus Christ was crucified at the Center of the World, where Adam had been created and buried, Christs' blood, flowing onto "Adam's head," baptized him and atoned for his sins.[12] And since the Savior's blood had atoned for the original sin, the Cross (= Tree of Life) becomes the source of the sacraments (symbolized by olive oil, wheat, the grape) and of medicinal herbs.[13] These mythological themes, elaborated by Christian authors, especially from the third century onward, have a long and complex prehistory: from the blood and the body of a sacrificed god or primordial being, wondrous plants grow. But it is important to emphasize at this point that these archaic scenarios and images, rehandled by Christian authors, enjoyed an unparalleled success in the religious folklore of Europe. Countless popular legends and songs tell of flowers and medicinal herbs that grow under the Cross or on Jesus'

11. See Eliade, *Patterns in Comparative Religion*, §§ 99 ff.; *Images and Symbols*, pp. 160 ff.

12. See, e.g., *The Book of the Cave of Treasures*, p. 53.

13. See the references in our study "La Mandragore et les mythes de la naissance miraculeuse," pp. 23 ff.

tomb. In Romanian popular poetry, for example, the Savior's blood produces wheat, holy oil, and the grapevine:[14]

And my flesh fell.
Where it fell
Good wheat came.

He drove in nails.
My blood spurted out,
And where it dripped
Good wine flowed.

From his sides flowed
Blood and water.
From the blood and the water—the vine.
From the vine—fruit.
From the fruit—wine:
The Savior's blood for Christians.

237. Toward "cosmic Christianity"

It is in one of the last chapters of the third volume that we shall study the significance of Christian folklore and its interest for the general history of religions. But it is necessary to point out now the role of what we have called the "universalization" of the Christian message through the instrumentality of mythological imagery and through a continual process of assimilation of the pre-Christian religious heritage. It should first be borne in mind that the majority of the symbols invoked (baptism, the Tree of Life, the Cross assimilated to the Tree of Life, the origin of the sacramental substances—olive oil, chrism, wine, wheat—from the Savior's blood) continue and develop certain symbols documented in normative Judaism or in the intertestamentary apocryphas. Sometimes (e.g., the Cosmic Tree, the Tree of Life) they are archaic symbols, already present in the Neolithic period and clearly valorized in the Near East from Sumerian culture on.

In other cases we have to do with religious practices of pagan origin, borrowed by the Jews during the Greco-Roman period (e.g., the ritual use of wine, the symbol of the Tree of Life in

14. The following texts are cited in "La Mandragore," pp. 24–26.

Jewish art, etc.).[15] Finally, a large number of the mythological images, figures, and themes that are employed by Christian authors, and that will become the favorite subjects of European popular books and religious folklore, derive from the Jewish apocrypha. In short, the Christian mythological imagination borrows and develops motifs and scenarios that belong to cosmic religiosity but that have already undergone a reinterpretation in the biblical context. In adding their own valorization, Christian theology and mythological imagination have only continued a process that had begun with the conquest of Canaan (see § 60).

In the language of theology, it could be said that, integrated into a Christian scenario, a number of archaic traditions gain their "redemption." What in fact we have here is a phenomenon of homologation of different and multiform religious universes. A similar process is found (as early as the end of antiquity, but especially in the High Middle Ages) in the transformation of certain gods or mythological heroes into Christian saints. We shall analyze the significance of the cult of saints and their relics further on (vol. 3, chap. 32). But one of the consequences of this cult must be borne in mind even now: the "Christianization" of pagan religious traditions—hence their survival in the framework of Christian experience and imagination—contributes to the cultural unification of the ecumene. To give only one example, the countless dragon-slaying heroes and gods, from Greece to Ireland and from Portugal to the Urals, all become the same saint: Saint George. It is the specific vocation of all religious universalism to go beyond provincialism.[16] Now as early as the third century, and everywhere in the Roman Empire, we see various tendencies toward autarchy and autonomy that threaten the unity of the Roman world.[17] After the collapse of urban civilization,

15. See E. Goodenough, *Jewish Symbols in the Greco-Roman Period*, vol. 6, pp. 136 ff., and vol. 12, pp. 123 ff. (religious use of wine); vol. 7, pp. 87 ff., and vol. 12, pp. 126 ff. (the Tree of Life). But the number of pagan symbols assimilated by Judaism is far longer: bull, lion, Victory, eagle, shell, bird, boat, etc.; see Goodenough's summary of vols. 7–11 in vol. 12, pp. 132–83.

16. Similar processes are found in India (Hinduization of aboriginal divine figures and cults), in China (especially in popular Taoism), in Judaism (in the period of the conquest of Canaan and in the Middle Ages), and in Islam.

17. See Roger Rémondon, *La crise de l'Empire romain* (1970), p. 322.

the process of homologation and unification of the pre-Christian religious traditions is destined to play a considerable part.

The phenomenon is important because it is characteristic of religious creativity of the folklore type, which has not engaged the attention of historians of religions. It is a creativity parallel to that of the theologians, the mystics, and the artists. We may speak of a "cosmic Christianity" since, on the one hand, the Christological mystery is projected upon the whole of nature and, on the other hand, the historical elements of Christianity are neglected; on the contrary, there is emphasis on the liturgical dimension of existence in the world. The conception of a cosmos redeemed by the death and resurrection of the Savior and sanctified by the footsteps of God, of Jesus, of the Virgin, and of the Saints permitted the recovery, if only sporadically and symbolically, of a world teeming with the virtues and beauties that wars and their terrors had stripped from the world of history.[18]

It must be added, however, that Christian folklore is also inspired by more or less heretical sources and that it sometimes ignores myths, dogmas, and scenarios that are of prime importance for theology. For example, it is significant that the biblical cosmogony vanished from European folklore. The only "popular" cosmogony known in southeastern Europe is dualistic in structure: it involves both God and the Devil.[19] In the European traditions in which this cosmogony is not documented, there is no cosmogonic myth.[20]

We shall return in volume 3 of this work to the problem of the survival, in European folklore, of figures and scenarios familiar to the Jewish, Christian, and heretical apocalypses and apocryphas. The persistence of this class of archaic traditions until the twentieth century emphasizes their importance in the religious universe of the rural populations. It is highly significant, for example, that a mythological motif that is abundantly invoked in Mandaeanism and Manichaeanism but whose origin is prob-

18. On "cosmic Christianity," see our book *Zalmoxis, the Vanishing God,* chap. 7, esp. pp. 125 ff., and vol. 3 of the present work.

19. This myth is referred to by some scholars as the "cosmic dive"; we have studied it in *Zalmoxis,* chap. 3, pp. 76–125.

20. This is the case in France; see Paul Sébillot, *Folklore de France* (1905), p. 183.

ably Sumerian still plays an essential part in the mythology of death and the funeral rituals of the Romanians and other peoples of eastern Europe. Mandaean and Manichaean writings speak of "customs houses" at each of the seven heavens and of the "customs officers" who examine the soul's "merchandise" (i.e., its religious works and merits) in the course of its heavenly journey.[21] Now in the religious folklore and funerary customs of the Romanians there is mention of a "road of death" through the seven "customs houses of the atmosphere" (*vămile văzduhului*).

We will list some Iranian symbols and scenarios that were assimilated by both Christian theology and Christian mythology. The Iranian idea of the resurrection of bodies was received with the Judaic inheritance. "The comparison of the body of resurrection to a heavenly garment is indubitably reminiscent of investitures that abound in Mazdaean theology. And the fact that the bodies of the just will shine is best explained by the Persian religion of light."[22] The imagery of the Nativity—the star or the pillar of light that shines above the cave—was borrowed from the Iranian (Parthian) scenario of the birth of the cosmocrator-redeemer. The Protogospel of James (18:1 ff.) tells of a blinding light that filled the cave in Bethlehem; when it began to depart, the Infant Jesus appeared. This is as much as to say that the light was consubstantial with Jesus or was one of his epiphanies.

But it is the anonymous author of the *Opus imperfectum in Matthaeum* who introduces new elements into the legend. According to him, the twelve magi-kings lived near the "Mount of Victories." They knew the secret revelation of Seth concerning the coming of the Messiah, and, every year, they climbed a mountain where there was a cave with springs and trees. There they prayed to God for three days, awaiting the appearance of the Star. It finally appeared in the form of a little child, and the child told them to go to Judaea. Guided by the Star, the magi-kings traveled for two years. Returned home, they told of the

21. See the texts cited by Geo Widengren, *Mesopotamian Elements in Manicheism,* pp. 82 ff. ("The Customers and the Merchandise"), and R. Murray, *Symbols of Church and Kingdom,* pp. 174 ff., 247 ff.

22. J. Duchesne-Guillemin, *La religion de l'Iran ancien,* p. 265 (English trans., p. 242).

prodigy they had witnessed, and, when the Apostle Thomas arrived in their country, they asked to be baptized.[23]

With some very suggestive developments, this legend is found again in a Syrian work, the *Chronicle of Zuqnîn*. There we learn that twelve "wisemen-kings" come from the land of "Shyr" (a corruption of Shyz, Zarathustra's birthplace). The "Mount of Victories" corresponds to the Iranian cosmic mountain, Hara Barzaiti, that is, to the *axis mundi* that connects heaven with earth. Hence it is at the "center of the world" that Seth hides the book containing the prophecy concerning the coming of the Messiah, and it is there that the Star announces the birth of the cosmocrator-redeemer. Now according to Iranian tradition, the *xvarenah* that shines above the sacred mountain is the sign announcing the Saoshyant, the redeemer miraculously born from the semen of Zarathustra.[24]

238. The flowering of theology

As we have already said, Christian theology, articulated during the Gnostic crisis of the second century, is essentially characterized by its fidelity to the Old Testament. Irenaeus, one of the earliest and most important Christian theologians, interprets the Redemption—that is, the Incarnation of Jesus Christ—as the continuation and completion of the work begun with the creation of Adam but obstructed by the Fall. Christ recapitulates the existential trajectory of Adam in order to deliver humanity from the consequences of sin. However, while Adam is the prototype of fallen humanity, doomed to death, Christ is the creator and exemplary model of a new humanity, blessed by the promise of immortality. Irenaeus seeks—and finds—antithetical parallels between Adam and Christ: the first was created from virgin soil, Christ is born of a virgin; Adam disobeys by eating the fruit of the forbidden tree, Christ obeys by allowing himself to be sacrificed on the tree of the Cross, etc.

23. *Patrologia Graeca*, vol. 57, cols. 637–38; see also Eliade, *The Two and the One*, pp. 50 ff., with bibliography.

24. See *The Two and the One*, pp. 52–54.

The doctrine of recapitulation can be interpreted as a twofold effort to assimilate, on the one hand, the biblical revelation in its totality and, on the other hand, to justify the Incarnation as the completion of the same revelation. The first structures of the sacred calendar, i.e., of liturgical time, continue Jewish institutions; but there is always the christological *novum*. Justin calls Sunday "the first day," connecting it at once with the Resurrection and with the creation of the world.

This effort to emphasize the universality of the Christian message by associating it with the sacred history of Israel—the one truly universal history—is made in parallel with the effort to assimilate Greek philosophy. The theology of the Logos—more precisely, the mystery of its Incarnation—gives speculation admittance to perspectives that were inaccessible within the horizon of the Old Testament. But this daring innovation was not without its dangers. Docetism, one of the earliest heresies, which was Gnostic in origin and structure, dramatically illustrates the resistance against the idea of the Incarnation. For the Docetists (the name comes from the Greek verb *dokeō,* "to seem," "to appear"), the Redeemer could not accept the humiliation of becoming incarnate and suffering on the Cross; according to them, Christ *seemed* to be a man because he had put on an appearance of the human form. In other words, the passion and death were suffered *by someone else* (the man Jesus or Simon of Cyrene).

Yet the Fathers were right in fiercely defending the dogma of the Incarnation. From the point of view of the history of religions, the Incarnation represents the last and most perfect hierophany: God completely incarnated himself in a human being both *concrete* and *historical* (that is, active in a well-defined and irreversible historical temporality) without thereby confining himself to his body (since the Son is consubstantial with the Father). It could even be said that the kenosis of Jesus Christ not only constitutes the crowning of all the hierophanies accomplished from the beginning of time but also *justifies* them, that is, proves their validity. To accept the possibility of the Absolute becoming incarnate in a historical person is at the same time to recognize the validity of the universal dialectic of the sacred; in other words, it is to recognize that the countless pre-Christian generations were not victims of an illusion when they proclaimed the presence of the sacred, i.e., of the divine, in the objects and rhythms of the cosmos.

The problems raised by the dogma of the Incarnation of the Logos recur, in aggravated form, in the theology of the Trinity. To be sure, the theological speculations had their source in the Christian experience. From the beginnings of the Church, Christians knew God in three figures: (1) the Father—creator and judge—who had revealed himself in the Old Testament; (2) the Lord Jesus Christ, the Risen One; and (3) the Holy Spirit, who had the power to renew life and bring about the Kingdom. But at the beginning of the fourth century, Arius, an Alexandrian priest, proposed a more consistent and more philosophical interpretation of the Trinity. Arius does not reject the Trinity, but he denies the consubstantiality of the three divine persons. For him, God is *alone* and *uncreated;* the Son and the Holy Spirit were created *later* by the Father, and so are inferior to him. Arius revived, on the one hand, the doctrine of the Christ-Angel, i.e., Christ identified with the archangel Saint Michael (a doctrine documented at Rome at the beginning of the second century), and, on the other hand, certain of Origen's theses that presented the Son as a secondary divinity. Arius' interpretation had some success, even among the bishops, but at the Council of Nicaea in 325 the creed rejecting Arianism was adopted. However, Arius' theology still had comparatively powerful defenders, and the controversy continued for more than half a century.[25] It was Athanasius (died 373) who elaborated the doctrine of the consubstantiality (*to homoousion*) of the Father and the Son, a doctrine summarized by Saint Augustine: *una substantia—tres personae*. All this was no mere controversy among theologians; the dogma of the Trinity was of the utmost concern to the people in general. For if Jesus Christ was only a secondary divinity, how was it possible to believe that he had power to save the world?

The theology of the Trinity never ceased to raise problems; from the Renaissance on, rationalistic philosophers declared themselves first of all by their antitrinitarianism (see vol. 3). However, the theology of the Trinity must be credited with hav-

25. Arianism was definitively conquered in 388.

ing encouraged daring speculations, by forcing Christians to escape from the bounds of daily experience and ordinary logic.[26]

The increasing sanctification and, in the last analysis, the deification of Mary are chiefly the work of popular piety. Toward the end of the first century, the date of the Gospel of John, the Church had already recognized the religious significance of Mary. On the Cross, Jesus said to his mother: " 'Woman, this is your son . . . .' Then to the disciple he said, 'This is your mother' " (John 19:25 ff.). The importance of Mary derives from her motherhood: she is Deipara, "she who gives birth to the God." The term is first documented at the beginning of the third century; but when the Monophysites[27] used it in a heretical sense, Deipara was replaced by a clearer term, Theotokos, "Mother of God." But it was always a *virgin* mother, and the dogma of the perpetual virginity of Mary was proclaimed at the Council of Ephesus.[28]

In this case, too, we can see the process of assimilating and revalorizing an archaic religious idea that is universally disseminated. In fact the theology of Mary, the Virgin Mother, takes over and perfects the immemorial Asiatic and Mediterranean conceptions of parthenogenesis, the faculty of self-fecundation, which was claimed by the Great Goddesses (for example, Hera; see § 93). Marian theology represents the transfiguration of the earliest and most significant homage paid, from the time of prehistory, to the religious mystery of womanhood. In Western Christianity the Virgin Mary will be identified with the figure of divine Wisdom. The Eastern Church, on the contrary, will develop, side by side with the theology of the Theotokos, the doctrine of celestial Wisdom, Sophia, into which the feminine figure of the Holy Spirit flowers. Many centuries later, sophianology will play for the intellectual elites of Eastern Christianity a part similar to Neo-Thomism in the renewal of Christian philosophy in the West.

26. From this point of view it can be compared to the metaphysics of Nāgārjuna (§ 189), to the Cabala, and to the methods of the Zen masters (see vol. 3).

27. A heretical movement (beginning of the fifth century) whose members thought that in Christ humanity and divinity are mingled in one entity (*physis*).

28. However, it is not until about the year 1000 that the dogma that the Virgin was conceived without sin is found in the West.

239. Between Sol Invictus and "In hoc signo vinces"

As we saw (p. 367), the Emperor Aurelian (270–75) had rightly grasped the importance of a solar theology, monotheistic in structure, for insuring the unity of the Empire. Thus he reintroduced the god of Emesa into Rome, but in doing so he took care to make radical changes in the god's structure and cult. The Syrian elements were deliberately eliminated, and service of the god was confined to Roman senators. The anniversary of the Deus Sol Invictus was set at December 25th, the "birthday" of all Oriental solar divinities.

The universalistic nature of the solar cult and theology was recognized, or foreseen, by the Greek and Roman disciples of Apollo-Helios, as well as by the worshipers of Mithra and the Syrian Baals. What is more, the philosophers and theosophers were, many of them, believers in a monotheism solar in structure. Indeed, the tendencies toward monotheism and universalism that are characteristic of the end of the third century become dominant in the fourth. Numerous religious syncretisms—the Mysteries, the rise of the Christian theology of the Logos, the solar symbolism applied at once to the emperor and to the *imperium*—illustrate the fascination exercised by the notion of the One and by the mythology of Unity.

Before his conversion, Constantine (306–37) was a disciple of the solar cult and saw in Sol Invictus the foundation of his Empire. The sun is plentifully represented on figured monuments, on coins, and in inscriptions. But unlike Aurelian, for whom Sol Invictus was the Supreme God, Constantine considered the sun the most perfect symbol of God. The subordination of the Sun to the Supreme God was in all probability the first consequence of his conversion to Christianity; but the idea had already been expressed by the Neo-Platonist Porphyry.[29]

The various testimonies do not agree as to the sign that Constantine saw before the decisive battle at the Milvian Bridge, in which his adversary, Maxentius, was killed. According to Lactantius, Constantine "was directed in a dream to cause *the heavenly sign* to be delineated on the shields of his soldiers, and so

29. See F. Altheim, *Der unbesiegte Gott*, chap. 5.

to proceed to battle. He did as he had been commanded, and he marked on their shields . . . the cipher of Christ'' (*De mortibus persecutorum* 44). But in his *Vita Constantini* (1. 28–29) Eusebius, bishop of Caesarea, tells a different story. According to him, Constantine said that

> about mid-day, when the sun was beginning to decline, he saw with his own eyes the trophy of a cross of light in the heavens, above the sun, and bearing the inscription *Conquer by this*. At this sight he himself was struck with amazement, and his whole army also . . . . He doubted within himself what the import of this apparition could be; . . . and in his sleep the Christ of God appeared to him with the same sign which he had seen in the heavens, and commanded him to procure a standard made in the likeness of that sign, and to use it as a safeguard in all engagements with his enemies.

The genuineness of these accounts is still in dispute, and there is dispute, too, whether the sign that Constantine saw was Christian or pagan.[30] However this may be, Constantine's conversion insured the official Christianization of the Empire. The first Christian symbols begin to appear on coins as early as 315, and the last pagan images disappear in 323. The Church receives a privileged judicial status, that is, the state recognizes the validity of the decisions of the episcopal court, even in civil affairs. Christians attain the highest offices, and restrictive measures against pagans increase in number. Under Theodosius the Great (379–95) Christianity becomes the state religion, and paganism is definitely forbidden; the persecuted become the persecutors.

Indeed, Christianity had proved its strength and vitality before the conversion of Constantine. About 300, at Antioch and Alexandria, the Christian community was the largest and best-organized religious group. Indeed, the antagonism between Church and Empire gradually lost its intransigence. The last apologists, Lactantius (240–ca. 320) and Eusebius of Caesarea (263–ca. 339), proclaimed that Christianity was the only hope of saving the Empire.

30. See the present position of studies in Benoit, *Le Judaïsme et le Christianisme antique*, pp. 308 ff.

The causes of the final triumph of Christian preaching are many and various. First of all were the unshakable faith and moral strength of Christians, their courage in the face of torture and death—a courage admired even by their greatest enemies, Lucian of Samosata, Marcus Aurelius, Galienus, Celsus. Furthermore, the solidarity of the Christians was unequaled; the community took care of widows, orphans, and the aged and ransomed those captured by pirates. During epidemics and sieges, only Christians tended the wounded and buried the dead. For all the rootless multitudes of the Empire, for the many who suffered from loneliness, for the victims of cultural and social alienation, the Church was the only hope of obtaining an identity, of finding, or recovering, a meaning for life. Since there were no barriers, either social, racial, or intellectual, anyone could become a member of this optimistic and paradoxical society in which a powerful citizen, the emperor's chamberlain, bowed before a bishop who had been his slave. In all probability, neither before nor afterward has any historical society experienced the equivalent of this equality, of the charity and brotherly love that were the life of the Christian communities of the first four centuries.

The most unexpected innovation, and one that had marked consequences for the religious, cultural, and social history of Europe, was monasticism, characterized by separation from the world and an extremely severe asceticism.[31] This phenomenon appeared in the third century, and not only in Egypt, as was believed until recently, but also, independently, in Palestine, Syria, and Mesopotamia.[32] Saint Anthony founded Egyptian monasticism, but it was Pacomius (ca. 290–347) who, in 320, organized monastic life in the desert of the Thebaïd (where, toward the end of the fourth century, there were some 7,000 monks). As Peter Brown observes, the monks had voluntarily

31. See A. J. Festugière, *Les moines d'Orient,* vol. 1, *Culture et Sainteté;* A. Vööbus, *History of Asceticism in the Syrian Orient,* vols. 1 and 2; J. Lacarrière, *Les hommes ivres de Dieu.*

32. It is true that Egyptian monasticism developed rapidly and, by virtue of its literature, which made it famous, exercised considerable influence.

chosen the "anti-culture"—the desert and the caves.[33] Their considerable prestige is the consequence, on the one hand, of their victory over the demons and, on the other hand, of their mastery of wild beasts. A new idea appears: these monks, true "saints," are strong enough to command devils and to affect God's will by their prayers. And in fact only the monks had the courage to resist some of the emperor's decisions. Perched on his pillar, Saint Simeon Stylites examined lawsuits, prophesied, performed cures, and reprimanded and advised high officials.

Toward the end of the fourth century a wave of violence committed by monks swept from Mesopotamia to North Africa: in 388 they burned a synagogue at Callinicum, near the Euphrates, and terrorized Syrian villages in which there were pagan temples; in 391 the Patriarch of Alexandria, Theophilus, summoned them to "purify" the city by destroying the Serapeum, the great temple of Serapis. During the same period they forced their way into the houses of pagans to look for idols. And in 415 a group of fanatical monks committed one of the most odious crimes known to history: they lynched Hypatia, the noble Alexandrian philosopher, whom her pupil, Bishop Synesius, termed "mother, sister, teacher, and benefactress" (*Ep.* 16).

In the East the bishops protected the monks in order to reinforce their own position; together, bishops and monks put themselves at the head of the people and dictated popular opinion. As Peter Brown observes, "these eccentrics transform Christianity into a religion of the masses."[34] This makes the accomplishment of their successors, the monks of the High Middle Ages, especially in the West, appear all the more surprising (see vol. 3).

240. The bus that stops at Eleusis

No historical event more effectively expresses the "official" end of paganism than the burning of the sanctuary of Eleusis in 396 by Alaric, king of the Goths. On the other hand, however, no

33. Peter Brown, *The World of Late Antiquity,* pp. 101 ff.; see also, by the same author, "The Rise and Function of the Holy Man in Late Antiquity."

34. Brown, "The Rise and Function of the Holy Man," p. 107.

other example better illustrates the mysterious process of occultation and continuity undergone by pagan religiosity. In the fifth century the historian Eunapius, himself an initiate into the Eleusinian Mysteries, relates the prophecy of the last legitimate hierophant. In Eunapius' presence, the hierophant predicts that his successor will be illegitimate and sacrilegious; he will not even be an Athenian citizen; still worse, he will be someone who, "consecrated to other gods," will be bound by his oath "to preside only at their ceremonies." Because of this profanation, the sanctuary will be destroyed, and the cult of the Two Goddesses will disappear forever.

And in fact, Eunapius goes on, a highly placed initiate into the Mysteries of Mithra (where he had the rank of *pater*) became hierophant. He was the last hierophant of Eleusis, for, soon afterward, Alaric's Goths made their way through the pass of Thermopylae, followed by "men in black," Christian monks—and the oldest and most important religious center in Europe was finally ruined.[35]

However, if the initiation ritual disappeared from Eleusis, Demeter did not abandon the site of her most dramatic theophany. It is true that, in the rest of Greece, Saint Demetrius had taken her place, thus becoming the patron of agriculture. But Eleusis knew, and still knows, a Saint Demetra, a saint who is unknown elsewhere and who has never been canonized. Until the beginning of the nineteenth century a statue of the goddess was ritually covered with flowers by the peasants of the village, for she insured the fertility of their fields. Then, in 1820, despite the armed resistance of the inhabitants, the statue was taken away by E. D. Clarke, who presented it to Cambridge University.[36] Again at Eleusis, in 1860 a priest told the French archeologist F. Lenormant the story of Saint Demetra: she was an old woman from Athens; a "Turk" carried away her daughter, but a brave *pallikar* succeeded in setting her free. And in 1928,

35. Eunapius, *Bioi sophistōn*, pp. 42 ff. (ed. Boissade, 1822); cf. G. E. Mylonas, *Eleusis*, p. 8; C. Kerényi, *Eleusis*, pp. 17–18.

36. J. C. Lawson, *Modern Greek Folklore and Ancient Greek Religion*, pp. 80 ff.

Mylonas heard the same story from an Eleusinian woman ninety years old.[37]

The most touching episode of the Christian mythology of Demeter took place at the beginning of February 1940, and it was recounted and commented on at length in the Athenian press.[38] At one of the bus stops between Athens and Corinth there came on board an old woman, "thin and dried up but with very big and keen eyes." Since she had no money to pay her fare, the driver made her leave the bus at the next stop—which was, precisely, Eleusis. But the driver could not get the motor started again; finally the passengers decided to chip in and pay the old woman's fare. She got back on board, and this time the bus set off. Then the old woman said to them: "You ought to have done it sooner, but you are egotists; and, since I am among you, I will tell you something else: you will be punished for the way you live, you will be deprived even of plants and water!" "She had not finished threatening them," the author of the article published in *Hestia* goes on, "before she vanished. . . . No one had seen her get out. Then the passengers looked at one another, and they examined the ticket stubs again to make sure that a ticket had indeed been issued."

To conclude, we will quote Charles Picard's well-taken observation: "I believe that even Hellenists in general will find it hard, in face of this story, not to summon up certain recollections of the famous Homeric Hymn, in which Kore's mother, disguised as an *old woman* in the house of the Eleusinian king Celeus, also prophesied and—in a fit of anger, reproaching men with their impiety—announced terrible catastrophes for the whole region."[39]

37. F. Lenormant, *Monographie de la voie sacrée éleusinienne,* pp. 399 ff.; Lawson, *Modern Greek Folklore,* pp. 81 ff.; Mylonas, *Eleusis,* p. 12.

38. We use the report published in *Hestia,* February 7, 1940, and translated by C. Picard, "Demeter, puissance oraculaire," pp. 102–3.

39. Picard, ibid., pp. 103–4.

Abbreviations

ANET	J. B. Pritchard, *Ancient Near Eastern Texts Relating to the Old Testament* (Princeton, 1950; 2d ed., 1955)
AO	*Acta Orientalia* (Leiden)
ArOr	*Archiv Orientální* (Prague)
ARW	*Archiv für Religionswissenschaft* (Freiburg and Leipzig)
BEFEO	*Bulletin de l'Ecole française d'Extrême-Orient* (Hanoi)
BJRL	*Bulletin of the John Rylands Library* (Manchester)
BMFEA	*Bulletin of the Museum of Far Eastern Antiquities* (Stockholm)
BSOAS	*Bulletin of the School of Oriental and African Studies* (London)
CA	*Current Anthropology* (Chicago)
ERE	*Encyclopaedia of Religion and Ethics,* ed. James Hastings
FFC	Folklore Fellows Communications (Hamina; later, Helsinki)
HJAS	*Harvard Journal of Asiatic Studies* (Cambridge, Mass.)
HR	*History of Religions* (Chicago)
HTR	*Harvard Theological Review* (Cambridge, Mass.)
IIJ	*Indo-Iranian Journal* (The Hague)

IPEK	*Jahrbuch für prähistorische ethnographische Kunst* (Berlin)
JA	*Journal Asiatique* (Paris)
JAFL	*Journal of American Folklore* (Boston and New York)
JAOS	*Journal of the American Oriental Society* (Baltimore)
JAS	*Journal of the Asiatic Society, Bombay Branch*
JIES	*Journal of Indo-European Studies* (Montana)
JNES	*Journal of Near Eastern Studies* (Chicago)
JRAS	*Journal of the Royal Asiatic Society* (London)
JRASB	*Journal of the Royal Asiatic Society of Bengal* (Calcutta)
JSS	*Journal of Semitic Studies* (Manchester)
NGWG	*Nachrichten von der Königlichen Gesellschaft der Wissenschaften zu Göttingen* (Göttingen)
OLZ	*Orientalische Literaturzeitung* (Berlin and Leipzig)
RB	*Revue Biblique* (Paris)
RE	Pauly-Wissowa, *Real-Encyclopädie der klassischen Altertumswissenschaft*
REG	*Revue des Etudes Grecques* (Paris)
RHPR	*Revue d'Histoire et de Philosophie religieuses* (Strasbourg)
RHR	*Revue de l'Histoire des Religions* (Paris)
SBE	*Sacred Books of the East*, 50 vols., ed. Max Müller (Oxford)
SMSR	*Studi e Materiali di Storia delle Religioni* (Rome)
VT	*Vetus Testamentum* (Leiden)
WdM	*Wörterbuch der Mythologie* (Stuttgart)
ZDMG	*Zeitschrift der deutschen morgenländischen Gesellschaft* (Leipzig)

Present Position of Studies: Problems and Progress. Critical Bibliographies

Chapter 16. The Religions of Ancient China

126. Especially deserving of mention among the numerous studies of the prehistoric cultures of China are: William Watson, *Early Civilization in China* (London, 1966), an excellent introduction; Li Chi, *The Beginnings of Chinese Civilization* (Seattle and London, 1957; 2d ed., 1968); Cheng Tê-k'un, *Archaeology in China,* vol. 1, *Prehistoric China* (Cambridge, 1959); William Watson, *Cultural Frontiers in Ancient East Asia* (Edinburgh, 1971), especially the first chapter, "Neolithic Frontiers in East Asia" (pp. 9–37); Carl Hentze, *Funde in Alt-China: Das Welterleben im ältesten China* (Göttingen, 1967), which summarizes the author's views presented in several earlier works; Ping-ti Ho, *The Cradle of the East: An Inquiry into the Indigenous Origins of Techniques and Ideas of Neolithic and Early Historic China, 5000–1000* B.C. (Hong Kong and Chicago, 1975).

On the discovery of the Chinese Neolithic (the Yang Shao culture), see J. G. Anderson, *Children of the Yellow Earth* (London, 1934). In his recent work, Ho maintains the autochthonous origin of Chinese agriculture, metallurgy, and writing; see his *Cradle of the East,* esp. pp. 341 ff. For his part, Li Chi, in accord with other archeologists, brings out certain Western (i.e., Mesopotamian) influences in the iconography of Anyang (*Beginnings of Chinese Civilization,* pp. 26 ff.). In any case it is certain that Chinese culture, like all other cultures, was progressively enriched by ideas and techniques that were Western, Nordic, or Meridional in origin. On the other hand, as has often been stated, China is "a window toward the Pacific," and the influence of the Chinese cosmological symbolism and its artistic expressions can be discerned in the religious art of certain peoples of Borneo, Sumatra, and New Zealand, as well as among the tribes of the northwest coast of America. See, inter alia, two studies of art in the Pacific area: Mino

Badner, "The Protruding Tongue and Related Motifs in the Art Style of the American Northwestern Coast, New Zealand, and China," and Robert Heine-Geldern, "A Note on Relations between the Art Style of the Maori and of Ancient China," both published in *Wiener Beiträge zur Kulturgeschichte und Linguistik* 15 (Vienna, 1966); see also Douglas Fraser, ed., *Early Chinese Art and the Pacific Basin: A Photographic Exhibition* (New York, 1968).

On the religious conceptions, see Hermann Koster, "Zur Religion in der chinesischen Vorgeschichte," *Monumenta Serica* 14 (1949–55): 188–214; Ping-ti Ho, *The Cradle,* pp. 279 ff.; Bernhard Karlgren, "Some Fecundity Symbols in Ancient China," *Bulletin of the Museum of Far Eastern Antiquities,* no. 2 (Stockholm, 1930), pp. 1–54; Carl Hentze, *Funde in Alt-China,* pp. 20 ff., 219 ff.; Hentze, *Bronzegerät, Kultbauten, und Religion im ältesten China der Shang-Zeit* (Antwerp, 1951); and Hentze, *Das Haus als Weltort der Seele* (Stuttgart, 1961). On the "death pattern," see Hanna Rydh, "Symbolism in Mortuary Ceramics," *BMFEA,* no. 1 (Stockholm, 1929), pp. 71–121.

127. On the Chinese Bronze Age cultures, see Cheng Tê-k'un, *Archaeology in China,* vol. 2, *Shang China* (Cambridge, 1960); Kwang Chih Chang, *The Archaeology of Ancient China,* pp. 185–225; and Watson, *Cultural Frontiers in Ancient East Asia,* pp. 38 ff. (esp. pp. 42 ff.).

On religious ideas, see Herlee G. Creel, *The Birth of China: A Study of the Formative Period of Chinese Civilization* (New York, 1937), pp. 174–216; Chang, *The Archaeology of Ancient China,* pp. 251 ff.; Cheng Tê-k'un, *Archaeology in China,* vol. 2, pp. 213 ff.; Hentze, *Bronzegerät, Kultbauten, und Religion;* W. Eichhorn, "Zur Religion im ältesten China," *Wiener Zeitschrift für indische Philosophie* 2 (1958): 33–53; F. Tiberi, "Der Ahnenkult in China," *Annali del Pontificio Museo Missionario Etnologico* 27 (1963): 283–475; Ping-ti Ho, *Cradle,* pp. 289 ff.; Tsung-tung Chang, *Der Kult der Shang Dynastie im Spiegel der Orakelinschriften: Eine paläographische Studie zur Religion im archäischen China* (Wiesbaden, 1970) (cf. the critique by Paul L. M. Serruys, "Studies in the Language of the Shang Oracle Inscriptions," *T'oung Pao* 60 [1974]: 12–120); M. Christian Deydier, *Les Jiaguwen: Essai bibliographique et synthèse des études* (Paris, 1976) (divinatory inscriptions on bone and on tortoise shells); David N. Keightley, "The Religious Commitment: Shang Theology and the Genesis of Chinese Political Culture," *HR* 17 (1978): 211–25.

On scapulamancy, see Eliade, *Shamanism: Archaic Techniques of Ecstasy,* trans. Willard R. Trask, Bollingen Series 76 (Princeton, 1972), p. 164, n. 97 (bibliography).

On the symbolism of the *t'ao-t'ieh* mask, see the works by Carl Hentze, especially *Bronzegerät . . . der Shang-Zeit,* pp. 215 ff., *Funde in Alt-China,* pp. 171 ff., 195 ff., and "Antithetische *T'ao-t'ieh*-motive," *IPEK* 23 (1970/73): 1–20.

No less significant is the symbolism of the cicada. Since its larva comes out of the ground (hence, it is a symbol of obscurity), the cicada is an emblem of resurrection; this is why it is put in the mouth of the corpse; see Carl Hentze, *Frühchinesischen Bronzen und Kultdarstellungen* (Antwerp, 1937), pp. 37 ff. Stylized delineations of cicadas are engraved on the tongue of the *t'ao-t'ieh* mask, the demon of darkness that created light and life (ibid., pp. 66 ff.).

128. On Chou culture, see Ch'eng Tê-k'un, *Archaeology in China,* vol. 3, *Chou China* (Cambridge, 1963); Kwang-Chih Chang, *The Archaeology of Ancient China,* pp. 256 ff., 263 ff.

On religion in the Chou period, see Ping-ti Ho, *Cradle,* pp. 322 ff.; Hentze, *Funde in Alt-China,* pp. 218 ff., and the works cited in the following two paragraphs.

The "classic books" present a dozen names of the Supreme God, among which the most famous are Shang Ti ("The Lord on High") and Huang Ti ("August Lord"). But at the basis of all these divine names are the appellatives Ti (Lord) and T'ien (Heaven). The celestial structure of the supreme god is evident: Shang Ti is all-seeing (*Shih Ching* 3. 1. 7. 1), he hears everything (5. 16. 3. 14); T'ien keeps watch over men (*Shu Ching* 4. 9. 1. 3), he sees and hears (3. 3. 5. 7), he is clairvoyant (*Shih Ching* 3. 3. 2. 11–12), his decree is infallible (*Shu Ching* 4. 3. 2. 5), he understands and observes everything (4. 8. 2. 3), etc. For translations of the *Shu Ching,* see vol. 3 of James Legge's *The Chinese Classics,* 5 vols. (London, 1861–72), and Bernhard Karlgren *Shu Ching: The Book of Documents* (Stockholm, 1950).

On the cult of the supreme celestial god, see B. Schindler, "The Development of Chinese Conceptions of Supreme Beings," *Asia Major: Introductory Volume* (1923), pp. 298–366; H. H. Dubs, "The Archaic Royal Jou Religion," *T'oung Pao* 47 (1958): 217–59; and J. Shih, "The Notion of God in the Ancient Chinese Religion," *Numen* 16 (1969): 99–138. According to Joseph Shih, Ti was a supreme god and T'ien a personal god. Under the Chou these two divine names were used indifferently to invoke the same god; see also, by the same author,

"Il Dio Supremo," in "La religione della Cina," *Storia delle Religioni* 5 (Turin, 1971): 539 ff.

In contrast to what is the case with other religions, books on the general history of Chinese religion are few. The most useful ones are L. Wieger, *Histoire des croyances religieuses et des opinions philosophiques en Chine depuis l'origine jusqu'à nos jours* (Hien-hien, 1917), a very personal work, to be consulted with caution; Jan J. M. de Groot, *The Religious System of China,* 6 vols. (Leiden, 1892–1910; reprinted Taipei, 1964), irreplaceable for its documentation; Marcel Granet, *La religion des Chinois* (Paris, 1922); Henri Maspéro, *Mélanges posthumes,* vol. 1: *Les religions chinoises* (Paris, 1950); C. K. Yang, *Religion in Chinese Society* (Berkeley, 1967), an important work, though not a general history of Chinese religion; D. H. Smith, *Chinese Religions* (New York, 1968) (but see the review by Daniel Overmyer, *HR* 9 [1969–70]: 256–60); Laurence G. Thompson, *Chinese Religion: An Introduction* (Belmont, 1969), which chiefly presents religious ideas and practices after the Han; Werner Eichhorn, *Die Religionen Chinas* (Stuttgart, 1973), an admirable restatement; and *Religion and Ritual in Chinese Society,* ed. Arthur P. Wolf (Stanford, 1974). A short but brilliant exposition has been provided by Max Kaltenmark, "La religion de la Chine antique" and "Le taoïsme religieux," in Henri-Charles Puech, ed., *Histoire des religions,* vol. 1 (1970), pp. 927–57, 1216–48.

Pertinent analyses of Chinese religious beliefs and institutions occur in the books by Marcel Granet, *Fêtes et chansons anciennes de la Chine* (1919), *Danses et légendes de la Chine ancienne* (1926), and *La pensée chinoise* (1934). See also Henri Maspéro, *La Chine antique* (1927; new ed., 1955).

On the Earth Mother, see Berthold Laufer, *Jade: A Study of Chinese Archaeology and Religion* (Chicago: Field Museum, 1912), pp. 144 ff. (against these views, see B. Karlgren, "Some Fecundity Symbols in Ancient China," pp. 14 ff.); Marcel Granet, "Le dépôt de l'enfant sur le sol: Rites anciennes et ordalies mythiques," *Revue archéologique* (1922), reprinted in the volume *Etudes sociologiques sur la Chine* (1953), pp. 159–202. According to Edouard Chavannes (*Le T'ai Chan: Essai de monographie d'un cult chinois* [Paris, 1910], esp. pp. 520–25), the personification of the Soil as a Great Earth Goddess would be a comparatively recent phenomenon: it seems to have taken place about the beginning of the Han dynasty, in the second century B.C.; before that date there would have been only local cults crystallized around gods of the soil (p. 437). But Granet has shown that these gods replaced very ancient feminine or "neuter" divinities who had preceded them. This is a widespread phenomenon; see Eliade, "La Terre-Mère et les hiérogamies cosmiques'' (1953), published in English as ''Mother Earth and the Cosmic Hierogamies,'' in *Myths, Dreams, and Mysteries: The Encounter between Contemporary Faiths and Archaic Realities,* trans. Philip Mairet (New York, 1960).

For a detailed analysis of the various provincial and marginal cultures that were integrated into Chinese culture, see Wolfram Eberhard, *Kultur und Siedlung der Randvölker Chinas* (supplement to vol. 36 of *T'oung Pao* [Leiden, 1942]); and Eberhard, *Lokalkulturen im alten China,* 2 vols. (vol. 1 was published as a supplement to vol. 37 of *T'oung Pao* [1943]; vol. 2 was published as *Monumenta Serica,* monograph no. 3 [Peking, 1943]). A corrected and enlarged version of the second volume of *Lokalkulturen* has been published under the title *The Local Cultures of South and East China* (Leiden, 1968).

On Chinese shamanism, see Eberhard, *The Local Cultures,* pp. 77 ff., 304 ff., 468 ff.; cf. Eliade, *Shamanism,* pp. 448 ff.; Joseph Thiel, ''Schamanismus im alten China,'' *Sinologica* 10 (1968): 149–204; John S. Major, ''Research Priorities in the Study of Ch'u Religion,'' *HR* 17 (1978): 226–43, esp. pp. 236 ff.

129. The most important cosmogonic texts have been translated by Max Kaltenmark, ''La naissance du monde en Chine,'' in *Sources Orientales,* vol. 1: *La naissance du monde* (Paris, 1959), pp. 453–68. The problem of Chinese mythology, especially that of cosmogonic myths, has been discussed, from different viewpoints, by these authors: Henri Maspéro, ''Légendes mythologiques dans le *Chou King,*'' *JA* 204 (1924): 1–100; Bernhard Karlgren, ''Legends and Cults of Ancient China,'' *Bulletin of the Museum of Far Eastern Antiquities,* no. 18 (1946), pp. 199–365 (irreplaceable for its rich documentation, but see the critique of Karlgren's method in the review by W. Eberhard, *Artibus Asiae* 9 [1946]: 355–64); Derk Bodde, ''Myths of Ancient China,'' in S. N. Kramer, ed., *Mythologies of the Ancient World* (New York, 1961), pp. 369–408; J. Shih, ''The Ancient Chinese Cosmogony,'' *Studia Missionaria* 18 (1969): 111–30; N. J. Girardot, ''The Problem of Creation Mythology in the Study of Chinese Religion,'' *HR* 15 (1976): 289–318 (critical analysis of some recent approaches).

On the myth of P'an Ku, see Maspéro, ''Légendes mythologiques,'' pp. 47 ff.; Edouard Erkes, ''Spuren chinesischer Weltschöpfungsmythen,'' *T'oung Pao* 28 (1931): 355–68; Eberhard, *The Local Cultures,* pp. 442–43; Bodde, ''Myths of Ancient China,'' pp. 382 ff.; Girardot, ''The Problem of Creation Mythology,'' pp. 298 ff.

On the cutting of communications between Earth and Heaven, see Maspéro, ''Légendes mythologiques,'' pp. 95–96; Maspéro, *Les reli-*

gions chinoises, pp. 186 ff.; Bodde, "Myths of Ancient China," pp. 389 ff.; and Eliade, *Myths, Dreams, and Mysteries,* pp. 59 ff.

On Nu-kua, see Bodde, pp. 386 ff. On the myth of Yü the Great, conqueror of the floodwaters, see Marcel Granet, *Danses et légendes,* pp. 466 ff., 482 ff.

On the origin and ceremonial structure of Chinese cities, see Paul Wheatley, *The Pivot of the Four Quarters: A Preliminary Inquiry into the Origins and Character of the Ancient Chinese City* (Chicago, 1971), pp. 30 ff., 411 ff., and passim; see also Werner Müller, *Die heilige Stadt* (Stuttgart, 1961), pp. 149 ff.

On cosmology and spatial symbolism, see Granet, *La pensée chinoise,* pp. 342 ff.; three works by Schuyler Camman, "Types of Symbols in Chinese Art," in *Studies in Chinese Thought,* ed. Arthur F. Wright (Chicago, 1953), pp. 195–221, "Evolution of Magic Squares in China," *JAOS* 80 (1960): 116–24, and "The Magic Square of Three in Old Chinese Philosophy and Religion," *HR* 1 (1961): 37–80; Eliade, "Centre du monde, temple, maison," in *Le Symbolisme cosmique des monuments religieux,* Série Orientale, no. 14 (Rome, 1957), pp. 57–82; Eliade, *The Myth of the Eternal Return: Cosmos and History,* trans. Willard R. Trask, Bollingen Series 46 (Princeton, 1965). Hermann Koster, *Symbolik des chinesischen Universismus* (Stuttgart, 1958), esp. pp. 14 ff., 48 ff.; R. A. Stein, "Architecture et pensée religieuse en Extrême-Orient," *Arts asiatiques* 4 (1957): 163–86; Stein, "L'habitat, le monde et le corps humain en Extrême-Orient et en Haute-Asie," *JA* 245 (1957): 37–74.

On the *ming-t'ang,* see Granet, *La pensée chinoise,* pp. 102 ff., 178 ff., 250 ff.; Stein, "Architecture et pensée religieuse," pp. 164 ff.; Koster, *Symbolik,* pp. 34 ff., 48 ff.

130. On the morphology of the various symbolisms of polarity and alternation, see our study "Prolegomenon to Religious Dualism: Dyads and Polarities," in *The Quest: History and Meaning in Religion* (Chicago, 1969), pp. 127–75. On polarity in Chinese cosmology, see Granet, *La pensée chinoise,* pp. 86 ff., 149 ff.; Carl Hentze, *Bronzegerät,* pp. 192 ff.; Hentze, *Tod, Auferstehung, Weltordnung* (Zurich, 1955), pp. 150 ff.; and Koster, *Symbolik,* pp. 17 ff.

In his analysis of the love songs preserved in the earliest "classic book," the *Shih Ching,* Marcel Granet has brought out the structure of the seasonal festivals celebrated by the peasants, probably from Neolithic times (see his *Fêtes et chansons anciennes de la Chine*). According to Kaltenmark, "They were chiefly the festivals of young people in connection with marriage festivals: the two sexual groups came from different villages by virtue of the principle of exogamy and engaged in poetic contests whose themes were obligatory and drawn from the ritual landscape. This was nearly always a landscape of water and mountains, and all of its elements were sacred. . . . [The festivals] corresponded to critical moments in peasant life, those in which the agriculturalists changed their way of life. The spring season scattered them in the fields, where they lived in small huts; in winter they were once again in the familial village. There is certainly a connection between the holy places of the peasant communities on the one hand and the mountains, rivers, and sacred woods of the classic ritual on the other; both were ancestral centers, and the chief sanctuaries of the feudal cult—the temple of the ancestors, the altars of the gods of the soil and of harvests—were only diversifications of the ancient holy places. In the same way, certain royal cult practices are only transpositions of the peasant festivals'' (Max Kaltenmark, ''Religion de la Chine antique,'' p. 952).

On the notion of Tao, see Granet, *La pensée,* pp. 300 ff.; Joseph Needham, *Science and Civilisation in China,* vol. 2 (1956), pp. 36 ff. (five volumes of this work have been published by Cambridge University Press; two more are in preparation); Koster, *Symbolik,* pp. 16 ff., 51 ff.; Ellen Marie Chen, ''Nothingness and the Mother Principle in Early Chinese Taoism,'' *International Philosophical Quarterly* 9 (1969): 391–405; Holmes Welch, *Taoism: The Parting of the Way* (Boston, 1957; rev. ed. 1965), pp. 50 ff.; Max Kaltenmark, *Lao tseu et le taoïsme* (Paris, 1965), pp. 30 ff.; Wang-tsit Chan, *The Way of Lao Tzu* (New York, 1963), pp. 31 ff.

On the cosmogonic fragments of the *Tao Tê Ching,* see Norman J. Girardot, ''Myth and Meaning in the *Tao te Ching:* Chapters 25 and 42,'' *HR* 16 (1977): 294–328, and the bibliography listed in §129.

On the ''Valley Divinity,'' ''the Obscure Female,'' see §132.

131. Confucius was the first to use his teaching as a method of spiritual and political reform. He did not give formal instruction but simply conversed with his disciples. At the age of fifty he was given a post in the administration of the kingdom, but he resigned soon afterward, when he realized that he had no power. Disappointed, he traveled for more than ten years through all the states of the kingdom. At the age of sixty-seven he yielded to the urging of his old disciples and returned to his native country, Lu, where he lived five years more.

Tradition ascribes a number of works to Confucius, especially the ''Classic Books,'' but it is very unlikely that he composed them, and it is even doubted if he edited them. A collection of his notes and conversations was published later by his disciples under the title *Lun Yu* ("Conversations," usually translated into English as *Analects*). We have used the translations by James Legge, *The Analects of Confucius* (new ed., New York, 1966); L. Giles, *The Sayings of Confucius* (new ed., New York, 1961), and W. E. Soothill, *The Analects* (London, 1958). See also F. S. Couvreur, *Entretiens de Confucius et de ses disciples* (new ed., Paris, n.d.); James R. Ware, *The Sayings of Confucius* (New York, 1955).

There is an abundant literature on Confucius. We mention: H. G. Creel, *Confucius and the Chinese Way* (New York, 1949; republished 1960); Lin Yutang, *The Wisdom of Confucius* (New York, 1938); Liu Wu-chi, *Confucius, His Life and Times* (New York, 1955); Etiemble, *Confucius* (Paris, 1956); Daniel Leslie, *Confucius* (Paris, 1962); J. Munro, *The Concept of Man in Early China* (Stanford, 1969), pp. 49–83 ("The Confucian Concept of Man"); Herbert Fingarette, *Confucius: The Secular as Sacred* (New York, 1972); and the selection of critical studies edited by Arthur F. Wright, *Confucianism and Chinese Civilization* (New York, 1967).

132. There are many translations of the *Tao Tê Ching* (thirty-six in English alone, published between 1868 and 1955). We are frequently reminded of Marcel Granet's observation concerning the translation by Stanislas Julien (1842): "perfectly conscientious, it is not unfaithful to the text, but neither does it make possible to understand it" (*La pensée chinoise,* p. 503, n. 1). We have used the translation by Arthur Waley, *The Way and Its Power* (London, 1934), for its literary value, and the translation by Wing-tsit Chan for the richness and precision of its commentary. But the portions cited in the text follow the translation of Max Kaltenmark, in his admirable little book *Lao tseu et le taoïsme* (Paris, 1963).

The works by Waley and Chan contain long introductions, which examine the numerous problems raised by the history of the text. See also Jan Yün-Hua, "Problems of Tao and the *Tao Te Ching,*" *Numen* 22 (1975): 208–34 (the author presents the latest investigations into early Taoism by Fung Yu-lan), and his "The Silk Manuscripts on Taoism," *T'oung Pao* 63 (1977): 66–84 (on the manuscripts recently discovered in a tomb dating from ca. 168). The commentary by Ho-shang-kung has been translated by Edouard Erkes, *Ho-shang-kung's Commentary on Lao-tse, Translated and Annotated* (Ascona, 1950).

Among the general presentations, we mention: Henri Maspéro, *Mélanges posthumes,* vol. 2: *Le taoïsme* (Paris, 1950); Fung Yu-lan, *History of Chinese Philosophy,* vol. 1 (Princeton, 1952), pp. 170 ff.;

Max Kaltenmark, *Lao tseu et le taoïsme;* Holmes Welch, *Taoism: The Parting of the Way;* Nicole Vandier-Nicolas, *Le taoïsme* (Paris, 1965); Etiemble, "En relisant Lao-Tseu," *Nouvelle Revue Française* 171 (1967): 457–76; and Herlee G. Creel, *What Is Taoism?* (Chicago, 1970).

A portion of the communications presented at the Colloquy on Taoism in Bellagio, September 7–14, 1968, has been published in *History of Religions* 9 (1969–70): 107–255; see, especially, Holmes H. Welch, "The Bellagio Conference on Taoist Studies," pp. 107–36, and Arthur F. Wright, "A Historian's Reflection on Taoist Tradition," pp. 248–55. On present orientations in the study of Taoism, see Norman J. Girardot, "Part of the Way: Four Studies on Taoism," *HR* 11 (1972): 319–37.

We list some recent studies: Donald Munro, "The Taoist Concept of Man," in *The Concept of Man in Early China* (Stanford, 1969), pp. 117–39; J. J. L. Duyvendak, "The Philosophy of Wu-Wei," *Asiatische Studien* 1 (1947): 81–102; Walter Liebenthal, "The Immortality of the Soul in Chinese Thought," *Monumenta Niponica* 8 (1952): 327–97; Max Kaltenmark, "Ling-pao: Note sur un terme du taoïsme religieux," *Bibliothèque de l'Institut des Hautes Etudes Chinoises* 14 (Paris, 1960): 551–88; Kimura Eiichi, "Taoism and Chinese Thought," *Acta Asiatica* 27 (1974): 1–8; Michel Strickmann, "The Longest Taoist Scripture," *HR* 17 (1978): 331–54. The relations between "philosophical Taoism," as it is expressed in the *Tao Tê Ching* and by Chuang Tzŭ, and "religious Taoism," or the search for immortality by various techniques of subtle physiology and by alchemy, are a problem that is still under dispute. Some authors insist on the differences that separate "philosophical Taoism" from the cult of immortality. According to these authors (for example, A. G. Graham, H. H. Welch, Fung Yu-lan), the first great period of philosophical Taoism was debased by the invasion of superstitions (magic and popular religion) and by Buddhist conceptions and practices. The result of this debasement is "Neo-Taoism" or the "Taoist religion." See, inter alia, Creel, *What Is Taoism?* pp. 1–24, 37 ff.; A. C. Graham, *The Book of Lieh-tzu* (London, 1960), pp. 10 ff., 16 ff. (see the critique of this position by K. Schipper in his review in *T'oung Pao* n.s. 51 [1964]: 288–92). On the other hand, French sinologists and their pupils (Granet, Maspéro, Max Kaltenmark, C. Schipper, Anna Seidel, etc.) bring out the structural likeness between the two "Taoist schools." For discussion of some recent works that illustrate these two methodological approaches see Norman Girardot, "Part of the Way: Four Studies on Taoism," pp. 320–24, and especially the article by N. Sivin, "On the Word 'Taoist' as a Source of Perplexity: With Special Reference to the Relations of Science and Religion in

Traditional China," *HR* 17 (1978): 303–30 (see pp. 313 ff. for Sivin's examination of some recent interpretations by Japanese scholars).

On Chinese conceptions of immortality, see Yang-shih Yu, "Life and Immortality in the Mind of Han China," *HJAS* 25 (1964–65): 80–82; Eliade, *The Two and the One,* trans. J. M. Cohen (Chicago, 1979); Ellen Marie Chen, "Is There a Doctrine of Physical Immortality in the *Tao Te Ching?*" *HR* 12 (1973): 231–49. Joseph Needham has emphasized the "magical, scientific, democratic, and politically revolutionary" character of Taoism (*Science and Civilisation in China,* vol. 2, p. 35); according to Needham, the Taoists were hostile not only to Confucianism but also to the whole feudal system (p. 100; cf. pp. 100–132). However, Sivin has expressed doubts concerning the justification for these statements; no one has been able to demonstrate the antifeudalism of the Taoists or their identification with the beginnings of a scientific movement; see his "On the Word 'Taoist,' " pp. 309 ff.

The writings of Chuang Tzŭ have been more than once translated into the chief European languages. The translation by James Legge, *The Writings of Kwan-zze* (*SBE,* vols. 39 and 40, London, 1891) is the best known. Now see Burton Watson, *The Complete Works of Chuang Tzu* (New York, 1968).

On Chuang Tzŭ, see Arthur Waley, *Three Ways of Thought in Ancient China* (London, 1939; reprinted New York, 1956), pp. 3–79; Yu-lan Fung, *Lao Tzu and Chuang Tzu: The Spirit of Chinese Philosophy* (London, 1947); A. C. Graham, "Chuang-tzu's Essay on Seeing Things as Equal," *HR* 9 (1969–70): 137–59.

133. On the Taoist techniques for obtaining physical immortality, see Henri Maspéro, *Le taoïsme,* pp. 89–116; Holmes Welch, *Taoism,* pp. 97 ff.; Max Kaltenmark, *Lao tseu et le taoïsme,* pp. 146 ff.

On the Taoist Immortals, see Lionel Giles, *A Gallery of Chinese Immortals* (London, 1948); Max Kaltenmark, *Le Lie-sien Tchouan: Biographies légendaires des Immortels taoïstes de l'antiquité* (Peking, 1953) (translation and commentary).

On the "freeing of the corpse," see H. Maspéro, *Le taoïsme,* pp. 98 ff.; H. Welch, *Taoism,* pp. 108 ff.

On the "magical flight" of yogis and alchemists, see Eliade, *Yoga: Immortality and Freedom,* trans. Willard R. Trask, Bollingen Series 56 (Princeton, 1969), pp. 414 ff.; Eliade, *Shamanism,* pp. 474 ff.; and Eliade, *The Forge and the Crucible: The Origins and Structures of Alchemy,* trans. Stephen Corrin (Chicago, 1979), pp. 190–93.

On the legend of the three sacred mountains that are set in the middle of the sea and that no one could approach, see Ssŭ-ma Ch'ien,

Mémoires, trans. Edouard Chavannes (Paris, 1967), vol. 3, pp. 436–37: "In former times . . . people could travel there: there are the Blessed and the drug that prevents death; there all beings, the birds and the quadrupeds, are white, and the palaces there are made of gold and silver; when those people were not yet there, they saw them from afar like a cloud; when they arrived there, the three sacred mountains were upside down under the water. . . . No one now has been able to arrive there" (see also vol. 2, pp. 152–53). These are countries that belong to a mythical geography, crystallized as the result of immemorial ecstatic experiences. Cf. the Hindu legends of the *ṛṣis* rising into the air to travel to the mysterious region in the North called Çvetadvïpa; so, too, the lake Anavatapta could be reached by those who possessed the supernatural power of flight; the Buddha and the *arhats* arrived at Anavatapta in the twinkling of an eye (see Eliade, *Yoga,* pp. 414 ff.).

The crane is especially the bird of the Immortals; it was believed to live for more than a thousand years and "could breathe with its neck bent, a technique that makes the breath flexible and that the Taoists imitate" (Kaltenmark, *Lao tseu,* p. 153). See also J. J. de Groot, *The Religious System of China,* vol. 4, pp. 232–33, 295, 395. On the dance of the cranes, see Granet, *Danses et légendes,* pp. 216 ff.

On the "Fields of Cinnabar" and the "Three Worms," see Maspéro, *Le taoïsme,* pp. 91 ff.; Welch, *Taoism,* pp. 106–9, 121, 130–32.

On the antiquity of respiratory practices in China, see Hellmut Wilhelm, "Eine Chou-Inschrift über Atemtechnik," *Monumenta Sinica* 13 (1948): 385–88.

On the technique of "nourishing the vital force," Henri Maspéro's article remains fundamental: "Les procédés de 'nourrir le principe vital' dans la religion taoïste ancienne," *JA* (1937): 177–252, 353–430; see also *Le taoïsme,* pp. 107–14. For a comparative analysis of Indian, Islamic, and Christian respiratory techniques (hesychasm in the last instance), see Eliade, *Yoga,* pp. 47–53.

"The importance of Embryonic Respiration lies in the fact that the human body is made of breaths. At the beginning of the world, the Nine Breaths mingled to form Chaos; when Chaos dispersed, they separated: the pure and subtle breaths rose and formed heaven, the impure and coarse breaths descended and formed earth. The first gods, the greatest ones, were spontaneously created from the knotting of the breaths; then lesser gods were produced and engendered. Later, the Yellow Emperor, Huang-ti, formed men by erecting earthen statues at the four cardinal points; he exposed them to all the breaths for three hundred years; when they were thoroughly penetrated, they were able to speak and move, and they gave birth to the various races of men.

Thus man's body is made from the impure breaths that formed the earth, but the vital breath that animates it is the pure breath that circulates between heaven and earth. For man to become immortal he must entirely replace the impure breaths in him by pure breaths; this is the goal of Embryonic Respiration. Whereas the ordinary man, subsisting on cereals, every day replaces the matter of his body by such gross matter, the Taoist, subsisting on breaths, replaces it by a purer and purer matter'' (Maspéro, *Le taoïsme,* p. 114).

The parallelism with the Orphic anthropogony and eschatology should be noted; see §181.

For the Taoists, the whole human body is filled with divinities and transcendent beings; see the description of this pantheon in Maspéro, *Le taoïsme,* pp. 116–37. It is possible to enter into relation with the gods by mystical meditation and by ecstasy (ibid., pp. 137–47).

For Taoist sexual techniques, see Joseph Needham, *Science and Civilisation in China,* vol. 2, pp. 146–52, and Akira Ishihara and Howard S. Levy, *The Tao of Sex: An Annotated Translation of the XXVIII Section of ''The Essence of Medical Prescriptions''* (Tokyo, 1968; new ed. New York, 1970). The techniques analyzed are not exclusively Taoist.

A text translated by Maspéro (''Les procédés,'' p. 385) gives the following description of ''making the semen return and repair the brain'': ''The principle . . . consists in copulating so that the Essence [i.e., the semen] is extremely agitated; [then] when it is about to come out, [the penis] is quickly seized behind the scrotum and in front of the anus by the two middle fingers of the left hand; it is squeezed tightly, and the breath is slowly expelled through the mouth while the teeth are gritted several times without the breath being held. Then, when the Essence is emitted, it cannot come out but instead returns from the Jade Stem [the penis] and rises to enter the brain. This procedure is transmitted from Immortal to Immortal; drinking blood, they swear not to transmit it at random.'' See also van Gulik, *Erotic Colour Prints of the Ming Period, with an Essay on Chinese Sex Life from the Han to the Ch'ing Dynasty,* B.C. *206*–A.D. *1644* (Tokyo, 1951), p. 78.

In the *Biography of the Real Man of Pure-Transcendence,* which Maspéro considers may date from the fifth century A.D., the method for returning the semen is included among the five recipes of the Immortal Master Chiang: ''It is necessary, by perfect meditation, to dismiss [every] external thought; then men and women can practice the method of Eternal Life. This procedure is absolutely secret: transmit it to none but sages! . . . Whenever one practices [this procedure], [one must] enter into meditation; first, consciousness of one's body, and consciousness of the external world, must be lost." After saying a prayer, "men keep [the mind fixed on] the kidneys, firmly preserving the Essence [i.e., the sperm] and distilling the Breath, which follows the spine and rises to the *Ni-hoan* [i.e., the Cinnabar Field situated in the head] against the current: this is what is called 'making return to the Origin,' *hoan-yuan;* women will keep [the mind fixed on] the heart, nourishing the spirits, distilling an immutable fire, making the Breath descend from the two breasts to the kidneys, whence it mounts by the spine and thus goes to the *Ni-hoan;* this is what is called 'transforming the real,' *hoan-chen.* After a hundred days one reaches Transcendence. If one practices [this procedure] for a very long time, one spontaneously becomes Real-Man and, living eternally, traverses the centuries. This is the method for not dying" (after the translation by Maspéro, "Les procédés," pp. 386–87).

On the "mysterious embryo" of the new immortal body, see Welch, *Taoism,* pp. 108 ff., 120 ff.

On the relations between Taoist techniques and Tantric Yoga, see Eliade, *Yoga,* pp. 264 ff., 413 ff.; Needham, *Science and Civilisation,* vol. 2, pp. 425 ff.; R. H. van Gulik, *Sexual Life in Ancient China* (Leiden, 1961), pp. 339 ff.; J. Filliozat, "Taoïsme et Yoga," *JA* 257 (1969): 41–88. See also Lu K'uan Yu, *Taoist Yoga: Alchemy and Immortality* (London, 1970), an English translation of a book by a modern author ("No evidence of Taoist origin or particular association is given," says Sivin in "On the Word 'Taoist,' " *HR* 17 [1978]: 319, n. 27).

134. For Chinese alchemy, the essential bibliography will be found in our books *Yoga,* pp. 284–90, and *The Forge and the Crucible,* pp. 193–95, and especially in Joseph Needham, *Science and Civilisation in China,* vol. 5, pt. 2 (1974), pp. 2 ff., 381 ff. The most important works are: A. Waley, "Notes on Chinese Alchemy," *BSOAS* 6 (1930): 1–24; Homer H. Dubs, "The Beginnings of Alchemy," *Isis* 38 (1947): 62–86; Nathan Sivin, *Chinese Alchemy: Preliminary Studies* (Cambridge, Mass., 1968) (see our review of this in *HR* 10 [1970]: 178–82); J. Needham, *Science and Civilisation,* vol. 5, pt. 3 (1976) (the history of alchemy will be continued in the two final volumes, now in preparation).

Among the translations of alchemical texts, we mention especially two articles by Lu-Ch'iang Wu and Tenney L. Davis, "An Ancient Chinese Treatise on Alchemy Entitled *Ts'an T'ung Ch'i,* Written by Wei Po-Yang about 142 A.D.," *Isis* 18 (1932): 210–89, and "Ko Hung on the Yellow and the White," *Proceedings of the American Academy of Arts and Sciences* 71 (1935): 221–84. This last work includes a translation of chapters 4 and 6 of the treatise by Ko Hung (*Pao P'u Tzu*). Chapters 1–3 are translated by Eugen Feifel in *Monumenta Serica* 6 (1941): 113–211 (see ibid., vol. 9, 1944, for a new translation of chapter 4, also by Feifel), and chapters 7 and 11 by T. L. Davis and K. F. Chen, "The Inner Chapters of *Pao-pu-tzu*," *Proceedings of the American Academy of Arts and Sciences* 74 (1940–42): 287–325. On the value of the translations of T. L. Davis and his collaborators, see J. Needham, *Science and Civilisation*, vol. 5, pt. 2, p. 6, and Nathan Sivin, *Chinese Alchemy*, p. 15. James R. Ware has provided a complete translation of the *Nei P'ien* of Ko Hung in *Alchemy, Medicine and Religion in the China of* A.D. *320: The "Nei P'ien" of Ko Hung* (Cambridge, Mass., 1966) (see our observations in *HR* 8 [1968]: 84–85). Sivin's *Chinese Alchemy*, pp. 145–214, contains an annotated translation of *Tan ching yao chueh* ("Essential Formulas from the Alchemical Classics"), a work ascribed to Sun Ssu-mo (sixth century A.D.). See also Roy C. Spooner and C. H. Wang, "The Divine Nine-Turn *Tan Sha* Method: A Chinese Alchemical Recipe," *Isis* 38 (1947): 235–42.

According to H. H. Dubs, the earliest document would date from 144 B.C.; in that year an imperial edict threatens public execution to all those who are caught counterfeiting gold (the text is reproduced by Dubs, "The Beginnings of Alchemy," p. 63). But as Needham has pointed out (*Science and Civilisation*, vol. 5, pt. 2, pp. 47 ff.), counterfeiting gold is not, properly speaking, an alchemical "method."

Dubs believes that the origin of alchemy is to be sought in the China of the fourth century B.C. According to him, alchemy could be born only in a civilization in which gold was little known and in which there was no knowledge of the methods of titration of the quantity of pure metal; the fact that in Mesopotamia these methods were well known as early as the fourteenth century B.C. makes the Mediterranean origin of alchemy improbable (Dubs, pp. 80 ff.). But this opinion has not been accepted by the historians of alchemy (see, inter alia, F. Sherwood Taylor, *The Alchemists* [New York, 1949], p. 75). Dubs (p. 84) thinks that alchemy was introduced into the West by Chinese travelers. However, according to Laufer, it is not impossible that "scientific" alchemy represents a foreign influence in China (Laufer, *Isis* [1929], pp. 330–31). On the penetration of Mediterranean ideas into China, see Dubs, pp. 82–83, nn. 122–23. On the probable Mesopotamian origin of the Chinese alchemical ideology, see H. E. Stapleton, "The Antiquity of Alchemy," *Ambix* 5 (1953): 15 ff. In a short discussion of the origin of Chinese alchemy, Sivin (pp. 19–30) rejects Dubs's hypothesis. The most radical critique has been provided by Needham (vol. 5, pt. 2, pp. 44 ff.), despite the fact that he too, though for entirely different reasons, maintains that alchemy is a Chinese creation. According to Needham, the culture of ancient China was the only milieu in which belief in an elixir against death, the supreme work of the chemist, could crystallize (pp. 71, 82, 114–15), and the two conceptions—that of the elixir and that of the alchemical manufacture of gold—were integrated for the first time in the history of China in the fourth century B.C. (pp. 12 ff., etc.). But Needham recognizes that the relation between gold and immortality was known in India before the sixth century B.C. (pp. 118 ff.).

In a recent article, N. Sivin has drawn attention to the "pan-Chinese" character of Taoist techniques and of alchemy; see his "On the Word 'Taoist' as a Source of Perplexity," pp. 316 ff. In the same article (pp. 323 ff.) Sivin aptly analyzes the importance of Ko Hung, regarded by the majority of scholars as "the greatest of all Chinese alchemical writers" (Needham).

Until recent years Western scholars regarded "external alchemy," or iatro-chemistry (*wai-tan*), as "exoteric" and regarded "internal [otherwise, yogic] alchemy" (*nei-tan*) as "esoteric." If this dichotomy is true for certain late authors such as Peng Hsiao (9th–10th centuries), in the beginning *wai-tan* "was as esoteric as its yogic counterpart" (Sivin, *Chinese Alchemy,* p. 15, n. 18). And in fact Sun Ssu-mo, the great iatro-chemist of the seventh century, representing "external alchemy," is entirely within the Taoist tradition; see the fragment cited in our *The Forge and the Crucible,* p. 110, after Sivin's translation in *Chinese Alchemy,* pp. 146–48.

For the alchemical symbolism of respiration and the sexual act, see R. H. van Gulik, *Erotic Colour Prints,* pp. 115 ff.

Not only Lao Tzŭ's death (see n. 109) but also his birth have been interpreted as a cosmogony; see Kristofer Schipper, "The Taoist Body," *HR* 17 (1978): 355–86, esp. 361–74.

On the deification of Lao Tzŭ, see Anna K. Seidel, *La divinisation de Lao tseu dans le Taoïsme des Han* (Paris, 1969); see also, by the same author, "The Image of the Perfect Ruler in Early Taoist Messianism: Lao tzu and Li Hung," *HR* 9 (1969–70): 216–47.

On Taoist movements messianic in structure, see Paul Michaud, "The Yellow Turbans," *Monumenta Serica* 17 (1958): 47–127; Werner Eichhorn, "Description of the Rebellion of Sun En and Earlier Taoist Rebellions," *Mitteilungen des Instituts für Orientforschung* 2 (1954): 325–52; Howard S. Levy, "Yellow Turban Religion and Rebellion at the End of the Han," *JAOS* 76 (1956): 214–27; R. A. Stein, "Remarques sur les mouvements du Taoïsme politico-religieux au IIe siècle ap. J.-C.," *T'oung Pao* 50 (1963): 1–78. See also the bibliographies for chapter 35 (vol. 3).

Chapter 17. Brahmanism and Hinduism

135. On the Hinduization of the subcontinent and the integration of local elements, see Eliade, *Yoga: Immortality and Freedom,* trans. Willard R. Trask, Bollingen Series 56 (Princeton, 1970), pp. 293 ff., 431 (bibliography); J. Gonda, *Les religions de l'Inde,* vol. 1 (Paris, 1962), pp. 236 ff., 268 (bibliography).

There is an extensive literature on the morphology and history of Hinduism. The most useful works are: L. Renou and Jean Filliozat, *L'Inde classique,* vol. 1 (1947), pp. 381–667; L. Renou, *L'Hindouisme,* Coll. "Que sais-je?" (1951); J. Gonda, *Les religions de l'Inde,* vol. 1, pp. 257–421; Anne-Marie Esnoul, "L'Hindouisme," in H.-C. Puech, ed., *Histoire des religions,* vol. 1 (1970), pp. 996–1104; and Esnoul, *L'Hindouisme* (1973) (an anthology).

See also J. E. Carpenter, *Theism in Mediaeval India* (London, 1926) (valuable for its documentation); J. Gonda, *Aspects of Early Viṣṇuism* (Utrecht, 1954); Gonda, *Change and Continuity in Indian Religion* (The Hague, 1964); Gonda, *Viṣṇuism and Śivaism: A Comparison* (London, 1970); Arthur L. Herman, *The Problem of Evil and Indian Thought* (Delhi, Varanasi, Patna, 1976), pp. 146 ff.; Stella Kramrisch, "The Indian Great Goddess," *HR* 14 (1975): 235–65, esp. pp. 258 ff. (the androgyne and the goddess) and pp. 263 ff. (Devī); J. C. Heestermann, "Brahmin, Ritual, and Renouncer," *Wiener Zeitschrift zur Kunde des Süd- und Ostasien* 11 (1964): 1–37; V. S. Agrawala, *Śiva Mahādeva, The Great God* (Benares, 1966); Madeleine Biardeau, *Clefs pour la pensée hindoue* (Paris, 1972); Wendell Charles Beane, *Myth, Cult, and Symbols in Śakta Hinduism: A Study of the Indian Mother Goddess* (Leiden, 1977), esp. pp. 42 ff., 228 ff.; Wendy Doniger O'Flaherty, *Asceticism and Eroticism in the Mythology of Śiva* (London, 1973).

See also the bibliographies for chapter 24 (§§191–94).

We shall present the different phases of Śivaism and Viṣṇuism in chapters 31 and 32 (vol. 3).

136. On the leitmotiv "deliverance from suffering," see Eliade, *Yoga,* pp. 31 ff.

On the analogies between the Indian symbolism of captivity and deliverance from bonds and certain aspects of Gnostic mythology, see Eliade, *Myth and Reality,* trans. Willard R. Trask (New York, 1963), pp. 114 ff. ("Mythologies of Memory and Forgetting").

137. On the continuity of Vedic ideas in the Upanishads, see F. Edgerton, "The Upanishads: What Do They Seek, and Why," *JAOS* 49 (1929): 97–121, esp. pp. 100 ff.

The general problem of continuity in Indian religion has been treated by J. Gonda, *Continuity and Change* (see esp. pp. 38 ff., 315 ff.).

Ananda K. Coomaraswamy has on numerous occasions brought out the "traditional" character of Indian metaphysics (in the sense of its independence from historical conjunctions). See his *Selected Papers,* vols. 1 and 2, edited by Roger Lipsey (Princeton, 1977).

138. On presystematic Vedānta, see the respective chapters in the histories of Indian philosophy by S. N. Dasgupta and S. Radhakrishnan; H. von Glasenapp, *Die Philosophie der Inder* (Stuttgart, 1949), pp. 129 ff.; William Beidler, *The Vision of Self in Early Vedānta* (Delhi, Patna, Benares, 1975), esp. pp. 104 ff., 227 ff.

We have examined (§ 82) the paradox of the "corporeal" ("mortal") and "incorporeal" ("immortal") *brahman* in the middle Upanishads; we also mentioned the mythological antecedents of this metaphysical speculation (§ 68). A similar tendency toward the *coincidentia oppositorum* is observable in Sāṃkhya philosophy, and especially the "teleological instinct" that moves the cosmic substance (*prakṛti*) to further the deliverance of spirit (*puruṣa*); see § 140. We add that the *coincidentia oppositorum* that characterizes the *brahman* (as totality of the real or the absolute Being) is also expressed in numerous myths, especially in myths that refer to the human condition. Thus, for example, the manifestations of evil (demons, monsters, etc.) emerge from the very body of the God (first of all from his excreta); in other words, evil, exactly like good, is of divine origin: it is an integral part of the divinity. See the Brāhmaṇic and Purāṇic myths cited and commented on by W. D. O'Flaherty, *The Origins of Evil in Hindu Mythology* (Berkeley, 1976), pp. 139 ff. It should be added that this motif is documented in other mythologies: the devil, or Death, is born from the spittle or the excrement or the shadow of the Creator; see Eliade, *Zalmoxis, the Vanishing God,* trans. Willard R. Trask (Chicago, 1972), pp. 82 ff. (Bulgarian legend); p. 83 (Mordvinian legend); p. 97 (Vogul myth).

139. The bibliography for the Sāṃkhya texts and their commentaries is listed in our book *Yoga: Immortality and Freedom,* pp. 377–79. To this, add Corrado Pensa's translation, *Īśvarakṛṣṇa, Sāṃkhya-kārikā con commento di Gauḍapāda* (Turin, 1960), and Anne-Marie Esnoul's translation, *Les strophes de Sāṃkhya (Sāṃkhya-kārikā),* with the commentary by Gauḍapāda (Paris, 1964) (Sanskrit text and annotated translation).

For the critical bibliography, see *Yoga,* p. 379. To this, add J. A. B. van Buitenen, "Studies in Sāṃkhya," *JAOS* 80 (1956): 153–57; 81 (1957): 15–25, 88–107; Pulinbihari Chakravarti, *Origin and Development of the Sāṃkhya System of Thought* (Calcutta, 1952); and Gerald James Larson, *Classical Sāṃkhya: An Interpretation of Its History and Meaning* (Delhi, Varanasi, Patna, 1969). Larson's book contains a critical review of the interpretations of the Sāṃkhya philosophy from Richard Garbe to S. Radhakrishnan (pp. 7–76).

On Sāṃkhya ideas in the Upanishads, see Eliade, *Yoga,* pp. 111 ff.; E. H. Johnston, "Some Sāṃkhya and Yoga Conceptions of the Śvetāśvatara Upanishad," *JRAS* 30 (1930): 855–78; Johnston, *Early Sāṃkhya* (London, 1937); J. A. B. van Buitenen, "Studies in Sāṃkhya," esp. pp. 88 ff., 100 ff.; Larson, *Classical Sāṃkhya,* pp. 99 ff.

On the ontological structure of the *puruṣa* (the "Self"), see *Yoga,* pp. 15 ff.; Larson, *Classical Sāṃkhya,* pp. 181 ff.

As we saw, the almost magical power of "gnosis" (*vidyā, jñāna*) is tirelessly praised in the Upanishads (see vol. 1, § 80). Indeed, it is solely by virtue of (esoteric) metaphysical knowledge that the *ṛṣis* succeed in destroying "ignorance" (*avidyā*) and obtaining liberation, that is, succeed in transcending the human condition. The quasi-magical force of "gnosis" can be compared on the one hand to the powers set in motion by rituals and on the other hand to the "marvelous powers" obtained by asceticism or by Yoga practices (see §§ 76 ff.). On this particular point, Sāṃkhya carries on the Vedic and Upanishadic tradition. F. Edgerton has cogently emphasized the "magical" character of knowledge in the Upanishads; see his *The Beginnings of Indian Philosophy* (London, 1965), pp. 22 ff. See also Corrado Pensa, "Some Internal and Comparative Problems in the Field of Indian Religions," in *Problems and Methods of the History of Religions* (Leiden, 1971), pp. 114 ff.

Meditation of the Sāṃkhya type has been analyzed by Gerhard Oberhammer, *Strukturen yogischer Meditation* (Vienna, 1977), pp. 17–56.

140. On the modalities and "development" of substance (*prakṛti*), see Eliade, *Yoga,* pp. 19 ff.

In respect to the emergence of the world, it is important to point out the difference between Sāṃkhya and Yoga. Whereas for Yoga the world comes into being because of ignorance of the real structure of spirit (see *Yoga Sūtra* 2. 23–24), the Sāṃkhya authors consider that the procession (*pariṇāma*) of substance (*prakṛti*) is animated by a "teleological instinct'' for ''the benefit of the *puruṣa*'' (*Sāṃkhya Kārikā* 31, 42, etc.; cf. Eliade, *Yoga,* pp. 26 ff.). This attempt of the Sāṃkhya philosophy to go beyond the dualism *puruṣa/prakṛti* can be compared to the speculations of the Upanishads—especially the middle Upanishads (*Katha, Śvetāśvatara, Maitri*)—on the two modalities of the *brahman:* ''spiritual'' and ''material,'' ''absolute'' and ''relative,'' etc. (see § 82; see also C. Pensa, ''Some Internal and Comparative Problems,'' pp. 109 ff.).

141. See the texts cited and commented on in Eliade, *Yoga,* pp. 35 ff., 88 ff.

142. On Yoga practices, their origin and history, see Eliade, *Yoga,* pp. 47–101 (techniques of autonomy); pp. 101–43 (Yoga and Brahmanism); pp. 143–59 (Yoga and Hinduism). On Patañjali and the texts of classic Yoga, see ibid, pp. 370–73. Also see ibid., p. 373, for a list of works on Yoga published down to 1954. We mention here the most important: three works by S. N. Dasgupta, *A Study of Patañjali* (Calcutta, 1920), *Yoga as Philosophy and Religion* (London, 1924), and *Yoga Philosophy in Relation to Other Systems of Indian Thought* (Calcutta, 1930); three works by J. W. Hauer, *Die Anfänge der Yoga-Praxis* (Stuttgart, 1922), *Der Yoga als Heilweg* (Stuttgart, 1932), and *Der Yoga: Ein indischer Weg zum Selbst* (Stuttgart, 1958); Alain Daniélou, *Yoga: The Method of Reintegration* (London, 1949); Jacques Masui, *Yoga, science de l'homme intégral* (Paris, 1953) (texts and studies published under the direction of Jacques Masui); P. Masson-Oursel, *Le Yoga* (Paris, 1954); T. Brosse, *Etudes expérimentales des techniques du Yoga,* with an introductory essay by J. Filliozat, ''La nature du Yoga dans sa tradition'' (Paris, 1963); Jean Varenne, *Le Yoga et la tradition hindoue* (Paris, 1973; English trans., by Derek Coltman, *Yoga and the Hindu Tradition* [Chicago, 1976]).

The *Yoga Sūtra,* with the commentaries by Vyāsa and Vācaspatimiśra, has been translated by J. H. Woods, *The Yoga-System of Patañjali* (Cambridge, Mass., 1914). Jean Varenne has translated *Huit Upanishads du yoga* (Paris, 1971), and a translation of the *Yoga-darśana Upaniṣad* is published in his *Le Yoga et la tradition hindoue* (pp. 232–55; Eng. trans., pp. 200–222).

The *Yoga Sūtra* consists of four chapters, or books (*pādas*). The first, containing fifty-one aphorisms (*sūtras*), is the ''chapter on yogic enstasis'' (*samāddhi-pāda*); the second, containing fifty-five aphorisms, is called *sādhana-pāda* (''chapter on realization''); the third, of fifty-five *sūtras,* treats of the ''marvelous powers'' (*vibhūti*). Finally, the fourth and last chapter, the *kaivalya-pāda* (*kaivalya* = isolation), has only thirty-four *sūtras* and probably represents a late addition.

Whatever Patañjali's date may be (second century B.C. or third or even fifth century of our era), the techniques of asceticism and meditation expounded by the author of the *Yoga Sūtra* are certainly of considerable antiquity; they are neither his discoveries nor those of his time; they had been tested many centuries before him. Moreover, it is not impossible that the original text of the *Yoga Sūtra* was rehandled more than once in order to adapt it to new "philosophical situations." This basic text was meditated on and commented on by numerous authors. The first work of this kind that is known to us is the *Yoga Bhāṣya* of Vyāsa (sixth–seventh centuries), a commentary later annotated (about 850) by Vācaspatimiśra in his *Tattvavaiśāradī*. These two texts are among the most important for an understanding of the *Yoga Sūtra*. See Eliade, *Patañjali and Yoga,* trans. Charles L. Markmann (New York, 1969), pp. 9 ff.

143. On the techniques of Yoga, see Eliade, *Yoga,* pp. 47–101; *Patañjali and Yoga,* pp. 61–122; J. Varenne, *Le Yoga et la tradition hindoue,* pp. 114–50.

On the "restraints" (*yamas*) and the bodily and psychic "disciplines," see Eliade, *Yoga,* pp. 48 ff.; Varenne, *Le Yoga,* pp. 121 ff.; Corrado Pensa, "On the Purification Concept in Indian Tradition, with Special Regard to Yoga," *East and West* n.s. 19 (1969): 1–35, esp. 11 ff.

On the yogic postures (*āsanas*) and the discipline of respiration (*prāṇāyāma*), see Eliade, *Yoga,* pp. 53–69, 384; *Patañjali and Yoga,* pp. 3–5, 65; Varenne, *Le Yoga,* pp. 126–33.

On yogic "concentration" (*dhāraṇa*) and "meditation" (*dhyāna*), see Eliade, *Yoga,* pp. 69–76, 384–85; Varenne, *Le Yoga,* pp. 141 ff.; Gerhard Oberhammer, "Strukturen yogischer Meditation," *Verl. der Österr. Akad. d. Wiss., Phil.-hist. Klasse* 322 (Vienna, 1977): 71 ff., 135 ff.

144. On the role of Īśvara in classical Yoga, see Dasgupta, *Yoga as Philosophy and Religion,* pp. 85 ff.; Eliade *Yoga,* pp. 76 ff. Absent from the *Ṛg Veda,* the *Sāma Veda,* and the *Yajur Veda,* Īśvara is cited six times in the *Atharva Veda*. But it is above all in the earliest Upanishads and in the *Bhagavad Gītā* that Īśvara proves to be the goal of all who seek deliverance; see J. Gonda, *Change and Continuity in Indian Religion* (The Hague, 1965), pp. 139 ff. (Īśvara in the *Atharva*

Veda); pp. 144 ff. (Īśvara in the Upanishads and the *Bhagavad Gītā*); and pp. 158 ff. (Īśvara in philosophy and in classic Yoga).

145. On the *siddhis,* or "miraculous powers," see S. Lindquist, *Die Methoden des Yoga* (Lund, 1932), pp. 169–82; Lindquist, *Siddhi und Abhiññā: Eine Studie über die klassischen Wunder des Yoga* (Uppsala, 1935); J. W. Hauer, *Der Yoga,* pp. 326 ff.; Eliade, *Yoga,* pp. 84 ff., 384 (bibliography); A. Janàček, "The Methodical Principle in Yoga according to Patañjali's Yogasūtra," *ArOr* 19 (1951): 514–67, esp. 551 ff.; C. Pensa, "On the Purification Concept in Indian Tradition," pp. 6 ff., 16 ff.

On *samādhi,* see Eliade, *Yoga,* pp. 79 ff.; Hauer, *Der Yoga,* pp. 336 ff.; Varenne, *Le Yoga,* pp. 169 ff.; Oberhammer, *Strukturen yogischer Meditation,* pp. 135 ff.

Aside from the Yoga "with eight members," as described by Patañjali (that is, the series of exercises and meditations, of "restraints" up to *samādhi*), Indian tradition also knows the "Yoga with six members" (*ṣaḍaṅga-yoga*). In this series, the first three "members" (*yama, niyama, āsana*) are lacking, but a "member" unknown to the Patañjalian tradition appears: *tarka* (literally "reasoning," but here having the meaning "supreme knowledge"). See A. Zigmund-Cerbu, "The Ṣaḍaṅgayoga," *HR* 3 (1963): 128, 134; C. Pensa, "Osservazzioni e riferimenti per le studio dello *ṣaḍaṅga-yoga,*" *Istituto Orientale di Napoli, Annali* 19 (1969): 521–28. This yogic system "with six limbs" played an important part in late Buddhism and in Tantrism; see vol. 3. See also Günter Grönbold, *Ṣaḍaṅga-yoga* (Inaugural diss., Munich, 1969), esp. pp. 118 ff. (*Kalācakra Tantra*); pp. 122 ff. (the series of masters said to have taught the *ṣaḍaṅga-yoga*).

146. On final deliverance and the condition of a *jīvan-mukta* ("one delivered in life"), see Eliade, *Yoga,* pp. 91 ff.; cf. Roger Godel, *Essai sur l'expérience libératrice* (Paris, 1951); Varenne, *Le Yoga,* pp. 162–63. "Since they are now placed, by definition, 'beyond good and evil,' these supermen need no longer take any account of earthly values; everything is permitted to them. As one might expect, there are many yogins who, claiming (or sincerely believing) that they have attained samadhi, then take advantage of that attainment in order to 'live in heaven' on earth. And metaphysically they are quite justified in doing so, insofar as their acts are all at once without cause and without effect. Without cause, because the jivan-mukta is by definition liberated from all desire (since all his vasanas have been destroyed); without effect, because the liberated soul can no longer be affected by karman. Any act in such a situation must therefore be a gratuitous act, and this is why it is said of the jivan-mukta that he is in a state of absolute solitude (kaivalya)'' (Varenne, *Yoga,* English trans., p. 138).

Chapter 18. The Buddha and His Contemporaries

147. Of the immense number of works dealing with the biography of Śākyamuni, we mention the most important: E. J. Thomas, *The Life of the Buddha as Legend and History* (London, 1927); A. Foucher, *La Vie du Bouddha d'après les textes et les monuments de l'Inde* (Paris, 1949); H. von Glasenapp, *Buddha: Geschichte und Legende* (Zurich, 1950). The historical value of the tradition has been analyzed by Ernst Waldschmidt, ''Die Überlieferung vom Lebensende des Buddha,'' *Abhandlungen der Akademie der Wissenschaften in Göttingen, Phil.-hist. Klasse,* 3d ser. nos. 29 and 30 (1944, 1948); E. Lamotte, ''La légende du Bouddha,'' *RHR* 134 (1947): 37–71; Lamotte, *Histoire du Bouddhisme indien, des origines à l'ère Śaka* (Louvain, 1958), pp. 16 ff.; André Bareau, ''La légende de la jeunesse du Bouddha dans les Vinayapiṭaka anciens,'' *Oriens Extremus* 9 (1962): 6–33; Bareau, *Recherches sur la biographie du Bouddha dans les Sūtrapiṭaka et les Vinayapiṭaka anciens,* vol. 1: *De la Quête de l'Eveil à la conversion de Śāriputra et de Maudgalāyana* (Paris, 1963); vol. 2: *Les derniers mois, le parinirvāṇa et les funérailles* (Paris: Ecole Française de l'Extrême-Orient, 1970); Bareau, ''The Superhuman Personality of the Buddha and Its Symbolism in the Mahāparinirvāṇasūtra of the Dharmaguptaka,'' in Joseph M. Kitagawa and Charles H. Long, eds., *Myths and Symbols: Studies in Honor of Mircea Eliade* (Chicago, 1969), pp. 9–21; Bareau, ''Le Parinirvāṇa du Bouddha et la naissance de la religion bouddhique,'' *BEFEO* 64 (1974): 275–99. The most recent interpretations have been analyzed by Frank E. Reynolds, ''The Many Lives of Buddha: A Study of Sacred Biography and Theravāda Tradition,'' in Frank E. Reynolds and Donald Capps, eds., *The Biographical Process* (The Hague, 1976), pp. 37–61. After referring to the methodological positions characteristic of scholars in the second half of the nineteenth century and the beginning of the twentieth—the ''myth-oriented'' (E. Sénart, H. Kern, A. K. Coomaraswamy) and the ''historicists'' (H. Oldenberg, T. W. and Caroline A. F. Rhys-Davids)—Reynolds analyzes some recent approaches that attempt to integrate the two viewpoints: that of ''myth'' and that of ''history.''

Benjamin I. Schwartz has cogently drawn attention to the fallacious character of the sociological interpretations of the rise of Buddhism and, in general, of soteriological movements: "If Buddhism did indeed arise within an urban commercial environment, as Prof. Thapar suggests, it hardly strikes us as a particularly 'bourgeois' philosophy. While she stresses the political and social doctrine of early Buddhism, one has the feeling that the heart of Buddhism does not lie there" ("The Age of Transcendence" in "Wisdom, Revelation and Doubt: Perspectives on the First Millennium B.C.," *Daedalus,* Spring, 1975, p. 4).

On the symbolism of the "Great Man" (*mahāpuruṣa*), see A. K. Coomaraswamy, "The Buddha's *cūḍā,* Hair, and *uṣṇīṣa,* Crown," *JRAS* 26 (1928): 815–40; Stella Kramrisch, "Emblems of the Universal Being," *Journal of the Indian Society for Oriental Art* 3 (Calcutta, 1935): 148–60; A. Wayman, "Contributions Regarding the Thirty-Two Characteristics of the Great Person," in the Liebenthal Festschrift, ed. K. Roy, *Sino-Indian Studies* 5 (Santiniketan, 1957): 243–60.

The theme of the "Seven Steps" recurs in the Nativity of Mary; see the Proto-Gospel of James, chap. 6, and the commentary by Henri de Lubac, *Aspects du Bouddhisme* (Paris, 1951), pp. 126–27.

The *boddhisattva*'s presentation in the temple has been compared to an episode in Pseudo-Matthew 23: "When Blessed Mary entered the [Egyptian] temple with the child, all the idols were flung to the ground." But the two stories prove to be unlike: the Egyptian idols are thrown down forever, for Christ abolishes the worship of false gods, but the Brāhmaṇic divinities prostrate themselves in homage to the future Savior; see Foucher, *La vie du Bouddha,* pp. 55 ff.

The episode of the *ṛṣi* Asita is related at length in *Lalita Vistara,* pp. 101 ff.; see the translation of the passage in Foucher, *La vie du Bouddha,* pp. 61–63. Foucher also gives the relevant iconography. Asita's prediction has been compared with the episode of the old Simeon taking the child Jesus in his arms and blessing God ("for mine eyes have seen the salvation which thou has prepared," Luke 2:8–20, 25–35); see Foucher's commentary, pp. 63–64. See also J. Brinktrine, "Die buddhistische Asita-Erzählung als sog. Parallele zum Darstellung Jesu im Tempel," *Zeitschrift für Missionswissenschaft und Religionswissenschaft* 38 (1954): 132–34; F. G. W. de Jong, "L'épisode d'Asita dans le Lalitavistara," *Asiatica: Festschrift E. Weller* (Leipzig, 1954), pp. 312–25; C. Regamey, "Encore à propos du Lalitavistara et de l'episode d'Asita," *Asiatische Studien* 27 (1973): 1–34.

148. On the quest for illumination, see A. Foucher, *La vie du Bouddha,* pp. 112 ff.

On the materialists (*Lokāyatas*), see the bibliography given in Eliade, *Yoga,* pp. 375–76. Add: Debiprasad Chattopadhyaya, *Lokāyata: A*

Study in Ancient Indian Materialism (New Delhi, 1959). On the temptation by Māra, see E. Windisch, *Māra und Buddha* (Leipzig, 1895), which includes translations of a large number of stories (pp. 87 ff.) and, on pp. 214 ff., a comparative analysis of the temptation of Jesus (Luke 4:1–13). The Buddhist sources on Māra are cited and commented on by J. Masson, *La religion populaire dans le Canon bouddhique pāli* (Louvain, 1942), pp. 103–13, and by E. Lamotte, *L'Enseignement de Vimalakīrti* (Louvain, 1962), pp. 204–5, n. 121. See also J. Przyluski, "La place de Māra dans la mythologie bouddhique," *JA* 210 (1927): 115–23; A. Wayman, "Studies in Yama and Māra," *IIJ* 3 (1959): 44–73, 112–31; T. O. Ling, *Buddhism and the Mythology of Evil* (London, 1962); J. W. Boyd, *Satan and Māra: Christian and Buddhist Symbols of Evil* (Leiden, 1975). G. Fussmann has recently shown that, in certain regions, Māra was an ancient supreme god; see his "Pour une problématique nouvelle des religions indiennes anciennes," *JA* 265 (1977): 21–70, esp. pp. 52 ff.

149. The sources for the illumination are listed by Foucher, *La vie du Bouddha,* pp. 363–64. For the comparative symbolism of the tree of the Awakening, see H. de Lubac, *Aspects du Bouddhisme,* pp. 55 ff. On the "divine eye" (*divya-cakṣu*), see the references to the texts of the Pali canon and to the later literature in E. Lamotte, *L'Enseignement de Vimalakīrti,* pp. 168–69, n. 57. The Pali and Sanskrit sources for the sermon at Benares are given by Lamotte, *Histoire,* vol. 1, p. 28, n. 1. On the rope trick used by the Buddha, see Eliade, *The Two and the One,* trans. J. M. Cohen (Chicago, 1979), pp. 166 ff. On the "marvelous powers," (*siddhis*) and their prohibition by the Buddha, see Eliade, *Yoga,* pp. 175 ff., and below, §159.

On the *arhats,* see A. Bareau, "Les controverses relatifs à la nature de l'Arhat dans le Bouddhisme ancien," *IIJ* 1 (1957): 241–50.

On the symbolism of the *cakravartin* ("universal sovereign"), see J. Auboyer, "The Symbolism of Sovereignty in India according to Iconography," *Indian Art and Letters* 12 (1938): 26–36; K. V. Soundara Rajan, "The Chakravarti Concept and the Chakra (Wheel)," *Journal of Oriental Research* (Madras) 27 (1962): 85–90. See also A. J. Prince, "The Concepts of Buddhahood in Earlier and Later Buddhism," *Journal of the Oriental Society of Australia* 7 (1970): 87–118.

On the earliest conversions, see A. Foucher, *La vie du Bouddha,* pp. 211–40, 368–71. The history of the first Buddhist community (*saṃgha*) is narrated in the *Mahāvagga* (translated by T. W. Rhys-Davids and Hermann Oldenberg in *Vinaya Texts,* vol. 1 [Oxford, 1881]).

150. The successive stages of the legend of the Buddha are analyzed by Lamotte, *Histoire,* pp. 718–56. See also the studies by E. Waldschmidt cited above, §147, and E. Burnouf, *Introduction à l'histoire du bouddhisme indien* (Paris, 1844). On the schism of Devadatta, see A. M. Hocart, "Buddha and Devadatta," *Indian Antiquary* 52 (1923): 267–72; 54 (1925): 98–99; E. Waldschmidt, "Reste von Devadatta-Episoden," *ZDMG* 123 (1964): 552 ff.; B. Mukherjee, *Die Überlieferung von Devadatta, der Widersacher des Buddha, in den kanonischen Schriften* (Munich, 1966); E. Lamotte, "Le Bouddha insulta-t-il Devadatta?" *BSOAS* 33 (1970): 107–15.

On the Buddha's last meal, see A. Bareau, "La nourriture offerte au Bouddha lors de son dernier repas," in *Mélanges de l'Indianisme . . . Louis Renou* (Paris, 1968), pp. 61–71; cf. Bareau, "La transformation miraculeuse de la nourriture offerte au Bouddha par le Brahmane Kasibhāradvāja," in *Etudes tibétaines dédiées à Marcelle Lalou* (Paris, 1971), pp. 1–10.

On the Buddha's funeral, see C. Vaudeville, "La légende de Sundara et les funérailles du Bouddha dans l'Avadānaśataka," *BEFEO* 53 (1964): 71–91.

On the Buddha's relics, see, J. Przyluski, "Le partage des reliques du Bouddha," *Mélanges Chinois et Bouddhiques* 4 (1935–36): 341–67; B. C. Law, "An Account of the Six Hair Relics of the Buddha (Chakesadhātuvaṃsa)," *Journal of Indian History* 30 (1952): 193–204; E. Waldschmidt, "Der Buddha preist die Verehrungswürdigkeit seines Reliquien," republished in the volume *Von Ceylon bis Turfan* (Göttingen, 1967), pp. 417–27.

151. On the ascetics and religious sectarians contemporary with the Buddha, see the bibliography given in Eliade, *Yoga,* p. 399. Add: J. Filliozat, *L'Inde classique,* vol. 2, pp. 511–16; E. Lamotte, *Histoire,* vol. 1, pp. 6 ff.

152–53. The most important translations of the Jain texts are: H. Jacobi, *Jaina Sūtras, SBE,* vols. 22, 45 (Oxford, 1887); W. Schubring, *Worte Mahāvīras,* vol. 14 of *Quellen zur Religionsgeschichte* (Göttingen, 1926); and Schubring, *Die Jainas,* fasc. 7 of *Religionsgeschichtliche Lesebuch* (Tübingen, 1927).

For bibliography and generalities, see C. L. Jain, *Jaina Bibliography* (Calcutta, 1945); L. Alsdorf, *Les études jaïna: Etat présent et tâches futures* (Paris, 1965); Jozef Deleu, "Die Mythologie des Jainismus," in *Wörterbuch der Mythologie,* vol. 2, pp. 207–84 (see ibid., pp. 212–13, for the Jain Canon). General studies: H. von Glasenapp, *Der Jainismus*

(Berlin, 1925); A. Guérinot, *La religion djaina* (Paris, 1926); E. Leumann, *Buddha und Mahāvīra* (Munich, 1926); W. Schubring, *Die Lehre der Jainas nach den alten Quellen dargestellt* (= *Grundriss der indoarischen Philologie und Altertumskunde,* vol. 3, pt. 7 [Berlin, 1935]); C. della Casa, *Il Gianismo* (Turin, 1962); C. Caillat, *Les expiations dans le rituel ancien des religieux jaina* (Paris, 1965); Caillat, "Le Jainisme," in H.-C. Puech, ed., *Histoire des religions,* vol. 1 (1970), pp. 1105–45); see also the bibliographies for §190.

It is above all the mythology of the twofold "nativity" of Mahāvīra that inspired Jain art and iconography; see W. N. Brown, *Miniature Paintings of the Jaina Kalpasūtra* (Washington, D.C.: Smithsonian Institution, 1934); T. N. Ramachandran, *Tiruparuttikuṇṛam and Its Temples* (Madras: Government Press, 1934); Ananda K. Coomaraswamy, "The Conqueror's Life in Jaina Painting," *Journal of the Indian Society of Oriental Art* 3 (Calcutta, 1935): 1–18.

On the light that illuminates the night of Mahāvīra's birth, see *Akārāṇga Sūtra* 2. 15. 7 (= *Gaina Sūtras,* pt. 1, trans. H. Jacobi, *SBE,* vol. 22 [Oxford, 1884], p. 191).

On the mythology and iconography of Parśva and the Tīrthaṃkaras, see Heinrich Zimmer, *Philosophies of India,* Bollingen Series 26 (Princeton, 1969), pp. 181–234; Jozef Deleu, "Die Mythologie des Jainismus," pp. 252–53, 270–73.

154. On Makkhali Gośāla and the Ājīvikas, see the bibliography given in Eliade, *Yoga,* p. 400. The most complete source for Gośāla is the Jain treatise *Bhagavatī.* The best monograph, which also uses Tamil sources, is the one by A. L. Basham, *History and Doctrines of the Ājīvikas: A Vanished Indian Religion* (London, 1951). The word *ājīvika* has been explained by the root *ājīva* ("way of life or profession of a class of beings"), but it could also derive from the expression *ā jīvāt,* "as long as life," a reference to the fundamental doctrine that postulated a large number of existences before obtaining deliverance.

Chapter 19. The Message of the Buddha

155. A large number of Pali texts are accessible in English translation. Among the most important are: *Dialogues of the Buddha* (*Dīgha Nikāya*), translated by T. W. and C. A. Rhys-Davids, 3 vols. (*Sacred Books of the Buddhists,* vols. 2–4) (Oxford, 1899–1921); *Further Dialogues of the Buddha* (*Majjhima Nikāya*), trans. by Lord Chalmers, 2 vols. (*Sacred Books of the Buddhists,* vols. 5–6) (Oxford, 1926–27);

The Book of Kindred Sayings (Saṃyutta Nikāya), trans. by C. A. F. Rhys-Davids and F. L. Woodward (Pali Text Society, Translation Series, nos. 7, 10, 13–14, 16) (London, 1917–30); *The Book of Gradual Sayings (Aṅguttara Nikāya)*, trans. by F. L. Woodward and E. M. Hare (P.T.S. Translation Series, nos. 22, 24–27) (London, 1932–36); *Minor Anthologies,* vol. 1: *Dhammapāda, Khuddakapāṭha,* trans. by T. W. Rhys-Davids (*Sacred Books of the Buddhists,* no. 7) (Oxford, 1931); *Minor Anthologies,* vol. 2: *Udāna, "Verses of Uplift," and Itivuttaka, "As It Was Said,"* trans. by F. L. Woodward (*Sacred Books of the Buddhists,* no. 8) (Oxford, 1935).

Among the most useful anthologies, we mention: H. C. Warren, *Buddhism in Translation* (Cambridge, Mass., 1896; republished several times); Edward Conze, *Buddhist Texts through the Ages* (Oxford, 1954; New York: Harper Torchbooks, 1964); E. Conze, *Buddhist Scriptures* (Harmondsworth, 1959); E. J. Thomas, *Early Buddhist Scriptures* (London, 1935); Lilian Silburn, *Le Bouddhisme* (Paris, 1977).

A bibliography of translations has been provided by André Bareau, "Le bouddhisme indien," in *Les Religions de l'Inde,* vol. 3 (Paris, 1966), pp. 240–43. See also ibid., pp. 227–34, "Histoire de l'étude du bouddhisme indien."

156. There is a quite extensive literature on the fundamental principles of the doctrine of the Buddha. The best overall treatments are by E. Conze, *Buddhism: Its Essence and Development* (Oxford, 1951; New York: Harper Torchbooks, 1959), pp. 11–69; Walpola Rahula, *L'Enseignement du Bouddha d'après les textes les plus anciens* (Paris, 1961); A. Bareau, "Le bouddhisme indien," pp. 13–82. See also M. Walleser, *Die philosophische Grundlage des älteren Buddhismus* (Heidelberg, 1904); Hermann Oldenberg, *Buddha: Sein Leben, seine Lehre und seine Gemeinde* (Berlin, 1881; 9th ed., 1921); Oldenberg, *Die Lehre der Upanishaden und die Anfänge des Buddhismus* (Göttingen, 1915); E. Lamotte and J. Przyluski, "Bouddhisme et Upaniṣad," *BEFEO* 32 (1932): 141–69; A. K. Warder, "On the Relationship between Early Buddhism and Other Contemporary Systems," *BSOAS* 18 (1965): 43–63.

157. On the formula of the twelve causes, see Surendranath Dasgupta, *A History of Indian Philosophy,* vol. 1 (Cambridge, 1922), pp. 84 ff.; A. Bareau, "Le bouddhisme indien," pp. 40 ff.; W. Rahula, *L'Enseignement du Bouddha,* pp. 79 ff.; B. C. Law, "The Formulation of the Pratītyasamutpāda," *JRAS* 104 (1937): 287–92; A. C. Banerjee, "Pratītyasamutpāda," *Indian Historical Quarterly* 32 (Calcutta, 1956):

261–64; Thera Narada, "Kamma, or the Buddhist Law of Causation," in D. R. Bhandarkar et al., eds., *B. C. Law Volume,* pt. 2 (Poona, 1946), pp. 158–75. See also L. de la Vallée-Poussin, *Bouddhisme: Etudes et matériaux: Théorie des Douze Causes* (Ghent, 1931).

On the doctrine of *anatta,* see L. de la Vallée-Poussin, *Nirvāṇa* (Paris, 1925); E. Conze, *Le Bouddhisme,* pp. 16 ff.; Conze, *Buddhist Thought in India* (London, 1962), pp. 34 ff.; W. Rahula, *L'Enseignement,* pp. 77 ff. See also Maryla Falk, "Nairātmya and Karman," in *Louis de la Vallée-Poussin Memorial Volume* (Calcutta, 1940), pp. 429–64.

On the problems raised by the earliest Buddhism, see Frank Reynolds, "The Two Wheels of Dhamma: A Study of Early Buddhism," in Bardwell L. Smith, ed., *The Two Wheels of Dhamma* (Chambersburg, Pa., 1972), pp. 6–30; see also Reynolds' "A Bibliographical Essay on Works Related to Early Theravāda and Sinhalese Buddhism," ibid., pp. 107–21.

158. An excellent history of Western interpretations of *nirvāṇa* has been provided by Guy Richard Welbon in *The Buddhist Nirvāṇa and Its Western Interpreters* (Chicago and London, 1968); see especially the chapters on Hermann Oldenberg (pp. 194–220), T. W. and C. A. F. Rhys-Davids (pp. 221–48), and the controversy between L. de la Vallée-Poussin and T. Stcherbatsky (pp. 248–96). For la Vallée-Poussin's first interpretation, see his *The Way to Nirvāṇa: Six Lectures on Ancient Buddhism as a Discipline of Salvation* (Cambridge, 1917), *Nirvāṇa* (Paris, 1925), and his article "Nirvāṇa" in *Indian Historical Quarterly* 4 (1928): 347–48. For Stcherbatsky's views, see his *The Central Conception of Buddhism and the Meaning of the Word "Dharma"* (London, 1923) and *The Conception of Buddhist Nirvāṇa* (Leningrad, 1927). However, after a long controversy, each of these two scholars became convinced by the interpretation of his antagonist; see T. Stcherbatsky, "Die drei Richtungen in der Philosophie des Buddhismus," *Rocznik Orjentalistyczny* 10 (1934): 1–37; L. de la Vallée-Poussin, "Buddhica," *HJAS* 3 (1938): 137–60.

Friedrich Heiler has examined the concept of *nirvāṇa* in terms of religious experience; see his *Die buddhistische Versenkung* (Munich, 1918).

On the "road to *nirvāṇa*" and the symbolism of initiation, see Eliade, *Yoga: Immortality and Freedom,* trans. Willard R. Trask, Bollingen Series 56 (Princeton, 1970), pp. 155 ff. On the relations between Yoga and Buddhism, see L. de la Vallée-Poussin, "Le bouddhisme et le Yoga de Patañjali," *Mémoires Chinois et Bouddhiques* 5 (Brussels, 1937): 223–42; Eliade, *Yoga,* pp. 162 ff. See ibid., pp. 395–96, for bibliographical indications; add: Gerhard Oberhammer, *Strukturen yogischer Meditation* (Vienna, 1977), pp. 102 ff.

159. On the Buddhist techniques of meditation, see Eliade, *Yoga,* pp. 162 ff., and the bibliographies given there (pp. 396 ff.); Grace Constant Lounsberry, *Buddhist Meditation in the Southern School* (London, 1950); E. Conze, *Buddhist Meditation* (London, 1956).

On the jhāyins and the dhammayogas, see L. de la Vallée-Poussin, "Musīla et Nārada," *Mémoires Chinois et Bouddhiques* 5 (1937): 189–222. On the "superknowledges" (*abhijñās*), see L. de la Vallée-Poussin, "Le Bouddha et les Abhijñās," *Le Muséon* 44 (1931): 335–42; Eliade, *Yoga,* pp. 177 ff., 398–99 (bibliography on the "miraculous powers").

160. On the *arhats,* see Eliade, *Yoga,* pp. 170 ff.; E. Conze, *Le Bouddhisme,* pp. 91 ff.; A. Bareau, "Le bouddhisme indien," pp. 60 ff., 123 ff. See also Isaline Horner, *The Early Buddhist Theory of Man Perfected: A Study of the Arhat* (London, 1936).

On the mystical structure of *asaṃskṛta,* see André Bareau, *L'Absolu en philosophie bouddhique: Evolution de la notion d'asaṃskṛta* (Thesis for the doctorat ès lettres, Paris, 1951).

On the images of the annihilation of the conditioned world ("the destruction of the house" by the Buddha, the Buddhist symbolism of "breaking out of the cosmic egg," and "the roof broken" by the *arhats*), see Eliade, *Images and Symbols: Studies in Religious Symbolism,* trans. Philip Mairet (New York, 1961), pp. 73–79, and "Briser le toit de la maison: Symbolisme architectonique et physiologie subtile," in *Studies in Mysticism and Religion, Presented to Gershom G. Scholem* (Jerusalem, 1967), pp. 131–39.

Chapter 20. Roman Religion

161. The immense literature on primitive Italy and the origins of Rome has been listed by Jacques Heurgon in his *Rome et la Méditerranée occidentale jusqu'aux guerres puniques* (1969), pp. 7–50. The work by Pietro de Francisci, *Primordia civitatis* (Rome, 1959), contains several chapters on the social structures and religious ideas of archaic Rome (pp. 197–405); useful for their documentation, these pages must, however, be read with caution (see the critique by G. Dumézil, *Revue Belge de philologie et d'histoire* 39 [1961]: 67 ff., and the observations by

Pierangelo Catalano, *Contributi allo studio del diritto augurale,* vol. 1 [Turin, 1960], pp. 402 ff., 542 ff.).

A first wave of Āryan-speaking peoples, acquainted with the metallurgy of copper and practicing cremation, settles in northern Italy in the second millennium; they are the authors of the so-called terramare civilization ("from *terra mar*[*n*]*a,* 'fat earth,' because of its wealth of organic matter, where the peasants traditionally came to get their fertilizers" [Heurgon, *Rome et la Méditerranée occidentale,* p. 64]). A second wave, toward the end of the second millennium, is that of the Villanovans: they use iron and put the ashes of the dead in large terracotta urns, buried at the bottom of a pit. At the beginning of the first millennium Latium was dominated by a civilization of the Villanovan type.

Deserving of mention among general histories are: A. Piganiol, *Histoire de Rome,* 5th ed. (Paris, 1962); G. de Sanctis, *Storia dei Romani,* vols. 1 and 2, *La conquista del primato in Italia,* 2d ed. (Florence, 1956–60); L. Pareti, *Storia di Roma,* vol. 1 (Turin, 1951); Robert E. A. Palmer, *The Archaic Community of the Romans* (Cambridge, 1970) (but this author criticizes Dumézil [see, e.g., p. 154] without having read him).

Since the work by G. Wissowa, *Religion und Kultus der Römer,* 2d ed. (Munich, 1912), which remains fundamental, several general accounts of the religion of royal and republican times have been published; see especially Cyril Bailey, *Phases in the Religion of Ancient Rome* (1932); Nicola Turchi, *La Religione di Roma antica* (1939); A. Grenier, *Les religions étrusque et romaine* (1948); Franz Altheim, *A History of Roman Religion,* trans. Harold Mattingly (London, 1938) (originally published as *Römische Religionsgeschichte* [Baden-Baden, 1931]); Jean Bayet, *Histoire psychologique et politique de la religion romaine* (1957; 2d ed., 1973); Kurt Latte, *Römische Religionsgeschichte* (1960) (but see the critique by A. Brelich, *SMSR* 32 [1961]: 311–54, and the numerous remarks by G. Dumézil in his book, next cited); Georges Dumézil, *La religion romaine archaïque* (1966; 2d ed., 1974; English translation, by Philip Krapp, *Archaic Roman Religion,* 2 vols., Chicago, 1970); Pierre Boyancé, *Etudes sur la religion romaine* (Rome, 1972).

A selection of Latin texts in translation will be found in *Religionsgeschichtliches Lesebuch,* fasc. 5 of K. Latte, *Die Religion der Römer und der Synkretismus der Kaiserzeit* (Tübingen, 1927), and in Frederick C. Grant, *Ancient Roman Religion* (New York, 1957). J. G. Frazer's translation, with commentary, *The Fasti of Ovid* (London, 1919), constitutes an unequaled mine of information.

On Italic, Paleo-Venetian, and Messapic religion and that of ancient Sicily, see the general treatment by Aldo Luigi Prosdocimi, "Le religioni dell'Italia antica," in *Storia delle religioni,* founded by P. Tacchi Venturi, edited by Giuseppe Castellani, 6th ed., vol. 2 (Turin, 1971), pp. 673–724 (good bibliography). See also F. Altheim, *A History of Roman Religion,* pp. 18–33.

On the Iguvine Tables found at Gubbio in Umbria, whose text describes in detail the rituals performed each year by a sacerdotal college (purification of the city and lustration of the people), see J. W. Poultney, *The Bronze Tables of Iguvium* (Baltimore, 1959) (edition of the text, with commentary); G. Devoto, *Tabulae Iguvinae,* 3d ed. (Rome, 1962) (text and commentary); G. Dumézil, "Les trois grands dieux d'Iguvium," in *Idées romaines* (1969), pp. 167–78 (an article first published in 1955); A. J. Pfiffig, *Religio Iguvina: Philologische und religionsgeschichtliche Studien zu den Tabulae Iguvinae* (Vienna, 1964).

On the mythology of Romulus and Remus, see Michael Grant, *Roman Myths* (London and New York, 1971), pp. 91 ff.; Jaan Puhvel, "Remus et Frater," *HR* 16 (1975): 146–57; and Bruce Lincoln, "The Indo-European Myth of Creation," *HR* 16 (1975): 137 ff.

In addition to the most popular version—his being carried away during a storm—another tradition reports that, because he became a tyrant, Romulus was killed by the senators; the tyrannicides then dismembered his body and carried away the pieces under their robes; see Dionysius of Halicarnassus, *Rom. arch.* 2. 56; Plutarch, *Romulus* 27; Ovid, *Fasti* 2. 497, etc. Puhvel compares this version with the dismemberment of Puruṣa, Ymir, and Gayōmart; in the Roman myth the episode was transferred from Remus to his twin brother, "because a man can be killed only once" ("Remus et Frater," p. 155).

On the cosmogonic meaning of the founding of cities, see Eliade, *The Myth of the Eternal Return: Cosmos and History,* trans. Willard R. Trask, Bollingen Series 46 (Princeton, 1965), pp. 18 ff.; Werner Müller, *Die heilige Stadt* (Stuttgart, 1961), esp. pp. 9–51 (Roma quadrata). On the symbolism of the augural sign (the twelve vultures seen by Romulus), see Jean Hubaux, *Les grands mythes de Rome* (1949), pp. 1–26; Eliade, *Myth of the Eternal Return,* pp. 133 ff.; Dumézil, *La rel. rom. arch.,* pp. 499–500 (English trans., pp. 502–4).

162. On the Indo-European heritage, see G. Dumézil, *L'héritage indo-européen à Rome* (1949) and, above all, *Mythe et épopée* (1968), vol. 1, pp. 259–437, which analyzes the traditions of the first four kings; see also Dumézil, *Les dieux souverains des Indo-Européens* (1977), pp. 158 ff. On the mythological model for the Sabine War, see

L'héritage, pp. 127 ff.; *Mythe et épopée,* vol. 1, pp. 290 ff.; *La rel. rom. arch.,* pp. 82 ff. On the Indo-European mythological motifs camouflaged in the "history" of Horatius and the Curiatii and in that of Cocles and Scaevola, see Dumézil, *Horace et les Curiaces* (1942) and *La rel. rom. arch.,* p. 90 (where the author's earlier works are listed). The two maimed men, Cocles and Scaevola ("Cyclops" and "Lefty") successively save Rome, beseiged by Lars Porsena, "the one paralyzing the Etruscan army by the dazzling glance of his eye, the other sacrificing his right hand before the Etruscan leader in an heroic act of perjury." This legend has its parallel in the Scandinavian pair of the one-eyed god and the one-armed god, Óðinn and Týr, of whom "the former, because he has sacrificed an eye, receives supernatural wisdom as compensation, while the other saves the gods by thrusting his right hand into the jaws of the demon-wolf" (Dumézil, *La rel. rom. arch.,* p. 90; English trans., pp. 75–76).

See Dumézil's discussion of H. J. Rose's theses (especially those set forth in "Numen and Mana," *HTR* 29 [1951]: 109–30) and those of H. Wagenwoort (*Roman Dynamism,* 1950), in *La rel. rom. arch.,* pp. 36 ff. (with the earlier bibliography). Dumézil has brilliantly analyzed a certain number of Roman religious concepts: *ius, credo* and *fides, augur, maiestas* and *gravitas,* in a series of studies republished in *Idées romaines* (1969), pp. 31–152. See also P. Grimal, " 'Fides' et le secret," *RHR* 185 (1974): 141–55.

163. On the particular character of the religious experience of the Romans, see Pierre Grimal, *La civilisation romaine* (1960), pp. 85 ff.; see also Dario Sabbatucci, "Sacer," *SMSR* 23 (1951–52): 91–101; H. Fugier, *Recherches sur l'expression du sacré dans la langue latine* (1963); R. Schilling, "Magie et religion à Rome," *Annuaire de l'Ecole Pratique des Hautes Etudes,* sec. 5 (1967–68), pp. 31–55.

On the religious function of prodigies, see J. Bayet, "Présages figuratifs déterminants dans l'antiquité gréco-latine," in *Hommages à F. Cumont* (Brussels, 1936), vol. 1, pp. 27–51, reprinted in Bayet, *Croyances et rites dans la Rome antique* (1971), pp. 44–63; R. Bloch, *Les prodiges dans l'antiquité classique* (1963); G. Dumézil, *La rel. rom. arch.,* pp. 584 ff. (see p. 590, n. 1, for bibliography). Livy (21. 62) reports the prodigies that occurred during the winter of ca. 218, one of the most dramatic of the Punic War. In the Forum boarium an ox had climbed by himself to the third story, from which he later threw himself down. Images of ships had burned in the sky. The temple of Spes had been struck by lightning. Juno's lance had moved of itself. In the country human phantoms clad in white had been seen far off.

Stones had rained in the Picenum, etc. Consulted, the Sibylline Books decreed nine days of sacrifices. The whole city was busy with the expiation of the portents: first, there were lustrations, followed by sacrifices; then an offering of gold weighing forty pounds was carried to the temple of Juno, and a bronze statue of the goddess was consecrated on the Aventine, etc. See E. de Saint-Denis, "Les énumérations de prodiges dans l'œuvre de Tite-Live," *Revue de philologie* 16 (1942): 126–42.

A list handed down by Varro enumerates the divine entities who governed the various moments of agricultural activity: Vernactor (for turning over fallow ground), Imporcitor (for plowing deep furrows), Institor (for sowing), Oburator (for surface digging), Occator (for harrowing), Sarritor (for weeding), Subruncinator (for second dressing), Messor (for harvest), Connector (for carting), Conditor (for storing), Promitor (for taking out of storage). The list comes from the *Libri iuris pontificii* by Fabius Pictor, cited by Varro in a text preserved by Servius (ad Vergil, *Georg*. 1. 21); see J. Bayet, "Les feriae sementinae," *RHR* 137 (1950): 172–206, republished in *Croyances et rites dans la Rome antique,* p. 184; see also Dumézil's remarks, *La rel. rom. arch.,* pp. 51 ff.

164. On the private cult, see A. de Marchi, *Il culto privato di Roma antica,* 2 vols. (1896–1903); Dumézil, *La rel. rom. arch.,* pp. 600–610. See also Gordon Williams, "Some Aspects of Roman Marriage Ceremonies and Ideals," *Journal of Roman Studies* 48 (1958): 16–29; G. Piccaluga, "Penates e Lares," *SMSR* 32 (1961): 81–87; J. M. C. Toynbee, *Death and Burial in the Roman World* (1971). On the Manes, see F. Bömer, *Ahnenkult und Ahnenglaube im alten Rom* (*ARW* Beiheft no. 1, 1943), and the bibliography given by Latte, *Römische Religionsgeschichte,* p. 100, n. 2.

The *lemures* that visit houses during the Lemuria festival in May are not identical with the *larvae,* which come to torment the living at any time of year; see Dumézil, *La rel. rom. arch.,* p. 373.

The dead also return on August 24, October 5, and November 8, when the *mundus*—the trench that gives access to the underground world—is opened. "When the *mundus* is open, it is as if the door of the grim infernal deities were open" (Varro, cited by Macrobius, *Saturnalia* 1. 16. 18). But the term *mundus* also designated the trench into which Romulus had thrown the "first-fruits of all things the use of which was sanctioned by custom as good and by nature as necessary," together with a small portion of the soil of each of his companions' native lands (Plutarch, *Romulus* 11. 1–4; Ovid, *Fasti* 4. 821–24). See Stefan Weinstock, "Mundus patet,'' *Rheinisches Museum* 45 (1930): 111–23; Henri Le Bonniec, *Le culte de Cérès à Rome* (1958), pp. 175–84; W. Müller, *Die heilige Stadt,* pp. 24–27, 33; Dumézil, *La rel. rom. arch.,* pp. 356–58 (Eng. trans. pp. 351–53).

The formula of *devotio* (Livy, 8. 9–10) is reproduced and commented on by Dumézil, *La rel. rom. arch.,* pp. 108 ff.

165. At Rome, as in every traditional society, the festivals sacralized time; this explains the importance of the calendar. On the Roman calendar, see A. Grenier, *Rel. étrusque et romaine,* pp. 94 ff.; J. Bayet, *Histoire psychologique,* pp. 89 ff. and 298 (bibliography); G. Dumézil, *Fêtes romaines d'été et d'automne* (1975).

On the seasonal festivals and their patron gods, see L. Delatte, *Recherches sur quelques fêtes mobiles du calendrier romain* (Liège, 1957); Dumézil, *La rel. rom. arch.,* pp. 339 ff. See also Giulia Piccaluga, *Elementi spettacolari nei rituali festivi romani* (Rome, 1965). On sacred places—the *pomerium* (the place of the walls) and the *templum* (the place consecrated by the *inauguratio*)—see Pierangelo Catalano, *Contributi allo studio del diritto augurale,* vol. 1, pp. 292 ff. (*pomerium;* see n. 177 for bibliography); pp. 248 ff., 205 ff. (*templum*).

On the priesthoods, see J. Marquart and T. Mommsen, *Handbuch der römische Altertümer,* 2d ed. (7 vols., 1876–86), vol. 3, pp. 234–415; Wissowa, *Religion und Cultus der Römer,* pp. 479–549; K. Latte, *Römische Religionsgeschichte,* pp. 195–212, 397–411; Dumézil, *La rel. rom. arch.,* pp. 567–83. On the *rex* and his relations with the major flamens, see Dumézil, ''Le *rex* et les *flamines maiores,*'' in *The Sacred Kingship* (Leiden, 1959), pp. 407–17. See also Dumézil, ''La préhistoire des flamines majeurs,'' *RHR* 118 (1938): 188–200 (reprinted in *Idées romaines,* pp. 156–66).

On the pontifical college and the *pontifex maximus,* see G. Rohde, *Die Kultsatzungen der römischen Pontifices,* Religionsgeschichtliche Versuche und Vorarbeiten, no. 25 (Giessen, 1936); J. Bleicken, ''Oberpontifex und Pontifikal-Collegium,'' *Hermes* 85 (1957): 345–66.

On the Vestals, see T. C. Worsfold, *The History of the Vestal Virgins of Rome,* 2d ed. (1934); G. Giannelli, *Il Sacerdozio delle Vestali romane* (Florence, 1933); F. Guizzi, *Aspetti juridici del sacerdozio Romano; il sacerdozio di Vesta* (1968).

On the augurs and the augural college, see A. Bouché-Leclercq, *Histoire de la divination dans l'antiquité,* vol. 4 (1882), pp. 160 ff.; Pierangelo Catalano, *Contributi allo studio dello diritto augurale,* vol. 1 (pp. 9–20, for critical discussion of the theories concerning the differences between *augurium* and *auspicium,* ranging from those of

Mommsen to I. M. J. Valeton and U. Coli; pp. 395–558, on the *rex* and augural law; pp. 559–74, on the Latin and Sabine *reges augures* and the Etruscan kings). See also Dumézil, *La rel. rom. arch.,* pp. 584–89.

The origin and history of the Sibylline Books are obscure. According to legend, they were acquired by Tarquin, who deposited them in the temple of Jupiter and appointed a commission of two members with the duty of consulting them—but only when ordered to do so and only for the sake of the state. In ca. 367 the permanent college of the *decemviri,* five patricians and five plebeians, was created. Whatever their origin may have been, the Books were already Hellenized when the Second Punic War increased their consultation. In ca. 213 the *carmina Marciana* were added to them. "Burned in Sulla's time along with the Capitol, reconstructed or forged anew by commissions sent to every place in the world where there were Sibyls, and particularly to Erythrae, expurgated under Augustus and transferred from Jupiter to Apollo, from the Capitol to the Palatine, revised once more under Tiberius, they were burned at the beginning of the fifth century of the Christian era by Stilicho. The college, which had been honored by the emperors, then disappeared" (Dumézil, *La rel. rom. arch.,* p. 594; English trans., p. 605). On the origin of the Sibylline Books, see also J. Gagé, *Apollon romain* (Paris, 1955), pp. 26–38, 196–204; cf. R. Bloch, "Les origines étrusques des Livres Sibyllins," *Mélanges A. Ernout* (1940), pp. 21–28.

On the sodalities, see Wissowa, *Religion und Cultus,* 550–64; Dumézil, *La rel. rom. arch.,* pp. 579 ff. On the *fetiales,* see Jean Bayet, "Le rite du fécial et le cornouailler magique" (1935; republished in *Croyances et rites dans la Rome antique* [1971], pp. 9–44). On the *ius fetiale,* see Dumézil, *Idées romaines,* pp. 63–78. On the Salii, see R. Cirilli, *Les prêtres-danseurs de Rome: Etudes sur la corporation sacerdotale des Saliens* (1913); Dumézil, *La rel. rom. arch.,* pp. 285–87, 581–82. On the twelve Fratres Arvales, see G. Wissowa, "Zum Rituel der Arvalbrüder," *Hermes* 52 (1917): 331–47; E. Norden, *Aus römischen Priesterbüchern* (1939), pp. 109–268; A. Pasoli, *Acta fratrum Arualium* (1950) (text and commentary).

The principal rite of the fetiales consisted in demanding reparation in the name of Rome; if he did not obtain satisfaction, the fetial returned and, after thirty-three days, ceremonially declared war by throwing a lance or a cornel branch on the enemy's soil (Livy, 1. 32. 5–14; etc.).

The Salii, "dancer-priests," ritually opened the season of war on March 1. They ran through the city and, at the consecrated places, indulged in contorted dances, at the same time singing a *carmen* (which had become incomprehensible by the time of the end of the Republic) in honor of the gods. At the close of each day of dancing there was a feast. From March 9 on, the rites became more spectacular; there were horse races, lustration of weapons and war trumpets, etc. In October the Salii celebrated the closing of the season of war by lustrations of arms (to spare the city the miasma of spilled blood). An attempt has been made to reconstruct the text of the *carmen saliare;* see L. Bayard, "Le chant des Saliens, essai de restitution," *Mélanges des sciences rel. des Facultés Catholiques de Lille* 2 (1945): 45–58.

The twelve Fratres Arvales had their cult center in the sacred wood of "the Goddess" (Dea Dia), 75 kilometers from Rome. The annual ceremonies were celebrated during three days in May: the first and the last at Rome, the second—and most important—at the cult center. In the sacred wood the Brothers immolated two pregnant sows (*porciliae,* outstanding symbols of fecundity) and ate the flesh. Then, crowned with ears of grain and veiled, they advanced to the temple in procession; in front of the sanctuary they passed the ears from hand to hand. After a vegetable meal, they shut themselves up in the temple and sang invocations to the Lares and to Mars. (The text of the *carmen arvale,* in a very archaic Latin, is hard to interpret.) The invocations were followed by a dance and by horse races. See Ileana Chirassi, "Dea Dia e Fratres Arvales," *SMSR* 39 (1968): 191–291.

On the Lupercalia, see L. Deubner, "Lupercalia," *ARW* 13 (1910): 481 ff.; A. K. Michels, "The Topography and Interpretation of the Lupercalia," *Trans. Amer. Phil. Assoc.* 54 (1953): 35–39 (with an extensive bibliography); M. P. Nilsson, "Les Luperques," *Latomus* 15 (1956): 133–36; Ugo Bianchi, "Luperci," *Dizionario Epigrafice di Antichità Romane,* vol. 4 (Rome, 1958), pp. 1–9; G. Dumézil, *La rel. rom. arch.,* pp. 352 ff. The name of the brotherhood certainly contains the name of the wolf, but the formation is obscure; see Dumézil, *La rel. rom. arch.,* p. 352 and n. 2. J. Gruber derives *lupercus* from a "lupo-sequos," i.e., "qui lupum sequitur" (*Glotta,* vol. 39, 1961). The brotherhood would be a *Männerbund* inherited from protohistory; see F. Altheim, *A History of Roman Religion,* pp. 206–17 (German ed., *Römische Religionsgeschichte,* vol. 1, pp. 131 ff.). A. Alföldi also considers the Luperci to be the vestige of a *Männerbund*—the brotherhood, in fact, that would have played a decisive part in the founding of the Roman state; see his *Die trojanischen Urahnen der Römer* (Rektoratsprogr. d. Univ. Basel für das Jahr 1956). For Kerényi, the Luperci represented at once wolves (the primitive form of the brotherhood, of Nordic origin) and goats (southern influence); see his "Wolf und Ziege am Fest der Lupercalia," in *Mélanges Marouzeau* (1948), pp. 309–17 (reprinted in *Niobe* [Zurich, 1949], pp. 136–47).

Plutarch (*Romulus* 21. 10) describes a rite of the initiatory type: after a sacrifice of goats, two youths of noble birth are brought before the Luperci; "some of them touch their foreheads with a bloody knife and others wipe the stain off at once with wool dipped in milk. The youths must laugh after their foreheads have been wiped."

The initiatory character of the brotherhood has been analyzed by G. Dumézil, *Le problème des Centaures* (Paris, 1929), pp. 203–22. Now see Gerhard Binder, *Die Aussetzung des Königskindes: Kyros und Romulus* (Meisenheim am Glan, 1964), pp. 90–115, esp. pp. 98 ff.

On the race of the two groups of Luperci, see G. Piccaluga, "L'aspetto agnostico dei Lupercalia," *SMSR* 33 (1962): 51–62.

On *februum,* Februarius, and Faunus, see Dumézil, *Le problème des Centaures,* pp. 195 ff.; A. Brelich, *Tre variazioni romane sul tema delle origini* (Rome, 1956), pp. 95–123; Binder, *Die Aussetzung des Königskindes,* pp. 80 ff.; Dumézil, *La rel. rom. arch.,* pp. 353 ff.

On sacrifices, see S. Eitrem, *Opferritus und Voropfer der Griechen und Römer* (1913); Wissowa, *Religion und Kultus,* pp. 380 ff.; Latte, *Römische Religionsgeschichte,* pp. 379–92.

Dumézil has brought out the structural analogy between the sacrifice of the *suovetaurilia* (comprising the immolation of pigs, ovines, and bulls), a sacrifice peculiar to the cult of Mars, and the *sautrāmaṇī,* offered to Indra; see his *Tarpeia* (1947), pp. 117–58, and *La rel. rom. arch.,* pp. 247–51.

On the ritual of the October horse, sacrificed to Mars, and the similarities with the *aśvamedha,* reserved for the warrior class (see § 73), see, most recently, Dumézil, *La rel. rom. arch.,* pp. 225–39, and his *Fêtes romaines d'été et d'automne,* pp. 179–219.

Later (end of the fifth century?), under the influence of the Etruscans (who, in fact, were following a Greek model), Rome saw the introduction of the *lectisternia,* characterized by the physical presence of the god to whom sacrifice was being offered. "To feed the god at the altar is the object of every sacrifice. To serve him a meal is another matter" (Dumézil, *La rel. rom. arch.,* p. 559; Eng. trans., p. 567). And in fact the god (i.e., his cult statue) lay on a bed near the table that was served for him. "The *lectisternia* were originally served outside of the temples: in this way men could see with their own eyes these protectors, who were ordinarily confined in a *cella*" (ibid.).

166. On the *di indigetes* and *divi novensiles,* see Wissowa, *Religion und Kultus,* pp. 18 ff., 43, and the sources cited by A. Grenier, *Les religions étrusque et romaine,* p. 152.

On the formula of *devotio* handed down by Livy (8. 9. 6), and against Latte (who sees a forgery by the *pontifex maximus*), see Dumézil, *La rel. rom. arch.,* pp. 108 ff.

On the archaic triad, see the treatment by Dumézil, *La rel. rom. arch.,* pp. 187–290, with the bibliography of his earlier works (most importantly: *Jupiter, Mars, Quirinus* [1941]; *Naissance de Rome* [1944]; *L'héritage indo-européen à Rome* [1948]; and *Mythe et épopée,* vol. 1 [1968], pp. 259–437). Wissowa had already drawn attention to the existence of the pre-Capitoline triad; see his *Religion und Kultus,* pp. 23, 133–34. According to Latte, the grouping is late and accidental (*Römische Religionsgeschichte,* pp. 37, 195, etc.); but see Dumézil's critique, *La rel. rom. arch.,* pp. 154 ff.

In the circumstances in which Jupiter appears to be agrarian or martial, allowance must be made for the *mode* of his interventions (Dumézil, *La rel. rom. arch.,* p. 193). "Politics and law, power and justice are united, at least ideally, at many points. Another element of the prestige of Jupiter, as of Zeus and the sovereign gods of Vedic India, Varuṇa and Mitra, is his role as witness, as guarantor, as avenger of oaths and pacts, in private as well as in public life, in commerce between citizens or with foreigners" (ibid., p. 190; Eng. trans., p. 179).

On Mars, see Dumézil, ibid., pp. 215–56. For a radically different orientation, see Udo W. Scholz, *Studien zum altitalischen und altrömischen Marskult und Marsmythos* (1970). On the October horse sacrifice, and, again, H. J. Rose's agrarianistic interpretations (in *Some Problems of Classical Religion: Mars* [Oslo, 1958], pp. 1–17), see Dumézil, *La rel. rom. arch.,* pp. 223–38.

On Quirinus, see Dumézil, *La rel. rom. arch.,* pp. 259–82, and A. Brelich, "Quirinus: una divinità romana alla luce della comparazione storica," *SMSR* 36 (1965): 63–119. Carl Koch has presented an anti-Dumézilian interpretation in "Bemerkungen zum römischen Quirinuskult," *Zeitschrift für Rel. und Geistesgeschichte* 5 (1953): 1–25.

On Vesta, see O. Huth, *Vesta: Untersuchungen zum indo-germanischen Feuerkult* (1943); A. Brelich, *Geheime Schutzgottheit von Rom: Vesta* (*Albae Vigiliae* n.s. 7 [Zurich, 1949]); Dumézil, "Aedes Rotunda Vestae," in *Rituels indo-européens à Rome* (1954), pp. 26–43, and other works summarized in *La rel. rom. arch.,* pp. 319–32.

On Janus, see L. A. Lackay, "Janus," *University of California Publications in Classical Philology* 15 (1956): 157–82; R. Schilling, "Janus, le dieu introducteur," *Mélanges d'archéologie et d'histoire de l'Ecole Française de Rome,* 1960, pp. 89–100; G. Capdeville, "Les épithètes cultuelles de Janus," ibid., 1973, pp. 395–436; Dumézil, *La rel. rom. arch.,* pp. 333–39.

On the Capitoline triad, see the general treatment in Dumézil, *La rel. rom. arch.*, pp. 291–317. See also U. Bianchi, "Disegno storico del culto Capitolino nell'Italia romana e nelle provincie dell'Impero," *Monumenti antichi dei Lincei* 8 (1949): 347–415, and Bianchi, "Questions sur les origines du culte capitolin," *Latomus* 10 (1951): 341–66.

On Juno, see Dumézil, *La rel. rom. arch.*, pp. 299–310, and also his "Junon et l'Aurore," *Mythe et épopée*, vol. 3 (1973), pp. 164–73. For the etymology of the name, see E. Benveniste, "Expression indo-européenne de l'éternité," *Bull. Soc. Linguistique* 38 (1937): 103–12. See also M. Renard, "Le nom de Junon," *Phoibos* 5 (1951): 131–43, and Renard, "Juno Historia," *Latomus* 12 (1953): 137–54.

On the festivals patronized by Juno, especially the Nonae Caprotinae and the Matronalia, see Dumézil, *La rel. rom. arch.*, pp. 301–13. See also J. Gagé, *Matronalia: Essai sur les organisations cultuelles des femmes dans l'ancienne Rome,* Coll. Latomus, no. 60 (1963).

On the etymology of the name Minerva, see A. Meillet, *De i.-e. radice *men, "mente agitare"* (1897), p. 47.

167. On the Etruscans, the essential information will be found in some recent publications: M. Pallottino, *Etruscologia,* 6th ed. (Milan, 1968); R. Bloch, *Les Etrusques* (1954); J. Heurgon, *La vie quotidienne chez les Etrusques* (1961); H. H. Scullard, *The Etruscan Cities and Rome* (London, 1967); L. Banti, *Il mondo degli Etruschi,* 2d ed. (Rome, 1969).

The "Etruscan question" is discussed in two articles by M. Pallottino, "Nuovi Studi sul problema delle origini etrusche," *Studi Etruschi* 29 (1961): 3–30, and "What Do We Know Today about the Etruscan Language?" *Intern. Anthropological Linguistic Review* 1 (1955): 243–53. See also two works by H. Hencken, *Tarquinia, Villanovans, and Early Etruscans* (Cambridge, Mass., 1968), vol. 2, pp. 601–46, and *Tarquinia and Etruscan Origins* (London, 1968).

On Etruscan religion, see the treatments by A. Grenier, "La religion étrusque" in his *Les religions étrusque et romaine* (Paris, 1948) (= *Mana* 2 [1948]: 3–79); R. Herbig, *Götter und Dämonen der Etrusker* (Heidelberg, 1948); F. Altheim, *A History of Roman Religion,* pp. 46–92, 485–94; Dumézil, *La rel. rom. arch.*, pp. 611–80; G. C. Giglioli and G. Camporeale, "La religione degli Etruschi," in G. Castellani, ed., *Storia delle Religioni,* 6th ed., rev. and enl., vol. 2 (1971), pp. 539–672 (good bibliographies on pp. 655–61, 670–72). The texts by classical authors are listed and analyzed by Giglioli on pp. 544–52, 652–54.

On the Asian origin of the Etruscans (Herodotus 1. 94) and the Lemnos inscriptions, see A. Piganiol, "Les Etrusques, peuple d'Orient,"

Cahiers d'histoire mondiale 1 (1953): 329–39; see also Dumézil, *La rel. rom. arch.*, pp. 614–19.

On the Etruscan gods and their *interpretatio graeca,* see G. Devoto, "Nomi di divinità etrusche," *Studi Etruschi* 6 (1932): 243–80 (Fufluns); 7 (1933): 259–66 (Culšanš); 14 (1940): 275–80 (Vertumno). See also L. Banti, "Il culto del cosidetto 'Tempio dell'Apollo' a Veii e il problema delle triadi etrusco-italiche," *Studi Etruschi* 17 (1943): 187 ff.; J. D. Beazley, "The World of the Etruscan Mirror," *Journal of Hellenic Studies* 69 (1949): 1–17; F. Messerschmidt, "Griechische und Etruskische Religion," *SMSR* 5 (1929: 21–32; Eva Fiesel, *Namen des griechischen Mythos im Etruskischen* (1928) (see E. Benveniste's observations, *Rev. Philol.* 56 [1930]: 67–75, and Dumézil's, *La rel. rom. arch.*, pp. 660–61); Dumézil, ibid., pp. 658–76.

In the sanctuary at Pyrgi (one of the ports of Caere), a Punic inscription has recently been discovered, together with tablets inscribed in Etruscan, dating from ca. 500. The Punic text contains the homage of the Etruscan king to the Phoenician goddess Astarte, assimilated to Uni (= Juno). This is another proof of the malleability of Etruscan theology, ready to receive a mythico-ritual formula of the Semitic world and homologize it with a national divinity. Cf. A. Dupont-Sommer, "L'inscription punique récemment découverte à Pyrgi (Italie)," *JA* 252 (1964): 289–302; the translation (p. 292) is reproduced and commented on by Dumézil, *La rel. rom. arch.*, pp. 665 ff. See the later bibliography in J. Heurgon, "The Inscriptions of Pyrgi," *Journal of Roman Studies* 56 (1966): 1–14, and G. Camporeale, in Castellani, ed., *Storia delle Religioni,* vol. 2 (1971), p. 671.

On techniques of divination, the book by A. Bouché-Leclercq, *Histoire de la divination dans l'antiquité,* vol. 4 (Paris, 1882), pp. 3–115, has not yet been replaced.

The contents of the different *libri* is presented and commented on in the three volumes by C. O. Thulin, *Die etruskische Disziplin,* vol. 1: *Die Blitzlehre* (Göteborgs Högskolas Årsskrift, no. 11 [1905], pp. i–xv, 1–128); vol. 2, *De Haruspicium* (ibid., no. 12 [1906], pp. 1–54); vol. 3, *Ritualbücher* and *Zur Geschichte und Organization der Haruspices* (ibid., no. 15 [1909], pp. 1–158).

Pliny's and Seneca's texts on the theory of thunderbolts depend on the same source (Caecina). Jupiter himself had at his disposal three different categories of thunderbolts. The other eight types of thunderbolts were manipulated by the gods corresponding to Juno, Minerva, Vulcan, Mars, and Saturn and to three other divinities who have remained unknown. See Bouché-Leclercq, *Histoire de la divination,* vol. 4, pp. 32–61; Thulin, *Die Blitzlehre,* pp. 47–68; A. Biedl, "Die Himmelsteilung nach der 'disciplina etrusca,' " *Philologus* n.s. 40 (1931): 199–214; A. Piganiol, "Sur le calendrier brontoscopique de Nigidius Figulus," *Studies . . . in Honor of A. C. Johnson* (1951), pp. 79–87; Piganiol, "Les Etrusques, peuple d'Orient," pp. 640–41; S. Weinstock, "Libri Fulgurales," *Papers of the British School at Rome* 19 (1951): 122–42; R. B. Bloch, *Les prodiges dans l'antiquité classique* (1963), pp. 149 ff.; Dumézil, *La rel. rom. arch.*, pp. 624–35. The analogies with Oriental doctrine and technique are also discussed by G. Furlani in two articles, "Il *bidental* etrusco e un' inscrizione di Tiglatpilesar I d'Assiria," *SMSR* 6 (1930): 9–49, and "Fulmini mesopotamici, ittiti, greci ed etruschi," *Studi Etruschi* 5 (1931): 203–31.

On the *libri haruspicini* and the bronze model from Piacenza, see Bouché-Leclercq, *Histoire de la divination,* vol. 4, pp. 61–74; Thulin, *Ritualbücher;* G. Furlani, "Epatoscopia babilonese ed epatoscopia etrusca," *SMSR* 4 (1928): 243–85; Furlani, "Mantica babilonese ed etrusca," *Tyrrhenica, Saggi di studi etruschi* (1957), pp. 61–76. For a comparative study, see *La divination en Mésopotamie et dans les régions voisines,* 14th Meeting of the International Assyriologists Association, 1967; J. Nougayrol, "Haruspicine étrusque et assyro-babylonienne," *Comptes Rendus de l'Acad. des Inscriptions,* 1955, pp. 508–17; Nougayrol, "Le foie d'orientation BM 50594," *Revue d'Assyriologie* 62 (1968): 31–50; E. Laroche, "Eléments d'haruspicine hittite," *Revue hittite et asianique* 12 (1952): 19–48; R. Bloch, "Liberté et détermination dans la divination romaine," *Studi in onore di Luisa Banti* (Rome, 1965), pp. 63 ff.; Bloch, "La divination en Etrurie et à Rome," in *La Divination,* vol. 1 (Paris, 1968), pp. 197–232.

The forty divinities whose names are inscribed on the bronze model of a liver found at Piacenza are probably grouped according to a certain order that it has not yet been possible to reconstruct. We have another classification of the pantheon, namely, the one transmitted by Martianus Minneus Felix Capella in his treatise *De nuptiis Philologiae et Mercurii* (1. 41–61). This is a late text (fifth century A.D.), full of Greek and Greco-Roman speculations; however, it is valuable for the clear and detailed presentation of the gods assigned to the sixteen celestial regions. (The chief source seems to have been the translation of the Etruscan rituals made by Nigidius Figulus, a contemporary of Cicero.) Thulin had no doubt that there was a correspondence between the divine personages inscribed in the sixteen divisions of the liver from Piacenza and Martianus Capella's sixteen regions (see his *Die Götter des Martianus Capella und der Bronzeleber von Piacenza* [Berlin, 1906]). But Stefan Weinstock has brought out the considerable contribution made by Hellenistic astrology; see his "Martianus Capella and the Cosmic System of the Etruscans,'' *Journal of Roman Studies* 36 (1946): 101–29. For an analysis of the first three *regiones,* that is, those of Jupiter, see Dumézil, *La rel. rom. arch.,* 672–76.

On demonology and funerary beliefs, see S. Weinstock, ''Etruscan Demons,'' in *Studi in onore di Luisa Banti,* pp. 345–50; C. C. van Essen, *Did Orphic Influence on Etruscan Tomb Paintings Exist?* (Amsterdam, 1927); van Essen, ''La Tomba del Cardinale,'' *Studi Etruschi* 2 (1928): 83–132; F. de Ruyt, *Charun, démon étrusque de la mort* (Brussels, 1934); M. Pallottino, ''Il culto degli antenati in Etruria ed una probabile equivalenza lessicale etrusco-latino,'' *Studi Etruschi* 26 (1958): 49–83; J. M. Blásquez, ''La Tomba del Cardinale y la influencia orfico-pitagorica en las creencias etruscas de ultratumba,'' *Latomus* 26 (1965): 3–39.

In certain tomb scenes a demon holds a book or a scroll or is writing on it. The few characters that it has been possible to decipher indicate the name and age of the dead person. It would seem that we have ''a sort of passport for the beyond'' (F. de Ruyt, *Charun,* p. 160). On the Egyptian analogies, see the bibliography for § 33 in volume 1.

168. On the triad of the Aventine, see H. Le Bonniec, *Le Culte de Cérès à Rome, des origines à la fin de la Republique* (Paris, 1958), and Dumézil, *La rel. rom. arch.,* pp. 379 ff. ''The Aventine cult is evidence of a victory of the plebs, resulting from one of the first of the many compromises which little by little were to assure that social class of political and religious equality. The classic pattern—the plebeian aediles holding office in the outbuildings of the temple and accumulating there the archives of the plebs, the texts of the plebiscites, and later, as a precautionary measure, duplicates of the senatus consulta of the rival order—would have been formed in the beginning of the fifth century, at the time of the foundation'' (Dumézil, p. 384; Eng. trans., *Archaic Roman Religion,* vol. 1, pp. 379–80). See also F. Altheim, *History of Roman Religion,* p. 250. It is probable that the association of three agrarian divinities, two of them female and one male, comes from Magna Graecia; see Dumézil, p. 448.

On the occasion of the Cerealia, in addition to the sacrifice of sows, a barbarous ''game'' was played: foxes were turned loose in the Circus ''with burning torches fastened to their backs'' (Ovid, *Fasti* 4. 679–82). The interpretation of this rite is in dispute; see Dumézil, p. 380.

On the etymology of Liber, see E. Benveniste, ''Liber et liberi,'' *Rev. etudes latines* 13 (1936): 52–58. On the cult, see A. Bruhl, *Liber pater, origine et expansion du culte dionysiaque à Rome et dans le monde romain* (Paris, 1953), esp. pp. 13 ff. The information on the Liberalia supplied by Saint Augustine, partly after Varro, is examined by Bruhl, pp. 17 ff. Franz Altheim maintains the Greek origin of the god Liber in his *Terra Mater* (Giessen, 1931), pp. 15 ff.; see Bruhl's critique, pp. 23 ff. On the *interpretatio graeca* of the Cerealia, see Jean Bayet, "Les 'Cerealia,' altération d'un culte latin par le mythe grec," *Revue Belge de philologie et d'histoire* 29 (1951): 5–32, 341–66; republished in *Croyances et rites dans la Rome antique* (1971), pp. 89–129.

On Greek influences, see Franz Altheim, *A History,* pp. 34 ff., 149 ff.; Dumézil, *La rel. rom. arch.,* pp. 450 ff. On Celtic influences, see Altheim, *History,* pp. 282 ff., 353 ff.

On Apollo, see J. Gagé, *Apollon romain: Essai sur le culte d'Apollon et le développement du 'ritus graecus' à Rome, des origines à Auguste* (Paris, 1955).

On Venus, see R. Schilling, *La religion romaine de Vénus depuis les origines jusqu'au temps d'Auguste* (Paris, 1954); Schilling replies, in "Les origines de la Vénus romaine," *Latomus* 17 (1958): 3–26, to A. Ernout's and P. Grimal's critiques of his views. See also Dumézil, *La rel. rom. arch.,* pp. 422–24, 471–74.

On the *evocatio,* see V. Basanoff, *Evocatio: Etude d'un rituel militaire romain* (Paris, 1947); R. Bloch, "Héra, Uni, Junon en Italie centrale," *Comptes rendus de l'Académie des Inscriptions* 117 (1972): 384–96. Other famous examples of *evocatio:* Vertumnus, "evoked" from the Volsinii in ca. 264, and the Punic Tanit from Carthage by Scipio Aemilianus in ca. 146 (Macrobius, *Sat.* 3. 9).

On the prodigies of ca. 207 listed by Livy, see J. Cousin, "La crise religieuse de 207 avant J.-C.," *RHR* 126 (1943): 15–41. Religion during the Second Punic War is brilliantly presented by Dumézil, *La rel. rom. arch.,* pp. 457–87. On the *transvectio* of Cybele, see H. Graillot, *Le culte de Cybèle, mère des dieux, à Rome et dans l'empire romain* (Paris, 1912), pp. 38 ff.; on the sodalities of the goddess and their political significance, see ibid., pp. 90 ff.; on her cult at Rome and in the provinces, see F. Cumont, *Les religions orientales dans le paganisme romain,* 4th ed. (1929), pp. 17 ff., 208 ff. See also T. Köves, "Zum Empfang der Magna Mater in Rom," *Historia* 12 (1963): 321–47; F. Bömer, "Kybele in Rom," *Rheinisches Museum* 71 (1964): 130–51.

The sources and critical bibliography for the prosecution of the Bacchanals are cogently analyzed by A. Bruhl, *Liber pater,* pp. 82–116; for a critique of this, see J. Bayet, "Le phénomène religieux dionysiaque" (= *Croyances et rites,* pp. 241–74). See also J. Festugière, "Ce que Tite-Live nous apprend des mystères de Dionysos," *Mélanges d'archéologie et d'histoire de l'Ecole Française de Rome* 66 (1954): 79–99; Latte, *Römische Religionsgeschichte,* p. 270, n. 5 (bibliography); Dumézil, *La rel. rom. arch.,* pp. 511–16.

Chapter 21. Celts, Germans, Thracians, Getae

169. For the prehistory of the Celts, see M. E. Marien, "Où en est la question des champs d'urnes?" *L'antiquité classique* 17 (1948): 413–44; E. Sprockhoff, "Central European Urnfield Culture and Celtic La Tène," *Proceedings of the Prehistoric Society,* 1955, pp. 257–81; P. Bosch-Gimpera, *Les Indo-Européens: Problèmes archéologiques,* trans. R. Lantier (Paris, 1961), pp. 241 ff.; G. Devoto, *Origini indoeuropee* (Florence, 1962), pp. 389 ff.; Stuart Piggott, *Ancient Europe* (Edinburgh, 1963), pp. 215 ff. (excellent bibliography, pp. 261–66); Piggott, *The Druids* (London, 1968), pp. 9–24; Richard Pittioni, "Das Mittel-Metallikum—Die Frühzeit der indogermanischen Einzelvölker Europas," *Anzeiger der Öst. Akad. der Wissenschaften, Phil.-hist. Klasse,* no. 5 (1972), pp. 14–29.

Of the considerable literature on the history and culture of the Celts, we mention H. Hubert, *Les Celtes,* 2 vols. (1932); A. Grenier, *Les Gaulois* (Paris, 1945); T. O'Rahilly, *Early Irish History and Mythology* (Dublin, 1946); T. G. E. Powell, *The Celts* (London, 1958); Jan de Vries, *Kelten und Germanen* (Berne and Munich, 1960); J. Philip, *Celtic Civilization and Its Heritage* (Prague and New York, 1962); C. F. C. Hawkes, "The Celts: Report on the Study of Their Culture and Their Mediterranean Relations, 1942–1962," in *Rapports et Commentaires, VIIIe Congrès International d'Archéologie Classique* (Paris, 1963), pp. 3–23; Nora Chadwick, *The Celts* (Harmondsworth, 1966) (but see Piggott, *The Druids,* p. 193); Anne Ross, *Pagan Celtic Britain: Studies in Iconography and Tradition* (London, 1967); Helmut Birkhan, *Germanen und Kelten bis zum Ausgang der Römerzeit* (Vienna, 1970), pp. 1–636; Jean-Jacques Hatt, *Les Celtes et les Gallo-Romains,* Series Archaeologia Mundi (Geneva, Paris, Munich, 1970) (excellent illustrations).

The Greek and Latin texts on Celtic religion have been edited by J. Zwicker, *Fontes historiae religionis celticae,* 3 vols. (Berlin, 1934–36); a selection, in a German translation, has been published by Wolfgang Krause in "Die Kelten," *Religionsgeschichtliches Lesebuch,* 2d ed. (Tübingen, 1929). See the bibliography of the other sources (Gallic inscriptions, sculptures, bronze statuettes, divine representations on decorated vases) in Paul-Marie Duval, *Les dieux de la Gaule* (Paris, 1976), pp. 129–30.

For general works on the religions of the Celts, see M.-L. Sjoestedt, *Dieux et héros des Celtes* (Paris, 1940; English trans., *Gods and Heroes of the Celts,* New York, 1976); J. Vendryès, "La religion des Celtes," in *Mana: Les religions de l'Europe ancienne,* vol. 3 (Paris, 1948), pp.

239–320 (good repertory of the gods); A. Rees and B. Rees, *The Celtic Heritage: Ancient Tradition in Ireland and Wales* (London, 1961); J. de Vries, *La religion des Celtes* (Paris, 1963; originally published as *Keltische Religion,* Stuttgart, 1961); Anne Ross, *Pagan Celtic Britain* (excellent bibliography, pp. 489–503); Françoise Le Roux, "La religion des Celtes," in *Histoire des religions* (Encyclopédie de Pléiade), vol. 1 (1970), pp. 780–840; Paul-Marie Duval, *Les dieux de la Gaule* (1976) (a revised and enlarged edition of the work published in 1957).

On the protohistorical sanctuaries and the symbolism of the sacred space, see K. Schwarz, "Zum Stand der Ausgrabungen in der Spätkeltischen Viereckshanze von Holzhausen," *Jahresbericht d. Bayerische Bodendenkmalpfl.* (1962), pp. 21–77; Piggott, *Ancient Europe,* pp. 230 ff. On the symbolism of the Center and "sacred geography" in medieval Ireland, see A. Rees and B. Rees, *The Celtic Heritage,* pp. 146 ff.

On the cult of skulls, see P. Lambrechts, *L'Exaltation de la tête dans la pensée et dans l'art des Celtes* (Bruges, 1954), and, especially, Anne Ross, *Pagan Celtic Britain,* pp. 94–171, figs. 25–86, and pls. 1–23 (see pp. 155 ff. on the continuation of the cult after the conversion to Christianity).

170. On the archaism of Celtic culture and its parallelism with ancient India, see G. Dumézil, *Servius et la Fortune* (1942); Myles Dillon, "The Archaism of Irish Tradition," *Proceedings of the British Academy* 33 (1947): 245–64; Dillon, "The Hindu Act of Truth in Celtic Tradition," *Modern Philology* 44 (1947): 137–40; Dillon, "Celt and Hindu," *Vishveshvaranand Indological Journal* 1 (1963): 1–21; J. E. Caerwyn Williams, "The Court Poet in Medieval Ireland," *Proc. Brit. Acad.* 57 (1971): 85–135. See also D. A. Binchy, "The Linguistic and Historical Value of the Irish Law Tracts," *Proc. Brit. Acad.* 29 (1943); C. Watkins, "Indo-European Metrics and Archaic Irish Verse," *Celtica* 6 (1963): 194 ff.; R. Schmidt, *Dichtung und Dichtersprache in indogermanischer Zeit* (Wiesbaden, 1967), pp. 61 ff. In his posthumous book, *Celts and Aryans* (Simla, 1975), Myles Dillon restudied the entire problem: morphology and syntax (pp. 32 ff.), court poetry and heroic tradition (pp. 52 ff.), social institutions (pp. 95 ff.), and religion (125 ff.). See also Hans Hartmann, *Der Totenkult in Irland* (Heidelberg, 1952); K. H. Jackson, *The Oldest Irish Tradition: A Window on the Iron Age* (Cambridge, 1964); H. Wagner, "Studies in the Origin of Early Celtic Tradition," *Eriu* 26 (1975): 1–26.

On social tripartition among the Celts, see G. Dumézil, *L'idéologie tripartite des Indo-Européens* (Brussels, 1958), p. 11: "If we reconcile the documents that describe the social condition of the decadent pagan Gaul that Caesar conquered with the texts that inform us concerning Ireland soon after its conversion to Christianity, there appears, under the **rīg* (the exact phonetic equivalent of Sanskr. *rāj-,* Lat. *rēg-*), a type of society constituted as follows: (1) dominating everything, stronger than frontiers, almost as supranational as the class of Brahmans, is the class of *Druids* (**dru-uid*), that is, of the 'Very Learned,' priests, jurists, depositaries of the tradition; (2) then comes the military aristocracy, sole owners of the soil, the Irish *flaith* (cf. Gallic *vlato,* Ger. *Gewalt,* etc.), properly 'power,' the exact semantic equivalent of Sanskr. *kṣatra,* essence of the martial function; (3) last are the stock breeders, the Irish *bó airig,* free men (*airig*), who are defined solely as owners of cows (*bó*).'' T. G. Powell has taken up Dumézil's demonstration (in *Jupiter, Mars, Quirinus,* pp. 110–23) in his study ''Celtic Origins: A Stage in the Enquiry,'' *Journal of the Royal Anthropological Institute* 78 (1948): 71–79; cf. Piggott, *The Druids,* p. 88.

And, as Dumézil remarks elsewhere, ''The Irish conceived the history of their island as a succession of invasions; the next-to-the-last invading people, that of the Tuatha Dé Danann, 'tribes of the goddess Dana,' is in fact composed of the old gods of paganism, especially those whom the Celts had inherited from their Indo-European ancestors.'' The general staff of the Tuatha Dé Danann is made up of the following: the great god Dagda, devoted to high Druidic magic; Ogma, the champion god; Lug (''the god of all trades''); Dian Cecht, the physician; and Goibniu, the blacksmith. The third function in its most necessary form, agriculture, the supplier of food and wealth, was represented by the preceding inhabitants of the island, the Fomòrs, ''demonic beings whom the Tuatha Dé Danann conquered, killed for the most part, and domesticated the rest. And it was at the end of this war, at their famous victory of Mag Tuired, that the invading Tuatha Dé Danann decided to leave the leader of the conquered folk alive, in return for his revealing the secrets that were to insure the agricultural and pastoral prosperity of Ireland'' (G. Dumézil, *Mythe et épopée,* vol. 1 [1968], p. 289; see also note 1 for references to earlier works). Jan de Vries has followed Dumézil's interpretation in his *La religion des Celtes,* pp. 157 ff. See also Myles Dillon, *Celts and Aryans,* pp. 96 ff.

For other examples of Irish epic traditions involving the trifunctional structure, see *Mythe et épopée,* vol. 1, pp. 602–12 (''Le trio des Machas''); pp. 616–23 (''Les trois oppressions de l'île de Bretagne''). The structural analogies between the myth of the successive ''queens Medb'' and that of the Indian Mādhavī, daughter of the universal king Yayāti, have been analyzed in chapter 5 of *Mythe et épopée,* vol. 2 (1971), pp.

331–53 (this volume of *Mythe et épopée* has been translated into English by Alf Hiltebeitel under the title *The Destiny of a King* [Chicago, 1973]). See also "The Well of Nechtan," *Mythe et épopée,* vol. 3 (1973), pp. 27–34.

On the value of Caesar's testimony, see the useful but overly critical work by Michel Rambaud, *L'Art de la déformation historique dans les Commentaires de César,* 2d ed., rev. and enl. (Paris, 1966), especially the pages on religion (pp. 328–33). "By his picture of Gallic religion, the proconsul, conqueror of Gaul and grand pontiff at Rome, suggested the policy that he followed" (p. 333).

On the so-called "giant Jupiter" columns, see Werner Müller, *Die Jupitergigantensäulen und ihre Verwandten* (Meisenheim am Glan, 1975), with a rich bibliography (pp. 113–27). On the symbolism of the wheel, see ibid., pp. 46 ff.; see also A. Ross, *Pagan Celtic Britain,* pp. 347 ff., 475 ff.; R. Pettazzoni, "The Wheel in the Ritual Symbolism of Some Indo-European Peoples," in his *Essays on the History of Religions* (Leiden, 1954), pp. 95–109; J. J. Hatt, "Rota flammis circumsepta, à propos du symbole de la roue dans la religion gauloise," *Revue archéologique de l'Est* 2 (1951): 82–87.

On Dagda, see J. Vendryès, "La religion des Celtes," p. 263; F. Le Roux, "Notes sur le Mercure celtique," *Ogam* 4 (1952): 289 ff.; J. de Vries, *La religion des Celtes,* pp. 45 ff.

On Lug, see Vendryès, "La religion des Celtes," pp. 278, 313; de Vries, *La religion des Celtes,* pp. 58 ff.; P.-M. Duval, *Les dieux de la Gaule,* pp. 27 ff.; R. Pettazzoni, "Il dio gallico a tre teste," in *L'onniscienza di Dio* (Turin, 1955), pp. 286–316; R. Lantier, in *Wörterbuch der Mythologie,* pt. 2, pp. 132 ff., 138 ff., 141 ff.

On the Gallic Mars, see J. de Vries, *La religion des Celtes,* pp. 64 ff.; P. Lambrechts, *Contributions à l'étude des divinités celtiques* (Bruges, 1942), pp. 126 ff.; E. Thevenot, *Sur les traces des Mars celtiques entre Loire et Mont Blanc,* Dissertationes archaeologicae Gandenses (Bruges, 1955); F. Benoit, *Mars et Mercure: Nouvelles recherches sur l'interprétation gauloise des divinités romaines* (Aix-en-Provence, 1959).

On Ogmios, see Françoise Le Roux, "Le dieu celtique aux liens: de l'Ogmios de Lucien à l'Ogmios de Dürer," *Ogam* 12 (1960): 209–34, who also discusses earlier works; J. de Vries, *La rel. des Celtes,* pp. 73–79; P.-M. Duval, *Les dieux de la Gaule,* pp. 79–82. According to M. L. Sjoestedt, Ogma's name "shows a non-Gaelic phonetics and must be explained as a borrowing from the Gallic Ogmios" ("Légendes épiques irlandaises et monnaies gauloises," *Etudes Celtiques* 1 [1936]: 7). On the other hand, the name Ogmios appears to be borrowed from

Greek *ogmos,* "line, row, furrow"; but this divine name of Greek origin conceals a Celtic religious reality.

The god Ogma is called "father of the ogams," alphabetical characters used especially in the 360 funerary inscriptions found chiefly in Ireland and Wales and dating from the fifth and sixth centuries; see J. Vendryès, "L'écriture ogamique et ses origines," *Etudes Celtiques* 4 (1939): 83–116 (with a rich bibliography). On the arithmetical use of these signs, see L. Gerschel, "Origine et premier usage des caractères ogamiques," *Ogam* 9 (1959): 151–73. See, most recently, James Carney, "The Invention of the Ogam Cipher," *Eriu* 26 (1975): 53–65.

On "Apollo," see J. Vendryès, "La religion des Celtes," pp. 261 ff., 287 (divinities associated with Apollo); F. Le Roux, "Introduction à une étude de l'Apollon Celtique," *Ogam* 12 (1960): 59–72; J. de Vries, *La religion des Celtes,* pp. 79–86.

On "Minerva," see J. Vendryès, "La religion des Celtes," pp. 261 ff.; J. de Vries, *La religion des Celtes,* pp. 86 ff.

171. On the Gallic gods mentioned by Lucan, see P.-M. Duval, "Teutates, Esus, Taranis," *Etudes Celtiques* 8 (1958–59): 41–58; Duval, "Le groupe de bas-reliefs des 'Nautae Parisiaci,' " *Monuments Piot* 48 (1956): 78–85; E. Thevenot, "La pendaison sanglante des victimes offertes à Esus-Mars," in *Hommages à Waldemar Déonna* (Liège, 1957), pp. 442–49; J. de Vries, *La religion des Celtes,* pp. 53 ff., 105 ff.; Françoise Le Roux, "Les chaudrons celtiques à l'arbre d'Esus: Lucain et les scholies Bernoises," *Ogam* 7 (1955): 33–58; Le Roux, "Taranis, dieu celtique du Ciel et de l'orage," *Ogam* 10 (1958): 30–39; 11 (1959): 307–24; Anne Ross, "Esus et les trois 'grues,' " *Etudes Celtiques* 9 (1960–61): 405–38; J. J. Hatt, "Essai sur l'évolution de la religion gauloise," *Revue des études anciennes* 67 (1965): 80–125 (systematic reconstruction, not convincing).

The medieval glosses preserved in *Commenta Bernensis* are contradictory. Teutates is identified with Mercury and, in another place, with Mars; Esus with Mars and Mercury, Teutates with Dis Pater and Jupiter.

On the theme of the Irish king who, trapped in a burning house, is finally drowned in a vat, see Clémence Ramnoux, "La mort sacrificielle du Roi," *Ogam* 6 (1954): 209–18.

For a linguistic and historico-cultural analysis of Taranis, see H. Birkhan, *Germanen und Kelten,* pp. 311 ff.

On Cernunnos, see P. P. Bober, "Cernunnos: Origin and Transformation of a Celtic Divinity," *American Journal of Archaeology* 55 (1951): 13–51; J. de Vries, *La religion des Celtes,* pp. 112 ff. (with bibliography); Anne Ross, *Pagan Celtic Britain,* pp. 180 ff. On the Val

Cammonica engraved scene, see F. Altheim and E. Trautmann, "Keltische Felsbilder der Val Cammonica," *Mitteilungen des Deutschen Archaeologischen Instituts, röm. Abt.*, 54 (1939): 1 ff. On the religious symbolism of the stag, see Eliade, *Zalmoxis, the Vanishing God,* trans. Willard R. Trask (Chicago, 1972), pp. 147 ff. (with bibliography); Otto Höfler, *Siegfried, Arminius und die Symbolik* (Heidelberg, 1960), pp. 32 ff. and notes 66–94; Helmut Birkhan, *Germanen und Kelten,* pp. 453–57. On rites involving stag masks in Christian Europe, see Waldemar Liungman, *Traditionswanderungen: Euphrat-Rhein,* FFC no. 118 (Helsinki, 1937), p. 735 ff.

On the *Matres* and *matronae,* see Vendryès, "La religion des Celtes," pp. 275 ff., 288, n. 9; de Vries, *La religion des Celtes,* pp. 122 ff.; P.-M. Duval, *Les dieux de la Gaule,* pp. 55 ff.; Anne Ross, *Pagan Celtic Britain,* pp. 265 ff.

M. L. Sjoestedt has emphasized the importance of the ritual union of the god-chief and the mother goddess on New Year's Day (*Samain*), when "the Celtic year is reborn"; this *hieros gamos* was "the guarantee of the ever-reborn vitality of the tribe" (*Dieux et héros des Celtes,* p. 57). The theme of the *hieros gamos* between the Irish sovereign and the territorial goddess (epiphany of Terra Mater) has been fully treated by Celtic scholars. See, most recently, Proinsias Mac Cana, "Aspects of the Theme of King and Goddess in Irish Literature," *Etudes Celtiques* 7 (1956): 76–114, 356–413; 8 (1958): 59–65; Rachel Bromwich, "Celtic Dynastic Themes and the Breton Lays," *Etudes Celtiques* 9 (1960): 439–74; Ross, *Pagan Celtic Britain,* pp. 292 ff. See also the works by A. C. L. Brown and A. K. Coomaraswamy cited below.

F. R. Schröder was the first to call attention to a passage in the *Topographia Hibernica* (ca. 1185) of Geraldus Cambrensis in which it is related that among the Kenelcunil, a tribe of Ulster, the king copulates with a white mare in the presence of his subjects. The mare is then killed, its flesh is cooked, and, from the contents of the pot, a bath is made ready for the king. He then shares out the meat and drinks the liquid in which he has bathed; see Schröder, "Ein altirischer Krönungsritus und das indogermanischen Rossopfer," *Zeitschrift für keltische Philologie* 16 (1927): 310–12. Schröder compared this ritual of royal consecration with the *aśvamedha* (see § 73). The problem was then taken up again, from Dumézil's point of view, by Jaan Puhvel in "Aspects of Equine Functionality," in his *Myth and Law among the Indo-Europeans* (1970), pp. 159–72 (but see Dumézil, *Fêtes romaines d'été et d'automne,* pp. 216–19).

On Epona and Rhiannon, see H. Hubert, "Le mythe d'Epona," *Mélanges Vendryès* (Paris, 1925), pp. 187 ff.; P. Lambrechts, "Epona et les Matres," *L'Antiquité classique* 19 (1950): 103 ff.; Jean Gricourt, "Epona-Rhiannon-Macha," *Ogam* 6 (1954): 25–40, 75–86, 165–88 (the myth of Rhiannon, Breton equivalent of Epona, corresponds in Ireland to the myth of Macha). Like Gricourt, Puhvel holds that the territorial goddesses originally had hippomorphic features; see his "Aspects," pp. 165 ff. Dumézil had recognized in the three Machas a seeress, a woman warrior, and a peasant mother; in other words, they represented the three social functions: that of the priest, the warrior, and the peasant; see his "Le trio des Machas," *Mythe et épopée,* vol. 1, p. 603.

In one of the versions of "the horrible old woman and the young hero," the fairy (= goddess) explains the meaning of the kiss that brings about her metamorphosis: "As at first thou hast seen me ugly but in the end beautiful, even so is royal rule. Without battles it may not be won, but in the end, to anyone, it is comely and handsome" (trans. by Ananda Coomaraswamy in "On the Loathly Bride," *Speculum* 20 [1945]: 391–404 [a comparative study of this theme, making use principally of Indian sources]). A. C. L. Brown has amply analyzed the theme of the "horrible fairy who represents sovereignty" in the Breton Grail romances; see chapter 7 of his work *The Origin of the Grail Legend* (Cambridge, 1943).

On the religious importance of woman among the Celts and the ancient Germans, see Helmut Birkhan, *Germanen und Kelten bis zum Ausgang der Römerzeit,* pp. 487 ff.

172. Most of our information on the status and ceremonies of the Gallic Druids goes back to Posidonius' *History* (book 23). The work is lost, but Strabo (ca. 63 B.C.–A.D. 21), Diodorus Siculus (who wrote between 60 and 30 B.C.), Athenaeus (second century A.D.), and Julius Caesar (who also had access to other sources) reproduced and summarized long passages from it. J. J. Tierney has succeeded in identifying these borrowings in his study "The Celtic Ethnography of Posidonius," *Proceedings of the Royal Irish Academy* 60 (1959–60): 180–275 (the texts are published on pp. 225–46, followed by an English translation, pp. 247–75). On Posidonius' importance for the ethnology of the Celts, see also Arnaldo Momigliano, *Alien Wisdom: The Limits of Hellenization* (Cambridge, 1975), pp. 67 ff.

We also have some information transmitted by Pliny (*Nat. Hist.* 16. 249) and some commentaries by several late authors (first–fourth centuries A.D.), which, to use Nora Chadwick's expression, make up "the Alexandrine tradition"; see her *The Druids* (Cardiff and Connecticut, 1966); see also Stuart Piggot, *The Druids* (1968), pp. 88 ff.

There is a large literature on the Druids, most of it unusable. The book by T. D. Kendrick, *The Druids: A Study in Keltic Prehistory* (London, 1927), must be mentioned for its ultra-positivist point of view; according to this author, the Druids were "wizards" (see the pertinent observations by Françoise Le Roux, "Contribution à une définition des druides," *Ogam* 12 [1960]: 475–86, esp. pp. 476 ff.). The following may be consulted: Jan de Vries, "Die Druiden," *Kairos* 2 (1960): 67–82; de Vries, *La religion des Celtes,* pp. 212 ff.; F. Le Roux, *Les Druides* (Paris, 1961); Nora Chadwick, *The Druids;* S. Piggott, *The Druids* (all these works include more or less complete bibliographies; Piggott's book, pp. 123 ff., also contains the history of the romantic image of the Druids, which dates from the seventeenth century).

The information given by Caesar is the most valuable because, during his consulate in Gaul, he had personally become aware of the spiritual authority and political power of the Druids. Moreover, there were many people in Rome who knew Gaul and could therefore inhibit any exaggerations on his part.

The vernacular literatures of Great Britain and Ireland make up an inestimable source for a knowledge of the Druidic order. See the works by Myles Dillon, D. A. Binchy, J. E. C. Williams, and K. H. Jackson, cited above (§170), and Françoise Le Roux, *Les Druides*. The differences recorded by some classic authors between Druids, bards, and *vates* is not documented among the insular Celts (see Le Roux, pp. 14 ff.).

Caesar writes that the doctrine of the Druids "was discovered in Britain and was transferred thence to Gaul, and today those who would study the subject more accurately journey, as a rule, to Britain to learn it" (*De Bello Gal.* 6. 13. 11 ff.). This observation has inspired several extravagant hypotheses (some of them are mentioned by de Vries, *La rel. des Celtes,* pp. 218–20). But the Druidic order is a Celtic institution inherited—in Gaul as in Great Britain—from a common past; de Vries analyzes the reasons that seem to lie behind Caesar's statement.

Caesar adds that people came from everywhere to "the consecrated spots in the land of the Carnutes" to have their disputes settled. But since the suits of individuals were usually dealt with by the Druids of their own community, it is likely that Caesar's reference is to political conflicts between tribes. The assembly at the *locus consecratus* constituted a "supranational" court of final appeal; see Hubert, *Les Celtes,* vol. 2, p. 227; de Vries, *La rel. des Celtes,* pp. 215–16.

On the prohibition against committing the sacred tradition to writing, see M. Winternitz, *Geschichte der indischen Literatur,* vol. 1 (Leipzig, 1908), p. 31; G. Dumézil, "La tradition druidique et l'écriture, le Vivant et le Mort," *RHR* 122 (1940): 125–33; S. Gandz, "The Dawn of Literature," *Osiris* 7 (1969): 261 ff. On oral transmission in Ireland, see D. A. Binchy, "The Background to Early Irish Literature," *Studia Hibernica* 1 (1961): 21 ff.; A. Rees and B. Rees, *The Celtic Heritage,* pp. 20 ff.

On the *locus consecratus* and temples, see F. Le Roux, *Les Druides,* pp. 108 ff.; J. de Vries, *La rel. des Celtes,* pp. 201 ff. (with bibliography); R. Lantier, in *Wörterbuch der Mythologie,* pt. 2, pp. 147 ff. On the cult, see de Vries, pp. 228 ff. (sacrifices), pp. 233 ff. (festivals); Lantier, pp. 151 ff.

On the various meanings of human sacrifice, see Eliade, *Zalmoxis,* pp. 48 ff.

On the analogies between the religious conceptions of the Celts and those of the Geto-Dacians, see §§178–79.

173. For interpretation of the Scandinavian rock designs, see O. Almgren, *Nordische Felszeichnungen als religiöse Urkunden* (Frankfort, 1934) (the Swedish edition appeared in 1926); Peter Gelling and Hilda Ellis Davidson, *The Chariot of the Sun and Other Rites and Symbols of the Northern Bronze Age* (New York, 1969), pp. 9–116.

The principal sources for Germanic religion are brought together, in German translation, by W. Baetke in *Die Religion der Germanen in Quellenzeugnissen* (1937). The original texts are published by F. R. Schröder, *Quellenbuch zur germanischen Religionsgeschichte* (1933). The best edition, with commentary, of Tacitus' short treatise has been provided by Rudolph Much, *Die "Germania" des Tacitus* (Heidelberg, 1937; 2d ed., 1959).

There is a brief analysis of the medieval sources—the Eddas, the Sagas, the *Edda* of Snorri Sturluson (ca. 1179–1241), and the *Gesta Danorum* of Saxo Grammaticus (born 1150)—in the work by E. O. G. Turville-Petre, *Myth and Religion of the North* (London, 1964), pp. 1–34, 287–90, 321–23 (and, on pp. 321–23, bibliographical information concerning various editions and translations).

We have used the translations by F. Wagner, *Les poèmes héroïques de l'Edda* (Paris, 1929), and *Les poèmes mythologiques de l'Edda* (Liège, 1936). See also C. A. Mastrelli, *L'Edda* (complete translation, with a full commentary) (Florence, 1952); Jean I. Young, *The Prose Edda of Snorri Sturluson: Tales from Norse Mythology* (Berkeley, 1964); Henry Adams Bellows, *The Poetic Edda* (New York, 1968).

The best general presentations are those by Werner Bentz, "Die altgermanische Religion," in W. Stammler, *Deutsche Philologie im Aufriss* (1957), cols. 2467–2556; by Jan de Vries, *Altgermanische*

Religionsgeschichte, 2 vols., 2d ed. (Berlin, 1956–57), and by Turville-Petre, *Myth and Religion of the North* (1964). Pertinent analyses will be found in Helmut Birkhan, *Germanen und Kelten bis zum Ausgang der Römerzeit,* esp. pp. 250–343 (the celestial god among the Germans and the Celts).

Georges Dumézil has several times undertaken the comparative study of Germanic religion from the Indo-European point of view; see, especially, his *Les dieux des Germains* (1959; English trans. by Einar Haugen, *Gods of the Ancient Northmen,* University of California Studies in Comparative Folklore and Mythology, no. 3, Berkeley, 1974); his *Loki* (1948; a second, revised, edition was published in German in 1959); his *La Saga de Hadingus* (1953; a new, enlarged, edition of this work, entitled *Du mythe au roman,* was published in 1970; this has been translated into English by Derek Coltman under the title *From Myth to Fiction: The Saga of Hadingus,* Chicago, 1973); and his *Les dieux souverains des Indo-Européens* (1977), pp. 86 ff. See also Edgar Polomé, "The Indo-European Component in Germanic Religion," in Jaan Puhvel, ed., *Myth and Law among the Indo-Europeans* (Berkeley, 1970), pp. 55–82; Uno Strutynski, "History and Structure in Germanic Mythology: Some Thoughts on Einar Haugen's Critique of Dumézil," in C. G. Larson, ed., *Myth in Indo-European Antiquity* (Berkeley, 1974), pp. 29–50 (cf. Edgar Polomé, "Approaches to Germanic Mythology," ibid., pp. 51–65).

An entirely different orientation is that of Karl Helm, *Altgermanische Religionsgeschichte,* vol. 1 (1913); vol. 2, pts. 1 and 2 (1937–53); cf. the methodological discussion with Dumézil (bibliographical indications, *Les Dieux des Germains,* p. 38). See also Peter Buchholz, "Perspectives for Historical Research in Germanic Religion," *HR* 8 (1968): 111–38 (resistance to Dumézil's approach, p. 114, n. 7); W. Baetke, *Das Heilige im Germanischen* (1942); R. L. M. Derolez, *Les dieux et la religion des Germains* (French trans., Paris, 1962; originally published in Dutch, Roermond, 1959); H. R. Ellis Davidson, *Gods and Myths of Northern Europe* (Harmondsworth, 1964).

In a series of studies Alois Closs has presented Germanic religion from the point of view of historical ethnology; see his "Neue Problemstellungen in der germanischen Religionsgeschichte," *Anthropos* 29 (1934): 477–96; "Die Religion des Semnonenstammes," *Wiener Beiträge zur Kulturgeschichte und Linguistik* 4 (1936): 549–674; "Die Religion der Germanen in ethnologischer Sicht," in *Christus und die Religionen der Erde,* vol. 2 (Vienna, 1951), pp. 271–366; "Historische Ethnologie und Germanistik: Das Gestaltproblem in der Völkerkunde," *Anthropos* 51 (1956): 833–91.

On cosmogony, see F. R. Schröder, "Germanische Schöpfungsmythen," *Germanisch-Romanische Monatsschrift* 19 (1931): 1–26, 81–99; Jan de Vries, *Altgermanische Religion,* vol. 2, pp. 359–71; de Vries, "*Ginnungagap,*" *Acta Philologica Scandinavica* 5 (1930–34): 41–66. See also Kurt Schier, "Die Erdschöpfung aus dem Urmeer und die Kosmogonie der Völospá," in *Märchen, Mythos, Dichtung: Festschrift Friedrich von der Leyen* (Munich, 1963), pp. 303–34 (a comparative study, making use of very full documentation); Bruce Lincoln, "The Indo-European Myth of Creation," *HR* 15 (1976): 121–45; and the bibliographies given for §§ 73, 75, 76.

On the creation of the first human couple, see J. de Vries, *Altgermanische Religion,* vol. 1, pp. 268 ff.; K. Helm, "Weltwerden und Weltvergehen in altgermanischen Sage, Dichtung, und Religion," *Hessische Blätter für Volkskunde* 38 (1940): 1–35 (rich bibliography); Otto Höfler, "Abstammungstraditionen," in *Reallexikon der germanischen Altertumskunde,* vol. 1, pp. 18–29. On anthropogony from trees, see G. Bonfante, "Microcosmo e macrocosmo nel mito indoeuropeo," *Die Sprache* 5 (1959): 1–8.

174. The principal sources for the war between the Aesir and the Vanir are: *Völuspá* 21–24; *Skâldskaparmâl,* chap. 4; *Ynglinga Saga* 1. 2. 405; and Saxo Grammaticus, *Gesta Danorum* 1. 7. They have been translated and commented on by Dumézil in his *Tarpeia* (1947), pp. 253–69, and his *Les dieux des Germains,* pp. 10–14. The interpretation of this war as a "historization" of an Indo-European mythological poem was given by Dumézil in *Tarpeia,* pp. 247–91; *Loki* (1948), pp. 97–106; *L'Héritage indo-européen à Rome* (1949), pp. 125–42; and *Les dieux des Germains,* pp. 3–37. This interpretation has been accepted by J. de Vries, *Altgermanische Religion,* vol. 2, pp. 208–14, and by W. Betz, *Die altgermanische Religion,* col. 2475.

On Óðinn-Wodan, see the treatments by J. de Vries, *Altgermanische Religion,* vol. 2, pp. 27–106, by W. Betz, cols. 2485–95 (these two works contain excellent bibliographies), and by Dumézil, *Les dieux des Germains,* p. 40–64. See also Dumézil, *Les dieux souverains des Indo-Européens,* pp. 189–99; Turville-Petre, *Myth and Religion of the North,* pp. 35–74; Derolez, *Les dieux et les religions des Germains,* 70–91; and Davidson, *Gods and Myths of Northern Europe,* pp. 48–72, 140–57. A psychological interpretation was recently proposed by Richard L. Auld, "The Psychological and Mythic Unity of the God Odhinn," *Numen* 33 (1976): 144–60. In his book *Contribution to the Study of Odhin, Especially in His Relation to Agricultural Practices in Modern Popular Lore,* FF Communications no. 94 (Helsinki, 1931),

Jan de Vries has shown the danger of explaining ancient Germanic religion by the help of folklore (see esp. pp. 62–63).

The Romans homologized Óðinn-Wodan with Mercury, and the Germans translated *dies Mercurii* by "day of Wodan." The reasons for this homologation are not clear. The fact has been adduced that Óðinn, like Mercury, was the protector of traders. In addition, Mercury was supremely the psychopomp, and Óðinn ended by assimilating the function of god of the dead. But what makes the two most akin is their "spiritual" faculties, and especially their mastery of magical powers and their relations with occult techniques (cf. § 92). On Óðinn hanging from the cosmogonic tree, see A. G. Hamel, "Odhinn Hanging on the Tree," *Acta Philologica Scandinavica* 7 (1932): 260–88; Konstantin Reichardt, "Odin am Galgen," in *Wächter und Hüter: Festschrift für Hermann J. Weigand* (1957), pp. 15–28. Óðinn's self-sacrifice and his acquisition of occult wisdom have been analyzed by Jere Fleck, "Odhinn's Self-Sacrifice—A New Interpretation, I: The Ritual Inversion," *Scandinavian Studies* 43 no. 2 (1971): 119–42; "II: The Ritual Landscape," ibid. 43 no. 4 (1971): 385–413.

On the cult of Óðinn-Wodan, see J. de Vries, *Altgermanische Religion,* vol. 2, pp. 48 ff., and Turville-Petre, *Myth and Religion of the North,* pp. 64 ff., 70 ff. On human sacrifices in honor of Óðinn, see Turville-Petre, pp. 48 ff., and James L. Sauve, "The Divine Victim: Aspects of Human Sacrifice in Viking Scandinavia and Vedic India," in *Myth and Law among the Indo-Europeans* (Berkeley, 1970), pp. 173–91.

On shamanism among the ancient Germans, see Eliade, *Shamanism: Archaic Techniques of Ecstasy,* trans. Willard R. Trask (Princeton, 1964), 379 ff. Add: Peter Buchholz, *Schamanistische Züge in der altisländischen Überlieferung* (Inaugural diss., Saarbrücken, 1968); Alois Closs, "Der Schamanismus bei den Indoeuropäern," *Gedenkschrift für Wilhelm Brandenstein* (Innsbruck, 1968), pp. 289–302, esp. pp. 298 ff.; Karl Hauck, *Goldbrakteaten aus Sievern* (Munich, 1970), pp. 444 ff. Against the "shamanistic" interpretations of Óðinn, see Jere Fleck, "The Knowledge-Criterion in the *Grímnismál:* The Case against 'Shamanism,' " *Arkiv för nordisk filologi* 86 (1971): 49–61.

The sources for Sleipnir, the horse with eight legs, and for the two ravens are analyzed by de Vries, *Altgermanische Religion,* vol. 2, pp. 63 ff., and by Turville-Petre, *Myth and Religion of the North,* pp. 57 ff. See also Davidson, *Gods and Myths of Northern Europe,* pp. 145 ff.

On the *seiðr,* see Eliade, *Shamanism,* pp. 385 ff., and Peter Buchholz, *Schamanistische Züge,* pp. 43 ff.

For the other versions of the myth of Kvasir, see Derolez, *Les dieux et les religions des Germains,* pp. 87 ff., and Turville-Petre, *Myth and Religion of the North,* pp. 45 ff.

On Yggdrasill, the cosmic tree, and the symbolism of the center of the world, see de Vries, *Altgermanische Religion,* vol. 2, pp. 380 ff.; Eliade, *Shamanism,* pp. 380. Cf. Turville-Petre, *Myth and Religion of the North,* p. 279.

Like the Spinners (Klōthes) or the Moirai (see § 87), the Norns "spin" men's destinies (see Eliade, *Patterns in Comparative Religion,* trans. Rosemary Sheed [London and New York, 1958], § 58). The names designating destiny (Old Norse *urð,* Anglo-Saxon *wyrd,* German *wurd*) are close to the Latin *vertere,* "to turn." On destiny, the goddess of destiny, and the Norns, see J. de Vries, *Altgermanische Religion,* vol. 1, pp. 267 ff.

175. On *wut,* "fury," and its Indo-European analogues—Celtic *ferg,* the *menos* of the Homeric heroes—see G. Dumézil, *Horace et les Curiaces* (Paris, 1942), pp. 16 ff. On initiations of young warriors in the Indo-European societies, see Dumézil, ibid., pp. 34 ff.; cf. Eliade, *Rites and Symbols of Initiation: The Mysteries of Birth and Rebirth,* trans. Willard R. Trask (New York, 1965), pp. 81 ff. On the *berserkir* see the bibliographies given ibid., pp. 174–82, notes 1–11. Add: Klaus von See, "Berserker," *Zeitschrift für deutsche Wortforschung* n.s. 2 (1961): 129–35; A. Margaret Arendt, "The Heroic Pattern: Old Germanic Helmets," in *From Old Norse Literature and Mythology: A Symposium,* ed. Edgar C. Polomé (Austin, Tex., 1969), pp. 130–99; Eliade, "The Dacians and Wolves," in *Zalmoxis,* pp. 16–20; Mary R. Gerstein, "Germanic *Warg:* The Outlaw as Werwolf," in G. J. Larson et al., eds., *Myth in Indo-European Antiquity* (Berkeley, 1974), pp. 131–56.

On ritual lycanthropy, see *Zalmoxis,* pp. 14 ff.

On the analogies between the *berserkir* and the young *hamatsas*—the members of the Cannibal Society among the Kwakiutl—see Dumézil, *Horace et les Curiaces,* pp. 42 ff.; Eliade, *Zalmoxis,* pp. 16 ff.

On the Valkyries and Valhalla, see the documentation and bibliography in de Vries, *Altgermanische Religion,* vol. 2, pp. 58 ff.; cf. H. R. Ellis Davidson, *Gods and Myths,* pp. 61 ff.

176. On Týr (*Tiwaz, Ziu), see de Vries, *Altgermanische Religion,* vol. 2, pp. 13 ff. Germanists generally dwell on Týr's function as a war god; see Derolez, *Les dieux et les religions des Germains,* pp. 107 ff.; Davidson, *Gods and Myths,* pp. 57 ff. On Týr's juristic aspect and his relations with the peaceful assemblies (*thinge*) of the Germans, see de

Vries, vol. 2, pp. 13 ff.; Dumézil, *Les dieux des Germains,* pp. 68 ff.; and Dumézil, *Les dieux souverains,* pp. 196 ff.

In chapter 9 of his *Germania,* Tacitus writes that the chief gods are Mercury, Mars, and Hercules, that is, Wodan-Óðinn, Týr (Tiwaz), and Thór (Donar). In chapter 39, in his presentation of the Semnones, the chief tribe of the people of the Suebi, the Roman historian relates that at a particular time the delegates of the Suebi gather in a sacred wood; there they immolate human victims to a god whom Tacitus calls *regnator omnium deus.* For a century scholars have tried to prove that this supreme god was either Týr or Wodan; see the history of the controversy in R. Pettazzoni, "Regnator omnium deus," *Essays on the History of Religion* (Leiden, 1954), pp. 136–50; the Italian text appeared in *SMSR* 119–20 (1943–46): 137 ff.; cf. Hildebrecht Hommel, "Die Hauptgottheiten der Germanen bei Tacitus," *ARW* 37 (1941): 144–73; J. de Vries, *Altgermanische Religion,* vol. 2, pp. 32 ff.; Eliade, *Images and Symbols: Studies in Religious Symbolism,* trans. Philip Mairet (New York, 1952), pp. 103 ff. Pettazzoni (p. 145) rejects the identifications with Týr or Wodan; for him, the reference is to the impersonal *numen* of the sacred forest. It must, however, be taken into account that the Suebi were the most important tribe of the Herminones, an eponym derived from the name Irmin-Hermin (see A. Closs, "Die Religion des Semnonenstammes," pp. 653 ff.). Now Rudolf of Fulda, author of the *Translatio S. Alexandri,* composed between 863 and 865, writes that the Saxons venerated a tall wooden column, called in their language Irminsul and in Latin *universalis columna,* for it supports the whole world. (See other references to Irmin and Irminsul in R. Meissmer, "Irminsul bei Widukind von Corvey," *Bonner Jahrbücher* 139 [1934]: 34–35; Heinz Löwe, "Die Irminsul und die Religion der Sachsen," *Deutsches Archiv für Geschichte des Mittelalters* 5 [1942]: 1–22.) So Irmin was a celestial god; in fact, a number of archaic peoples represent their celestial and supreme god in a column that, symbolically, supports the Sky. Following other authors, H. Löwe (p. 15) identifies Irmin with the *regnator omnium deus.* It follows that the Germans worshiped a celestial and supreme deity named Irmin or Tiwaz-Ziu (cf. H. Hommel, "Die Hauptgottheiten," p. 151), a god who was later supplanted by Wodan-Óðinn. See the excellent analysis by Werner Müller, *Die Jupitergigantensäulen und ihre Verwandtes* (Meisenheim am Glan, 1975), esp. pp. 88 ff.

On Thór, see de Vries, *Altgermanische Religion,* vol. 2, pp. 107 ff., and Dumézil's *Les dieux des Germains,* pp. 67 ff., *L'idéologie tripartite des Indo-Européens,* pp. 54 ff., and *Heur et malheur: Aspects mythiques de la fonction guerrière chez les Indo-Européens* (1956), pp. 69

ff. (English translation by Alf Hiltebeitel, *The Destiny of the Warrior* [Chicago, 1970], pp. 89 ff.). See also Turville-Petre, *Myth and Religion of the North,* 75 ff.; F. R. Schröder, "Thor, Indra, Herakles," *Zeitschrift für deutsche Philologie* 76 (1957): 1 ff.; and H. R. Ellis Davidson, "Thor's Hammer," *Folklore* 74 (1963).

The bibliography on Baldr is immense; see, first of all, J. de Vries, *Altgermanische Religion,* vol. 2, pp. 214–38; W. Betz, *Die Altgermanische Religion,* cols. 2502–8; G. Dumézil, *Les dieux des Germains,* pp. 93 ff.; Otto Höfler, "Balders Bestattung und die nordischen Felszeichnungen," *Anzeiger der Österreichischen Akademie der Wissenschaften, Phil.-hist. Klasse* 88 (1951): 343–72; Turville-Petre, *Myth and Religion of the North,* pp. 196 ff. The interpretation of Baldr as a genius of agrarian fecundity, proposed by Mannhardt and Frazer, has been revived by F. R. Schröder, "Balder und der zweite Merseburger Spruch," *Germanisch-Romanische Monatsschrift* 34 (1953): 166–83; the theory has been criticized by J. de Vries, "Der Mythos von Balders Tod," *Arkiv för Nordisk Filologi* 70 (1955): 41–60 (but de Vries's interpretation—Baldr's death as myth, corresponding to a ritual of initiation for young warriors—has not been accepted by Dumézil; see his *Les dieux des Germains,* p. 104). For an exhaustive analysis of the theme of the *mistilteinn,* see Jonathan Z. Smith, "When the Bough Breaks," *HR* 12 (1973): 342–72, esp. pp. 350–70. Since S. Bugge, several scholars have found likenesses between Baldr and Christ; see Derolez, pp. 126 ff.; Turville-Petre, pp. 119 ff. For Dumézil, Baldr takes over the function of Týr ("that degenerate Scandinavian Mithra"); see his *Les dieux des Germains,* p. 93.

For another god of the Aesir, Heimdallr, the documentation is fragmentary. He is the watchman of the gods and is endowed with clairvoyance; he was born of nine mothers. There is an enmity between Heimdallr and Loki, and at the end of the world they will kill each other. The sources for Heimdallr are analyzed by B. Pering, *Heimdall* (1941); cf. J. de Vries, *Altgermanische Religion,* vol. 2, pp. 238 ff.; de Vries, "Heimdallr, dieu énigmatique," *Etudes germaniques* 10 (1955): 257–68. The book by Ake Ohlmarks, *Heimdall und das Horn* (Uppsala, 1937), should be consulted for its ample documentation; his naturalistic explanation (Heimdall = the sun; the horn = the moon) is naïve. Dumézil interprets Heimdallr as a "first god," analogous to Vāyu and Janus; see his "Remarques comparatives sur le dieu scandinave Heimdallr," *Etudes Celtiques* 8 (1959): 263–83.

177. On the Vanir gods, see J. de Vries, *Altgermanische Religion,* vol. 2, pp. 163–208, 307–13; W. Betz, *Die Altgermanische Religion,* cols. 2508–20; Dumézil, *Les dieux des Germains,* pp. 117–27; Turville-Petre, *Myth and Religion of the North,* pp. 156–79, 325 (bibliography).

On Nerthus-Njörð, see Helmut Birkhan, *Germanen und Kelten,* pp. 544 ff.; E. Polomé, "A propos de la déesse Nerthus," *Latomus* 13 (1954): 167 ff.; G. Dumézil, *La Saga de Hadingus, du mythe au roman* (1953); in the new, enlarged edition, *Du mythe au roman* (1970), the author shows that Hadingus is an epic plagiarism from Njörð and his myths; see also his "Njördhr, Nerthus et le folklore scandinave des génies de la mer," *RHR* 147 (1955): 210–26, a study reprinted in *Du mythe au roman,* pp. 185–96 (Eng. trans., *From Myth to Fiction,* pp. 215–29).

On Freyr and Frigg, see the bibliography for the Vanir gods and the treatments by J. de Vries (vol. 2, pp. 302 ff.), Derolez (pp. 139 ff.), and Davidson (*Gods and Myths of Northern Europe,* pp. 92–127).

There is an extensive literature on Loki. The theories put forward up to 1931 have been examined by J. de Vries, *The Problem of Loki, FFC* no. 110 (Helsinki 1933), pp. 10–22; see also de Vries, *Altgermanische Religion,* vol. 2, pp. 255 ff. De Vries compares Loki to the "trickster," a characteristic figure of North American mythology. F. Ström, in *Loki: Ein mythologisches Problem* (Gothenburg, 1956), sees in this god a hypostasis of Óðinn, his "foster brother." Using documents of Scandinavian folklore, A. B. Rooth concludes that the original figure of Loki was the spider (*Locke* in dialectal Swedish); see his *Loki in Scandinavian Mythology* (Lund, 1961). See also de Vries, "Loki . . . und kein Ende," *Festschrift für F. R. Schröder* (Heidelberg, 1959), pp. 1 ff.; Alois Closs, "Loki und die germanische Frömmigkeit," *Kairos* 2 (1960): 89–100. Georges Dumézil has treated the problem in an important book, *Loki* (1948), a second edition of which, considerably altered, appeared in German in 1959; see also his *Les dieux des Germains,* pp. 94 ff. Dumézil has adduced a Caucasian parallel to the drama that opposes Loki to Baldr: the wicked Syrdon succeeds in having the handsome hero Sozryko killed by a seemingly harmless stratagem; see *Loki,* pp. 169 ff.

On the Scandinavian eschatological myth, the Danish scholar Axel Olrik has published a book that is extremely valuable for its abundant documentation: *Ragnarök: Die Sagen vom Weltuntergang,* trans. W. Ranisch (Berlin, 1922). According to Olrik, the conception of the Ragnarök would have been influenced by certain Causasian myths and by Persian and Christian eschatologies. R. Reitzenstein attributed an important role to Manichaean influences; see his "Weltuntergangsvorstellungen" in *Kyrkohistorisk Årsskrift* 24 (1924): 129–212, and his "Die nordischen, persischen und christlichen Vorstellungen vom Weltuntergang,'' in *Vorträge der Bibliothek Warburg 1923–24* (Leipzig and Berlin, 1926): 149–69. But Dumézil has shown that what is really involved is the Indo-European eschatological myth documented in India (the *Mahābhārata*), in Iran, and in Scandinavian tradition; see his *Les dieux des Germains,* pp. 212 ff. Cf. Stig Wikander, "Germanische und indo-iranische Eschatologie," *Kairos* 2 (1960): 83–88. On the Ragnarök, see also J. de Vries, *Altgermanische Religion,* vol. 2, pp. 397 ff.; J. S. Martin, *Ragnarök* (Assen, 1972).

Ideas concerning postmortem existence and the mythology of death are analyzed by G. Neckel, *Walhall: Studien über germanischen Jenseitsglauben* (Dortmund, 1931); H. R. Ellis, *The Road to Hel* (Cambridge, 1943); and R. T. Christiansen, *The Dead and the Living* (1946).

Pertinent observations on the initiation of warriors, the destiny of the hero, and the paganism-Christianity symbiosis will be found in a study by H. Margaret Arendt, "The Heroic Pattern: Old Germanic Helmets, Beowulf, and the Grettis Saga," in *From Old Norse Literature and Mythology: A Symposium,* ed. Edgar C. Polomé (Austin, Tex., 1969), pp. 130–99.

On the Gosforth cross, see K. Berg, "The Gosforth Cross," *Journal of the Warburg and Courtauld Institutes* 21 (1951): 27 ff. (excellent photographic reproductions).

On Germanic royalty, Otto Höfler has published a suggestive and extremely learned book, *Germanische Sakralkönigtum,* vol. 1: *Der Runenstein von Rök und die germanische Individualweihe* (Tübingen, 1953); see also his article in *The Sacral Kingship* (Leiden, 1959), pp. 664 ff. See the review by J. de Vries, in *Germanisch-Romanische Monatsschrift* 34 (1953): 183 ff., and our observations in *Critique* 83 (1954): 328 ff. The importance of the runic inscription on the Rök monument lies in the fact that its author, Varin, guardian of a sanctuary, "consecrates" his son not to a god—a custom well documented in Germanic traditions—but to a king, Theodoric, king of the Goths. Now Varin erects the monument in Sweden, but Theodoric had reigned in Italy, at Verona, *several centuries earlier.* "But," the text of the inscription states, Theodoric "still decides the fate of battles." He intervenes in battles fully armed, shield on shoulder, riding his charger. Theodoric was not only a king who, during his lifetime and after his death, had known glory and apotheosis; for the whole Germanic world he had become a mythical personage, and, under the name Diederich of Berne, he was still popular in the nineteenth century and even in the twentieth. These facts were well known. But the Rök inscription proves that it is no longer a matter of "literature" or folklore but of a *living* religious belief; in other words, when he erected his monument,

Varin performed a *ritual,* which implied belief in the *sacredness of the king.*

On Germanic royalty, see also K. Hauck, "Herrschaftszeichnen eines Wodanistischen Königtums," *Jahrbuch für fränkische Landesforschung* 14 (1954): 9–66; J. de Vries, "Das Königtum bei den Germanen," *Saeculum* 7 (1956): 289–310.

178. On the protohistory and history of the Thracians, see the treatment in Joseph Wiesner, *Die Thraker* (Stuttgart, 1963). The work by W. Tomaschek, "Die alten Thraker," *Sitzungsberichte der Akad. Wien* 130 (1893) remains fundamental. Scattered but useful information concerning certain religious ideas will be found in recent works on the Thracian language, first of all those by D. Dečev, *Die thrakischen Sprachreste* (Vienna, 1957); I. I. Russu, *Limba Traco-Dacilor,* 2d ed. (Bucharest, 1963); C. Poghirc, ed., *Thraco-dacica* (Bucharest, 1976); Poghirc, *Studii de tracologie* (1976).

Raffaele Pettazzoni has presented an overall view in "La religione dell'antica Tracia," in *Serta Kazaroviana* (= *Bulletin de l'Institut Archéologique Bulgare* 16 [Sofia, 1950]: 291–99, a study published in an English translation, "The Religion of Ancient Thrace," in Pettazzoni's *Essays on the History of Religions* [Leiden, 1954], pp. 81–94). See also Furio Jesi, "Su Macrobe *Sat.* I. 18: Uno schizzo della religione tracica antica," *Studii Clasice* 11 (Bucharest, 1969): 178–86.

On the Thracian cult of Ares, see Wiesner, *Die Thraker,* pp. 101 ff. and notes 36 ff. On Bendis-Artemis, see ibid., pp. 106 ff. and the sources cited in notes 48 ff.

On Zbelsurdos, see G. Seure, "Les images thraces de Zeus Keraunos: Zbelsurdos, Gebeleïzis, Zalmoxis," *REG* 26 (1913): 225–61; A. B. Cook, *Zeus,* vol. 2, pt. 1 (Cambridge, 1925), pp. 817–24.

On the Thracian "Dionysus," chapter 8 of the work by Erwin Rohde, *Psyche: The Cult of Souls and Belief in Immortality among the Greeks,* has not been surpassed. (The original edition, *Psyche: Seelencult und Unsterblichkeitsglaube der Griechen,* was published in 1894. We cite the English translation by W. B. Hillis, published in 1925.) See also Wiesner, *Die Thraker,* pp. 102 ff.

Under the name of Sabazius, the cult of the Thracian "Dionysus" spread as far as Africa (as early as the fourth century B.C.); see Charles Picard, "Sabazios, dieu thraco-phrygien: Expansion et aspects nouveaux de son culte," *Revue archéologique* 2 (1961): 129–76; see also M. Macrea, "Le culte de Sabazius en Dacie," *Dacia* n.s. 3 (1959): 325–39; E. Lozovan, "Dacia Sacra," *HR* 7 (1968): 215–19.

On the syncretistic cult of Sabazius ("the hand of Sabazius," the assimilation with Yahweh, etc.), see W. O. E. Oesterley, "The Cult of Sabazios," in *The Labyrinth,* ed. S. H. Hooke (London, 1925), pp. 115–58.

On the Thraco-Getan ascetics and contemplatives, see Eliade, *Zalmoxis,* pp. 61 ff.

The representations of the "Hero on Horseback" in Bulgaria have been inventoried by Gavril I. Kazarow in his *Die Denkmäler des thrakischen Reitergottes in Bulgarien,* 2 vols., Dissertationes Pannonicae (Budapest, 1938). See also his "Zum Kult des thrakischen Reiters in Bulgarien," *Wissenschaftliches Zeitschrift der Karl Marx Universität* 3 (Leipzig, 1953–54): 135–37; C. Picard, "Nouvelles observations sur diverses représentations du Héros-Cavalier des Balkans," *RHR* 150 (1956): 1–26; and R. Pettazzoni, "The Religion of Ancient Thrace," pp. 84 ff.

179. The Geto-Dacians descend directly from the Thracians of the Bronze Age. They extended well beyond the present frontiers of Romania. Recent excavations have brought to light Geto-Dacian sites as far east as the Dniester, south as far as the Balkans, and north and west as far as Hungary, southeastern Slovakia, and Serbia. In the first century B.C., under King Boerebista, the Dacian state attained its greatest power. But the Romans, who had made their way into the Balkan Peninsula toward the end of the third century, reached the Danube in the days of Augustus. The second important Dacian king, Decebalus, successfully fought off the Romans under Domitian in 89 but was conquered by Trajan's legions in two bloody wars (101–2, 105–7) and committed suicide. Dacia was then transformed into a Roman province. From the ample bibliography on the protohistory and history of Dacia, we mention: Vasile Pârvan, *Getica* (Bucharest, 1926); Pârvan, *Dacia: An Outline of the Early Civilization of the Carpatho-Danubian Countries* (Cambridge, 1928; see also the Romanian translation of this work by Radu Vulpe, 4th ed. [Bucharest, 1967], containing important additions and critical bibliographies by the translator [pp. 159–216]); Hadrian Daicoviciu, *Dacii* (Bucharest, 1965); H. Daicoviciu, *Dacia de la Buerebista la cucerirea romană* (Bucharest, 1972); R. Vulpe, *Aşezări getice în Muntenia* (Bucharest, 1966); I. H. Crişan, *Burebista şi epoca sa* (1975). On the expansion of the Thracians and the Geto-Dacians and their relations with the Scythians, see M. Dušek, "Die Thraker im Karpatenbecken," *Slovenska Archaeologia* 22 (1974): 361–428.

According to Strabo (7. 3. 12), the Dacians were originally named *daoi*. A tradition preserved by Hesychius informs us that *daos* was the

Phrygian word for "wolf." Thus the early Dacians called themselves "wolves" or "those who are like wolves." Now the wolf was the exemplary model of the warrior: imitation of the wolf's behavior and external appearance was characteristic of military initiations and of the secret warrior brotherhoods. See Eliade, "The Dacians and Wolves," in *Zalmoxis,* pp. 5–20.

On the religious beliefs of the Geto-Dacians see I. I. Russu, "Religia Geto-Dacilor: Zei, credinţe, practici religioase," *Annuarul Institutului de Studii Clasice* 5 (Cluj, 1947): 61–137, and the bibliography given in our *Zalmoxis,* p. 22, n. 1.

On Gebeleïzis, see *Zalmoxis,* pp. 51–55, and the bibliographies given in notes 87–97. Add: C. Poghirc, "Considérations philologiques et linguistiques sur Gebeleïzis," *Academia Litterarum Bulgarica,* vol. 2: *Thracia* (Serdicae, 1974), pp. 357–60. The author proposes (p. 359) to read this divine name as **Nebeleizis,* the first part of which is close to Greek *nephelē,* Lat. *nebula,* Anglo-Saxon *nifol,* meaning "cloud, stormy sky," while the second part means "god."

On Zalmoxis, see the bibliography given in our *Zalmoxis,* p. 22, n. 1. See ibid., pp. 24 ff., for the analysis of the mythico-ritual scenario that can be detected in Herodotus 4. 94–96.

On the Greek ecstatics, thaumaturges, and "shaman-philosophers," with whom numerous scholars have compared Zalmoxis, see *Zalmoxis,* pp. 34–42.

From Jakob Grimm to Neckel and Jan de Vries, some Germanists have compared the theme of Zalmoxis' occultation with the death of Freyr, god of fertility, but the comparison is not necessarily valid; see *Zalmoxis,* pp. 47–48.

Hippolytus (*Philosophoumena* 2. 25) reports a legend according to which Zalmoxis would have propagated the Pythagorean doctrine among the Celts, which once again proves the importance attributed to the tradition that defined the religion of Zalmoxis by belief in the immortality of the soul. H. Hubert has compared Druidism with the Thracian and Geto-Dacian brotherhoods; see his *Les Celtes depuis l'époque de la Tène,* p. 283. It is above all the importance of the high priest, the belief in immortality, and a sacred science of the Druidic initiatory type that suggest Geto-Dacian parallels. Moreover, certain Celtic influences must be considered, since the Celts inhabited the western parts of Dacia for some time; see Parvân, *Getica,* pp. 461 ff.; Parvân, *Dacia, Civilizaţiile antice din ţările carpato-danubiene,* 4th ed. (Bucharest, 1967), pp. 103 ff., 183 ff.; H. Daicoviciu, *Dacii,* pp. 61 ff.

On the *Getica* of Jordanes, see Eliade, *Zalmoxis,* pp. 64 ff. and note 127. Add: Norbert Wagner, *Getica: Untersuchungen zum Leben des Jordanes und zur frühen Geschichte der Goten* (Berlin, 1967).

On the "observatory-temples" of Sarmizegetuza and Costeşti, see C. D. Daicoviciu, "Le problème de l'état et de la culture des Daces à la lumière des nouvelles recherches," in *Nouvelles études d'histoire présentées au Xe Congrès de sciences historiques* (Bucharest, 1955), pp. 126 ff.; Hadrian Daicoviciu, "Il Tempio-Calendario dacico di Sarmizegetuza," *Dacia* n.s. 4 (Bucharest, 1960): 231–54; H. Daicoviciu, *Dacii,* pp. 194 ff., 210 ff.

On the later history of Zalmoxis in the mythologizing historiography of the Middle Ages (the Getae are confused with the Goths, etc.), see Eliade, *Zalmoxis,* pp. 70 ff.

Chapter 22. Orpheus and Pythagoras

180. The texts have been edited by O. Kern, *Orphicorum Fragmenta* (Berlin, 1922); translations of some of the texts can be found in W. K. C. Guthrie, *Orpheus and Greek Religion* (London, 1935; 2d ed., 1952), pp. 59 ff., 137 ff., and in G. Arrighetti, *Frammenti Orfici* (Turin, 1959). A good edition of the Orphic hymns is G. Quandt's *Orphei Hymni* (Berlin, 1941), and a partial translation, with full commentary, has been made by G. Faggin, *Inni Orfici* (Florence, 1949). See also G. Dottin, *Les "Argonautiques" d'Orphée* (Paris, 1930).

Critical analysis of the sources, from radically different points of view, has been undertaken by Guthrie, *Orpheus,* pp. 29 ff., and by I. M. Linforth, *The Arts of Orpheus* (Berkeley, 1941), passim. R. Böhme, *Orpheus, der Sänger und seine Zeit* (Berne and Munich, 1970), has once again made a meticulous examination of the earliest textual data. See also K. Ziegler, "Orphische Dichtung," in the Pauly-Wissowa *Realencyklopädie,* vol. 28 (1942), cols. 1321–1417.

A complete bibliography of modern works down to 1922 was compiled by Kern for his *Orphicorum Fragmenta* (pp. 345 ff.); this was updated to 1941 by Martin P. Nilsson in "Early Orphism and Kindred Religious Movements," *Opuscula Selecta,* vol. 2 (Lund, 1952), note 1, pp. 628–30 (this article is an enlarged version of an article published in *HTR* 28 [1935]: 181–230). For recent research, see K. Prümm, "Die Orphik im Spiegel der neueren Forschung," *Zeitschrift für Katholische Theologie* 78 (1956): 1–40. From the large literature on Orpheus and Orphism, we mention: E. Mass, *Orpheus: Untersuchungen zur griechischen, römischen, altchristlichen Jenseitsdichtung und Religion*

(Munich, 1895); Otto Kern, *Orpheus: Eine Religionsgeschichtliche Untersuchung* (Berlin, 1920); A. Boulanger, *Orphée: Rapports de l'orphisme et du christianisme* (Paris, 1925), esp. pp. 17–67; Vittorio Macchioro, *Zagreus: Studi intorno all'orfismo* (Florence, 1930) (to be consulted with caution); P. Boyancé, *Le culte des Muses* (1937), pp. 33–61; Nilsson, "Early Orphism"; Nilsson, *Geschichte der griechischen Religion,* 3d ed., vol. 1 (1967), pp. 678–99; 2d ed., vol. 2 (1961), pp. 246–431 (the complete second edition has been translated into English under the title *A History of Greek Religion* [New York, 1964]); Guthrie, *Orpheus and Greek Religion;* Guthrie, *The Greeks and Their Gods* (Boston, 1968), pp. 307–32; Guthrie, *A History of Greek Philosophy,* 4 vols. (Cambridge, 1975); Linforth, *The Arts of Orpheus;* E. R. Dodds, *The Greeks and the Irrational* (Berkeley, 1951), pp. 146 ff.; R. Pettazzoni, *La religion dans la Grèce antique* (Paris, 1953), pp. 108–31; Louis Moulinier, *Orphée et l'orphisme à l'époque classique* (Paris, 1955); Dario Sabbatucci, *Saggio sul misticismo greco* (Rome, 1965), pp. 69–126; Walter Burkert, "Orpheus und die Vorsokratiker," *Antike und Abendland* 14 (1968): 93–114; Burkert, *Griechische Religion der archäischen und klassischen Epochen* (Stuttgart, 1977), pp. 440–47 ("Orpheus und Pythagoras").

Orpheus' Thracian origin, already maintained by Strabo and Plutarch, has been adopted again by E. Rohde (*Psyche*), by E. Mass (*Orpheus*), and by P. Perdrizet (*Cultes et mythes du Pangée,* 1910). But A. Boulanger has discerningly observed that "the most characteristic features of Orphism—consciousness of sin, need of purification and redemption, infernal punishments—have never been found among the Thracians" (*Orphée,* p. 47, n. 1). See also R. Böhme, in *Annales Univ. Saraviensis* 6 (1956): 3 ff. A. J. van Windeken suggests that the "Hyperboreans" were originally a religious group with Orphic tendencies before they were defined as a mythical people; see his "Hyperboréens," *Rheinisches Museum* 100 (1957): 164–69.

M. Detienne has recently put forward a new reading for the myth of the loss of Eurydice in "Orphée au miel," *Quaderni Urbinati di Cultura Classica,* no. 12 (1971), pp. 17 ff. The murder of Orpheus was a favorite subject of fifth-century painters; see Guthrie, *Orpheus,* pp. 64–65, and fig. 4, pl. IV, and Moulinier, *Orphée et l'orphisme,* p. 14, n. 2 (listed according to Sir John Beazley's catalogue, *Attic Red-Figured Vase-Paintings,* Oxford, 1942).

181. On the Platonic myth of the soul, shut up in the body (*sōma*) as in a tomb (*sēma*), and its relations with Orphism, see the analyses and commentaries, made from different points of view, in the following works: Guthrie, *Orpheus,* pp. 214 ff.; Guthrie, *The Greeks and Their Gods,* pp. 311 ff.; Linforth, *The Arts of Orpheus,* pp. 147 ff. and passim; Perceval Frutiger, *Les mythes de Platon* (Paris, 1930), pp. 259 ff.; F. Cumont, *Lux Perpetua* (Paris, 1949), pp. 245 ff.; and Moulinier, *Orphée et l'orphisme,* pp. 24 ff.

On the "Orphic life," see Guthrie, *Orpheus,* 263–66; Dodds, *The Greeks and the Irrational,* pp. 149 ff.

On Orphic mysticism, see Dario Sabbatucci, *Saggio sul misticismo greco,* pp. 41 ff. On the meaning of Orphic vegetarian practices, see Guthrie, *Orpheus,* pp. 197 ff.; Sabbatucci, pp. 69 ff.; Marcel Detienne, "La cuisine de Pythagore," *Archives de sociologie des religions,* no. 29 (1970), pp. 141–62; Detienne, *Les jardins d'Adonis* (Paris, 1972), pp. 85 ff. and passim (English trans., *The Gardens of Adonis,* New York, 1976).

The documents concerning the Orphic theogonies and cosmogonies are translated and commented on by Guthrie, *Orpheus,* chap. 4; Alderinck, *Crisis and Cosmogony: Post-Mortem Existence in the Eleusinian and Orphic Mysteries* (Ph.D. diss., University of Chicago, 1974), chap. 6. See also R. Mondolfo, "Intorno al contenuto dell'antica teogonia orfica," *Rivista di filologia classica* 59 (1931): 433–61; F. Dümmler, "Zu orphische Kosmologie," *Archiv f. Gesch. d. Phil.* 7 (1948).

For analogies with the Phoenician and Egyptian cosmogonies, see two articles by Ugo Bianchi, "Protogonos," *SMSR* 28 (1957): 119 ff., and "Le dualisme en histoire des religions," *RHR* 159 (1961): 26 ff., and S. Morenz, *Die Aegypten und die altorphische Kosmogonie* (1950).

In his book *Die Trennung von Himmel und Erde: Ein vorgriechischer Schöpfungsmythos bei Hesiod und den Orphiker* (Tübingen, 1942; reprinted, Darmstadt, 1968), pp. 85 ff., Willibald Staudacher distinguishes two original Orphic cosmogonies, the first based on the motif of Night (Eudemus and Plato, *Timaeus* 40c and 41a), the other on the theme of the primordial Egg (Aristophanes, *The Birds* 650–731; also Hieronymus and Hellanicus); these two traditions were amalgamated in the cosmogony of the Orphic *Rhapsodies.* The Derveni Papyrus, discovered in 1962, has revealed an independent theory, glorifying the cosmogonic power and absolute sovereignty of Zeus. This papyrus has been edited by S. C. Kapsomenos and translated into German by Walter Burkert in "Orpheus und die Vorsokratiker: Bemerkungen zum Derveni-Papyrus und zum pythagoreischen Zahlenlehre," *Antike und Abendland* 13 (1967): 93–114 (translation, pp. 94–96), and by R. Merkelbach in "Der orphische Papyrus von Derveni," *Zeitschrift für Papyrologie und*

Epigraphik 1 (1967): 23–30. An English translation, with commentary, has been provided by Alderinck in *Crisis and Cosmogony,* chap. 6.

On the myths of the Titans struck by Zeus's thunderbolts, see §124 in vol. 1 of the present work. The birth of men from the Titans' ashes has given rise to countless controversies. Nilsson (*Geschichte der griechischen Religion,* vol. 1, pp. 686 ff.) accepts the antiquity of the myth; on the other hand, Linforth (*Arts,* p. 331) holds that we have no convincing element to determine the age of the tradition. Moulinier's hypercriticism (*Orphée,* pp. 44 ff.) arrives at a completely negative result: "It is Plutarch who first . . . saw that the myth of the Titans devouring Dionysus refers to our own birth: men who eat flesh will be punished as they were" (p. 59, referring to *De esu carne* 996e, Kern, *Orph. Frag.,* no. 210, p. 231). On the other hand, Dodds says that, taking into account *all* references to the myth, "I find it hard to resist the conclusion that the complete story was known to Plato and his public" (*The Greeks and the Irrational,* p. 156; cf. p. 176, notes 132 and 135). Dodds allows a certain importance to Xenocrates' testimony. For discussion of this passage, see P. Boyancé, "Xenocrates and the Orphics," *Rev. des études anciennes* 50 (1948): 218–25. J. C. G. Strachan ("Who Did Forbid Suicide at *Phaedo* 62b?" *Classical Quarterly* n.s. 20 [1970]: 216–20) derives Xenocrates' fragment from an Orphic source. In any case, Olympiodorus states that Plato's work "is filled with echoes of the writings of Orpheus" (ad *Phaed.* 70c; Kern, *Orph. Frag.,* no. 224). See also H. Jeanmaire, *Dionysos,* pp. 391 ff. Ugo Bianchi interprets the myth of Zagreus and the passage in Plato's *Laws* 701c–d on "the old nature of the Titans" as an "antecedent sin," committed by superhuman beings in a time preceding human existence; see his "Péché originel et péché antécédent," *RHR* 170 (1966): 118 ff.

182. On the Orphic underworlds, see Kern in *RE,* s.v. "Mysterien," col. 1287; Cumont, *Lux Perpetua* (Paris, 1949), pp. 245 ff.; M. Treu, "Die neue 'orphische' Unterweltbeschreibung und Vergil," *Hermes* 82 (1954): 24–51. On Orphic eschatology, see Guthrie, *Orpheus,* pp. 164 ff., 183 ff.; R. Turcan, "L'âme-oiseau et l'eschatologie orphique," *RHR* 155 (1959): 33–40; Walter Burkert, *Lore and Science in Ancient Pythagoreanism* (Cambridge, Mass., 1972), pp. 125 ff. (original edition: *Weisheit und Wissenschaft* [Nuremberg, 1962]).

On the Platonic theory of reincarnation, see two articles by R. S. Bluck, "The *Phaedrus* and Reincarnation," *American Journal of Philology* 79 (1958): 156–64, and "Plato, Pindar and Metempsychosis," ibid., pp. 405–14.

The Orphic origin of the gold plates found in Italy and Crete, generally accepted until about 1930, has been disputed by U. von Wilamowitz-Moellendorff, *Der Glaube der Hellenen,* 2 vols. (Berlin, 1931–32), vol. 2, pp. 202 ff.; A. Boulanger, "Le salut selon l'Orphisme," *Mémorial Lagrange* (Paris, 1940), p. 71; Boulanger, *Orphée et l'orphisme,* p. 23; C. Picard, "Remarques sur l'Apologue dit de Prodicos," *Revue archéologique* 6th ser. 42 (1953): 23; G. Zuntz, *Persephone: Three Essays on Religion and Thought in Magna Graecia* (Oxford, 1971), pp. 318 ff. (but see the critique by R. Turcan, *RHR* 183 [1973]: 184). It is now agreed to call the plates "Orphico-Pythagorean"; see, inter alia, Konrad Ziegler, "Orphische Dichtung," *RE,* vol. 18, cols. 1386–88; Guthrie, *Orpheus,* pp. 171–82; Cumont, *Lux Perpetua,* pp. 248, 406; Burkert, *Science and Lore in Ancient Pythagoreanism,* p. 113, n. 21 (with bibliography).

The texts inscribed on the gold plates have been edited by Diels-Krantz, *Die Fragmente der Vorsokratiker,* vol. 1, sec. 1B, Frags. 17–21, and by Kern, *Orph. Frag.,* no. 32. See also the English translations by Gilbert Murray, "Critical Appendix on the Orphic Tablets," in J. E. Harrison, *Prolegomena to the Study of Greek Religion* (Cambridge, 1903; 2d ed., 1922), pp. 664–66, and Guthrie, *Orpheus,* pp. 172 ff. The best edition of the gold plates—which he considers to be Pythagorean in origin—and the strictest analysis of the texts have been provided by Günther Zuntz in *Persephone: Three Essays on Religion and Thought in Magna Graecia,* pp. 275–393.

On the "thirst of the dead," see André Parrot, *Le "Refrigerium" dans l'au-delà* (Paris, 1937); Eliade, "Locum refrigerii . . . ,"*Zalmoxis* 1 (1938): 203–8; T. Gaster, *Thespis* (1961), pp. 204 ff.; Zuntz, *Persephone,* pp. 370 ff.

On "forgetting" and "memory" in ancient Greece, see Eliade, *Myth and Reality,* trans. Willard R. Trask (New York, 1963), pp. 119 ff., using the article by J. V. Vernant, "Aspects mythiques de la mémoire en Grèce," *Journal de psychologie* 56 (1959): 1–29; cf. Marcel Detienne, *Les maîtres de vérité dans la Grèce ancienne* (Paris, 1967), pp. 9–27 ("La mémoire du poète"), and pp. 125 ff. (very extensive bibliography).

"An exile by the will of the gods and a wanderer"—so Empedocles presented himself. "For already have I once been a boy and a girl, and a bush and a bird, and a sea fish" (*Purifications,* frag. 117). Speaking of Pythagoras, Empedocles described him as "a man knowing an extraordinary number of things," for, "when he reached out with all his thoughts, he would see easily every one of all the things that are in the ten, or even twenty, lifetimes that one lived as a man" (ibid., frag. 129); cf. Ettore Bignone's commentary, *Empedocle* (Turin, 1926), pp.

483 ff. The Indian yogins and *ṛṣis* remembered some of their previous existences, but the Buddha alone knew them *all*. This is a way of saying that only the Buddha was omniscient; see Eliade, *Yoga*, pp. 180 ff. The fact that shamans also claim to remember their former existences indicates the archaism of the practice; see Eliade, *Myths, Dreams, and Mysteries: The Encounter between Contemporary Faiths and Archaic Realities*, trans. Philip Mairet (New York, 1960), pp. 51–52.

The essentials of the legend of Aristeas of Proconnesus are reported by Herodotus (4. 14). Left for dead in his city, he was met on the road to Cyzicus. After seven years he was said to have reappeared at Proconnesus, bringing with him an epic poem in which he narrated his adventures: "possessed by Phoebus," he traveled as far as to the Issidones, where he was told about their neighbors, the Arimaspes ("men who are said to have but one eye") and the Hyperboreans. He disappeared for the second time, but Herodotus adds that 240 years later he appeared in Metaponte, in southern Italy, and ordered the inhabitants to build an altar to Apollo and, beside the altar, to erect "a statue bearing the name of Aristeas of Proconnesus." He told them that in the form of a crow he had accompanied Apollo when the god once visited Metaponte. "This said, he disappeared." Let us note some distinctly shamanic features: ecstasy that can be confused with death, bilocation, appearance in the form of a crow. On Aristeas, see the bibliographies given in Eliade, *Zalmoxis, the Vanishing God*, trans. Willard R. Trask (Chicago, 1972), p. 37, n. 44, and Burkert, *Lore and Science*, pp. 147–49. J. D. P. Bolton, in his book *Aristeas of Proconnesus* (Oxford, 1962), presents a "historicistic" interpretation of the legend. Another legendary personage, Hermotimus of Clazomenae, had the power to leave his body for many years. During this long ecstasy he journeyed far, and on his return he predicted the future. But one day, when he was lying inanimate, his enemies burned his body, and his soul never returned after that (see *Zalmoxis*, p. 37, n. 45).

Certain "shamanic" features can be identified in the legends of Epimenides of Crete, of Phormion, and of Leonymus (see *Zalmoxis*, pp. 37–38; Burkert, *Lore and Science*, p. 152). Some scholars have added the names of Parmenides and Empedocles. H. Diels had already compared Parmenides' mystical journey, described in his poem, to the ecstatic journeys of Siberian shamans; the subject was taken up again, with various arguments, by Meuli, Morrison, Burkert, and Guthrie (see *Zalmoxis*, p. 38 and notes 48–50). As for Empedocles, Dodds writes that his fragments represent "the one first-hand source from which we can still form some notion of what a Greek shaman was really like" (*The Greeks and the Irrational*, p. 145). This interpretation has been rejected by Charles H. Kahn: "Empedocles' soul does not leave his body like that of Hermotimus and Epimenides. He does not ride on an arrow like Abaris or appear in the form of a raven like Aristeas. He is never seen in two places at the same time, and does not even descend to the underworld like Orpheus and Pythagoras" ("Religion and Natural Philosophy in Empedocles' Doctrine of the Soul," *Archiv für Geschichte der Philosophie* 42 [1962]: 3–35, esp. pp. 30 ff.). However, Empedocles is known for certain magical powers: he can control storms and bring rains (frag. 111; see other references in Burkert, *Lore and Science,* pp. 153–54). This practice is characteristic of Turkish, Mongol, and Icelandic shamans; see John Andrew Boyle, "Turkish and Mongol Shamanism in the Middle Ages," *Folklore* 83 (1972): 184 ff.; Stefan Einarsson, "Harp Song, Heroic Poetry . . . ," *Budklavlen* 42 (1965): 25–26. We add that this is a practice that goes beyond the sphere of shamanism *stricto sensu.*

For Pythagorean "shamanism," see Burkert, pp. 120 ff. (with an ample bibliography); J. A. Philip, *Pythagoras and Early Pythagoreanism* (Toronto, 1966), pp. 159 ff.; M. Detienne, *La notion de Daimon dans le pythagorisme ancien* (Paris, 1963), pp. 60 ff.

On the differences between the two categories of Pythagoreans—the *acousmatici* (held to be "inferior") and the *mathematici* (representing the Master's esoteric knowledge)—see Burkert, *Lore and Science,* pp. 166 ff., 192 ff. See also M. Detienne, "Des confréries de guerriers à la société pythagoricienne," *RHR* 163 (1963): 127–31.

The existence of an Orphic "sect" or of Orphic conventicles, accepted by Guthrie, *Orpheus,* pp. 203 ff., and by Cumont, *Lux Perpetua,* pp. 240, 244, 405–6, has been disputed by Festugière (in agreement with Gruppe and Wilamowitz) in his study "L'Orphisme et la légende de Zagreus," *Revue Biblique* 44 (1935): 366–96. Yet we may compare the Orphic "secret groups" to the no less secret associations of Tantric adepts.

183. From the extensive bibliography on Plato's myths, we single out Karl Reinhardt, *Platons Mythen* (Bonn, 1927); Perceval Frutiger, *Les mythes de Platon* (Paris, 1930); P. M. Schuhl, *Etudes sur la fabulation platonicienne* (Paris, 1947); Ludwig Edelstein, "The Function of the Myth in Plato's Philosophy," *Journal of the History of Ideas* 10 (1949): 463 ff.; W. J. W. Koster, *Le mythe de Platon, de Zarathoustra et des Chaldéens* (Leiden, 1951); Paul Friedländer, *Plato,* vol. 1 (Princeton, 1958; 2d ed., 1969), pp. 171–212.

On Pherecydes of Syros and the probable Oriental influences on his cosmology and anthropology, see M. L. West, *Early Greek Philosophy and the Orient* (Oxford, 1971), pp. 1–75.

On beliefs in celestial immortality, the ancient sources and modern critical studies have been admirably analyzed by Walter Burkert, *Lore and Science in Ancient Pythagoreanism,* pp. 358 ff. Louis Rougier's interpretation, *L'Origine astronomique de la croyance pythagoricienne en l'immortalité céleste des âmes* (Cairo, 1935), according to which the origin of the idea is not to be sought in religious imagination but in "Pythagoras' astronomical revolution" (pp. 21 f.), is critically examined and rejected by Burkert, *Lore and Science,* p. 358, n. 41.

On the similarities between the philosophies of Pythagoras and Plato, see Burkert, pp. 43 ff., 53 ff., 81 ff. On the *Timaeus* interpreted as a Pythagorean document, see ibid., pp. 64 ff., 84 ff. The possible Oriental influences on Plato are discussed by Joseph Bidez, *Eos, ou Platon et l'Orient* (Brussels, 1945), chaps. 5 and 9, and by Julia Kerschensteiner, *Platon und der Orient* (Stuttgart, 1945), pp. 147 ff., who argues against them.

We observed above (p. 201 and n. 46) the analogy between one of Plato's images ("the wings of the soul") and Indian thought. We add that, for Plato, as for Sāṃkhya-Yoga and Vedānta, the so-called "virtues" lose their value beside the supreme faculty of the soul, which is to contemplate the Eternal (*Rep.* bk. IV, 428 ff.). The duty of the perfect sage is to perfect his inner life in order to gain liberation. The highest knowing, applied to true Being, leads to liberation; to know God is to become divine.

We must point out a rather unexpected parallel to *anamnēsis.* Like Plato (*Meno* 81), the Australian Aranda also believe that to *know* is to *remember.* During his initiation the novice learns the myths that narrate the activities of the totemic ancestors, who lived at the beginning of time. He next learns that he himself is the reincarnation of one of these ancestors. In the mythology of a particular hero he discovers his own fabulous biography, his exploits during the primordial period. Certain material objects (rocks, *tjurungas,* etc.) are proofs of his earlier and glorious existence on earth. (For Plato, too, external objects help the soul to recover the knowledge that it possessed during its supraterrestrial existence.) Among the Aranda the supreme initiatory act consists in the revelation, by the novice's father, of the mystical identity between the young man and the sacred object (*tjurunga*). "Young man, see this object. This is your own body. This is the tjilpa ancestor you were when you used to wander about in your previous existence. Then you sank down to rest in the sacred cave nearby" (T. G. H. Strehlow, quoted in Eliade, *Australian Religions: An Introduction* [Ithaca, N.Y., 1973], pp. 98–99).

On another occasion we outlined the process of erosion of Greek myths (*Myth and Reality,* pp. 152 ff.). We quote some fragments from Xenophanes (born ca. 565): ''Homer and Hesiod say that the gods do all manner of things which men would consider disgraceful: adultery, stealing, deceiving each other.'' He cleverly criticizes the anthropomorphism of the gods: ''If cattle and horses or lions had hands, or were able to draw with their hands and do the works that men can do, horses would draw the forms of gods like horses, and cattle like cattle, and they would make their bodies such as each had themselves.''

Yet the mythology of Homer and Hesiod continued to interest the scholars of the whole Hellenistic world. But the myths were no longer accepted literally: now ''hidden meanings,'' ''undermeanings'' (*hyponoiai;* the term *allēgoria* was used later) were sought in them. By means of the allegorical method, developed especially by the Stoics, Homer and Hesiod were ''saved'' in the eyes of the Greek elites, and the Homeric gods were able to retain a high cultural value. Another method, euhemerism, contributed to saving the Homeric pantheon and mythology. At the beginning of the third century B.C. Euhemerus published a romance in the form of a philosophical journey, *Hiera anagraphē* (Sacred History), whose success was immediate and considerable. Euhemerus believed that he had discovered the origin of the gods: they were ancient kings who had been deified. This offered another ''rational'' possibility of preserving Homer's gods. They now had a ''reality'': it was historical (more precisely, prehistoric) in nature; the myths represented a confused memory, or a memory transfigured by imagination, of the deeds of the primitive kings.

It is important to add that the ''mythology of the soul'' articulated by Plato has never lost its power of attraction. But the allegorical interpretation of certain Platonic myths has been of interest only to scholars.

184. For a general presentation of the life and work of Alexander, see W. W. Tarn, *Alexander the Great,* 2 vols. (Cambridge, 1948; the first volume was reprinted in 1956; the second volume includes a study of the sources and a number of appendices); A. R. Burn, *Alexander the Great and the Hellenistic World,* 2d rev. ed. (New York, 1962); F. Schachermeyr, *Alexander der Grosse: Ingenium und Macht* (Vienna, 1949); F. Altheim, *Alexander und Asien: Geschichte eines geistiges Erbe* (Tübingen, 1953); R. D. Milns, *Alexander the Great* (London, 1968); Peter Green, *Alexander the Great* (London, 1970; 2d ed., rev.

and enl., under the title *Alexander of Macedon,* Harmondsworth, 1974); Robin Lane Fox, *Alexander the Great* (London, 1973). The works by Peter Green and R. L. Fox include extensive critical bibliographies; in addition, they provide analyses of the historiographic presuppositions of Droysen, Tarn, and some other biographers of Alexander. The volume *Alexander the Great: The Main Problems* (Cambridge, 1966), ed. C. T. Griffith, contains a number of previously published studies written by the most competent specialists; see, especially, the contributions by C. A. Robinson, E. Badian, and G. Walser (Walser's article—"Zur neueren Forschung über Alexander den Grossen," pp. 345–88—was originally published in 1956). See also J. R. Hamilton, *Plutarch: Alexander—A Commentary* (Oxford, 1969).

For the general history of the period, see P. Jouguet, *L'Impérialisme macédonien et l'hellénisation de l'Orient* (Paris, 1926); G. Glotz, P. Roussel, and R. Cohen, *Histoire grecque,* vol. 4: *Alexandre et l'hellénisation du monde antique* (Paris, 1938; 2d ed., 1945); M. Rostovtzeff, *Social and Economic History of the Hellenistic World,* 3 vols. (Oxford, 1941; rev. ed., 1953).

On Hellenistic civilization, see W. W. Tarn, *Hellenistic Civilisation* (London, 1927; 3d ed., revised by the author and G. T. Griffith, 1952); Moses Hadas, *Hellenistic Culture: Fusion and Diffusion* (New York, 1959); Hadas, "From Nationalism to Cosmopolitanism," *Journal of the History of Ideas* 4 (1943): 105–111; and Carl Schneider, *Kulturgeschichte des Hellenismus,* vol. 2 (Munich, 1969)—a monumental work, including an exhaustive bibliography (pp. 989–1106). Schneider distinguishes four periods in the history of Hellenistic civilization: (1) until ca. 280 B.C., a time characterized by the appearance of the first Hellenistic universal god, Sarapis, and by the beginnings of the cult of the great gods, worshiped as protectors of dynasties, etc.; (2) the time between ca. 280 and ca. 220, the most brilliant period of Hellenism; (3) the time of eschatological tensions and uneasiness (ca. 220–168), characterized by the rise of apocalyptic literature, of Egyptian and Asiatic mysteriosophic cults, and of Dionysianism; (4) the Roman conquest, from ca. 168 to ca. 30, a time during which many temples were destroyed or pillaged and their priests were deported, etc., but the Hellenistic religious traditions survived in the initiatory centers: Eleusis, Samothrace, Andania, Delos (pp. 770–72); see also the final synthesis (pp. 963–88).

On the Near East in the Hellenistic period, see Samuel K. Eddy, *The King Is Dead: Studies in the Near Eastern Resistance to Hellenism, 334–31 B.C.* (Lincoln, 1961), and F. E. Peters, *The Harvest of Hellenism:*

A History of the Near East from Alexander the Great to the Triumph of Christianity (New York, 1970).

On the deification of sovereigns, see below, § 205.

On the spread of Greek education, see H. I. Marrou, *Histoire de l'éducation dans l'antiquité* (Paris, 1948; 2d ed., 1965), pp. 139 ff.; W. W. Tarn, *Hellenistic Civilisation,* pp. 268 ff.; M. Hadas, *Hellenistic Culture,* pp. 59 ff.; C. Schneider, "Jugend und Erziehung," in his *Kulturgeschichte des Hellenismus,* vol. 1.

The encounter between biblical Judaism and Hellenistic "enlightenment" will be analyzed in chapter 25, especially § 202. See also Tarn, *Hellenistic Civilisation,* pp. 210 ff.; Hadas, *Hellenistic Culture,* pp. 30 ff., 72 ff.

The bibliography for religion in the Hellenistic period is given in chapter 26, §§ 205–10.

As W. W. Tarn puts it: "The philosophy of the Hellenistic world was the Stoa; all else was secondary" (*Hell. Civ.,* p. 326). The texts have been edited by H. von Arnim, *Stoicorum veterum fragmenta,* 4 vols. (1903–5, 1924; republished, Stuttgart, 1968); Italian translation by N. Festa, *Frammenti degli Stoici antichi* (1932–35; republished, Hildesheim, 1971), and by R. Anastasi, *I Frammenti morali di Crisippo* (Padua, 1962); French translation by E. Bréhier, *Les Stoïciens* (Paris, 1962); see also the German translation by M. Pohlenz, *Stoa und Stoiker* (Zurich, 1950).

The fundamental work remains the one by M. Pohlenz, *Die Stoa,* 2 vols. (Göttingen, 1948–49; 2d ed., 1964; Italian translation, Florence, 1967). See also J. M. Rist, *Stoic Philosophy* (Cambridge, 1969); C. Rodis-Lewis, *La morale stoïcienne* (Paris, 1970); R. Hoven, *Stoïcisme et stoïciens face au problème de l'au-delà* (Paris, 1971); and the bibliographies listed by Léon Robin, *La pensée grecque et les origines de l'esprit scientifique* (new ed., 1973), pp. 477–78, and by P. M. Schuhl, ibid., pp. 501–3.

Epicurus' fragments have been collected by Hermann Usener, *Epicurea* (1887; republished Rome, 1963). See also C. Arrighetti, *Epicuro: Opere* (original texts and Italian translations) (Turin, 1960). From the extensive critical literature it is important for our purpose to cite the work by A. J. Festugière, *Epicure et ses dieux* (1946; 2d ed., 1968).

On the Cynics, see the essential bibliography in L. Robin, *La pensée grecque,* pp. 464–65.

In the Hellenistic period the philosophy of Aristotle enjoyed chiefly a scientific reputation, but in the Middle Ages it will have considerable influence on the Christian, Islamic, and Jewish theologies. Aristotle's metaphysics is also reminiscent of Sāṃkhya-Yoga. Man is made up of the body (*sōma*), the soul (*psychē*), and the mind (*nous*), that "whereby the soul thinks and judges" (*De anima* 429a23). The mind exists from all eternity and it "must come into a being in the male from outside" (*De generatione animalium* 736b20). The mind is transcendent to man's living organism, which it directs while remaining inaccessible to psychic influences: it is "something more divine and is unaffected" (*De anima* 408b29). In fact, the *nous* resembles God, who is, for Aristotle, the absolute, unconditioned, eternal reality; being "motionless," God's activity is purely spiritual (*Eth. Nic.* 1178b7–22; *De caelo,* 292b4 ff.). Similarly, the mind's only activity consists in thinking. The human personality is not determined by the mind. Undifferentiated and equal to itself, the mind has no relation with the personalities to which it is attributed. Having no birth, it does not experience death (*De caelo* 279b20). When death comes, the *nous* recovers its previous condition. But it is impossible for us to know, or even to imagine, the modality of this disincarnate existence, for the mind has neither any rational activity nor any memory; the predicate that can be attributed to it is that of *being* (*De anima* 408b18 ff.). Consequently, in the beyond, man cannot feel a desire to liberate himself, and belief in immortality no longer makes sense. It is precisely this part of Aristotle's doctrine that gave rise to countless controversies in the Middle Ages.

We will once again emphasize the analogies with, on the one hand, the speculations of the Upanishads and Vedānta on the nature of the *ātman* and, on the other hand, the structure and destiny of the *puruṣa* in Sāṃkhya-Yoga (see §141). However, there is a capital difference between Aristotle's doctrine and the Indian metaphysical systems; for the latter, the deliverance of the spirit (*ātman, puruṣa*) implies both consciousness of self and bliss (cf. *sāccitanānda*).

On Alexander and India, see H. G. Rawlinson, *Intercourse between India and the Western World,* 2d ed. (New York, 1972); A. K. Narain, "Alexander and India," *Greece and Rome* 12 (1965): 155–65; F. F. Schwartz, "Neue Perspective in den griechisch-indischen Beziehungen," *Orientalistische Literaturzeitung* 67 (1972): 18 ff.

On the earliest cultural contacts between India and the West, see the bibliography listed in Eliade, *Yoga: Immortality and Freedom,* trans. Willard R. Trask, Bollingen Series 76 (Princeton, 1964), pp. 431–32; add F. F. Schwartz, "Candragupta-Sandrakottos: Eine historische Legende in Ost und West," *Das Altertum* 18 (1972): 85–102; H. Scharff, "The Maurya Dynasty and the Seleucids," *Zeitschrift für vergleichende Sprachforschung* 85 (1971): 211–25. The article by F. F. Schwartz, "Arrian's *Indike* on India: Intention and Reality," *East and West* 25

(1975): 180–200, discusses the most recent contributions to the study of this problem.

On the traditions concerning Alexander's conversations with Brahmans, see Friedrich Pfister, "Das Nachleben der Überlieferung von Alexander und den Brahmanen," *Hermes* 68 (1941): 143–69; Günther C. Hansen, "Alexander und die Brahmanen," *Klio* 43–45 (1965): 351–80; J. D. M. Derrett, "Greece and India: The *Milindapañha,* the Alexander-Romance, and the Gospels," *Zeitschrift für Religions- und Geistesgeschichte* 19 (1967): 33–64; Derrett, "The History of 'Palladius' on the Races of India and the Brahmans," *Classica et Mediaevalia* 21 (1960): 64–135.

Chapter 23. History of Buddhism and Jainism

185. There is an extensive bibliography on Buddhism and the history of the Buddhist sects. The essential works are listed in the following volumes: three works by L. de la Vallée-Poussin, *Le dogme et la philosophie du Bouddhisme* (Paris, 1930), *Nirvāṇa* (1925), and *La morale bouddhique* (1927); two works by E. Conze, *Buddhism: Its Essence and Development* (Oxford, 1951), and *Buddhist Thought in India* (London, 1962); Sukumar Dutt, *The Buddha and Five After Centuries* (London, 1957); E. Frauwallner, *Die Philosophie des Buddhismus* (Berlin, 1956); E. Lamotte, *Histoire du bouddhisme indien,* vol. 1, *De l'origine à l'ère Śaka* (Louvain, 1958); A. Bareau, "Le Bouddhisme Indien," in *Les religions de l'Inde,* vol. 3 (Paris, 1966), pp. 7–246 (pp. 234–43, bibliography).

On the literature of the Sūtras in the Pali language, see the account by J. Filliozat in L. Renou and J. Filliozat, *L'Inde classique* (1949), vol. 2, pp. 323–51; A. Bareau, "Le Bouddhisme Indien," pp. 30–40. On the formation of the canon, see Lamotte, *Histoire,* vol. 1, pp. 155–209.

At the Council at Rājagṛha, the two collections of texts—*Sūtra Piṭaka* and *Vinaya Piṭaka*—were recited in chorus by all the participants. According to some traditions, the *Abhidharma Piṭaka,* the "Basket of the Supreme Doctrine" (or "Quintessence of the Doctrine") was recited in the same way, so that the complete canon, the *Tripiṭaka,* was already organized at that period; but this is improbable (see Bareau, "Le Bouddhisme Indien," p. 27).

On the importance of Śāriputra, see A. Migot, "Un grand disciple du Bouddha, Śāriputra," *BEFEO* 46 (1954): 405–54.

On Ānanda, see the references to the sources in G. P. Malalasekera, *Dictionary of Pāli Proper Names,* 2 vols. (London, 1937–38), vol. 1, pp. 249–68.

On Upāli, who knew the Discipline by heart, see the documents cited by E. Lamotte, *L'Enseignement de Vimalakīrti* (Louvain, 1962), pp. 170–71, n. 62.

On the councils, see J. Przyluski, *Le concile de Rājagṛha* (Paris, 1926–28), although some of his hypotheses—e.g., Ānanda's interdiction as the vestige of a rite of expelling the scapegoat—are improbable; A. Bareau, *Les premiers conciles bouddhiques* (Paris, 1955); M. Hofinger, *Etude sur le concile de Vaiśālī* (Louvain, 1946); E. Lamotte, *Histoire du bouddhisme indien,* vol. 1, pp. 297–319; E. Frauwallner, *Die buddhistische Konzilien, ZDMG* 102 (1952): 240–61; see also Charles S. Prebish, "A Review of Scholarship on the Buddhist Councils," *Journal of Asian Studies* 33 (1974): 230–54; Janice J. Nattier and Charles S. Prebish, "Mahāsāṃghika Origins: The Beginnings of Buddhist Sectarianism," *HR* 16 (1977): 237–72.

On differences in the canon, see A. Bareau, in *Les religions de l'Inde,* vol. 3, pp. 84 ff.

On the appearance of differing sects, see Lamotte, *Histoire,* vol. 1, pp. 571–602; A. Bareau, *Les sectes bouddhiques du Petit Véhicule* (Saigon, 1955); N. Dutt, *Early Monastic Buddhism,* vol. 2 (Calcutta, 1945), pp. 47–206; and Prebish, "Mahāsāṃghika Origins." See also T. O. Ling, *Buddhism and the Mythology of Evil: A Study in Theravāda Buddhism* (London, 1962).

186. On India in the time of Alexander the Great and the Maurya Empire, see L. de la Vallée-Poussin, *L'Inde aux temps des Mauryas et des barbares* (Paris, 1930); E. Lamotte, "Alexandre et le Bouddhisme," *BEFEO* 44 (1945–50): 147–62; A. K. Narain, *The Indo-Greeks* (Oxford, 1957); W. W. Tarn, *The Greeks in Bactria and India,* 2d ed. (Cambridge, 1951).

On Aśoka, see J. Bloch, *Les inscriptions d'Aśoka* (Paris, 1950); Lamotte, *Histoire,* pp. 319–40; A. Bareau, *Les sectes bouddhiques,* pp. 35–55. Przyluski's work, *La légende de l'empereur Aśoka dans les textes indiens et chinois* (Paris, 1923), is still useful for its excellent translation of the texts. Filliozat has this to say: "At the height of his power, Aśoka was the greatest prince of his times. Neither the Rome of the middle of the third century B.C. nor the Egypt of the Ptolemies attained the greatness and power of the Indian empire; the Seleucid kingdom yields to pressure from the Parthians, China is still struggling against the Ch'in dynasty that is to give it its unity. If Aśoka remained unknown to all these peoples despite the efforts he made in the direction of the West, it is because in his time none of them could or would see anything but itself in history. His power, however, is not his only title to fame; very few princes have had the intelligence to bring to government the inspiration of a liberal religion with as much moderation as he'' (*L'Inde classique,* vol. 1, pp. 220–21).

On the Greek-Aramaic bilingual inscription found at Kandahar, see D. Schlumberger, L. Robert, A. Dupont-Sommer, and E. Benveniste, ''Une inscription bilingue gréco-araméenne d'Aśoka,'' *JA* 246 (1958): 1–48. On two other recently discovered inscriptions, see D. Schlumberger, ''Une nouvelle inscription grecque d'Aśoka,'' *Comptes rendus des séances de l'Académie des Inscriptions et Belles Lettres* 109 (1964): 1–15; A. Dupont-Sommer, ''Une nouvelle inscription araméenne d'Aśoka trouvée dans la vallée du Lagman (Afganistan),'' ibid. 115 (1970): 15.

187. On the *stūpa* and the cult of relics, see M. Benisti, ''Etude sur le *stūpa* dans l'Inde ancienne,'' *BEFEO* 50 (1960): 37–116; A. Bareau, ''La construction et le culte des *stūpa* d'après les Vinayapiṭaka,'' ibid., pp. 229–74; S. Paranavitana, ''The *stūpa* in Ceylon,'' *Memoirs of the Archaeological Survey of Ceylon,* vol. 5 (Colombo, 1946); Akira Hirakawa, ''The Rise of Mahāyāna Buddhism and Its Relation to the Worship of Stūpas,'' *Memoirs of the Research Department of Toyo Bunko* 22 (1963): 57–106. John Irwin has shown that Aśoka's pillars carry on a long religious tradition, dominated by a cosmological symbolism comparable to that of Mesopotamia; see his '' 'Aśokan' Pillars: A Reassessment of the Evidence,'' *Burlington Magazine* 65 (1973): 706–20; 66 (1974): 712–27; 67 (1975): 631–43.

On the *caitya,* see V. R. Ramchandra Dikshitar, ''Origin and Early History of Caityas,'' *Indian Historical Quarterly* 14 (1938): 440–51, and the bibliography given in Eliade, *Yoga,* p. 426.

On the symbolism of Buddhist temples, Paul Mus's great work *Barabudur,* 2 vols. (Hanoi, 1935), remains irreplaceable.

On the origin and development of the image of the Buddha, see A. K. Coomaraswamy, ''Indian Origin of the Buddha Image,'' *JAOS* 46 (1926): 165–70, and his ''Origin of the Buddha Image,'' *Art Bulletin* 9 (1927): 1–42; P. Mus, ''Le Bouddha paré. Son origine indienne. Śākyamuni dans le Mahāyānisme moyen,'' *BEFEO* 28 (1928): 153–280; O. C. Gangoly, ''The Antiquity of the Buddha-Image, the Cult of the Buddha,'' *Ostasiatische Zeitschrift* n.s. 14 (1937–38): 41–59; E. Benda, *Der vedische Ursprung des symbolischen Buddhabildes* (Leipzig,

1940); B. Rowland, "Gandhāra and Late Antique Art: The Buddha Image," *American Journal of Archeology* 46 (1942): 223–36; Rowland, *The Evolution of the Buddha Image* (New York, 1963).

On the continuity of Vedic symbolism in Buddhist images, see Paul Mus, "Etudes indiennes et indochinoises," *BEFEO* 29 (1929): 92 ff.; A. Coomaraswamy, "Some Sources of Buddhist Iconography," in *Dr. B. C. Law Volume* (1945), pt. 1, pp. 1–8; and Coomaraswamy "The Nature of Buddhist Art," in his book *Figures of Speech or Figures of Thought* (London, 1946), pp. 161–99, esp. pp. 180 ff. On the analogies between representations of the Buddha and of Christ in the first to fifth centuries, see Benjamin Rowland, "Religious Art East and West," *HR* 2 (1962): 11–32. According to Rowland, it is a matter of the common inheritance of a symbolism that goes back to a far earlier period. Christ and the Buddha are presented as primarily teachers (inheriting the Greek orator's toga), or they are endowed with solar symbolism and with gigantic proportions, in order to show their transcendental nature. See also Rowland's "Buddha and the Sun God," *Zalmoxis* 1 (1938): 69–84.

On monastic life, see Nalinaksha Dutt, *Early Monastic Buddhism,* rev. ed. (Calcutta, 1960); Charles Prebish, *Buddhist Monastic Discipline: The Sanskrit Prātimokṣa Sūtras of the Mahāsāṃghikas and the Mūlasarvāstivādins* (Pennsylvania, 1975).

On the literature of the *Abhidharma Piṭaka,* see L. de la Vallée-Poussin, "Documents d'Abhidharma, traduits et annotés," pt. 1, *BEFEO* 30 (1930): 1–28, 247–98; pts. 2–5 were then published in *Mélanges chinois et bouddhiques* 1 (1932): 65–125; 6 (1937): 7–187; Mahathera Nyanatiloka, *Guide through the Abhidharma-Piṭaka,* 2d ed. (Colombo, 1957); A. Bareau, "Le Bouddhisme Indien," pp. 93–106. See also H. V. Guenther, *Philosophy and Psychology in the Abhidharma* (Lucknow, 1967); *L'Abhidharmakośa de Vasubandhu,* translated by La Vallée-Poussin, 6 vols. (Paris, 1923–31).

It must be noted, however, that the *Abhidharma* set out not to encourage speculation but to clarify the mind by the help of a consistent philosophical theory. Its ultimate purpose, then, was soteriological.

188. For the chronology and the literature of the *Prajñāpāramitā,* as well as the bibliography on it, see the excellent presentation by Edward Conze, *The Prajñāpāramitā Literature* (The Hague, 1960), which also includes a list of translations into European languages. Conze himself has published several volumes of translations from it; see his *Selected Sayings from the Perfection of Wisdom* (London, 1955).

On the Mahāyāna, see E. Conze, *Buddhist Thought in India* (London, 1962), pp. 195–237; A. Bareau, "Le Bouddhisme Indien," in *Les religions de l'Inde,* vol. 3, pp. 141–99; Bareau, *L'Absolu en philosophie bouddhique* (Paris, 1951); E. Lamotte, "Sur la formation du Mahāyāna," *Festschrift Friedrich Weller* (Leipzig, 1954), pp. 377–96. The most important translations of Mahāyāna texts into European languages are listed by A. Bareau, "Le Bouddhisme Indien," pp. 242–43.

According to Mahāyāna tradition, after the death of the Blessed One the disciples met at Rājagṛha under the leadership of Mahākāśyapa and compiled the "Three Baskets"; during this time the great *boddhisattvas* ascended Mount Vimalasvabhāva and, with the help of Ānanda, compiled the Mahāyāna Sūtras. These were deposited in hiding places among the Devas, the Nāgas, and the Gandharvas. It was not until five hundred years after the *parinirvāṇa,* when the Law was in decline, that Nāgārjuna found, in the Nāgas' palace, seven baskets filled with Mahāyāna Sūtras. In ninety days he memorized them and began communicating them to laymen. On this fabulous tradition, see Lamotte, *L'Enseignement de Vimalakīrti,* pp. 67–68.

On the *boddhisattva,* see, most recently, W. Rahula, "L'Idéal du Bodhisattva dans le Theravāda et le Mahāyāna," *JA* 259 (1971): 63–70. In the first centuries of our era, the Mahāyāna authors speak of *śrāvakas, pratyekabuddhas,* and *boddhisattvas.* A *śrāvaka* (literally, "disciple") practices the Buddha's teaching and finally attains *nirvāṇa;* a *pratyekabuddha* (individual Buddha) realizes *nirvāṇa* himself but is not able to reveal the truth to others, as a fully awakened Buddha does. A *boddhisattva* is a person who is capable of attaining *nirvāṇa* but who renounces it for the good of others (Rahula, pp. 65–66).

There are analyses of the various *boddhisattvas* in E. Conze, *Le bouddhisme,* pp. 123 ff.; A. Bareau, "Le Bouddhisme Indien," pp. 169 ff.; J. Rahder, *Daśabhūmikasūtra et Boddhisattvabhūmi* (Paris, 1962); L. de la Vallée-Poussin, *Vijñaptimātratāsiddhi,* vol. 1, pp. 721–42; and especially the translation (with full commentary) by Etienne Lamotte, *L'Enseignement de Vimalakīrti.*

On Maitreya, see H. de Lubac, *Amida* (Paris, 1955), pp. 82 ff., and the texts cited and commented on by E. Lamotte, *L'Enseignement de Vimalakīrti,* pp. 189–92, note 89. On Mañjuśrī, see, most recently, E. Lamotte, "Mañjuśrī," *T'oung Pao* 48 (1960): 1–96.

On Avalokiteśvara, see M.-T. de Mallmann, *Introduction à l'étude d'Avalokiteśvara* (Paris, 1948); H. de Lubac, *Amida,* pp. 104 ff. A certain number of scholars (Sylvain Lévi, Sir Charles Eliot, J. Przyluski, Paul Pelliot, Mlle de Mallmann) have brought out the Iranian elements in Avalokiteśvara; see the discussion in H. de Lubac, *Amida,* pp. 237 ff. But the Indian antecedents are not lacking; see J. Filliozat's remarks in *JA* 239 (1951): 81 and *RHR* 137 (1950): 44–58.

On Amitābha and Sukhāvatī, see de Lubac, *Amida,* pp. 32–48, 78–119, and passim.

The article by P. Demiéville cited in note 13, "Version chinoise . . . ," appeared in *BEFEO* 24 (1924), and in an offprint of 258 pages.

None of the other Buddhas has the greatness and efficacity of Amitābha. Later, all these Buddhas and *boddhisattvas* are described as accompanied by gods, especially Brahmā and Indra, and by various feminine personifications of Prajñāpāramitā or of the Tārās (goddesses whose name means "Star" and "Savior" [fem.]). This new Buddhology continues the pre-Mahāyānist theories of the supramundane nature of the Buddhas. It seems to have been definitely constituted by Asaṇga in the fourth century; see *Vijñaptimātratāsiddhi,* trans. L. de la Vallée-Poussin, vol. 2, pp. 762–813; Paul Demiéville, ed., *Hobogirin: Dictionnaire encyclopédique du Bouddhisme d'après les sources chinoises et japonaises* (Tokyo, 1929), fasc. 2, pp. 174–85.

The "Buddha fields" (*buddha kṣetras*) are the countless universes in which the compassion of a Buddha is manifested. Pure, impure, and mixed universes are distinguished. Our universe, Sahā, is presented as dangerous and wretched, yet it is there that Śākyamuni attained perfect enlightenment. But, "pure or impure, the *buddha-kṣetras* are all 'Buddha lands' and, as such, perfectly pure. The distinction between pure and impure fields is wholly subjective. The Buddhas transform an impure land into a pure land and vice versa at will" (Lamotte, *L'Enseignement,* p. 399). See also the article *Butsudu* in *Hobogirin,* pp. 198–203.

The cult of Buddhas and *boddhisattvas* includes various kinds of homage and praise, an effort to think of them continually, requests to be reborn one day as a perfect Buddha, but, most of all, repetition of their names, a method that became very popular in India and in all the countries to which the Mahāyāna spread. The doctors have discussed the respective virtues of these two methods: *faith* in a Buddha and *ritual repetition of his name.* As matter of fact, these two Mahāyānist innovations have a long prehistory in India, and, in their "popular" guise, conceal strictly enunciated ideas of the effectiveness of sacred words and "thoughts of compassion." See also Frank E. Reynolds, "The Several Bodies of the Buddha: Reflections on a Neglected Aspect of Ṭheravāda Tradition," *HR* 16 (1977): 374–89.

189. On Nāgārjuna and Mādhyamika, see the bibliographies in Frederick J. Streng, *Emptiness: A Study in Religious Meaning* (Nashville, 1967), pp. 237–45. On Nāgārjuna's life, see ibid., pp. 237–38, and the bibliography listed by E. Lamotte in the Introduction to his *Le Traité de la grande vertu de sagesse de Nāgārjuna (Mahāprajñāpāramitā-śāstra)*, 2 vols. (Louvain, 1944, 1949), vol. 1, pp. xi–xiv. Lamotte has shown that, for Kumārajīva and his school, Nāgārjuna falls between 243 and 300 A.D. (*L'Enseignement de Vimalakīrti,* p. 76). On Nāgārjuna's works and the works that have been attributed to him, see Streng, *Emptiness,* pp. 238–40. The *Mūlamādhyamaka Kārikā* and *Vigrahavyārtanī* are translated by Streng, pp. 181–227; Lamotte's *Traité* contains a translation of chapters 1–30 of the Chinese version by Kumārajīva. Probably the work contains supplements added by Kumārajīva. Translations of other works into European languages are listed by Streng, pp. 238–40. The text of the *Mādhyamika Kārikā* is included in the Sanskrit, Tibetan, and Chinese commentaries on the work. The commentary by Candrakīrtī (*Prasannapadā*) is by far the most valuable. The twenty-seven chapters of the *Prasannapadā* have been translated into German, English, and French by various authors (Stcherbatsky, S. Schayer, E. Lamotte, J. de Jong, and J. May; see Streng, p. 240). J. May, *Candrakīrtī Prasannapadā Mādhyamakavṛtti: Douze chapitres traduits du sanskrit et du tibétain* (Paris, 1959), deserves special mention.

On Nāgārjuna's philosophy, see F. I. Stcherbatsky, *The Conception of Buddhist Nirvāṇa* (Leningrad, 1927), pp. 1–68; La Vallée-Poussin, "Réflexions sur le Mādhyamaka," *Mélanges chinois et bouddhiques* 2 (1933): 1–59, 139–46; T. R. V. Murti, *Central Philosophy of Buddhism* (London, 1955), together with J. May's remarks, *IIJ* 3 (1959): 102–111; Richard H. Robinson, *Early Mādhyamika in India and China* (Madison and London, 1967), pp. 21–70; and, especially, Streng's *Emptiness,* pp. 43–98, 139–52.

190. For a short history of the Jaina canon and church, see L. Renou, *L'Inde classique,* vol. 2, pp. 609–39. For Jaina philosophy, see O. Lacombe, ibid., pp. 639–62, and the bibliographies given above, §152. Add: Y. R. Padmarajiah, *A Comparative Study of the Jaina Theories of Reality and Knowledge* (Bombay, 1963). See also Mrs. S. Stevenson, *The Heart of Jainism* (Oxford, 1915); S. B. Deo, *A History of Jaina Monachism from Inscriptions and Literature* (Poona, 1956); R. Williams, *Jaina Yoga: A Survey of the Medieval Śrāvakācāras* (London, 1963); U. P. Shah, *Studies in Jaina Art* (Benares, 1955); V. A. Sangave, *The Jaina Community: A Social Survey* (Bombay, 1959).

Chapter 24. The Hindu Synthesis

191. The text of the *Mahābhārata* is now accessible in the critical edition published under the editorship of Vishnu S. Sukthamkar and S. K. Belvalkar: *The Mahābhārata: For the First Time Critically Edited* (Poona: Bhandarkar Oriental Research Institute, 1933–66).

The English translations by P. C. Roy (Calcutta, 1882–89) and by M. N. Dutt (Calcutta, 1895–1905) are still useful, but now the reader should consult the version begun by the late J. A. B. van Buitenen. Before his recent death, van Buitenen had translated books 1 through 5 of the *Mahābhārata* (University of Chicago Press, 1973–78), and he had completed his translation of the *Bhagavad Gītā* (now published; see below, § 194).

For the history of interpretations of the poem, see Alf Hiltebeitel, *Kṛṣṇa and the Mahābhārata: A Study in Indian and Indo-European Symbolism* (Ph.D. diss., University of Chicago, 1973), pp. 134–90. Among the most important contributions, we mention those of Adolf Holtzmann (the younger), *Das Mahābhārata und seine Theile,* 4 vols. (Kiel, 1892–93); E. W. Hopkins, *The Great Epic of India: Its Character and Origin* (1901); Joseph Dahlmann, *Die Genesis des Mahābhārata* (Berlin, 1899); G. J. Held, *The Mahābhārata: An Ethnological Study* (London and Amsterdam, 1935); V. S. Sukkhamkar, *The Meaning of the Mahābhārata* (Bombay, 1957); Georges Dumézil, *Mythe et épopée,* vols. 1 and 2 (Paris, 1968, 1971); Alf Hiltebeitel, *The Ritual of Battle: Krishna in the Mahābhārata* (Ithaca, N.Y., 1976). J. Bruce Long has recently published an annotated bibliography, *The Mahābhārata: A Select Annotated Bibliography,* South Asia Occasional Papers and Theses, no. 3 (Cornell University) (Ithaca, N.Y., 1974).

In 1947 Stig Wikander showed in an article (in Swedish) that the gods who were the fathers of the Pāṇḍavas formed a well-structured Vedic or pre-Vedic group and that the heroes' collective marriage corresponds to a theologem related to the same divine grouping. The article—"La légende des Pāṇḍava et la substructure mythique du Mahābhārata"—was translated and annotated by Georges Dumézil in *Jupiter, Mars, Quirinus,* vol. 4 (Paris, 1948), pp. 37–53, 55–85. Now see Dumézil, *Mythe et épopée,* vol. 1, pp. 42 ff. (The first part of the book—pages 31–257—is devoted to an analysis of the *MBh* from the viewpoint of Indo-European mythology.)

192. On the analogies between the *MBh* and the Iranian and Scandinavian eschatologies, see G. Dumézil, *Mythe et épopée,* vol. 1, pp.

218 ff.; Stig Wikander, "Germanische und Indo-Iranische Eschatologie," *Kairos* 2 (1960): 83–88.

Dumézil's studies are discussed by Madeleine Biardeau, "Etudes de mythologie hindoue: Cosmogonies purāṇiques," *BEFEO* 55 (1969): 59–105, esp. pp. 97–105; see also *Annuaire de l'Ecole des Hautes Etudes,* sec. 5 (1969–70), pp. 168–72, and Alf Hiltebeitel, *Krishna and the Mahābhārata,* chap. 27, and "The Mahābhārata and Hindu Eschatology," *HR* 12 (1972): 95–135; cf. Hiltebeitel, *The Ritual of Battle,* pp. 300–309.

On the *pralaya* in the epic, see Biardeau, "Etudes," *BEFEO* 57 (1971): 17–89; on *bhakti* and *avatāra,* see "Etudes," ibid. 63 (1976): 111–263.

See also David Kinsley, "Through the Looking Glass: Divine Madness in the Hindu Religious Traditions," *HR* 13 (1974): 270–305.

193. On Sāṃkhya and Yoga ideas in the *Mahābhārata,* see Eliade, *Yoga: Immortality and Freedom,* trans. Willard R. Trask (Princeton, 1969), pp. 146 ff., and the bibliographies given there, p. 144, n. 1, and p. 392. In one of his interminable didactic discourses Bhīṣma affirms that "Sāṃkhya and Yoga each praises its method as the best means (*kāraṇa*) . . . . I consider both these teachings true. . . . They have in common purity, suppression [of desires], and compassion for all beings; . . . but the opinions [*darśanas*] are not the same in Sāṃkhya and in Yoga" (*MBh* 13. 11043 ff.). To be sure, the reference is to a presystematic stage of the two *darśanas.* Sāṃkhya is not presented as the method for distinguishing and separating the spirit (*puruṣa*) from psychomental experience, which is the point of departure for Īśvara Kṛṣṇa's system.

194. There is an immense literature on the *Bhagavad Gītā;* see some bibliographical indications in Eliade, *Yoga,* p. 394; see also J. Bruce Long, *The Mahābhārata: A Select Annotated Bibliography,* pp. 16–19. We cite the translation by Emile Sénart (Paris, 1922). Indispensable among recent translations with commentaries are those by Franklin Edgerton (Harvard University Press, 1952), by R. C. Zaehner (Oxford University Press, 1969), and by J. A. B. van Buitenen, *The Bhagavadgītā in the Mahābhārata* (University of Chicago Press, 1981).

On yogic technique in the *Bhagavad Gītā,* see Eliade, *Yoga,* pp. 159 ff.

195. On the "separation" of the celestial essence, obtained by sacrifice (*yasna*), see G. Gnoli, "Lo state di 'maga,' " *Annali dell'Istituto*

Orientale di Napoli n.s. 15 (1965): 105–17, and the other works by the same author cited in § 104. See also Eliade, "Spirit, Light, and Seed," in *Occultism, Witchcraft, and Cultural Fashions* (Chicago, 1976), pp. 108–9 (= *HR* 11 [1971]: 18 ff.).

On the alternation of antagonistic principles, see Eliade, "Prolegomenon to Religious Dualism," chap. 8 of *The Quest: History and Meaning in Religion* (Chicago, 1969).

Chapter 25. The Ordeals of Judaism

196. The history of the Jewish people after the Exile has inspired many studies. We mention some recent works: K. Galling, *Studien zur Geschichte Israels im persischen Zeitalter* (Tübingen, 1964); E. Bickerman, *From Ezra to the Last of the Maccabees: Foundations of Post-Biblical Judaism* (New York, 1962); I. L. Myres, "Persia, Greece and Israel," *Palestine Exploration Quarterly* 85 (1953): 8–22. For a general view of the religious history, see Georg Fohrer, *History of Israelite Religion* (Nashville and New York, 1972), pp. 330–90.

On Deutero-Isaiah, see, most recently, the extremely valuable book by P. E. Bonnard, *Le Second Isaïa, son disciple et leurs éditeurs (Isaïa 40–68)* (Paris, 1972).

Iranian influences have been identified in certain passages of Deutero-Isaiah. Thus, for example, Is. 50:11 speaks of those who are "setting light to a fire," an expression equivalent to the Avestan term *athravan*. See the bibliography in David Winston, "The Iranian Component in the Bible, Apocrypha, and Qumran," *HR* 5 (1966): 187, n. 13. Still more obvious is the Iranian influence in chapters 44 and 45, whose resemblance to the "Cylinders of Cyrus" and to *Yasna* 44 has been observed; see Morton Smith, "II Isaiah and the Persians," *JAOS* 83–84 (1963): 415–21, and the bibliography cited by Winston, p. 189, n. 17.

On the Songs of the Servant, see I. Engnell, "The ʿEbed Yahweh Songs and the Suffering Messiah in 'Deutero-Isaiah,' " *BJRL* 31 (1948): 54–96; C. Lindhagen, *The Servant Motif in the Old Testament* (Uppsala, 1950); J. Lindblom, *The Servant Songs in Deutero-Isaiah* (1951); C. R. North, *The Suffering Servant in Deutero-Isaiah* (1942; 2d ed., London, 1956), and his commentary in *The Second Isaiah* (Oxford, 1965); H. A. Rowley, *The Servant of the Lord* (London, 1952); S. Mowinckel, *He That Cometh* (New York, 1955), pp. 187–260; and W. Zimmerli and J. Jeremias, *The Servant of God,* 2d ed. (London, 1965).

197. On the prophet Haggai, see Théophane Charry, O.F.M., *Agée–Zacharie–Malachie,* Coll. "Sources bibliques" (Paris, 1969); F. Hesse, "Haggai," in A. Kuschke, ed., *Verbannung und Heimkehr* (Rudolph Festschrift) (Tübingen, 1961), pp. 109–34; K. Koch, "Haggais unreines Volk," *Zeitschrift für die alttestamentliche Wissenschaft* 79 (1967): 52–66.

On Zechariah, see T. Charry, *Agée–Zacharie–Malachie;* K. Galling, *Studien,* pp. 109–26; Otto Eissfeldt, *The Old Testament: An Introduction* (English translation) (Oxford and New York, 1965), pp. 429–40 (with an extensive bibliography on pp. 429, 762).

On the developments in the eschatology, see G. Hölscher, *Der Ursprung der jüdischen Eschatologie* (Giessen, 1925); P. Volz, *Die Eschatologie der jüdischen Gemeinde in neutestamentlichen Zeitalter,* 2d ed. (Tübingen, 1934); G. Fohrer, "Die Struktur der alttestamentlichen Eschatologie," in his *Studien zur alttestamentlichen Prophetie* (Berlin, 1967), pp. 32–58. See also the bibliography cited for § 198.

198. On the biblical conceptions of the Messiah, see H. Gressmann, *Der Messias* (Göttingen, 1929); A. Bentzen, *King and Messiah* (London, 1955; translation of *Messias, Moses redivivus, Menschensohn,* Zurich, 1948); L. E. Browne, *The Messianic Hope in Its Historical Setting* (1951); H. Ringgren, "König und Messias," *Zeitschrift für die alttestamentliche Wissenschaft* 64 (1952): 120–47; T. W. Mason, *The Servant–Messiah* (Cambridge, 1952); S. Mowinckel, *He That Cometh,* pp. 280 ff.; Joseph Klausner, *The Messianic Idea in Israel from Its Beginning to the Completion of the Mishnah* (New York, 1955); G. Fohrer, *Messiasfrage und Bibelverständnis* (1957). See also the bibliography cited for § 203. For the rabbinic conceptions, see G. F. Moore, *Judaism in the First Centuries of the Christian Era* (Cambridge, Mass., 1927, 1930; republished 1971), vol. 2, pp. 349 ff.; Gershom Scholem, *The Messianic Idea in Judaism* (New York, 1971), pp. 1–78.

On the relations between the royal ideology of the great Oriental monarchies and the mythical motif of the King-Redeemer among the Israelites, see G. Widengren, "Early Hebrew Myths and Their Interpretation," in S. H. Hooke, ed., *Myth, Ritual and Kingship* (Oxford, 1958), pp. 168 ff., and Widengren, *Sakrales Königtum im Alten Testament und im Judentum* (Stuttgart, 1955), pp. 30 ff.

199. The history of the composition of the Pentateuch is complicated. For the present postion of studies and bibliography see O. Eissfeldt, *The Old Testament,* pp. 155–240, and ibid., pp. 241–300, for textual analysis of the earliest historical books (Joshua, Judges, Samuel, Kings).

The chronology of Ezra and Nehemiah presents numerous problems; see J. Wright, *The Date of Ezra's Coming to Jerusalem* (London, 1947); Wright, *The Building of the Second Temple* (London, 1958); A. Gelston, "The Foundations of the Second Temple," *VT* 16 (1966): 232 ff.; H. Rowley, "The Chronological Order of Ezra and Nehemiah," in *The Servant of the Lord* (London, 1952), pp. 131 ff.; Rowley, "Nehemiah's Mission and Its Historical Background," *BJRL* 37 (1955): 528 ff.; H. Cazelles, "La mission d'Esdras," *VT* 4 (1954): 113 ff.; S. Mowinckel, *Studien zu dem Buche Ezra-Nehemia,* 3 vols. (Oslo, 1964–65); F. Michaeli, *Les livres des Chroniques, d'Esdras et de Néhémie* (Neuchâtel, 1967). According to Kellermann, followed by Morton Smith, Ezra preceded Nehemiah; see U. Kellermann, *Nehemiah: Quellen, Überlieferung und Geschichte,* supplement 102 to *Zeitschrift für die alttestamentliche Wissenschaft* (Berlin, 1967); "Erwägungen zum Problem der Esradatierung," *Zeitschr. für die alttest. Wiss.* 80 (1968): 55 ff.; Morton Smith, *Palestinian Parties and Politics That Shaped the Old Testament* (New York and London, 1971), pp. 120 ff. For the history of the text, see O. Eissfeldt, *The Old Testament,* pp. 541–59.

During Ezra's and Nehemiah's mission the opposition takes shape between the "parties" of the exclusivists (or "nationalists") and the syncretists (or "universalists"). To be sure, the opposition existed before the Captivity, but it acquires a political character in the period of Ezra and Nehemiah.

The short Book of Jonah, composed in the fourth century, admirably illustrates the "universalist" tendency: God sends the prophet to Nineveh to announce that the city will be destroyed because of the wickedness of its inhabitants. But since the Ninevites repent, Yahweh renounces punishing them. In other words, *Yahweh cares for all peoples*. (Some authors have seen the same spirit in the Book of Ruth.) But the denomination "universalist" could equally well be applied to the partisans of *assimilation* (religious, cultural, racial). This syncretistic tendency, which was already popular at the time of the monarchy, will reach its height in the Hellenistic period.

200. For the history of Palestine during the Hellenistic period see S. Lieberman, *Greek in Jewish Palestine* (New York, 1942); Lieberman, *Hellenism in Jewish Palestine* (New York, 1950); F. M. Abel, *Histoire de la Palestine depuis la conquête d'Alexandre jusqu'à l'invasion arabe,* vol. 1: *De la conquête d'Alexandre jusqu'à la guerre juive* (1952). An excellent general view has been presented by Victor Tcherikover, *Hellenistic Civilization and the Jews* (New York, 1970) (translated from the Hebrew). See also W. W. Tarn, *Hellenistic Civilisation,* 3d ed. (1952; republished, New York, 1961), chap. 6: "Hellenism and the Jews" (pp. 210 ff.); Samuel K. Eddy, *The King Is Dead: Studies in the Near Eastern Resistance to Hellenism, 334–31 B.C.* (Lincoln, Neb., 1961), esp. pp. 183–256.

For religious history, the book by W. Bousset and H. Gressmann, *Die Religion des Judentums im späthellenistischen Zeitalter,* 3d ed. (Tübingen, 1926; republished 1966), still retains all its value. The problem was brilliantly treated in the learned work by Martin Hengel, *Judentum und Hellenismus* (1968; 2d ed., Tübingen, 1973); we cite the English translation by John Bowden, *Judaism and Hellenism: Studies in Their Encounter in Palestine during the Early Hellenistic Period,* 2 vols. (Philadelphia, 1974). Marcel Simon and André Benoit have given an excellent synthetic presentation of the question, supported by a good bibliography, in *Le Judaïsme et le Christianisme antique, d'Antiochus Epiphane à Constantin* (Paris, 1968).

Morton Smith has brought out the antiquity and importance of Greek influence in Palestine, both in Jerusalem (where a Greek garrison resided from 320 to 290 and again in 218 and 199) and in the villages; see his *Palestinian Parties,* pp. 57 ff. Martin Hengel furnishes a supplementary documentation in *Judaism and Hellenism,* vol. 1, pp. 6–106; vol. 2, pp. 2–71 (chap. 1, "Early Hellenism as a Political and Economic Force"; chap. 2, "Hellenism in Palestine as a Cultural Force and Its Influence on the Jews").

On the personification of Wisdom (*hokmā*) and its analogies in the Oriental Wisdom literatures, see W. Schencke, *Die Chokma (Sophia) in der jüdischen Hypostasenspekulation* (Christiania, 1913); P. Humbert, *Recherches sur les sources égyptiennes de la littérature sapientiale d'Israël* (Neuchâtel, 1929); W. Baumgartner, "Die israelitische Weisheitsliteratur," *Theologische Rundschau* n.s. 5 (1933): 258–88; J. Fichtner, *Die altorientalische Weisheit in ihrer israelitisch-jüdischen Ausprägung* (Giessen, 1933); H. Ringgren, *Word and Wisdom* (Lund, 1947); W. F. Albright, "Some Canaanite-Phoenician Sources of Hebrew Wisdom," in *Wisdom in Israel and the Ancient Near East,* suppl. to *VT* 3 (1955): 1–15; G. von Rad, *Wisdom in Israel* (Nashville and New York, 1972; the German edition dates from 1970); H. Conzelmann, "The Mother of Wisdom," in *The Future of Our Religious Past,* ed. J. M. Robinson (London and New York, 1971), pp. 230–43; Hengel, *Judaism and Hellenism,* vol. 1, pp. 153 ff.; vol. 2, pp. 97 ff.

201. On the Qoheleth, see J. Pederson, "Scepticisme israëlite," *RHPR* 10 (1930): 317–70; R. Gordis, *Koheleth: The Man and His World* (New York, 1951); K. Galling, *Die Krisis der Aufklärung in Israel* (Mainzer Universitätsreden, 1952); H. L. Ginsburg, *Studies in Koheleth* (New York, 1960); H. Gese, "Die Krisis der Weisheit bei Koheleth," in *Les sagesses du Proche-Orient Ancien: Travaux du Centre d'histoire des religions de Strasbourg* (Paris, 1963), pp. 139–51; O. Loretz, *Qoheleth und der alte Orient* (Freiburg, 1964); M. Dahood, "Canaanite-Phoenician Influence in Qoheleth," *Biblica* 33 (1952): 30–52; Dahood, "Qoheleth and Recent Discoveries," ibid. 42 (1961): 359–66; David Winston, "The Book of Wisdom's Theory of Cosmogony," *HR* 11 (1971): 185–202; R. Braun, *Koheleth und sein Verhältnis zur literarischen Bildung und Populärphilosophie,* supplement 130 to *Zeitschrift für die Alttestamentliche Wissenschaft* (Erlangen, 1973); M. Hengel, *Judaism und Hellenism,* vol. 1, pp. 115–29, and the bibliographies listed in vol. 2, pp. 77–87 (notes 51–162). For the historical analysis of the text, see Eissfeldt, *The Old Testament,* pp. 491–99.

On Ben Sirach, see the annotated translation by G. H. Box and W. O. E. Oesterley in R. H. Charles, *Apocrypha and Pseudepigrapha of the Old Testament* (Oxford, 1913), vol. 1, 268–517. For historical analysis of the text, with an extensive bibliography, see Eissfeldt, *The Old Testament,* pp. 595–99. Our interpretation is much indebted to Martin Hengel, *Judaism and Hellenism,* vol. 1, pp. 130–55; vol. 2, pp. 88–96.

Ben Sirach's approach presents certain analogies with Stoic conceptions; first, the certainty that the world and human existence develop according to a plan determined by God (see §184). In addition, Sirach shares with Stoicism the idea that the cosmos is infused with a rational power, which is, precisely, the divinity; see M. Pohlenz, *Die Stoa,* 2d ed. (Göttingen, 1964), vol. 1, p. 72. Then, too, Zeno's philosophy comes out of a Semitic religious vision that has much in common with the thought of the Old Testament (see ibid., p. 108). Thus the assimilation of Stoic ideas by the Jews, from Ben Sirach and Aristobulus to Philo, was in fact a return to an Oriental heritage (see Hengel, *Judaism and Hellenism,* vol. 1, pp. 149, 162). However, the importance of Greek influences must not be exaggerated. The parallels between the celebrated chapter 24 of Ben Sirach and the aretalogies of Isis have long been recognized. W. L. Knox observed "a startling affinity [of the personified Wisdom] to a Syrian Astarte with the features of Isis" ("The Divine Wisdom," *Journal of Theological Studies* 38 [1937]: 230–37; the passage quoted occurs on p. 235). See also

H. Ringgren, *Word and Wisdom,* pp. 144 ff.; H. Conzelmann, "The Mother of Wisdom," in J. M. Robinson, ed., *The Future of Our Religious Past,* pp. 230–43; and Hengel, vol. 1, pp. 158 ff.; vol. 2, pp. 101 ff. (supplementary bibliography in n. 331). It is not impossible that the cult of Isis was known in Jerusalem in the third century and that the Jewish schools of Wisdom transferred the aretalogy of Isis-Astarte to divine Wisdom; see Hengel, vol. 1, p. 258. But, as we have already observed (p. 258), Wisdom is not the *paredros* (associate) of God but comes out of his mouth. See W. Schencke, *Die Chokma (Sophia) in der jüdischen Hypostasenspekulation;* J. Fichtner, *Die altorientalische Weisheit in ihrer israelitisch-jüdischen Ausprägung;* Fichtner, "Zum Problem Glaube und Geschichte in der israelitisch-jüdischen Weisheitsliteratur," *Theologische Literaturzeitung* 76 (1951): 145–50; J. M. Reese, *Hellenistic Influence on the Book of Wisdom and Its Consequences* (Rome, 1970); B. L. Mack, *Logos und Sophia: Untersuchungen zur Weisheitstheologie im hellenistischen Judentum* (Göttingen, 1973).

It is important to note that, between the third century B.C. and the second century of our era, similar conceptions are documented not only in the Oriental-Hellenistic world but also in Buddhist and Hindu India; we witness the religious and mythological personification of "knowledge" (*prajña, jñāna*) as the supreme means of liberation. The process will continue in the Middle Ages, both in India and in Christian Europe (see vol. 3).

The grandiose undertaking of the translation of the Pentateuch, an enterprise unequaled in antiquity, had provided the possibility for a Jewish literature composed directly in Greek, and in ca. 175–70, Aristobulus, the first Jewish "philosopher," wrote a didactic and apologetic work addressed to the young sovereign Ptolemy VI Philometor. To judge from the fragments of it that have been preserved, the author propounded a daring theory, which was to be frequently restated later: Jewish doctrine, as formulated in the Bible, represents the one true philosophy; Pythagoras, Socrates, and Plato were acquainted with it and borrowed its principles; when the Greek poets and philosophers speak of "Zeus," they are referring to the true God. "For all philosophers agree that, concerning God, we ought to hold pious opinions, and to this, especially, our system gives excellent exhortation" (quoted by Eusebius, *Praeparatio Evangelica* 13. 12. 7 f.). However, the wisdom of Moses is proclaimed to be definitely superior to Greek philosophical doctrines because it is of divine origin; see Hengel, vol. 1, pp. 163 ff., and the references he cites in vol. 2, pp. 106–10, notes 375–406.

Soon afterward, the author of the *Letter of Aristeas* still more clearly expresses the tendency to assimilate the biblical idea of God to the Greek (i.e., "universalist") conception of the divinity. The Greeks and the Jews "worship the same God—the Lord and Creator of the Universe . . . , though we call him by different names, such as Zeus or Dis" (*Arist.* 15–16). Greeks learned in philosophy were held to have long professed monotheism. In conclusion, the author considers Judaism identical with Greek philosophy. See the English translation and the commentary by M. Hadas, *Aristeas to Philocrates: Jewish Apocryphal Literature* (New York, 1951), and the edition by A. Pelletier, *Lettre d'Aristée à Philocrate,* Sources Chrétiennes, no. 89 (Paris, 1962); cf. V. Tcherikover, "The Ideology of the Letter of Aristeas," *HTR* 51 (1958): 59–85; Hengel, vol. 1, p. 264; vol. 2, p. 176.

202. For the history of Palestine between Antiochus IV Epiphanes and Pompey, see the bibliography cited above for § 200. Add three works by E. Bickerman, "Un document relatif à la persécution d'Antiochus IV Epiphane," *RHR* 115 (1937): 188–221, *Der Gott der Makkabäer* (Berlin, 1937), and "Anonymous Gods," *Journal of the Warburg Institute* 1 (1937–38): 187–96; B. Nazar, "The Tobiads," *Israel Exploration Journal* 7 (1957): 137–45, 229–38; J. A. Goldstein, "The Tales of the Tobiads," in *Christianity, Judaism, and Other Greco-Roman Cults: Studies for Morton Smith,* vol. 3 (Leiden, 1975), pp. 85–123.

For the persecutions by Antiochus and the war of liberation, see the sources cited in note 31. In the last analysis, the "reform" that Antiochus sought—inspired by the philhellenes—aimed at transforming Jerusalem into a Greek *polis;* see Hengel, vol. 1, p. 278. Recent translations of and commentaries on the Books of Maccabees are F. M. Abel, *Les Livres des Maccabées,* 2d ed. (Paris, 1949); S. Zeitlin, *The First Book of Maccabees* (New York, 1950); Zeitlin, *The Second Book of Maccabees* (1954); and J. G. Bunge, *Untersuchungen zum zweiten Makkabäerbuch* (Bonn, 1971). For critical analyses and bibliographies, see Eissfeldt, *The Old Testament,* pp. 576–82, 771.

On the identification of Yahweh with Greek conceptions of God, see Hengel, vol. 1, 261 ff.; add Marcel Simon, "Jupiter–Yahvé: Sur un essai de théologie pagano-juive," *Numen* 23 (1976): 40–66. It is important to note that the first testimonies by Greek authors—Hecataeus of Abdera, Theophrastus, Megasthenes, Clearchus of Soli—presented the Jews as a people of "philosophers"; see the analysis of the sources in Hengel, vol. 1, pp. 255 ff.

O. Plöger has demonstrated that the *hassidim* have a long history; the movement is documented in the third century, and it may be presumed to have begun under the Persian domination; see his *Theocracy and Eschatology* (Oxford, 1968), pp. 23 ff., 42–52. Also on the *hassidim*, see Hengel, vol. 1, pp. 175 ff.; vol. 2, 118 ff.

On Jewish apocalyptic literature and thought, see W. Bousset, *Die jüdische Apokalyptik* (Berlin, 1903); P. Volz, *Die Eschatologie der jüdischen Gemeinde im neutestamentlichen Zeitalter,* 2d ed. (Tübingen, 1934); H. H. Rowley, *The Relevance of Apocalyptic,* 3d ed. (London, 1950); Rowley, *Jewish Apocalyptic and the Dead Sea Scrolls* (London, 1957); S. B. Frost, *Old Testament Apocalyptic: Its Origins and Growth* (London, 1952); Rudolph Mayer, *Die biblische Vorstellung vom Weltentbrand* (Bonn, 1956); D. S. Russell, *The Method and Message of Jewish Apocalyptic* (London, 1964); H. D. Betz, "Zum Problem des religionsgeschichtlichen Verständnisses der Apokalyptik," *Zeitschrift für Theologie und Kirche* 63 (1966): 391–409; Hengel, vol. 1, pp. 181 ff.

On the Book of Daniel, see R. H. Charles, *A Critical and Exegetical Commentary on the Book of Daniel* (Oxford, 1929); W. Baumgartner, "Ein Vierteljahrhundert Danielforschung," *Theologische Rundschau* n.s. 11 (1939): 59–83, 125–44, 201–28; L. S. Ginsburg, *Studies in Daniel* (New York, 1948); A. Bentzen, *Daniel,* 2d ed. (Tübingen, 1952); O. Eissfeldt, *The Old Testament,* pp. 512–29 (valuable bibliography, pp. 512–13, 768–69); André Lacoque, *Le Livre de Daniel* (Neuchâtel and Paris, 1976).

On the theme *vaticinia ex eventu,* see E. Osswald, "Zum Problem der *vaticinia ex eventu,*" *Zeitschrift für die alttestamentliche Wissenschaft* 75 (1963): 27–44.

On Iranian influences in the Book of Daniel, see I. W. Swain, "The Theory of the Four Monarchies: Opposition History under the Roman Empire," *Classical Philology* 35 (1940): 1–21; David Winston, "The Iranian Component in the Bible, Apocrypha, and Qumran: A Review of the Evidence," *HR* 5 (1966): 189–92. The problem of Oriental influences is discussed by Hengel, vol. 1, pp. 181 ff. It should be emphasized that a number of themes already occur in the Prophets.

On the "Great Year," see Eliade, *The Myth of the Eternal Return: Cosmos and History,* trans. Willard R. Trask, Bollingen Series 46 (Princeton, 1965), pp. 134 ff.; B. L. von Waerden, "Das Grosse Jahr und die ewige Wiederkehr," *Hermes* 80 (1952): 129–55.

On the four kingdoms and the four beasts, see H. H. Rowley, *Darius the Mede and the Four World Empires in the Book of Daniel* (Cardiff, 1935), pp. 161 ff.; W. Baumgartner, "Zu den vier Reichen von

Daniel 2," *Theologische Zeitschrift* 1 (1945): 17–22; A. Daquot, "Sur les quatre Bêtes de Daniel VII," *Semitica* 5 (1955): 5–13.

203. On the syndrome of the end of the world, see Eliade, *The Myth of the Eternal Return,* pp. 112 ff. See also the bibliography on apocalyptic given for § 202 and T. F. Glasson, *Greek Influence in Jewish Eschatology, with Special Reference to the Apocalypse and Pseudepigrapha* (London, 1961).

On the resurrection of bodies, see R. H. Charles, *Eschatology* (1899; republished New York, 1963), pp. 78 ff., 129 ff., 133 ff.; P. Volz, *Eschatologie;* A. Nicolainen, *Der Auferstehungsglaube in der Bibel und ihrer Umwelt* (1944); E. F. Sutcliffe, *The Old Testament and the Future Life* (1946); R. Martin-Achard, *De la mort à la résurrection d'après l'Ancien Testament* (1956); K. Schubert, "Die Entwicklung der Auferstehungslehre von der nachexilischen bis zur frührabbinischen Zeit," *Biblische Zeitschrift* n.s. 6 (1962): 177–214.

The Iranian doctrine of resurrection is clearly documented in the fourth century B.C.; see Theopompus, Frag. 64, in F. Jacoby, *Fragmente der griechischen Historiker* (Berlin, 1929); see also §112 in vol. 1 of the present work.

The apocrypha and pseudepigrapha of the Old Testament have been translated by R. H. Charles and his collaborators in the second volume of *Apocrypha and Pseudepigrapha* (Oxford, 1913). We have followed their translations of 4 Esdras, 1 Enoch, the Psalms of Solomon, the Testament of the XII Patriarchs, and the Syriac Apocalypse of Baruch. We have also consulted J. T. Milik, *The Books of Enoch* (1976), and Pierre Bogaert, *L'Apocalypse syriaque de Baruch,* 2 vols. (1969). See also A. M. Dennis, *Introduction aux Pseudépigraphes grecques de l'Ancien Testament* (Leiden, 1970).

On the "Son of Man," see the analytical bibliography in E. Sjöberg, *Der Menschensohn im äthiopischen Henochbuch* (Lund, 1946), pp. 40 ff.; add: S. Mowinckel, *He That Cometh,* pp. 346–450; C. Colpe, in *Theologisches Wörterbuch zum Neuen Testament,* vol. 8, pp. 418–25; J. Coppens, *Le Fils de l'Homme et les Saints du Très-Haut en Daniel VIII, dans les Apocryphes et dans le Nouveau Testament* (Bruges and Paris, 1961); F. H. Borsch, *The Son of Man in Myth and History* (Philadelphia, 1967). For the meanings of the expression "Son of Man" in the New Testament, see § 221.

On Satan, see Bousset and Gressmann, *Die Religion des Judentums im späthellenistischen Zeitalter,* pp. 332 ff.; Ringgren, *Word and Wisdom,* pp. 169 ff. (with bibliography); B. Reicke, *The Disobedient Spirits and Christian Baptism* (Copenhagen, 1948); B. L. Randelini, ''Satana nell'Antico Testamento,'' *Bibbia e Oriente* 5 (1968): 127–32.

On the ascension of Enoch, see G. Widengren, *The Ascension of the Apostle and the Heavenly Book* (Uppsala, 1950), pp. 36 ff.

The rabbinic texts and the *midrashim* referring to the New Testament are translated and commented on by H. L. Strack and P. Billerbeck in *Kommentar zum Neuen Testament aus Talmud und Midrash,* 6 vols. (Munich, 1922–61).

On Iranian influences in the apocrypha and pseudepigrapha, see D. Winston, ''The Iranian Component in the Bible, Apocrypha, and Qumran,'' *HR* 5 (1966): 192–200.

204. On apocalyptic as defense against the terror of history, see Eliade, *The Myth of the Eternal Return,* pp. 112 ff.

On the tradition of Enoch, see three works by P. Grelot, ''La légende d'Hénoch dans les Apocryphes et dans la Bible,'' *Recherches de science religieuse* 46 (1958): 5–26, 181–210, ''La géographie mythique d'Hénoch et ses sources orientales,'' *RB* 65 (1958): 33–69, and ''L'eschatologie des Esséniens et le Livre d'Hénoch,'' *Revue de Qumran* (1958–59): 113–31; see also J. T. Milik, ''Problèmes de la littérature hénochique à la lumière des fragments araméens de Qumran,'' *HTR* 64 (1971): 333–78.

On the Pharisees, see W. L. Knox, *Pharasaism and Hellenism in Judaism and Christianity,* vol. 2: *The Contact of Pharasaism with Other Cultures* (London, 1937), and, especially, L. Finkelstein, *The Pharisees,* 2 vols. (1938; 3d ed., Philadelphia, 1962). See also Hengel, vol. 1, pp. 169–75 (''Wisdom and Torah in Pharisaic and Rabbinic Judaism''), J. Neusner, *The Rabbinic Traditions about the Pharisees before 70,* 3 vols. (Leiden, 1971), and W. B. Davies, *Torah in the Messianic Age and for the Age to Come,* Journal of Biblical Literature Monograph Series, no. 7 (1952).

On Jewish proselytism, see W. Braude, *Jewish Proselyting,* Brown University Studies, no. 6 (Providence, 1940), and Hengel, vol. 1, pp. 168 ff. (with recent bibliography).

Hengel rightly observes that Judaism exercised its greatest historical influence during the Hellenistic-Roman period. ''Both its fight for freedom against the Seleucids and its bitter struggle with Rome are probably unique in the ancient world'' (vol. 1, p. 309). Unique, too, was the effort to proselytize that was imitated and continued by primitive Christianity. However, the "ontology of the Torah" and the strict legalism of the Pharisees ended, on the one hand, in halting the missionary effort and, on the other hand, in the tragic misunderstanding in regard to Christianity. The small Judaeo-Christian community managed to maintain itself in Palestine with great difficulty and only by observing the Torah. The accusation of syncretistic-Hellenistic apostasy still influences Jewish interpretations of Paul in our own day (Hengel, vol. 1, p. 309, mentioning J. Klausner, L. Baeck, and H. J. Schoeps; cf. Hengel, vol. 2, p. 205, n. 315). For H. J. Schoeps, for example, Paul is "a Jew of the Diaspora, alienated from the faith of his fathers" (*Paul* [London, 1961], p. 261). Citing this passage, Hengel remarks (vol. 1, p. 309) that strict and apologetic understanding of the Torah, so unlike the message of the Prophets, was irreconcilable with the universal eschatological proclamation of the Gospels and must have been ignored. For the defenders of the Torah, however, the Christians looked like the Jewish renegades who, between ca. 175 and 164, urged apostasy and assimilation (ibid., p. 314).

Chapter 26. Hellenistic Syncretism and Creativity

205. The religions of the Hellenistic period are presented in the excellent work by Carl Schneider, *Kulturgeschichte des Hellenismus,* vol. 2 (Munich, 1969), pp. 838 ff. (on the foreign gods, with an extensive bibliography). See also the texts translated and commented on by F. C. Grant, *Hellenistic Religion: The Age of Syncretism* (New York, 1953). The work by Karl Prümm, *Religionsgeschichtliches Handbuch für den Raum der altchristlichen Umwelt* (Freiburg im Breisgau, 1943), contains a general treatment, supplemented by a valuable bibliography, of religious realities in the Hellenistic and Roman period. See also W. W. Tarn, *Hellenistic Civilisation* (London, 1927; 3d rev. ed., 1952); two works by A. D. Nock, *Conversion: The Old and the New in Religion from Alexander the Great to Augustine of Hippo* (Oxford, 1933), and *Essays on Religion and the Ancient World,* 2 vols. (Oxford, 1972); Johannes Leipoldt and Walter Grundmann, *Umwelt des Urchristentums,* vol. 1 (Berlin, 1965), esp. pp. 68 ff., 101 ff.; and three works by V. Cilento, *Trasposizioni dell'antico: Saggi su le forme della grecità al suo tramonto* (Milan and Naples, 1961–66), *Comprensione della religione antica* (Naples, 1967), and *Studi di storia religiosa della tarda antichità* (Messina, 1968).

On religious syncretism, see R. Pettazzoni, "Sincretismo e conversione," in *Saggi di storia delle religioni e della mitologia* (Rome, 1946), pp. 143–51; Helmer Ringgren, "The Problem of Syncretism," in *Syncretism,* ed. Sven S. Hartman (Stockholm, 1969), pp. 7–14; A. S. Kapelrud, "Israel's Prophets and Their Confrontation with the Canaanite Religion," ibid., pp. 162–70; J. van Dijk, "Les contacts ethniques dans la Mésopotamie et les syncrétismes de la religion sumérienne," ibid., pp. 171–206; Jan Bergman, "Beitrag zur *Interpretatio Graeca:* Aegyptische Götter in griechischer Übertragung," ibid., pp. 207–27; *Le syncrétisme dans les religions grecque et romaine,* Travaux du Centre d'Etudes Supérieures spécialisé d'Histoire des Religions à Strasbourg (Paris, 1972); Geo Widengren, "Cultural Influence, Cultural Continuity, and Syncretism," in *Religious Syncretism in Antiquity: Essays in Conversation with Geo Widengren,* ed. B. Pearson (Missoula, Mont., 1975), pp. 1–20; F. Dunand and P. Lévêque, eds., *Les syncrétismes dans les religions de l'antiquité: Colloque de Besançon, 1973* (Leiden, 1975).

On astrology and astral fatalism, see Karl Prümm, *Religionsgeschichtliches Handbuch für den Raum der altchristlichen Umwelt,* pp. 404 ff. (with the earlier literature); A. J. Festugière, *La Révélation d'Hermès Trismégiste,* vol. 1 (1944), pp. 89–122; three works by Franz Cumont, *Astrology and Religion among the Greeks and the Romans* (New York, 1912), *L'Egypte des astrologues* (Brussels, 1973), and *Lux Perpetua* (1949), pp. 303 ff.; H. Ringgren, ed., *Fatalistic Beliefs* (Stockholm, 1967), especially Jan Bergman's study, "I Overcome Fate, Fate Harkens to Me," pp. 35–51; C. Schneider, *Kulturgeschichte des Hellenismus,* vol. 2, pp. 907–19.

In the Roman period the fashion for horoscopes became general at Rome as well as in the Empire. Augustus published his horoscope, and coins were struck with the image of Capricorn, his zodiacal constellation.

The mythology and theology of the seven planets have left their traces in the seven days of the week, the seven angels of the Apocalypse, the notion of seven Heavens and seven Hells, the ritual stairway of seven steps in the cult of Mithra, etc.

For the cult of sovereigns, see E. Bickerman, "Die römische Kaiserapotheose," *ARW* 27 (1929): 1–24; Lily R. Taylor, *The Divinity of the Roman Emperor* (Middletown, 1931); Mac Evance, *The Oriental Origin of Hellenistic Kingship* (Chicago, 1934); D. M. Pippidi, *Recherches sur le culte impérial* (Bucharest, 1939); Pippidi, "Apothéose impériale et apothéose de Pérégrinos," *SMSR* 20 (1947–48): 77–103; Karl Prümm, *Religionsgeschichtliches Handbuch,* pp. 54–66 (with an extensive bibliography); L. Certaux and J. Tondriau, *Le culte des souverains dans la civilisation hellénistique* (Paris, 1958); *Le culte des souverains dans l'Empire romain,* Entretiens sur l'antiquité classique, no. 19 (Vandoeuvres and Geneva, 1973).

The literary sources for the Mysteries have been published by N. Turchi, *Fontes mysteriorum aevi hellenistici* (Rome, 1923). Despite its apologetic tendency, Karl Prümm's work, *Religionsgeschichtliches Handbuch,* pp. 215–356 ("Die Mysterienkulte in der antiken Welt") remains indispensable for its documentation and bibliography. A selection of iconographic monuments has recently been published by Ugo Bianchi in his *The Greek Mysteries* (Leiden, 1976).

Comprehensive studies on the Mystery religions are those by R. Reitzenstein, *Die hellenistischen Mysterienreligionen nach ihren Grundgedanken und Wirkungen,* 3d ed. (1927); N. Turchi, *Le religioni misteriosofiche del mondo antico* (Rome, 1923); R. Pettazzoni, *I Misteri: Saggio di una teoria storico-religiosa* (Bologna, 1924); S. Angus, *The Mystery Religions and Christianity* (London, 1925); H. R. Willoughby, *Pagan Regeneration: A Study of Mystery Initiation in the Graeco-Roman World* (Chicago, 1929); F. Cumont, *Les religions orientales dans le paganisme romain,* 4th ed. (1929; English trans., *Oriental Religions in Roman Paganism,* New York, 1911); A. Loisy, *Les Mystères païens et le mystère chrétien,* 2d ed. (Paris, 1930).

See also *The Mysteries: Papers from the Eranos Yearbooks* (New York, 1955); Eliade, *Rites and Symbols of Initiation: The Mysteries of Birth and Rebirth* (New York, 1958), pp. 109 ff.; A. D. Nock, "Hellenistic Mysteries and Christian Sacraments," *Mnemosyne* 4th ser. 5 (1952): 117–213; reprinted in *Early Gentile Christianity and Its Hellenistic Background* (New York: Harper Torchbooks, 1964), pp. 109–46; R. Merkelbach, *Roman und Mysterium in der Antike* (Munich and Berlin, 1962); P. Lambrechts, "L'Importance de l'enfant dans les religions à mystères," *Latomus* 28 (1957): 322–33; G. Freymuth, "Zum Hieros Gamos in den antiken Mysterien," *Museum Helveticum* 21 (1964): 86–95; F. Cumont, *Lux Perpetua* (Paris, 1949), pp. 235 ff.; L. Bouyer, "Le salut dans les religions à Mystères," *Revue des sciences religieuses* 27 (1953): 1–16. See also the bibliographies given below, §§ 206–8.

206. On Dionysus in the Hellenistic milieu and in the Greco-Roman period, see U. von Wilamowitz-Moellendorff, *Der Glaube der Hellenen,* vol. 2 (1932), pp. 261 ff.; H. A. Jeanmaire, *Dionysos: Histoire du culte de Bacchus* (Paris, 1951), pp. 417 ff. (bibliographies on pp. 497 ff.); C. Schneider, *Kulturgeschichte des Hellenismus,* vol. 2, pp. 800–810, 1097 ff. (bibliography); M. P. Nilsson, *The Dionysiac Mysteries in the Hellenistic and Roman Age* (Lund, 1957); Nilsson,

Geschichte der griechischen Religion, vol. 2, 2d rev. ed. (1961), pp. 360–67 (Eng. trans., *History of Greek Religion,* 2d ed. [New York, 1964], pp. 205–10); R. Turcan, *Les sarcophages romains à représentation dionysiaque: Essai de chronologie et d'histoire religieuse* (Paris, 1966).

On the Infant Dionysus, see D. Costa, "Dionysos enfant, les bacchoi et les lions," *Revue archéologique* 39 (1952): 170–79; Turcan, *Les sarcophages romains,* pp. 394 ff. On the apotheosis of Semele, see P. Boyancé, "Le disque de Brindisi et l'apothéose de Sémélé," *Revue des études anciennes* 44 (1942): 195–216; Nilsson, *The Dionysiac Mysteries,* pp. 4 and 14; P. Boyancé, "Dionysos et Sémélé," *Atti della Pontificia Accademia Romana di Archeologia* 38 (1965–66): 79 ff.

On initiations into the Dionysiac Mysteries, see the bibliography in Schneider, *Kulturgeschichte des Hellenismus,* p. 1101. See especially F. Matz, *Dionysiakē teletē: Archäologische Untersuchungen zum Dionysos-Kult in hellenistischer und römischer Zeit* (1964); G. Zuntz, "On the Dionysiac Fresco in the Villa dei Misteri at Pompeii," *Proceedings of the British Academy* 49 (1963): 177–202; three works by R. Turcan, "Un rite controuvé de l'initiation dionysiaque," *RHR* 158 (1960): 140–43, "Du nouveau sur l'initiation dionysiaque," *Latomus* 24 (1965): 101–19, and *Les sarcophages romains,* pp. 408 ff.; P. Boyancé, "Dionysiaca: A propos d'une étude récente sur l'initiation dionysiaque," *Revue des études anciennes* 68 (1966): 33–60.

On the role of caves in the cult of the Dionysiac *thiasoi,* see P. Boyancé, "L'Antre dans les mystères de Dionysos," *Rendiconti della Pontificia Accademia di Archeologia* 33 (1962): 107–27; Claude Bérard, *Anodoi: Essai sur l'imagerie des passages chthoniens,* Bibliotheca Helvetica Romana no. 13, Institut Suisse de Rome (1947), pp. 58 ff., 144 ff.; Bérard, in *Mélanges d'histoire ancienne et d'archéologie offerts à Paul Collart* (Lausanne, 1976), pp. 61–65.

See also F. Cumont, *Etudes sur le symbolisme funéraire des Romains* (1942), pp. 370 ff., and Cumont, *Lux Perpetua,* pp. 250 ff.

207. For short accounts of the Phrygian Mysteries, see R. Pettazzoni, *I Misteri,* pp. 102–49; A. Loisy, *Les Mystères païens,* pp. 83–120; F. Cumont, *Les religions orientales,* pp. 43–68, 220–30; K. Prümm, *Religionsgeschichtliches Handbuch,* pp. 255–63 (with the earlier bibliography); C. Schneider, *Kulturgeschichte des Hellenismus,* vol. 2, pp. 856 ff.

The written sources (literary and epigraphic) for the cult of Attis have been collected and commented on by H. Hepding, *Attis, seine Mythen und sein Kult* (Giessen, 1903). The book by H. Graillot, *Le culte de Cybèle, Mère des Dieux, à Rome et dans l'Empire Romain*

(Paris, 1912), remains indispensable. The first volume of the *Corpus Cultus Cybelae Attisque,* by M. J. Vermaseren, was published in 1977. The same author has published *The Legend of Attis in Greek and Roman Art* (Leiden, 1966) and *Cybele and Attis: The Myth and the Cult,* translated from the Dutch by A. M. H. Lemmers (London, 1977); this last work contains an extensive bibliography. See also P. Lambrechts, *Attis: Van herdersknaap tot god* (Brussels, 1962) (on pp. 61–74 there is a summary in French).

On the protohistory of Kubaba-Cybele, see R. Eisler, "Kubaba-Kybele," *Philologus* 68 (1909): 118–51, 161–209; E. Laroche, "Koubaba, déesse anatolienne, et le problème des origines de Cybèle," in *Eléments orientaux dans la religion grecque ancienne* (Paris, 1960), pp. 113–28; Vermaseren, *Cybele and Attis,* pp. 13–24; Dario M. Cosi, "La simbologia della porta nel Vicino Oriente: Per una interpretazione dei monumenti rupestri frigi," *Annali della Facoltà di lettere e Filosofia* 1 (Florence, 1976): 113–52, esp. pp. 123 ff.

On the cult of Cybele and Attis in the Roman period, see P. Boyancé, "Sur les mystères phrygiens: 'J'ai mangé dans le tympanon, j'ai bu dans la cymbale,' " *Revue des études anciennes* 37 (1935): 161–64; J. Carcopino, "La réforme romaine du culte de Cybèle et d'Attis," in *Aspects mystiques de la Rome païenne* (Paris, 1942), pp. 49–171; P. Lambrechts, "Les fêtes 'phrygiennes' de Cybèle et d'Attis," *Bulletin de l'Institut d'Histoire Belge de Rome* 27 (1952): 141–70; E. van Doren, "L'Evolution des mystères phrygiens à Rome," *Antiquité classique* 22 (1953): 79–88; Charles Picard, "Les cultes de Cybèle et d'Attis," *Numen* 4 (1957): 1–23; P. Romanelli, "Magna Mater e Attis sul Palatino," *Hommages à Jean Bayet,* Coll. Latomus, no. 70 (Brussels, 1964), pp. 619–26; A. Brelich, "Offerte e interdizioni alimentari nel culto della Magna Mater a Roma," *SMSR* 36 (1965): 26–42; D. Fishwick, "The Cannophori and the March Festival of Magna Mater," *Transactions and Proceedings of the American Philological Association* 97 (1966): 193–202; Dario M. Cosi, "Salvatore e salvezza nei Misteri di Attis," *Aevum* 50 (1976): 42–71.

The controversy over the meaning and ritual function of the *pastos* (cubiculum) is summarized by Vermaseren, *Cybele and Attis,* p. 117.

On the *taurobolium,* see R. Duthoy, *The Taurobolium: Its Evolution and Terminology* (Leiden, 1969), with the earlier literature.

A. Loisy (*Mystères païens,* p. 110) has drawn attention to a myth reported by Clement of Alexandria (*Protrept.* 2. 15) which serves as a commentary on the formula "From the tambourine I have eaten . . . ; the room I have entered": Zeus by a trick copulated with the Mother of the gods (Cybele); then, "to pacify her wrath when she learned that he had abused her, he threw a ram's testicles into her lap as if he had mutilated himself to expiate his offense. Arnobius, reporting this myth, says that Zeus had turned himself into a bull to copulate with the Mother."

On the Galloi, see Vermaseren, *Cybele and Attis,* pp. 98 ff., and the literature cited there, pp. 200 ff. On castration as identification with the divinity, see Michel Meslin, "Réalités psychiques et valeurs religieuses dans les cultes orientaux, Ier–IVe siècles," *Revue historique* 512 (1974): 295 ff.

On the relations between the Phrygian Mysteries and Christianity, see M. J. Lagrange, "Attis et le christianisme," *RB* 16 (1919): 419–80; Lagrange, "Attis ressuscité," *RB* 36 (1927): 561–66; A. Loisy, *Les Mystères païens,* pp. 108 ff.; Vermaseren, *Cybele and Attis,* pp. 180 ff.

See also Hugo Rahner, "Christian Mysteries and Pagan Mysteries," in *Greek Myths and Christian Mystery* (London and New York, 1963), pp. 1–45, and the bibliography given in § 205, above.

208. On the Egyptian Mysteries, see F. Cumont, *Les religions orientales,* pp. 69–94, 231–48; A. Loisy, *Les Mystères païens,* pp. 121–56; K. Prümm, *Religionsgeschichtliches Handbuch,* pp. 268–80; Georges Nagel, "The 'Mysteries' of Osiris in Ancient Egypt," in Joseph Campbell, ed., *Pagan and Christian Mysteries: Papers from the Eranos Yearbooks,* trans. Ralph Manheim and R. F. C. Hull (New York, 1963), pp. 119–34 (the French text was published in the *Eranos-Jahrbuch* for 1944); Curt Schneider, *Kulturgeschichte des Hellenismus,* vol. 2, pp. 840 ff.

On Serapis, see P. M. Fraser, "Two Studies on the Cult of Sarapis in the Hellenistic World," *Opuscula Atheniensia* 3 (1960): 1–54; Fraser, "Current Problems Concerning the Early History of the Cult of Sarapis," ibid. 7 (1967): 23–45; Ruth Stiehl, "The Origin of the Cult of Sarapis," *HR* 3 (1963): 21–33; Ladislav Vidman, *Isis und Sarapis bei den Griechern und Römern* (Berlin, 1970); J. E. Stambaugh, *Sarapis under the Early Ptolemies* (Leiden, 1972); W. Hornbostel, *Sarapis: Studien zum Überlieferungsgeschichte, den Erscheinungsformen und Wandlungen der Gestalt eines Gottes* (Leiden, 1973).

On Herodotus and the Egyptian Mysteries, see A. B. Lloyd's commentaries in *Herodotus, Book II,* 2 vols. (Leiden, 1975–76).

There is an extensive literature on the cult of Isis and its dissemination in the Roman Empire. See R. Merkelbach, *Isisfeste in Griechisch-römischer Zeit: Daten und Riten* (Meisenheim am Glan, 1963); M. Münster, *Untersuchungen zur Göttin Isis* (Berlin, 1968); R. E. Witt, *Isis in the Graeco-Roman World* (London and Ithaca, 1971) (on the whole a disappointing book); S. K. Heyob, *The Cult of Isis among Women in the Graeco-Roman World* (Leiden, 1975). See also R. Harder, "Karpokrates von Chalkis und die memphitische Isispropaganda," *Abhandlungen der Preussischen Akademie der Wissenschaften, Phil.-Hist. Klasse* 1943:14 (Berlin, 1944); D. Vandebeek, *De interpretatio Graeca van de Isisfigur,* Studia hellenistica no. 4 (Louvain, 1946).

Among recent publications on the dissemination of the cult, we mention G. Grimm, *Zeugnisse aegyptischer Religion und Kunstelemente im römischen Deutschland* (Leiden, 1969); P. F. Tchudin, *Isis in Rom* (Aarau, 1962); Tam Tinh Tram, *Le culte d'Isis à Pompéi* (Paris, 1964); Françoise Dunand, *Le culte d'Isis dans le bassin oriental de la Méditerranée,* 3 vols. (Leiden, 1973); M. Malaise, *Les conditions de pénétration et de diffusion des cultes égyptiens en Italie* (Leiden, 1972).

On the aretalogies of Isis, see D. Müller, "Aegypten und die griechischen Isis-Aretalogien," *Abhandlungen der Sächsischen Akademie der Wissenschaften, Phil.-hist. Klasse* 53:1 (1961); Jan Bergman, *Ich bin Isis: Studien zum memphitischen Hintergrund der griechischen Isisaretalogien* (Uppsala, 1968); cf. Jonathan Smith's observations in *HR* 11 (1971): 236 ff. (also see ibid., n. 10, pp. 241–42, for an extensive bibliography).

On initiation into the cult of Isis, see M. Dibelius, "Die Isisweihe bei Apuleius und verwandte Initiationsriten," in *Botschaft und Geschichte* (Tübingen, 1965), vol. 2, pp. 30–79 (a study first published in 1917); V. von Gonzenbach, *Untersuchung zu den Knabenweihung im Isiskult* (Bonn, 1957); J. Gwyn Griffiths, *Apuleius of Madauros: The Isis Book* (Leiden, 1975). See also J. Baltrušaitis, *La Quête d'Isis: Introduction à l'égyptomanie: Essai sur la légende d'un mythe* (Paris, 1967).

209. The Hermetic texts have been edited and translated by A. J. Festugière and A. D. Nock, *Hermès Trismégiste,* 4 vols. (Paris, 1945–54). The English translation of the Hermetic texts by W. Scott and A. S. Ferguson, *Hermetica,* 4 vols. (Oxford, 1924–36), valuable for its notes and commentaries, should be consulted cautiously, since the authors worked from a poor text.

An excellent presentation and review of studies and problems has been provided by Jean Doresse, "L'Hermétisme égyptianisant," *Histoire des religions,* vol. 2 (Paris, 1972), pp. 430–97 (see also pp. 433–41 for an inventory of texts). The fundamental work by Festugière, *La Révélation d'Hermès Trismégiste,* 4 vols. (Paris, 1944–54), remains indispensable. The same author has collected a certain number of studies—among them, "L'Hermétisme" (1948) and "Hermetica" (1938)—

in the volume *Hermétisme et mystique païenne* (1967). See also K. Prümm, *Religionsgeschichtliches Handbuch,* pp. 540–605; G. van Moorsel, *The Mysteries of Hermes Trismegistos* (Utrecht, 1955); Hugo Rahner, *Greek Myths and Christian Mystery* (London and New York, 1963), pp. 190 ff.

The texts of popular Hermetism have been analyzed at length, interpreted, and translated in part in Festugière's *La Révélation d'Hermès Trismégiste,* vol. 1: *L'Astrologie et les sciences occultes*. On the alchemical structure of the creation of souls in the treatise *Korē Kosmou,* see the article by Festugière published in *Pisciculi* (Münster, 1939), pp. 102–16, and reprinted in *Hermétisme et mystique païenne,* pp. 230–48.

The writings of philosophical Hermetism belong to various literary genres. The *Poimandres* is an aretalogy, that is, a narrative of a miraculous manifestation (*aretē*) of the divinity (here, the divine Nous); there are also fragments of cosmogony and didactic *logoi* (see Festugière, *Révélation,* vol. 2, pp. 28 ff.). Treatises I and XIII describe the experience of a divinization, and it is especially these two treatises that contain the revelation of Hermetic salvation (see Festugière, *Hermétisme et mystique païenne,* pp. 34 ff., 38 ff.).

The optimistic theology is expounded in Treatises V, VII, and IX of the *Corpus Hermeticum,* and the pessimistic doctrine is presented in Treatises I, IV, VI, VII, and XIII. But sometimes the orientations coexist in the same book. The Egyptian affinities of the *Corpus Hermeticum* have been brought out by Reitzenstein in R. Reitzenstein and H. H. Schaeder, *Studien zum antiken Synkretismus* (Leipzig and Berlin, 1926), pp. 43–44; Philippe Derchain, "L'authenticité de l'inspiration égyptienne dans le *Corpus Hermeticum,*" *RHR* 161 (1962): 172–98; Martin Krause, "Aegyptisches Gedankengut in der Apokalypse des Asclepius," *ZDMG,* supplement, 1 (1969): 48–57; and by Jean Doresse in "Hermès et la gnose: A propos de l'*Asclepius* copte" and, most recently, "L'Hermétisme égyptianisant," pp. 442–50.

Certain influences from Jewish sources have also been detected. *Corpus Hermeticum,* Treatise I, cites Genesis; see C. H. Dodd, *The Bible and the Greeks* (1935), pp. 99 ff.; Scott, *Hermetica,* vol. 1, pp. 54 ff. See also Marc Philonenko, "Une allusion de l'*Asclepius* au livre d'Hénoch," in *Christianity, Judaism and Other Greco-Roman Cults: Studies for Morton Smith,* vol. 2 (Leiden, 1975), pp. 161–63.

The *Poimandres* has been studied by R. Reitzenstein, *Poimandres: Studien zur griechisch-ägyptischen und frühchristlichen Literatur* (Leipzig, 1904); Festugière, *Révélation,* vol. 4, pp. 40 ff.; Hans Jonas, *The Gnostic Religion* (1958; 2d rev. ed., 1963), pp. 147–73; E. Haenschen, *Gott und Mensch* (Tübingen, 1965), pp. 335–77. The Gnostic library of Nag Hammadi has yielded a collection of Hermetic texts in the dialect of Upper Egypt, among them several long fragments of a proto-*Asclepius;* see three works by J. Doresse, "Hermès et la gnose: A propos de l'*Asclepius* copte," *Novum Testamentum* 1 (1956): 54–59; *Les livres secrets des gnostiques d'Egypte* (Paris, 1958), pp. 256 ff.; and "L'Hermétisme égyptianisant," p. 434.

210. The existence of Hermetic brotherhoods has been maintained by R. Reitzenstein, *Poimandres,* pp. 248 ff. (on the "Poimandres-Gemeinde"), and accepted by Geffcken, *Der Ausgang des griechisch-römischen Heidentums* (Heidelberg, 1920), pp. 20 ff. See the critique of this hypothesis by Festugière in *La Révélation d'Hermès Trismégiste,* vol. 1, pp. 81–84, and in *Hermétisme et mystique païenne,* pp. 37–38.

On the transposition of cult Mysteries into literary Mysteries, see Festugière, *L'idéal religieux des Grecs et l'Evangile,* pp. 116–32; *La Révélation,* pp. 82 ff.; *Hermétisme et mystique païenne,* pp. 103 ff. See also A. D. Nock, "The Question of Jewish Mysteries," *Gnomon* 13 (1937): 156–65, republished in *Essays on Religion and the Ancient World* (Oxford, 1972), vol. 1, pp. 459–68.

On Hermetic "initiation," see G. Sfameni Gasparro, "La gnosi ermetica come iniziazione e mistero," *SMSR* 36 (1965): 53–61; Henry and Renée Kahane, *The Krater and the Grail: Hermetic Sources of the Parzival* (Urbana, 1965), pp. 40 ff.

On the relations between Hermetism and Essenism, see F. M. Braun, "Essénisme et Hermétisme," *Revue Thomiste* 54 (1954): 523–58; see also, by the same author, "Hermétisme et Johanisme," ibid. 55 (1955): 22–212; 56 (1956): 259–99.

The Hermetic literature of the Sabaeans is analyzed by Scott, *Hermetica,* vol. 4, pp. 248–76 (the author has drawn chiefly on the two volumes by D. A. Chwolsohn, *Die Ssabier und Ssabismus* (St. Petersburg, 1856]); see also Festugière and Nock, *Hermès-Trismégiste,* vol. 4, pp. 145–46; J. B. Segal, "The Sabian Mysteries," in E. Bacon, ed., *Vanished Civilizations* (New York and London, 1963), pp. 201–20.

On Arabic Hermetic literature, see L. Massignon's appendix in the first volume of *La Révélation d'Hermès Trismégiste,* pp. 384–99, and Henry and Renée Kahane, *The Krater and the Grail,* pp. 116–22.

In the twelfth century, after a spate of translations of Arabic works, Hermetism began to be known in Europe; see H. and R. Kahane, pp. 130 ff. The Hermetic influence on the *Parzival* of Wolfram von Eschenbach and the derivation of the term *graal* (cup, vessel, basin) from the vocable *kratēr* have been brought out by the Kahanes in *The Krater and the Grail,* passim. See also, by the same authors, "Hermetism in the Alfonsine Tradition," *Mélanges offerts à Rita Lejeune* (Gembloux, 1969), vol. 1, pp. 443–45. The Kahanes' results have been accepted by Henry Corbin, *En Islam iranien,* vol. 2 (1971), pp. 143–54.

On the Latin translation of the *Corpus Hermeticum* and its importance in the Renaissance, see Frances A. Yates, *Giordano Bruno and the Hermetic Tradition* (Chicago, 1946), and the third volume of the present work.

211. For a general view of alchemy, see Eliade, *The Forge and the Crucible: The Origins and Structures of Alchemy,* trans. Stephen Corrin, 2d ed. (Chicago, 1979) (originally published in 1962). On Hellenistic alchemy, see ibid., pp. 146 ff. and the bibliography given on pp. 217–21. Among recent works, we mention A. J. Festugière, *La Révélation d'Hermès Trismégiste,* vol. 1 (1944), pp. 216–82; three works by F. Sherwood Taylor, "A Survey of Greek Alchemy," *Journal of Hellenic Studies* 50 (1930): 103–39, "The Origins of Greek Alchemy," *Ambix* 1 (1937): 30–47, and *The Alchemists* (New York, 1940); Robert P. Multhauf, *The Origins of Chemistry* (London, 1966), pp. 103–16; W. J. Wilson, "The Origins and Development of Greco-Egyptian Alchemy," *Ciba Symposia* 3 (1941): 926–60; and J. Lindsay, *Hellenistic Alchemy* (London, 1970).

As for technical recipes for metallurgy and the craft of the goldsmith, already documented in the sixteenth century B.C. (in, for example, the Ebers Papyrus), they certainly comprised a hierurgical context, for in the traditional societies operations were paralleled by a ritual. The Leiden and Stockholm papyri, containing purely "chemical" recipes (on these, see, most recently, Multhauf, *The Origins of Chemistry,* pp. 96 ff., with the recent bibliography), were found in a tomb at Thebes beside Magical Papyruses XII and XIII (published by Preisendanz). R. G. Forbes has cited many examples of a "secret language" used in Mesopotamia for writing down recipes for the manufacture of glass (as early as the seventeeth century B.C.) and for synthetic lapis lazuli, as well as for medical recipes; see his *Studies in Ancient Technology,* vol. 1 (Leiden, 1955), p. 125. The oft-repeated warning in Mesopotamian medical texts of the seventh century B.C.—"He who knows may show to him who knows, but he who knows may not show to him who knows not"—is already found in recipes for manufacturing glass in the Kassite period, ten centuries earlier; see Forbes, p. 127. Hellenistic alchemical literature abounds in objurations and oaths forbidding the communication of esoteric mysteries to the profane. Ostanes "veiled the mysteries as cautiously as [he did] the pupils of his eyes; he ordered that they were not to be imparted to disciples who were not worthy of them''; other examples are in J. Bidez and F. Cumont, *Les mages hellénisés* (Paris, 1938), vol. 2, pp. 315 ff. The obligation to preserve the secrecy of the *opus alchymicum* remained in force from the end of the ancient world down to our day. Besides, communication of ''trade secrets'' by means of writing is an illusion of modern historiography. If there is a literature that has claimed to ''reveal secrets,'' it is certainly the literature of Tantrism, but in this sizable mass of writings we never find the practical indications that are indispensable to *sadhana:* in the decisive moments, the assistance of a master is necessary, if only to verify the authenticity of the experience.

H. E. Stapleton holds that the origin of Alexandrine alchemy must be sought not in Hellenistic Egypt but in Mesopotamia, at Harran; it is there that he places the author of the *Treatises of Agathodaimon,* a text probably written in the year 200 B.C. and so, according to Stapleton, before *Physika kai Mystika;* see his ''The Antiquity of Alchemy,'' *Ambix* 5 (1953): 1–43. This hypothesis, which, among other things, explains the rise of Arabic alchemy, is still in dispute. In a series of recent studies H. J. Shepard has seen in Gnosticism the chief source of the alchemical mystique; see his ''Gnosticism and Alchemy,'' *Ambix* 6 (1957): 86–101, and the bibliography given in Eliade, *The Forge and the Crucible,* pp. 217–21.

C. G. Jung commented on the visions of Zosimus in his study ''The Visions of Zosimus,'' trans. R. F. C. Hull, in *The Collected Works of Carl G. Jung,* Bollingen Series 20, vol. 13 (Princeton, 1954). The original text of the ''Visions'' is in M. Berthelot, *Collection des anciens alchimistes grecs* (Paris, 1888), pp. 107–12, 115–18. There is also an English translation by F. Sherwood Taylor in *Ambix* 1 (1937): 88–92. *Separatio* is expressed in alchemical terms of the dismembering of a human body; see Jung, ''The Visions of Zosimus,'' p. 87, n. 111. On the ''torture'' of the elements, see ibid., p. 105. See also Eliade, *Shamanism: Archaic Techniques of Ecstasy,* trans. Willard R. Trask (Princeton, 1964). On the transmutation of matter into spirit, see C. G. Jung, *Psychology and Alchemy,* trans. R. F. C. Hull, *Collected Works,* vol. 12, 2d ed. (1968).

Chapter 27. New Iranian Syntheses

212. For good accounts of the political and cultural history of the Parthians, see Franz Altheim, *Alexandre et l'Asie* (Paris, 1954), pp.

275 ff. (originally published as *Alexander und Asien,* Tübingen, 1953); R. Ghirshman, *Parthes et Sassanides* (Paris, 1962); I. Wolski, "Les Achémenides et les Arsacides," *Syria* 43 (1966): 65–89; Wolski, "Arsakiden und Sasaniden," *Festschrift für Franz Altheim* (Berlin, 1969), vol. 1, pp. 315–22.

All of the general presentations of Iranian religious history cited in volume 1 of the present work, in the Critical Bibliographies, § 100, pp. 464–66, include chapters on the Parthian period. See, especially, J. Duchesne-Guillemin, *La religion de l'Iran ancien* (Paris, 1962), pp. 224 ff. (English trans., by K. M. JamaspAsa, *The Religion of Ancient Iran,* Bombay, 1973); four works by G. Widengren, *Les religions de l'Iran* (Paris, 1968), pp. 201 ff. (originally published as *Die Religionen Irans,* Stuttgart, 1965); *Iranisch-semitische Kulturbegegnung in parthischer Zeit* (Cologne and Opladen, 1960); "Juifs et Iraniens à l'époque des Parthes," *VT,* suppl., 4 (1957): 197–240; and "Iran and Israel in Parthian Times," *Temenos* 2 (1966): 139–77. See also Stig Wikander, *Feuerpriester in Kleinasien und Iran* (Lund, 1946).

On the *Oracles of Hystaspes,* see Widengren, *Les religions de l'Iran,* pp. 228 ff.; J. Bidez and F. Cumont, *Les mages hellénisés* (Paris, 1934), vol. 1, pp. 228 ff. John R. Hinnells considers that these oracles are in agreement with Zoroastrian theology; see his "The Zoroastrian Doctrine of Salvation in the Roman World," in *Man and His Salvation: Studies in Memory of S. C. F. Brandon* (Manchester, 1973), pp. 146 ff. Cf. F. Cumont, "La fin du monde selon les mages occidentaux," *RHR* 103 (1931): 64–96.

On royalty in the Arsacid period and initiatory symbolism in the fabulous biography of Mithradates Eupator, see Widengren, "La légende royale de l'Iran antique," *Hommages à Georges Dumézil* (Brussels, 1960), pp. 225–37, and *Les religions de l'Iran,* pp. 266 ff.

213. On the archaic structure of Zurvan, see G. Widengren, *Hochgottglaube im alten Iran* (Uppsala, 1938), pp. 300 ff.; see also his *Religions de l'Iran,* pp. 244 ff., 314 ff. The texts on Zurvan have been translated and commented on by R. C. Zaehner, *Zurvan, A Zoroastrian Dilemma* (Oxford, 1955); see also, by the same author, *The Teachings of the Magi* (London, 1956). In addition to the works by Zaehner, Widengren, and Duchesne-Guillemin we mention, from the immense literature on Zurvanism, M. Molé, "Le problème zurvanite," *JA* 247 (1959): 431–70; Ugo Bianchi, *Zamān i Ohrmazd: Lo zoroastrismo nelle sue origini e nella sua essenza* (Turin, 1958), pp. 130–89; Gherardo Gnoli, "Problems and Prospects of the Studies on Persian Religion," in U. Bianchi, C. J. Bleeker, and A. Bausani, eds., *Problems and Methods of the History of Religions* (Leiden, 1971), pp. 85 ff.

On the cosmogonic myths, disseminated from Eastern Europe to Siberia, in which God's adversary plays a part, see Eliade, *Zalmoxis, the Vanishing God: Comparative Studies in the Religions and Folklore of Dacia and Eastern Europe,* trans. Willard R. Trask (Chicago, 1972), pp. 76 ff. (the Iranian legends are analyzed on pp. 106–12).

The myth transmitted by Eznik, *Against the Sects* (translated by Zaehner, *Zurvan,* pp. 438–39) goes on to relate that Ohrmazd, after creating the world, did not know how to make the sun and the moon. Ahriman did know, and talked of it to the demons: Ohrmazd must sleep with his mother to create the sun and with his sister to make the moon. A demon hastened to communicate the formula to Ohrmazd (see Eliade, *Zalmoxis,* p. 107 and notes 80–81). Now, as Widengren has shown (*Religions de l'Iran,* p. 321), the Magi were known for their incestuous practices. The continuation of the myth preserved by Eznik contains a contradiction, for Ohrmazd, who had shown himself to be the "successful creator" ("all that Ohrmazd created was good and straight"), suddenly proves unable to complete his creation; he exhibits the "mental fatigue" that is characteristic of certain types of *dii otiosi* (see *Zalmoxis,* pp. 87 ff. and passim). This episode was probably introduced as an etiological myth to justify the conduct of the Parthian Magi.

214. We shall study the religions of the Sassanid period in volume 3 (see also below, § 216). A good account will be found in Widengren, *Les religions de l'Iran,* pp. 273 ff., and in Duchesne-Guillemin, *La religion de l'Iran ancien,* pp. 276 ff. It must not be forgotten, however, that several conceptions that are documented only in late texts go back to the Achaemenid period; see, inter alia, G. Widengren, "The Problem of the Sassanid Avesta,'" in *Holy Book and Holy Tradition,* ed. F. F. Bruce and E. G. Rupp (Manchester, Eng., 1968), pp. 36–53.

On the doctrine of millennia and the formula of the three times (*aršōkara, frašokara,* and *maršokara*), see H. S. Nyberg, "Questions de cosmogonie et de cosmologie mazdéennes," *JA* 214 (1929): 193–310; 219 (1931): 89 ff.; and Nyberg, *Die Religionen des alten Iran* (Leipzig, 1938), pp. 380 ff. On limited time and the role of the luminaires, see M. Molé, *Culte, mythe et cosmologie dans l'Iran ancien* (Paris, 1963), pp. 395 ff.

215. On the two creations, see, in addition to the books by Nyberg, Duchesne-Guillemin, Zaehner, and Widengren, s.v. *mēnōk* and *gētik,* G. Gnoli, "Osservazioni sulla dottrina mazdaica della creazione,"

Annali dell'Istituto di Napoli n.s. 13 (1963): 180 ff.; S. Shaked, "Some Notes on Ahreman, the Evil Spirit, and His Creation," in *Studies in Mysticism and Religion Presented to Gershom G. Scholem* (Jerusalem, 1967), pp. 277–34; Shaked, "The Notions *mēnōg* and *gētīg* in the Pahlavi Texts and Their Relation to Eschatology," *Acta Orientalia* 32 (1971): 59–107; Mary Boyce, *A History of Zoroastrianism,* vol. 1 (Leiden, 1975), pp. 229 ff. See also Henry Corbin, "Le Temps cyclique dans le mazdéisme et dans l'ismaëlisme," *Eranos-Jahrbuch* 20 (1955): 150–217; R. Zaehner, *The Dawn and Twilight of Zoroastrianism* (London, 1961).

216. The sources for the myth of Gayōmart are partly translated and commented on in A. Christensen, *Les types du premier homme et du premier roi dans l'histoire légendaire des Iraniens* (Leiden and Uppsala, 1971–74), vol. 1, pp. 19 ff.; S. S. Hartmann, *Gayōmart, étude sur le syncrétisme dans l'ancien Iran* (Uppsala, 1953) (unconvincing); and M. Molé, *Culte, mythe et cosmologie,* pp. 280 ff., 409 ff., 447 ff.

There are good discussions of Gayōmart by Duchesne-Guillemin, *La religion de l'Iran ancien,* pp. 208 ff., 324 ff.; Zaehner, *Dawn and Twilight,* pp. 180, 232, 262 ff.; M. Molé, *Culte, mythe et cosmologie,* pp. 484 ff. (critique of Hartmann's thesis). K. Hoffmann has brought out the similarities to a semidivine Vedic personage, Mārtāṇḍa ("mortal seed"), in "Mārtāṇḍa and Gayōmart," *Münchener Studien zur Sprachwissenschaft* 11 (1957): 85–103.

On the macrocosmos-microcosmos theme and its relations with the cosmogony and with Gayōmart, see Anders Olerud, *L'idée de macrocosmos et de microcosmos dans le "Timée" de Platon* (Uppsala, 1951), pp. 144 ff., and Ugo Bianchi, *Zamān i Ohrmazd,* pp. 190–221 (see pp. 194 ff. for a critique of Olerud).

Jewish circles provide similar speculations in regard to Adam. A text of the *Sibylline Oracles* (3. 24–26), dating from the second or first century B.C., explains the name of Adam as a symbol of the cosmos: A = *anatolē,* East; D = *dysis,* West; A = *arktos,* North; M = *mesēmbria,* South. See also the *Book of the Slavic Enoch* (in R. H. Charles, *The Apocrypha* [Oxford, 1913], vol. 2, p. 449); the alchemist Zosimus, *Authentic Commentaries,* sec. 11, translated by Festugière in his *La Révélation d'Hermès Trismégiste,* vol. 1 (Paris, 1944), p. 269.

On the myth of men-plants born from the semen of an innocent being that is sacrificed or hanged, see Eliade, "Gayōmart et la Mandragore," in *Ex Orbe Religionum: Studia Geo Widengren Oblata,* vol. 2 (Leiden, 1972), pp. 65–74.

According to an earlier tradition preserved in the *Bundahišn,* Gayōmart fiercely resisted the attackers and, before succumbing, caused considerable losses among them. In Manichaean mythology, the Primordial Man, Gēhmurd (Gayōmart), headed the resistance against the Evil One's attack; see G. Widengren, "The Death of Gayōmart," in J. M. Kitagawa and C. H. Long, eds., *Myths and Symbols: Studies in Honor of Mircea Eliade* (Chicago, 1969), p. 181. See also, by the same author, "Primordial Man and Prostitute: A Zervanite Motif in the Sassanid Avesta," *Studies in Mysticism and Religion Presented to Gershom G. Scholem,* pp. 337–52.

On Gayōmart as Perfect Man, see M. Molé, *Culte, mythe et cosmologie,* pp. 469 ff. According to Molé, the "Mazdaean Macranthropos is not Gayōmart; rather, he appears as a manifestation of Ohrmazd" (p. 410).

The various expressions for the imperishable element in man (*ahū,* "life"; *urvan,* "soul"; *baodhah,* "knowledge"; *daēnā* and *fravashi*) are analyzed by Duchesne-Guillemin, *La Religion de l'Iran ancien,* pp. 327 ff., who also mentions the essential bibliography.

On the saviors to come and the final renovation, see Duchesne-Guillemin, pp. 343–54 (there is a brief analysis of the contradictions in the eschatology, pp. 352–53); G. Widengren, *Les religions de l'Iran,* pp. 127 ff.; Molé, *Culte, mythe et cosmologie,* pp. 412 ff., and the bibliographies given in vol. 1 of the present work, pp. 471–73 (§§111–12).

217. The two volumes by Franz Cumont, *Textes et monuments figurés relatifs aux Mystères de Mithra* (Brussels, 1896, 1898), still remain indispensable. The same author has published a short summarizing book, *Les Mystères de Mithra* (Brussels, 1900; 3d ed., 1913); see also his *Les religions orientales dans le paganisme romain,* 4th ed. (Paris, 1929), pp. 131 ff., 270 ff. (both works are available in English translation). Cumont's last work on Mithraism, probably finished in May 1947, three months before his death, was not published until 1975: "The Dura Mithraeum," translated and edited by E. D. Francis in *Mithraic Studies,* ed. J. R. Hinnells (Manchester, 1975), pp. 151–214. A critical analysis of Cumont's interpretation has been provided by R. L. Gordon, "Franz Cumont and the Doctrines of Mithraism," ibid., pp. 215–48. Stig Wikander had already criticized Cumont's reconstruction in the first fascicle (the only one published) of his *Etudes sur les Mystères de Mithra* (Lund, 1950); but see Widengren's observations in *Stand und Aufgaben der iranischen Religionsgeschichte* (Leiden, 1955), pp. 114 ff.

The corpus of inscriptions and monuments has been published by M. I. Vermaseren, *Corpus Inscriptionum et Monumentorum Religionis Mithricae,* 2 vols. (The Hague, 1956, 1960). See, by the same author, *Mithras, the Secret God* (London and New York, 1963) (translated from the Dutch).

There are brief accounts in A. Loisy, *Les Mystères païens et le mystère chrétien,* 2d ed. (1930), pp. 157–98; R. Pettazzoni, *I Misteri* (Bologna, 1924), pp. 220–81; J. Duchesne-Guillemin, *La religion de l'Iran ancien,* pp. 248–56; G. Widengren, "The Mithraic Mysteries in the Greco-Roman World, with Special Regard to Their Iranian Background," in *La Persia e il mondo greco-romano* (Academia Nazionale dei Lincei, 1966), pp. 433–55 (with references to the author's earlier publications); R. C. Zaehner, *The Dawn and Twilight of Zoroastrianism,* pp. 128 ff. See also K. Prümm, *Religionsgeschichtliches Handbuch für den Raum der altchristlichen Umwelt* (Freiburg im Breisgau, 1943), pp. 281 ff.

The proceedings of the first International Congress of Mithraic Studies, which was held in Manchester in 1971, have been published under the editorship of John R. Hinnells: *Mithraic Studies* (Manchester, Eng., 1971). The second Congress was held in Teheran in 1975. See also *The Journal of Mithraic Studies* for the years 1975 ff.

In several of his works G. Widengren has brought out the Iranian elements present in the Mysteries of Mithra; see, most recently, "The Mithraic Mysteries," passim. R. Merkelbach has identified other features of Iranian origin; see his "Zwei Vermutungen zur Mithrasreligion," *Numen* 6 (1959): 154–56. On the enthronement of the Parthian king and the Armenian traditions concerning Meher, see G. Widengren, *Iranisch-semitische Kulturbegegnung in parthischer Zeit,* pp. 65 ff.; S. Hartmann, *Gayōmart,* p. 60, n. 2, p. 180, and note 6. Cf. Eliade, *Zalmoxis,* pp. 28 ff.

In his study "Mithra-Verehrung, Mithras-Kult, und die Existenz iranischer Mysterien" (*Mithraic Studies,* pp. 378–405), Carsten Colpe limits the origin of the Mysteries to the region of Pontus and Commagene; he sees the cult as a politically oriented syncretistic one, of comparatively recent date (second century A.D.).

For the episodes featuring Mithra and the bull *before* the immolation, see Duchesne-Guillemin, *La religion de l'Iran ancien,* p. 250, and M. I. Vermaseren, *Mithras, the Secret God,* pp. 79 ff.; these adventures are depicted almost exclusively on the monuments of Central Europe, between the Rhine and the Danube.

On Cautes and Cautopates, see, most recently, Leroy A. Campbell, *Mithraic Iconography and Ideology* (Leiden, 1968), pp. 29 ff., and

Martin Schwartz, "Cautes and Cautopates, the Mithraic Torch Bearers," in *Mithraic Studies,* pp. 406–23; these two studies cite the most important items of the earlier literature.

In the representations of the sacrifice of the bull, Mithra has his head turned, "as if looking behind him and often with a strangely sad expression; usually a crow, to the left, leans toward him; the figure of the Sun is often in the left-hand corner, and, to the right, that of the Moon; below, springing toward the blood spouting from the wound, is a dog, also a snake; a scorpion pinches the testicles of the dying beast and stings them with its tail; an ant sometimes joins the gathering; or else, below the bull, a krater is depicted, and a lion appears to be guarding it or drinking from it, while, elsewhere, the snake seems to be doing likewise. . . . The bull's raised tail ends in a tuft of ears of corn; there are even monuments in which, instead of blood, such ears spout from the bull's wound" (Loisy, *Les Mystères païens,* pp. 185–86, summarizing Cumont).

From the considerable bibliography on Mithra the bull-slayer, we mention Vermaseren, *Mithras, the Secret God,* pp. 67 ff., and also his "A Unique Representation of Mithras," *Vigiliae Christianae* 4 (1950): 142–256; L. A. Campbell, *Mithraic Iconography,* pp. 247 ff.; John R. Hinnells, "Reflections on the Bull-slaying Scene," in *Mithraic Studies,* pp. 290–312 (the author rejects Cumont's interpretation, according to which the animals present at the sacrifice of the bull—the dog, the snake, and the scorpion—would represent the conflict between Good and Evil).

For the sacrifice of animals on the occasion of the Mithrakana among the Zoroastrians of Iran, see Mary Boyce, "*Mihragan* among the Irani Zoroastrians," in *Mithraic Studies,* pp. 106–18.

On the seven grades of Mithraic initiation, see F. Cumont, *Textes et monuments figurés,* vol. 1, pp. 314 ff.; G. Widengren, "The Mithraic Mysteries," pp. 448 ff.; and Campbell, *Mithraic Iconography,* pp. 303 ff. For a long time the second grade was read *cryphius* instead of *nymphus*. However, though no manuscript of Jerome (*Ep. ad Laetam* 107. 10) has *cryphius,* this term is documented in the Mithraic inscriptions of San Silvestro; see Bruce M. Metzger, "The Second Grade of Mithraic Initiation," in his *Historical and Literary Studies: Pagan, Jewish, and Christian* (1968), pp. 25–33. See also W. Vollgraff, "Les cryfii des inscriptions mithraïques," *Hommage à Waldemar Deonna* (Brussels, 1957), pp. 517–30.

As for the initiation described by a fourth-century author (Pseudo-Augustine, *Quaest. vet. et novi Test.* 114. 12), some scholars hesitate to consider it authentic; see F. Saxl, *Mithras: Typengeschichtliche*

Untersuchungen (Berlin, 1931), p. 67, n. 2. But Prümm (*Handbuch,* p. 290) and J. Leipold (in J. Leipold and W. Grundmann, *Die Umwelt des Christentums,* vol. 3 [Berlin, 1967], p. 35) agree with Loisy (*Les Mystères païens,* p. 183) that this text contains a description of real initiatory ordeals.

The frescoes of the mithraeum at Capua have recently been reproduced in color by M. I. Vermaseren in his *Mithraica,* vol. 1: *The Mithraeum at Sa. Maria Capua Vetere* (Leiden, 1971). See also, by the same author, *Mithraica,* vol. 2: *The Mithraeum at Ponza* (1974).

218. There is an extensive bibliography on the dissemination of the Mysteries of Mithra in the Roman Empire. See F. Cumont, *Textes et monuments figurés,* and M. I. Vermaseren, *Corpus Inscriptionum.* See also Vermaseren's *Mithraica;* W. Blawatsky and G. Kochelenko, *Le culte de Mithra sur la côte septentrionale de la Mer Noire* (Leiden, 1966); V. J. Walters, *The Cult of Mithras in the Roman Provinces of Gaul* (Leiden, 1974); G. Ristow, *Mithras in römischen Köln* (Leiden, 1974); C. M. Daniels, "The Role of the Roman Army in the Spread of the Practice of Mithraism," *Mithraic Studies,* pp. 249–74; Nicolae Mitru, "Mithraismul în Dacia," *Studii Teologice* (Bucharest) 2d ser. 23 (1971): 261–73.

R. Merkelbach holds that the Mithraic cosmogony was inspired by Plato's *Timaeus.* See his "Die Kosmogonie der Mithra-Mysterien," *Eranos-Jahrbuch* 34 (1966): 249 ff. See also R. Turcan, *Mithras Platonicus: Recherches sur l'hellénisation philosophique de Mithra* (Leiden, 1975).

A comparative analysis of cult meals in antiquity has been provided by J. P. Kane, "The Mithraic Cult Meal in Its Greek and Roman Environment," *Mithraic Studies,* pp. 313–51 (see esp. pp. 341 ff.). See also A. D. Nock, "Hellenistic Mysteries and Christian Sacraments," *Mnemosyne* 4th ser. 5 (1952): 177–213 (reprinted in Nock, *Essays on Religion and the Ancient World* [Oxford, 1972], pp. 791–820), and the bibliography given below, § 220.

On the testimony of the Christian apologists, see Carsten Colpe, "Die Mithrasmysterien und die Kirchenväter," in *Romanitas und Christianitas: Studia I. H. Waszink* (Amsterdam and London), pp. 29–43.

Chapter 28. The Birth of Christianity

219. The majority of works on Jesus of Nazareth, which have been increasing in number ever more rapidly since the beginning of the nineteenth century, are of interest chiefly for the ideology and methodology of their authors. A detailed critical history of the works that appeared from Hermann E. Reimarus (1779) to Wilhelm Wrede (1901) will be found in the book by Albert Schweitzer, *Von Reimarus zu Wrede: Eine Geschichte der Leben-Jesu-Forschung* (Tübingen, 1906; 6th ed., 1951); we have used the English translation, *The Quest of the Historical Jesus* (1910), republished in 1968, with an introduction by James M. Robinson valuable for its analysis of some later studies (Maurice Goguel, R. Bultmann, Karl Barth, F. Buri, etc.).

We mention some recent works: G. Bornkamm, *Jesus von Nazareth* (Stuttgart, 1956; English trans., *Jesus of Nazareth,* New York, 1961); Ethelbert Stauffer, *Jesus: Gestalt und Geschichte* (Bern, 1957); J. Jeremias, *Das Problem des historischen Jesus* (Stuttgart, 1960; English trans., *The Problem of the Historical Jesus,* Philadelphia, 1964); H. Conzelmann, G. Eberling, E. Fuchs, *Die Frage nach dem historischen Jesus* (Tübingen, 1959); V. Taylor, *The Life and Ministry of Jesus* (London, 1954); C. H. Dodd, *The Founder of Christianity* (London and New York, 1970). See also J. Moreau, *Les plus anciens témoignages profanes sur Jésus* (Brussels, 1944); E. Trocmé, *Jésus de Nazareth vu par les témoins de sa vie* (Paris, 1971); F. Trotter, ed. *Jesus and the Historians* (Colwell Festschrift) (Philadelphia, 1968); W. Kümmel, "Jesusforschung seit 1950," *Theologische Rundschau* 31 (1966): 15 ff., 289 ff.

The earliest "Lives of Jesus," from the Gospels to Origen, are analyzed by Robert M. Grant, *The Earliest Lives of Jesus* (New York, 1961). For information transmitted by sources other than the Gospels, see Roderic Dunkerley, *Beyond the Gospels* (Harmondsworth, 1957). Joseph Klausner has approached the problem from the point of view of Judaism; see his *Jesus of Nazareth,* translated from the Hebrew (London, 1925), and *From Jesus to Paul,* translated from the Hebrew (New York, 1943). There is a good general presentation of Jesus and the birth of Christianity, with bibliographies and state of studies, by Marcel Simon, in M. Simon and A. Benoit, *Le Judaïsme et le Christianisme antique* (Paris, 1968), pp. 33 ff., 81 ff., 199 ff. See also Robert M. Grant, *Augustus to Constantine* (New York, 1970), pp. 40 ff.; Norman Perrin, *The New Testament: An Introduction* (New York, 1974), pp. 277 ff.

The disciples of John the Baptist continued to form a separate sect, a rival to the Christian community. See M. Goguel, *Jean-Baptiste* (Paris, 1928); J. Steinmann, *St. Jean Baptiste et la spiritualité du désert* (Paris, 1955); J. Daniélou, *Jean-Baptiste, témoin de l'Agneau* (Paris, 1964); J. A. Sint, "Die Eschatologie des Täufers, die Täufergruppen und die Polemik der Evangelien," in K. Schubert, ed., *Von Messias zum Christos* (Vienna, 1964), pp. 55–163.

On the miracles of Jesus and their relations with Hellenistic magic and theurgy, see L. Bieler, *Theios aner,* 2 vols. (Vienna, 1935, 1936); H. van der Loos, *The Miracles of Jesus* (Leiden, 1965); O. Böcher, *Christus Exorcista* (Stuttgart, 1972); G. Petzke, *Die Traditionen über Apollonius von Tyana und das Neue Testament* (Leiden, 1970); Morton Smith, "Prolegomena to a Discussion of Aretalogies, Divine Men, the Gospels, and Jesus," *Journal of Biblical Literature* 40 (1971): 173–99; J. Hull, *Hellenistic Magic and the Synoptic Tradition* (Naperville, Ill., 1974); Jonathan Z. Smith, "Good News Is No News: Aretalogy and Gospel," in Jacob Neusner, ed., *Christianity, Judaism and Other Greco-Roman Cults: Studies for Morton Smith,* vol. 1 (Leiden, 1974), pp. 21–38. See also below, p. 533.

The Greek and Semitic sources for Jesus' relations with the Pharisees have been translated and commented on by John Bowker, *Jesus and the Pharisees* (1973).

On the reign of Herod Antipas, see H. Hoehner, *Herod Antipas* (Cambridge, 1972). On the Zealots and their relations with Jesus and Judaeo-Christianity, see the suggestive but controversial book by S. C. F. Brandon, *Jesus and the Zealots* (Manchester, 1967). According to Marcel Simon, the ideal of the Zealots is "that of a theocracy, whose inauguration must doubtless coincide with that of the messianic time or be the prelude to it . . . . The strength of their religious convictions is incontestable. It is what animates their nationalism" (Simon and Benoit, *Le Judaïsme et le Christianisme antique,* p. 214).

On the trial of Jesus, see *The Trial of Jesus: Cambridge Studies in Honour of C. F. D. Moule,* ed. E. Bammel (London, 1970). See also A. Jaubert, "Les séances du sanhédrin et les récits de la passion," *RHR* 166 (1964): 143–63; 167 (1965): 1–33. A penetrating and original analysis of the Resurrection has been provided by A. Ammassari, *La Resurrezione, nell'insegnamento, nelle profezie, nelle apparizioni di Gesù,* 2 vols. (Rome, 1967, 1976).

220. On Jesus' preaching concerning the imminence of the Kingdom of God, see T. W. Manson, *The Teaching of Jesus* (Cambridge, 1931; 2d ed. 1937); N. Perrin, *The Kingdom of God in the Teaching of Jesus* (London, 1963); Perrin, *Rediscovering the Teaching of Jesus* (New York, 1967), pp. 54–108 (annotated bibliography, pp. 249 ff.).

On the Kingdom as already *present,* see E. Käsemann, "The Problem of the Historical Jesus," in *Essays on New Testament Themes* (London, 1964), pp. 15–47, N. Perrin, *Rediscovering the Teaching of Jesus,* pp.

85 ff. (analysis, with commentary, of recent exegeses), and M. Simon, in *Judaïsme et Christianisme,* pp. 85 ff.

On the Eucharist, see Oscar Cullmann, *Le culte dans l'Eglise primitive* (Paris, 1945), pp. 12 ff.; K. G. Kuhn, "Repas cultuel essénien et Cène chrétienne," in *Les manuscrits de la Mer Morte: Colloque de Strasbourg* (1957), pp. 85 ff.; Jean Daniélou, *Théologie du Judéo-Christianisme* (Tournai, 1958), pp. 387 ff. (English trans. by John A. Baker, *The Theology of Jewish Christianity,* vol. 1 of *A History of Early Christian Doctrine* [Philadelphia, 1977]); M. Simon, in *Judaïsme et Christianisme,* pp. 184 ff. For a comparative study, see A. D. Nock, *Early Gentile Christianity and Its Hellenistic Background* (New York, 1964), pp. 109–46. See also Nock's article "Hellenistic Mysteries and Christian Sacraments," *Mnemosyne* 4th ser. 5 (1952): 177–214.

There is a significant difference between the spectacular cures, exorcisms, and miracles performed by Jesus and the similar exploits documented in the Hellenistic traditions (e.g., by Apollonius of Tyana) and the Jewish tradition (some examples from the Babylonian Talmud are cited by Perrin, *Rediscovering the Teaching of Jesus,* p. 135). Jesus always insists on "*the faith that saves*" (see Mark 5:34, 10:52; Luke 7:50, 17:19, etc.). After he cured the boy possessed by a devil, the disciples asked Jesus: "Why were we unable to cast it out?" "Because you have little faith," he answered. For "if your faith were the size of a mustard seed you could say to this mountain, 'Move from here to there,' and it would move; *nothing would be impossible for you*" (Matt. 17:19–20; cf. Luke 17:6). Now, as has been observed, this valorization of faith is completely absent from Hellenistic literature and from the traditions collected in the Babylonian Talmud; see Perrin, *Rediscovering the Teaching of Jesus,* pp. 130–42, and the recent works cited there, p. 130, n. 1, and p. 131, nn. 1–6, etc.

221. On the birth of the Church and on the Acts of the Apostles as a historical source, see J. Dupont, *Les problèmes du Livre des Actes d'après les travaux récents* (Louvain, 1950); E. Haenchen, *Die Apostelgeschichte* (Göttingen, 1956); E. Trocmé, *Le Livre des Actes et l'histoire* (Paris, 1957).

On the community in Jerusalem, see the studies by L. Cerfaux, collected in *Recueil Lucien Cerfaux,* vol. 2 (Gembloux, 1954), pp. 63–315; P. Gaetcher, *Petrus und seine Zeit* (Innsbruck, 1957); O. Cullmann, *Peter: Disciple, Apostle, Martyr* (1962; English translation of the second edition, revised and enlarged, of *Petrus* [1960]). On the relations between the primitive Church and normative and sectarian Judaism, see E. Peterson, *Frühkirche, Judentum, und Gnosis* (Vienna,

1959); H. Kosmalas, *Hebräer, Essener, Christen* (Leiden, 1959); M. Simon, *Verus Israel* (Paris, 1948; 2d ed., 1964).

The Book of Acts scarcely mentions the leader of the first Christian community in Jerusalem, James, "the brother of the Lord" (Gal. 1:19), whom Paul opposed (Gal. 2:12). His relations with rabbinic Judaism are obvious (he did not drink wine, never shaved, spent his life in the Temple, etc.). Since James's party finally disappeared after the war of 66–70, the memory of him faded away. But other documents (the Gospel of the Hebrews, the Gospel of Thomas, the Pseudo-Clementines, etc.) present James as the most important personage in the Church; see S. G. F. Brandon, *The Fall of Jerusalem and the Christian Church* (London, 1951), pp. 126–54; J. Daniélou, *Nouvelle histoire de l'Eglise,* vol. 1 (Paris, 1963), pp. 37–38.

On Judaeo-Christianity, see H. J. Schoeps, *Theologie und Geschichte des Judenchristentums* (Tübingen, 1949); Jean Daniélou, *Théologie du Judéo-Christianisme,* esp. pp. 17–101; M. Simon et al., *Aspects du Judéo-Christianisme: Colloque de Strasbourg* (Paris, 1965). There is a good general presentation in M. Simon and A. Benoit, *Le Judaïsme et le Christianisme antique,* pp. 258–74. Add: M. Simon, "Réflexions sur le judéo-christianisme," *Christianity, Judaism . . . : Studies for Morton Smith,* vol. 2 (Leiden, 1975), pp. 53–76 (critical examination of some recent works). Judaeo-Christianity was characterized by its exclusive attachment to observance of the Jewish Law—a fidelity that was later expressed, in M. Simon's words, in "a sort of fossilization. Certain Judaeo-Christians became heretics by the mere fact that they remained apart from the doctrinal evolution of the Great Church and did not accept, or simply ignored, the enlargements and enrichments that Christian dogma experienced in relation to the simple primitive kerygma, especially from the time when Greek thought lent it its framework and concepts. . . . Their aversion to Paul, so characteristic of their position, was doubtless motivated by his attitude toward the Law. But by the same token, it kept them apart from Christological developments, of which Pauline thought constitutes the point of departure. In doctrine as on the plane of observance, they remained the immobile heirs of the primitive community. They were, so to speak, negative heretics, heretics by default" (Marcel Simon, in *Le Judaïsme et le Christianisme antique,* p. 270).

The reasons given by the Jews for rejecting Christianity are examined by D. R. A. Hare, *The Theme of Jewish Persecution of Christianity in the Gospel according to St. Matthew* (Cambridge, 1967), pp. 1–18.

222. For two generations, the interpretations of the conversion and theology of Saint Paul were dominated, on the one hand, by too strict a distinction between Palestinian and Hellenistic Judaism and, on the other hand, by overly personal evaluations of these two forms of Judaism. Thus, for example, Albert Schweitzer contrasted Saint Paul, whom he held to have been an adherent of the Palestinian religious structure, to Saint John, who was completely integrated into the tradition of Hellenistic Judaism; see A. Schweitzer, *Die Mystik des Apostel Paulus* (Tübingen, 1930; English trans., *The Mysticism of Paul the Apostle,* New York, 1968); while a Jewish exegete, C. J. G. Montefiore, ranked Paul among the uprooted members of the Diaspora; had he known the pure and superior Judaism of Palestine, Montefiore concluded, Paul would never have accepted the Gospel (*Judaism and St. Paul* [London, 1914]). Similar positions are defended by Joseph Klausner, *From Jesus to Paul,* translated from the Hebrew by W. F. Stinespring (London, 1943; republished, New York, 1961), and by S. Sandmel, *A Jewish Understanding of the New Testament* (New York, 1956), pp. 37–51, and H. J. Schoeps, *Paulus* (Tübingen, 1959).

But recent researches have shown, on the one hand, the profound Hellenistic influence on the rabbinic ideology and vocabulary and, on the other hand, the presence of Semitic concepts in the Hellenistic writings. The old dichotomy between Palestinian and Hellenistic Judaism is no longer tenable (see the bibliographies for §§ 200, 204). By the same token, the opposition between the two forms of Christian religiosity, Pauline and Johannine—an opposition brilliantly elaborated by A. Schweitzer—disappears. See W. D. Davies, *Paul and Rabbinic Judaism: Some Elements in Pauline Theology* (London, 1948; paperback, New York, 1967, with a new introduction, "Paul and Judaism since Schweitzer," pp. vii–xv). In obeying the call of the resurrected Christ, Paul did not consider himself an apostate. But he redefined the true nature of Israel and the Law from the point of view of a Jew who had just discovered the Messiah in Jesus Christ. For Paul, what thenceforth characterized the "people of God" was no longer obedience to the Law but faith in the Christ. It was in a sense the fulfillment of Jewish religious universalism; for, by virtue of the Christ-Messiah, the "people of God" could accomplish the universal reconciliation ("neither Greek nor Jew nor man nor woman," etc.) and prepare the renewal of the world, the "New Creation."

From the very extensive recent literature, we mention M. Dibelius and W. G. Kümmel, *Paulus,* 2d ed. (Berlin, 1956; English trans. of the first ed., *Paul,* New York, 1953); J. Dupont, *Gnosis: La connaissance religieuse dans les Epîtres de Saint Paul* (Louvain, 1949); A. D. Nock, *St. Paul,* 3d ed. (London, 1948); L. Cerfaux, *La théologie de l'Eglise suivant Saint Paul,* 2d ed. (Paris, 1948); W. C. Van Unnik, *Tarsus or Jerusalem* (London, 1952); E. Earle Ellis, *Paul and His Recent Interpreters* (Grand Rapids, Mich., 1961); Ellis, "Paul and His Opponents: Trends in the Research," *Christianity, Judaism . . . : Studies for Morton Smith,* vol. 1, pp. 264–98, esp. pp. 284 ff.; J. W. Drane, *Paul, Libertine or Legalist: A Study in the Theology of the Major Pauline Epistles* (London, 1975); K. Stendhal, *Paul among Jews and Gentiles* (Philadelphia, 1976); E. P. Sanders, *Paul and Palestinian Judaism* (Philadelphia, 1977). See also the discussion of some recent theses in the study by W. D. Davies, "Paul and the People of Israel," *New Testament Studies* 24 (1977): 4–39; G. Bornkamm, *Paul,* trans. D. G. M. Stalker (New York, 1971; original German edition, *Paulus* [Stuttgart, 1969]).

223. For translations of the Dead Sea manuscripts, see, among others, T. H. Gaster, *The Dead Sea Scriptures in English Translation* (New York, 1956); G. Vermes, *The Dead Sea Scrolls in English* (Harmondsworth, 1962); J. Carmignac et al., *Les textes de Qumran traduits et annotés,* 2 vols. (Paris, 1961, 1963). See also A. S. van der Ploeg, *Le Rouleau de la Guerre: Traduit et annoté avec une introduction* (Leiden, 1969); Y. Yadin and C. Rabin, *The Scroll of the War of the Sons of Light against the Sons of Darkness* (London and New York, 1962). A number of texts will also be found translated, with commentaries, in the works by J. M. Allegro, F. M. Cross, A. Dupont-Sommer, etc.

Among the general presentations, the most useful are J. M. Allegro, *The Dead Sea Scrolls* (Harmondsworth, 1956); Y. Yadin, *The Message of the Scrolls* (London, 1957); H. Bardtke, *Die Sekte von Qumran* (Berlin, 1958; 2d ed., 1961); F. M. Cross, Jr., *The Ancient Library of Qumran and Modern Biblical Studies* (New York, 1958; 2d rev. ed., 1961); O. Cullmann, J. Daniélou, et al., *Les manuscrits de la Mer Morte: Colloque de Strasbourg* (Paris, 1958); R. K. Harrison, *The Dead Sea Scrolls: An Introduction* (New York, 1961); A. Dupont-Sommer, *Les écrits esséniens découverts près de la Mer Morte* (Paris, 1959; 2d ed., 1965; English trans. by G. Vermes, *The Essene Writings from Qumran,* Oxford, 1961); E. F. Sutcliffe, *The Monks of Qumran as Depicted in the Dead Sea Scrolls* (London, 1960); H. Ringgren, *The Faith of Qumran: Theology of the Dead Sea Scrolls* (Philadelphia, 1963).

The bibliography of publications on the Qumran manuscripts down to the beginning of 1957 has been published by C. Burchard, *Bibliographie zu den Handschriften vom Toten Meer* (Berlin, 1957). The author has continued to bring it up to date in the *Revue de Qumran*. There is a selected list of publications (1951–64) in A. Dupont-Sommer, *Les écrits esséniens,* 2d ed., pp. 442–44; see also R. K. Harrison, *The Dead Sea Scrolls,* pp. 151–58.

On the relations of Qumran with Christianity, see J. Daniélou, *Les manuscrits de la Mer Morte et les origines du christianisme* (Paris, 1956); K. Stendhal, ed., *The Scrolls and the New Testament* (New York, 1957); H. Kosmala, *Hebräer, Essenen, Christen* (Leiden, 1959); L. Mowry, *The Dead Sea Scrolls and the Early Church* (Chicago, 1962); J. van der Ploeg et al., *La secte de Qumran et les origines du Christianisme* (Bruges and Paris, 1959); M. Black, *The Scrolls and Christian Origins* (Edinburgh and New York, 1961); Black, *The Scrolls and Christianity* (London, 1969); J. H. Charlesworth, ed., *John and Qumran* (London, 1972). See also F. Nötscher, *Zur theologischen Terminologie der Qumranischen Texte* (Bonn, 1956); W. D. Davies, " 'Knowledge' in the Dead Sea Scrolls and Matthew 11:25–30," in *Christian Origins and Judaism* (Philadelphia, 1962), pp. 31–66; J. Jeremias, *Die Abendmahlsworte Jesu,* 2d ed. (Göttingen, 1949), pp. 58 ff.

On the relations of Qumran with Iran, see K. G. Kuhn, "Die Sektenschrift und die iranische Religion," *Zeitschrift für Theologie und Kirche* 49 (1952): 296–316; H. Michaud, "Un mythe zervanite dans un des manuscrits de Qumran," *VT* 5 (1955): 137–47; David Winston, "The Iranian Component in the Bible: Apocrypha and Qumran—A Review of the Evidence," *HR* 5 (1966): 183–216; S. Shaked, "Qumran and Iran: Further Considerations," *Israel Oriental Studies* 2 (1972): 433–46; Richard N. Frye, "Qumran and Iran: The State of Studies," *Christianity, Judaism . . . : Studies for Morton Smith,* vol. 3 (Leiden, 1975), pp. 167–73 (rather skeptical in regard to the arguments of David Winston and other scholars, Frye nevertheless accepts Shaked's thesis; see pp. 172–73).

On the *pesher* method of interpretation, see the bibliography in Cross, *The Ancient Library of Qumran,* p. 218, n. 38; add Lawrence H. Schiffman, *The Halakha at Qumran* (Leiden, 1975). On the war between the two Spirits, see Y. Yadin and C. Rabin, *The Scroll of the War,* pp. 29 ff. and passim; H. S. van der Ploeg, *Le Rouleau de la Guerre;* Cross, *The Ancient Library,* pp. 210 ff. (n. 25, bibliography); S. Shaked, "Qumran et Iran," pp. 437 ff.

On the figure of the Paraclete, see the excellent comparative study by O. Betz, *Der Paraklet: Fürsprecher im häretischen Spätjudentum, im Johannes-Evangelium, und in neugefundenen gnostischen Schriften* (Leiden and Cologne, 1963).

224. On Rabbi Johanan ben Zakkai, see the monographs by Jacob Neusner, *Life of Rabbin Yohanan ben Zakkai* (Leiden, 1962) and *Development of a Legend: Studies in the Traditions concerning Yohanan ben Zakkai* (Leiden, 1970). Add: N. Sed, "Les traditions secrètes et les disciples de Rabbin Yohanan ben Zakkai," *RHR* 184 (1973): 49–66.

On the consequences of the destruction of the Temple, see G. F. Moore, *Judaism in the First Centuries of the Christian Era,* 2 vols. (Cambridge, Mass., 1927, 1930), vol. 1, pp. 93 ff.; vol. 2, pp. 3 ff., 116 ff.; cf. Judah Goldin, "On Change and Adaptation in Judaism," *HR* 4 (1965): 269–94; Jacob Neusner, *From Politics to Piety: The Emergence of Pharisaic Judaism* (Englewood Cliffs, N. J., 1973); Sheldon R. Isenberg, "Power through Temple and Torah in the Greco-Roman Period," *Christianity, Judaism . . . : Studies for Morton Smith,* vol. 3, pp. 24–52.

On the consequences of the catastrophe of the year 70 for Christianity, see L. Gaston, *No Stone on Another: Studies in the Significance of the Fall of Jerusalem in the Synoptic Gospels* (Leiden, 1970); N. Perrin, *The New Testament,* pp. 40 ff., 136 ff.

On the relations between Christians and Jews, see Robert A. Kraft, "The Multiform Jewish Heritage of Early Christianity," *Christianity, Judaism . . . : Studies for Morton Smith,* vol. 3, pp. 174–99; Wayne A. Meeks, " 'Am I a Jew?' Johannine Christianity and Judaism," ibid., vol. 1, pp. 163–86; see also G. W. Bruchanam, "The Present State of Scholarship on Hebrews," ibid., pp. 299–330. On the relations between Christians and Jews in the Roman Empire, see Marcel Simon, *Verus Israel.*

On the delay in the parousia, see Norman Perrin, *The New Testament: An Introduction,* pp. 40–51, 197–98, and A. L. Moore, *The Parousia in the New Testament* (Leiden, 1966).

On the origin of Christology, see R. H. Fuller, *The Foundation of New Testament Christology* (London, 1965); Martin Hengel, *Der Sohn Gottes: Die Entstehung der Christologie und die jüdisch-hellenistische Religionsgeschichte,* 2d rev. ed. (Tübingen, 1977; English trans. by John Bowden, *The Son of God,* Philadelphia, 1976); C. F. D. Moule, *The Origin of Christology* (New York, 1977).

There is an extensive literature on the theology of the New Testament. See, especially, N. Perrin, *The New Testament* (pp. 353–59, bibliography), and Rudolf Bultmann, *Theology of the New Testament,* 2 vols. (English translation; New York, 1951, 1955) (a penetrating and personal work, but it includes critical bibliographies: vol. 1, pp. 357–68; vol. 2, pp. 253–60).

Indispensable for the problems discussed in this chapter are Gerhard Delling et al., *Bibliographie zur jüdisch-hellenistischen und intertestamentarischen Literatur: 1900–1970,* 2d ed. (Berlin, 1975).

Chapter 29. Paganism, Christianity, Gnosis

225. On the penetration of Oriental cults into Rome and the Roman Empire, see F. Cumont, *Les religions orientales dans le paganisme romain,* 4th ed. (Paris, 1929; English trans., *Oriental Religions in Roman Paganism,* paperback); A. D. Nock, *Conversion: The Old and the New in Religion from Alexander the Great to Augustine of Hippo* (Oxford, 1933; 2d ed., 1961), pp. 66 ff., 99 ff., 122 ff.; see also the bibliographies given above for §§ 205–8.

On the *Sibylline Oracles,* see the bibliography cited in § 165 and A. Peretti, *La Sibilla babilonese nella propaganda ellenistica* (Florence, 1942); A. Kurfess, *Die Sibyllinische Weissagungen* (Munich, 1951); V. Nikiprowetski, *La Troisième Sibylle* (Paris and The Hague, 1970), esp. chap. 6, "La Doctrine," pp. 71 ff.; John J. Collins, *The Sibylline Oracles of Egyptian Judaism* (Missoula, Mont., 1974) (see esp. pp. 101 ff. on the doctrine of the Great Year in the Hellenistic world). On apocalyptic and its relations with the schools of Wisdom, see the bibliography given for §§ 202–4; add J. Z. Smith, "Wisdom and Apocalyptic," in *Religious Syncretism in Antiquity: Essays in Conversation with Geo Widengren* (Missoula, Mont., 1975), pp. 131–56; John J. Collins, "Cosmos and Salvation: Jewish Wisdom and Apocalyptic in the Hellenistic Age," *HR* 17 (1977): 121–42.

On the *Fourth Eclogue,* see E. Norden, *Die Geburt des Kindes* (Berlin, 1924); J. Carcopino, *Virgile et le mystère de la IVe Eglogue* (Paris, 1930; rev. ed., 1943); Henri Jeanmaire, *La Sibylle et le retour de l'âge d'or* (Paris, 1939).

The two myths on the destiny of Rome are examined by Jean Hubaux, *Les grands mythes de Rome* (Paris, 1945), and Eliade, *The Myth of the Eternal Return: Cosmos and History,* trans. Willard R. Trask, Bollingen Series 46 (Princeton, 1965), pp. 133 ff.

On the Pax Augusta, see Charles Norris Cochrane, *Christianity and Classical Culture* (Oxford and New York, 1940; rev. and enl. ed., 1944), pp. 1–26.

On Augustus' religious reforms, see Franz Altheim, *A History of Roman Religion,* trans. Harold Mattingly (London, 1938), pp. 321–410 (originally published as *Römische Religionsgeschichte,* Baden-Baden, 1931).

226. An excellent synthesis on the Imperial period has been provided by Robert M. Grant, *Augustus to Constantine: The Thrust of the Christian Movement into the Roman World* (New York, 1970).

On the cult of sovereigns, see the bibliography for § 205.

On the relations between the Church and the Empire, see E. Peterson, *Der Monotheismus als politisches Problem* (Leipzig, 1935); G. Gittel, *Christus und Imperator* (Stuttgart and Berlin, 1939); E. Stauffer, *Christus und die Cäsaren,* 2d ed. (Hamburg, 1952); J. M. Hornus, *Evangile et Labarum: Etude sur l'attitude du christianisme primitif devant les problèmes de l'Etat, de la guerre, et de la violence* (Geneva, 1960).

There are good syntheses on the confrontation between Christianity and the classical tradition in C. N. Cochrane, *Christianity and Classical Culture,* 2d ed. (1944), and H. Chadwick, *Early Christian Thought and the Classical Tradition* (Oxford, 1966). See also W. Jaeger, *Early Christianity and Greek Paideia* (Cambridge, Mass., 1962); J. Carcopino, *De Pythagore aux Apôtres* (Paris, 1956). The work by Pierre de Labriolle, *La réaction païenne,* 5th ed. (Paris, 1942), remains very useful.

On conversion to Christianity, see A. D. Nock, *Conversion,* pp. 187 ff., 297 ff. (sources and bibliography); Gustave Bardy, *La conversion au christianisme durant les premiers siècles* (Paris, 1949); A. Tuck, *Evangélisation et catéchèse aux deux premiers siècles* (Paris, 1962); Paul Aubin, *Le problème de la "conversion": Etude sur un thème commun à l'hellénisme et au christianisme des trois premiers siècles* (Paris, 1963).

On the expansion of Christianity, the work by A. von Harnack, *Mission und Ausbreitung in der ersten drei Jahrhunderten,* 4th ed. (Leipzig, 1924), remains irreplaceable (an English translation is available, entitled *The Mission and Expansion of Christianity in the First Three Centuries*); see also R. Liechtenhan, *Die urchristliche Mission* (Zurich, 1946); Jean Daniélou and Henri Marrou, *Nouvelle histoire de l'Eglise,* vol. 1: *Des origines à Grégoire le Grand* (1963), pp. 112–340.

On the persecutions, see P. Allard, *Histoire des persécutions,* 3d ed., 5 vols. (Paris, 1903–8)—out of date but still very useful; H. C. Babut, *L'Adoration des empereurs et les origines de la persécution de Dioclétien* (Paris, 1916); H. Grégoire, *Les persécutions dans l'Empire romain* (Brussels, 1951; 2d ed., enl., 1964); J. Moreau, *Les persécutions du christianisme dans l'Empire romain* (1956), an excellent synthesis; W. H. C. Frend, *Martyrdom and Persecution in the Early Church*

(Oxford, 1965); G. E. M. de Ste. Croix, "Why Were the Early Christians Persecuted?" *Past and Present* 26 (1961): 6–31. See also N. H. Baynes, "The Great Persecution," *Cambridge Ancient History,* vol. 12 (1939), pp. 646–77; G. E. M. de Ste. Croix, "Aspects of the Great Persecution," *HTR* 47 (1954): 75–113.

The most important apologists are Theophilus of Antioch (ca. 180), author of a treatise *To Autolycus;* the Syrian Tatian (ca. 165); Tertullian, whose *Apologeticum* was composed in 197; Minucius Felix, author of *Octavius;* and, especially, Justin Martyr.

On the apologists, see M. Pellegrino, *Gli Apologetici del II° secolo,* 2d ed. (Brescia, 1943); Pellegrino, *Studi sull'antica Apologetica* (Rome, 1947); E. R. Goodenough, *The Theology of Justin Martyr* (Jena, 1923); W. H. Shotwell, *The Exegesis of Justin* (Chicago, 1955); P. Prigent, *Justin et l'Ancien Testament* (1964).

From the enormous literature on the apostolic tradition, we cite R. P. C. Hanson, *Tradition in the Early Church* (London, 1963), and M. Pellegrino, *La tradizione nel Cristianesimo antico* (Turin, 1963). The Catholic point of view is represented by, inter alia, A. Deneppe, *Der Traditionsbegriff* (Münster, 1947), and Yves Congar, *La tradition et les traditions* (Paris, 1960). For the position of Protestant theology, see O. Cullmann, *La Tradition* (Neuchâtel and Paris, 1953); E. Flessemann van Leer, *Tradition and Scripture in the Early Church* (Assen, 1954); and G. G. Blum, *Tradition und Sukzession: Studien zum Normbegriff des apostolischen von Paulus bis Irenäus* (Berlin, 1963); see also A. Ehrhardt, *The Apostolic Succession in the First Two Centuries of the Church* (London, 1953) (Anglican position).

Georg Kümmel has recently retraced the history of New Testament research in his book *Das Neue Testament: Geschichte der Erforschung seiner Probleme* (1970; English trans., *The New Testament: The History of Investigation of Its Problems,* Nashville and New York, 1972; extensive bibliography, pp. 407–65). For a short exposition see R. M. Grant, *The Formation of the New Testament* (London, 1965); the same author has published a fuller book, *Historical Introduction to the New Testament* (New York and Evanston, 1963). See also A. Riesenfeld, *The Gospel Tradition and Its Beginnings* (London, 1957), and the bibliographies cited in §§ 221 ff., above.

227. The sources on esotericism (= secret teachings and rites) in normative Judaism and in the Judaic sects—among the Essenes, the Samaritans, and the Pharisees—are listed by Morton Smith, *Clement of Alexandria and a Secret Gospel of Mark* (Cambridge, Mass., 1973), pp. 197–99; this work is valuable for its considerable documentation, but the author's thesis—concerning the initiatory baptism practiced by Jesus and the libertine practices that invoked the authority of that secret tradition—has been generally rejected by the exegetes. See ibid., pp. 199 ff., for analysis of the sources on Jesus' secret teaching.

On Jewish esotericism, see two works by G. Scholem, *Jewish Gnosticism, Merkabah Mysticism, and Talmudic Tradition* (New York, 1966), and "Jaldabaoth Reconsidered," *Mélanges H.-C. Puech,* pp. 405–21; Jean Daniélou, *Théologie du Judéo-christianisme* (Paris, 1957), pp. 121 ff. (English trans., *The Theology of Jewish Christianity,* 1977); See also Morton Smith, "Observations on *Hekhalot Rabbati,*" in *Biblical and Other Studies,* ed. A. Altmann (Cambridge, Mass., 1963), pp. 142–60; James M. Robinson, ed., *Jewish Gnostic Nag Hammadi Texts* (Berkeley, 1975).

Father Jean Daniélou has examined the sources of Christian esotericism in his study "Les traditions secrètes des Apôtres," *Eranos-Jahrbuch* 31 (1962): 199–215. According to him, "the esoteric traditions of the Apostles are the continuation of a Jewish esotericism that existed in the time of the Apostles and that concerns the very definite domain of the secrets of the celestial world" (p. 211). See also G. Quispel, "Gnosis and the New Sayings of Jesus," *Eranos-Jahrbuch* 38 (1969): 261–95.

On Christian Gnosis, see J. Dupont, *Gnosis: La connaissance religieuse dans les Epîtres de Saint Paul* (Louvain, 1949); Stanislas Lyonnet, "Saint Paul et le gnosticisme: L'Epître aux Colossiens," in *Le origini dello Gnosticismo* (contributions to the Messina Colloquium) (Leiden, 1967), pp. 531–38; H. J. Schoeps, *Aus frühchristlicher Zeit* (Tübingen, 1950); Schoeps, *Urgemeinde, Judenchristentum, Gnosis* (Tübingen, 1956); H. B. Bartch, *Gnostisches Gut und Gemeindetradition bei Ignatius von Antiochen* (Gütersloh, 1940). See also M. Simonetti, *Testi gnostici cristiani* (Bari, 1970), and the bibliography cited for § 221.

228. Investigations of Gnosis and Gnosticism have made significant progress during the past forty years; however, the origin of the current known by the name of "Gnosticism" is not yet solved. For Adolf Harnack, Gnosticism—as it appears in the second century of our era—represents a radical Hellenization of Christianity ("eine akute Hellenisierung des Christentums"). This is, furthermore, the thesis of the Christian theologians—first of all, Irenaeus of Lyons and Hippolytus of Rome—for whom Gnosticism was a diabolical heresy, produced by a deformation of Christian doctrine under the influence of Greek philosophy. But in a book that still remains fundamental, *Hauptprobleme* *der Gnosis* (Göttingen, 1907), Wilhelm Bousset proposes a completely contrary explanation: analyzing the specifically Gnostic themes (dualism, the notion of the Savior, the ecstatic ascent of the soul) from a comparative point of view, he credits them with an Iranian origin. For Bousset, then, Gnosticism is a pre-Christian phenomenon that also actually included Christianity. R. Reitzenstein developed and clarified this hypothesis in several works, the most important of which is *Das iranische Erlösungsmysterium* (Leipzig, 1921). Reitzenstein reconstructs the Iranian myth of the "saved Savior," whose most articulate expression is in the "Hymn of the Pearl" in the Acts of Thomas (see § 230). The Iranian origin of Gnosis, criticized by certain Orientalists and historians of religions, has been accepted, corrected, and brought up to date by G. Widengren; see especially his study "Les origines du gnosticisme et l'histoire des religions" (*Le origini dello Gnosticismo,* pp. 28–60), where the Swedish scholar also examines other more recent hypotheses.

The work by Hans Jonas, *The Gnostic Religion: The Message of the Alien God and the Beginnings of Christianity* (Boston, 1958; enl. ed., 1963), is fundamental for its penetrating analysis of the "Gnostic phenomenon." Jonas is the first historian of philosophy to study Gnosticism, after H. Leisegang and Simone Pétrement; but Leisegang's *Die Gnosis* (Leipzig, 1924; 3d ed., 1941; French trans., *La Gnose,* 1951) is useful chiefly for its long quotations from texts, and Simone Pétrement's work has as its title *Le dualisme chez Platon, les gnostiques, et les manichéens* (Paris, 1947). As regards the beginnings of the Gnostic movement, Jonas distinguishes two types of Gnosis, derived from two different cultural milieux: Syro-Egyptian and Iranian (this hypothesis is criticized by Widengren in "Les origines du gnosticisme," pp. 38 ff.).

The book by Robert M. Grant, *Gnosticism and Early Christianity* (New York, 1959), is an excellent introduction, valuable for its pertinent analyses of several Gnostic systems. Grant explains the appearance of Gnosticism by the crisis of Jewish apocalyptic thought after the catastrophe of the 70s. This hypothesis, accepted by Father Jean Daniélou (among others), has been criticized by, inter alia, Jacob Neusner, "Judaism in Late Antiquity," *Judaism* 15 (1966): 236 ff.

For Gilles Quispel, Gnosis is a universal religion (see his *Gnosis als Weltreligion* [Zurich, 1951]), but the different Gnostic systems of the second century derive from Jewish and Judaeo-Christian apocalyptic speculations (see his articles collected in *Gnostic Studies,* 2 vols. [Leiden, 1973]). Henri-Charles Puech's important contributions to the history and phenomenology of Gnosis, published from 1934 on in various learned journals and in the *Annuaire du Collège de France,* have recently been collected and published under the title *En quête de la Gnose,* vol. 1: *La Gnose et le Temps;* vol. 2: *Sur l'Evangile selon Thomas* (Paris, 1978). We must mention especially his studies on Plotinus, on the phenomenology of Gnosis, and on Gnosis and time (vol. 1, pp. 55–116, 185–214, 215–70).

An up-to-date restatement has been provided by R. McL. Wilson, *The Gnostic Problem* (London, 1958), where he analyzes particularly the Jewish and Christian elements present in the various Gnostic schools. See also his contribution to the Messina Colloquium, "Gnosis, Gnosticism, and the New Testament" (*Le origini dello Gnosticismo,* pp. 511–27).

The participants in the international Messina Colloquium on the origins of Gnosticism undertook carefully to delimit the meanings of the terms *Gnosis* and *Gnosticism;* "Gnosticism" designates "a certain group of systems of the second century A.D., which everyone agrees to denominate thus." But "Gnosis," on the contrary, means "a knowledge of divine mysteries, but a knowledge restricted to an elite" (*Le origini dello Gnosticismo,* p. xxiii). On the occasion of the Messina Colloquium it was possible to observe once again the number and variety of the hypotheses concerning the "origins" of Gnosticism. In his study "Perspectives de la recherche sur les origines du gnosticisme" (ibid., pp. 716–46), Ugo Bianchi sketched a morphology of Gnostic themes, at the same time analyzing their geographical distribution and their possible historical relations. See also, by the same author, "Le problème des origines du gnosticisme" (ibid., pp. 1–27).

Among the numerous communications to the Messina Colloquium we mention those of H. Jonas, "Delimitation of the Gnostic Phenomenon—Typological and Historical" (ibid., pp. 90–108); A. Bausani, "Lettere iraniche per l'origine e la definizione tipologica di Gnosi" (pp. 251–64); G. Gnoli, "La gnosi iranica: Per un impostazione del problema" (pp. 281–90), principally an examination of Manichaeanism; R. Grahay, "Eléments d'une mythopée gnostique dans la Grèce classique" (pp. 323–39); M. Simon, "Eléments gnostiques chez Philon" (pp. 359–76); H. Ringgren, "Qumran and Gnosticism" (pp. 379–88); H. J. Schoeps, "Judenchristentum und Gnosis" (pp. 528–37); and G. Quispel, "Makarius und das Lied von der Perle" (pp. 625–44).

On Plotinus and Gnosis, see the study by H.-C. Puech, *En quête de la Gnose,* vol. 1, pp. 55–116; on the relations between Platonic dualism (especially in Plotinus' interpretation) and Gnostic dualism, see E. R. Dodds, *Pagan and Christian in an Age of Anxiety: Some Aspects of*

Religious Experience from Marcus Aurelius to Constantine (Cambridge, 1965), pp. 24 ff., 83 ff.

The discovery of Gnostic manuscripts in a jar at Nag Hammadi in Upper Egypt and the eventful history of their acquisition, deciphering, and publication have been told by Jean Doresse, *Les livres secrets des gnostiques d'Egypte,* vol. 1: *Introduction aux écrits gnostiques coptes découverts à Khenoboskion* (Paris, 1958), pp. 133 ff. (English trans., *The Secret Books of the Egyptian Gnostics,* New York, 1972), and, with previously unknown details, by John Dart, *The Laughing Savior* (New York, 1976). See also James R. Robinson, "The Jung Codex: The Rise and Fall of a Monopoly," *Religious Studies Review* 3 (1977): 17–30. The complete edition, *The Facsimile Edition of the Nag Hammadi Codices,* was completed in 1976. Critical editions of certain texts, accompanied by translations and commentaries, have been published progressively since 1956, but the only complete translation (unfortunately without notes and commentaries) is the one published under the direction of James M. Robinson, *The Nag Hammadi Library* (New York, 1977).

The library discovered at Nag Hammadi has given rise to countless studies. See David M. Scholer, *Nag Hammadi Bibliography, 1948–1969* (Leiden, 1971), and the annual reports of developments published in the periodical *Novum Testamentum.* An extremely learned analysis of the new publications—critical editions, translations, and contributions to the history and exegesis of the texts—has been provided by Carsten Colpe in "Heidnische, jüdische, und christliche Überlieferung in den Schriften aus Nag Hammadi," *Jahrbuch für Antike und Christentum* 16 (1973): 106–26; 17 (1974): 109–25; 18 (1975): 144–65; 19 (1976): 120–38.

Among works devoted to analysis and interpretation of the new texts, we mention: W. C. van Unnik, *Newly Discovered Gnostic Writings* (Naperville, Ill., 1960); Alexander Böhlig, *Mysterion und Wahrheit* (Leiden, 1968), pp. 80–111, 119–61; Martin Krause, ed., *Essays on the Nag Hammadi Texts in Honour of Alexander Böhlig* (Leiden, 1972); M. Tardieu, *Trois mythes gnostiques: Adam, Eve, et les animaux d'Egypte dans un écrit de Nag Hammadi* (Paris, 1974). See also the studies by Henri-Charles Puech collected in his work *En quête de la Gnose,* vol. 2: *Sur l'Evangile selon Thomas.* The same volume contains (pp. 11–32) a translation of the Gospel according to Thomas (published for the first time, with apparatus criticus and commentary, in 1959). Another translation, thoroughly annotated, has been provided by Jean Doresse in *L'Evangile selon Thomas, ou les Paroles Secrètes de Jésus* (Paris, 1959). See also the excellent commentary by J. E.

Menard, *L'Evangile selon Thomas* (Leiden, 1975). On this important text, see further, Robert M. Grant, *The Secret Sayings of Jesus* (New York, 1960); R. McL. Wilson, *Studies in the Gospel of Thomas* (London, 1960); B. Gartner, *The Theology of the Gospel of Thomas.*

One of the most discussed texts, and one that has been translated several times, is The Gospel of Truth; see the translation by W. W. Isenberg in R. M. Grant, *Gnosticism,* pp. 146–61, and the one by George W. MacRae in J. M. Robinson, *The Nag Hammadi Library,* pp. 37–49.

On the Gospel of Philip (= *Nag Hammadi Library,* pp. 131–51, trans. W. W. Isenberg), see R. McL. Wilson, *The Gospel of Philip* (London, 1962); J. E. Menard, *L'Evangile selon Philippe* (Paris, 1967).

Several anthologies of Gnostic texts, translated and annotated, have been published during the past fifteen years. We mention Robert M. Grant, *Gnosticism: A Source Book of Heretical Writings from the Early Christian Period* (New York, 1961), and Werner Foerster, *Die Gnosis,* 2 vols. (Zurich, 1969, 1971; English trans., ed. R. McL. Wilson, *Gnosis: A Selection of Gnostic Texts, Coptic and Mandaean Sources,* 2 vols., Oxford, 1972, 1974).

229. On Simon Magus, see Grant, *Gnosticism and Early Christianity,* pp. 70–96; H. Leisegang, *La Gnose,* pp. 48–80; L. Cerfaux, "Simon le Magicien à Samarie," *Recherches de science religieuse* 27 (1937): 615 ff.; L. H. Vincent, "Le culte d'Hélène à Samarie," *Revue Biblique* 45 (1936): 221 ff.; H. Jonas, *The Gnostic Religion,* pp. 103–111, 346 (bibliography).

On the origins of the legend of Doctor Faustus, see E. M. Butler, *The Myth of the Magus* (Cambridge, 1948); Gilles Quispel, "Faust: Symbol of Western Man," *Eranos-Jahrbuch* 35 (1966): 241–65 (reprinted in *Gnostic Studies,* vol. 2 [Leiden and Constantinople, 1973], pp. 288–307).

Marcion's work, the *Antitheses,* is lost, but the substance of it is known to us from Tertullian's treatise *Adversus Marcionem.* Numerous orthodox writers composed attacks on Marcionism—for example, Justin, Irenaeus, and Dionysius of Corinth.

The book by Adolph von Harnack, *Marcion: Das Evangelium vom fremden Gott,* 2d ed. (Leipzig, 1924), has not been surpassed. See also E. G. Blackmann, *Marcion and His Influence* (London, 1948); H. Leisegang, *La Gnose,* pp. 185–91; Hans Jonas, *The Gnostic Religion,* pp. 130–46; Grant, *Gnosticism and Early Christianity,* pp. 121 ff.

On heterodox Judaeo-Christianity, see J. Daniélou, *Théologie du Judéo-Christianisme* (Tournai, 1958), pp. 68–98; on Cerinthus, see ibid., pp. 80–81. On Carpocrates, see Leisegang, *La Gnose,* pp. 136–75;

Wilson, *The Gnostic Problem,* pp. 123 ff.; and Grant, *Gnosticism and Early Christianity,* pp. 142 ff.

On Valentinus and his school, see F. M. Sagnard, *La gnose valentinienne et le témoignage de saint Irénée* (Paris, 1947); A. Orbe, *Estudios valentinianos,* 4 vols. (Rome, 1955–61), a most learned comparative study of the Gnostic and Christian theologies; and H. Jonas, *The Gnostic Religion,* pp. 174–205. See also the bibliography given above on the Gospel of Truth. Among the writings that belong to the Valentinian school, mention must be made of the treatise *De Resurrectione* (*Epistula ad Rheginum*); we use the translation and commentary by Malcolm Lee Peel, *The Epistle to Rheginos: A Valentinian Letter on the Resurrection* (Philadelphia, 1969). This short text (fewer than eight pages) is especially important because it is the first Gnostic document from Nag Hammadi devoted to individual eschatology (i.e., the death and postexistence of the person).

Valentinus is the only Gnostic teacher the names of whose disciples are known. One of them, Heracleon, composed the first commentary on John's Gospel; Origen replied to him by writing his own commentary. In fact, these disciples developed Valentinus' system in such a way that it is hard to determine the outline of his original doctrine. On the different expressions of the Valentinian theology, see R. Grant, *Gnosticism and Early Christianity,* pp. 134 ff.

On the libertine Gnostic sects, first of all the Phibionites (whose orgies were described by Epiphanius, *Panarion,* 26. 1. 1 ff.), see Stephen Benko, "The Libertine Gnostic Sect of the Phibionites according to Epiphanius," *Vigiliae Christianae* 2 (1967): 103–19; Alfonso M. de Nola, *Parole segrete di Gesù,* p. 80–90; Eliade, *Occultism, Witchcraft, and Cultural Fashions* (Chicago, 1976), pp. 109 ff., 139–40.

The Gnostic sect of the Mandaeans still survives in a small community of 13,000–14,000 believers in southern Iraq. Their name derives from the term *mandāyē* ("Gnostics"). We have a large number of works: the two *Ginzās* ("treasures"), the Book of John, and a canonical book of prayers and other cult texts, all obtained especially thanks to the enthusiasm and energy of Lady E. S. Drower. It is probable that the religious practices (first of all, baptism and the requiem Mass), as well as the theology of the Mandaeans, go back to a very ancient time, preceding the preaching of Jesus Christ. However, the origin and history of the sect are still inadequately known. Probably it represents a heretical Jewish sect, opposed to orthodox Judaism and strongly influenced by Gnostic and Iranian ideas. As Kurt Rudolph writes: "It is a branch, organized in a baptismal sect, of the Judaeo-Syrian Gnostic current, which has become a closed community in life and language and has preserved to our day most valuable documents of a vanished belief.'' There is a considerable literature (texts and critical studies); see E. S. Drower, *The Mandaeans of Irak and Iran* (Oxford, 1937; reprinted Leiden, 1962); K. Rudolph, ''Mandäische Quellen,'' in W. Foerster, ed., *Die Gnosis,* vol. 2 (Zurich, 1971), pp. 171–418; Rudolph, *Die Mandäer,* 2 vols. (Göttingen, 1960–61). See also Rudolph's general presentation, ''La religion mandéenne,'' in H.-C. Puech, ed., *Histoire des religions,* vol. 2 (Paris, 1972), pp. 498–522.

230. The ''Hymn of the Pearl'' has given rise to a long-continued controversy. The Iranian origin of the myth has been maintained especially by R. Reitzenstein, *Das iranische Erlösungsmysterium* (Bonn, 1921), pp. 72 ff.; G. Widengren, ''Der iranische Hintergrund der Gnosis,'' *Zeitschrift für Religions- und Geistesgeschichte* 4 (1952): 105 ff.; and Widengren, *Religionsphänomenologie* (Berlin, 1969), pp. 506 ff. Good analyses will be found in Jonas, *The Gnostic Religion,* pp. 116 ff.; Erik Peterson, *Frühkirche, Judentum, und Gnosis* (Rome and Freiburg, 1959), pp. 204 ff.; Alfred Adam, *Die Psalmen des Thomas und das Perlenlied als Zeugnisse vorchristlicher Gnosis* (Berlin, 1959); H.-C. Puech, *En quête de la Gnose,* vol. 2, pp. 118 ff., 231 ff. See also A. T. J. Klijn, ''The So-Called Hymn of the Pearl,'' *Vigiliae Christianae* 14 (1960): 154–64; G. Quispel, *Makarius, das Thomasevangelium, und das Lied von der Perle* (Leiden, 1967).

On the symbolism of the pearl in archaic and Oriental cultures, see Eliade, *Images and Symbols,* trans. Philip Mairet (New York, 1961), pp. 130–50; M. Mokri, ''Les symboles de la Perle,'' *JA* 248 (1960): 463–81. As for the pearl identified with Christ by Christian theologians, see C. M. Edsman, *Le baptême de feu* (Leipzig and Uppsala, 1940), pp. 190 ff.; Eliade *Images and Symbols,* pp. 148 ff.

The legends of Matsyendranāth and his amnesia are analyzed in our book *Yoga: Immortality and Freedom,* trans. Willard R. Trask (Princeton, 1969), pp. 314 ff.; see the bibliography of sources there, pp. 421–22. The themes of exile, captivity in a foreign country, and the messenger who wakes the prisoner and urges him to set forth are found in a little work by Suhrawardi, *Recital of Occidental Exile,* brilliantly analyzed by Henry Corbin in his *En Islam iranien,* vol. 2 (1971), pp. 270–94.

On the myth of the ''saved Savior,'' see the works by R. Reitzenstein and G. Widengren cited above; see also the criticisms put forward by C. Colpe, *Die religionsgeschichtliche Schule* (Göttingen, 1961).

On the specifically Gnostic images and symbols, see Hans Jonas, *The Gnostic Religion,* pp. 48–99; G. MacRae, ''Sleep and Awakening in Gnostic Texts,'' in *Origini dello Gnosticismo,* pp. 496–510; H.-C.

Puech, *En quête de la Gnose,* vol. 2, pp. 116 ff. See also Eliade, *Myth and Reality,* trans. Willard R. Trask (New York, 1963), pp. 127 ff.

231. The history of Manichaean studies constitutes an important chapter in the history of ideas in Europe; we need but call to mind the philosophical interest and the impassioned controversies aroused by the *Histoire critique de Manichée et du Manichéisme,* 2 vols. (Amsterdam, 1734–39), by Isaak de Beausobre, and by Bayle's articles in his *Dictionnaire;* see J. Ries, "Introduction aux études manichéennes: Quatre siècles de recherches," *Ephemerides Theologicae Lovanienses* 33 (1957): 453–82; 35 (1959): 362–409. On works published in the twentieth century, see H. S. Nyberg, "Forschungen über den Manichäismus," *Zeitschrift für neutestamentliche Wissenschaft* 34 (1935): 70–91; Raoul Manselli, *L'eresia del male* (Naples, 1963), pp. 11–27. The best general exposition remains the book by H.-C. Puech, *Le Manichéisme: Son fondateur, sa doctrine* (Paris, 1949); the notes (pp. 98–195) make up an excellent documentation. The same author presents a new synthesis in the chapter "Le Manichéisme" in H.-C. Puech, ed., *Histoire des religions,* vol. 2 (1972), pp. 523–645. See also G. Widengren, *Mani und der Manichäismus* (Stuttgart, 1962) (we cite the English translation, *Mani and Manichaeism* [London and New York, 1965]); O. Klima, *Manis Zeit und Leben* (Prague, 1962); François Decret, *Mani et la tradition manichéenne* (Paris, 1974). Still to be consulted with profit are A. V. W. Jackson, *Researches in Manichaeism, with Special Reference to the Turfan Fragments* (New York, 1932); A. H. Schaeder, "Urform und Fortbildungen des manichäischen Systems," *Vorträge der Bibliothek Warburg 1924–25* (Leipzig, 1927), pp. 65–157; U. Pestalozza, "Appunti sulla vita di Mani," *Reale Istituto Lombardo di Scienze e Lettere* 2d ser. 67 (1934): 417–79; reprinted in *Nuovi Saggi di Religione Mediterranea* (Florence, 1964), pp. 477–523. For the bibliography of recent works, see L. J. R. Ort, *Mani: A Religio-Historical Description of His Personality* (diss., Leiden, 1967), pp. 261–77; Puech, "Le Manichéisme," pp. 637–45.

The episode of the voice heard by Patek has been transmitted to us by Ibn an-Nadîm (*Fihrist,* pp. 83–84, trans. Flügel). On the baptismal sect to which Patek was converted, see the discussion of the sources in Puech, *Le Manichéisme,* pp. 40–42 and nn. 146–56; G. Widengren, *Mani,* pp. 24–26.

The recent discovery of a Greek Codex whose Syriac origin goes back to the fifth century enables us to identify the baptismal sect: it is that of the Elchasaites, a Judaeo-Christian Gnostic movement founded by Elchai during the reign of Trajan. See A. Heinrichs and

L. Koenen, "Ein griechischer Mani-Codex," *Zeitschrift für Papyrologie und Epigraphik* 5 (1970): 97–216; Hans J. W. Drijvers, "Die Bedeutung des Kölner Mani-Codex für die Manichäismusforschung," in *Mélanges . . . Henri-Charles Puech* (1974), pp. 471–86; Gilles Quispel, "Mani the Apostle of Jesus Christ," *Epektasis: Mélanges . . . Cardinal Jean Daniélou* (1972), pp. 667–72; R. N. Frye, "The Cologne Greek Codex about Mani," *Ex Orbe Religionum* (Festschrift for G. Widengren), vol. 1, pp. 424–29; F. Decret, *Mani,* pp. 48 ff.

Mani consigned the two revelations to his book *Shābuhragān* (see al-Bîrûni, *Chronology of Ancient Nations,* trans. Edward Sachau [London, 1879], p. 190). According to the testimony of a Coptic *Kephalaion,* Mani received a single revelation at the age of twelve years: the Holy Spirit, the Paraclete promised by Jesus, descended and revealed to him the long-hidden "mystery," that is, the conflict between Light and Darkness, the origin of the world, the creation of Adam—in short, the essentials of what will later become the Manichaean doctrine; see *Kephalaia* (=H. J. Polotsky, *Manichäische Handschriften,* vol. 1 [Stuttgart, 1934], chap. 1, pp. 14–15).

On the date of the conversation with Shapur I, see Puech, *Le Manichéisme,* p. 46 and notes 197–84; the date April 9 was calculated by S. H. Taqizadeh. On Mani's last journey, see W. B. Henning, "Mani's Last Journey," *BSOAS* 10 (1942): 941–53. As for certain atrocious details of Mani's death (he was flayed alive, etc.), their authenticity seems to be suspect; see Puech, pp. 54–56.

232. Mani's writings have been analyzed by P. Alfaric, *Les écritures manichéennes,* 2 vols. (Paris, 1918–19; on the later discoveries and the publications of F. W. K. Müller, E. Chavannes, P. Pelliot, W. B. Henning, et al., see Puech, *Le Manichéisme,* pp. 144 ff. (nn. 240 ff.); Puech in *Histoire des religions,* vol. 2, pp. 547 ff.; and Widengren, *Mani und der Manichäismus,* pp. 151–53; see also Ort, *Mani,* pp. 32 ff. Aside from *Shābuhragān,* dedicated to Shapur and composed in Middle Persian, Mani wrote, in Syriac or in Eastern Aramaic, "The Living Gospel," "The Book of Mysteries," the "Pragmateia" (or "Treatise"), "The Treasure of Life," "The Book of Giants," and the "Letters" (Puech, *Le Manichéisme,* p. 67 and n. 262). Among the texts attributed to the prophet, the most important are the *Kephalaia,* or "Chapters." Some texts, translated and commented on, will be found in A. Adam, *Texte zum Manichäismus* (Berlin, 1954); C. R. C. Allberry, *A Manichaean Psalm-Book* (Oxford, 1954); H. J. Polotsky, *Manichäische Homilien* (Stuttgart, 1934); H. J. Polotsky and A. Böhlig, *Kephalaia* (Stuttgart, 1940); and F. Decret, *Mani,* pp. 58 ff. and passim.

233. The myth is presented by Puech, *Le Manichéisme,* pp. 74–85, Widengren, *Mani,* pp. 43–69, and Hans Jonas, *The Gnostic Religion,* 2d ed. (Boston, 1963), pp. 209–31. While insisting on the Iranian character of Manichaeanism (see also *Les religions de l'Iran,* pp. 331–41), G. Widengren has pertinently analyzed the Mesopotamian antecedents of certain personages and episodes in the myth; see his *Mesopotamian Elements in Manichaeism* (Uppsala, 1946), pp. 14–21, 25, 53 (the "Mother of Life"), pp. 31 ff. (the "Prince of Darkness"), pp. 74 ff. (the "Messenger"), etc. See also W. B. Henning, "Ein manichäischer kosmogonischer Hymnus," *NGWG* 10 (1932): 214–28; Henning, "A Sogdian Fragment of the Manichaean Cosmogony," *BSOAS* 12 (1948): 306–18; A. V. W. Jackson, "The Doctrine of the *Bolos* in Manichaean Eschatology," *JAOS* 58 (1938): 225–34; Hans W. Drijvers, "Mani und Bardaisan: Ein Beitrag zur Vorgeschichte des Manichäismus," *Mélanges . . . Henri-Charles Puech,* pp. 459–69.

On the "Prince of Darkness," see the important study by H.-C. Puech, "Le Prince des Ténèbres et son Royaume," in *Satan* (Paris, 1948), pp. 136–74. On the episode known as "the seduction of the Archontes," see F. Cumont, *Recherches sur le Manichéisme,* vol. 1 (Brussels, 1908), pp. 54–68, and Puech, *Le Manichéisme,* p. 172 (n. 324). On the equivalence light, spirit, and *semen virile,* see Eliade, "Spirit, Light, and Seed," *HR* 11 (1971): 1–30 (now chap. 6 in *Occultism, Witchcraft, and Cultural Fashions* [Chicago, 1976]). For the myth of the origins of plants from the semen of a primordial being, see Eliade, "La Mandragore et les mythes de la 'naissance miraculeuse,' " *Zalmoxis* 3 (1940–42): 3–48; Eliade, "Gayōmart et la Mandragore," *Ex Orbe Religionum,* vol. 2, pp. 65–74; Eliade, "Adam, le Christ et la Mandragore," *Mélanges . . . H.-C. Puech,* pp. 611–16.

234. The image of Jesus Patibilis and, above all, the idea that making bread constitutes a sin since it implies "torturing" grain (see Puech, *Le Manichéisme,* p. 96) are reminiscent of certain archaic beliefs that are an integral part of agrarian religiosity (see §§11 ff.).

On the dissemination of Manichaeanism, see U. Pestalozza, "Il manicheismo presso i Turchi occidentali ed orientali," *Reale Istituto Lombardo di Scienze e Lettere* 2d ser. 57 (1934): 417–79 (republished in *Nuovi Saggi di Religione Mediterranea,* pp. 402–75); G. Messina, *Cristianesimo, Buddhismo, Manicheismo nell'Asia Antica* (Rome, 1947); H. S. Nyberg, "Zum Kampf zwischen Islam und Manichäismus," *OLZ* 32 (1929): 425–41; O. Maenchen-Helfen, "Manichaeans in Siberia," *University of California Publications in Semitic Philology* 11 (1951): 311–26; M. Guidi, *La lotta tra l'Islam ed il Manicheismo* (Rome, 1927);

W. B. Henning, "Zum zentralasiatischen Manichäismus," *OLZ* 37 (1934): 1–11; Henning, "Neue Materielen zur Geschichte des Manichäismus," *ZDMG* 40 (1931): 1–18. The book by E. de Stoop, *Essai sur la diffusion du manichéisme dans l'Empire Romain* (Ghent, 1909), is out of date; see the more recent bibliographies in Puech, *Le Manichéisme,* p. 148, n. 257, and Widengren, *Mani,* pp. 155–57. See also P. Brown, "The Diffusion of Manicheism in the Roman Empire," *Journal of Roman Studies* 59 (1969): 92–103; F. Decret, *Aspects du manichéisme dans l'Afrique romaine* (Paris, 1970). For bibliographies on the so-called "Neo-Manichaean" movements, see vol. 3, chap. 36.

Chapter 30. The Twilight of the Gods

235. On Hebrew religious thought, see Claude Tresmontant, *Essai sur la pensée hébraïque* (Paris, 1953); on the biblical structure of Christian theology, see, by the same author, *La métaphysique du christianisme et la naissance de la philosophie chrétienne* (Paris, 1961), pp. 21 ff. On the theme "in the image and likeness" of God, see J. Jervell, *Imago Dei, Gen. I, 26 f., im Spätjudentum, in der Gnosis, und in den paulinischen Briefen* (Göttingen, 1960).

On the controversies concerning the definition of "orthodoxy," see Walter Bauer, *Rechtglaubigkeit und Ketzerei im ältesten Christentum* (Tübingen, 1939; 2d ed., 1964; English translation, *Orthodoxy and Heresy in Earliest Christianity,* 1971); E. H. W. Turner, *The Pattern of the Christian Truth* (London, 1954); A. Benoit, in M. Simon and A. Benoit, *Le Judaïsme et le Christianisme antique* (Paris, 1968), pp. 289–90. In this book, Benoit remarks (p. 300): "It is necessary henceforth to renounce a simplistic and monolithic view of Christian origins. Though always appealing to faith in Christ, Christianity did not express it in a single and identical way: it is enough to think here of the different theologies that are found in the New Testament itself: Pauline theology, Johannine theology . . . ."

236. On aquatic symbolism and mythology, see Eliade, *Patterns in Comparative Religion,* trans. Rosemary Sheed (New York, 1958), §§ 64, 65; *Images and Symbols,* trans. Philip Mairet (New York, 1961), pp. 151 ff. On the symbolism of Christian baptism, see J. Daniélou, *Sacramentum futuri* (Paris, 1950), pp. 13–20, 55–85; Daniélou, *Bible et liturgie* (1951), pp. 29–173; Hugo Rahner, *Greek Myth and Christian Mystery* (London, 1963), pp. 69–88.

On the symbolism of the androgyne in primitive Christianity and among the Gnostics, see Eliade, *The Two and the One,* trans. J. M. Cohen (Chicago, 1979), pp. 103 ff.; add: A. di Nola, *Parole segrete di Gesù* (Turin, 1964), pp. 60 ff.; Wayne A. Meeks, "The Image of the Androgyne: Some Uses of a Symbol in Earliest Christianity," *HR* 13 (1974): 165–208 (ample bibliography); Derwood Smith, "The Two Made One: Some Observations on Eph. 2:14–18," *Ohio Journal of Religious Studies* 1 (1973): 34–54; Robert Murray, *Symbols of Church and Kingdom: A Study in Early Syriac Tradition* (Cambridge, 1975), pp. 301 ff. A good anthology of texts has been provided by Ernst Benz, *Adam: Der Mythus des Urmenschen* (Munich, 1955). Among contemporary authors, we mention the Catholic theologian Georg Koepgen, *Die Gnosis des Christentums* (Salzburg, 1939), who considers not only Christ but also the Church and priests androgynous (pp. 316 ff.). For Nicholas Berdyaev, too, the perfect man of the future will be androgynous, as Christ was; see his *The Meaning of the Creative Act* (English translation, 1955), p. 187 (originally published in 1916).

On the symbolism of the Cosmic Tree and the "center of the world," see Eliade, *Patterns in Comparative Religion,* §§ 99 ff.; *Images and Symbols,* pp. 42 ff. On the symbolism of the Cross as Cosmic Tree or Tree of Life, see the references given in *Images and Symbols,* pp. 161 ff.; add H. Rahner, *Greek Myth and Christian Mystery,* pp. 46–68 ("The Mystery of the Cross").

On "Adam's head" buried on Golgotha and baptized by the Savior's blood, see *The Book of the Cave of Treasures,* translated from the Syriac by E. A. W. Budge (London, 1927), p. 53.

On the legends of miraculous plants springing up under the Cross, see Eliade, "La Mandragore et les mythes de la 'naissance miraculeuse,' " *Zalmoxis* 3 (1940–42): 3–48 (bibliographical notes, pp. 44–45), and Eliade, "Adam, le Christ et la Mandragore," *Mélanges . . . H.-Ch. Puech* (Paris, 1974), pp. 611–16.

On the legend of the origin of the grapevine from the Savior's blood, see Eliade, "La Mandragore," pp. 24 ff.; N. Cartojan, *Cărtile populare in literatura romăneascâ,* 2d ed., vol. 2 (1973), pp. 113 ff.

On legends concerning the origin of the chrism ("medicine of life") in Syriac literature, in Mandaeanism, and in Manichaeanism, see G. Widengren, *Mesopotamian Elements in Manichaeism* (Uppsala, 1946), pp. 123 ff., and Robert Murray, *Symbols of Church and Kingdom,* pp. 95 ff., 320 ff.

On the circulation of similar legends (Seth and the Cross, the search for oil and the chrism, etc.) in the West, see Esther Casier Quinn, *The Quest of Seth for the Oil of Life* (Chicago, 1962).

237. The long and complex process of assimilating pagan religious iconography and its symbolism by Judaism during the Hellenistic and Roman period has been brilliantly presented by Edwin R. Goodenough in the twelve volumes of his opus magnum: *Jewish Symbols in the Greco-Roman Period* (New York, 1953–65). See also Morton Smith, "The Image of God: Notes on the Hellenization of Judaism, with Especial Reference to Goodenough's Work on Jewish Symbolism," *BJRL* 40 (1958): 473–512.

On "cosmic Christianity," see Eliade, *Zalmoxis, the Vanishing God,* trans. Willard R. Trask (Chicago, 1972), chap. 7.

On the dualistic cosmogonies documented in the folklore of eastern Europe, see *Zalmoxis,* chap. 3.

The problem of the Iranian contribution to Christianity has been briefly presented by J. Duchesne-Guillemin, *La religion de l'Iran ancien* (Paris, 1962), pp. 264 ff. (see p. 264, nn. 2–3, for bibliography).

The earliest Christian sources that place the Nativity in a cave are the Proto-Gospel of James (18:1 ff.) and Justin Martyr and Origen. Justin attacked the initiates into the Mysteries of Mithra, who, "instigated by the devil, claimed to perform their initiations in a place that they called *spelaeum*" (*Dialogue with Tryphon,* chap. 78). This attack proves that as early as the second century Christians perceived the analogy between the Mithraic *spelaeum* and the cave in Bethlehem.

On the *Opus imperfectum in Matthaeum* and the *Chronicle of Zuqnin,* see Ugo Monneret de Villard, *Le leggende orientali sui Magi evangelici* (Rome, 1952), pp. 62 ff.; G. Widengren, *Iranisch-semitische Kulturbegegnung in parthischer Zeit* (Cologne and Opladen, 1960), pp. 70 ff.; Eliade, *The Two and the One,* trans. J. M. Cohen (Chicago, 1979), pp. 52 ff.

238. The early rise of Christian theology is the subject of a considerable bibliography. See some bibliographical indications in J. Daniélou and H. Marrou, *Nouvelle histoire de l'Eglise,* vol. 1, pp. 544–55. We mention here J. Daniélou, *Message évangélique et culture hellénistique aux IIe et IIIe siècles* (Tournai, 1961; English trans., *The Gospel Message and Hellenistic Culture,* Philadelphia, 1977); M. Werner, *Die Entstehung des christlichen Dogmas problemgeschichtlich dargestellt,* 2d ed. (Tübingen, 1954); H. A. Wolfson, *The Philosophy of the Church Fathers* (Cambridge, Mass., 1956); E. F. Osborn, *The Philosophy of Clement of Alexandria* (Cambridge, 1957); J. Daniélou, *Origène* (Paris, 1950); H. de Lubac, *Histoire et Esprit: L'intelligence de l'Ecriture d'après Origène* (Paris, 1950); H. Crouzel, *Théologie de l'image de Dieu chez Origène* (Paris, 1956); A. Houssiau, *La Christologie de saint*

Irénée (Louvain, 1955); A. Benoit, *Saint Irénée: Introduction à l'étude de sa théologie* (Paris, 1960); R. P. C. Hansen, *Origen's Doctrine of Tradition* (London, 1954); C. Tresmontant, *La métaphysique du christianisme et la naissance de la philosophie chrétienne* (Paris, 1961).

On Arius and the Council of Nicaea, see H. Marrou in *Histoire de l'Eglise,* vol. 1, pp. 290 ff., 551–53 (bibliography); W. Telfer, "When Did the Arian Controversy Begin?" *Journal of Theological Studies* (London) 47 (1946): 129–42; 48 (1949): 187–91.

On Mariology, see F. Braun, *La mère des fidèles: Essai de théologie johannique* (Paris, 1953); J. Galot, *Mary in the Gospel* (1964); Karl Rahner, *Mary, Mother of the Lord* (1958); E. Schillebeeckx, *Mary, Mother of the Redemption* (1964); H. C. Graef, *Mary: A History of Doctrine and Devotion,* 2 vols. (1963, 1966).

239. On Sol Invictus and the solar religion, see F. Altheim, *A History of Roman Religion,* trans. Harold Mattingly (London, 1938), pp. 466 ff.; Altheim, *Der unbesiegte Gott* (Hamburg, 1957), esp. chaps. 5–7; and G. H. Halsberghe, *The Cult of Sol Invictus* (Leiden, 1972).

On the conversion of Constantine and his religious policy, see A. Piganiol, *L'empereur Constantin* (Paris, 1932) (the author sees a syncretist in Constantine); A. Alföldi, *The Conversion of Constantine and Pagan Rome* (Oxford, 1948); W. Seston, *Dioclétien et la Tétrarchie* (Paris, 1946); H. Kraft, *Konstantins religiöse Entwicklung* (Tübingen, 1955). See also the works by F. Altheim cited above, especially *Der unbesiegte Gott,* chap. 7. A good synthesis has been provided by André Benoit in M. Simon and A. Benoit, *Le Judaïsme et le Christianisme antique,* pp. 308–34, and he remarks (p. 328) that, "Whatever the case may be concerning the precise meaning and origins of the sign seen by Constantine, it is clear that historians will tend to explain it in terms of their general understanding of the Constantinian question. For those who think that Constantine definitely sided with Christianity in 312, the sign can only be Christian (see, among others, Alföldi and Vogt). Those who think that Constantine did not side with Christianity in 312 regard the sign as either pagan or Christian and used to rally believers (see Grégoire). Finally, those who hold that, beginning in 312, Constantine evolves in a syncretistic perspective consider the sign ambiguous, polyvalent, able simultaneously to express paganism and Christianity."

On the history of Christianity in the fourth century, see the synthesis by Henri Marrou in J. Daniélou and H. Marrou, *Nouvelle histoire de l'Eglise,* vol. 1: *Des origines à Saint Grégoire le Grand* (Paris, 1963), pp. 263–72, 547–59 (bibliographies).

On the relations between Christianity and paganism, see P. de Labriolle, *La réaction païenne,* 5th ed. (Paris, 1942); E. R. Dodds, *Pagan and Christian in an Age of Anxiety: Some Aspects of Religious Experience from Marcus Aurelius to Constantine* (1965); A. Momigliano, ed., *The Conflict between Paganism and Christianity in the Fourth Century* (Oxford, 1963), especially the contributions by H. I. Marrou, "Synesius of Cyrene and Alexandrian Neoplatonism" (pp. 125–50), and by H. Bloch, "The Pagan Revival in the West at the End of the Fourth Century" (pp. 193–218). Finally, see Peter Brown, *The World of Late Antiquity: From Marcus Aurelius to Muhammad* (London, 1971), pp. 34 ff.

On the origins and earliest developments of monasticism, see H. Marrou, in Daniélou and Marrou, *Nouvelle histoire de l'Eglise,* vol. 1, pp. 310–20 (bibliography, pp. 553–55); A. Vööbus, *A History of Asceticism in the Syrian Orient,* vol. 1: *The Origin of Asceticism: Early Monasticism in Persia;* vol. 2: *Early Monasticism in Mesopotamia and Syria* (Louvain, 1958, 1960); D. Chitty, *The Desert a City* (Oxford, 1966); Peter Brown, "The Rise and Function of the Holy Man in Late Antiquity," *Journal of Roman Studies* 61 (1971): 80–101, and chap. 8 of his book *The World of Late Antiquity.* See also the annotated translations provided by A. J. Festugière, *Les moines d'Orient,* 4 vols. (Paris, 1961–66), and the richly illustrated work by Jacques Lacarrière, *Les hommes ivres de Dieu* (Paris, 1961).

240. The fragment of Eunapius' *Bioi sophistōn* on the last legitimate hierophant's predictions has been translated by C. Kerényi, *Eleusis* (New York, 1967), pp. 17–18; see also George E. Mylonas, *Eleusis and the Eleusinian Mysteries* (Princeton, 1961), p. 8.

On pagan survivals at Eleusis, see F. Lenormant, *Monographie de la voie sacrée eleusinienne* (Paris, 1864), vol. 1, pp. 398 ff. (the legend of Saint Demetra narrated by Lenormant has been translated into English by A. B. Cook, who added a bibliography; see Cook's *Zeus,* vol. 1 [1914], pp. 173–75). See also John Cuthbert Lawson, *Modern Greek Folklore and Ancient Greek Religion: A Study of Survivals* (Cambridge, 1910; reprinted New York, 1964), pp. 79 ff. On the episode of February 7, 1940, see Charles Picard, "Demeter, puissance oraculaire," *RHR* 122 (1940): 102–24.

Index